THE GREATEST SPORTING FAMILY IN HISTORY

The Blue And Black Brothers

TERRY BREVERTON

DEDICATION

For Cenydd Owen Williams, b.1938 - Cardiff First XV Centre, Outside Half 1956-57 to 1962-63; 115 appearances, 20 tries; RAF XV1959-62, Combined Services XV, tour of Rhodesia and Kenya 1962; Barbarians Centre vs Cardiff and Leicester; St. Helens Rugby League 1963-69 Centre, Full Back, Wing 108 appearances 34 tries.

For Mair Olwen Phillips, formerly Williams, b.1936 – who grew up with her late sisters Dilys Myfanwy Jones, Enid Mary Pritchard and Joan Beryl Roberts in the rugby-mad household of 11 Moy Road.

For the late Elwyn Rhys Williams 1939-2022, 'a fabulous person', a blind-side wing forward who could play in the backs. Wales Under-15s, Captain Cardiff Youth 1957-58, Wales Youth, Wales Under-23s 1962, Wales Final Trial 1962, 339 games Cardiff First XV 1958-59 to 1972-73, 44 First team tries, and over 100 games for Cardiff Athletic. Taff's Well Player-Coach 1973-74 to 1977-78 'The Silver Years' with 3 District Cups and the Silver Ball Trophy, playing with brother Tony. Glamorgan Wanderers Coach 1978-1981, Cardiff Youth Coach 1981-1984, Taff's Well Coach 1985-88. 'Loving husband and father of two children and three grandchildren. A gifted rugby player who did his talking on the pitch.'

For the late Gwyn, Bleddyn, Bryn, Vaughan, Lloyd and Tony Williams.

For the late Donald Richard 'Don' Llewellyn (1933-2021), winner of several BAFTA awards; film producer, director and editor; local historian; Pentyrch RFC captain and president; honoured by the Gorsedd of Bards in 2018 for his contribution to his community; possibly the last speaker of the Gwenhwyseg south-east Welsh dialect.

For the late Dyfed Evans, Books Council of Wales, Llanbadarn Fawr, a fellow rugby aficionado.

For the late Colin Howe, a wonderful Cardiff prop, playing 261 games from 1952-1963

ACKNOWLEDGEMENTS

I have been so lucky, writing a book about a club and game that both are special to me, and enjoying every minute, despite the coronavirus problem kicking off just as I was starting research. This meant that personal interviews and library research were put on hold for almost two years, with my suffering long-Covid and two bouts of Covid putting it back even more. However, I was very fortunate in contacting men who were my heroes as a youngster – Cenydd Williams, Alun Priday and the late Colin Howe. And, with great gratitude, Cardiff Rugby Club's former fly-half Gabe Servini and Taff's Well's former scrumhalf Carey Collings helped me throughout. The late, great Don Llewellyn was an inspiration regarding Pentyrch's traditional rivalry with Taff's Well.

Lynne Barry thankfully untangled the genealogies of the Williams, Roberts and Tamplin families. Thanks to Mike Roberts who worked upon the family trees, digitised them and gave me information upon his father Roy Roberts MM, the uncle of the Williams brothers, who played with the older brothers. Also gratitude to Peter Thomas, the former player and author of the hugely entertaining and informative Taff's Well R.F.C. history.

The book relies extensively upon three brilliant resources – it would have been absolutely impossible without them:

D.E. 'Danny' Davies: *Cardiff Rugby Club – 'The Greatest' – 100 Years at Cardiff Arms Park: History and Statistics 1876-1975* (1975)

Don Llewellyn and Gerald Edwards: *The Williams Family (More than a Rugby Dynasty), The Garth Domain* No.26 December 2004

Peter Thomas: 1887-1987 - *A View from the Garth – One Hundred Years of Taff's Well Rugby* (1987)

CONTENTS

PREFACE

This book should have been written in 1980, when memories were still fresh of this wonderful achievement. In fact, if the brothers had been from England, France, or any other major rugby-playing country, that would have happened. Thus, it would have been better, with many individuals and the brothers themselves contributing. However, this is still a 'long' book, and one written over forty years ago would have had to be published in two or three volumes to do justice to Cardiff and their careers with that club, Taff's Well and Wales. The research and writing were virtually halted for over two years by the coronavirus outbreak, during which some playing colleagues of the brothers passed on. This is an amazing, and unique story which can never be replicated in any sport. I repeat, it is not 'quite unique', 'very unique' or any similar description – it is simply unique.

Any mistakes are my own and can be corrected quickly, as the book is available print-on-demand, as well as being stocked by bookshops and the Books Council of Wales - Cyngor Llyfrau Cymru. The writer and poet Dave Lewis, of Publish and Print, Pontypridd (publishandprint.co.uk) was of immense help, formatting the book and its tables and photographs – I cannot speak too highly of his professionalism. The book was 'too big' for my usual publishers, so I have used Publish and Print's services under my own imprint, Glyndŵr Publishing, to make it available at a reasonable price. The work could have been a quarter of the size, but that would not have given justice to two great clubs and hundreds of wonderful players, at a time when rugby was a much different – and amateur – sport. And their achievements over half a century need to be placed into context, to prove their worth. One can honestly posit that if these eight brothers had been English, or perhaps Scottish or Irish – or French, Australian, South African or New Zealanders, they would have been honoured in their countries and known world-wide. Growing up in relative poverty in a tiny village, living through the Second World War, and playing for what was acknowledged in their time as 'the greatest rugby club in the world' for a span of 40 years, they need to be remembered – **in all of sporting history, no other family will EVER COME CLOSE to the Williams brothers**.

INTRODUCTION

'*Between ourselves, we consider that our matches against Wales and England are secondary affairs. Our primary aim is to beat Cardiff.*' Bob Stuart, New Zealand captain, speech to Cardiff Rotary Club 16 November 1953 five days before the match

The definitions of 'hero', and 'unique', have changed in this author's lifetime. This book is about a sporting family – 'unique' in the literal sense. The eight brothers in this book, and their playing partners, were, and always will be 'heroes' to this author. Imagine, if you will, the Real Madrid football team, at the height of its powers in the global game, having eight brothers from a poor family playing for them, sometimes with four of those brothers at the same time. Or imagine Juventus, Barcelona, Liverpool – the Chicago Bulls – the New South Wales cricket team – the New England Patriots - or any world-class club in any team sport. It is unimaginable, but in another, full-contact, sport it happened. And this at a time when substitutes were not allowed – there were no 'squads' of perhaps 40 professional players, all hoping to play, just 15 amateurs playing for enjoyment. Injured players generally played on, being shifted to a position, usually the wing, with less chance of contact. And international caps were very rare – there were between 3 and 4 international matches every season, depending upon whether France were allowed to play, plus every few years a game for Cardiff and Wales against one of the major touring sides, New Zealand, South Africa and Australia.

In what was always acknowledged as '*the greatest rugby club in the world*', eight brothers from the small nearby village of Taff's Well played for Cardiff. What is astonishing is that the careers of the three eldest were severely damaged by the Second World War, when club and international games were suspended for over six years. Another three of the brothers had to serve more than two years of National Service in the Armed Forces. The youngest, Elwyn and Tony were too young for National Service. Their uncle Roy Roberts and cousin Bill Tamplin, who played with the older brothers, also served in the war. Many readers hopefully will have heard of the peerless Bleddyn Williams, who captained both Wales and Cardiff to beat the touring New Zealanders in 1953, when England, Ireland, Scotland and another 24 representative and club teams failed to do so. The tourists' only draw was at Swansea 6-6. Bleddyn was Cardiff captain in 1949-50 and Cardiff vice-captain in 1947-48, 1948-49 and 1950-51. He played for Wales 22 times, being universally regarded as the best centre in world rugby, playing in all five tests in the British Lions' 1950 tour of Australia and New Zealand. His career was hampered by the war, and as mentioned there were very few international games in his era.

All the brothers played for Taff's Well School and the village club. Bleddyn's younger brother Lloyd Williams also captained Wales, playing 13 times for the national team, and captained Cardiff in 1960-61 and 1961-62, having been vice-captain in 1958-59. Vaughan Williams played for Cardiff Athletic, then London Welsh First XV during his National Service, then for Neath First XV and Cardiff Athletic again. Elwyn Williams captained Cardiff Youth, played for Wales Youth and Wales Under-23s, had a final Welsh Trial, and would have played for Wales, but for breaking his leg at the height of his powers. The same applies to the Barbarian Cenydd, certain to be picked for Wales at outside half or centre, who instead was lured to rugby league's St. Helens. The youngest, Tony Williams ended his long career with Cardiff Firsts, to enjoy captaining the brilliant Cardiff Athletic team of 1972-73 and 1973-74. Bleddyn, Cenydd, Lloyd and Tony all played for the Barbarians, an unsurpassable record for a family, only equalled by the Biggs brothers of Cardiff. The two brothers who turned to rugby league, Gwyn pre-war and Cenydd post-war, joined the outstanding teams of their eras, Wigan and St Helens. Another brother, Bryn was away in the army during the war years, when Bleddyn trained as a fighter pilot and switched to gliders for the invasion of Europe. However, Bryn played alongside Bleddyn in Cardiff Athletic and the First XV. Gwyn, regarded as the greatest of the brothers, was almost killed in the war. Aged 17 when he played against New Zealand, he kept secret that he 'went North' to pay for Bleddyn's public school fees at Rheidol (Rydal) in North Wales, costing him many a Welsh cap, in Bleddyn's estimation. Theirs is the most astonishing story, of hardship, resilience, but most of all enormous talent and matching humility.

There were no substitutes in their era, from the eldest boy Gwyn Williams playing in 1934-35, as Cardiff's youngest ever player, until 1969. Mike Gibson replaced Cardiff's Barry John in the British Lions' First Test against South Africa in 1968, the first official injury replacement in a test. The first Five Nations injury substitute was by Scotland in 1969, with up to two now being allowed. Not until 1996 were three tactical substitutions allowed. In 2012 five replacements were allowed – for any reason, and now up to eight players can be replaced, with South Africa often using six men, 'the Bomb Squad', to beef up a tiring pack. This, wrongly, allows teams with greater resources to swing a game in the second half. Most commentators agree that too many subs are spoiling the game.

This author was privileged to see the youngest four brothers play many times, often together, when rugby was a strictly amateur (and far more attractive) sport. During their playing careers, and for almost a century, Cardiff was THE team that all touring countries wanted to play, and has supplied more players to Wales and the British Lions than any other club. (Josh Adams and Josh Navidi were the 61st and 62nd Cardiff 'Lions', in South Africa in 2021). To play for their reserves, the affectionately termed

4

'Rags' was a terrific achievement for any player, who could then hope for a series of performances to impress the senior team, and then dream of his Cardiff 'cap' with 20 appearances in a season for the First XV. This is not just the story of the most incredible sporting brothers, but of probably the greatest achievement in sporting history by siblings. The magical aura of Gwyn, Brinley, Vaughan, Bleddyn, Elwyn, Cenydd, Lloyd and Tony is vanishing, as seven of these great players have passed on, and there are fewer and fewer of us who remember the glorious days of the most famous club in rugby.

1950-51 Bleddyn Williams in British Isles (Lions) shirt

Where does one start? As noted, this book is arriving four decades too late. And there is far too much to write about. The brothers played a total of 1,480 times for the Cardiff First XV, and hundreds of games for the second team, helping develop new players. We must also note that each one of them also played for their village of Taff's Well – has there ever been any record approaching this in any field of sport? They all played in what was then an amateur game, juggling full-time work and family commitments, with up to 45 games in a season. The brothers were all noted for gentlemanly conduct, admired by both fellow players and opponents. Yet they are now virtually unknown, even in Wales. They played their first senior games for their local village, Taff's Well, with four (Bryn, Vaughan,

Elwyn and Tony) later re-joining the club, so the brothers' history with Cardiff RFC is intermingled with that of Taff's Well and its players. And the Williams boys were surrounded by some fabulous players, famous in their time, some of whom have been able to contribute their memories to this publication. Thus, along with other players from Taff's Well and surrounding villages, I have also attempted to paint a portrait of some of these players. For instance, Bleddyn Williams played for Cardiff alongside his brothers Brinley (Bryn) and Lloyd, and also his uncle Roy Roberts of Taff's Well and his cousin Bill Tamplin of Risca. He just missed out on playing with brother Cenydd, but from 1945-46 to his retirement in 1954-55, Bleddyn also played for Cardiff with John Llewellyn and Doug Jones (Taff's Well), Ray Bale and Alun Priday (neighbouring Tongwynlais) and Basil Evans, Glyn Williams and Derek Murphy from 'over the hill' Pentyrch.

There were eight Williams brothers and four sisters, brought up in a small, rented, terraced house, with a working-class father. Arthur Williams was a coal-tipper down at Cardiff Docks, who had to work all hours, and their mother Nell (formerly Roberts), looked after the family of fourteen. At this time, in England, Scotland and Ireland, rugby was very much a public school or grammar school game. Even now the English national team has a very substantial proportion of privately educated players. In Wales, it seemed like the bigger forwards were working class men, steelworkers, miners, farmers etc., while the smaller backs were more likely to be teachers, doctors and professionals with a better education. However, only Gwyn and Elwyn Williams were forwards, being the tallest of the brothers, while the other six were comfortable playing in various positions in the threequarters. Then again, in rugby league Gwyn often played on the wing as well as loose forward, and Elwyn could easily play in the centre if any back was injured. Danny Davies' magnificent centenary celebration book 'Cardiff Rugby Club – "The Greatest": History and Statistics 1876-1975' thankfully covers all their playing careers, from which I have taken a list of the eight leading Cardiff first-team appearances, up to the end of their time with the club.

1 Howard Norris 413 (14 seasons, 1958-59 to 1971-72) – prop, Wales.

2 Alun Priday 410 (14 seasons, 1952-53 to 1965-66) – fullback, Wales – it would have been more, but a Bridgend player ended his career by breaking his jaw in foul play.

3 **Elwyn Williams** 339 (15 seasons, 1958-59 to 1972-73) – wing forward, was set to play for Wales but broke his leg, losing 55 appearances. A new coach, overly impressed by New Zealand forward play, wanted forwards who looked for contact instead of directly playing the ball to the backs, so cut his appearances from 38 a year to 3 or 4 for four seasons, or Elwyn would have led the chart, possibly breaking the 450+ mark.

4 J.D. Evans 338 (10 seasons, 1951-52 to 1960-61) – prop, Wales.

5 Geoff Beckingham 331 (10 seasons, 1948-48 to 1957-58) – hooker, Wales.

6 **A.D. 'Tony' Williams** 328 (15 seasons, 1959-60 to 1973-74) – centre, outside-half.

7 D.J. 'Dai' Hayward 325 (10 seasons, 1957-58 to 1966-67) – flanker, Wales.

8 **Lloyd Williams** 310 (12 seasons, 1952-53 to 1963-64) – scrumhalf, outside-half, Cardiff and Wales captain. (All were forwards except Alun Priday, Tony and Lloyd Williams.)

The great centre Bleddyn Williams could not begin playing until the 1945-46 season, aged 21, when he scored 30 tries in 21 games, but still played 183 times. He missed perhaps close to 100 Cardiff games because of war, and many because of injury, while playing in up to 3 International Trials a year, 22 times for Wales, and captaining the British Lions. Gwyn Williams played 103 times from 1934-35 to 1938-39, when he joined Wigan Rugby League, the **best** league team of that time, and was severely injured at war. Cenydd Williams, an outside-half but mainly a centre like Bleddyn, Tony, Bryn and Vaughan, played 115 times between 1956-57 and 1962-63 before joining St Helens Rugby League, again then the **best** rugby league side in the world.

One of the Williams brothers played for Cardiff in every full season from 1934-35 to 1973-74 – a period of 40 years! And this was not just for any rugby club – it was *'the world's greatest club'.* Of the four youngest brothers Lloyd, Cenydd, and Elwyn played together for 4 years from 1958-59 to 1962-63. With Tony, all four appeared together in 1961-62 and 1962-63, until Cenydd joined the brilliant St. Helens Rugby League team, owing to the efforts of the legendary Alex Murphy. Elwyn and Tony left in 1973 and 1974 to win honours for their home team, Taff's Well.

The Williams boys played 1,480 times for Cardiff Firsts, to which we should add the familial appearances of their uncle Roy Roberts and cousin Bill Tamplin, to make a total of 1,747 First Team matches, plus many more games for Cardiff Athletic. Roy Roberts' career was on either side of the war, where he won the Military Medal, from 1936-37 to 1948-49, yet he made 150 appearances for Cardiff and then went on to captain Pontypridd. The Wales international captain Bill Tamplin played alongside Roberts in Cardiff's second row, making 252 appearances from 1945-46 to 1952-53. Both were fine kickers. (In those days, with a heavy leather mud-coated ball, most kickers were big forwards who had the necessary strength to hoof a dead-weight rain-sodden leather ball using the toe of the boot.)

But amazingly, there was another family of 8 brothers and 4 sisters, the Turnbulls, from the previous era just overlapping with the Williams – six of these brothers played for Cardiff and two for Wales, one captaining Wales. However, this was a rich family, unlike the Williams clan. Maurice Turnbull played cricket for England and rugby for Wales, and has been called *'Wales' most outstanding all-round sportsman'*. The Turnbulls were a truly remarkable sporting family, so they are added to the book, along with other bands of brothers who played for the *'Blue and Blacks'*. I have to add Bleddyn's mentor the Cambridge Blue Wilf Wooller – another man who has been called *'Wales' best all-round sportsman'* – excellent at rugby, football and cricket. Wooller was Cardiff and Wales rugby captain, later captain of Glamorgan cricket, played 18 times for Wales, and in 1935 he was inspirational in the Welsh victory over the All Blacks. He also scored a hat-trick for Cardiff City football club. 'Wilf' was captured by the Japanese, which ended his rugby career. A legend, Wooller played with Gwyn and Bleddyn, and massively influenced Bleddyn's career. There are excellent books upon Bleddyn Williams, Maurice Turnbull and Wilfred Wooller. However, this is a book also about fellow players, at both Taff's Well and Cardiff – rugby is a team game, and some of these great teammates of the brothers must also be mentioned in some detail.

To emphasise, in these days of no substitutes, if an injured player could hobble, he went out on the wing. Otherwise, he was carried off. Thus, the chance of getting a game for a top-class club was very, very difficult. And if selected, one had to perform well in **every** game. Great Cardiff players like Geoff Beckingham realised that they had to play at their very best in each game in order to be selected for the next. No-one wanted to miss a game, in case their replacement played so well that they were relegated to the second team, the Athletic. It was even worse with internationals. In Wales, the so-called 'Big Five' selectors were often guilty of bias, in trading off the selection of players, in order to get 'their' players selected from the club or region with which they had close ties. And sometimes Wales only played three internationals in a season, when France was suspended from the Five Nations Championship, instead of today's overload of a constant merry-go-round of visits and tours and competitions. An international career, with so few games, and so few men involved, was several times as difficult to achieve as today.

Because of Cardiff's influence on the game, and their high number of international players, their history is interlinked with that of the national team. From 1883-1910, the Home Nations Championship meant that there were just three internationals a year, expanded to four from 1919-1931 when France joined to form the 'Five Nations.' However, France was excluded from 1932 to 1939, but there was a return to four fixtures from 1940-1999 upon its return. Since 2000, with Italy's admission, the Six Nations ensures five games a year for each team. Upon alternate years Wales plays the 'Blues', Scotland, France and Italy, away. The fixtures away against England and Ireland every other year make it difficult to achieve a Triple Crown or Grand Slam in those years, likewise with France away. As regards games against the 'Big Three' Southern Hemisphere teams, in the period of this book, international games were played at home against New Zealand 7 times: - 1905-06, 1924-25, 1953-53, 1963-64, 1967, 1972-73 and 1974; South Africa 7 times - 1906-07, 1912-13, 1931-32, 1951-52, 1960-61, 1966-67, 1969-70; and Australia 6 times - 1908-09, 1939-40, 1947-48, 1957-58, 1966-67, 1973. Taking away the two war periods of 13 years when no matches could be played, from 1905 to 1973 there were in 20 major visiting teams in 55 years, i.e. roughly every three years there would be an extra international game to add to the three or four per year. Now it is averaging thirteen games a year, weakening club sides, and with international 'windows' halting club fixtures and helping drive away supporters.

There is now an absurd number of international matches, of increasingly devalued games, which are played each year for extra financial benefit to the respective Rugby Unions, but which lead to many long-term injuries. In the days of Gareth Edwards and Barry John, and then Phil Bennett, the same team picked itself for virtually every game – four games a season, and five every few years against a touring team. To have an international cap meant that you were a truly special player. However, the number of international matches played by Wales each year from 1999 until November 2021 has been 14, 8, 11, 11, 16, 12, 11, 11, 15, 11, 10, 12, 17, 13, 12, 11, 13, 13, 10, 11, 16, 10 and 12. That is 280 games in 23 years, around 12 hard internationals a year, plus for some players brutal British Lions tours every four years. Players are taller, bigger and fitter than in amateur days. Players from the 1950s would be dwarfed by their modern counterparts, with modern top-class three-quarters being bigger and heavier than most of yesterday's forwards. In 1955, the average player's body mass was 84.8 kg (13st 5lb). In 1995, the game turned professional, and by 2015 the average weight had risen to 105.4 kg (16st 8lb), an increase of 24.3%. Today, the average size of a professional rugby player in Europe is 102 kg (16 stone 9 pounds) in weight and 1.87 metres (6ft 1in) in height. The average size of a forward now is 112.55kg (17st 10lbs) and 1.90m (6ft 2in) and the average size of a back is 91.7kg (14st 6lb) and 1.83m (6ft). The biggest increase has been in the backs. At the 2015 Rugby World Cup, the Welsh backs had the potential to be heavier on average than the New Zealand forwards who played in the 1987 tournament. In New Zealand, between 1974 and 2014, research revealed the average height and weight of backs increased by four inches and around 2 stone 3 pounds (14kg). The switch to professionalism prompted advances in fitness and conditioning, and the increased weight is increasingly striking. England's 1991 team, considered big by the standards of the day, then weighed 14st 8lb (94.3kg) on average, compared with 16st 6lb (105.8kg) in 2019.

Because hookers stopped striking for the ball, as no penalties were given for crooked feeds into a scrum, English hookers have seen the biggest weight increase across the Six Nations since 1995, with an increase of 16.5

per cent in 25 years. Some hookers are now taller and bigger than their props, as they no longer have to strike for the ball. Research tells us that the average impact force at the hit of a scrum is 10,850 Newtons. To compare, a knockout punch is 3,000 Newtons. All sides in the Six Nations have seen a major increase in the size of their forwards. France usually dominates the heaviest pack contest, with its forwards in 2020 called the 'heaviest pack in history,' weighing in at over 18 stone average per player. However, the England pack in 2021 weighed 952kg, almost 19 stone per forward. The game is turning into American Football, where ferocious hard contact is more appreciated than non-contact skills. The point is that, in the past, it was much more difficult to be selected for international matches, unlike today's match-day squads of 23 players who all expect to play. Also, today's concentration upon full contact in training, and match contact between much bigger and probably over-trained players has led to far more harmful collisions, with players sometimes being out of the game for up to two years with injuries.

1936-37 Gwyn Williams is 2nd left seated middle row. Les Spence is captain

However, this is the story of a far better, more attractive game, of an overlapping, intricate network of people and events, telling the story of eight brothers, also of Taff's Well RFC, its surrounding rugby clubs like Pentyrch and Tongwynlais, and of Cardiff RFC and of Welsh rugby during the brothers' four decades of playing. We have to place the importance of Taff's Well Rugby Club in the first appearances of Gwyn Williams, soon playing as a seventeen-year-old for Cardiff against the All Blacks in 1935, through all the brothers' playing careers, up to Elwyn and Tony ending at Cardiff, then winning trophies with Taff's Well and then Elwyn finishing coaching in 1988. We have 40 years of the brothers playing for Cardiff, plus another 14 with Elwyn coaching Taff's Well, Glamorgan Wanderers, Cardiff Youth, being asked to coach Cardiff, and then coaching Taff's Well again. And remember, the Second World War and National Service affected the rugby of six of the brothers, with only the youngest two, Elwyn and Tony missing military duties. Additionally, we have to 'prove' that Cardiff was indeed the *'greatest rugby club'* in the world – it was certainly the most famous - and place its importance to the Welsh team. Thus the narrative begins in the nineteenth century, with more detailed Cardiff RFC information from the 1930s with Gwyn Williams playing, to Tony Williams joining his brother Elwyn for two seasons at Taff's Well in 1974. Taff's Well RFC is covered from its formation, up to Elwyn retiring from coaching the team.

I hope the book is not too confused. The problem is giving justice to far too many great men, who played for the love of sport, not money, and gave spectators terrific entertainment, on far poorer pitches, much removed from the Crash-Bang-Wallop which passes for the overly vicious rugby of today. With international teams now averaging over 16 stone per man, perhaps the term *'thugby'* is more apt, with the Australian coach Eddie Jones urging his England team to be more *'brutal'* and to *'crush'* the opposition in every game. For Cardiff RFC, before 'modern' rugby, the emphasis was always upon a non-contact game, moving the ball in thrilling, passing movements, like flowing cavalry attacks if the pitch was good enough. It was *'the Cardiff way'*, and it attracted the finest backs to the Arms Park. They knew that on reasonable pitches they would have the opportunity to participate. The Cardiff forwards' job was to get the ball out to the half-backs, who, unless there was an opportunity to break, would quickly pass to the centres for the wings to have a run. And Cardiff's best wings, such as Maurice Richards and Gerald Davies, began their careers as centres, determined not to 'die' with the ball. Unfortunately, the state of early pitches often militated against such a strategy, with the 'best' games being in Autumn and Spring.

Today the game is a contact sport, much admired for 'big hitters', played by massive men, where the ball may move a yard of so forwards or backwards, in over 20 phases of possession. It rarely flows – it is often like trench warfare with some players making 25 tackles per game. The spectators and commentators who 'love' it are often those that admire boxing, other blood sports, and more often people who have never played rugby. It is no wonder that there are fewer and fewer people attracted to play or watch such a violent game, that is incredibly difficult to explain. The Rugby Union 'Laws' book in the 1960s had about 12 pages. Now it

11

runs to 160. Past players, without exception to my knowledge, are dismayed by the modern game. In the past, the ball went 'straight' into the middle of the scrum, both hookers 'struck' for it, and the scrum hardly ever collapsed except in muddy conditions. The referee never gave instructions, unlike today's performing arts, where the ball is placed in the second row and the scrum immediately wheels or collapses several times. In a recent Irish international, 25 minutes of the allotted 80 were taken up with scrummaging. In my lifetime, lines-out (they were never line-outs in the past) were taken almost immediately, to pre-arranged line-out calls, compared to today's huddled conferences and time-wasting. There was far more time in active play – watch any Welsh international game from the 1970s and 1980s, with skills of side-step, swerve, change of pace, dummy, different weights of pass etc. on display. Compare that to today's boring top-class fare of trench warfare interspersed with 'kickfests', interminable scrums, line-out conferences and the like. That is not the rugby of the past. And there will be no rugby of the future, if there are not weight restrictions upon teams and sensible laws. The game must be made easier to understand, to attract players and spectators. This is a book about a different time, different people and a different game – indeed, a better time, better people and a better game. In mini-rugby, New Zealand children are allocated to teams by size, not age, so fewer drop out when contact tackling comes into the game. (I would put an average weight limit of international teams at 15 stone, which would make for better rugby, and reduce the number of substitutes to three, not eight).

And were Cardiff truly 'the greatest'? In club games, against the cream of England and Wales, and sometimes Scotland and Ireland, and the Southern Hemisphere 'Big Three', just read on, checking the number of tries for and against in every season. The Cardiff game was treated as an international by touring teams, who always fielded their strongest side. Cardiff defeated Australia in all four games in the time this book covers, scoring 12 tries to five. Cardiff beat South Africa in 1907, 17-0, but then lost 7-6, 13-5, 11-9, 13-0 and 17-3. The 11-9 defeat saw a perfectly good try disallowed, and the 13-0 was a disgraceful game where Cardiff played most of the game with 14 men and three badly injured players for most of the game. (I was there…) Against New Zealand, games were lost 10-8 (by a dreadful mistake), 16-8, 20-5, 6-5 (Cardiff scoring the only try) and 20-4. However, in 1953 Bleddyn Williams led Cardiff and Wales to defeat the All Blacks, their only losses in 29 matches in the British Isles.

CHAPTER 1 - THE WILLIAMS FAMILY OF TAFF'S WELL

There has always been confusion about the relationship of Bill Tamplin to the Williams brothers and sisters, resolved below thanks to Lynne Barry (see sources). It makes sense to place the children in order, as it was a large family, and include the children's parents, their uncle Roy Roberts and second cousin, Bill Tamplin who are integral to their story. Thus, this short section may seem a little 'boring' compared to the rest of the contents of the book, but it will help future researchers into this unique family. I have included family trees of the Williams, Roberts and Tamplin families in Chapter 48, kindly researched and collated by Lynne Barry. Some death dates are missing, as many records do not contain details of other Christian names on death certificates, and Williams is such a popular surname that too much time would be spent finding the correct person/date.

*Arthur and Nell Williams, with Tony, Bleddyn, Cenydd,
Elwyn, Lloyd, Vaughan, Bryn and Gwyn*

THE PARENTS

Mary Ellen 'Nellie or Nell' Roberts born September 1898 in Risca.
Her parents were Edward (Ted) George Roberts and Susan Roberts, née Lewis. 'Ted' Roberts played rugby for Risca in the Monmouthshire League before moving to Taff's Well for work, and where he also played rugby, becoming a formative force in the early years of the rugby club. Over 26 years 'Nell' had 12 children who survived: 1915 (girl), 1918 (boy), 1921 (boy), 1923 (boy), 1926 (girl), 1928 (girl), 1931 (boy), 1933 (boy), 1935

(girl), 1938 (boy), 1940 (boy) and 1941 (boy).

Arthur Lougher Williams b.1891, Cardiff
His brother Philip Williams, b. 1874, played for Taff's Well and Cardiff Athletic, and like the brother's grandfather, Ted Roberts, influenced the Williams brothers in their aptitude for rugby.
Parents Charles Williams and Susan Williams, née Griffiths.

Married 1 March 1915, when Arthur was a trooper in the Glamorgan Yeomanry, aged 23, living at Kings Road Cardiff, and 'Nell' was in Gwaelod-y-Garth. His father was a dock labourer and her father a collier.

THE CHILDREN – 8 boys, 4 girls

Dilys Myfanwy Williams b. 5 October 1915 registered 9 November.
Born when her mother Nellie/Nell Williams was just 17. Dilys was born at her mother's parents' house, 5 Bristol Terrace in nearby Gwaelod-y-Garth, Pentyrch parish. Her grandmother Susan Roberts was present at the birth. Dilys was the only child not born in Taff's Well. At the time Arthur Williams's rank or profession was given as '*Trooper, Glamorgan Yeomanry, Colliery Proprietor's Clerk*'. Dilys married Stanley G. Jones, miner at Ty Nant Colliery in 1934.

Gwyn Glyndwr Williams b.20 May 1918, registered 18 June. D.15 February 1997. His mother's name on the birth certificate was now given as 'Nellie' Williams, formerly Roberts. He was born at 11 Moy Road, Taff's Well. His father Arthur was now registered as Private 100096 Machine Gun Corps, and was still away fighting until 11 November 1918, now Armistice Day, so Nellie informed the birth. Gwyn married Eunice M. Williams in the third quarter of 1941, registered in East Glamorgan.

Brinley ('Bryn') Edward Lougher Williams b.23 December 1920, registered 1 Feb 1921. D.7 April 2011, aged 90, in Cardiff. His father Arthur Williams was now registered as a Coal Tipper on Cardiff Docks. Bryn married a local girl, Elizabeth Phillips in 1939 in Pontypridd.

Bleddyn Llewellyn Williams 22 February 1923 - 6 July 2009. The middle name is missing on Bleddyn's birth certificate. Married Violet J. Harry in 1944 in Cardiff. She was 'a lovely girl', according to Mair Williams and others who knew her. Children - Bleddyn Ashley, Lynne Gamblin and Leslie Anne Morgan.

Enid Mary Williams b.10 December 1925, registered March 1926 married Dilwyn Pritchard in East Glamorgan in 1944, but he died aged 40.

14

Enid watched every Cardiff game she could.

Joan Beryl Williams b.20 May 1928 married David R 'Goff' Roberts, a miner at Ty Nant Colliery, in East Glamorgan in 1944.

'The Clan' – Gwyn, Cenydd, Lloyd, Bryn, Tony, Vaughan, Bleddyn and Elwyn

Vaughan Ronald Williams b. 3 August 1931, registered September. D. 4th quarter of 2005, aged 74. His aunt Ada Lancaster (nee Roberts) was present at the birth. Married Marjorie G. Gummer in 1968 in East Glamorgan. A son Huw, in Porthcawl.

Lloyd Hugh Williams 19 October 1933 – 25 February 1997 M. first Anne E. Ambler 1958 in Cardiff; 2nd marriage to Lyn. His name was usually spelt Huw in later years.

Mair Olwen Williams 14 January 1936 (registered 5 March 1956) married Brian P. Phillips, who worked in Forgemasters, in 1962. Mair worked in Cardiff's Hamadryad Hospital. Her father, after a few years being registered as a Coal Tipper, is now a Coal Weigher. Nell William's sister, Ada Lancaster (b.1901) was registered as being present at the birth, and living at 62 Cardiff Road, Taff's Well.

Cenydd Owen Williams was born 20 July 1938, at 10 Moy Road, according to the birth certificate, whereas all his siblings except Dilys were registered at 11. His name is spelt Cenydd on the birth certificate, but he has always spelt it Cennydd. (Either would be correct. All articles and programmes use one 'n', so I have kept that spelling). One of twins, a brother did not survive long. Arthur Williams is now a Coal Tipper again. 'Cen' married Margaret J. Phillips, known as Jean, from Rhydfelen in 1961. Their son Gregory died aged 41, and grandson Dan's mother died of cancer aged 37.

Elwyn Rhys Williams born 6 November 1939, D. 31 August 2022. Married Anne Humphrys in 1962, who was *'a fabulous person'* according to Mair. Anne was the sister of John Humphrys of Cardiff, the television and radio interviewer/presenter and writer. Mair said Elwyn was also 'excellent at golf.' Elwyn looked after his wife and mother-in-law, as both developed dementia. Later, Elwyn, like his brothers Lloyd and Tony, also succumbed to the illness.

Anthony 'Tony' David Williams 1 February 1941 – 3 September 2014
Tony's mother Nell was now 43, and there was a 26-year gap between the eldest sibling, Dilys, and Tony. Children - Eifion Lloyd and Cenydd Hywel (named after brothers Lloyd and Cenydd), grand-daughter Cerys Ellen. He married Euronwy Morfydd Emmanuel in East Glamorgan in 1962.

All the brothers and sisters at Tony's wedding

RELATIVES who played for Cardiff with the brothers – their brief biographies are included in the text:

William (Bill) Ewart Tamplin 10 May 1917 (registered 12 June) – 20 October 1979

Bill was born at 12 Dixon's Place, Risca, Rogerstone District, Monmouthshire. His parents were (the same name) William Ewart Tamplin (snr.) and Mabel Ann Lewis, who married in Newport in 1918. Mabel's sister Susan Lewis was 11 years older, and married Ted Roberts of Taff's Well, the father of Roy Roberts. Susan Roberts (née Lewis) was the grandmother of the Williams brothers and sisters, with the first child Dilys being born in her house in Gwaelod-y-Garth. Thus Bill Tamplin snr. and Nell Roberts were first cousins, Bill Tamplin jnr. and the Williams boys were second cousins. Bill was also a nephew of Roy Roberts. On his birth certificate, his father's rank and profession were Private, 3rd Battalion South Wales Borderers, also a Colliery Timberman.

Leslie Roydon (Roy) Roberts MM 3 June 1917 – 9 November 1988
Roy was the younger brother of Nell Williams, née Roberts, the Williams boys' mother, and the son of Ted Roberts, a driving force in Taff's Well RFC, who had previously played Monmouthshire League rugby for Risca. Roy's older sister Nell was born in September 1891, and Roy almost 26 years later in June 1917. Nell's second child Gwyn Williams was born in May 1918, so was almost the same age as his uncle Roy Roberts, who played rugby for Cardiff pre-war with Gwyn Williams and post-war with Bleddyn Williams and Bill Tamplin. Susan Lewis was the first wife of Ted Roberts. Roy Roberts' son Mike remembers, '*She had died probably before I was born and I only briefly remember my grandfather's second wife who we knew as 'aunty', because she was Susan's sister. 'Aunty' died circa 1951, after which dad, mum, my sister & myself moved in with grandfather* (Ted Roberts, in Taff's Well), *in order to look after him.*'

'*SPORTING FAMILIES – 8 WILLIAMS… – Two Welsh Skippers – two R.L. stars'*

In Cardiff and Wales hooker Geoff Beckingham's scrapbooks (- kindly loaned by *rugbyrrelics.com*, there is a torn-out piece from the *South Wales Echo*, Saturday 8 June 1968. Entitled *Sporting Families*, the headline is '*8 WILLIAMS'* but the rest of the heading is missing. The sub-heading is '*Two Welsh Skippers – two R.L. stars.*' The sixth brother to play for Cardiff, Cenydd, had just turned professional. The last two brothers were to finish playing for Cardiff in 1973 and 1974, and both returned to play for their village team Taff's Well. I repeat the entire article by Malcolm Lewis, to give readers a flavour of what this book is about – brilliance – eight siblings who dazzled spectators – and who were humble participants in a unique event. One hears presenters and people on TV talking about 'very unique', 'quite unique' and 'most unique' events/people or whatever. They have a problem with language. Unique has come to mean 'exceptional' or rare or distinctive – but its real meaning is unreplicable.

17

Something that has never happened, ever. A single event or happening that can never happen again. Try to imagine eight brothers, with no money behind them, from a small rented terraced house that they shared with their parents and four sisters, all playing for what was in their era, recognised as '*the greatest club in the world*'. It was a purely amateur and physical sport, in careers broken for four of them by six years of war and for two of them by over two years of national service, yet they still managed 1,480 games for Cardiff First XV, and two captained Wales. This is not 'truly' unique, not 'really' unique – it is UNIQUE. One hopes that if you read this following newspaper report from 1962, you will be enthused to read the rest of the book. I loved writing it, and I hope that comes across. The paragraphing, headlines, capitals and bold sections are taken exactly from the article.

'*From the modest home in Moy Road, Taff's Well, has sprung a remarkable family of eight brothers. All of them have played rugby for Cardiff; two have captained Wales and two have won fame elsewhere by going North to play with distinction in Rugby League.*

The Williams brothers hardly need any introduction. In order of seniority, Gwyn, Brinley, Bleddyn, Vaughan, Lloyd, Cenydd, Elwyn and Tony have put Taff's Well on the rugby map and made their family name ring around the world. All have shown an uncanny instinct for mastering the basic skills and applying them with intelligence and finesse.

BLEDDYN, the holder of 22 Welsh caps and the most famous of the brothers, is a prime example of the way they have striven for perfection. As a centre he had no equal. Beautifully balanced and the possessor of a wonderful jink, he was in a class of his own. His perfectly delivered passes and octopus-like tackles contribute to the all-round brilliance of his play.

Powerful

He captained both Cardiff and Wales, as did LLOYD, whose big and strong build made him the most powerful scrum half of his time. Lloyd's football ability was such that he made a good job of playing at outside half for Cardiff for a time. By the end of his playing career, he had made more than 300 appearances for the club which he now serves as a member of the committee.

One by one, the family graduated through the local village school of Ffynnon Taf bordering the River Taff. There they came under the expert tuition of coach Del Harris, who did so much in giving them their early grounding and maintaining the steady flow of the Williams clan into the Cardiff club.

GWYN began it all in 1935 by playing at wing forward for Cardiff against the famous All Blacks at the tender age of 17 years! What is more he helped them beat the famous tourists. (The passage is emboldened, as in the text, but Cardiff actually lost that match.)

Tragic end

Even at that age he was an outstanding player, but Wales did not see the best of him, because within a few years he had signed for Wigan for about £400. There he played for the Wales Rugby League team, only for his brilliant career to be cut short by the war and a terrible injury, while serving in the North African desert. His courage and fortitude pulled him through, but his playing days were tragically finished and he is now quietly living in Swanage, Dorset.

BRINLEY was the next to arrive at Cardiff. He could play either at outside half or centre and appeared for the club before and after the war. He also had a spell with Cross Keys before returning to his home club of Taff's Well where he served them both as a player and a committee-man. He still lives in the village and works as a salesman.

After Bleddyn came VAUGHAN, another big and strong centre. He played with Lloyd in the "Rags" before leaving to turn out for Neath and then Pontypridd. He, too, ended his playing days with Taff's Well, where he is running a fruit and fish-mongery business.

CENYDD moved down the valley and sprang up through the Cardiff Youth and Athletic sides. Able to fit in at outside half or centre with equal skill, he was recognised by the Barbarians and was in the running for a Welsh cap when he elected to go North. He collected £6,000 from St. Helens for his signature in 1962 and is still playing for them.

ELWYN emerged as the second brother to play in the pack. Winning Welsh schoolboy and youth caps, he became a cultured blind-side wing forward for Cardiff. He was singled out for Welsh under-23 honours and also had a Welsh trial, but had the misfortune to break a leg two seasons ago and this has hampered his development.

The last of the line is TONY, who is most probably the most wily of the brothers since Bleddyn. Like the Rydal-trained Bleddyn, he went to a public school – Christ College, Brecon – and the rigorous training he underwent there polished him into an astute performer. Centre is his best position, although he has helped Cardiff on a number of occasions at outside half. He has that wonderful Williams knack of doing the right thing at the right time, and had he been blessed with a little more speed he would have played for Wales by now.

Triple bid

Indeed it is only by the narrowest of margins that the Williams family have failed to join the select company of the Gould and Jones families, who have each provided Wales with a set of three brothers. Who knows? - they may yet do it. Elwyn and Tony still have years of rugby ahead of them.

The thick strain of rugby in the family comes from the mother's side. She is of Monmouthshire stock. Her father, Ted Roberts, played for Risca in the Monmouthshire league and her nephew is former Cardiff and Wales forward Bill Tamplin. Roy Roberts, who also played for Cardiff, is another *member of the family.'* (Roy was their mother Nell Roberts' younger brother). *'It is a sore point with father, a retired coal-trimmer, that he cannot boast of a similar rugby tree on his side of the family. The best he can do is that he had a brother who played in a Mallett Cup final!'* (Actually, Arthur Williams was a coal tipper not a trimmer, the latter being a job with a drastically reduced life-span, breathing in dust, while balancing ('trimming') loads of coal being tipped into the holds of ships for export and for fuel. Arthur's brother Philip, 16 years older, played for Taff's Well and Cardiff Athletic and encouraged the brothers. The Mallett Cup, dating from 1894, is the oldest cup competition in Wales). *'Not that he ever worries about it. What with eight sons, besides four daughters, Dilys, Enid, Joan and Mair, he heads a family of which he can be proud.'*

In Fred Croster's long profile of Lloyd Williams, May 1968, later in this book, he ends with a description of the brothers and their parents: 'From their humble beginning in Moy Road, Taff's Well, just alongside the main road, have come all the Williams players who have earned fame on the rugby fields of the world.

No. 1 was elder brother Gwyn. He was an outstanding forward, played for Cardiff when they played the All Blacks in 1935 in 1935. He was only 16 when he joined the Club and started the flow, down the river, to the famous ground on its banks. Gwyn, tall, curly-haired, good-looking, went North to Wigan in 1937; played for Wales Rugby League and then left when war broke out. During the war he was very seriously wounded in North Africa, left for dead, very nearly did die and had experiences too dreadful to recount. Happily fully recovered now, Gwyn left the County Hall where he worked for a number of years, and is settled comfortably at Swanage.

No. 2 was Bryn - he was an outside half or centre; started off with Taff's Well, then went to Cardiff, played for the 1sts and the "Rags", before and after the war; then went to Cross Keys, then back to play for Taff's Well again and spent a number of years on their committee when his playing days were over. Still about, still living locally, Bryn, always smiling, is never far away when there is the smell of a rugby ball in the air.

No. 3 was the immortal Bleddyn. So much has been said about this "Prince of Three quarters", that anything I say will only be superfluous. I will only add that I have known Bleddyn for 26 years and still marvel at the man.

No. 4 was Vaughan - another centre: Vaughan, big, strong, with the unmistakable Williams stamp, started again with Taff's Well, went down to the Arms Park, played for the "Rags", then went to Neath, then back to Pontypridd and ended his playing career back at Taff's Well, where it all started. Vaughan is still local and looks as fit as ever. Also played for the Welsh Guards (B.O.A.R.)

No. 5 was Lloyd, the subject of this profile, which has been such a pleasure to write.

No. 6 was Cenydd - from Taff's Well, straight down to Cardiff Youth, then to the "Rags", then the 1sts, then the Baa-Baas, was well in the running for a Welsh Cap as a centre with tremendous ability and potential. Strong, determined, as were they all, Cenydd then went North to St. Helens. Mixed fortune there, mainly due to a severe knee injury, but is happily now fully recovered, doing well again and thoroughly enjoying life. Cenydd also played for the R.A.F. and the Combined Services.

No. 7 was Elwyn - a forward, only the second, but what a good one, and one able to play in the backs whenever the occasion called, as it often did when someone was injured. Elwyn was capped for the Welsh Schoolboys in the second row, then went to Cardiff Youth, earned his Welsh Youth Cap; went on to play for the "Rags", then established himself for the 1sts, as one of the outstanding blind-side wing forwards. He played for Wales Under-23s against Canada, has a very good Welsh Trial, was unfortunate not to be selected, then when at his peak broke his leg against London Welsh. Is recovered now, playing hard and determined to "Get back in". A fine 7's player.

No. 8 Tony - played for Cardiff Schools under-11's as an outstanding outside half. Gained a scholarship to Christ College, Brecon. Here he came under A.T. "Akka" Thomas, former Cardiff pre-war wing, coaching rugger at Brecon then, now back in Cardiff, on the committee; former chairman and co-founder of the Youth Section. Tony benefited greatly here - in one memorable Llandovery "Battle", he earned Brecon a draw by tacking Colin Elliot, their "Star" O/H, out of the game. Tony came then to Cardiff Youth, then Welsh Youth, then the "Rags", then the 1sts, acting captain at this very moment and one of the finest Club players Cardiff have ever had. Was bitterly disappointed at non-selection for the Australian game. Suffered then, as he was considered for the O/H position, not centre, where he has been such a wonderful servant.' (Also, Tony was only just back after a long injury lay-off). 'Was the player of the 7's at Newport recently in the Memorial Tournament, won the Final of the Snelling Sevens for Cardiff last year and contributed so much to Cardiff's consistently fine displays. The proud father of a very young son, he has recently measured him for his first pair of boots.

No.9 - I nearly automatically went on. Has there ever been such an array of talent - all from the same stock and all with allegiance to the Cardiff Club? I think it's wonderful.

All this talent must inevitably be in the blood, as although father, now 75, was not a well-known player himself, he had a brother who played in a Cardiff Mallet Cup Final. Mother, although now aged 70, still takes active, proud, interest, as both have throughout all the years. Mother's sister was the sister of Bill Tamplin, another whose name will never die; Roy Roberts of the same great Cardiff era is her own brother, thus the young Uncle of the Williams boys. Roy still looks as well as ever, and is still "Around". Tom Roberts was another good player, as was cousin Ray. There was also Ted who seemed destined to become a great forward until he sadly died in 1937 at the age of only 21.

1939-40 Gwyn Williams and Roy Roberts
at the back of 11 Moy Road

These "Roberts", the relations on that wonderful Mother's side, could well have inherited their talent from Grandfather "Ted" Roberts, who, at the age of 87, still takes considerable interest and is still an active Taff's Well character. In his day, he played for Risca, prominent always in the Monmouthshire League. Is it any wonder that Taff's Well could so aptly be called "Williams Town"? The wonder is that, despite their fame, they all stay close to their birthplace in spirit and body; are still attached in the way that seems to belong to Welsh families particularly.' This is the story to be told, but we first have to explain why Cardiff held the peak position amongst rugby clubs – across the world - for a century.

CHAPTER 2 - CARDIFF'S IMPORTANCE TO THE GAME

FROM THE BEGINNING - THE FIRST GOLDEN ERA FOR CARDIFF AND WALES – THE FOUR THREE-QUARTER SYSTEM – 1907 – CARDIFF'S GREATEST WIN? - THE UNIQUE 'TWO FIRST TEAMS' EXPERIMENT 1926-27 to 1930-31 – THE FIRST 'GOLDEN ERA' FOR CARDIFF AND WALES - A BRIEF SUMMARY OF THE CLUB'S HISTORY TO THE 70s

'... *pass out to half backs at once, and so get the ball away from your opponents' forwards as quickly as possible.*' - paragraph from a newspaper report of 1883, from *One Hundred Years of Scarlet*, by Gareth Hughes - a lesson that seems to be sadly forgotten.

1884-85 Cardiff team

Cardiff Rugby Football Club was founded in 1876 following the amalgamation of two clubs – Glamorgan, and Cardiff Wanderers. The first competitive game was played away against Newport, at Wentloog Marshes on 2 December 1876. The first home fixtures were played at Sophia Gardens, but the club soon moved two hundred yards to Cardiff Arms Park, in the grounds of the old Cardiff Hotel, and the venue was named after the local Cardiff Arms public house, There were complaints about the original club strip of black, with white skull and crossbones on the front, presumably because pirates had sinister connotations. However, in training Thomas Williams Rees always wore his Gonville & Gaius College, Cambridge colours. These were adopted, Cambridge Blue and Black, with Cardiff becoming known through their history as the 'Blue and Blacks'. The colours were worn until the disastrous advent of regional rugby from 2003 until 2021.

Crowds were declining, and an experiment was made for 2003-2004, putting four regions at the pinnacle of the Welsh game. The move was bitterly opposed by other clubs and their supporters, and did not halt the decline in attendances and players. Very basically, Cardiff became the 'Blues'; Llanelli the 'Scarlets'; Newport were now the Newport-Gwent 'Dragons', and then just the 'Dragons'/'Dreigiau'; and Neath and Swansea were merged to become the Neath-Swansea 'Ospreys', later the 'Ospreys'/'Gweilch' playing in Swansea.

The renamed Cardiff 'Blues' usually wore pastel blue and navy, with a none too imposing pink away strip for some years, worn with a notable lack of success. Regional results in leagues and cups have been dismal, despite the success of the national team. Thankfully, Cardiff has now reverted to becoming Cardiff Rugby/Rygbi Caerdydd, with the Blues feeder club, Cardiff, regaining its former name of Cardiff RFC, the much-loved former 'Rags', and both playing primarily in their traditional blue and black.

Danny Davies calls 1876-77 to 1884-85 *'the Foundation Years'* of Cardiff, building up to *'the Golden'* or *'Supreme Period'* of around 1905-06 to 1908-09. In 1881 the first Welsh international match took place, with four players from Cardiff. The Welsh Rugby Football Union was formed on 12 March 1881 at the Castle Hotel, Neath. Domestically Cardiff won the South Wales Challenge Cup on 12th March 1881 against Llanelly (as then spelt). The competition was disbanded shortly afterwards due to persistent problems with the crowd. A Cardiff second team was organised in 1881-82, and in 1884-85 to 1885-86, were unbeaten, scoring 512 points to 29. This indicated the strength of players wishing to play for the team, and hopefully move on up to the Firsts. In 1884 Cardiff's Frank Hancock initiated the four three-quarters system, so there were now 7 backs and 8 forwards, a move that eventually revolutionised the game. 1885-86 was referred to as *'Hancock's Year'* with 26 wins and 1 loss, scoring 533 points to 18 – it was an amazing passing team, which only lost the last match to Moseley because of Hancock's dictum of only scoring tries. He warned his players never to attempt drop goals, only tries were to be scored. The ethos remained for decades.

In that year, the team scored no penalties, dropped goals nor goals from a mark, just 133 tries against 4 (3 by Moseley and 1 by

Gloucester). Cardiff had beaten Moseley 11-5 away, scoring 3 tries to 1, but succumbed 10-3 at home, 2-1 on tries, Hancock refusing to take kicks to win the game. Gloucester scored the other try at home, just losing to 2 tries, 6-3, but Cardiff won 32-0 at home, scoring 8 tries, 4 converted. Newport were beaten by 13 tries, 3 converted, 36-0 and 23-0. In the final game of the previous season, Swansea were beaten 30-0, Cardiff scoring 6 tries and a dropped goal, and winning the previous 3 fixtures. Cardiff again won all four Swansea fixtures in 1885-86, not dropping a point. Neath suffered 8 tries in one game, Llanelli 10 tries, strong Northern England clubs were beaten, and W.M. Douglas scored 4 tries against Newport in one game, repeated by Bleddyn Williams in 1947-48. The team weaved what was called *'Blue and Black Magic'*, led by a *'Messiah'*, Frank Hancock. To be fair, only 9 of 27 games were away fixtures at this time. In the other 24 games, against teams like Swansea, Newport, Llanelli, Harlequins, Castleford, Dewsbury, Moseley, Liverpool, London Welsh and Neath, Cardiff did not concede a single point. From this period, for the duration of this book, over a century, Cardiff were *'the team to beat'* and always drew large crowds across England and Wales.

Frank Hancock's last season was 1885-86, when they played Cirencester away and home, winning 23-0 and 25-0, and scoring 12 tries in the process, 6 converted. In the first Cirencester game, on 31 October 1885, he caused a sensation when he threatened to send off one of his own team, for attempting a drop goal, disobeying his strict orders. However, the strict disciplinarian had retired by next season, when Cardiff won 19-0 away and 40-0 at home, ratcheting up 13 tries, 8 converted... plus... a drop goal. The final game in official fixtures with Cirencester was won 46-3 in October 1887, with Cardiff scoring 10 tries, 8 converted, against a try. Cirencester, after losing 35-1 on tries in 5 games, were dropped from the fixture list as Cardiff went about constantly strengthening it. Other teams also wanted to strengthen their fixtures and attract crowds by asking Cardiff for regular matches.

On the international scene, Wales could hardly muster a team for the first international against England in 1881, borrowing two players from the crowd and playing most of the game with 13 men. Wales lost the next four games to England, then drew at Stradey Park. Then in February 1890, Wales travelled to Dewsbury, and on a muddy pitch with driving sleet favouring forwards, at last adopted the hugely successful *'Cardiff system'*. Wales now employed eight forwards and four three-quarters against England's nine forwards and three three-quarters. Wales thereby won its first derby in eight attempts. There followed 2 losses, a win, 3 losses, a win and a loss before the underdogs came good. Wales won the next 5 games, then drew away in 1904, then won another 5 successive matches, going unbeaten for 11 games against England. Four Cardiff players were among the 1890 team for the first win against England: William Bancroft

(Swansea); Percy Lloyd (Llanelli), Arthur 'Monkey' Gould (Newport, captain), Richard Garrett (Penarth), David Gwynn (Swansea); Charles Thomas (Newport), William Stadden (Cardiff); William Williams (Cardiff), Alec Bland (Cardiff), David Evans (Cardiff), Jim Hannan (Newport), William Thomas (London Welsh), Steve Thomas (Llanelli), William Bowen (Llanelli), John Meredith (Swansea).

After a few years 'settling in', Cardiff were attracting better players, and beating teams from across Wales and England, with the intention of playing clean, fast, flowing, running and passing rugby. The team started to take pride in having the strongest possible fixture list, playing the best teams in England and Wales, and sometimes Irish and Scottish sides. Cardiff always tried to eschew penalties in order to score tries, to entertain spectators, and **changed the nature of the sport**. At this time, rugby was a forwards-driven game, with forward 'dribbling', close-control kicking, of the ball along the ground, much admired. However, Cardiff became the first team to play with seven 'backs', and the system over the years was adopted by all other teams. From that time onwards, *'the Cardiff Way'* was to move the ball out to the wings as quickly as possible. They attracted crowds wherever they played.

Actually, the adoption of 'the Cardiff System' heavily involved the Cardiff wing Thomas 'Tom' Williams, who was Cardiff's top try scorer in 1881-82, with 7 tries in 13 matches. There were only 22 games that season and the next highest try scorer had 3. It was a forward dominated game then. Tom left for Pontypridd for a year, where he won a cap, before coming back to Cardiff in 1883-84. Williams fell ill in 1884, and short of players, Cardiff had asked Frank Hancock to play, who touched down twice, the only scores of the match. On Williams' recovery, the Cardiff club could not choose between Williams, their fastest three-quarter, and Hancock, and did not want to lose either. As a compromise Cardiff decided to play both, dropping a player from the pack to accommodate four threequarters, rather than the traditional three, changing the formation of their rugby team. This formation was trialled by Wales, with Hancock as captain in 1886, and adopted by the international side in 1888, before becoming a worldwide tactic that continues to this day. In 2010 Cardiff gained IRB recognition when the four three-quarters/seven-backs initiator, **Frank Hancock, and the club were inducted into the IRB Hall of Fame**. Cardiff was the first club side (and currently one of only two clubs) to have been thus honoured. 'Immortals' such as Gwyn Nicholls, Rhys Gabe, Percy Bush, Wilfred Wooller, Dr Jack Matthews, Bleddyn Williams, Cliff Morgan, Gerald Davies, Barry John, Gareth Edwards, Rob Howley and Dai Young have all been Cardiff stalwarts, and Cardiff has provided more players to the Welsh team and the British Isles/British Lions than any other club.

By 1890, Cardiff were a power in the land, with Swansea and Newport their closest rivals. The first colonial touring team, the Maoris, had been beaten in 1888-89, and in the following year four Cardiff players were in the first Welsh team to beat England. In 1891 the Barbarians were formed and their continuing fixtures with Cardiff were crucial to their survival. In 1892-93 Cardiff's T.W. Pearson scored 40 tries, a record that stood until Bleddyn Williams' 41 in 1947-48. In 1951, Col. T.W. Pearson was asked for his greatest memory and recalled, *'On February 11th, 1893, my year as captain of Cardiff, we met and defeated Graham's Newport "Invincible" team. They had gone through 1891-1892 unbeaten and up to that day in February 1893, were still unbeaten. We won, and I remember as a skipper being carried off the field amidst great excitement.'* Nearby Newport have always been Cardiff's greatest rivals, and have the best record against the club of all teams, albeit a losing one. To be fair, Newport have rarely had the resources of the larger city.

1897, Cardiff v Newport

'The Prince of Three-quarters', Cardiff's Gwyn Nicholls began playing centre for Wales on 1 January 1894 and was to captain the side in the *Golden Era* of Welsh rugby that followed, until around 1910. In the 1905-1906 season, Swansea and Newport were each beaten 4 times by Cardiff. There was **only one defeat**, to New Zealand on Boxing Day 10-8, owing to a silly mistake by the Cardiff star, international Percy Bush. On 9 December 1905, against Blackheath in London, the Welsh Rugby Union asked Cardiff to play Teddy Morgan of London Welsh and Willie Llewellyn of Penygraig, alongside Gwyn Nicholls and Rhys Gabe in their three-quarter line, as that was the line-up selected against New Zealand the following Saturday. Cardiff's fullback H.B. 'Bert' Winfield was also to

play, along with Cardiff's Percy Bush receiving his first cap as outside-half. The 'Original All Blacks', then known simply as *'The Originals'* were the first New Zealand national rugby union team to tour outside Australasia, touring the British Isles, France and the United States in 1905–1906. They defeated every English side that they faced, and managed narrow wins against four Welsh clubs, and in 30 matches and 5 tests only lost once – to Wales. They scored 976 points and conceded only 59, setting the standard for future All-Blacks sides. The tour saw the first use of the All-Blacks name, establishing New Zealand's reputation as a world-class rugby nation. The All-Blacks had beaten Australia 14-3, Scotland 12-7, Ireland 15-0 and England 15-0. Wales were unbeaten also, thrashing England 25-0, beating Scotland 6-3 and Ireland 10-3.

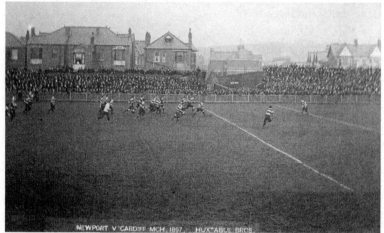

1897 Newport – Cardiff – Forward foot rush at Rodney Parade

In the Wales game, the Welsh anthem *Mae Hen Wlad fy Nhadau* (Land of my Fathers), was sung for the first time at Cardiff Arms Park by the players and fans, in response to the *haka*. Tom Williams, a Llwynypia solicitor, had played for his hometown, then Pontypridd and Cardiff, winning his only cap in Wales's first win against Ireland, in Dublin in 1882. Now a national selector (and uncle of Willie Llewellyn), he wrote to the *Western Mail* hoping that the Welsh would respond to the Maori war chant. The 2nd Battalion Band of the Welsh Regiment played *'Men of Harlech'* as the teams entered the Arms Park, then the *haka* was performed. The Welsh players lined up in the centre of the field, and captain Teddy Morgan led the players in singing the anthem, <u>the first time a national anthem had been sung at a sporting event</u>.

It was Triple Crown Wales against the All Blacks, the team that had never been beaten, EVER. Cardiff's Gwyn Nicholls told his team before the game: '*Gather round, men. The eyes of the rugby world are on Wales today. It is up to us to prove that the Old Country (Hen Wlad in the Welsh anthem) is not quite barren of a team that is capable of giving New Zealand at least a hard fight. Every man in possession must be put down, ball and all. As for the forwards, you already know what to do to get the loose head. Come on! Let's get out!'* It is hard to realise, but there were no team coaches, training or tactical talks – the players made their own way to the ground on match day and met up in the changing room. The match was, somewhat later, controversial. Wales went ahead with a try by Teddy Morgan, then the All Blacks thought they'd scored claiming that Deans was dragged back from over the line. Subsequent interviews with participants seem to verify that Deans was halted two or three feet from the line. J.B.G. Thomas in *'Taff's Acre'* scotches the claim decisively as a *Daily Mail* concoction that no-one believed at the time, and the referee later wrote in a letter *'Deans did not score.'* Deans was also supposed to have uttered the last words on his death bed *'I did score'*, but he was in a coma for a long time before that moment. New Zealanders still believe they won... It was called *'the Match of the Century'*.

1904-05 Cardiff lost at Newport 7-5, 19 November 1904.
They would not lose to Newport again for 15 games

Regarding the great victory, Cardiff supplied 5 of the 7 backs: H.B. 'Bert' Winfield (Cardiff); William 'Willie' Morris Llewellyn (Llwynypia) right wing; captain Gwyn Nicholls (Cardiff) right centre; Rhys Gabe (Cardiff) left centre; Teddy Morgan (London Welsh/Cardiff) right centre; Percy Bush (Cardiff) outside half; Dicky Owen (Swansea) scrumhalf and Cliff Pritchard of Pontypool as 'extra back' or *'rover'*. *Rugbyrelics.com* has a *'1905 All Blacks jersey swapped with Welsh player Cliff Pritchard after the match. Pritchard was the Welsh 'Rover', the man who supplied the pass to Rhys Gabe who fed Teddy Morgan who scored the try. According to the local newspaper the Pontypool Free Press, Pritchard caught the train home to Pontypool and when he arrived in the station at 11.23 pm he was expecting it to be deserted. The station however was packed with well-wishers. They then carried him shoulder high through the streets. It is thought he was wearing this jersey on his lap of honour around Pontypool.'*

Cardiff captain in 1907-08, Rhys Gabe
scored 11 tries in 24 games for Wales

We must mention here, the unique talents of Willie Llewellyn, (1 January 1878 - 12 March 1973), born in Tonypandy, who attended Christ College, Brecon and Bloomsbury Pharmaceutical College. His playing career encompassed Ystrad Rhondda, Llwynypia 1895-1900, London Welsh 1900-1906 (captain in 1900, 1901, 1902) concurrently with Newport 1903-1905, and he was noted in the All Blacks 1905 programme playing for Llwynypia. From 1906 he played for Penygraig. Llewellyn captained Wales in 1905 and London Welsh in 1902, being responsible for reviving that team's fortunes. Returning to Wales after college, Llewellyn joined first class club, Newport, where he stayed four seasons. Llewellyn toured with the British Isles to Australasia in 1904 and won three Triple Crown trophies in 1900, 1902 and 1905. Llewellyn made his debut for

Wales against England in 1899, alongside Billy Bancroft and Gwyn Nicholls, scoring four tries. He played 20 times for Wales, a virtually automatic choice from 1899 to 1905, and scored 16 tries. In 1904 Llewellyn played in 4 Tests, 3 in Australia and 1 in New Zealand, scoring 4 tries against Australia. A forgotten rugby hero.

1907-08 Louis Meredith Dyke was born in Cardiff, educated at Christ College, Brecon, a Barbarian and Welsh international

There was widespread criticism of Willie's selection to play the All Blacks at Cardiff in 1905, as he was thought too old to play on the wing (he was 27), and was now playing for the second-class club Penygraig, but he tackled his opposite number Wallace out of the game. And now we come to a recurring problem in Welsh rugby – partisan selectors – although it worked out this time. A solicitor from Llwynypia, Thomas Williams, was Willie's uncle. Tom Williams was the man mentioned above, who had been indirectly responsible for the four three-quarter 'Cardiff system'. Tom Williams had one Welsh cap and played for Cardiff, then Pontypridd and then Cardiff, playing 53 times between 1880-81 and 1886-87 for the club. After he retired from playing, Williams was made a national selector from 1901 until 1908, regarded as *'the most influential Welsh selector of the day'*. In 1905, Williams was at the centre of the selection of the Welsh team, and a Llwynypia rugby man picked his Llwynypia rugby nephew. In the same year, Willie Llewellyn opened a pharmacy in his birth town of Tonypandy. It seems that during the 1910 Tonypandy Riot the rioters left Willie's pharmacy untouched, while wrecking other shops.

The New Zealand game was also notable in that it was the <u>first ever international to have numbered jerseys</u>, and it was not until 1922, in the Wales-England game, when both teams wore numbered jerseys. However, for some years Wales never had a number 13 in their team, and some teams

31

numbered from the full-back as number 1, and some from the fullback as number 15. In Wales the fullback was therefore sometimes 16. For some unknown reason, Wales changed from numbers to letters in the away Scottish game in 1932, and persisted until the 1950s. Cardiff's great fly-half Cliff Jones was lettered F in the 1930s, while the wonderful Cliff Morgan, in the same position was a 6 in the 1950s, and the identification of that position is memorable for the 10 on Cardiff's Barry John, Newport's David Watkins and Llanelli's Phil Bennett in the 1970s. (Leicester and Bristol had letters on their shirts until the 1990s. Numbering from A, prop, to O, fullback, the Leicester front row was known for decades as 'the ABC Club.')

Boxing Day 1905 saw Cardiff play the unbeaten 'Originals' and Davies records the match as '*a battle of the giants... Cardiff were playing at their brilliant best. Described as an exhilarating game, Cardiff's passing movements were superb, the visitors rugged and stern in defence, as yet unbeaten except by Wales in twenty-seven matches. Cardiff took the lead in the first half when John Brown direct from a line-out threw to Percy Bush, from whom the ball went to Gibbs, to Gabe and then to Gwyn Nicholls who scored a fine try in the corner for Winfield to convert with a splendid kick. New Zealand equalised before half time with a try by "Mons" Thomas and W. J. Wallace converted. In the second half the All Blacks took the lead most fortuitously, when from an injudicious kick ahead by Seeling one of their forwards, from thirty yards out the ball crossed our line but it was well covered by Percy Bush who merely had to touch it down to minor it. Although eyeing Nicholson a New Zealand forward following up, Bush hesitated, and as the ball canted awkwardly, Nicholson made a spring and touched it down for a try, for Wallace to easily convert and the All Blacks to lead by 10-5.*

The crowd was shocked, and Bush was shamed but played brilliantly afterwards in an effort to save the game, and towards the end Cardiff scored another great try after a grand passing movement when the ball went from Dicky David the scrum half, to Bush, to Gibbs, to Nicholls who put Ralph Thomas our wing over in the corner. Could Winfield convert and so save the game? Alas his kick, an excellent one, just missed, and New Zealand had won by 10 points to 8. Their captain Dave Gallagher said Cardiff was the best club side the tourists had met, but that was no consolation to Percy Bush whose lapse was to haunt him for the rest of his days. I suppose that if the unfortunate incident had happened in these modern days, our critics would have opined that Percy Bush was trying to take the 'mickey' out of the All Blacks.' Cardiff lost to a mistake by one of their greatest players, and a successful conversion would have given a draw.

In the season, Cardiff only lost this of 32 games, scoring 513 points against 86 (10 by New Zealand) and 136 tries against 24. In modern points, scoring would be 753-124, an average match score of 26-4. Cardiff only scored 7 dropped goals and 2 penalties all season. But for Bush's error, or Bert Winfield's missed conversion, it would have been an 'Invincible' season. Davies writes that any type of reward had to be sanctioned by the WRU: *'Our most successful season. was duly celebrated with a complimentary smoking concert held at the Park Hotel Cardiff on the evening of 29th September 1906. Subsequently, presentations were made to twenty-one players, the Welsh Rugby Union had sanctioned a club value of £2.2.0d. per player which was supplemented by public subscription. The presentations took the form of 18 ct. gold watches suitably inscribed, which were supplied by Messrs. T. W. Long of 2 St. Mary Street, Cardiff.'* In January 1906, Wales had beaten England at Twickenham 16-3, 4 to 1 on tries, and on 3 February Scotland lost in Cardiff 9-3, 3-0 on tries. Wales then lost the chance of the Triple Crown in Belfast, scoring 2 tries to 3 and losing 11-6. Hopes were high on 6 December for the South Africa game, being played in Swansea, but the Springboks scored 3 tries, winning easily 11-0. Nicholls was injured, but it was thought that Wales had not played so poorly for ten years. But the undefeated Springboks had yet to face Cardiff.

Cardiff's Greatest Win?
Charley Arthur had been Cardiff wing and captain in 1889-90, and became the club historian, writing, *'The South Africans had, as everybody knows, beaten every club, county and country except Scotland, and had caused consternation by beating Wales.* **Cardiff was their best fixture**, *and to Cardiff everyone looked to beat them, so that one Welsh team should stay their triumphant career.'* Cardiff, after all, had scored 9 tries, including a hat-trick by wing Johnnie Williams, against the Barbarians. Cardiff had been missing their stars Bush and Gabe in the game on Boxing Day 1906, and still won 35-0, having also scored 9 tries to win 38-0 in April 1906. The previous season of the 38-0 victory, 1905-06 was called by Davies *'Cardiff's greatest ever season'.* A week after demolishing the Baa-Baas yet again, upon New Year's Day, 1907, South Africa came up against that brilliant Cardiff team. The great Rhys Gabe played in the centre with Gwyn Nicholls, outside the British touring team and Wales outside-half Percy Bush. The South African vice-captain Paddy Carolin claimed that Cardiff *'decided the only way they could beat us was to play 8 backs.'* In 27 games, the Springboks had conceded few tries, beating Ireland, Wales, Newport, Llanelli et al, and were pre-match favourites. However, Glamorgan with Cardiff players had only lost 6-3 in front of 40,000 at the Arms Park.

Carolin described the state of the Arms Park pitch. *'Owing to a hard frost the ground was covered with straw, and this was not removed when the thaw came. It looked as if a rived had overflowed the ground which was literally a sea of mud at least a foot deep. A strong wind blew from end to end, and to add to our misery we lost the toss and had to face it.'* However, the touring team's pack had no misgivings – 8 men bigger and better trained than the 7 Welsh forwards – in deep mud – no problems. There followed *'a marvellous exhibition of running rugby'*, although Cecil Biggs limped off the field. A long pass from a scrum out to Gwyn Nicholls, a swerving run and a classic centre's try, converted by Bert Winfield. 5-0. Biggs returned to the field, but was a passenger with torn knee ligaments, and limped off again. Cardiff's Fred Smith was knocked out in a heavy tackle. Cecil's brother Reggie, playing 'rover', took the ball in a line-out and dribbled into the wind to touch down. 8-0. Just before half-time, Cardiff were attacking and the Springboks were penalised for offside, Winfield scoring from the touchline with a ball that must have weighed – who knows? Older former players will remember the weight of a leather ball when saturate. 11 – 0. Cardiff ran off the field to change their jerseys in the 5-minute half-time break. Could 14 men and a passenger hold out against the wind in the second half? 30,000 soaking wet spectators could only hope.

Dr. BUIST, J. POWELL, J. CASEY, W. NEILL, J. BROWN, A. BRICE, GIL EVANS (Referee), J. DAVIES.
H. B. WINFIELD, C. F. BIGGS, G. NORTHMORE, P. F. BUSH, Capt. R. T. GABE, E. G. NICHOLLS, R. DAVID.
Cardiff XV., 1906-7.   R. A. GIBBS, J. L. WILLIAMS, F. SMITH.   **"Springboks'' Vanquishers.**

1926-27 Cardiff v Springboks

Carolin wrote, *'Owing to the wind it was next to impossible to clear our lines and gain relief by kicking and at half-time, when Cardiff led by 11 points to nil, we had all more than enough... Under such conditions we could never have beaten any side, let alone such a **magnificent side** as Cardiff fielded.'* The crowd sang the *National Anthem* as Cecil Biggs returned to the field for a second time after half-time, his leg heavily strapped and a passenger, but his courage inspired Cardiff. The home team defended desperately, with Winfield, Nicholls and Bush managing to achieve distance with their relieving kicks into the gale. South Africa missed two penalties, and changed tactics, resorting to handling, but the icy wind forced mistakes. In midfield, Bush and Gabe combined to give Johnnie Williams a clear run at the line – 14-0. The Western Mail reported: '*There was no longer any doubt as to the result, Cardiff being **infinitely the superior team and outplaying their opponents at all points with only 14 men**. Towards the end, the Cardiff pack made headway into the Springboks' 25, where their fullback failed to gather a loose ball. Gabe dribbled past him, regathered off his toes and dived over to score. Winfield had no chance with either conversion. New Year's Day 1907 – 1 goal, three tries and a penalty - 17-0 to Cardiff on a morass of a pitch. It was the 28th and final match of the Springboks 29-game British tour, before they smashed France 55-6 in an unofficial international in Paris. Scotland had beaten them 6-0 and England drew 3-3.

In 1951 'Rusty' Gabe recalled his favourite match. '*Wales has never beaten the South Africans, but Cardiff has. That famous match took place on New Year's Day in 1907, on a ground which was a veritable quagmire. The Cardiff passing was truly wonderful and the truth of this can be believed only by those who saw it. Two days before, the match against Old Merchant Taylors was abandoned because the ground was waterlogged. The try-getters against South Africa were Gwyn Nicholls, Reggie Gibbs, Johnny Williams, and myself. Bert Winfield kicked a penalty goal, the final score being 17 points to nil.*' In a tour of 29 games, the Springboks lost to Cardiff, conceding 4 tries, and in horrible weather only also lost to Scotland 6-0 and drew with England at Crystal Palace 3-3. Ireland had been beaten in Belfast 15-12. Cardiff were far better than Wales, who lost 11-0 at St. Helen's. In the previous two games before Cardiff, the Springboks had beaten Monmouthshire 17-0 and Llanelli 16-3. In 27 games, they had piled up 540 points and conceded 56, averaging 20 points to 2 per match. 14 sides had failed to score a point against them.

Cardiff scored four tries to nil in a mud-bath. It could easily have been 6 tries – wing Johnny Williams dropped a pass early on, with a clear run to the line, and later in the first half, after Cardiff had scored two tries, he could have scored but fumbled the ball. Any older reader who watched Cardiff in the 1950s and 60s will know what a horrible morass the Arms Park became on a wet winter, with a howling gale hammering in from the West, over the terrace and along the length of the ground. Percy Bush was in no doubt why Wales lost 11-0 and Cardiff won 17-0: '*Transcending easily all of the hundreds of famous games, in which I had the privilege to sport the dear old "Blue and Black", the one against our most-looked-forward-to visitors of this season, I rate our most famous game against the original "Springboks" on the Park, New Year's Day, 1907. Up to that date, the South Africans had been beaten only once* (in 27 matches, to Scotland). *A month before the match, they had humiliated Wales at Swansea by 11 points to nil! So that our glorious victory not only put Wales back on the map, with a bang, but also proved my claim that the*

Welsh side at Swansea was badly selected. It was a dreadful day. Gales of wind and unceasing thick sheets of rain, from the river-end. This did not prevent our winning by 17 points to nil, and avenging the dignity placed upon Gwalia, at Swansea!' Club historian Charley Arthur reported, *'No Cardiff team ever played better, or achieved so great renown, and the best man on the field, as he had been so many times before, was Gwyn Nicholls. He never played a better game in his life, and never scored a better try than the one he opened Cardiff's score with.'* These years were excellent for Cardiff. Despite a 'poorish' year in 1913-14, their try scoring record in 11 seasons from 1903-04 to 1913-14 was 1,043-285.

Cardiff played Cork's Constitution Club on 29 April 1907, with Percy Bush starring, and in the excitement before the game, the *Cork Examiner* described Cardiff as *'the finest club team in the world'*. Cardiff won 19-3, and the same paper called their performance *'a piece of perfection, a faultless piece of mechanism, and they seem incapable of erring, except by accident.* Cardiff wing Johnny Williams had scored a magnificent try against South Africa, and was selected for his first cap, against England, on 12 January 1907, in a team with 5 new caps. The *London Express* commented that Williams and others were selected because a lack of choice, the Welsh team being *'unexceptional.'* It is thought that there was a record low attendance for a Welsh international. However, *'unexceptional'* Wales beat England at St. Helen's 22–0, scoring 6 tries, through Brown, Gibbs, Maddock (2) and Williams (2), all points coming from Cardiff players, with Gibbs converting two. However, Wales then lost to Scotland away 6-3, with the Scots 8 forwards hammering out the win against the Welsh 8 backs system. Service was resumed against Ireland, with Wales including seven Cardiffians. Bush, Gabe and Jones scored tries and Williams achieved a hat-trick to win 29-0, 26 of the points coming from Cardiff players. 51 of Wales 54 points were scored by Cardiff men. Cardiff kept supplying most players to the national side, and Wales were unbeaten in 1908 and 1909.

In 1907-08, Wales won the Triple Crown for the 5th time, with Cardiff supplying 5 players against Ireland and France, and 7 against England and Scotland. Cardiff players scored 60 of Wales points, with Reggie Gibbs scoring 4 tries against France, and dropping the ball over the line to just miss a record 5 tries in an international. Cardiff faced Australia on 28 December 1908, and Australia suffered the biggest defeat of their tour, 24–8, Williams providing two tries, the backs getting another 3, and Percy Bush converting a try, dropping a goal and kicking a penalty. In the modern points system, Cardiff scored 36 points. The Australia Rugby Union had asked their team, on its first European tour, to perform a 'war cry' before the game, something akin to the New Zealand haka, and the team reluctantly did so. However, forewarned, Percy Bush advanced towards the tourists crouching and holding a spear and shield, supposedly relics from Rorke's Drift. Before the game, the Australians gave themselves the nickname of Wallabies, preferring it to *Waratahs* or *Wallaroos*. Since then, they have always been known as the Wallabies, and never beat Cardiff in six attempts, although the later Cardiff Blues have lost to them.

Danny Davies points out that, '*but for our Captain's singular lapse against the All Blacks of 1905, Cardiff would have achieved victories over the first four visiting colonial teams, e.g. the Maoris, 1888, one goal, one try to one try; the South Africans (1907) 17 points to nil; New Zealand (1905) – lost instead of won, and now the Australians, by 26 points to 8. These encounters indicated the remarkable strength of Cardiff Rugby Club up to World War 1.*' Interestingly, there was for many years a division between the lighter backs being professional men and the forwards being manual workers. Only in the 1960s and 1970s did this distinction fade. In the 1905 Welsh backs, only scrumhalf Dicky Owen had a manual job. His Cardiff fly-half Percy Bush was a student who would enter consular service in Nantes. On the wings, Teddy Morgan was a doctor and Willie Llewellyn a chemist. The Cardiff fullback Bert Winfield was in business with his Cardiff centre team-mate Gwyn Nicholls. The other centre was Cardiff schoolmaster Rhys Gabe.

Cardiff finished the season as Welsh Champions, and a wonderful attacking Wales team won the **Grand Slam in 1908, 1909 and 1911**, and not then until 1950, 1952, 1971, 1976, 1978, 2005, 2008, 2012, 2019 (missing by two points in Paris in 2021). Wales won the Triple Crown in 1893, 1900, 1902, 1905, 1908, 1909, 1911, 1950, 1952, 1965, 1969, 1971, 1976, 1977, 1978, 1979, 1988, 2005, 2008, 2012, 2019, 2021. As an aside, despite the poor performances of Welsh regions, the Welsh international record since 2005 has been utterly remarkable, despite constant criticism in the national press. There have been 7 Triple Crowns in this period, with Wales winning 4, Ireland 2 and England 1. There have been 8 Grand Slams, with Wales winning 4; Ireland 2, and England and France 1 apiece. In 2021, Wales narrowly missed out on a fifth, by 3 points away in Paris. The press called us 'lucky' to win the Championship in that year, but Wales were missing around 15 squad players through injuries. Of the 17 Six Nations Championships in this time, Wales won 6, France 3, Ireland 4 and England 4. England has 17 times the number of registered players as Wales.

For the season 1908-09, Percy Bush's Cardiff fixture list was missing games for the Saturdays when he and Wales played Australia, England, Scotland and Ireland, but contains games against: Cardiff & District; Neath 2, Bristol 2, Newport 4, Swansea 2, Gloucester 2, Pontypool 2, Leicester 2, Moseley 2, Blackheath 2, Llanelly 2, Australia, Glamorgan League, Penarth, Bordeaux (away), Devonport Albion 2, London Welsh and the Barbarians 2 – one on Boxing Day and one at Easter. In the match programme against Moseley on 7 November 1908, *'The Week's Football Gossip'* by 'Blindside' noted that Cardiff had lost its unbeaten record to Leicester the week before because of *'Mr Referee... Cardiff were in the Cart-wright through the game.'* Terry Holmes was to experience the same refereeing in his last away game for Cardiff in Leicester, but fashioned a win by scoring tries from distance with no opportunity to blow the whistle. (I was there...)

In 1874, the O'Neill family from Cork was emigrating to the USA when their little ship foundered in the Irish Sea, but it managed to turn and limp into Milford Haven. After the awful experience, they instead moved to Cardiff, where their son, known to all as 'Billy Neill', was born. The second row was the first forward to make over 200 appearances for Cardiff (204), over 11 seasons, scoring 17 tries. Billy won 11 caps for Wales, only losing one game against Ireland, and was a regular when Wales became the first team to win a Grand Slam in 1908. He then turned professional with Warrington, winning rugby league caps for Wales. 1908-1909 had seen the first appearance of Robert Francis 'Bobby' Williams of Tongwynlais, neighbouring Taff's Well, who made 159 appearances for Cardiff until 1919-1920. There were no games during the Great War, or in 1918-19. Davies calls him a *'popular and plucky fullback. It was not generally known that Williams overcame the handicap of playing minus three fingers on one hand and partially paralysed one on the other. What we do for rugby!'* Born in Canton, Cardiff, and one of 17 children, Williams started working on Cardiff Docks aged 14, but was injured at work, losing three fingers, with two paralysed on the other hand. He had played for Canton RFC from 1906. Bobby won his Welsh cap in his second season of 1910-1911, playing 30 games for Cardiff. The disabled Bobby Williams played for Wales, and 28 times for Cardiff in 1912-13. He was Cardiff vice-captain and played 32 times for Cardiff in the following year. In his first international, South Africa won 3-0, and then he was in the Cardiff team beaten 6-3. In 1913-14 he played against Scotland, England and Ireland and was selected against France, but *could not take time off work for the trip.* As a Barbarian, Bobby played twice against Leicester. One doubts if any player had disabilities ever close to those of Bobby, yet played for a truly great team, and his country. Cardiff's Joe Pugsley had a fitting name for a rugby hooker, playing 162 times between 1905-06 and 1910-11. Pugsley, a name resurrected in *The Addams Family*, won the first of his 7 caps in 1910, heading North to Salford in 1911 and winning a Wales rugby league cap in that year.

In the 1908-1909 season, Cardiff had been criticised for spending £300 on an away game against Stade Bordelaise U. C. (Bordeaux). In that season, in its 13 games up to playing Cardiff, Bordeaux had been by far the best team in France, twice beating Toulouse, Paris and Lyons, winning a local championship three times, and scoring 218 against 24 points. Its only

38

losses in 13 games had been 3-0 to Edinburgh University and 9-6 to the British Army. Bordeaux had been 10 times in the Provinces Final since its formation in 1898, and had won the French Championship six times, including the four consecutive years before the Cardiff game. They were the best team in France by a mile. Let me enlighten you, in terms of travelling to Bordeaux and back in those days. Cardiff, with hardly any committee men, no coach and no trainer – the latter two jobs did not exist until well after WW2 - left Cardiff by rail at 10am on Thursday 18 February. They reached Paddington in 3 hours – the journey varies from 2 hours to 2 hours 40 minutes today, 133 years later. The joys of progress... The team left for Charing Cross, where they took Great Western Rail buses at 2.20pm, arriving in Folkestone at 4pm, only just in time for a mad rush carrying their kit and suitcases, for the 4.10 boat. They reached Boulogne at 5.40 (French time), leaving at 6.17pm precisely by train for Paris, arriving at 9.15pm, where buses took the players to the Hotel St. Petersbourg. After over 12 hours of travel, supper was served at 11.50pm. With probably 4-5 hours of sleep, after a 6.45am breakfast, the team left Paris at 7.30, arriving in Bordeaux at 4.48pm, a journey of over 10 hours. Here the Grand Hotel Français bus met the train, and they had hardly any time before dinner at 5.30 and supper at 11.00. A second long day of travel. On Saturday 20th there was breakfast at 9.15, lunch at 1.30pm, and kick-off was at 4pm, following around 22 hours travel by rickety buses, early trains and a boat in the previous two days. The exhausted Cardiff players, buoyed by an excellent lunch, put on a show, on 20 February 1909, scoring 5 tries, three converted, to a goal to smash the crack French team 21-5. (In modern scoring 31-7.) Gwyn Nicholls scored a hat-trick. The game was followed by a grand dinner at 7.30 and supper at 11. The next two days, the journey was repeated, arriving after 5 days away, back in Cardiff at 9.15pm on Monday 22 February. Then the players had to find their own way home.

In this year of 1908-09, Cardiff was the best team in Britain, with doubles over Bristol, Gloucester, Blackheath, Moseley and the Barbarians. Friendlies like that at Bordeaux were not included in their official record. The team won 26, lost 3 and drew 2 games, scoring 79 tries against 33. Cardiff beat Newport three times but the fourth game in March was abandoned because of frost and snow. There are reports of 30,000 spectators for these local derbies. The Baa-Baas were beaten 6-3 on Boxing Day, and 22-0 in better weather at Easter, with 3 converted tries, a try and a drop goal. Cardiff were Welsh champions, despite Ronnie Gibbs and Johnny Williams missing much of the season away on tour, and some retirements such as Rhys Gabe.

In the next season, 1909-1910, there was a record crowd of 20,000 Rodney Parade, with Newport unbeaten. Newport's pack contained 5 present and 3 future internationals, and they were led by the great scrumhalf Tommy Vile. Davies records it in 1974: '... *unfortunately, the match turned out to be one of the roughest of the 113 matches between the clubs... Cardiff's victory by three splendid tries by Spiller to one goal, one penalty goal was tarnished by the other less pleasing events in the game. There were many fouls, there was kicking, punching, throttling on the ground, late tackling and so on which involved many injuries and stoppages.'* A player from each side was sent off, and it was reported that '*the game has not been equalled for ferocity and fouling since the Rugby game was introduced into Wales'*. Davies writes that from his personal experience, playing for Cardiff as outside-half, '*I have no doubt that this dirty game was responsible for engendering bad feeling and intense rivalry between these two great clubs which lasted well into the twenties.*'

Joe Pugsley was Cardiff and Wales hooker
until 1911 when he turned to Salford rugby league

Police Sergeant William 'Billy' Spiller played centre for Cardiff and Wales and remembered: '*I think my most famous match was against Newport away in 1909-1910 season; Johnny Williams was captain. We broke Newport's record by 9 points to 8, and I scored three tries. We had a great reception by our supporters after the match and on our return to Cardiff we were shouldered from the station to the Queen's Hotel.*' Cardiff drew the final Newport game 0-0, and then thrashed the Barbarians on 27 December 1909, 10 tries to nil, Reggie Gibbs scoring 4 tries but Cardiff missed every conversion, 5 in front of the posts, using 6 kickers. (Kicking was never a priority for the team. For decades they scored more tries every season, while their opponents kicked more penalties). That 30-0 game would be 50-0 today, and with a kicker, 70-0. In the season Cardiff scored 115 tries to 34, scoring 470 points to 144 in 36 games. In 1909-10, 7 Cardiff players were chosen for Wales. All four three-quarters – Gibbs, Dyke, Spiller and Williams were from Cardiff – with Bush at outside-half, against Ireland. Williams scored another hat-trick, with Gibbs and Dyke a try apiece and a dropped goal by Bush, for Cardiff players to score all Welsh points in a 19-3 win.

In 1910, Wales beat France 49-14, with Reggie Gibbs scoring 3 tries, Hopkin 'Hop' Maddock 2, Morgan 2, and Trew, Gronow and Jones also touching down. Wales scored 2 tries to England's 2 at Twickenham, but dropping Cardiff players Johnny Williams and Louis Dyke, lost 11-6. Scotland were beaten 4-0 on tries 14-0, with Spiller and Cardiff hooker Joe Pugsley touching down. At Lansdowne Road, Johnny Williams and Dyke were returned to the team, Dyke and Gibbs touching down and Williams getting another hat-trick, to win 19-3, 5 tries to 1. England topped the International Championship by a point over Wales. **But for the wrong selection against England, Wales would have won Triple Crowns and Grand Slams in an unbelievable four successive seasons, 1908-1911**.

Cardiff's three-quarter line of Reggie Gibbs, Louis Dyke, Billy Spiller and Johnny Williams was picked intact for Wales on only four occasions: March 1910 beating Ireland 19-3 away; February 1911 beating Scotland away 32-10; February 1911 beating France away 15-0; and March 1911 defeating Ireland at Cardiff 16-0 – 82-13 on points. There is something special about club partnerships in international games, especially as there was no team training until the 1970s, for individuals to 'blend'. There was another Grand Slam for Wales in 1911, and against Scotland the Cardiff threequarters scored 29 of Wales' 32 points. Gibbs, Spiller, Dyke and Williams were supreme for Wales, and would have played in all four internationals except Dyke was replaced by Fred Birt of Newport for the first match against England. Wales beat England 15-11 at Swansea, after which Birt was dropped for Dyke. In Scotland, Wales won 32-10 (47-13 in today's scoring), in France 15-0 and in Cardiff Ireland lost 16-0. Wales scored 78 against 21 points. The scores were made up of Wales – 18 tries (4 converted); 1 drop goal; 2 pens – France/Scotland/England/Ireland – 4 tries (1 converted); 1 drop goal. Of the opposition's 4 tries, England scored 3 at Swansea. Cardiff hooker Joe Pugsley made that game safe with Wales' fourth try. Cardiff scored 3 of the 4 tries against England; 7 of 8 vs Scotland, with a Reggie Gibbs hat-trick; 1 of 3 vs France; and 1 of 3 vs Ireland, making 12 of 18 Welsh tries. As well as hooker Joe Pugsley, the Cardiff three-quarters of Reggie Gibbs, Billy Spiller, Louis Dyke and Johnny Williams featured in all three Grand Slam games.

Reggie Gibbs was Cardiff captain, and against Moseley away in January 1911 scored 4 of Cardiff's 15 tries and kicked 9 goals for a total of 30 points in Cardiff's 63-3 victory (93-5 today). Cardiff had only won the previous encounter 43-3 at home, scoring 11 tries. Cardiff's Sergeant 'Billy Spiller' was a Barbarian and in 1911 was called *'the player of the season'* and *'the best centre in the country'*. He played 10 times for Wales and 184 games for Cardiff between 1905-06 and 1913-14, and as a Barbarian, scored 30 points against the hapless Moseley in the same year that Cardiff scored 26 tries against them. So well was he playing, that he was to follow the internationals Gwyn Nicholls (1903-04, his fourth season as captain), Cecil Biggs (the third family member to captain the team after Norman Biggs 1893-94 and Selwyn Biggs 1897-98), Rhys Gabe, Percy Bush, Johnny Williams, Reggie Gibbs and Louis Dyke to captain the team in 1912-13. After 10 caps, Cardiff hooker Joe Pugsley went North to join Salford, in the era of contested scrums. Remember that Cardiff were losing players to injury, three Welsh trials a year, international appearances, charity games and representative games. However, their record when supplying so many players to the Welsh team was as follows, with 605 tries (averaging over 100 per season) being scored against 173:

	Pl	W	L	D	G	T	DG	P	Pts	vs	G	T	D	P	Pts
05-06	32	29	1	2	47	71	11	7	513		6	14	2	2	86
06-07	30	25	3	2	40	52	6	8	404		7	13		1	83
07-08	31	26	4	1	27	58	7	2	343		15	19		1	130
08-09	31	26	3	2	38	41	11	5	372		12	21	3	1	138
09-10	36	22	7	7	39	76	8	5	470		16	18	2		144
10-11	36	29	6	1	52	64	6	3	485		9	23	3	3	135
	196								2587						716

In this period, the Barbarians were played twice a year, Cardiff winning 11 of the 12 games. In 1911-12 Louis Dyke led the team to 6 losses in 39 games, three of which were lost 3-0, scoring 407-116 on points; tries 100-27. All the losses were away, giving Cardiff an unbeaten home record. Doubles were achieved over Leicester and Bristol, and the Barbarians were beaten twice, 19-0 and 16-9, 9-2 on tries. In February 1912 Cardiff played Stade Français away, having previously beaten them 44-8 (8-1 on tries) at home in 1905. (In 1906 Cardiff had also travelled to play a Combined French XV, in effect France, and beaten them 27-5, 7-1 on tries). In the away return game against Stade Français at Parc des Princes in February 1912, Cardiff won 19-3, but the match was remarkable for another reason. The great French Cubist painter Robert Delaunay, whose painting of the Eiffel Tower sold for almost 6 million dollars in 2012 at Christies, produced three paintings of *'L'Equipe de Cardiff'* depicting action scenes from the match, played in front of *'a huge concourse of spectators'*. The paintings were exhibited in Berlin and one is in Eindhoven and one in the

Musée d'Art Moderne in Paris. How many rugby – or football – or any sporting teams – are depicted by famous painters in great art galleries, anywhere in the world?

New stands were celebrated before the first game on 5 October 1912, making the Arms Park the finest ground in the country, with a capacity of 25,000. Unfortunately, Cardiff succumbed to a dropped goal to Newport, losing 4-0. Billy Spiller's 1912-13 team scored 439-124 points, and 99-22 on tries but lost 10 of 37 games. These losses, however, were generally by very small margins: Penarth 7-5 (H); Newport 4-0 (A); Swansea 3-0 (A); Neath 9-5 (A); Swansea 6-0 (H); Newport 23-10 (A, with 14 men as Spiller was off hurt); Devonport Albion 7-5 (A) and South Africa 7-6 (H). The Barbarians were defeated 18-5 and 10-0, 6-1 on tries. The Springboks could not score a try, but had a drop goal worth 4 and a penalty to win 7-6 against Cardiff's penalty and try, a reverse score today of 8-6 to Cardiff, of course. Captain Billy Spiller was top try scorer with 18.

1913-14 Crowd at Arms Park for a Newport match

The final pre-war season of 1913-14 was poor, losing many players, thus losing 14 and drawing 1 of 38 games, but they still won 73-47 on tries. In 1913-14 Percy Bush returned from playing for Nantes and played the first four games, scoring 3 tries, but returned to France. The Barbarians were beaten twice, and on 12 November 1913 there was a Past vs. Present match to raise funds for the Senghenydd Colliery disaster. The final death toll of the explosion on 14 October 1913 was 440 men and boys, the worst mining disaster in the history of the British coalfields. The 950 men on the day shift at the Universal Colliery, Senghenydd had just began work when a huge explosion ripped through the workings. The blast was so powerful that it sent the two-ton cage shooting up the Lancaster Shaft into the headgear. An inquiry could not determine the cause although it was agreed that methane gas ('firedamp') was involved. It soon became apparent that there had been a number of violations of the 1911 Coal Mines Act. In May 1914 the mine manager, Edward Shaw, faced 17 charges while the colliery owners, the Lewis Merthyr Coal Company, faced 4 charges. Edward Shaw was convicted of 8 of the charges and fined £24 - leading a local newspaper to publish the headline *'Miners' Lives at 5½p each'*. The owners were convicted of the *single charge* of not fitting reversible ventilation fans and were fined £10 with £5.25 costs. Of the disaster victims, 60 were younger than 20 years old, and 8 of those were only 14 years old. The disaster left 205 widows, 542 children and 62 dependent parents. This was the second explosion at the Universal Colliery: in 1901, 81 men had died.

The disabled Bobby Williams, mentioned previously, was vice-captain in 1913-14, being awarded a club blazer, playing 32 games and for Wales, in a year which Davies calls *'the End of a Great Era'*. Bobby was appointed club captain for 1914-1915 but no games were played that season, with war impending. He was one of four Cardiff players in a Wales team that lost 26-10 to the Barbarians in a charity game in 1915. We know about Gabe, Nicholls, Bush etc. but one hardly known Cardiff player shines through the pre-war period. **John Lewis (Johnnie) Williams** was a wonderful successor to Tom Pearson on the Cardiff wing. He was born in Whitchurch, Cardiff, educated at Cowbridge Grammar School, scored 3 tries on his debut in 1903 and scored 150 tries in 199 games for Cardiff. Williams was a British Isles test player, and played when Cardiff beat the Springboks 17-0 in 1907 and the Wallabies 24-8 in 1908, scoring tries in both games. In his first season for Cardiff (1903-1904), he partnered Rhys Gabe in the centre, each scoring 10 tries, and was in the Cardiff team that beat the All Blacks in 1905. In that season, 1905-06, the left centre scored 35 tries. Cardiff used to play the Barbarians twice a season, and in 12 of those games from 1904 to 1910 he scored 15 tries. In 1909-10 he was club captain. Also a fly-half or wing, he scored 17 tries in 17 internationals, a record that stood until 1978, when Gareth Edwards scored 20 tries in 50 tests. He won the Grand Slam in 1908, 1909 and 1911. Williams still has the record of tries per international, and in a forward-dominated era.

Captain John Lewis Williams of the Welch Regiment was fatally wounded in the massed attack at Mametz Wood from 7-12 July 1916 during the Battle of the Somme, dying on the last day. The 38th (Welsh) Division (an amalgamation of South Wales Borderers, Royal Welch Fusiliers and Welch Regiment troops) had to take a well-defended area of woodland near the village of Mametz. *'Most of these troops were in the Welsh 'Pals' Battalions with many inexperienced in combat, facing battle-hardened Prussian troops defending the wood. The initial attack on the eastern edge of the wood began on the 7th of July 1916, with dug-in*

44

German machinegun positions causing heavy casualties. The attacking Welsh troops were pinned down in the open with little cover. Thus, this first attack broke down 300 yards away from the treeline. A second assault took place on the southern edge of the wood on the 10th. Two days of hard fighting followed, with artillery bombardments from both sides decimating the trees and creating hails of lethal shrapnel and splinters. The defenders had to be flushed out of their positions with Mills bombs (grenades), and there was close-quarter fighting. By the 12th of July the entire wood was in the hands of the Welsh; they had suffered some 4,000 men killed or wounded.' (- sourced from *neverforgetyourwelshheroes.org*, website run by the Royal Welsh Regimental Museum). Military intelligence expected an easy attack, not aware that the woods were full of artillery, machine-gun emplacements, trenches and barbed wire. It was an achievement, albeit a massacre, ever to cross the 400 years of open ground to the woods, let along take them.

The poet Siegfried Sassoon and writer/poet Robert Graves, both of the Royal Welch, had met at the Battle of Loos and also fought in the battle, and it scarred both for life. Graves was so badly injured it was expected he would die, and suffered from shell-shock. His wonderful *'Goodbye To All That'* is an account of his experiences. This author's favourite poet, along with Idris Davies, is another survivor of Mametz Wood, David Jones - another Welch Fusilier, who wrote a vivid description of the fighting in his masterpiece *'In Parenthesis'* (1937), in which we read: *'And here and there and huddled over, death-halsed to these, a Picton-five-feet-four paragon of the Line, from Newcastle Emlyn or Talgarth in Brycheiniog, lying disordered like discarded garments or crumpled chin to shin-bone like a Lambourne find.'* The Welsh artist Christopher Williams painted *The Welsh at Mametz Wood* at the request of David Lloyd George, then Secretary of State for War. The painting is well worth seeing in the National Museum of Wales in Cardiff, as he studied the battlefield with survivors. Robert Graves described the wood immediately after the battle: *'It was full of dead Prussian Guards, big men, and dead Royal Welch Fusiliers and South Wales Borderers, little men. Not a single tree in the wood remained unbroken.'* In modern times, Owen Sheers with his 2000 poem *Mametz Wood* memorably records: *'This morning, twenty men buried in one long grave, a broken mosaic of bone linked arm in arm, their skeletons paused mid dance-macabre...'*

Ellis Humphrey Evans, 'Hedd Wynn', who died at Passchendaele in 1917, was posthumously awarded the Bard's Chair in that year, the chair being draped in black at the Birkenhead National Eisteddfod. He was another Welch Fusilier as was Frank Richards, who in 1933 published his classic account of the war from the standpoint of the regular soldier, *'Old Soldiers Never Die'*, *'a brilliant insight into the life of a soldier in the early stages of the twentieth century'*. It was written with the unaccredited assistance of Robert Graves, was an instant success and has never been out of print since. The author makes no apology for this non-rugby section, incidentally – the more we can be reminded of how disgusting war is, the better. And poetry is a wonderful medium for the expression of such futility. Further details on Johnnie Williams and the losses of rugby players in war can be found in Gwyn Prescott's book 'Call Them to Remembrance'.

1917 Cardiff Ladies

Games were suspended for five years, and many other Cardiff players had volunteered to serve, led by their Welsh international captain and Barbarian, W.J. 'Billy' Jenkins. Various matches were played for charity, including one in April 1915 when the Barbarians beat Wales 26-10. A New Zealand Army team played 13 games in Wales, drawing with Cardiff 0-0 in March 1919, before 10,000 spectators, and beating Wales 6-3 in April. The Club raised almost £2,000 for charities, while running an overdraft of £2,080. In December 1917, we have the **first photograph of a female rugby team** – Cardiff Ladies. During the War some women's charity games were organised, the most well documented taking place at Cardiff Arms Park on 16 December 1917, when Cardiff Ladies lost to Newport Ladies 6–0. The Cardiff team mainly worked for Hancocks Brewery in Cardiff, and wore protective headgear, decades before their male counterparts. Maria Eley played full-back for Cardiff, and remained a keen player, probably the oldest women's rugby player until she married her husband, Hector, and concentrated on bringing up eight children. She attributed her longevity to a love of rugby and an aversion to cigarettes and alcohol. She chaired the senior citizens club at her native Cogan, Penarth for 24 years and was still calling Bingo until she was 101, dying in Cardiff in 2007 at the age of 106.

The First World War had a major effect on the club, as Johnnie Williams had died at the Battle of the Somme, and many other players returned wounded or simply too old to play rugby. Cardiff had to turn to younger talent for their team, and the *'wondrous'* Jim Sullivan made his first appearance for Cardiff aged 16 in October 1920, making 38 appearances in that season. In December 1920, just after his 17th birthday, he became the **youngest player** to ever appear for the Barbarians, but in June 1921 he signed for professional rugby league club Wigan, beginning a new trend of Welsh union players 'going north' to play rugby league. In 1920, there were 250,000 colliers in Wales, but the end of demand for coal for steam ships, and for manufacturing for war meant that half a million men left Wales looking for work. Not only were rugby clubs denuded of players, but of the 21 players used by Wales when they shared the championship, 5 turned professional. In the depression of the 1920s and 1930s, many players headed North, not only to be offered employment but to be paid for playing rugby – it was a semi-professional game until the 1970s. Indeed, there were so many Welsh players at Wigan in the 1930s that the team became known as 'Wigan Welsh'.

We must mention here the state of the Cardiff Arms Park. Cardiff often preferred playing their open brand of rugby away. The England great Wavell 'Wakers' Wakefield wrote in his autobiography, of the 1922 England-Wales match: '... *we had a rude shock down at Cardiff when Wales beat us by 2 goals and 6 tries to two tries. The Cardiff ground has a reputation for muddiness but on that day it excelled itself. It was simply a squelching morass and football was impossible. It was most difficult to stand up at all, a difficulty which the Welshmen overcame by having phenomenally long studs in their boots, longer studs than I have ever seen, and I imagine they had considerably outgrown the regulation size.'* The 28-6 Welsh victory of 6 tries and 2 conversions against 2 tries, in today's terms, with all tries being converted, would be 56-14. Wales, unusually, had 8 new caps, including a vicar from Llanelli, the Rev. J.G. Stephens. There we no new caps in the England team. But for a 9-9 away draw in Scotland in 1922, Wales would have won another Grand Slam.

A year later at Twickenham in 1923, an English forward Leo Price scored from their kick off at the start of the game. The ball swirled in the wind, was missed by the Welsh defenders, and Price grabbed it and tried a drop at goal. It narrowly missed and the Welsh expected to ball to roll dead, but the strong wind held it up and Price fell on the ball. Not a Welsh hand touched it. England won by that try and a dropped goal to a try, 7-3. England were fairly determined. One Welsh player had stitches under a gashed left eye, another had three teeth knocked out, another was a passenger with badly bruised ribs from a kick and Thomas 'Codger' Johnson (Cardiff captain in 1924-25) was laid out by a kick on the head. At least the England try-scorer has a Welsh surname. Four years later, in 1926, a friend sent *'Wakers'* a telegram saying *'Good luck to you all. Mind you wear your galoshes'* before the game. This writer thought galoshes must be wellies, but checked on Wikipedia – *'Galoshes, also known as dickersons, gumshoes, overshoes or rubbers, are a type of rubber boot that is slipped over shoes to keep them from getting muddy or wet.'* That would be quite interesting in more modern times, ensuring that you had packed your rubbers before a game.

Codger Johnson

Davies terms 1919-20 to 1935-36 *'the Restoration or Rebuilding Period'*. (The Cardiff seasons relevant to the Williams brothers, from 1931 to 1975, follow from Chapter 5.) Dr. Tom Wallace, who played 155 times for Cardiff between 1919-20 and 1924-25 recalled: *'The match I remember is a Cardiff v. Newport match at Newport in 1923, not for the quality of the game, but for the tenseness and excitement of the game, both for players and spectators. Newport was unbeaten. I was Captain and got my head cut open after about twenty minutes; I was taken away to be mended and returned to find Tom (Codger) Johnson being carried off severely injured and to find that the late Arthur Cornish had scored a wonderful try'.* 'Codger' Johnson made 187 appearances for Cardiff from 1920-21 to

1926-27. As noted previously, Newport games were the most important of the season except for international touring teams. Thomas Albert 'Codger' Johnson grew up in Cardiff docks and was a ship's chandler who joined after a season with Penarth. He was Cardiff captain in 1924-25 and was top scorer with 25 tries in that season. Usually a wing, he played 12 times for Wales as wing or full back.

Swansea's Rowe Harding won 17 caps as centre for Wales between 1923 and 1928. In 1984 he recalled 'Codger' only too well: *Playing as I did in an era when Welsh international rugby was at an all-time low and when Cardiff were, as they have been ever since, Swansea's bogy side, most of the events that remain in my memory of Cardiff Arms Park in the twenties are tinged more with sadness than with joy. The first concerns a game between Cardiff and Swansea when I came across from the left wing to tackle 'Codger' Johnson in full flight. Nothing in that, you might think; but when I add that 'Codger' wore a gumshield like a professional boxer and carried that spirit on to the field you will understand why I count myself lucky to escape unscathed from the tackle… my first International match at Cardiff Arms Park was not until 1923. Before it I met the legendary Gwyn Nicholls, prince of centre three-quarters and one of the gentlest and most charming of men.*' There is a contemporary photo of Cardiff players having their usual meal of kippers after training, in the Arms Park Pavilion, a tradition of the 1920s. For the younger reader, kippers are cold-smoked, split and gutted herrings. Sounds awful, tastes fab. Herrings, if hot-smoked whole are known as bucklings; if cold-smoked whole, as bloaters. These particular nourishing delicacies were Cardiff kippers, when Cardiff had a great trawler fleet – those of Cardiff, Newport, Barry, Penarth, Swansea and Milford were virtually wiped out in WW2, along with most of their merchant shipping.

In November 1924, Cardiff played '*the Invincibles*,' the All Blacks who won all their 32 games on tour. They very fortunately won against Cardiff 16-8, and a week later easily beat Wales at Swansea 19-0. Harry Bowcott, the Cambridge Blue, Cardiff, Barbarians and Wales centre, played 8 times for Wales and in all 5 tests in 1930 for Great Britain (later named the British Lions) against Australia and New Zealand. He watched the Cardiff-All Blacks game, before he went up to Cambridge and wrote: '***The club match of the season, if not the decade***, *drew a 40,000 crowd, the gates being closed half an hour before the start. The All Blacks had won all 19 of their previous games including the first International of the tour in Dublin (and would go on to win 32 out of 32 obtaining the much-desired scalp of Wales at Swansea). Against Cardiff they were lucky to score 16 points, their opponents equally unlucky not to get more than eight. The home forwards outplayed their opponents, but the New Zealand midfield defended too well to allow penetration by the Blue and Black three-quarters. There was criticism of the referee, Captain A.S. Burge, who*

49

failed, it was said, to notice two knock-ons before Andrew White's try converted by that prince of players Mark Nicholls. He also disallowed a pushover try claimed by Cardiff in the second half.'

The small Cardiff outside-half Danny Davies recorded: *'These Second All Blacks proved to be invincible and were to win all 32 matches by 838 points to 116, but they were flattered by their win over Cardiff, as a try by Porter their captain, converted by Mark Nicholls, was allowed after a couple of palpable knocks on with some of us hesitating for the referee's whistle to blow; and again our pack – which had a really magnificent day and out-fought the All-Blacks in the second half claimed a pushover try; but referee Captain A.S. Burge of Penarth was of course the solo judge. Our backs somehow lacked penetration. I remember mainly two items of mine, a dropped pass after a most promising heel from the pack; and tackling George Nepia the famous All Blacks full-back, frontally, as he was charging through to convert defence into an attacking movement, a tackle we both really felt. "Bobbie" Delahay our scrum half scored Cardiff's try and Dr. Tom Wallace converted it and kicked the penalty goal.'* That particular game was one of the greatest memories of Cardiff's number eight, Tom Lewis of Gwaelod-y-Garth, Pentyrch and Taff's Well.

In 1924, Arthur Cornish and Danny Davies were invited on the British Isles tour to South Africa. Cornish was not released from school duties, and Davies could not go because of work. Cardiff captain Danny Davies had a final Welsh trial but no cap, and went on to become Cardiff chairman for 20 years, on the WRU for 16 years and WRU President in 1961. Without his years of research leading to his *'Cardiff Rugby Club, the Greatest'*, this book would have been impossible. Recounting their Easter 1924 tour of Wales, H. Waddell is recorded upon the Barbarians website: *'We had a very strong side just before the British tour to South Africa later that year, including great players like Voyce, Blakiston, Arthur Young, J. C. R. Buchanan, and it included three members of the famous Oxford three-quarter line - Ian Smith, George Aitken and John Wallace. I was naturally very nervous. I had never been to Wales. Cardiff, Swansea and Newport were just great names to me. The first game I played for the Barbarians was against Cardiff with a side including all of those mentioned and we eventually scrambled home 23-18 and promptly lost to Swansea on Monday 11-9. One of the attractions of the tour is that, whereas Sunday can be a dull day, thanks to the hospitality and kindness of the Penarth Golf Club, we have the freedom of the course and everybody has to play whether he has played golf before or not. Curiously enough, those who have never played before always seem to enjoy it best. We play with one bag to four players. Shot about, and it can be very exciting. You can very often win a hole in double figures. For many years we spent Easter at the Esplanade Hotel, Penarth, presided over by Mr. King and later by Mrs. King. She loved gay young men. (Younger readers please note* that up to 40 years ago 'gay' meant 'light-hearted and carefree'.) *She didn't mind noise. She charged us practically nothing. She didn't object to unusual emblems appearing overnight on the flagpole and she was quite unperturbed and amused when an Irishman drove four or five cattle into the hotel lounge uttering cries of encouragement to the mystified animals. You could get three helpings of every course and if you came in late, you cooked your own.'*

After the Second World War, some Baa-Baas after midnight managed to manoeuvre a cow up six flights of stairs to the top floor. Before breakfast, the manager said that there would be no recriminations if the cow could be taken back to its place of origin. Unfortunately, the guilty parties had to carry the beast, as cattle cannot, and will not descend steps. A.I. Voyce recalled a game: *'I stayed at the Esplanade Hotel, Penarth, several times. What fun we had! We used to dance around the table after the soup was served. I never saw one bowl of soup spilt - we were a gentle lot - good with our feet. your own bacon and eggs. It was a wonderful place for a touring side.'* Ralph Bond Sweet-Escott, a Penarth resident, played for Cardiff 148 times between 1889-90 and 1895-96, often with his two brothers. He also played half-back for Wales and was a founder-member of the Baa-Baas, and seems to have been responsible for the Penarth seafront Esplanade Hotel becoming the base for the nomadic Barbarians. From their first game with Penarth in 1901, the *'Esp'* became the place the Barbarians called home. (The grand Edwardian building was sadly demolished, having been burnt out by a fire in 1977 - with four different sources – to be replaced by an unremarkable block of flats).

Taff's Well was always a steady source of players for Cardiff – it was their local first-class club. Pontypridd was slightly nearer but had no fixtures with Cardiff between 1931 and 1960, and playing for Cardiff was a more prestigious and 'bigger' club. Men who played regularly for Cardiff and the Athletic could nearly always be found jobs around the city, which was a major pull for players, especially in the 30s Depression. Cardiff was not designated the Capital of Wales until 1955, and its northern suburb, Llandaff, is one of the oldest cathedrals in Britain, along with St. David's, Bangor and St. Asaf. All are older than the English cathedrals. 'Ponty' came good in the 1970s but even then lost the wonderful Tommy David to Llanelli, who went to play for a marvellous team. From 1920-21 to 1923-24, Phil Rowlands of Taff's Well played 44 times for Cardiff, and Taff's Well's great captain Fred Porter helped out on 5 occasions in 1925-26 and 1926-27. Tom Lewis of Taff's Well turned out for Cardiff no less than 260 times from 1923-24 to 1932-33, in that last year captaining the team. Taff's Well's Glamorgan policeman Fred Lee played 68 games for Cardiff between 1924-25 and 1927-28. His brother Trevor, another policeman, played 12 times from 1925-26 to 1929-30. Fred Lee was Cardiff captain in 1925-26, scoring 5 tries in that season. In 1926-27, an incredible four sets of brothers played for the Firsts, the Lees, plus Kevin and Bernard Turnbull (of whom more later); Tom and Jim Burns, and Dai and Llewellyn Williams. This must be a record for a first-class club. In September 1926, fullback Trevor Lee set an unbeatable record against Cardiff and District. With 12 conversions and a penalty he converted 13 of 14 kicks, the fourteenth hitting an upright. Cardiff scraped home 66-10 in their traditional opening game, but Trevor was not assured of a regular first team place and transferred to first team rugby at Penarth, returning to play for Cardiff three years later.

Such was Cardiff's power in attracting players that they began running **two First XVs for 5 Years**, so in 1926-27, so 82 First Team games were played in the season, 47 by the 'A' First XV and 35 by the 'B' First XV. Between them they lost 27 games, but the policy still lasted for five seasons. Davies informs us that '*on the day that Wales played Ireland on 12th March 1926, Walter Morgan, a former neat scrumhalf from Taff's Well, played in the Cardiff First XV against Mountain Ash, dropping a goal, and also against Glamorgan Wanderers scoring a try. Subject for a quiz?*' Morgan played 14 times for the firsts from 1920-21 to 1925-26. In 1926-27 over the Easter period, the 'A' Firsts beat the Barbarians on Easter Saturday 16-8, won again on Easter Monday and Tuesday, but lost on the Wednesday – 4 games in 5 days. The 'B' Firsts on that weekend played Torquay, Exeter and Ebbw Vale in 4 days. 1926-27 saw Cardiff's highest points total on record, 666 in 43 games, including 157 tries, a total not to be approached until Bleddyn Williams' wonderful season of 1945-46, with 661 points in 41 games, 149 tries.

However, there were complaints from Leicester, Aberavon, Coventry and others that Cardiff was not playing its strongest team against them. For the 10 November 1928 away Leicester game, which Leicester won 8-5, Cardiff played their strongest team against Newport, winning 12-6. In the return fixture at the Arms Park, Leicester lost 8-5, while Cardiff also won away at Gloucester 10-5, that same afternoon. Disgruntled at twice facing a Cardiff 'B' First XV, from that season, 1928-29, Leicester cut off fixtures until 1945-46, a time when every team in the land wanted a fixture with Cardiff to swell their gate receipts. The best teams wanted the best opposition both in order to improve their teams and attract better players. Other, lesser, teams were happy facing the 'B' Firsts, as it meant that they had beaten the mighty Cardiff. At the end of 1930-31, the experiment was discontinued. Incidentally, all the 'B' XV fixtures are included in Cardiff's official statistics, e.g., in 1929-30, 'the other Side' only won 5 out of 27 games, skewing Cardiff's record deleteriously for these five seasons.

A major highlight every year was the Easter game against the Barbarians, and C. D. Aarvold was asked about their 1928 game: '*I seem to remember playing golf at Penarth one Sunday and drinking a pint of beer on the next tee after winning a hole. We had some difficulty getting down to breakfast one year, because someone had thought it right to remove the iron railings from the sea front, and in the quiet of the night had dragged a long length of them up the stairs and along the corridors of the hotel in which we stayed, a highly complicated manoeuvre and very difficult to unravel, and the perpetrators were never discovered. Yet the discipline maintained by Emile de Lisa and Haigh-Smith and Hughie was marvellous to behold - Penarth, Swansea, Cardiff and Newport were reasonably tough opponents to deal with in five days, and an ability to move at a fast speed was a useful asset, both on and off the field. An invitation to join the Baa-Baas on their Easter tour was seldom ever refused. I personally still wear a somewhat crocked nose as a mark of the glory and the fun of it all.'*

In the years heading towards WW2, Davies notes that *'Cardiff were reinforced by some brilliant youngsters, some of whom gained Blues for Cambridge or Oxford, Caps for Wales, and some – the Captaincy of Cardiff. The Turnbulls, that great player and gentleman, John Roberts, his brother W. (Bill) Roberts, the Bowcotts, Ronnie Boon – another grand wing, with "Percy Bush like" cheekiness and versatility; Syd Cravos, Frank Williams and others. The versatile half-back, Bobbie Delahay was elected skipper for 1926-27, and with plenty of talent available the Committee "in its wisdom" decided on the experiment of "running" two "First XVs." This experiment became the subject of debate for years, and the reversion to a First XV and an Athletic XV in 1931-32 was, no doubt, much in deference to the feelings of many first-class Clubs, two of whom, for example, would find themselves playing Cardiff on the same day. Who amongst us, for example relished defeats on the same day, by Blackheath and Maesteg for example, or by Northampton and Ebbw Vale?'*

During this period the 'A team' played London Irish on 26 December 1928, Scotland's Watsonians on 27 December and travelled to play Lansdowne in Dublin the day after. They beat Lansdown 21-3, 5-0 on tries and were honoured by a celebratory dinner in Jury's Hotel in the evening. For anyone interested the Starter was tomato soup; then a Fish course – Boiled Turbot or Lobster; followed by a Joint of Roast Mutton & Jelly with Peas & Potatoes; Sweet was Apple Turnover or Fruit Salad; ended by Coffee. Cardiff had defeated London Irish 16-0, scoring 4 tries; and Watsonians 19-0 (5 tries); and Lansdowne 21-3 (5 tries). Thus, in three days they beat three first-class sides by 14 tries to 1 penalty, 56-3 on points. In February 1930, Bernard Turnbull, one of the six brothers who played for Cardiff, played for Wales alongside three other Cardiff threequarters, Louis Dyke, Gwyn Davies and Ronnie Boon, losing 12-9 at Murrayfield. In the 11-0 win at Stade Colombes in March 1930. Wales had two teenagers in the pack, its oldest member was a 25-year-old second row, and the team had an average age of 22 years and 109 days, the youngest on record. The 1930s are covered in more detail in Chapters 5 to 14 as the first Williams brother, Gwyn, joined the club.

A Brief History of Cardiff and its Players to the 1970s

During wartime, the Club arranged as many charity games as possible, with rugby league players participating alongside union players, and the Committee worked to ensure that a team would be up and running for the 1945-46 season. Davies writes: *'From the very resumption, the Team played with such co-ordination and speed that it was soon the talk and following of the Rugby World. It revitalised the game! Cardiff was its healthy heart! In this latest era, 1945-46 to 1950-51, there is no question that the brilliant standard of play equalled the greatest years of the Golden Era – many aver that it was superior! The names of the players are too fresh in your memory to be repeated here, and their individual achievements are still new, but, it must be said that the Club produced some brilliant leaders: Dr. Jack Matthews, Haydn Tanner, Bleddyn Williams, W.E. (Bill) Tamplin, and a combination of the finest exponents of the Rugby game in their supporting players.*

In the House of Commons it was stated that "Cardiff is undoubtedly the finest rugby club" (L.J. Callaghan, M.P., Cardiff South). 661 points were scored in Dr. Jack's first year; Bleddyn 30, and Dr. Glyn Jones 28 tries. All matches won until Boxing Day when we were defeated by the Kiwis by a 3 points to 0 defeat, to be later avenged in the seven-a-side at Twickenham. Another successful season, 1946-47, followed. Bill Tamplin kicked 52 goals, and Lyn Williams' Athletic XV lost only one match.

Then followed 1947-48, perhaps the greatest of all in terms of play and results. Haydn Tanner moulded his rugby craftsmen into an almost perfect attacking machine, indeed I would say his own ability reached a peak in the process; 803 points scored; 39 out of 41 matches won; Bleddyn's club record of 41 tries established; the Australians beaten by 11 points to 3. All this despite the drain on the club for Welsh Trials (then three a year, in season) *and International matches. Years 1948-49 to 1950-51 were all excellent. The Club formed a Youth XV in support of the W.R.U. formation; it lost but one game under Peter Owen in its first year. Friendly ties were made with the French Clubs at Nantes and Cognac; a Past vs. Present XV produced £1,400 for the Cardiff Royal Infirmary. The Athletic XV, under Len Evans, broke the "Rags" Record with a total of 636 points in 1948-49. A French referee, Louis Murail, officiated for a Cardiff-London Welsh match on the park; Billy Cleaver retired; 48,500 spectators at the Cardiff v. Newport game, February 7th, 1951; the old Park churned up badly in the 1950-51 season; it has now been thoroughly repaired; highest honours have been bestowed upon out players and officials, and young Cliff Morgan was capped against France on his 21st birthday... perhaps these written words will have reminded the readers of a pleasant memory or two, and the great place Cardiff Rugby Club holds in the Rugby World.'* (Davies was writing in September 1951).

In 1953, Dave Phillips wrote in the *South Wales Echo* of Bleddyn captaining Cardiff to beat New Zealand – '*For 80 minutes we saw the traditional skill and fire of what has rightly been called "the greatest Rugby Club in the World", countered by the all-action enthusiasm of a determined All Black side who tried everything in their power to whittle down Cardiff's half-time lead of five points in a storming grand-stand finish.*' In the years before the War, the eldest Williams brother Gwyn was playing with his uncle Roy Roberts for Cardiff. Roy Roberts (1936-37 to 1948-49) also played after the War in the second row, with his nephew Bleddyn Williams and Bleddyn's cousin Welsh international Bill Tamplin (1945-46 to 1952-53). During and after the War, the brothers Vaughan and Brinley Williams ('Bryn' 1949-50) played intermittently for the club in unofficial matches, as did Bleddyn (1945-46 to 1954-55). Then came Lloyd, the fifth brother, who played from 1952-53 to 1963-64, initially alongside Bleddyn, and then with the three youngest brothers Cenydd (1956-57 to 1962-63); Elwyn (1958-59 to 1972-73) and Tony (1959-60 to 1973-74). **For 41 years, these brothers played continuously for Cardiff**, some making appearances for charity matches in WW2.

Indeed, the four youngest brothers played together several times before Lloyd retired. Gwyn left to join the greatest rugby league club of the 1930s, Wigan, and Cenydd joined its equivalent in the 60's, St Helens. The brothers played 1,480 times for Cardiff Firsts, in the years before no substitutes, and in the years when Cardiff were regarded as the best rugby club in the world. The book encompasses not only the Taff's Well Williams brothers, their uncle Roy Roberts, their cousin Bill Tamplin, but the Taff's Well and Cardiff rugby clubs, and the players around them.

In the 125 years of playing from 1876-77 to 1990, Cardiff have had two losing seasons, in the nineteenth century. In 1881-82, 22 games were played, 8 won, 10 lost and 4 drawn. In 1891-92, 13 games were won, 14 lost and 4 drawn. The club never came even close to a losing season thereafter. Cardiff's iconic home has always been the Cardiff Arms Park, originally the ground of both Cardiff cricket and rugby clubs, and the venue is known across the world. In 1912 the first stand was erected, and several stands and terraces have developed the famous ground. In October 1966, the world's first floodlit game was held at Cardiff Arms Park, with Cardiff RFC beating the Barbarians 12-8. Until 1969 Cardiff and Wales played their home matches on the same pitch, but in the 1969-70 season, the National Ground project established a new stadium for international matches, with Cardiff fixtures switched to the original cricket ground on the Arms Park site, which is still the current site for Cardiff RFC.

Only 20 years later, the ugly concrete monolith now known as the National Stadium, was replaced by the more attractive Millennium (Principality) Stadium. The decision by visiting teams to play with the roof open in bad weather is disliked by all those sitting near the numerous exits, as a cold wind funnels through and chills one to the marrow. I know well

55

wrapped-up people who have at left half-time. There has never been any survey of customer satisfaction with the new stadium, with its monopoly pricing of alcohol and poor choice of food, nor of the dissatisfaction of rugby supporters having to stand up and sit down, as beer is transported along rows of seats constantly during games. Watching a game is no longer for the cognoscenti who have played the game, and wish to watch it, but for men and women wishing for a drinking interlude between hostelries. (This is 'grumpy old man-speak', you will be aware).

Cardiff Rugby Club continues to play at the adjoining Cardiff Arms Park, as did the regional team Cardiff Blues from 2003 to 2021. In 1888 Cardiff beat the New Zealand Maoris, the first rugby touring team, and Cardiff has beaten all the major touring teams, with Australia never having beaten Cardiff RFC in six attempts. In more recent times, Cardiff were Heineken Cup finalists in 1996, domestic Cup champions on seven occasions, in 1981, 1982, 1984, 1986, 1987, 1994 and 1997, Welsh League champions in 1995 and won the Welsh/Scottish league title in 2000. In 2003 Regional rugby was introduced to Wales and the professional players started to play in a new team and in a new league. The Cardiff Blues team became the standard bearer for the City's professional team. Cardiff RFC then formed part of the Welsh pyramid system hopefully feeding players into the top level of Regional rugby. The formation of the Welsh Premiership in 2003 allowed players an opportunity to showcase themselves to Regional teams, and several players from Cardiff RFC have gone on to play not only at Regional level but also in internationals and for the British Lions.

Cardiff's contribution to rugby in general and Wales in particular has been immense, and it is worthwhile mentioning here its international importance. This book attempts to place Cardiff RFC in its acknowledged 'greatest' position over the years up to the end of the last Williams brother's playing career with them, in 1974, as well as tell their lives and the story of the rugby club and village of their birth, Taff's Well. In fact, the 'Golden Eras' of Cardiff coincided with the first three of Wales - 1908, 1909, 1911 (first era); 1950, 1952 (second era) and 1971-79. 1971 was the beginning of the third 'Golden Era' for the club, with the world's greatest half-back pair, Barry John and Gareth Edwards, and the superb wings John Bevan and Gerald Davies. All were first choice Test players for the British Lions, and of incredible importance for Welsh success in the 1970s.

There was a wonderful period in the 1970s, when Wales played superb attacking rugby. There were five Triple Crowns, in 1971, 1976, 1977, 1978 and 1979 (- the 'QuadTriple Crown' according to my Grogg statuette of a Welsh player), with the 1971, 1976 and 1978 successes contributing to Grand Slam successes. The 1979 Triple Crown also secured the Championship outright. Cardiff's three-quarter quartet played in all games when available. 1971 began with an easy home win at the National Stadium against England. Welsh wings John Bevan scored a try and Gerald

Davies bagged two, with John Taylor converting two, JPR Williams scoring a penalty and Barry John dropping two goals (- this was before he became a recognised penalty taker). 22-6 to Wales, 3-1 on tries and supporters were optimistic heading to Scotland. 'I was there', in the words of Max Boyce, in what has been called *'The greatest Five Nations match of all time'*. Wales *'refused to pick a first-choice goalkicker preferring to stick with their attacking team and sink Scotland on try-count.'* It was the idea of the coach Clive Rowlands, to force the team to play attacking rugby. Can anyone think of such an attitude today?

John Taylor, with the last kick of the game, converted from the touchline for Wales to win 19-18. *Walesonline* reported *'"There's been a whole lot said about that conversion and one thing was I only took it because Barry John was concussed in the process of scoring his try," said Taylor. "Two weeks before Scotland I had kicked two from the right-hand touchline against England. I had missed the conversion of Gareth Edwards' try from a similar spot earlier on at Murrayfield but I can tell you now I was always delegated to take that last kick."*

Keith Jarrett had gone north a year or two earlier and Clive Rowlands was asked by journalists on the eve of the game, "Do you know who's going to take the penalties?". Clive in typical fashion replied: "No but I can tell you who's going to take the conversions though.". "He was setting out his stall because like England a fortnight earlier, we weren't going to play a specialist kicker. JPR was not much of a place kicker and Barry had never kicked much at goal before then. It was just one those quirky things and he turned out to be a great kicker. We decided to mix and match and anything out on the right-hand side of the field, I was going to take it because I was a left-footer and tended to draw the ball in a bit." And on his date with destiny, what was going through Taylor's mind as he made his mark in the Murrayfield soil? "In some ways the pressure was off me because it was wide out and I was certainly fully aware I was going to be a villain or a hero in front of 105,000 rugby fans lining the pitch," he added. "It was then the magnitude of the kick hit home and I was thinking to myself: 'My God this is a biggie'. "The atmosphere that day at Murrayfield or on any game when we went to Edinburgh, was just incredible. That bank on the far side from where I was kicking from was the only part of Murrayfield those days where you could pay on the gate. That's why all the miners and steelworkers in the 70s took the week off and went up there. There were certainly more Welshmen than Scotsmen over there judging by the roar when the kick went over. I was trying to just keep my emotions in check running back after that kick."' This writer was there with a bunch of friends, heading to the game after 'one last pint' and saw everyone streaming past us back towards town. The ground was full and the gates were shut. Ah well, led by a Scots mate, eight of us vaulted over and began legging it up the huge grassy bank, avoiding the steps and stewards. The largest lad, a Liverpudlian was lagging behind, not helped by a policeman hanging on to his foot. We formed a quick human chain and dragged him up while he removed the officer with his other foot.

In the game, Scotland had scored two tries and four penalties, to Wales' <u>five</u> tries, with only the last and one other being converted. Try scorers were Taylor, and Cardiff's contingent of Davies (two), John and Edwards. Next up was Ireland, who with the benefit of Mike Gibson as a kicker, had just won at Murrayfield 17-5. In Cardiff, Gibson kicked Ireland's three penalties, but again Cardiff players scored all the tries, Gerald Davies achieving another brace on the wing, and scrumhalf Edwards equalling him with a pair. Barry John at last took over the regular goal-kicking, converting only one of the four tries, but kicking two penalties and a dropped goal – 23-9 to Wales. The team travelled to and France for the first Grand Slam since 1952. Again, the Cardiff quartet were crucial to the win. Unbeaten France scored a converted try, but Edwards and John scored tries, with John converting one for a momentous 9-5 win.

Grogg of Gerald Davies

The **1971 Grand Slam** points table gave Wales, despite missing many, many kicks, a points difference of 72-38 = +34; followed by France +1;

Ireland – 5; England -14 and Scotland – 17. Has there ever been a table like that in rugby? Wales easily were the most attractive side, winning on tries 14-3 (3-1 England; 5-1 Scotland; 4-0 Ireland; and 2-1 France. **Of the 14 tries scored, John Taylor of London Welsh bagged one, but 13 were scored by the four Cardiff players in the team!** Gerald Davies scored 2 tries in each of the first three games; John Bevan scored one, Barry John two and Gareth Edwards four. Only 5 of 14 tries were converted, 3 by John Taylor and 2 by Barry John. Other points came from a penalty by JPR Williams, 3 pens by Barry John, and John dropped 3 goals. Not only did the Cardiff contingent score nearly all the tries, 13 out of 14, but Barry John contributed another 17 points with kicks. Apart from John Taylor's 4 conversions and a try, and JPR's penalty, equalling 14 points, **59 of Wales' 73 points were scored by their four world-class Cardiff players**. Points scored by players were Barry John (not kicking for first two games) 26pts; Gerald Davis 18 pts; Gareth Edwards 12pts; John Taylor (London Welsh) 11pts; John Bevan 3 pts; and JPR Williams (London Welsh) 3pts. Wales scored 14 tries; 5 conversions (10 missed!); 4 penalties and 3 dropped goals. Can any other team point to an end of a winning season score of 14 tries (5 converted), 4 pens and 3 dropped goals? This was a time when rugby was interesting to watch and play, not like today's mixture of 'kickfest' and trench warfare played by giants.

Wales did not travel to Ireland in 1972 because of IRA threats, and this would, in this author's eyes, have been another Triple Crown and Grand Slam. Away to England, JPR Williams scored a try, with Barry John converting and kicking two penalties, to win 12-3, a penalty by Hillier. At home to Scotland, the visitors scored a try among their 12 points, but Wales amassed two tries by Gareth Edwards and others by Gerald Davies, Roy Bergiers and John Taylor, with Barry John converting three and kicking three penalties of the Welsh total of 35 points (45 in today's scoring). Wales then beat France with tries by John Bevan and Gerald Davies and four penalties by Barry John, to two penalties, winning 20-6 in Cardiff. They scored 8-1 in tries in the three games, with Cardiff players being responsible for 54 points of the 67-21 total.

CHAPTER 3 – TAFF'S WELL – A BRIEF HISTORY

This short chapter is included to give the reader a feeling for the home of the brothers. The River Taff (Afon Tâf) begins as two rivers in the Brecon Beacons. The Tâf Fawr (Big Taff) rises below the peak of Corn Du, south-west of Pen y Fan Mountain, flowing southerly through a steep-sided valley. The Tâf Fechan (Smaller Taff) rises south of Pen y Fan, forming reservoirs, to form a confluence near Merthyr Tydfil. From Merthyr, the Taff is joined by the River Cynon at Abercynon, and by the River Rhondda at Pontypridd, then flows through Taff's Well, and six miles onwards south to Cardiff, skirting the Millennium Rugby Stadium and magnificent Cardiff Castle. Its exit into the Severn Sea (Môr Hafren, Bristol Channel), like that of the nearly adjacent River Ely, now forms a massive freshwater lake behind the barrage and seawater locks at Cardiff Bay.

1913 Taff's Well Youth XV, Dai Millward captain

The Rhondda Valley had many coal pits and engineering works, so from the time of the Industrial Revolution to the destruction of the coal industry in the 1960s, the Taff was a terribly polluted river. To carry coal, limestone and iron ore to the port of Cardiff, the Glamorganshire Canal, a stupendous feat of engineering, was authorised in 1790. In 1796 it was written: '*The canal is brought through mountainous scenery with wonderful ingenuity.*' From Merthyr to Taff's Well to Cardiff Docks, the canal was 25 miles long, and dropped 542 feet, with 50 locks, but sadly only traces remain after railways, then roads, superseded it. Taff's Well, where the Taff Valley narrows, grew into an important railway junction during the mid-to late nineteenth century, when Cardiff was a major global exporter of coal. Tragically, the A470 dual carriageway, heading north out of Cardiff via Merthyr to Conwy/Llandudno was built over much of the canal.

Over the years, many Taff's Well rugby players, including Elwyn Williams, worked for Forgemasters in the village. From the Taff's Well RFC Facebook site, in June 2019 we read: '*South Wales Forgemasters -*

The end of a Glorious Industrial Era. Today, the Forgehammer that synched with our bodily biorhythms, fell for the very last time as an eerie silence surrounded the village of Taff's Well. The last rites were carried out by two colleagues, who having drop-forged the last component, turned to shake hands and began to contemplate life without the metronomic beat that had become so much a part of their, and our lives. From a once mighty workforce of 450, the last remaining twelve employees clocked off the final shift, the remnants of an institution which started in 1938 and become a source of employment for thousands of people over its working life. The iconic Forgemasters site will be demolished to make way for the £100 million train depot development, totally reshaping the landscape and erasing any physical trace of the contribution it made to the social and economic way of life in Taff's Well. As part of our historical village project theme, we will be keeping the memory of the Forgemasters alive with a forthcoming project.' In the 10-acre Garth Works and Estate site, where the main 200,000 sq ft Forgemasters operation, with its 5-ton hammer, closed in the 1980s, there are now several small business units.

Taff's Well (Ffynnon Tâf) had a population of just 3,672 in the 2011 Census, and the town stretches alongside the River Taff, hemmed in by the Taff and Garth Mountain to the west, and the A470 bypass to the east. The old 'Cardiff Road' runs through the town, parallel to the A470 for a few miles north, squeezed in the valley, to the small town of Nantgarw. Nantgarw Colliery was shut down in 1986, throwing 573 people out of work. Twin shafts had been sunk in 1911 to reach the coal seam at a depth of more than 2,600 feet in 1915, placing them 2,000 ft below sea level. Nantgarw was at the time the deepest pit to be sunk in the South Wales Coalfield. The village also deserves mention for the survival of the Nantgarw Tradition of Welsh Folk Dance, with hammer and stick, as well as the famous Nantgarw Porcelain (1813-1820) which can be seen in the Nantgarw Chinaworks Museum. From Taff's Well, sometimes referred to as the *'Gates to the Valleys,'* one can see the amazing red spires of Castell Coch, a Norman castle built in 1081, further fortified from 1267-1277, but destroyed by the Welsh in 1314. Restored by William Burgess between 1875 and 1891, although he died before completion, it has been called '*one of the greatest Victorian triumphs of architectural composition.*'

The actor David Jason spent much time in Taff's Well, and the BBC TV comedy series *Open All Hours,* in which he starred with Ronnie Barker, was based upon Arthur's shop in the town. The shop was dismantled and sent to the St Fagan's Museum of Welsh Life. Taff's Well also recently featured in the Sky sitcom *Stella* Starring Ruth Jones, when the post office in nearby Nantgarw was a filming location in the series. The best views in the area are from Garth Mountain (Mynydd y Garth), known locally as 'The Garth', which overlooks the village. It was the inspiration for the book and 1995 film '*The Englishman Who Went Up a Hill but Came Down a Mountain.'* Hugh Grant was typically type-cast as the star in a charming story. Christopher Monger, a Taff's Well native, wrote the book and directed the film. There are four Bronze Age tumuli (burial mounds, about 4,000 years old) on top of the Pennant Sandstone Garth, but the adjoining Lesser Garth has almost been destroyed by iron ore mining and limestone quarrying. The valley and the lower slopes of the Garth, facing Taff's Well, were formerly full of small coal mines which fed the great ironworks over the river from Taff's Well. The Garth stands above both Taff's Well and Tongwynlais, but from Pentyrch on the other side of the hill the climb is much easier. Sitting higher on the hillside, Pentyrch is less linear than Taff's Well and Tongwynlais, with a far higher percentage of Welsh speakers.

Taff's Well Park (Parc Ffynnon Tâf) is the site of a once-famous thermal spring, bringing visitors from far and wide in the years 1840-1914. It enjoys temperatures which average a tepid 21.6 degrees C, and the well is Wales's only natural thermal spa. It may have been a religious site, and it is said that floods in 1799 laid bare Roman masonry adjoining the well. In 1891 the healing well was enlarged, because of increasing visitor numbers, but by 1929 had fallen into disuse. It was resurrected in the 1930s, with a new swimming pool incorporating the spa, heated by the spring. The Williams brothers learned to swim there, but in 1960 another flood sadly destroyed the baths.

Let us drift back to 1861, to read what *'The Book of South Wales'* tells us of the village, just 26 years before its rugby club was formed. After describing Castell Coch, and on a journey to Newbridge (Pontypridd), Mr. and Mrs. Hall write: *'Resuming the Taff Vale Railway, having journeyed eight miles from Cardiff, we alight at a singularly picturesque railway station, TAFF'S WELL, to visit one of the most remarkable of all the relics of old times to be found in the Principality. We are now in a great mining district; the hills above us produce the iron and coal that make the district "rich" and give its true power to Great Britain. The mountain before us is the GARTH MOUNTAIN; at its foot is an iron foundry of great extent, around which are collected the dwellings of labourers. The object to which we direct special attention is "the Well", on the left bank of the river; the hill and the cottages being on the other side. Taff's Well has long been famous for the cure of many diseases – rheumatism especially. It stands in a field, close to the water's edge – so close as to be frequently overflowed. Several springs are bubbling from the earth; they are tepid, and have a slight mineral tinge: only one of them is enclosed, and that is encompassed with sheets of iron. At all hours of the day or night, there are ailing and decrepid (sic) persons, men, women and children, all waiting a "turn" to bathe. Women must bathe here as well as men, and when a bonnet is hung on the outside, it is a sign that the gentler sex have possession. As but two, or at most three, can find room in the bath inside, it is obvious that persons taking relief must wait sometimes for hours before they can gain right of entrance... From our inquiries, we have reason to conclude that the waters do relieve, and in some cases, banish chronic disorders.'* Later a stone building was erected around the well, and the tepid waters used to fill a swimming pool. It is said that the 'healing well' was used by the Romans, and almost certainly from the 5th century onwards was dedicated to a British saint, but cannot as yet receive funding for restoration, along with the reinstatement of the swimming pool.

It would be remiss of me not to mention another claim to fame of the town. The ten-member Taff's Well & Nantgarw Community Council hit the national press in 2010, being criticised by the Wales Audit Office, for breaching financial and corporate governance regulations with its financial records. It was described as *'The Worst Run Council in Wales'* (despite very stiff competition), with calls for the *'wholesale sacking'* of the members for breaching *'financial and corporate governance regulations because of its "inadequate" financial records, supporting paperwork and minutes between 2002 and 2006'*. Nothing happened – this is Wales, after all, and the council was merely following the template laid down by its superiors in power in Cardiff Bay.

CHAPTER 4 - TAFF'S WELL RUGBY CLUB and its FIRST WELSH INTERNATIONAL – TOM LEWIS

Quoted excerpts, except where notified, courtesy of David Peter Thomas: *'A View from the Garth – One Hundred Years of Taff's Well Rugby'* 1984

Taff's Well RFC was founded in 1887 and was successful in gaining membership to the Welsh Football Union (later the WRU) in 1900. St. Peter's RFC in Cardiff reports on its website: *'For the 1890/91 season.... Opponents included Barry Dock and Railways, Red Rose (Taff's Well), Cardiff Rangers, Barry Rovers, Llandaff Yard, Nantgarw, Cardiff Stars, Roath Windsor and Cardiff Albion. The team travelled to away games by public transport, either train or bus, and met at the stations.'* The first game played by the then small town of Cardiff was in 1874, but a form of the game predated that, with a drunken bloodbath of a game, between little Llanwenog and Llandysul on Christmas Day 1719, being recorded by the *Western Mail*. Rugby as we know it probably first appeared in Wales at St David's College, Lampeter in 1850.

The Welsh Rugby Union was probably founded in Swansea in 1880, but there is no written record remaining. The team representatives were thought to have been from Cardiff, Chepstow Haverfordwest, Llandaff (now part of Cardiff), Llanelli, Neath, Newport, Pontypridd and Swansea. A year later, in March 1881, eleven clubs met in the Castle Hotel, Neath to form what would be accepted as a Welsh rugby union. The twelve founding clubs of the WFU (Welsh Football Union), as it was then known, were Cardiff, Brecon, Swansea, Lampeter, Llandeilo, Llandovery, Llanelli, Merthyr, Newport, Bangor, Pontypool and what is regarded as the oldest rugby club in Wales, Neath RFC, who had representatives attending, but seem to have been accidentally omitted as being present.

Clubhouse, 2022

Many rugby players have moved from Taff's Well down to Cardiff to further their playing careers over the last 120 years, and the club was later a 'feeder club' for the regional team, Cardiff Blues from 2003 to 2021. To briefly explain, Cardiff rugby club was renamed Cardiff Blues (Gleision Caerdydd) in 2003, under a reorganisation of major clubs into four regions in Wales. This has not been a success in the country. The reserve team, Cardiff Athletic, the 'Rags', then became Cardiff Rugby Club, a feeder into the Blues. In 2021 it was announced that the Blues would be thankfully extinguished, with that team being renamed Cardiff Rugby/Rygbi Caerdydd, and Cardiff being renamed Cardiff RFC. The club is returning to its traditional colours of Cambridge Blue and Black. The tiny village and rugby club of Taff's Well has produced **three Welsh captains** (Bleddyn Williams, Lloyd Williams, Steve Fenwick), six Welsh internationals (the above plus Harry Rees, Tom Lewis and Ian 'Ike' Stephens) and **three British Lions** (Bleddyn Williams, Steve Fenwick and Ian Stephens). Bleddyn played in 3 of 4 tests in New Zealand and Australia in 1950, missing one through injury, and captaining the Lions. Steve

Fenwick played all four Lions tests in New Zealand in 1977. Ike Stephens toured with the Lions to South Africa in 1980 and New Zealand in 1983. Dozens of Taff's Well players have gone on to play top class rugby. This is not an unreasonable record for a place with a population of under 4,000.

On the other side of the Garth Mountain is Pentyrch, traditionally the greatest local rivals of Taff's Well rugby. Another local rival team, only formed in 1946, Llantwit Fardre also adjoins the Garth, on the other side to Taff's Well, and like Pentyrch and Taff's Well was a feeder club for Cardiff Blues. Tom Lewis, the Welsh cap, played for both Pentyrch and Taff's Well, and the Pentyrch club has also recently produced Harry Rhys Robinson (Cardiff Blues and Wales). Taff's Well's first recorded game took place at Pentyrch RFC, in 1887, which Taff's Well won by two goals, four tries and seven minors to nil. (A minor was a point gained when the opposition grounded the ball behind their own line.) Until 1891, a try scored one point, a conversion two. For the next two years, tries scored two points and conversion three. In 1893, the modern pattern of tries scoring more was begun, with three points awarded for a try, two for a kick. The number of points from a try increased to four in 1971 and five in 1992.

Proximity to Nantgarw to the north and Tongwynlais to the south gave a good supply of players from their teams to Taff's Well over the years, just as Taff's Well lost many of their better players to greater clubs. From 1882 the village began playing more games against new teams springing up in Cardiff and District, and in 1890, upon joining the equivalent of what is now the Welsh Rugby Union, they adopted a blue and black strip. In that year the player Dai Chislett caught a runaway horse, and they drew 0-0 at Tredegar before a crowd of 1,200 to 1,300. Dai was *'the life and soul of the team… songster, comedian and Powder-Hall sprinter*. Dai's son Ivor followed him in his role of club entertainer and was prominent in this guise in the 1920s, while his grandsons Arthur Chislett and Colin Johns, kept up the family tradition in recent years. Dai Chislett is remembered in his later life as "The man who kept the bicycle shop in the village." He was a very colourful character.'*

*The indefatigable sportswriter Brian Lee reminisced in *Wales Online*, 19 January 2015: '*Once one of the great events of the sporting calendar, the Welsh Powderhall Handicap sprint attracted up to 40,000 spectators to Taff Vale Park, Pontypridd. Professional sprinters from all over the world competed in this famous 130-yard handicap foot race. It was first held in 1903 when it was billed as 'The Great Welsh Sprint'. Boxers such Peerless Jim Driscoll and Jimmy trained their own schools of sprinters, running to their orders. Some athletes put lead in their spiked shoes to slow them down so that they could obtain good handicap marks. They were given a weekly wage and the best of food and drink. And before the big event they would spend months away from home with their masseurs and trainers who would put them through their paces. Mike 'Jake' Crowley, who played for*

Cardiff RFC between 1909 and 1920, wore a leaded belt to hoodwink the handicapper. He made one of the greatest killings in the history of the race when he won in 1912. The man behind the deception was Peerless Jim Driscoll himself and he gave Jake a gold watch and £800 to go with the £100 prize money he had won. (Driscoll had presumably laid many bets).

Before he competed in the 1923 event, Cardiff's Pat Barry had run in races all over Wales without winning a single heat, just to convince the handicapper that he had no chance of winning. He was given the limit 20 yards start and the bookmakers made him the rank outsider at 100-1. He coasted home in a very fast time. When Bryn Davies won in 1929 he was given a hero's welcome, as he had fulfilled his ambition of being the first man from Pontypridd to win. In 1930, following a big row between the promoters, two "Welsh Powderhalls" were held both claiming to be the official one, at Taff Vale Park and Caerphilly.' With the dispute, Depression and oncoming War, the event faded away.

However, Dai Chislett was not in the same league as another Taff's Well player, Tom Davies, who appeared in the inaugural game at Taff's Well in 1887. He was: 'a very well-known runner in South Wales. He made a lot of money from his sprinting. On September 8th, 1900, he took on E. Long of Cardiff over 200 yards at the Treforest Running Ground for a prize of £15. On the rugby field Tom was a consistent scorer for Taff's Well. His training schedule included drinking glasses of egg and sherry in the Castle under the watchful eye of Fred Harris. In fact, Fred was very strict about what his players should drink and insisted that they trained on "Smith's Football Stout."' For fifty years from around 1890, the Castle Hotel became the heart of the club. A large advertisement in The Pontypridd Observer in 1900 promotes: THE RHONDDA COMEDIAN and CHAMPION TAMBOURINE SOLOIST OF ENGLAND AND WALES, will be pleased to meet some of his old and new friends at the CASTLE HOTEL...TAFF'S WELL ... cyclists accommodated, and parties catered for... FRED HARRIS – CASTLE HOTEL – TAFF'S WELL ... PAINTING and DECORATING Done at very Reasonable Charges.'

Obviously one of the first marketing men, Fred challenged the world to a tambourine championship, and with no takers he could argue that he was the 'World Tambourine Champion'. That title followed his main billing as 'The Rhondda Comedian.' He was the rugby club secretary in 1900 and wrote match reports for the local press, with games being played behind his hotel (which acted as changing rooms and clubhouse), in the grandly named Castle Grounds. Fred was what we call in Wales 'a character', always performing somewhere or other, and 'in June 1900 he arranged a Grand Cycle Carnival, one of the biggest processions ever seen in the village.' Monies raised went to the 'Reservist Fund', and he recruited Taff's Well players to form the Taff's Well Company of the 3rd Volunteer Battalion, to potentially fight the Boers. Harris used the Castle as 'the *meeting place for rugby, cricket and cycling clubs'* and it was also used for Smoking Concerts and fund-raising events. Fred, as secretary of the rugby club, was also responsible for obtaining membership of the WRU-equivalent in 1890, and was greatly missed when he moved down to Cardiff to become a painter and decorator, or 'scenic painter' as he called it.

Apart from the Chisletts, *'Several families began appearing for the team, the first being Frank Bunn (1900-1921), Donald Bunn (1925-27), Gordon Bunn (1954-86) and Huw Bunn (1984-).'* Frank Bunn, club treasurer, used to bare-knuckle fight for money behind the Castle Hotel, while the spectators made bets. Many pairs of brothers played for the club, and sons followed fathers. For the purposes of our story, in 1910 an imposing figure is that of Ted Roberts in the team photograph. His son Roy was to play for the club, Cardiff and Wales. His daughter Nell married Arthur Williams, and they had eight sons and four daughters. Ted's son Roy Roberts (of whom much more later) was the thus the uncle of the eight Williams brothers who played for Cardiff, playing many times alongside the eldest Gwyn, and also with Brinley and Bleddyn Williams. The Williams's mother Nell had a sister, who gave birth to their cousin, Welsh international captain 'Bill' Tamplin, who played alongside Roy Roberts and Bleddyn for Cardiff.

In 1900 Mrs. Delaney, who had a hosiery shop in Pontypridd, had presented the team with a set of brand-new blue and black jerseys, but it seems the team had been known as 'Red Rose', perhaps from an emblem. World War I halted games until 1919, when blue and black was changed to a blue and white team strip. In 1922 all white kit was used (until 1970), giving the team the nickname of 'The Lilywhites'. Frank Bunn began playing again at the age of 44, and the outside-half Gwyn ('Top Shop') Williams returned to play for the club. He had played outside-half and scrumhalf with great success for Penarth and 12 times for Cardiff before the War, and had refused all efforts by Cardiff to retain him. After two seasons, he emigrated to farm in South Africa, but returned for the 1925-26 season, the club's best player for years. Ted Roberts was now on the Taff's Well rugby committee, after many years of playing.

According to the club history: *'It has been said that without Taff's Well there would be no Cardiff. Geographically, this is perfectly true. This small Glamorganshire village spread along the mainly eastern and, to a lesser extent, western banks of the River Taff, is in a unique position. At this point the river passes through a narrow gap between the Garth and Wenallt mountains. The builders of the Taff's Well Railway were grateful for this Taff's Well and Tongwynlais gap for, without it, the route to the coalfields of the Rhondda valleys would have been inaccessible. It was why Cardiff became a coal-exporting port.'* (Barry was a tiny village until the railway came there, making Barry at one stage the busiest coal-exporting port in the world. The railway succeeded the canal bringing coal and iron ore down to Barry, Penarth and Cardiff docks, of course. A main road threaded south through the village, and finally the A470 dual carriageway linked Cardiff, bypassing many towns heading north to Merthyr Tydfil.)

'*In rugby terms, Taff's Well seems to be in a geographical vacuum. In valley eyes we are regarded as a Cardiff club, while the Cardiff clubs see us as a valleys club. We are therefore in a unique position. The club is a mix of both cultures where the accents of Nantgarw and Taff's Well, resembling those of the valleys, blend with the Cardiff tones of the Tongwynlais boys. As a result, one week our players can be harangued in Ystrad Rhondda as "Cardiff Bastards" and the next week denigrated in Llandaff (the Cathedral city in north Cardiff) as "Cardiff Bastards". In fact, of course, we are really just "Taff's Well Bastards".*' Until the Great War, Tongwynlais had been the main local rival, but now that mantle fell upon Pentyrch, over the Garth. Don Llewellyn, a Pentyrch rugby stalwart, former TV producer and historian, was from a family that lived in the small, isolated village for centuries. He reminded me that Pentyrch even in the 1960s still had many native Welsh speakers, whereas Taff's Well had lost most of the language. To Pentyrch players, Taff's Well was always referred to as '*Yr Ochor Draw'*, 'The Other Side' (of the Garth) Better than 'something Bastards', one presumes, and a salute to the natural politeness of the Welsh.

Dai Millward, a founder member of the Referees' Society, had become Taff's Well club secretary in 1908, a position he held for forty years, working for the WRU when he retired as an accountant, and trying to guide Taff's Well until his death in 1969. The club president, Harry Field, allowed his shop to be the club HQ and his wife often washed the team's shirts. In 1922-23, playing at home on Rhiw Ddar field, the team were unbeaten all season. Harry Field treated '*The Invincibles'* to a supper at Barry's Hotel in Cardiff. Dai Millward worked wonders pushing people to watch the club, as each fourpence ticket was the only income the club had for shirts, balls, travelling etc. The arrival of Phil Rowlands from Cardiff had considerably strengthened the team. The excellent captain in this great season, Bleddyn Thomas, had married Dai Millward's daughter. He was followed as captain by Trevor Phillips of nearby Gwaelod-y-Garth, whose cousins Arthur and Phil played alongside him.

Ted Roberts (the Williams mother's father) supported every match, and his son Tom Roberts began playing full-back, selflessly switching to hooker and wing-forward when another full-back returned to play for the team. As mentioned, the younger son, Roy, also played for Taff's Well and Cardiff alongside his nephew Gwyn, the oldest Williams boy. Tom Lewis played for Taff's Well school, which won the Cardiff and District Sports Cup in 1920. His brother Bill had been a Pentyrch player before the war, and he wanted Tom to join him at that club for the 1920-21 season.

However, his injuries were too severe to continue playing, so he wrote to the committee that he had to retire soon, and they dropped him for the next game. For some reason they left out Tom Lewis also, so he came straight back to Taff's Well in January 2021 and played for the rest of the season. Tom was a miner at Nantgarw Colliery, and Sergeant 'Wacky' Thomas of Taff's Well convinced him to join the police force. The only two men on duty one day in Canton Police Station, Cardiff, were Tom Lewis and P.C. Rowlands, father of Keith Rowlands, later to be a great Cardiff, Wales and Lions player.

'*Deputy Chief Constable John Jones came to the station and asked Tom if he was playing that day. Tom explained that he had joined Penylan (in Cardiff) and as they only played away games there were quite often free Saturdays. Tom, in fact had filled in some of these Saturdays with games for Taff's Well. The Deputy Chief Constable informed P.C. Lewis that Cardiff Reserves were playing on the Arms Park and "ordered" him to report for the match. This he did and began a long career that was to lead him to international fame and also the captaincy of the Cardiff Club. On arrival for that first game he was welcomed by Phil Rowlands, then captain of the "Rags" and himself a Taff's Well man.* (Phil Rowlands also played 44 times for Cardiff Firsts between 1920-21 and 1923-24). *Today in his eighties Tom Lewis bears the stamp of a no nonsense and resilient man. In his prime, whether on the field or on the beat, he would not have been a man to treat lightly. We at Taff's Well honour him as "The first of the Few". As he himself says: "On many occasions I've teased Bleddyn that I was the first Taff's Well man to be capped by Wales."'* Tom Lewis captained Cardiff in 1932-33, playing the most games (40), the year that the club supplied 10 players for Wales' three international matches.

THE FIRST WELSH CAPTAIN FROM TAFF'S WELL - THOMAS 'TOM' WILLIAM LEWIS 7 June 1902 – 31 May 1994

Born in Gwaelod-y-Garth, just across the river from Taff's Well, after WWI he played for Pentyrch, then Taff's Well from 1920. A miner, he joined the police force and from 1922-23 played for Penylan in Cardiff and then was a regular for Cardiff from 1923-1924. Originally a number 8, Tom played prop 260 times until 1932-33, his year of his Cardiff captaincy, and claimed that in all that time he only played three times for the Athletic. His 21 tries were exceptional for a forward in those days. He was in the Cardiff team in 1924 which was thought very unlucky to lose to the 'Invincible' New Zealand team. He said '*I used to play my rugby with the thought that my place was never secure with Cardiff. In that way I tried to produce my best in every game*'. A regular in Glamorgan Police sides in the 1920s and early 30s, he once captained the British Police against the

Army, and played for Crawshay's XV, and for Glamorgan County four times.

Tom was told only two hours before the England game in 1926, that he had replaced Bridgend's Steve Lawrence. On 16 January, Lewis was one of 8 new Welsh caps at the Arms Park, and Rowe Harding's inexperienced team drew 3-3. Cardiff scrum-half Bobby Delahay had a perfectly good try in the closing minutes disallowed by an Irish referee – a constant bane in Welsh matches. Lewis was capped again against England at Twickenham in 1927. Wales lost 11-9, down to 14 men for most of the match, as Newport's Dai Jones was injured in the first fifteen minutes. (Substitutes were not allowed until 1968, when up to two were allowed, and only when a doctor had certified that the injured player should not play on.) Lewis's last game was for Ossie Male's team against Scotland, in 1927 Five Nations Championship, Wales losing at home 5-0. He recalled '*Conditions were worse than when Wales played the Springboks last December (1961). We were ankle deep in mud and you couldn't tell a Scotsman from a Welshman. I've often wondered since how the selectors managed to recognise me enough to drop me.*' He gave up rugby aged 31, moving to Rhiwbina Garden Village in Cardiff in 1935, and retired as a PC in C Division, Lansdowne Road Police Station until retirement in 1949, when he became a Civil Servant in Llanishen. (Note: Wikipedia states Tom Lewis joined Cardiff from Pentyrch, but it was from Taff's Well; it says he played No.8 when he was a prop; it says he was born in Llantwit Fardre, which may be right until I can check records, but it seems to be Taff's Well/Gwaelod-y-Garth; it claims he was born in 1904, when it seems to have been 1902).

A full-page article in the *Where Are They Now* series in the *South Wales Echo* 4 March 1961, is titled '*Tom Lewis – a famous son of Gwaelod-y-Garth.*' The subtitle is '*Sent Off – Tom Still Pleads "Not Guilty!"*'. Malcolm Lewis reported that he '*even today protests his innocence over the incident that led to marching orders. In spite of an appeal to the Welsh Rugby Union for a personal hearing, the union refused to grant it. Instead, they harshly doled out two months' suspension for an offence he swears he did not commit... He says "I was going away from a line-out at Newport when I put my hand out to ward off a tackle. The next thing I knew the referee, Mr. Cornfield, of Glynneath, told me to leave the field for alleged striking. It was one of those matches where the referee lost his grip on the game. The crowd were over-excited, and everything was out of proportion... The reason I let the matter drop was because I was in the Police Service and the Chief Constable advised me to do nothing about it... That game was the first and last match controlled by Mr. Cornfield. But it left me with the reputation of being a bad boy. Mind you, I'm no angel. I was a front-row forward and we had to know how to give it and take it in those days. But we didn't do anything viciously.*' In 1941 '*he made the*

70

magnificent gesture of presenting his collection of rugby memorabilia to Pentyrch RFC, which had been his first club. He said: "I have long forgiven the old parish for dropping me in 1920 and forcing me to go to Taff's Well!"'. It was just as well, as all of Taff's Well's memorabilia was destroyed in a clubhouse fire in 1999.

At Taff's Well, Tom Lewis played alongside the 'Fighting Mapstones', the brothers Charlie and Chris. In boxing, *'Charlie had turned professional in the early 1920s and was good enough to fight for the British Lightweight Championship, when he lost to "Seaman" Watson over 20 rounds. At this time Charlie and Chris were staunch members of Glandwr Chapel and boxing was not really acceptable in this strict chapel community. To avoid embarrassment, they both fought under the pseudonym of Stone instead of Mapstone'*. The loss to Watson was not surprising. Tommy 'Seaman' Watson (1908-1971) had been in the Royal Navy, where he was lightweight champion turning professional in 1925, and only losing 9 of 123 fights. He moved down a weight and was British Featherweight Champion from 1932-34. He won a fight in the States, earning a shot at the World Junior Lightweight Championship against the Cuban 'Kid Chocolate' at Madison Square Garden, but lost on points over 15 rounds. He moved back to Lightweight and then became a referee.

'Chris Mapstone won the Welsh Featherweight championship at the A.B.A. finals of 1922. Later he fought eight professional contestants. Then, when Jimmy Wilde was preparing for his world title fight with Pancho Villa, Chris Mapstone was approached and taken on as a sparring partner. This showed the high standing that Chris had achieved at a time when there were many fine flyweights in Wales. Chris kept his fighting exploits for the ring and his displays at scrumhalf for Wales showed his exemplary temperament.' I can find no record of him playing for Wales, but it would be remiss not to mention one of the world's greatest boxers here. There is no exaggeration, and this author met *'The Tylorstown Terror'* as a boy when Jimmy Wilde (1892-1969) had retired to Barry. His only losses occurred when fighting above his weight and injured. With the longest unbeaten streak in boxing history, he went 103 fights before his first loss. Wilde had a record of 139 wins, 3 losses, 1 draw and 5 no-contests, with an impressive 99 wins by knockout.

This author's *100 Greatest Welshmen* gives Wilde as much justice as possible in a few thousand words, but he was utterly unique. As a child he worked down the same coal pit as his father, and aged 16 started boxing in fairground boxing booths, fighting and beating much bigger men. In 1910, aged 18, he left Tylorstown Colliery, married and had a son. By now he had been fighting professionally for four years, winning hundreds of bouts, some against men weighing five stone more. William James 'Jimmy' Wilde (1892-1969) was only 5 foot 2 inches, and known as *'The Mighty Atom'*. He was so frail-looking and white that he was also called *'The*

Ghost with a hammer in his hand', *'The Indian Famine'* and *'The Furious Freak.'* His best fighting weight was 6 stone 10lbs, and Gilbert Odd wrote in *Boxing News*, 4 April 1969: *'He came in at a time when flyweights were plentiful and competition extremely high. Never made 8st in his fighting life!'* His first 'official' fight was in 1919 and his career was disrupted by the 1914-18 War, but he went undefeated in 103 successive bouts in Britain. Of his 132 wins, 99 were by knock-out, and he only lost 3 fights, two when he should not have fought, being ill against the great Pancho Villa for the world title, and against Pete Herman, a heavier bantamweight. With the longest unbeaten streak in boxing history, *Ring Magazine*, named him both the 3rd greatest puncher of all time, and **the greatest flyweight of all time**, and rated him as the 13th greatest fighter of the 20th century. In 1990, he was elected to the inaugural class of the International Boxing Hall of Fame and was ranked as the top flyweight of all-time by the International Boxing Research Organization in 2006. Like the Williams brothers, Wilde is hardly known – a truly wonderful man - I feel blessed having met him.

Fred Lee, the Taff's Well village policeman, like Tom Lewis was chosen for the final Welsh trial in 1926. Fred was reported as being *'the best forward on the field'* in Cardiff's game against the Maoris in 1927. However, he is recorded as 'Frank' Lee in Danny Davies' epic book upon Cardiff, playing 68 First team games from 1924-28. Dai Millward was still working hard for Taff's Well, and passed his W.R.U. referee exam to become a well-known top-level referee. With pitch problems, Taff's Well only played away games in 1930, with Fred Porter, Reg Field, Del Harris, Iorrie Jones and Bob Lewis being the heart of the team. Del Harris taught Roy Roberts, Gwyn Williams and the older Williams boys, and helped Gwyn's convalescence after his war wound. The eldest Williams brother, Gwyn, left the Taff's Well XV to join Cardiff in 1934, becoming possibly the youngest player in history for their First XV. His uncle Roy Roberts also joined Cardiff from Taff's Well in 1934, making 150 first-team appearances between 1936 and 1949, when he joined Pontypridd and became their captain. One wonders what Roy's record would have been without the war.

Peter Thomas records: *'At this time the young Roy Roberts, son of Ted and brother of Tom, began to show his potential. Such potential, in fact, that Roy followed the Taff down to Arms Park in 1934 and played for Cardiff until the outbreak of World War Two. Joining the Welsh Guards, he was to distinguish himself and was awarded the Military Medal in Germany in 1944. With the cessation of hostilities, Roy Roberts returned to play for Cardiff until 1949. In that year he transferred to Pontypridd and gave them sterling service until his retirement in 1953. Today Roy remembers with pride that he played with the Cardiff "greats" such as Tanner, Cleaver, Bleddyn Williams and Jack Matthews.*

"BOB' and "FATTY"

With Roy in the team of the 30s was R.W.C. "Bob" Lewis, a man who held Taff's Well dear to his heart from the time he joined the club till his death in 1983. During the 30s, the numbers playing at the club enabled Dai Millward to establish a regular Third XV and he used this team as a means of "blooding" the youngsters. Roy Roberts was one of these boys. Another was Roy's cousin (actually his nephew) Gwyn "Fatty" Williams. Even when he was as young as 14, Gwyn did not resemble a young boy. He had the physique of a young man and could compete with the senior players on equal terms. During these years of Depression, rugby was a welcome relief to the stresses of everyday life. The playing membership had increased rapidly and the club was a happy one, led by one of the most popular men and captains in our history. As is often the case with big men, Fred Porter was essentially a gentle man. Jessie Jones, Iorrie's wife, remembers him with great affection as a man who was kind to children and polite to ladies. Fred never seems to have made an enemy.

A product of the first "Lilywhites" of post-war years (the team had changed their strip from blue and black), Fred developed into a fine line-out forward and was asked on many occasions to turn out for Cardiff. Indeed, he played enough games for "The Rags" to gain his Athletic Cap. Primarily, however Fred was a Taff's Well man and remained so until the end of his days.' A Football Echo pen-picture of 'A Popular Captain', dated 10 September 1932, notes that he had played for Taff's Well Juniors, and was 'a sterling forward, with the heart of a lion. Porter is adept in opening up the game with forward movements, yet notwithstanding this attribute he is a strong scrummager. Cardiff RFC have discovered his value and have called upon him to assist them on several occasions.' Fred Porter played 22 times for Cardiff Firsts, and many times for the Athletic, from 1925-26 to 1927-28.

Ray Bale from the 'Ton' (Tongwynlais) was another Taff's Well player who played for Cardiff Firsts, on no less than 176 occasions, from 1934-35 and 1948-49. He was yet another player, like Roy Roberts and his nephews Gwyn, Brinley and Bleddyn Williams, whose career was affected by war. By 1939 the club at Taff's Well was thriving. There is a photo there of Dai Millward in the Taff's Well Junior RFC team in 1910-11 and another as captain of the Youth Team in 1913. In 1939 he was still involved in all club activities. The club history, 1887-1987, records: 'By 1939 his dream had come true – Taff's Well R.F.C. was an institution in the village. It had tradition and history, and as a result the club survived the war and is healthy today.' In 1961 Dai Millward stepped down from Club Secretary, having nurtured the club for forty years, as well as refereeing hundreds of games, to join the WRU, and a special presentation dinner was held. The baton was passed to Alan 'Rugger' Jones for another twenty years until 1981, when ill health intervened. The unpaid job was then passed around

73

until in 1986, 'Rugger', now retired and with more time to help, took up the post once more. The post-war story of Taff's Well RFC is continued in a later chapter.

CHAPTER 5 - BEFORE WORLD WAR TWO

CARDIFF RFC IN THE 30s - CARDIFF SEASON 1930-31 - THE LAST SEASON WHEN CARDIFF RAN TWO FIRST XVs

P43 W27 L13 D3 - Points 544-283 - Tries 139-58, Pens 9-11
(Cardiff players in each season from Taff's Well, Pentyrch and Tongwynlais will now be noted after each season heading:
Tom Lewis, Taff's Well, played 260 games from 1923/24 to 1932/3, Iorwerth 'Shoppy' Evans, Pentyrch played 6 times for the Firsts and many games for the Athletic.

This book would be far too long if we recorded more of Cardiff's brilliant history. Thus, we will begin with more detail in 1930-31, with the famous Turnbull and Bowcott brothers, leading up to 1934-35 season with the 16-year-old Gwyn Williams joining the First XV. If Gwyn played in the game against Cardiff and District noted as being on 1 September 1934, he would have been 16 years 3 months and 12 days. Two seasons later, his mother's much younger brother Roy Roberts joined Gwyn in the Cardiff pack.

There is a purpose in placing the try and penalty totals above, in that one can see that Cardiff always heavily outscores the opposition over a season in tries, but its **penalty ratio is far, far less**. For instance, on the ratio of tries for, to tries against, Cardiff should have converted over twice as many penalties as its opponents, instead of fewer. The team always preferred to run the ball, rather than kick it, and the ethos held through the dawning of professionalism until the rise of the four Welsh regions. Even in the early days, when a try was only worth one point, Cardiff captains instructed their teams to go for tries instead of 3-point penalties and dropped goals. The importance of penalties has increased every year, for instance in 1930-31, a somewhat mediocre season for Cardiff, in 43 games they scored 3.2 tries per game and only 0.2 penalties. In 1952-53, in 37 games with a brilliant team, there were 3.8 Cardiff tries per game, and 0.67 penalties. In 38 games in 1964-65, Cardiff achieved 4.1 tries per match, and 0.8 penalties. In 1974-75 Cardiff played 51 times, scoring an average 2.6 tries per match, but penalties had risen to 1.2, six times the 1930-31 average.

These penalty contribution figures rise inexorably, not just because the ball and pitches and kickers are better, but because there are so many penalties – for so many offences - in the modern game. And if games were refereed to the letter of the law, e.g. scrum-halves were to be penalised for feeding the ball crookedly into the scrum, there would be even more penalties. Many modern 'laws' have been introduced to increase the amount of time the ball is in play, but that time is now far worse than in the 1970s. Also, much of 'ball in play' time is spent in perhaps over 20 phases of battering possession, with a few yards being achieved. Modern rugby is nowhere near as entertaining as in the 1960s-1980s, as any former player will attest.

Back to 1930-31. The centre Bernard Turnbull, a Cambridge Blue with 6 Welsh caps, was captain, and he chose Syd Cravos as vice-captain. The three-quarter G. V. Wynne Jones ('Geevers', a businessman and later a famous rugby columnist), joined from Bristol for a couple of seasons, and played 40 games for the Firsts between this season and 1936-37. Emlyn Jenkins, a scrum half/outside half from Treorchy, played 16 consecutive first-team games before sadly turning professional. (Davies writes that he only played eight games). Les Spence, a back row forward who was later to play 267 times and captain Cardiff, also joined. Les was later to be imprisoned by the Japanese, along with Cardiff's Ken Street and Wilf Wooller. After 6 seasons and 178 games, Bernard Turnbull's brother Kevin moved to London for business interests. The half backs Maurice Bowcott and Howard Poole were selected for the British Lions' tour to New Zealand and Australia, so were unavailable to Cardiff until November. Cardiff's team included Taff's Well's Tom Lewis, with fullback back Tommy Stone; backs R. W. Boon, G. V. Wynne Jones, John Roberts and Iorwerth Evans; half-backs Howard Poole and H. M. Bowcott; forwards Norman Fender, Tom Lewis, R. Barrell, Archie Skym, Geoff Babbage, A. Clarke, V. R. Osmond and I. Williams.

On New Year's Day 1931, Cardiff had been invited by the French Rugby Federation to play its 'Probables' side, playing as France 'B', but **in effect the international side**, at Toulouse. After a long journey by train and boat, Cardiff were the first club to play a French national side, but lost 14-11. (There was a break in international rugby relations between the Home Unions and France which lasted until 1947, but well into the 1960s there was professionalism in French rugby, with rugby league in that country being amateur). However, they had played a Combined French XV back in 1906, winning 27-5, 7-1 on tries. Cardiff first played Stade Français back in 1905. Cardiff has played Auvergne 6 times; Bressane (Bourg en Bresse); Cognac 4 times; Club Athletique Paris; a Combined French XV; France B; Lyonnaise Selection twice; Bordeaux; Stade Français twice; Nantes 4 times; Nantes-Cognac twice; and Paris University. Of the 26 games, 21 were away, with 14 won, 5 lost and 2 drawn.

1,800 miles and two days later, at Bristol both teams scored 2 tries but Bristol converted theirs, a tired Cardiff team losing 10-6. Cardiff struggled to use their better backs in these games, with bad weather and unpleasant pitches. They lost 13-3 away at Aberavon after a match with Bridgend was cancelled, and scored 2 tries to 2 at London Welsh but lost 13-8. At Gloucester in February, Cardiff lost 6-4 and went down 3-0 at Newport. There were no bad defeats, except that at Aberavon, the other four games being lost by a total of 14 points, all away from home. In this bad weather, games were also called off against Plymouth Albion and Neath. In March, Cardiff beat Plymouth Albion away 23-8 (5-1 on tries), and in the April rearranged game at home, Cardiff scored 9 tries to a penalty to beat Plymouth Albion 31-3. Hard pitches always suited the team and its preference for three-quarter play. In November, Cardiff had beaten Blackheath 25-0 (7 tries, 2 converted), and in December achieved almost the same result with 7 unconverted tries against Watsonians, 21-0. In April yet again 7 tries were scored, Coventry losing 27-3. The rearranged April game with Neath at the Arms Park saw a wonderful 'end of season' affair, 6 tries to 3, with Cardiff winning 26-16.

Top try scorers were Barry's Ronnie Boon 23 (with 4 vs Watsonians), Graham Jones 18, G. V. Wynne Jones 15, H. M. Bowcott 13 and John Roberts 11. Tommy Stone kicked 33 goals and scored 2 tries. The Barbarians game was an equal 3-3 on tries, but the Baa Baas converted one to win 11-9. It was Cardiff's only home loss. First XV caps were awarded to Geoff Babbage, Emlyn Jenkins, G. V. Wynne Jones and Les Spence. Wales drew the first game at Twickenham 11-11, before beating Scotland 13-8 (H), France 35-3 (H) and Ireland 15-3 (A), winning the Championship but narrowly missing a Grand Slam. In the England game, the Irish (it had to be) referee at half-time added 2 points to England's score, over-ruling both touch judges who, in a better position, rules that a conversion had been missed. With 3 minutes left, the aforesaid referee ruled 'feet across' in a scrum and England scored the penalty that prevented a first Welsh win at 'Twickers' for many years. (For non-Welsh readers, we have had such a problem with Irish officiating that Max Boyce wrote a song featuring a 'blind Irish referee'. In the win against Scotland, the Welsh pack leader Watcyn Thomas, later to captain Wales in 1933 to their first win at Twickenham, played most of the game with a fractured collarbone.

The two 'First XVs' Cardiff experiment had started in 1926-27, with 82 games being played, 47 by the 'A' Firsts and 35 by the 'B' Firsts. Over Easter 1927, Cardiff 'A' beat the Baa-Baas 16-8 on Saturday; Harlequins 16-13 on Monday; Bradford 20-6 (6 tries) on Tuesday and lost to Northampton 18-6 on Wednesday. No wonder. In the same period, the 'Other XV' lost to Torquay 13-3, beat Exeter 19-13 and lost to Ebbw Vale 22-13. Although there were 27 losses, the Committee carried on with the trial. In 1928-29, teams began to complain, including Leicester, Northampton and Aberavon, that Cardiff was not playing its strongest team. In 1930-31, the 'Other XV' won only 12 of 30 games, and the experiment was at last discontinued. The 5-year 'two first teams' experiment seems to be **unique in any sport**. As all fixtures were counted as first team games, all the trial succeeded in achieving was worsening Cardiff's historical playing record. The Arms Park pitch was still dreadful for most of the season, being used for many representative games, and Cardiff also used to train upon it twice a week. When I say 'train', the players organised it themselves, throwing a ball about. Forwards and backs trained separately, led by a senior player. There were neither gym faculties nor coaching. Often players could not make it because of work requirements. A major problem was that the surface was below the higher tidal levels of the adjacent River Taff – and of course Wales suffers from a surfeit of rain. Ireland receives more rain from the prevalent Atlantic Westerlies but have rather imaginatively, and successfully, marketed their nation as 'the Emerald Isle.'

CHAPTER 6 - CARDIFF SEASON 1931-32

CARDIFF LOSE to the SPRINGBOKS, NEWPORT RIVALRY

Tom Lewis, TW; Iorwerth 'Shoppy' Evans, Pentyrch (appearances are not available for pre-war years)

P43, W25, L16, D2 - Points 451-281 - Tries 102-56, Pens 11-12

Scrumhalf Howard Poole and fly-half Harry Bowcott were captain and vice-captain, and both had played for the British Lions on tour to New Zealand and Australia in 1930. London Irish were defeated 29-3 (7 tries again) on Boxing Day, and Harlequins 24-10 (5-1 on tries) on Easter Monday, with wins against Coventry 22-3 (5-0 on tries) and Guys Hospital 22-0 (6 tries). Coventry won the return match in Cardiff 8-3, with Cardiff short of players. If the reader permits a short digression on Cardiff's eternal biggest club fixture - deadly rivals Newport were beaten three times, but were the better team in the final game, winning 10-5. It is interesting that on several occasions one of these clubs has won the first three of four, but then cannot win the fourth for a clean sweep. It means that much, not to 'get a whitewash'.

In 1931-32, Danny Davies points out that '*16 losses were a lot, despite the fact that nine of them were by merely five points or less. It was Swansea, under captain Jack Rees their forward, who really chastened us because they won all the four matches. They could boast of at least 7 international forwards in their club, Tom Day, Will Davies, Watkyn*

77

Thomas, D. Thomas, I Parker, as well as Eddie Long and Joe White: they could call upon Claude Davey, Jim Dark and J. Idwal Rees in their backs.' Cardiff generally played the All Whites four times a season from 1889-90 to 1938-39, beating them 4 times in 1884-85, 1905-06 and 1936-37.

Howard Poole lost form and was dropped, with the acting captaincy going to Harry Bowcott. Poole played in a Lions Test against New Zealand, but somehow was never picked for Wales. Henry Morgan Bowcott (1907-2004) was a Cardiff High School product and Cambridge Blue, and later President of the WRU. Bowcott was chosen to join the Lions on their tour of New Zealand and Australia in 1930, and played in 20 of the 27 matches, including all 5 Tests. The next year Harry Bowcott was Wales captain, and played for Wales 8 times. Cardiff's Ronnie Boon scored all the Welsh points in the famous 1933 win at Twickenham, but *'it was Bowcott's kicking during the second half of the match that ensured that the English were unable to get back into the game.'* Scrum-half Poole's replacements were a third Turnbull brother, Maurice J. Turnbull, and another Bowcott brother, J. E. 'Jackie' Bowcott, both taking turns partnering fly-half Harry Bowcott. The role of these and other brothers in Cardiff RFC is given later in this book. With a Cambridge Blue for hockey and cricket, Maurice Turnbull played rugby and hockey for Wales and cricket for England. The oldest brother Bernard, a centre, was Cardiff captain twice, a Barbarian, a Cambridge Blue, and played for Wales 6 times. Jackie Bowcott also gained his Cambridge Blue and while there played scrumhalf to Cardiff's Cliff Jones.

By the mid-1930s Cardiff was recognised as having the strongest fixture list of all clubs, but with games being played upon the three Welsh Trial days each season, and persistent calls for International players from the team, sometimes when Cardiff was also playing, results were not wonderful. Every season was easily a winning one, but Cardiff were to enter another 'purple patch' before war broke out. In 1933, Cardiff's wing Ronald Winston 'Ronny' Boon (1909-1998), from Barry, not only scored a try and dropped goal, all the Welsh points in the team's first win at Twickenham after a 23-year wait, but also scored a try against the Springboks for Cardiff. A Welsh AAA sprint champion, he played cricket for Glamorgan, gained 12 Welsh caps and played for 10 seasons for Cardiff before war broke out, putting an end to his great rugby career at the age of 28.

The problem in this season was in a fairly new set of forwards. The great Norman Fender had turned professional having made 112 appearances since 1927-28. Hooker D. J. 'Don' Tarr played 23 times in this, his only season for Cardiff, and is remembered having broken his neck playing for Wales against New Zealand in December 1935. Cardiff had beaten the first South African touring team 17-0 in 1907. In 1912 the Springboks scraped home 7-6 by a dropped goal – 4 points and a penalty 3 points, to a try and penalty. The third game was eagerly awaited on 21 November 1931. Cardiff's *'equalising try towards half time was a brilliant effort in which the ball had travelled from Maurice Turnbull to Bowcott, B. R. Turnbull, Graham Jones and finally to Ronnie Boon who scored in the corner from where Tommy Stone converted.'* It seems that South Africa played an astute tactical kicking game, whereas Cardiff, true to the team ethos, ran the ball in poor conditions.

It was Harry Bowcott's most memorable game, and he remembered in 1951: *'Against the Springboks in 1931, our surprising scrummaging superiority, our readiness to play open rugby, determined defence, a grand Cardiff try, Tommy Stone's magnificent conversion and South Africa's sound, if somewhat unattractive, all-round display of aggressive football – these immediate recollections all combined to make this a memorable game. Not a victory, we lost by 13 pts. to 5, not even a moral victory, but assuredly a game enjoyed by all fortunate to play that perfect afternoon.'* Wales were beaten by SA 8-3. Top try scorers were A. T. Thomas 15, Graham Jones 14, H. M. Bowcott 10. Davies records: *'One of our best and most popular threequarters, John Roberts, went to China as a missionary in January of the season'*, after 101 first-team games. The five-foot six-inch full-back Tommy Stone kicked 37 goals and scored 3 tries, playing no fewer than 42 out of 43 games.

France did not play in the Five Nations, and Wales beat England at Swansea in 1932, 12-5, with a try and drop goal by Cardiff's Boon, and a conversion and penalty by Penarth's Jack Bassett. Scotland were then beaten at Murrayfield, 6-0, with another Boon try and a Bassett penalty. In the last game of the season, at Cardiff, Wales were expected to take the Triple Crown for the first time in 21 years. However, Ireland won 12-10, marking Jack Bassett's last appearance for Wales, and he was widely blamed for losing the game. He 'failed badly' but not until some days later was it disclosed that he had broken a bone in his ankle in the fifteenth minute, and played on in excruciating agony, there being no substitutes. He missed two tackles which gave Ireland two tries, and kicking with his broken ankle, missed a conversion to draw the game.

NEWPORT RIVALRY

With Newport just a few miles east across the coast, this has always been a bitterly contested local Derby. In 1896-97 Cardiff had lost three Newport games, then scraped home 3-0 away. Yet in the following year 1897-98, Cardiff won all four 20-9 (6-2 tries), 18-0 (4-0 tries), 8-3 (2-1 tries) and 18-0 (4 tries) – 16-3 on tries immediately after a season where Newport were the better side! In 1988-89 Cardiff won three, scoring 6 tries to 2, but lost at Newport 9-5, a try apiece. In 1900-01, it was Newport's turn again to be disappointed, winning three before a Cardiff win away 10-0, with Newport scoring 7 tries in the series to Cardiff's 6. In 1901-02 the situation was reversed, Cardiff winning three tight games 7-5, 7-4, 6-4 then Newport winning in Cardiff 10-0 – the same away win that Cardiff achieved in the previous season. In 1905-06 Cardiff achieved its second 'quadruple', winning 17-3, 14-6, 10-3 and 20-5. In 1906-07 Cardiff won two, with high hopes, but then drew two. In 1907-08 Cardiff won 7-3, 6-3 and 6-3, drawing the last game at home 3-3. 1908-09 saw another three wins for Cardiff, but the final game at Newport was abandoned in foul conditions.

Four of five consecutive games between February 2012 and February 2013 were drawn, to demonstrate how bitterly contested was this greatest series of Derby games in world rugby. 1913-14 saw Cardiff lose 12-8, 3-0 and 11-5 before a home 3-0 win. Games were restarted in 1919-20, and the years 1922 and 1923 saw another four draws in five consecutive games, before in 1929-30 Cardiff won three and lost the last, a feat repeated in 1931-32. In 1938-39 Cardiff again won three 11-5, 13-0 and 7-0, but drew 0-0 at home in the last game. In 1947-48, Bleddyn William's Cardiff team won the 'grand slam' for a third time, having won three and drawn one in the previous season, winning 7-2 on tries. The 'slam' was emphatic: 29-0, 12-0, 8-5 and 19-3 – 14 tries to 1! The next season, Cardiff again won the first two, drew one and won the last game. In 1949-50, three games were won, but again Newport spoiled the celebrations, winning the last game, in Cardiff, 8-0. Up until this game, Cardiff had won 13 and drawn 2, **unbeaten in 15 consecutive games** against 'the old enemy'. It was a *golden era* for the club.

However, in 1950-51, the boot was on the other foot – a strong Newport side won 8-3, 8-6 and 8-3 before Cardiff forced a 3-3 away draw. The shock affected Cardiff positively and in 1951-52 they won a fourth '*slam*', 11-3, 6-5, 6-3 and 11-6, and in 1953-54 won 3 and drew 1, but out of sequence. In 1955-56 Newport again won the first 3 games, but Cardiff scraped a win away 10-9 in the last game. It is strange how many final games have been won 'away' to save face in these great fixtures. In 1958-59 Newport won the first three matches 11-0, 9-8 and 19-5, before only drawing 0-0 at Cardiff, and in 1959-60 won two games, then drew and then won – the quadruple has always been so close for them. In 1963-64 it was Cardiff's turn to win the first three games 14-6, 3-0, 8-5 before drawing 11-11 at home. In 1968-69 Newport won two games before a frost cancellation, then won again, but Cardiff drew 9-9 in the final game. However, the next season Cardiff won, drew, won and won. Cardiff came so close in 1972-73, winning 18-14, 24-3, 19-10 and losing 7-6. Up until 1973-74, in the 4-game series, Newport had won 3 and failed in the last game 7 times, and Cardiff had won 3 and failed to win 4 on 11 occasions. Thus Cardiff won four Grand Slams against their closest rivals, while Newport came agonisingly close on several occasions.

CHAPTER 7 - CARDIFF SEASON 1932 – 1933

'THE WONDER TEAM' - 'THE SCORING MACHINE' - WALES WIN AT TWICKENHAM for the FIRST TIME, with SIX CARDIFF PLAYERS

Tom Lewis, Taff's Well, Cardiff No.8 and captain, played 40 games in this, his last season, and played 260 times for the Firsts between 1923-24 and 1932-33. 3 Welsh caps.

P43, W23, L17, D3 - Points 532 – 321 - Tries 122-66, Pens 6-9

This was the fifth successive season where Cardiff were outscored on penalties but easily scored the most tries. The Taff's Well PC, Tom Lewis was captain, and he chose Wales centre Bernard Turnbull as vice-captain. Cardiff won their first seven matches, then lost away to Blackheath 6-3 in September. Dannie Davies recorded: *'By November, the press were calling Cardiff 'The Wonder Team', as they reported 'Cardiff's scoring machine' owing to the number of tries being scored.'* In November, Cardiff beat Blackheath 18-8; scored 7 tries against Neath 31-5; 6 tries vs. Newport 24-0; and Llanelli, who had gone 14 matches unbeaten, were defeated 8-5 on 26 November 1932. On Christmas Eve 1932, Cardiff also took Llanelli's unbeaten home record 17-5. On Boxing Day, after a day's rest, Cardiff scored 10 tries against London Irish to win 47-0. London Welsh were thrashed by 9 tries to 3, 41-13, on the same day that Cardiff had 6 men in the Welsh team that beat England away. The great P.C. Archie Skym played prop 212 times from 1928-29 to 1936-37 before moving to play for Llanelli, and recalled his most memorable game in 1951: *'One of the most enjoyable matches I played in was against Gloucester at the Arms Park on October 15th, 1932, when we won 16-0. Playing in the front row of a very good pack, with Maurice Turnbull at our heels, I scored two tries. One of these came at the end of the match when I managed to keep up with A.H. Jones and Turnbull for half the length of the field before taking the final pass. I consider it the best game I played for the club, but I had my leg pulled for being too much of a "wing" forward!'*

The deeply disappointed former Cardiff captain and British Lion Howard Poole had joined nearby Penarth in the previous season, a club that has always been a source of Cardiff players. Cardiff played the *'Seasiders'* twice a season from 1886-87 until the 1969-70 season. Indeed, from December 1926 to April 1935, Cardiff won 11 times, Penarth 5, with 2 draws – Penarth was a good team. Chris Thau's excellent history of Penarth Rugby Club tells us that the visit to Cardiff on 10 December 1932 would be the first appearance of the season, for Penarth's illustrious Welsh international Jack Bassett, called *'the greatest fullback in the world'* after playing for the British Lions in New Zealand, Australia and South Africa. Bassett was to end his career at Cardiff, to join his brother Arthur, only playing five times for the Firsts, and enjoying a few seasons winding down with the 'Rags'.

Along with the annual Easter Barbarians game, the Cardiff fixtures were the highlights of the Penarth season, and Cardiff were undefeated at home since the season's start. Penarth visited on 10 December 1932, beating their hosts 5-3, replicating exactly their 1929 result. Penarth captain Trevor Lee, who had played just 12 times for Cardiff in 5 years to 1928-29, missed the whole season with a long-term injury. Full back Lee had set a record of 13 consecutive goals in one game for the Blue and Blacks – his one missed attempt hit a post - but could not gain a regular place, unlike his brother Fred, who played 68 games for Cardiff. For the Penarth win against Cardiff, Penarth had Howard Poole, now playing outside half, the returning Alf 'Snowy' Clark (with prematurely white hair), who had just joined after playing 81 times in two seasons for Cardiff, and also Jack Bassett on the pitch. Penarth had just beaten Pontypool 4-3, and won at Newport 9-0, and were to defeat Bridgend. Cardiff then won in Penarth by the same score 5-3, as Penarth had beaten them. Penarth had also beaten Aberavon in November, and Aberavon were determined to avenge their defeat, a couple games after Penarth had played Cardiff. They won by 'vigorous' methods, and several Penarth players *'intimated that they would not take part in another game against Aberavon'*. The next season, Penarth beat Llanelli, London Welsh, Swansea, Newport and Pontypool, and did the double over Aberavon, then the committee cancelled further fixtures against the Aberavon 'Wizards'.

Acting captain Alf Clark recorded the Cardiff game in his contribution to Penarth's 75th anniversary rugby programme in 1955. *'You will remember at that period, Cardiff had swept all before them with their famous three-quarter line, then called "the scoring machine". Llanelli had come up the previous week with the fixed intention of taking Cardiff's ground record and I think there were very few people who considered Penarth had the slightest chance of humbling the might Cardiff. However, our pack was composed of the front row and five sprightly lads who all acted, as winging forwards. The plan worked. Immediately the Cardiff pack heeled the ball, the Penarth pack broke up and clogged the Cardiff scoring machine.'* Chris Thau tells us that at a line-out on the Cardiff line, Bryn Davies *'got the ball and dived over, with Edwards converting the try. The Cardiff "scoring machine" of AH Jones, Graham Jones, W Roberts and Cyril Cross went into overdrive trying to break through.'*

Alf Clark continues, *'However, the Penarth defence stood up manfully to their task and presented an impenetrable wall, especially with Howard Poole and Billy Goodman playing one of their best games of the season and Bassett as alert and safe and sound as ever. The pace was fast and furious and so well did Penarth play that with a little bit of luck at least a couple more tries might have been registered.*' Thau reports '*Imagine the delight of the former Cardiff players in the Penarth team, in particular Howard Poole, kicked out of the Arms Park in controversial circumstances the previous season. The final act of a rampant Penarth before Christmas, without Bassett, nursing a bad cold, was a 12-try, 44-0 demolition of Glamorgan Wanderers.*' There is an excuse for Cardiff, however. Along with first choice Wales backs Ronny Boon and Bernard Turnbull, most of the Cardiff team were involved in the three Probables vs. Possibles trial matches for the Wales team in December and January.

In season 1932-33, **Cardiff supplied 10 players to the Welsh team**, as following:

England: R. W. Boon, H. M. Bowcott, I. Isaacs, A. H. Jones, Archie Skym and M. J. Turnbull. (21 January)

Scotland: I. Isaacs, A. H. Jones, Archie Skym (M.J. Turnbull was selected but injured; H.M. Bowcott was selected but asked to stand down to allow a Swansea half-back pairing). (4 February)

Ireland: R. W. Boon, H. M. Bowcott, R. Barrell, Graham Jones, Archie Skym, M.J. Turnbull and Lew Rees. (11 Mar) Some sources note the prop Archie Skym as being a Llanelli player. However, having played in all four games for Wales in 1927-28, he was never chosen by Llanelli in 1928-29, so had joined Cardiff and played another 16 times for Wales.

It is interesting in that these 6 games between the 4 Home Nations were 'spread' over 10 weeks, to maximise interest. Today's professional era cannot allow for such a spread of fixtures, when international games were played upon 21 Jan, 4 Feb, 11 Feb, 11 Mar, 18 Mar and 1 Apr. With the current Six Nations, and beserk plans to add other countries, there now has to be an international 'window', where first class club rugby is abandoned, and there can be four internationals upon the same weekend, played at different times to suit commercial interests and television audiences.

Davies writes: '*The full back and fly-half Tommy Stone also deserved a Welsh cap. Barry's Ronnie Boon, known as the 'cheeky chappie' for his instinctive breaks, scored all Welsh points, a try and a drop goal, as **Wales won at Twickenham for the first time in 23 years**, 7-3. Against Ireland away, Cardiff's Harry Bowcott (now with London Welsh because of a job move) scored one of the best tries seen in international Rugby for years, but Wales lost 10-5 away, and Scotland beat Wales in our only home match 11-3.*' Wilf Wooller, soon to join Cardiff, played in the first two games for Wales while still representing Rydal School, and in the final game represented Colwyn Bay RFC.

Cardiff's results had tailed off because of the usual three international trials, internationals and injuries, with some senior players only managing 14 games. The brilliant outside half and Cambridge Blue C.W. 'Cliff' Jones played only three times, and his career was blighted by injury, ending too early in 1939. Full-back Tommy Stone kicked 56 goals, playing in 39 matches. Tom Lewis, from Pentyrch, was Cardiff's number 8 and captain and played in the most matches, 40, before retiring at the season's end after 260 first-team games. His vice-captain Bernard Turnbull was one of the six Turnbull brothers who played for Cardiff, and also played his last season after 232 games, having been captain in 1927-28 and 1930-31. His brother, scrumhalf Maurice Turnbull was awarded his Cardiff cap, and was also to play for Wales.

CHAPTER 8 - CARDIFF SEASON 1933 – 1934

THE LOWEST POINTS SCORED SINCE THE GREAT WAR

Gwyn Williams TW (Cardiff Athletic); Harry Rees TW, 5 Wales caps

P44, W25, L 17, D2 - Points 387 – 302 - Tries 92-64, Pens 7-14

A poor year, but still the try-penalty anomaly prevailed for a sixth successive season, with Cardiff scoring more tries but their opponents scoring more penalties. After the heights of 1932-33, not one Cardiff player played for Wales, and 1933-34 was one of the club's worst for results. Nine of the Glamorgan Police Force played for Cardiff's 1st XV, and one would like to, but one is not apportioning blame here. Cardiff captain Graham Jones, with two Welsh caps, lost form, was dropped and was replaced as captain by his vice-captain Rhys Gabe-Jones, the outside half. Scrumhalf Maurice Turnbull, owing to injuries, played only 19 games, and Cardiff scored the lowest number of points since the Great War. Bridgend won at Cardiff for the first time in 25 years, completing a double. Llanelli won four out of four games, and Newport three out of four.

Against this dismal background, in April 1934, the Welsh Public and Secondary Schools played Yorkshire Public Schools, and seven of that Welsh team later played for Cardiff. The boys were Eddie Watkins (played 1934-39) – a great friend of Gwyn Williams; the wonderful Haydn Tanner (1946-49); H. O. Edwards (1935-39); T. Lyn Williams (1936-48); D. E. M. Coombs (1938-39); L. G. S. "Jumbo" Thomas (1937-1939); and Les Manfield (1939-49). Cardiff's new double-decker North Stand was opened on 20 January 1934 for the Wales-England game, allowing a record attendance of 50,000, with gate receipts of £9,000. Billot reports '*The Welsh selectors lost this before it had even started' with an **unbelievable 13 new caps** and skipper John Evans chosen out of position as hooker.*'

One expects that the 'Big Five' made a killing at betting shops. There had been silly selections in the previous loss to Ireland 10-5 in the last international of the previous year. For this game they dropped all the Cardiff players – Wilf Wooller (soon to join Cardiff), wonder try-scorer Ronnie Boon, Frank Williams, Graham Jones, Archie Skym, Maurice Turnbull and L.M. Rees. One replacement, D..D. Evans, seems to be Barry RFC's only cap. England won 9-0 by three tries to nil, a score this writer can only attribute to a lack of Cardiff players, *'wrth gwrs'* - of course. Wales went on to beat Scotland 13-6 away and Ireland 13-0 at St. Helen's. Viv Jenkins of Bridgend became the first Welsh fullback, in its 85 years of international, to score a try. The next was to be Keith Jarrett in 1967.

It seems that the young Gwyn Williams of Taff's Well had a fair few outings for Cardiff Athletic, and in the next season he was a First XV regular. Aged only 15, he had been described aged 14 as looking like a fully-grown 'big' man. Cardiff drew with the Barbarians 3-3 on tries, but kicking let them down and the score was 14-9. On the Barbarians' website, two players reminisce about the game. R. W. Shaw remembered *'That 1934 Easter tour was certainly the most exhausting rugby I have ever encountered. Saturday v Cardiff; Monday v Swansea; Tuesday v Newport. I was given slight relief on Tuesday by being played on the wing. This was the only game I ever played with eight backs and seven forwards. Why this was so I cannot recall. Whether it was an admin. error or a last-minute call-off of a forward and the only available replacement was a back. However, it was all good fun with too many backs cluttering up the field and spoiling many scoring opportunities. High jinks in Penarth. Great friendly opinion from all the local people in Penarth allowed some horseplay at the dance. Setting off of fireworks and the riding of a bicycle all on the dance floor were all accepted in the spirit in which these actions were done. I used to conduct the dance band for several years in succession. In retrospect, I cannot understand this as I was timber toned and couldn't play a musical instrument. It is quite amazing what beer can do!'*

CHAPTER 9 - CARDIFF SEASON 1934 – 1935

GWYN WILLIAMS IS A CARDIFF REGULAR, AGED 16

Gwyn Williams TW, played 103 games until joined Wigan in 1938; Harry Rees TW, 5 Wales caps; Ray Bale Tongwynlais

P46 W27 L14 D5. Pts 427-250. Tries 103-59, Pens 10-6

At the start of the season, the strongly built Gwyn Williams was just 16 years and 4 months, having eased through Cardiff trials. His brothers believe that Gwyn had appeared aged 15 for Cardiff Athletic. Just 6 foot tall, Gwyn appeared much bigger. A wing-forward, he was quick enough to play in the centre – as all his brothers did, even Elwyn, another wing-forward. When he moved to rugby league before the war, he played loose-forward (the equivalent of number 8, there being no wing-forwards in the 13-man code), sometimes centre and more often wing. After six successive seasons of having more penalties scored against them than Cardiff scored, the adverse at last happened. Still, 10 penalties to 103 tries was a reasonable ratio. Eleven Glamorgan County Police played during the season, giving the team a solid pack of forwards.

Gwyn Williams is furthest right, front row and played regularly for the Athletic from the age of 16 years and 4 months, winning his cap in 1934-35

Former miner, P.C. Archie Skym (1906-1970) was the third policeman to captain Cardiff, after Willie Spiller (1912-13) and Tom Lewis of Taff's Well (1932-33), and Skym also captained British Police. Skym began for Wales in the second row, then shifted to prop, and could play anywhere in the pack - but generally as a hard prop for Cardiff, making 212 appearances between 1928-29 to 1936-37. Skym was known as *'the Butcher'* for his amazing strength in lifting opposing props, not for any connections with the meat trade. He scored 32 tries for Cardiff, a high rate for a forward. Because of his father's religious beliefs, Skym was not allowed to play rugby as a boy, but during a nine-month miners' strike he joined his local club Drefach, for something to do. An adult when he started playing, he soon moved to Tumble Rugby Club, then on 26 December 1926 he was playing for Llanelli against London Welsh. A Barbarian, Archie Skym played twenty matches for Wales, his first cap being against England on 21 January 1928. He scored two tries in that game, and played in all four internationals that season.

For some odd reason Llanelli would not pick him to play at all in the 1928-29 season, so he did not play for Wales, and by February 1929 he left to join Cardiff to resume playing for Wales from 1930. (He must have back-chatted someone on the Llanelli committee – their loss.) In 1930 and 1931, he again played in every international, and also in 1931 in the 8-3 loss to South Africa. In 1932 and 1933 he played in 3 internationals each year as games with France were suspended, and in 1935 played for a fifth time against England. In 1933 he played in the Welsh team that finally beat England at Twickenham. In January 1935, against Swansea, Skym broke his ankle but stayed on the pitch for the entire game. The injury ended his international career and he retired from Cardiff at the end of the season.

Let us examine the French international ban in brief. Rugby was a strictly amateur game, especially among senior clubs in Britain. However, in France rampant professionalism and transfer fees were common, along with high levels of violence at club level – which still happens. By the early 1930s, aggression and brutality were witnessed in games against England and Wales, and in 1931, France was ejected from the Five Nations, until 1939. Marshal Petain ordered league and union to merge during the war. Rugby union in Britain, especially in Wales, was also under threat from rugby league at this time. More Welsh players had 'jobs', rather than the higher-paid 'occupations' of their English, Scottish and Irish counterparts. Because of the Depression and job insecurity, Wales was awash with rugby league scouts in the 1930s, which led to a paranoid backlash by the W.R.U. that lasted until the 1980s. Unacknowledged professionalism came back into French rugby union after the war, well before it was allowed under Rugby Union rules. I seem to remember in the 50s that union was paid in France and league amateur.

Maurice Turnbull retired after 13 matches, and Archie Skym could not play in the last 13 games, being replaced by diminutive but terrific fullback and outside half Tommy Stone as captain. '*This was a far better year for the club, coinciding with arrival of two new forwards in the back row: Eddie Watkins had just left Caerphilly Grammar School and Gwyn Williams, the first of the celebrated Taff's Well family of brothers who were to play for Cardiff and gain fame in the Rugby world; Jim Regan, a local boy, established himself as the club's hooker and was unfortunate to have "Bunner" Travers of Newport in his way for international caps. Archie Skym's pack was strong enough, but his backs, mostly young, failed to really establish themselves excepting Willie Reardon on the wing.*' Bleddyn Williams as a schoolboy watched and practised Tommy Stone's jink, sidestep and swerve to make him the player he became, widely acknowledging the fact.

Cardiff drew with Newport but won the next three games, but Swansea with the excellent half-backs Haydn Tanner (later of Cardiff) and Willie Davies, won three out of four games; and the four matches with Llanelli resulted in two wins each. *'Twelve matches in one season with the strongest rival clubs illustrated the strength of Cardiff's fixture list'*. Within three days of returning from the traditional Cornish tour, Cardiff lost its three Easter fixtures, against the Barbarians 20-5 (20 April); Harlequins 13-3 (22 April): and Coventry 5-3 (23 April). *'This was the first time to lose all our Easter matches, it was the penalty of bad fixture arrangement'*, according to Danny Davies. 3 games in 4 days against crack teams is never a good idea, but the Easter pile-up persisted for decades as money-spinners for the club. Wing Willie Reardon scored five tries in Cardiff's home win by seven unconverted tries (a record in top class rugby?) to one goal against Richmond and was top scorer with 21 touchdowns. Ronnie Boon scored 7 tries in just 6 matches. Among First XV caps were Eddie Watkins (43 games) and Ken Street (30). Ken, along with Wilf Wooller and Les Spence, was to be captured by the Japanese. At Twickenham, Cliff Jones made a dazzling break for Wooller to score the only try of the game in a 3-3 draw. Edgar Jones was a passenger for most of the match with a cracked rib, and England were awarded a penalty for offside in the last minutes by the referee – Irish, obviously. Centre Wooller and fly-half Cliff Jones were now at Cambridge University, and both scored tries in the 10-6 home win over Scotland, a game in which Jones was excellent before he went off with an elbow injury and the 14 men hung on. In Belfast, Wales lost to an Ireland team 9-3, their first championship since 1899.

Hubert Johnson's second term as captain of 'The Rags' saw him playing in all 30 games, in an unsettled season where no fewer than 82 players were called upon, of whom only 6 played in more than 15 games. Thus, only two qualified for Athletic XV caps, the hooker W. J. 'Bill' Hurley, and scrum half Geoff Nicholls, son of the illustrious Gwyn Nicholls. The 'Rags' had a reasonable season with a record of P30 – W16 – L11 – D3. They scored 302 against 164 points. Cardiff Firsts had a couple of losing seasons in their formative years in the nineteenth century, and not one since. The Athletic had one losing season in the nineteenth century, in 1892-93, with a W10 L12 D3 record. However, they scored 43 tries against 35, and 210 points against 107. Their only other losing season was dreadful, in 1929-30, with a record of W5-L19-D3, losing 282-198 on points and 68-45 on tries. From 1884-85, when we have records, these were the only two losing seasons. For the 1929-30 losing season by the Athletic, Cardiff were playing two First XVs, resulting that over 80 players had run-outs in the 'Rags'. It is an amazing record, of only losing this

88

season in the twentieth century, and that because the two Firsts system took their team away. Thus **both Cardiff and the Athletic had one losing season between them in the twentieth century**.

CHAPTER 10 - CARDIFF SEASON 1935 – 1936

GWYN WILLIAMS IS THE YOUNGEST PLAYER TO FACE THE ALL BLACKS – WALES BEAT THE ALL BLACKS

Gwyn Williams TW; Harry Rees TW, 5 Wales caps; Ray Bale Tongwynlais

P44, W23, L18, D3. Points 375-275. Tries 85-56, Pens 10-11

The popular outside half Tommy Stone was captain, and he asked forward Les Spence to be vice-captain. The great full back P.C. Jack Bassett (1905-89), a British Lion in 1930 on the New Zealand and Australia tour, had been acclaimed on that tour as *'the greatest full back in world rugby'*. At that time with Penarth R.F.C., he played in all 5 tests. Between 1929 and 1932 Bassett played for Wales 15 times, captaining them in 1931 to their first Five Nations Championship since 1922 with 3 wins and a draw. Jack was happy appearing with the 'Rags' to end his playing days. His younger brother Arthur (1914-1999) joined from Aberavon R.F.C., making 101 appearances for Cardiff Firsts from 1935-36 to 1938-39. As a wing, he scored 99 tries, a terrific scoring rate. In the Glamorgan County Police force, like his elder brother, Arthur Bassett played for Wales against England in 1934, winning three caps in 1935 and two caps in 1938. However, aged 25, he signed for Halifax Rugby League team in 1939, winning 3 Wales, and 2 Great Britain caps. Arthur Bassett was a great loss to Cardiff and Wales rugby union.

In a mixed season for Cardiff, a highlight was victory over the 'Baa-Baas' on Easter Monday by a try and dropped goal to one try, the Barbarians' first defeat after a run of 22 games during their South Wales tours. Cardiff had last beaten them in April 1930. It was Les Spence's favourite memory of playing for Cardiff: *'Cardiff were playing the Barbarians who included fourteen internationals in their ranks. Their back division was as follows: V.G.J. (Viv) Jenkins, C.V. Boyle, P. Cranmer, Wilf Wooller, K.C. Fyfe, Wilson Shaw, and W.R. Logan. The Cardiff backs were Tommy Stone, Arthur Bassett, J.J. Davies, D. Brown, A.H. Jones, and J. Bowcott. The "Baa-Baas" had not been defeated in Wales for six years, and with such a galaxy of talent at their disposal, it was merely a question of how many points they would score, said the critics. As history relates, Cardiff won the game by 7 points to 3. They scored a try by Bassett* (later to play for Cardiff), *who intercepted a pass from Wooller to Cranmer; a magnificent dropped goal by A.H. Jones, after Wooller had levelled the scores with a try. At the close a jubilant Tommy Stone was carried off shoulder-high by enthusiastic supporters. Every man in the Cardiff side had played himself to a standstill'.* Gwyn Williams was playing wing-forward, a regular fixture in the side, and Wilf Wooller was still a schoolboy at Rydal while making occasional appearances for Cardiff. Cardiff had commenced their Barbarian RFC fixtures in March 1891 and played them twice a year, from 1899-1900 to 1920-21. From the first Baa-Baas game until the last of the Williams boys playing for Cardiff, 1974-75, in 91 games, Cardiff won 58, lost 29 and drew 4, scoring 1,208 points to 708, 269 tries to 162.

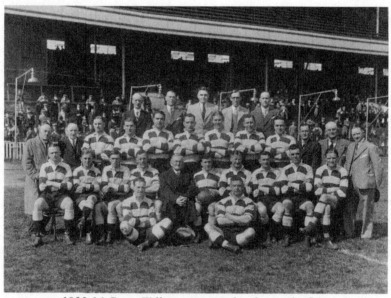

1935-36 Gwyn Williams is seated right, on the floor

Cardiff played New Zealand on 6 October 1935 and lost 20-5. The game was lost in the first half as the result of some bad mistakes by the Cardiff backs, and the team was losing 15-0 at half time. However, Cardiff played brilliantly in the second half, in which each side scored a converted try. The press reported it as the most thrilling match in which the All Blacks had so far played on tour. Wing forward Gwyn Williams was 17 years and 5 months, seemingly the youngest man ever to have played against the All Blacks.

Cardiff R.F.C. warmly congratulated Swansea when they beat New Zealand. We should mention Penclawdd's Haydn Tanner here, as he was a schoolboy at Gowerton Grammar School, when he played scrumhalf for Swansea against the All Blacks in 1935, Swansea winning. Tanner and his cousin, outside-half Willie Davies, had superb games. From the ESPN website we read: *'Haydn Tanner and Willie Davies, Sixth Formers from Gowerton Grammar School, plotted the downfall of the All Blacks. Swansea won 11-3 in front of 35,000 at St Helen's, and not only became the first non-international side to defeat the mighty All Blacks, but also the first club team to beat all three major touring sides. Their 11-3 triumph over New Zealand followed victories over Australia in 1908 and South Africa in 1912. All the points came in the first half, and the second, played in heavy rain, became a war of attrition in which the Swansea pack gave as good as they got, including in regular bouts of fighting that broke out. New Zealand's captain Jack Manchester begged the press, "Tell them we have been beaten, but don't tell them it was by a pair of schoolboys."'* From a Cardiff perspective, South Africa were beaten 17-0 in 1907, followed by an unlucky 7-6 loss in 1912, Cardiff scoring the only try, and an 11-9 loss in 1951, where Bleddyn said Cardiff lost the game, rather than SA won it. Australia were beaten in all four games from 1908 to 1966 – 24-4; 11-3; 14-11 and 14-8. Cardiff should have won against New Zealand in the 10-8 loss in 1908, recounted earlier in this book, but it took until Bleddyn's captaincy in 1953 to win, and also should have won in 1963, losing 6-5 by scoring a converted try against a drop goal and a penalty.

In December 1935, Haydn Tanner won his first cap, still not aged 19, becoming one of the youngest players to appear for Wales. Wales beat the All Blacks, and Tanner won 25 international caps, captaining Wales 12 times, despite a career interrupted for 6 years by WWII. There were no internationals from 1939 to 1947. He toured South Africa with the Lions in 1938 but played only one Test owing to injury. After the war he joined Cardiff, playing 78 times before retiring in 1949. Bleddyn Williams said *'Among all the scrum-halves I've seen and played with, he would reign supreme. He had a superb pass – the best I ever played with. His service was even better than Gareth Edwards.'*

In the Welsh defeat of the All Blacks on 21 December by 13-12, Eddie Watkins was Cardiff's only representative. Wilf Wooller and Cliff Jones also played but Wooller had not yet 'officially' joined the club, and Cliff Jones had only played in a few Cardiff matches because of his Cambridge law studies. The win was truly remarkable. Llandeilo's Don Tarr had joined Cardiff in 1931, playing in the 13-5 loss against South Africa. In 1933, the hooker decided to join his old classmate Claude Davey at Swansea, where they beat New Zealand. A Barbarian, Swansea's Don Tarr won his first and only Welsh cap in 1935 against the All Blacks. Huw Richards recalled: *'Wilfred Wooller, Wales's powerful big-striding centre, had been moved to the wing to accommodate the all-Swansea combination of Davey and all-round footballer Idwal Rees at centre, while seven clubs were represented in a pack in which another teenager, prop Eddie Watkins, was part of an all-debutant front-row.'*

Wales were 12-10 down with just ten minutes to go, when a loose scrum broke up to reveal Don Tarr lying motionless on the ground. The referee, Cyril Gadney, shouted for no one to touch the hooker and to wait for medical aid. The referee then insisted that Tarr be stretchered off in his prone position, saving his life. *"Tarr had broken his neck and sitting him up would have killed him."* Although Wales were losing and down to 14 men, they recovered strongly and after Rees-Jones scored a try, won 13-12. It was said to be **the most serious injury survived by a rugby player,** and for the rest of his life, his head was cocked to one side. Don Tarr only played one more game, for Ammanford in the years after, and became a Lieutenant-Commander in the Royal Navy in WW2. After the war, he taught GCE O and A-level physics in Cardiff High School, where the pupils nicknamed him 'Jack' Tarr. This was doubly clever, because 'jolly Jack Tar' was a nickname for sailors, and Swansea citizens were known as 'Swansea Jacks', from their sea-going clothes, tarpaulins tarred to provide some protection heavy weather at sea'. (I must here mention the wonderful Don Llewellyn, who helped with this book, and broke his neck playing for Pentyrch. After a suitable recuperation period he re-joined the team, playing as hooker for ten years, the most dangerous position for neck injuries when the scrum collapsed.)

As an aside, while Swansea's rugby team are known as 'Jacks', and we were 'city-slicker', 'fancy boy' or 'dock-rat' Cardiffians, the Llanelli side are still always referred to as 'Turks' or 'one-eyed Turks'. The wonderful *'The History of Wales'* Facebook site tells us: *'The possible origin of this nickname may refer to the 1800's when Llanelli was a thriving trading port and many Turkish seamen called to and settled in the town. Alternative theories include the fact that Llanelli's soldiers fought the Ottoman Turks during World War I or that the town's steel and tinplate workers used to wear rags around their heads, because of the intensive heat and sweat, which made them resemble Turkish nationals.'* One comment from Terry Chow, referring to an allegedly rough pub in the town, is *'It's because the Ottoman and Mamluk warriors were sent to the Moonraker on a Friday to learn how to handle themselves in battle.'* Trystan Lewis claims *'Turkish sailors owed Swansea docks money, they banned them from docking in Swansea and other South Wales docks stood by Swansea. Llanelli saw this as an opportunity to make new trade instead of sticking with the rest of South Wales. Turk wasn't a name given in good nature, after this is when the Llanelli and Turkish trade flourished.'* Finally, Neil Vaughan writes: *'I thought it was linked to the docks, years ago many UK/Welsh ports would not handle any cargo from Turkish ships. But Llanelli would and hence the name! I have been living in the Rhondda for 20yrs and my nickname has been Turk since my 1st pint here.'* A Cardiff friend bought one of those fashionable Jackapoo crossbreed dogs, also known as a Jackadoodle, a cross between a Jack Russel and a Poodle. He calls it a 'Do-a-Jack'. He was also wondering about keeping a turkey in his back garden for Christmas.

The wing Arthur Bassett scored most tries for Cardiff with 27, with A. H. Jones next highest with only nine. First XV caps were awarded to Jackie Bowcott, J. J. Davies, H. O. Edwards, Gwyn Porter and the young Gwyn Williams. Hubert Johnson became the first Athletic captain since 1891 to be appointed in three successive seasons, and his team Played 30; Won 21; Drew 3; and lost 6 games, with Jack Bassett sharing the goal-kicking and being awarded his Athletic cap. The Barbarians were beaten 7-3, and their player P. Cranmer reminisced, recorded on the Baa-Baas' website '*There was this attractive redheaded maid working at the Esplanade* (hotel in Penarth, their base for the Easter Tour) *so Wilf Wooller and I thought we'd better get more acquainted, so one evening we went to the servants' quarters, that house on the hill opposite the hotel entrance. All the lower doors were locked, but a half-opened window upstairs looked promising. There just happened to be a ladder lying on the ground, so we propped it up against the wall, but it could not stand the strain of our combined weight and we crashed, luckily feet first, through the cucumber frames below. No injury and we both played against Cardiff next day and won. Not so on another Saturday; Cardiff moved a wing, A. H. Jones, to fly half and he dropped a goal minutes before to make Cardiff the first club to beat the Baa-Baas on the Easter Tour for some time. It must have been after this match, back at the Esplanade, that I was leaning on a high-backed chair talking to the "Alikadoos"*, Some of the Cardiff players were there too, including Eddie Watkins, Cardiff and Wales 2nd row forward. He pushed me and I caught my lip on the top of the chair. Blood everywhere. Luckily Hughie Hughes was still about, though how he threaded the needle to stitch me up I'll never know, but he did, perfectly, and all Eddie said was "We couldn't do you on the field, Peter, so I've done you now!" When I used to go to Twickenham after I'd finished playing, the first person I used to see sitting at the bar in the International Room was Eddie Watkins. Lots of beer and no recriminations.*' *No, me neither. But *Wiktionary* helped out: '*A non-playing member of a rugby union club who helps in the running of the club by performing various roles, usually on match days. These roles are not committee positions but are essential if the club is to function properly.*' Every club needs them, at all levels, unsung heroes and usually former players.

GWYN'S UNCLE ROY ROBERTS GIVEN ATHLETIC CAP and **PLAYS FOR THE FIRSTS** - *'NO CLUB SIDE SHOULD BE AS GOOD AS CARDIFF'* - *'BLUE and BLACK MAGIC'* - *'THE BEST RUGBY CLUB IN THE COUNTRY'* - **TOMMY STONE** *'THE BEST FULL-BACK IN THE WORLD'*

Gwyn Williams TW; **Roy Roberts** TW (53 games pre-war and 97 games post-war); Harry Rees TW (169 games for Cardiff, 5 Welsh caps); Ray Bale Tongwynlais (108 pre-war games, 68 post-war)

P44, W36, L7, D1. Points 553-173. <u>Tries 118-28!</u> Pens 11-15

1936-37 was a good year, with 36 wins, 1 draw and 7 losses, incredibly scoring 118 tries to 28, over four tries to one, yet losing on penalties 15-11. Every loss was very close, and with luck the results would have been reversed, leading to an unbeaten season. Cardiff were Welsh Champions, and there is a celebratory team photo of Gwyn Williams sitting in the front row with Wilf Wooller, Arthur Bassett, Joe Regan, Ray Bale and captain Les Spence. Even better years were to follow, with Cardiff being by far the top team in Britain in the years leading up to and after World War II. Danny Davies tells us *'This was the season of Cardiff's recovery to equal some of her past glories, it was the most successful season since the end of the war. L. M. Spence was captain and he nominated Tommy Stone as vice-captain. Most of the previous season's players were available. Newcomers who joined the club were T. Lyn Williams, a versatile centre/outside half from Cardiff High School, W. Glyn Morgan a neat and diminutive scrum half from Penygraig, another member of the Turnbull family, Adrian, also a scrum half, and the two experienced international players C. W. "Cliff" Jones, at outside half and Wilfred Wooller the young but powerful-striding centre, a prodigious kicker of all goals. As a pair, the latter two made their debuts at the Cardiff Arms Park against Neath on 28th November, a match we won by 18 points* (3 converted tries and a penalty) *to nil.'* (I have usually avoided using goals for converted tries, as it can be confusing to the non-player).

Cambridge University's Cliff Jones was still studying law, and Wilf Wooller had gained work in Cardiff. They had played often together at Cambridge, developing moves between the small outside-half Jones and the 6-foot 3 inches centre Wooller, and knew each other's game inside out. Davies goes on: *'They had an inspiring influence on the rest of the team, their presence had an impact on gates at home and away. Of these two players, Jack Davis of the Newport "Argus" in his history of the Newport Club 1875-1960, wrote: "It is appropriate here to pay tribute to the effect this pair of great players had on Newport. Newport's Rugby had become to be dull, and support was dwindling, but the box office allure of Jones and Wooller boosted Newport's finances just when this was necessary. Their first visit to Newport drew a crowd of 13,000, the biggest for many years, and right up to the war Newport had reason to be thankful for the visits of those two personalities who have done so much for the game in so many ways."*

Sadly, Cliff Jones fractured his collarbone away at Swansea away in November, putting him out for the season, and Wilf Wooller was only available for 21 games because of injuries and internationals, but Les Spence captained a great team. Because of incidents in an away loss at Aberavon in 1932-33, fixtures had been broken off, but fixtures were officially resumed in 1936-37 in a tough away win, with the only score of the game, a try of course. Swansea were defeated four times, Newport and Pontypool three times, and Neath, Coventry and Plymouth Albion twice each. There was also a successful Midland tour, beating Coventry and Northampton, and a successful Cornish tour with wins over Plymouth Albion, Falmouth and Penzance. At Easter Cardiff easily beat the Barbarians 16-3. Davies records: *'In a footnote to our Barbarian victory, an Irish international who took part in the match pressed the view that* **"No club should be allowed to have such a good club side as Cardiff***... The margin of defeat in the seven matches lost was very close in every case, Bridgend (H) by 4 points to 3 (Cardiff scored a try to a drop goal), Gloucester (A) 13 points to 9 (one try, one drop, and two penalty goals to three tries from Cardiff), Llanelly 8 points to 6 (one goal, one try to two tries), Bristol (A) 5 points to 3 (a goal to a try), Newport (H) 8 points to 3 (two dropped goals to one try), Blackheath (A) 5 points to 4 (a goal to a dropped goal), and Llanelly (H) by 5 points to 3 (a goal to a penalty). It was understandable that the players' achievements should be recognized by the award to them of blazers by the club.'* Cardiff's aversion to taking penalties and missed conversions probably cost them the games – the try scores in these 7 losses were: **Cardiff first: 1-0, 3-1, 2-1, 1-1, 1-0, 0-1, 0-1 (=8-3).** Missing Cliff Jones badly, only in the last two games were Cardiff outscored on tries, 1-0 and 1-0. Harry Rees, Wilf Wooller and Eddie Watkins played in all three internationals (there was no France fixture), and international trials and injuries contributed to the losses – no wonder the club gave blazers, a rare event, to the players who came so close to an unbeaten season.

A terrific, highly-rated back row forward, Les Spence captained the team in 39 of their 44 matches. Wing Arthur Bassett again was leading try scorer with 22, then Wilf Wooller scored 15, and Les Spence with 12. Wilf and Les were to be captured together by the Japanese in WWII. Les Spence's 12 tries were a Cardiff record for a forward, unbeaten for 32 years until wing forward Mervyn John scored 13 in 1968-69, and back-row Roger

Lane equalled that in 1970-71. Our Gwyn Williams, the first of the Williams boys, scored 5 tries, and Wooller was awarded his cap. *For the eighth of nine seasons, Cardiff had now lost on the converted penalty count, although scoring up to six times more tries than the opposition.* It may be in this year that W.R.U. referee Fred Croster remembered an incident, in his article '*Magic Moments*' in *Welsh Rugby's* special issue celebrating Cardiff's centenary in 1976. '*Although a referee should always maintain a strict impartiality when on the field of play, I must admit that most of us have our own private opinion of the quality of players, clubs (even of certain Laws of the Game), so that my admiration for the Cardiff club is, perhaps, understandable. Having had the pleasure to be associated with this famous club since before the War, reflection brings back not only memories of great Arms Park occasions and personalities but also the realisation of what "Blue and Black Magic" means. To me it means something more than team-understanding and combination in the brilliant attacking movements for which the club is justly famed and also the camaraderie that exists among the players. Cardiff are famed for their sportsmanship and cherish their reputation for being a clean, sporting side.*

Occasionally they react (and believe me they can react with a vengeance) as was the case in one of my earliest memories of the club before the War. Centenary Year Chairman, Les Spence, and who better to receive this great honour) provided me with an unforgettable memory when, as a lad in the mid-thirties, I was watching with rapt attention a stirring, red-blooded encounter with the All-Whites of Swansea. Les, a fine wing forward unlucky not to be capped by his country which he later served as President of the Welsh Rugby Union, was causing all sorts of problems for the All Whites that day and soon became the target for special attention from the rugged Swansea forwards. One international (no names, no pack-drill, decided to take stern measures against the troublesome Cardiff flanker and stormed into action with a mighty swipe which laid out Les flat on the ground. Les Spence's great pal, then and now, is Wilfred Wooller and this must have been one of the very few occasions when Wilf, one of the greatest sportsmen of all time, lost his temper. He rolled up his sleeves and proceeded to chase his man all around the field, seeking vengeance against the miscreant who, doubtless, did not forget the attacking power (or the all-embracing tackling) of the great Cardiff and Wales centre for a long, long time!' Les and Wilf were to end up together in a Japanese prisoner-of-war camp, which effectively ended their rugby-playing days. One wonders whether it was this season, when Cardiff won all four Swansea encounters, 12-6, 19-9, 3-0 and 4-3, and Cardiff scored 8 tries to 1.

A Past vs. Present match was played in April, in aid of Cardiff Royal Infirmary, with the Present team winning 36-20, consisting of: Backs - D.

Brown; Arthur Bassett, T. J. Roberts; H. O. Edwards and Gwyn Porter; Half Backs - Cliff Jones and W. G. Morgan; Forwards - Ray Bale, J. Kelleher, Harry Rees, L. M. Spence, Roy Roberts, his nephew Gwyn Williams, Eddie Watkins and P.C. Ivor Heatley. We will hear much more of Les Spence, Roy Roberts, Eddie Watkins and Gwyn Williams. All of their careers were affected by the war, but Roy Roberts played 150 games for Cardiff from this season until 1948-49, when he left to captain Pontypridd. Les Spence had been a Cardiff player since 1930-31, playing his 267th game in 1939-40, but capture by the Japanese ended his rugby career. Prop Eddie Watkins played 151 times from 1934-35 to 1939-40, but the Welsh international later left for Wigan rugby league along with his great friend Gwyn Williams.

Wales lost away to England, Wilf Wooller's unconverted try worth 3 points against 4 points for England's drop goal, surely a moral victory. Viv Jenkins missed his kick to touch, the ball bouncing off an England back into the hands of the English wing, H. Sever. From the touchline, 40 yards out, Sever kicked his first ever drop goal. Wales lost 5-3 away to Ireland, when the ball hit the referee and the Welsh players stopped, expecting the whistle, and Ireland scored. They then suffered an unexpected loss at home to Scotland, 13-6. Welsh forwards were on the small side and not of the same calibre as their backs. England won the championship with scores of 4:3 (H); 9-8 (H to Ireland) and 6-3 (A at Scotland). In scoring 19:14 in 3 games, England won by a total points difference of 5, yet if Wales and Ireland had converted a try apiece, the All-Whites would have finished 3rd in the table. Rugby is a strange game – even now the greatest attraction of the Six Nations is that every season there are 'upsets'. Of the international season, Davies tells us *'Three players, Tommy Stone and Horace Edwards of Cardiff, and Charlie J. Anderson a forward from Maesteg, were to suffer a cruel blow in the matter of a Welsh cap. V. G. G. Jenkins full-back, Claude Davey centre, and Trevor Williams of Cross Keys had been chosen for the Welsh team against Ireland for 13th March but had to withdraw owing to injuries and they were replaced by the Cardiff and Maesteg players in the order named here. Alas, on the way to Belfast, the Welsh party ran into such a severe blizzard that the match was not played and it had to be re-arranged for 3rd April. The Welsh selectors decided to adhere to their original selection for it, and the unfortunate Stone, Edwards and Anderson never played for Wales. Tommy Stone, disappointed in many ways turned professional and joined the Barrow club. He was one of Cardiff's most loyal players, having played for the ex-schoolboys' teams in the early twenties, then on to Cardiff's senior teams, and for the First XV alone played no less than 317 times.'*

TOMMY STONE – 'THE BEST FULL BACK IN THE WORLD'
We should remember the 5ft. 2ins Tommy Stone, who had joined from

Llandaff North, in a little more detail – Bleddyn Williams freely admitted that he copied his devastating sidestep and jink from Tommy and practised it intensively. Tommy could play outside half, centre or full back, and was Cardiff Vice-Captain in 1934-34, Captain in 1935-36 and Vice-Captain again in 1936-37. Adrian Stone in 2009 wrote an extensive illustrated article for *The Rugby History Society*, from which the following is taken - (*www.therugbyhistorysociety.co.uk/tstone*) In 1913, a newspaper article '*Little child in dire peril*' recounted 3-year-old Tommy playing and being rescued from the Glamorgan Canal in Cardiff. A workman sprinted 300 yards to dive in and pull Tommy out, but he had been in the water for 4 minutes and was unconscious… '*while a messenger went for the doctor, artificial respiration was resorted to by several men who had hastened to the scene. For an hour their efforts met with no success but when they were almost giving up hope they noticed twitching in one of the little boy's eyes and doubled their efforts. A little later the doctor arrived and the boy was taken into his home. An hour later the doctor reported that due to his good constitution the child was out of danger.*'

There follows an account of his exploits for Highfield School, with one report reading: '*Prior to to-day's game, Stone, the Highfield centre had scored 95 points for 9 games played and his 7 points this morning made his total so far this season 102, a very creditable performance. Tom Stone's try was easily the best. He was the outstanding boy on the field and should be a strong candidate for international honours again this season.*' And in another match '*Last Saturday Highfield met St. Albans in the Ingram Rees Cup and ran out winners by 48 points to nil. Tom Stone, who should be an absolute certainty for a Welsh* (schoolboy) *cap this season, scored eight tries and converted two.*' In another account, by the game against St. David's he had gained his cap: '*Highfield had had the better of the exchange in the opening half, but failed to press home their advantage. Early in the second half Tom Stone, the Welsh international full back playing at centre in this game, dropped a pretty goal which decided the match.*' This was the final for the Cardiff Schools Rugby Shield at the Cardiff Arms Park, which was '*productive of scenes almost without parallel in the history of schoolboy rugby. A small rowdy element amongst the spectators made its presence felt during the game and especially so, at the conclusion of the game… the decision did not please the section already referred to, and there ensued scenes which were a disgrace to the fair name of the sport, and which might have had serious results. As it was the referee was roughly handled by hooligans, before he could obtain assistance and he was escorted off the field by members of the scholastic profession. The boys of the winning side were also subjected to maltreatment and a stone was thrown at Tommy Stone whose dropped goal gave Highfield the victory and was carried off shoulder high by his colleagues.*'

Reports of his games of 'brilliance' for Cardiff Boys follow: '*The outstanding player was Tommy Stone, the schoolboy international full back who played in the unusual position, for him, as outside half.*' In the Welsh Schoolboys' Trial, '*Tom Stone, Probables full back, is the captain of the undefeated Highfield school team. For his school he plays centre three-quarter but as Cardiff's full back he has made himself famous. He was reserve full back for Wales last season and is well in the running for his cap again this season.*' Tommy gained his Welsh Schoolboys Cap in 1924. He joined Cardiff RFC as a full back in 1928-29, the '*Best Rugby Club in the Country*', and in a 5-0 win against Newport: '*In the opening minutes of the half, Stone electrified the crowd of 20,000 with an amazing run, in which he covered 60 yards after fielding the ball in his own 25. The full back darted clean through the opposition, but when he finally passed, a Newport man snapped up the ball. Stone's brilliant effort, however paved the way for a Cardiff score, and this was obtained in the next movement when A T Thomas dashed over in the corner after B R Turnbull had paved the way.*' Tommy was a regular for Cardiff at just 19 years old, and his outstanding displays over the years had the press calling for him to be capped by Wales.

One report reads '*At the end of the match the name of T. Stone, Cardiff's full back, was on the tongue of most of the spectators. He gave a scintillating display, and without exaggeration might be said to have played the principal part in Cardiff's victory. His positioning and fielding were perfect and he kicked a good length with excellent judgement, but it was the manner in which he eluded would-be tacklers and gained large slices of ground by clever running, which was the feature of his play... The outstanding Cardiff player was Stone the full back. His touch finding was perfect and his try which resulted from a run almost the length of the field ending in a clever punt over an opponent's head was a great effort. Final score Gloucester 3 Cardiff 15 points.*' Some reports call Tommy 'superb' and 'magnificent' and a 'hero'. He played for Glamorgan and the Barbarians, and the Cardiff-Springboks match report reads: '*Little Stone with a Great Heart... Critical Match... Interesting contrasts are provided in the Cardiff team. The forwards, who include such famous Welsh caps as A Skym and B Barrel average 18 stone, but the full back, T Stone, is at 5 foot 2 inches the smallest man playing first class rugby in this position. Stone is, however, strong and sturdy, a plucky tackler and a good kicker...*

Twice in the first half, when Cardiff were the better side, a sprinter might have rounded off the attack, while on a third occasion, a minute or two before the interval, Stone (who played his best game of the season and did not suffer in comparison with Brand) with the assistance of Barrel and Skym, ran for over half the length of the field and failed to find a speedy man on the right flank to accept a pass when all the defence had been left behind... Cardiff as a team played nobly and Stone and Boon played heroically... Little full back's amazing pluck, went down to rushes of giant forwards. Although Cardiff did not beat the South Africans, they made them go all out to win by 2 goals and one try to 1 goal. Over 30,000 spectators attended. The man who caught the most, though was Stone, Cardiff's diminutive full back. He did not miss-field a single ball and went down to rushes in plucky style. On this display he must be the best full back in Wales to-day. Final score Cardiff 5 South Africa 13.'

Tommy had played 317 games for Cardiff and was extremely disappointed with not being picked for Wales – even Newport supporters were writing to the press complaining of his non-selection. In a Final Trial he inspired the Possibles to a 15-10 victory. A report reads: *'Tommy Stone, the Cardiff full back deserves a glance. There are of course Scourfield, Bayliss and Bassett ready to hand; Stone has one advantage over these three; his former experience as a fly-half makes him a much more constructive back than any of them. I am tending to the opinion that **the great full back of the future is going to be a very real part of the attack**. Full backs ignore attack too much. Someone will arise one day and alter that.'... 'There must be some prejudice in the selector's minds against Stone, perhaps they are fearful of his audacity, preferring stodgy efficiency, but if the little Cardiff full back ends his career without winning a Welsh cap it will be possible to say with perfect truth that he is one of the finest uncapped men who has ever played. When we remember the questionable credentials of so many internationals honoured even in Stone's time, we cannot but sympathise with a grand little player.'*

After 9 seasons as outside half, and later full back, Tommy had had enough, signing for Barrow in the League on 20 March 1937. *'"The scouts had been after me for years"* he explained *"and in my disappointment in not playing in Ireland I thought I might as well get something out of the game, so I signed for Barrow at a fee of £300."* He turned out to be one of Barrow's most costly buys. After no more than a dozen games for the rugby league club he strained the ligaments in his knee and was unable to play another game of rugby... Cheery and imperturbable Tommy, his chubby face constantly creased with an engaging grin, has only one regret about his rugby career - that he did not turn professional earlier. *"I was 27 years old when I went north and that was too late"* he points out. *"I could have gone as a youngster to either Leeds or Salford for £560 but my father was very ill and I thought it better to stay at home."'*

G. V. Wynne Jones wrote in 1974 *'Tommy was ahead of his time. It is a matter of getting the right mixture of individualism and discipline. If I had a son who was keen to be a three-quarter, I would want him to watch Wilf Wooller but learn from Bleddyn Williams. Wilf was the great individualist, the completely natural player. Bleddyn was a player who did all the orthodox things well, who could play the team game to perfection and then decide the match with one magnificent sidestep... The changes in the game today would have appealed to the people I played within the 1930's. Tommy Stone would have been in J P R's class as an attacking full back. Tommy who started as a fly half was regarded as too much of a risk as an international full back because he came up with his threequarters too often. They'd have said the same thing about J P R had he been playing then. Now he is rightly regarded as the best full back in the world.*' The author realises that the book is about the Williams Brothers, but some of their wonderful playing partners, such as Tommy, have been long forgotten. Their lives and amateur playing careers, holding down full-time jobs and trying to take time off work for some games, is a lesson for professional players in all sports – especially football – 'soccer' for American readers.

CHAPTER 12 - CARDIFF SEASON 1937 – 1938

WILF WOOLLER AND GWYN WILLIAMS PLAY - PRAISE FROM NEWPORT: *'A BRILLIANT SIDE... A BIGGER ATTRACTION THAN ANY OTHER CLUB IN THE KINGDOM'*

Gwyn Williams TW; **Roy Roberts** TW; Harry Rees TW; Ray Bale Tongwynlais (games played per season are not available pre-WW2)

P46, W38, L6, D2. Points 580-260. <u>Tries 120-42</u>, Pens 18-28

The club captain was Welsh international A.H. Jones, and Arthur chose former Taff's Well player and international Harry Rees as vice-captain. For 1937-38, Cardiff had a settled team, and played wonderful rugby, and with only one 'easy' fixture, the traditional first game 'warm-up' on 1 September against Cardiff and District. For modern readers, official leagues as such did not exist. The attraction of playing for, and watching, clubs was the strength of the fixture list. Cardiff, throughout its history, took pride in only playing the best clubs in England and Wales, and sometimes Scotland, Ireland and France. On 18 September 1937, Cardiff won at Bristol 14-6, 2 tries to 1. For the home game, on 30 October, the team was: 'Forwards from H - R. Bale; I - J. Regan; J - W.E.N. Davies; K – Harry Rees; L – L.M. Spence; M. Selby Davies; N – Gwyn Williams; O – E. Watkins; P – Ivor Williams. Backs A – Tom Williams (fullback); E – Arthur Basset (left wing); D – Wilfred Wooller (left centre); C – H.O. Edwards (right centre); B - A.H. Jones (captain) (right wing); F – Cliff Jones (outside half); G - W.G. Morgan (scrum half). Cardiff won 15-12, scoring 4 tries to 1. Pre-war individual scores are uncertain unless one has

101

a programme, and the programme is marked with a T against Les Spence, Cliff Jones, Wilf Wooller and Arthur Bassett, and a PG against Wilf Wooller.

The Newport home programme of 13 November 1937 praised Cardiff highly: '*even before return of W. Wooller and Cliff Jones Cardiff had a brilliant side... **Cardiff a bigger attraction than any other club in the Kingdom at Newport**.*' Cardiff beat Llanelli and Swansea three times, did the double against Bridgend, Bristol, Neath, Harlequins and Richmond, and won all three matches on the Cornish tour. Cliff Jones remembered the Swansea game: '*On Saturday, 27th November, 1937, Cardiff played at home the powerful Swansea team which included, inter alia, the brilliant Tanner and Davies at half-back, Idwal Davies and Powell in the three-quarter line and Long, E. Morgan, Payne and Hunt in the forwards. The game was beautifully open and Cardiff won a resounding victory to the extent of 21 pts. – 3. In retrospect, one wonders how WE overcame such formidable opposition by so great a margin – at the same time, no doubt Swansea were wondering how THEY were trounced. Such is the inherent beauty and glory of William Webb's legacy. Long may it flourish on the Arms Park and elsewhere*'. The previous season Cardiff had achieved the quadruple over a fine Swansea team, scoring 8 tries to 1. After losing the first Swansea game of the 1937-38 season, 7-0 to a drop goal and a penalty, Cardiff won the next three 21-3, 6-0 and 8-7, scoring 5 tries to 2. These four Swansea fixtures every season stopped after WW2, moving to two a season.

Cardiff beat Newport 11-3 home, and 13-6 away and drew two games, away at Newport 3-3, and with the Barbarians 8-8. A tight match was then lost at home to Newport 6-5, a try apiece. Of the four Newport matches, Cardiff won two, drew one and lost one, with a total points score of 32-18, 4 tries to 2 in very close games. The only other defeats were also all away: 7-0 at Swansea, 6-0 at Blackheath, 7-0 at Llanelli, 11-3 at Coventry and the biggest, at Aberavon 16-6, for which there is a real excuse. As mentioned previously, because of foul play – and a referee with visual problems - fixtures with Aberavon had been broken off from 1933-34 until 1936-37. However, in 1951 Cardiff captain A.H. Jones recalled his most memorable game, when captain in April 1938, '*I remember when I scored three tries against Newport from half-way, thanks to my centre, but I also recall even more vividly the game I lost against Aberavon. Owing to previous keen play, it was the first game for a number of seasons and the team had been warned by the Committee that play was to be clean and open. At half-time, as captain, I was approached by my forwards and asked if it would be in order for them to 'protect' themselves during the second half. I said "No!"; if they gave it, we must take it. Thank goodness it turned out to be one of the best games seen there that year, although I lost the game by giving them a try in the last minute.*'

Such was the strength in depth of the club, that the Athletic XV also achieved its best record since 1910-11. **It was P35, W30, L3, D2. Points 469-129**. The Athletic XV almost achieved an invincible season, unbeaten after 21 matches until they met Newport United on 19 February 1938. Danny Davies recollects that Cardiff: *'lost by 6 points to five as the result of a very fluky try by the Black and Ambers. It arose this way: one of the Newport men attempted a dropped goal, it was a poor effort and the ball veered to the right and almost to touch in goal. A crocked Athletic centre had been transferred to the wing position and it was he who limped vainly in his attempt to stop the Newport player from making a desperate, though successful dive for a try only one yard from the dead ball line.'*

The great prop Stan *'Buttons'* Bowes made his debut for the Rags, along with back row forward Tom Holley, both gaining their Athletic caps next season. Tom Holley was an unpaid attendant/masseur/trainer to the club in the 1950s-60s, and this writer remembers him with affection. At this time, most youngsters had to make do with 'scrumped' (stolen) apples as their only fruit, and a tangerine wrapped in silver paper inside their Christmas stockings (- actually dad's long woollen socks). At half-time, players always stayed on the pitch for 5 minutes before the restart, and Tom always took the teams plates of quartered oranges. He then used to bring any remaining sections to myself and school friends on the North Terrace half-way line. The best fruit I have ever tasted. For my sins, in the days before social media, I was not even aware that Tom had served Cardiff well as a player, and that his career was shortened by seven years because of the war. The extension of half-time from 5 to 15 minutes has allowed players more resting time, so fewer gaps owing to fatigue exist, and there is less open play. It is now a 23-man instead of a 15-man game, basically shortening the careers of many players, because of the brutality of the modern game. These days, South Africa have a habit of picking 6 forwards in their 8 reserves, who come on fresh as daisies after 50 to 60 minutes, with the sole intent of smashing the opposition forwards, and any backs who get in their way.

For a third successive year Arthur Bassett topped the list of scorers with 28 tries, and rugby league scouts were constantly circling the successful wing. Gwyn Porter scored 18 tries, H. O. Edwards 13 and Wilf Wooller 10. Wilf also set up a club record of 9 dropped goals this season, beating his 7 in the previous year, also set by Percy Bush in 1908-09 and Danny Davies in 1922-23. Barry John and Wooller each scored 30 drop goals for Cardiff, but the record is still held by Percy Bush, who dropped 35 during 1902-14. The back row forward Ivor Williams gained a British Lions tour to South Africa in 1938. Thus far, Cardiff have supplied 75 British Lions, a total unmatched by any other club. 21 ex-Cardiff players have also played rugby league for Great Britain, some like Maurice Richards and John Bevan accomplishing both.

Wales beat England 14-8 at Cardiff, with Aberavon's breakaway forward Alan McCarley scoring a try. Cliff Jones, Eddie Watkins and Bill Clement needed treatment for injuries. Against Scotland, Eddie Morgan suffered a fractured rib after 12 minutes, and went off, and Wooller was also injured. Wing forward McCarley then scored two first-half tries at Murrayfield, but the Scots won 8-6 in controversial manner, as English referee Cyril Gadney penalised Taff's Well's Welsh prop Harry Rees for lying on the ball when he was semi-conscious. Rees later said '*Haydn Tanner was lying underneath me, unconscious.*' That penalty goal cost Wales the Triple Crown, as they went on to beat Ireland 11-5 at Swansea. Referees in Wales in recent years have been sponsored by Specsavers, I will say no more. It was Cardiff fly-half Cliff Jones' last international, aged only 24. Wooller, Harry Rees, Arthur Basset and Watkins also played. Police Sergeant Harry Rees had gained his Cardiff 1st XV cap in 1933-34 with 31 appearances, and the prop was vice-captain in 1937-38. He captained Glamorgan County and the British Police, and played first against Scotland in 1937, winning five caps.

CHAPTER 13 - CARDIFF SEASON 1938 – 1939

GWYN WILLIAMS AND FOUR CARDIFF PLAYERS HEAD NORTH - 'WILF' WOOLLER IS CAPTAIN – CARDIFF LIFT THE MIDDLESEX SEVENS – CARDIFF WIN THE UNOFFICIAL WELSH CHAMPIONSHIP FOR THE THIRD YEAR IN A ROW– BRYN AND BLEDDYN WILLIAMS PLAY FOR CARDIFF ATHLETIC- GWYN NICHOLLS DIES - 1905 AND ALL THAT: CARDIFF'S FIRST SUPERSTAR

Gwyn Williams TW, 103 games; **Bryn Williams** played 10 games for Cardiff Athletic, and brother **Bleddyn Williams** (aged 15 and 16) 4 games for Athletic, playing together against Ebbw Vale; **Roy Roberts** TW; Harry Rees TW; Ray Bale Tongwynlais

P42, W31, L5, D6. Points 512-188. <u>Tries 107-35</u>, Pens 19-13

In *Welsh Rugby* November 1971, we read of Wooller's captaincy: '*The success of Wilf's second year was extraordinary inasmuch as five star players went North – Gwyn Williams, Alban Davies, Arthur Bassett, Eddie Watkins and Jim Regan. Much of this was due to the "Rags" under Ken Street. In his side were the inimitable Stan Bowes, E.R. Knapp, L. Arnold, Bryn Williams and E. Jones, plus Tom Holley, still serving the club. **Bryn*** *the second eldest Williams brother, was to lose most of his playing career, away in the army for six years, but was to briefly partner Bleddyn in the Firsts after the war.*' We must mention Tom Holley here, as he was given a Castella Award in Cardiff's Centenary Year, 1977, for 'outstanding services to rugby'. In *Welsh Rugby*, February 1977, we read: '***Castella Award*** *– Deep in the bowels of the prestigious Cardiff Arms Park North Stand complex, is tucked away a rather special meeting place for rather special rugby men. It is the "Players' and Officials' Bar", strictly restricted for their after-match privacy where eating, drinking and chatting can be undisturbed. This was the scene for our Award this month. Cardiff had just beaten Neath, another notch in the centenary year victory belt. Sitting, talking, strictly a teetotaller, totally unaware of what was going to happen, was the recipient to be. The only ones in the know were Les Spence, the club chairman and former W.R.U. President; Alun Priday, the secretary; Lyn Williams, the vice-chairman and the duty committeeman for the day; Hubert Johnson, the doyen and Athletic Club president, and Fred Croster who had made the arrangements. At an appropriate moment, order was called – a very unusual happening in this holy of places – and the reason for the occasion explained.*

When Tom Holley's name was announced and he was asked to come forward, it was an emotional moment with, it seemed certain, tears in his eyes. Hubert Johnson, in his own so dignified inimitable manner, added stature to the occasion. Les had stepped down as a typical gesture. By a remarkable coincidence Hubert – not in on the secret until just before – let it be known that only that same afternoon he had been commenting upon the wonderful service that Tom had rendered throughout the years. That service, since his playing career before the last war, meant 40 years plus with the Cardiff club. After his war service, his playing days were over and he began his long and remarkable career as a trainer extraordinary. Home and away, week after week, month after month, year after year, Tom was always there to prepare "his Lads" before the match, on the touchline, come rain or shine, during the match, and then attend to the wounded and wanting when the game was over.

The names of those who have benefited from his hands could read like the veritable Hall of Fame of our game. In addition to the legendary star-studded Cardiff players – but all came alike – there were no exceptions or "special cases". Throughout the years Tom Holley has cared for every touring country to come to our shores; and invitations to the distant lands from whence they came have been regularly forthcoming. The Cambridge XV for the Varsity match is just another example of those who seek his services. As Tom said in his emotion-charged reply, although these had been an honour, it was always for his club, Cardiff, that he had accepted, but to receive this honour now, so unexpected, in this Cardiff centenary year meant so much more that he could say no more.' Tom Holley, a newsagent in Rhiwbina, Cardiff, was never paid for his services, just his travel expenses upon submitting receipts. A wonderful man, and I, with David Mathews and Tim Jeffries-Jones, still remember those half-time oranges.

This was another terrific season, with the fewest number of defeats since 1908-09. 25-year-old Wilfred Wooller, 6 foot 3 inches tall and over 15 stone was in his international prime as a centre, in the days before we had big centres like Jamie Roberts and today's giants. Chosen captain, he selected the forward W. E. N. 'Wendy' Davis as his vice-captain. Wilf had gained senior Welsh caps while still at Rydal School, where he stayed on an extra year to get into Cambridge, where he was capped as a Blue. Wilf captained Wales three times in 1938-39 to win the Home Nations Championship, the 3-0 loss at Twickenham preventing a Triple Crown. An excellent kicker, he scored 163 points for Cardiff in this season, and was also noted for his bowling and batting for Cambridge and Glamorgan. Five men from Taff's Well played for Cardiff in this last full season before the war – three of the Williams brothers, their uncle Roy Roberts and Harry Rees – along with Ray Bale from Tongwynlais, just across the Taff. Incidentally, Jack Matthews, soon to join Cardiff and begin his lifelong friendship with Bleddyn Williams, played in the Final Welsh Trial at Swansea, the last occasion 'caps' were awarded for a final trial.

Sadly, five of Cardiff's best players 'went North', the first being Gwyn Williams after 17 matches. His friend Eddie Watkins almost immediately followed him to Wigan after 21 matches. Watkins had won 8 Welsh caps and was in the Wales team that beat the 1935 All Blacks. Cardiff's excellent hooker Jim Regan also left for Huddersfield after 18 games. Gwyn, Watkins and Regan all won Welsh rugby league caps. Alban Davies, a terrific full-back prospect from Cross Keys, and the exceptional wing Arthur Bassett left Cardiff after 17 games. In Rugby League, Alban Davies while at Huddersfield gained 2 caps for Wales, with more to come. Arthur Bassett at Halifax had won 6 Welsh caps at union, then won 3 caps for Wales rugby league, and was a star for Great Britain in their 1946 Australasia tour.

In the full season, Cardiff won three and drew once against both Newport and Llanelli. Bridgend won both games, 4-3 (dropped goal to a try, with modern scoring Cardiff would win 5-3) and 3-0. At Gloucester Cardiff lost 8-6 away, at Swansea the club lost 19-14, and the Barbarians won 11-6. Just 16 judiciously allotted points would have given Cardiff an unbeaten season. In just 17 games before heading North, Arthur Bassett with 23 was the top try scorer for the fourth year running. Wilf Wooller was next with 12 and Gwyn Porter 11 (plus 5 for the Rags). Wooller's 163 points included 12 dropped goals, a record for the number kicked in any one season. Wooller recounted the Swansea game of March 1938. Cardiff had lost there by 7-0 to a penalty and dropped goal, then won at home 21-3 (3 tries to 1) and 6-0 (2 tries) before the final meeting of the season. Dropped goals were still worth 4 points: '*I would like to recall a great moment, and not a great game. It occurred in the last few seconds of a hard-fought Cardiff/Swansea game at St. Helens in 1938. Swansea led 6 points to four.* (Actually 7-4, a try and a drop goal). *A scrum under the Swansea posts brought the code word "wrong" and Shorty Morgan at scrumhalf, ignoring the out-half, flung a pass directly behind the scrum to me. I dropped for goal and the ball hit the upright, fell onto the crossbar, bounced twice and went over. The final whistle went. Cardiff had won by 8 points to 6.'* (Actually Cardiff scored two drop goals to scrape home 8-7 on 19 April 1938).

In this season we see more of Gwyn Williams' brothers Brinley ('Bryn') and Bleddyn, playing for Cardiff Athletic. Brinley was a centre, and Bleddyn, playing fly half or centre, made 10 and 4 appearances respectively, with both turning out for Taff's Well when available. Bleddyn was 15, and then 16 from 22 February 1939. The Athletic captain was the prop Ken Street, who had gained his First XV cap in 1934-35. His team's record was P32, W21, L8, D3, Points 317-165. In April 1939, Cardiff was invited as a guest club to join the Middlesex County Seven-a-Side Tournament. In a *Wales Online* article from March 2011, 91-year-old Graham Hale recalled how Cardiff were the only Welsh-based club to lift the trophy: '*Only our captain, Wilf Wooller, had ever played in Sevens before, as it was not played in Wales and it appears he was in the Sale side that had won in 1936... I was a centre then and with Wilf at outside-half, we had Gwyn Porter outside me and Willie Davies, the brother of the Wales prop Cliff, playing scrumhalf, though he was really an outside-half. Willie was a splendid player but turned professional soon afterwards. In the forwards were Selby Davies, Evan Jones and Les Spence, while Wilf dropped the Wales forward "Wendy" Davis, as Wilf said he was too slow. Selby, Wendy and I had all been at Cardiff High School. We had a small practice and the next day (22 April 1939) we caught the train to Twickenham. We had never seen a Sevens match and watched the first one from the grandstand, the ground was full. We opened against the good St. Mary's Hospital side and the referee said we had two minutes left and we were losing 6-0.*

We ran down field and I was clear, but for some reason I stopped and dropped a goal. It was four points then and a try was three. It was the only drop goal I ever attempted! From the kick-off we got the ball and when I received it, I was again clear and scored to make it 7-6. I don't think we attempted the conversion. Cardiff then beat the Met Police 5-3 and then Birkenhead Park 8-5 in the semi-final. The BBC broadcast had broken down and those in the Cardiff club were resigned to the team losing. However, Cardiff met London Scottish in the final. Wilf was always loud off the pitch, but quiet on it. He had sat with me watching the Scotland fly-

half Logie Bruce Lockhart run rings round their opponents. He said that if I got Lockhart low, he would take him and the ball high. We did and won 11-6. We caught the train home with Wilf running down the platform as it was going. We got in the club that night and nobody knew we had won the splendid Kinross Arber Trophy. It was a great day to remember.' It was to be the first of Cardiff's successes in winning seven-a-side tournaments, with the Cardiff Royal Infirmary benefiting to the extent of £96.3s.11d. Like other Cardiff stalwarts Les Spence, Wilf Wooller and Ken Street, Graham Hale joined the army during the war and became a POW, Graham in North Africa and the others after Singapore.

Cardiff had experienced a revival in the late 1930s. Scrumhalf Howard Poole, although never capped for Wales, had been selected to play for the Lions in 1930, as was Ivor Williams in 1938. Cardiff also won the unofficial Welsh championship in 1937, retaining the title in 1938 and 1939. In the three last full seasons before the War, we see that 1936-37 was a fine season - 44P; 36W; 7L; 1D – all losses were close, and Cardiff scored 118 tries to 28, as usual losing on penalties 15-11. Then came the even better season of 1937-38 (not including unofficial games, of which there were several every season): 46P; 38W; 6L; 2D – 120-42 was the try count, but again losing the penalty count 28-18. Arthur H. Jones was captain, winning 2 Welsh caps and playing 158 times from 1932-33 until war halted his career. 1938-39 saw continued improvement, of 42 matches, winning 31, losing 5 and drawing 6, 107 tries against just 35, and scoring 512 points to 188. There were then just three games in 1939-40, all won.

Les Spence's captaincy in 1936-37 had kicked off the resurgence, and by the time of WW2 Cardiff had almost reached the standards of its Golden Era. Davies records in the *1951 Souvenir Programme* of Cardiff against the British Lions: *'With Cliff Jones, W. Wooller, Arthur Bassett among the backs, Arthur Skym, "Wendy" Davies, Eddie Watkins and Co., in the pack we had an excellent run of success. In 1937-38, Arthur Bassett scored 28 tries. The "Rags" under V.R. Osmond, had the best season between the wars. In 1938-39 Wooller scored 163 points and established a new Club record of 12 Drop Goals. In these three seasons we had much the better of the "arguments" with our Newport and Swansea friends, and Swansea in fact were beaten four rimes in 1936-37. The Middlesex Seven-a-Side Tournament was won at the first time of asking... We had entertained high hopes of a very successful season for 1939-40, but World War II came along and games were suspended after 2nd September 1939.'* The three great periods for Cardiff teams in the time covered by this book were the early 1900s, the late 1930s and the immediate post-war years. Cardiff were the unofficial *Western Mail* Welsh Championship winners in 1899, 1907, 1909, 1910, 1937, 1938, 1939, 1947, 1949, 1951, 1955, 1956 and 1959. Middlesex 7s winners: 1939. Gala Sevens winners: 1964. Snelling Sevens winners: 1955, 1966, 1969, 1972, 1976, 1977.

GWYN NICHOLLS (15 July 1874 – 24 March 1939)

Erith Gwyn Nicholls was a centre and became known as the *'Prince of Threequarters.'* He began playing in the Cardiff Firsts from 1893, **playing for 18 seasons**, captaining the side for four of six seasons from 1898-89 to 1903-04. His first cap was in 1896, but in 1897 and 1898 Wales were excluded from playing internationals because of 'the Gould Affair.' Touring Australia with the British Isles team in 1899, he was the only Welsh player with the means to go on tour. Gwyn played 24 times for Wales between 1896 and 1906, including ten matches as captain, and captained the Triple Crown winning side of 1902. He announced his retirement from international rugby, but returned to captain Wales in the renowned 1905 win against New Zealand, and was in the team which lost to South Africa in 1906. In 1923, trying to rescue a doctor, who had saved two girls from drowning at Weston-Super-Mare, Gwyn then made it to shore but almost died and his health never recovered. In 1939, he died in Dinas Powys, the village just west of Cardiff. Immediately efforts began for a memorial, but war halted progress. However, on Boxing Day 1949 the Gwyn Nicholls Memorial Gates were officially opened at Cardiff Arms Park by his great friend and teammate Rhys Gabe. They now stand outside Cardiff's ground, next to the Principality Stadium. In November 2005 Gwyn Nicholls was inducted into the International Rugby Hall of Fame.

CF10 website: 1905 AND ALL THAT: CARDIFF'S FIRST SUPERSTAR

The CF10 Arms Park Rugby Trust website has some marvellous cuttings on Gwyn Nicholls. (https://cf10rugbytrust.org/blog/1905-and-all-cardiff%E2%80%99s-first-superstar). *'Few better expositions of the modern scientific passing game have been given in London than was displayed by the Cardiff back division. If there was one man more than another to whom Cardiff owed their victory it was undoubtedly the international centre, E. G Nicholls, the pivot upon which the whole back machinery worked. Both in defence and in attack he was the most prominent man on the side, and it was in a great measure through his judgment that Huzzey, on the wing, was provided with so many opportunities of scoring.'* (*Daily Mail,* December 1898)

On the British Isles tour in Australasia, we read *'Mail advices received this morning from Australia state that Gwyn Nicholls, the international three-quarter, has obtained widespread popularity in the Colonies. His play has not only delighted the spectators, but his general demeanour on the field has been everywhere admired.'* (*Evening Express* 20 September 1899). *'Of the three-quarters, Gwyn Nicholls has almost throughout been **the shining star** - in fact, I should not be erring if I stated that his play has*

109

caused little less than a sensation over here. Equally at home both in defence and attack, he has all along played a most unselfish game, on several occasions without the least hesitation, handing over the ball with the line perhaps at his very mercy.' (*South Wales Daily News* 10 October 1899). *'Gwyn Nicholls nearly didn't play against the 1905 All Blacks. He might have stayed in Australia in 1899 after the tour which first established him as a global rugby star... He had been due to return to Wales to take up his rightful role as Cardiff captain that autumn. October came and went. There was still no sign of Nicholls. People in Cardiff were quietly beginning to panic. Cardiff, without Gwyn Nichols, is like the play of "Hamlet" with the prince left out, i.e. not worth much.'* (*South Wales Daily Post* 14 October 1899).

'When he finally returned, on 13th of January 1900, a crowd of hundreds met him at Cardiff Central Station and stormed onto his train as it pulled in. Nicholls slipped away through the crowd but was spotted. The horse-drawn cab carrying him and his friends (including Bert Winfield, the Cardiff fullback and Gwyn's business partner) was stopped and the horses uncoupled. 50 admirers then took hold of the cab and hauled it down Westgate Street to the cheers of passers-by. They arrived at the Grand Hotel opposite the Arms Park where Gwyn's brother Sydney was the proprietor.' (*The Western Mail* 15 January 1900). By 1902, Gwyn was Welsh captain and led the nation to a third championship. In 1904, Nicholls wanted to retire and marry, having in the previous 16 months been injured four times, and prevented from playing in four internationals. He broke his collarbone at Blackheath; then badly damaged his knee at Llanelli; then had a *'slight concussion of the brain'*; and had to retire from a game with a broken rib. Thus Gwyn gave up his captaincy of Cardiff, rarely played and had practically given up the game. However, *'it is only on a few occasions that he has appeared in the football arena this season... He was, if not now, the greatest centre of the day, and one who commands universal respect, not only as a player, but as one of the best sportsmen.'* (*Evening Express* 11 March 1905). In an emergency, Wales called him up for the 1905 Ireland game. Wales denied Ireland the Championship and won Wales another triple crown.

'Nicholls then was determined to finally draw the line under his rugby career with some ceremony. He was a man who felt the need to make it abundantly clear that no matter what anyone said, his battered body would not be subjected to more "serious football". Perhaps because he knew what was on the horizon, and the challenge that awaited Cardiff and Wales. The New Zealand All Blacks team had been encountered by Nicholls's clubmates Percy Bush, Rhys Gabe and Arthur Harding on the 1904 British Isles tour. Whereas they'd dazzled the Australians, in New Zealand they'd more than met their match. They lost to New Zealand and were battered by Auckland. Now the original All Black touring team were

110

coming north. If anyone had been in any doubt of the challenge faced by British and Irish teams, they were soon quelled by the way the All Blacks dominated all comers. In the first match, Devon (who had been favourites) were beaten 55-4. The All Blacks wouldn't concede another point for six matches. The next game against Cornwall was won 41-0. Bristol were also beaten 41-0. Northampton were beaten 32-0. Leicester 28-0. By the time Durham managed to only lose 16-3, just scoring points against the All Blacks was considered a triumph. The team were a sensation. After sweeping aside every team in England and dispatching Scotland and Ireland, a crowd of 100,000 would watch them hammer the English national team 15-0 at Crystal Palace. Plans were being made in Wales. The All Blacks weren't going to be allowed to march through the Welsh clubs and annihilate the national side as they had in the rest of Britain. Bush, Gabe and the others who had faced them the previous year felt they knew how to beat them. But they'd need Gwyn Nicholls.' (- CF10 website).

'Gwyn Nicholls has been invited to play and many thousands will be delighted to know that he will once again come to the assistance – one was almost tempted to say the rescue - of Wales, as he did at Swansea against Ireland, when the Triple Crown was in danger of crossing the Irish Channel on the Ides of March. Of course, there will be much speculation for some time to come as whether the doyen of Welsh three-quarters will put on the jersey again, but it may be taken as a certainty once and for all that he will make his appearance in his old position against the wearers of the silver fern'. (*Evening Express* 10 November 1905). *'When the Welshmen fielded with Gwyn Nicholls at the head -he carried a gigantic leek - the applause was deafening. The Colonials sang their war song, after which the Welshmen gave a rendering of "Hen Wlad fy Nhadau", the chorus of which went with a merry swing, with something like forty thousand voices holding forth.'* (*The Cambrian* 22 December 1905).

With Wales having won the Triple Crown, and New Zealand having won 27 matches in a row, scoring profusely, the *haka* had been performed. The Welsh team began singing *Mae Hen Wlad Fy Nhadau* in response and the 47,000-strong crowd joined in with both verses. The song was popular, but **that event transformed it into the National Anthem**. It was the first time a National Anthem had been sung before a sporting fixture. Incredibly, it was recorded, along with the *haka*, the Welsh players leaving the changing rooms, the crowd singing *Sospan Fach,* and the teams lining up facing each other. It can be viewed on Twitter, as an excerpt from *Game of the Century* via the APSM Rugby Channel.

'Although people had travelled from around Britain to attend the game, the bulk of the crowd that day were Welsh-speaking Welshmen. On a patch of land carved out by the English engineers of the Industrial Revolution, they were now claiming the game brought to Wales by English public schoolboys as their own. Just as the New Zealanders were touring to

111

establish themselves as masters of a game created in "the old country", the Welsh were adopting rugby as an expression of national pride. It was a clash between the best of Europe and the best of the Southern hemisphere. **It was nothing short of a world championship.** *In many ways, it was the true start of the phenomenon of international rugby. The first quarter was brutal. Witnesses years later would still say it was one of the fiercest games they'd seen. Wales gradually began to have the upper hand and were creating chances. With ten minutes left of the first half, Wales had a scrum on the All Black 22. Owen, the scrum half ran to the right. Bush, Nicholls and Willie Llewellyn drifted with him and the All Black defence followed. But it was a ploy. Owen threw a long pass left to Cliff Pritchard. Pritchard beat his man and passed to Rhys Gabe, who drew the last man and put Teddy Morgan away down the left wing.' 'The next moment Arthur Gould was dancing on the Press table waving his hat and shouting; "The fastest Rugby sprinter in the world! – Teddy Morgan has scored!" It may be said that in those days the Welsh Rugby Union did not know how to treat the Press; instead of reporters being given seats in the covered stand, they were placed at trestle tables inside the ropes, exposed to wind and rain, and occasionally to invasions by spectators who scaled the fences. Where Arthur Gould came from, I do not know, but there he was dancing the dance of triumph.'* (WJ Townsend Collins, writing in 1948).

'Wales were ahead three points to nil at halftime. Then the onslaught began. The All Black forwards took control and with a monopoly on possession, hammered the Welsh line for most of the second half. Nicholls led his men in 40 minutes of aggressive defence against the increasingly desperate New Zealand attacks. Finally, the All Black centre Bob Deans broke the Welsh defence and sprinted for the line. He was brought down short and would claim to have scored. The referee said no, and Wales breathed again. A kicking duel followed, ending with Winfield finding touch in the New Zealand 22. New Zealand's last chance had gone. The final whistle was blown'. *'The greatest match in football history has been fought and won by Wales. Many international matches have been classed as great games, but the struggle between New Zealand and Wales at the Cardiff Arms Park, on Saturday now claims the premier position. It was a spectacle never to be forgotten, the huge crowd of spectators and the tremendous enthusiasm shown both tended to make the occasion a brilliant one. It was the finest match I have ever had the pleasure of witnessing, and the equal of it may never be seen again.'* (*The Cambrian.* 22 December 1905)

'Six days later, the New Zealanders would get their chance for revenge on Cardiff Arms Park. After beating Glamorgan 9-0 and Newport 6-3, they would face the Blue and Blacks of Cardiff rugby club. Percy Bush's Cardiff side were unbeaten and included five of the team that had beaten the All Blacks on the 16th. Confidence was high.' *'Not for a dozen years have*

112

Cardiff had so clever a back division as this season, particularly as the three-quarter line will be strengthened to-day by the inclusion of the prince of centres, Gwyn Nicholls. At half, Percy Bush may be accepted as clever enough to outwit any opponent he may have to contend against, and R. A. Gibbs, the arch-spoiler, will be a perpetual thorn in the sides of the New Zealand backs. At inside-half R. David is very little less clever than R. M. Owen. In combined and skilful back play the Cardiff men ought certainly to be superior to their opponents. From every standpoint the prospects for Cardiff today are very rosy. The gates of the ground will be opened at 10.30 a.m., and there will be about 100 police, mounted and foot, on duty to control the crowd.' (*Evening Express* 26 December 1905). '*The crowd that gathered at Cardiff Arms Park that day was even greater than at the international. People swarmed into the city to see if Cardiff could repeat the feat of the national side. From an early hour the city was besieged by tens of thousands of visitors from all parts of South Wales and from more distant districts in England as well, and by eleven o'clock, when the gates of the Cardiff Arms Park were opened, there was tremendous pressure on the somewhat limited means of entrance to the ground. Excursion trains were run from all points of the compass, and the crowd, imbued with the Holiday Spirit, was even more demonstrative than that of the ever to be remembered 16th of December. By a quarter past one the ground was so packed in all parts that the head constable advised Mr. C. S. Arthur (the Cardiff secretary) to close the gates. So closely packed were the people on the shilling stand that there was an absence of that dangerous swaying which threatened so much danger on the occasion of the international match.*' (*Evening Express* 26 December 1905).

'*Nicholls would score the first try of the game after being put through a gap by Gabe. But the match was tied 5 all at halftime. In the second half, Cardiff were in the ascendancy and narrowly missed several chances to score, before Percy Bush made the mistake which would haunt him for the rest of his days. With the ball practically in his possession over his own goal-line, he dallied with it, when a child might have touched it down by simply putting one hand on it, and the next moment he found, to his mortification, that a New Zealand forward had dashed up and scored a try.* (*Evening Express* 27 December 1905). '*The softest of tries had given the All Blacks the lead. Cardiff would continue to create chances but the All Black defence was as aggressive as the Welsh defence had been a week before. A late try for Ralph Thomas in the corner made the score 10-8. But Winfield's conversion to draw the match narrowly missed. It is doubtful whether the Colonial defence has ever been so thoroughly beaten as it was by the scoring of this second try - every man in the Cardiff back division handling the ball, and Ralph Thomas putting on the finishing touch by bounding over in the corner. This try, as I have already remarked, fully deserved to save Cardiff the game, but the fortunes of the day were on the side of the Colonials.* (*Evening Express* 27 December 1905).

'*The following year, another formidable touring team would head for the British Isles. The first Springboks, like the All Blacks, caused a sensation. Nicholls once again came out of retirement to captain Wales against the tourists. But this time, age seemed to be catching up with him. South Africa won 11-0 at St Helens in Swansea and it was to be the last appearance in red for Nicholls and several others. After the game, the South Africans were dismissive.'*... '*A month after the humiliation in Swansea, Nicholls would face the Springboks once more. On New Year's Day 1906 they faced Cardiff at the Arms Park... History doesn't record whether Gwyn Nicholls read the newspapers, or the interviews that wrote him off as being too old. What history does record is that on the night before the game, Percy Bush was woken by the sound of heavy rain falling against his bedroom window. Looking outside to see the Welsh rain pounding the city streets, he thought of the effect the rain would be having on the clayish Arms park soil and how different it would be to the hard, dry pitches of South Africa. Advantage Cardiff. Percy Bush slept soundly that night.* **What followed was what remains perhaps the greatest win by a club team over any international team**. *Early on, Nicholls carved through the Springboks to open the scoring with a try. Three more followed for the Blue and Blacks as Cardiff beat the South Africans 17-0.'*... '*Yesterday the capital of Wales made history by coming to the rescue of national prestige, and Cardiff, to the lasting credit of the club, inflicted such a defeat upon the Springboks as to rehabilitate Wales in the eyes of the whole sporting world. In that defeat there was not the slightest suggestion or semblance of flukiness or of luck.* **It was decisive; it was thorough; it was complete; it was triumphant**. (*Evening Express* 2 January 1907). '*In the Cardiff Arms Park mud, Gwyn Nicholls at the age of 31 had played his greatest game. A career which might have ended 8 years earlier rough riding in Australia, had brought Gwyn Nicholls victory over the All Blacks and now the Springboks. In the Red of Wales and now in the Blue and Black of his beloved Cardiff, he had beaten the world. Perhaps in the pavilion after that match, as they sat in their muddy blue and black jerseys, there would have been a knowing look between Nicholls, Winfield, Gabe and Bush. The men who had beaten the All Blacks and now the Springboks. They must have known that the cheers at Cardiff Arms Park that day would follow them for the rest of their lives, and beyond. They had made themselves immortal'* (all italicised quotes from the CF10 website).

CHAPTER 14 - CARDIFF SEASON 1939-40

'HITLER INTERFERES IN WOOLLER'S SECOND TERM AS CAPTAIN'

Bleddyn Williams (Athletic) TW; **Bryn Williams** (Athletic) TW; **Roy Roberts** TW; Jack Russell TW; Ray Bale Tongwynlais

P 2, W 2, L 0, D 0. Points 54-19. Tries 12-2, Pens 0-3 (- Davies)
P 3, W 3, L 0, D 0. Points 82-25 (Davies' omits the game with Penarth on 23 December 1939, Cardiff winning 28-6).

One has to love Danny Davies' in his history of Cardiff RFC for this season, where he headlined in capitals the nuisance value of one of the most evil and mendacious morons in world history - *'HITLER INTERFERES IN WOOLLER'S SECOND TERM AS CAPTAIN'*. Davies records that: *'The 1939-40 season was the most fateful one in the club's history. Wilfred Wooller was the captain appointed by the members for a second term, he nominated Les Spence as his vice-captain. Ken Street for the Athletic XV was also appointed for a second term. These three players had enjoyed life together, particularly as Rugger men, and together, they were destined to share in the tragedies and miseries of war.'* All three suffered terribly – Wilf and Les survived Japanese imprisonment but with wasted muscles could never properly play rugby again, and Ken Street, with 74 Cardiff appearances and many more as its captain and playing for the 'Rags', died as a POW. We must pause and remember other Cardiff players who were lost in the war. As well as Maurice Turnbull, recounted later, the club lost Pat Cox (4 first team appearances 1934-1937), Cecil R. Davies (6 games 1928-30 to 1934-35), Frank Gaccon (105 games 1908-09 to 1919-20), Ken Jones (11 games 1936-37 to 1937-38), Trevor Ransome (6 games 1934-35 to 1935-36), Howard Roblin (2 games 1938-39 to 1939-40) and V. Neil Taylor (1 game 1939-40).

After three superb seasons, Cardiff had been expecting another great year, as Cliff Jones was now available after his studies, the excellent Welsh international Les Manfield had joined, and the Williams' uncle Roy Roberts was a real power in the pack. Don Llewellyn reminisced that Roberts was *'the best forward never to play for Wales'*. However, only three first team matches were played, and one by the Rags. On 1 September 1939, Cliff Jones dislocated an elbow against Cardiff and District and never played again in any serious match. Two games were squeezed in before war was declared. Cardiff and District were beaten 34-10 (3 converted tries, 5 tries and a drop goal, to a try, a drop goal and a penalty). The following day, 2 September, Bridgend had a try and two penalties against 4 tries (two converted) and a drop goal, to lose 20-9. The try count was 12-2, with Cardiff Firsts as usual hardly bothering with penalty kicks at goal (18-2 on tries if we include the strong 'Rags' victory, 23-0 at Llanharan, 6 tries). A later game on 29 December was also played to give spectators a chance to see rugby in the traditional holiday season, Cardiff beating Penarth 28-6, recorded in Penarth's history, but not in Cardiff's. The season had been incredibly promising, but an Austro-Hungarian, variously known as Hiedler, Hüttler, Hitler or Huettler, and the son of a bastard, had '*interfered*'. The only upside of the only 'just war' in this person's lifetime was that both the 1ˢᵗ XV and the Athletic had their only official unbeaten seasons. Thus the season ended, '*not with a bang but a whimper*'. Or rather a whimper followed by a horror show.

A recent book stated that from 1923 to 1939 there were an average of 10 policemen in the Cardiff team – this is difficult to research these days, especially if 'Rags' and reserve team players are included. However, it goes to show that the side could well have been more law-abiding than others in that era... (Although having been double spear-tackled by Manchester and Stockport Police and ending up in hospital, with recurring pains almost 60 years later, I now retract that last hypothesis).

CHAPTER 15 - THE WAR YEARS 1939 – 1945

OUTBREAK OF SECOND WORLD WAR - ROY ROBERTS, BLEDDYN AND GWYN WILLIAMS PLAY IN WARTIME INTERNATIONALS - THE TURNBULL BROTHERS - LES SPENCE AND WILF WOOLLER CAPTURED – GWYN WILLIAMS BADLY INJURED IN NORTH AFRICA – GWYN WILLIAMS - PLAYER PROFILE - FAMILY MEMORIES OF GWYN – THE ALLURE OF RUGBY LEAGUE by Keith Bowen - THE GREAT JIM SULLIVAN

Bleddyn Williams TW; **Brinley 'Bryn' Williams** TW; **Roy Roberts** TW; Jack Russell TW, Tom Rees – scrumhalf Llantwit Fardre; Ray Bale – Tongwynlais; all played unofficial games for Cardiff during wartime, plus representative games.

In the programme for the 75ᵗʰ anniversary match in 1951 against the Lions, J.B.G. Thomas wrote of Cardiff captains, '*In 1933-34 Graham Jones and Gabe-Jones shared the honour and they were followed by three stalwarts who were real club men in Archie Skym, Tommy Stone, and Les Spence. A.H. Jones came next and then the magnetic Wilf Wooller. The latter was to have led the side in 1939-40, but Hitler declared War, and Wooller and*

116

his men went off to fight. For a time, they were able to assist the Club in carrying on, but when the battle became serious, it was left to the new and comparatively unknown players like J. Matthews, B.L. Williams (Bleddyn), W. Darch, C. Davies, D. St. John Rees, Glyn and Hubert Jones. They did their job well and when the side started its first official season after the war – the tradition and spirit was there – besides the nucleus of a very good side. Messrs Riches, Cornish and Jenkins ran the Club during the War, and it must have given them great delight to see the manner in which their boys ran up big scores in the immediate post-war years.'

Blue and Black Bravura

The smiling-through philosophy of the Second World War as portrayed by South Wales Echo *and* Evening Express *cartoonist J. C. Walker in January 1941, after a German land-mine had wrecked the north stand.*

Many local sportsmen joined the 77th A.A. Regiment, Royal Artillery quartered in Penylan, Cardiff. Wilfred Wooller, his vice-captain Les Spence and Ken Street joined. With several service units stationed near Cardiff, wartime games were arranged to help charities. Many Cardiff players participated, including the above three, Ray Bale, Selby Davies, Graham Hale, Cliff Jones, E. 'Ianto' Jones, E. R. Knapp, Les Manfield, Gwyn Porter, Roy Roberts, Dr. Ron Tipple, L. G. S. 'Jumbo' Thomas, Godfrey 'Gogga' Williams, and T. Lyn Williams. Upon 9 March 1940 Wales played England in a game for war-time charities at Cardiff Arms Park. Wilf Wooller was captain and from Cardiff E. R. Knapp, H. O. Edwards, Les Manfield and W. E. N. 'Wendy' Davis took part. More than

40,000 attended the Arms Park and England won. Thankfully it was an unofficial match. For almost 7 years, from 11 March 1939 until 18 January 1947, Wales did not play a full international match, but they did play 'international' games, that never brought full caps to the 50 or so players who took part in them. The games, like many others, including Cardiff fixtures, were played to raise money for charity and hospitals in these terrible years. What would Bleddyn Williams' record have been if war had not interrupted six years of his Cardiff rugby career?

Cardiff Arms Park suffered from two bombs, the worst being a landmine explosion on 2 January 1941, which landed just behind the goal line at the west end. It caused much structural damage to the North and South stands, and to the West terrace. Wilf Wooller's 77th Heavy Anti-Aircraft ('Ack-Ack') Unit was initially engaged in South Wales coastal and port defences, but in December 1941 was sent to Java. In 1942 a train load of its personnel was involved in a terrible train crash, which caused the deaths of 21 officers and other ranks, including Bomber Sergeant-Major Ken Street. Street had played fly-half for Penarth in the early 1930s, and played against the Barbarians in 1934, before joining Cardiff, where he made 74 appearances for the Firsts from 1934-35 to 1938-39. Such was his popularity that he was elected captain of Cardiff Athletic XV in both 1938-39 and 1939-40. Commissioned officer Wooller and Battery Sergeant Major Les Spence also became prisoners of war of the Japanese.

There were two Red Cross Charity internationals between Wales and England in 1939-1940, with Cardiff players E.R. Knapp, W.E.N. (Wendy) Davies, Les Manfield and Wilf Wooller playing at Cardiff. In the return at Gloucester, they all played again, less the unavailable Knapp. Bridgend's Jack Matthews also played at Gloucester and joined Cardiff during the war. 'Wendy' Davies also played for England and Wales against Scotland and Ireland. Services internationals were played in wartime to help the war effort and raise money for charities, with Rugby League players allowed to combine with Union players. In the Services Internationals, Wales reigned virtually supreme, in 1942 beating England 17-12 and 11-7 at Swansea and 9-3 at Gloucester. In the first Swansea match, league players included Gwyn Williams (Bleddyn's older brother), Alan Edwards, Gus Risman, Syd Williams, Willie Davies and Trevor Foster. In 1943 Wales hammered England 34-7 at Gloucester and won again 11-9 at Swansea, with the 20-year-old Bleddyn (R.A.F. and Cardiff) making his senior (unofficial) Welsh debut, playing in both games. In 1945, England were defeated 28-11 at Swansea and 24-9 at Gloucester but also won 20-8 at Gloucester. Wales won the series 7-1.

In the Wales vs England Services Internationals, 1941-42 to 1944-45, Cardiff players involved for Wales, with their service and opponents in brackets, were Captain Duncan A. Brown (Army: 1943); A.D.S Bowen (Navy: twice 1945); Alban Davies (Cardiff then RL, Army: 1943, twice

1944); W.E.N. Davies (Army: twice 1942, 1943); Les Manfield (RAF: twice 1942); J. Regan (Army 1942); W.E. Tamplin (Pontypool then Cardiff, Army: twice 1943, twice 1944, 1945); H. Tanner (Swansea then Cardiff, Army: twice 1942, twice 1943, twice 1944, twice 1945); F. Trott Penarth then Cardiff, Army: twice 1945); E. Watkins (RAF: twice 1945).

Wales played 8 Victory Internationals in 1945-46 but no caps were awarded, unfortunately. Cardiff players selected were W.B. Cleaver – France (2); Kiwis; England, Ireland, Scotland; Billy Darch - France, Kiwis; Cliff Davies - England, Ireland, Scotland, France; Graham Hale - France, Kiwis, England; Maldwyn James France, Scotland, England, Ireland; Glyn Jones - France, England, Ireland; H. Elvet Jones - England, Ireland, Scotland, France (this is a different Elvet Jones to the Llanelli international who also played in these games); Les Manfield – France (2), Kiwis, England (2), Scotland (2), Ireland; Jack Matthews – France (2), England, Scotland (2); Bill Tamplin – England; H. Tanner, then joining Cardiff from Swansea – England, Ireland, Scotland, France; Frank Trott, then joining Cardiff from Penarth – Scotland, England; Bleddyn Williams - Kiwis, England, Scotland (2), Ireland, France. His later partnership in the war years with Gus Risman, born in Cardiff, brought up in Barry, was a huge part of Bleddyn's rugby education, and Bleddyn often paid tribute to his expertise.

Among the many charity matches played at Cardiff, F/O Bleddyn Williams, his uncle Lieut. W. E. ('Bill') Tamplin, Petty Officer Stan Bowes of Llandaff/Cardiff and 'Bunner' Travers, the Newport, Wales and Lions hooker appeared in Sir Robert Webber's XV, against a South Wales XV, on 13 January 1945. The South Wales XV included the Wigan 'great' Jim Sullivan; the future Cardiff scrum-half Lieut. Haydn Tanner; Willie Jones the Glamorgan cricketer; with F/O Hubert Johnson of the R.A.F. Regiment and Flight-Lieutenant Arthur Rees among the forwards. From Portmanmoor Road (an echo of its former Welsh name, Porth Maen Mawr) in Splott, after 38 games for Cardiff in 1919-20 to 1920-21, fullback Jim Sullivan had joined Wigan to become a true legend in Rugby League, scoring 4,883 points in a career that spanned 25 years. He was 16 when he joined Cardiff, he or Gwyn Williams their youngest player on record, and in December 1920, aged 17 years and 26 days, became the youngest Barbarian, playing against Newport. Sullivan holds the world record for the most first team appearances in Rugby League, making 928 first team appearances. He was captain-coach of the great Wigan team from 1932 until retiring in 1946, and was instrumental in luring Gwyn Williams to 'go North', aged just 17. There is a photograph of Jim Sullivan welcoming Gwyn to the club. In the match, the 41-year-old Sullivan knocked Bleddyn out cold. That night, in the Cardiff Cottage Hotel in St Mary Street, Jim was asked why he did it. He answered: *'I had never seen him play, but had read of his side-step. I don't buy those!'* Bleddyn will have told Jim of

Gwyn's terrible war injury. Bleddyn also played for Taff's Well vs Pentyrch in a War charity match, the local derby, and was tackled by Cliff Llewellyn. Don Llewellyn told me that Cliff was forever referred to after in the village of Pentyrch as *'the man who tackled Bleddyn'*.

THE TURNBULL BROTHERS

What is it about Cardiff that has given us sporting clusters of greatness? The latest is three boys who knew each other at Whitchurch High School and decided to specialise in different sports. Many of us know the terrific story of Geraint Howell Thomas, b.1986, who won cycling's hardest race, the Tour de France in 2018, plus two Olympic Gold Medals and three World Championship medals. Even in 2022, unfavoured because of his age, just 36, he was placed third in the Tour de France. Then there is the soccer star Gareth Frank Bale, b.1989, twice PFA Players' Player of the Year, Premier League Player of the Season, youngest captain of Wales, who in 2013 joined Real Madrid for a world record fee of £85.3 million. Wales all-time top goal-scorer, he guided Wales to the semi-final 2-0 loss to the eventual winners Portugal. (Sadly, Wales were missing their two other best players, Joe Allen and Aaron Ramsey). In 2014 Bale scored the winning goal in the Champions League Cup Final, and also scored and assisted in a 2-0 win to take the UEFA Super Cup. He won the Champions League Final again in 2016, and 2017 saw a FIFA Club World Cup victory. In the 2018 UEFA Champions League Final, Bale scored two goals, first a truly spectacular overhead kick and then a long-distance strike, resulting in a 3–1 victory over Liverpool, to help Real Madrid win their thirteenth Champions League trophy. Bale became the first substitute to score twice in a Champions League final and was named Man of the Match. He scored over 100 goals for Real Madrid, despite a series of injuries. His performances – he always turns out for Wales if fit – helped Wales qualify for the 2022 Qatar World Cup.

Finally we come to rugby, in the shape of Sam Kennedy-Warburton, b.1988, a Cardiff, Wales and British Lions rugby captain on two tours (the youngest-ever Lions captain, aged just 24), who holds the record for the most Wales caps as captain. For the Lions against Australia in 2013, Clive Woodward considered his performance in the second Test *'the most outstanding performance I have ever seen from a Lion.'* What do they have in common? Arguably, at their peaks these Whitchurch, Cardiff friends, within a few years of each other became the best Cyclist, Footballer and Rugby Player in the World.

My apologies for that digression in recounting that particular success story, but the Cardiff-born Turnbull brothers almost match the Williams boys of Taff's Well for sporting achievement, in that 7 of 8 played for Cardiff. Indeed, both families consisted of 8 sons and 4 daughters, but the

Turnbulls were very much in the higher classes of Cardiff society. Theirs is a story that is little-known and deserves a much longer retelling than is possible here. A well-known Catholic family, most of the boys, like their father, attended Downend Catholic boarding school in Bath, participating in hockey, rugby and cricket. When home in Cardiff, most of the boys played rugby for 'The Rocks', St. Peter's RFC founded in 1888, where many Catholic boys preferred to play (https://stpetersrfc.co.uk/snr/home/). The eldest boy, Bernard R. 'Lou' Turnbull (1904-1984), achieved the most rugby honours, being a Cambridge Blue, Barbarian, and gaining six Welsh caps. In his first game, against Ireland in a heavy defeat in 1925, he scored Wales' only try. In 1927 he captained Wales at Twickenham, but Wales played most of the game with 14 men, after Dai Jones was carried off after 15 minutes with a fractured shoulder bone. Scrum-half Wick Powell was knocked unconscious by an English forward. Wales scored two tries and a penalty to a converted try, a goal from a mark and a penalty but lost 11-9. In today's scoring, a 10-10 draw. 'Lou' Turnbull commented '*I think we were unlucky*'. A strong centre and excellent tackler, Bernard was twice Cardiff captain, 1927-27 and 1930-31, and vice-captain 1932-33. He played 232 times, scoring 54 tries between 1923-24 and 1932-33. In February 1930, Bernard played alongside three other Cardiff threequarters, Louis Dyke, Gwyn Davies and Ronnie Boon, losing 12-9 at Murrayfield. In 1931, Bernard played for Cardiff against South Africa, alongside his brother Maurice and Ronnie Boon, Archie Skym, Tommy Stone and captain Harry Bowcott. Cardiff lost 13-5, but the sports journalist 'Old Stager' reported: '*B. R. Turnbull was the best centre on the field, ubiquitous in defence and valiant in attack.*'

The next eldest was K.P.J. Turnbull, Kevin, who played at forward for Cardiff 178 times from 1923-24 to 1929-30, and was vice-captain in 1928-29. In Danny Davies' year of captaincy in 1925-26, he calls Kevin '*a fine prop and dribbling forward.*' Next in line was the famous Maurice Turnbull, who I shall defer to last in this section. The fourth brother was the forward Colin L. Turnbull, who could only play in the 1933-34 season, playing one game for the Firsts and 13 for the Athletic, before having to devote all his time to farming in the Vale of Glamorgan. Then, brother number 5 was T.R. 'Tommy' Turnbull, who played from 1933-34 to 1938-39, gaining an Athletic cap, playing for the Firsts 4 times and the Rags 30 times, before the war halted his career. The sixth brother, Adrian D. Turnbull was a scrumhalf like Maurice, playing from 1937-39 and then in 1946-47. He played in 45 matches, including 8 for the Firsts, and was highly regarded, but his career and the war prevented his progression. Thus 6 brothers played 488 times for Cardiff Firsts and many times for the Athletic. Another brother, Gerard, joined the Army in India, so was unavailable to play. C.B. Turnbull is listed as having a First XV appearance in 1927-28, and he was probably the seventh brother to play for Cardiff.

MAJOR MAURICE J. L. TURNBULL 16 March 1906 – 5 August 1944
'WALES' MOST COMPLETE ALL-ROUND SPORTSMAN'
Played for Glamorgan County Cricket Club as a schoolboy 1924
Glamorgan Cricket captain 1930-39
Cambridge Blue in cricket, rugby and hockey
England cricket debut vs New Zealand 1930
Toured with England cricket team to New Zealand in 1929-30 and South Africa in 1930-31. Last Test vs India 1936
1931-32 first season for **Cardiff** as scrumhalf, 62 games until 1934-35
1932 Glamorgan County rugby
1933 debut for **Wales**, with Harry Bowcott of Cardiff his fly-half, in Wales' first win at Twickenham
Wales hockey
Welsh squash champion
Cricket Test Selector 1938-39
'The only man to have played cricket for England and rugby for Wales'
Major First Battalion Welsh Guards

And now we come to '*Maurice Turnbull - Wales' most complete all-round sportsman*', the title of a long article by Graeme Brown posted on 1 August 2019, for the Roath Local History Society: *'The 5th of August will see the 75th anniversary of the death of Major Maurice Turnbull of the Welsh Guards in Normandy. He was 38 years old and in the words of the eminent Cricket historian, author and friend of our society Andrew Hignell "remains the most complete all-round sportsman Wales has ever produced". The evidence is compelling. He is the only sportsman to play Test cricket for England and rugby union for Wales. He represented Wales at hockey and squash and was Welsh Champion in the latter. He played cricket for Glamorgan between 1924-39 and was the Captain and Secretary in a tumultuous decade for the club. He was a Test Selector and captained Cambridge University. He played hockey and rugby for Cambridge University. His club rugby was primarily with Cardiff, but he also appeared for St Peters and London Welsh. He represented Glamorgan and Somerset at the oval ball game.'* The full article is available at: (https://roathlocalhistorysociety.org/2019/08/01/maurice-turnbull-wales-most-complete-all-round-sportsman/). Andrew Hignell's '*Turnbull: A Welsh Sporting Hero*', like his '*The Skipper- A Biography of Wilf Wooller*', is a wonderful read.

Maurice Joseph Lawson Turnbull was brought up at 101 Penylan Road, Cardiff. A Cambridge Blue at cricket, rugby and hockey, he played for

London Welsh and 65 times for Cardiff between 1931 and 1935, retiring on medical advice after several injuries. Scrum-halves and fly-halve were really 'targeted' in those days, with wing-forwards having far more freedom. He played hockey for Cambridge University, Cardiff and Wales and was Welsh squash champion. In cricket, Maurice played for Glamorgan as a schoolboy in 1924. The season was termed *'Turnbull's year'* in the *Wisden Cricket Annual,* as he averaged 85. He captained Cambridge in 1929 and Glamorgan from 1930 until 1939. Maurice passed 1,000 runs in a season ten times and hit double-centuries three times. He toured Australia and New Zealand in 1929-30 and South Africa in 1930-31, and also represented England against the West Indies and India at home. He was a Test selector 1938-39, Words cannot do justice to his achievements, but Graeme Brown writes: *'1932/33 would be Maurice's finest rugby season in which he achieved the distinction of a Welsh rugby cap to go alongside his England cricket sweater. He was in the words of Danny Davies Cardiff rugby historian "a crafty and resourceful scrum half". The selectors had decided to select a new exciting backline for the opener game of the championship against England which included Wilf Wooller and Viv Jenkins, future Glamorgan cricketers under Maurice. They considered Turnbull and Bowcott the best options to unleash them. The Welsh fans travelled in hope rather than anticipation, considering that Wales had not won at Twickenham since the ground had opened in 1909. Wales recorded a famous victory 7-3 with the backline excelling. Maurice sustained injuries to the jaw and neck from a robust English pack and was **unable to eat solids** at the post-match dinner. Nonetheless as he slurped his soup he no doubt reflected that despite the pain, he was glad to be playing rugby rather than cricket this winter. Across the world Jardine was winning the Ashes for England but threatening the stability of the Empire in The Bodyline series...'*

As a Major in the 1ˢᵗ Battalion of the Welsh Guards, Maurice took part in the Normandy landings in 1944. Brown tells us: *'He crossed the Channel to Normandy on 18 June. The battalion moved inland towards Caen passing scenes of devastation. Maurice's company were directed to provide support to the Americans in the Bocage, an area of small fields and narrow lanes. On the evening of 5 August, tanks and foot soldiers of the SS tank division were spotted advancing south of the village of Montchamp. Unfortunately, the anti-tank equipment and the bulk of British troops were situated north of the village and Maurice was isolated, and had lost radio communication with HQ. Maurice believed the best chance of repelling the counterattack was take out the leading tank, stalling the advance in the confined lanes. He led his men alongside the hedge and was about to order the attack when the Germans troops opened fire and the tank's gun pushed through the hedge to join them. Maurice was killed instantly. Others of the company were either killed or injured and a hasty retreat ordered.*' Maurice's body was rescued from the battlefield by Sergeant Fred Llewellyn, and his personal possessions were sent home to his family. On 7 September 1939, 4 days after war broke out, he had married Elizabeth Brooke, and they had three children, Sara, Simon and Georgina. Maurice was laid to rest at the military cemetery in Bayeux.

LESLIE 'LES' M. SPENCE MBE 1 January 1907-1988

267 games, backrow forward, for Cardiff 1930-31 to 1939-40 – 39 tries
Cardiff Vice-Captain 1935-36 chosen by Tommy Stone
Cardiff Captain 1936-37, chose Tommy Stone as vice-captain
1936-37 set try-scoring record for a forward – 12 tries
In the winning team at the Middlesex Sevens 1939
Cardiff Vice-Captain 1939-40, chosen by Wilf Wooller (Davies writes that W.E.N. 'Wendy' Davies also was vice-captain for this 3-match season)
1942, along with Wilf Wooller, captured by the Japanese
Chairman of Cardiff RFC from 1956/57 to 1976/77
President of the WRU 1973-74
Joint Secretary of Glamorgan County Cricket Club
He instigated a tour of Japan by the Wales rugby team in 1975 with the aim of reconciliation through sport. (Cardiff and Pontypridd Schools play every Boxing Day for the Les Spence Cup).
Memorial Gates were erected near the Arms Park for Les Spence
Les Spence played in the same Cardiff pack as Gwyn Williams and Eddie Watkins, that lost to the All Blacks in 1935. 'Les' had been a mainstay of the Cardiff side from 1930, and his contribution is mentioned throughout the text, and he was still playing, indeed vice-captain, aged 32 when war broke out. With other local sportsmen he joined the 77th Heavy Anti-Aircraft Regiment. A large number of the Cardiff rugby team joined, along with Glamorgan cricketers and Cardiff City footballers. Les was posted to the Far East but was captured, with his comrades, in Java in 1942. Spence was with Wilf Wooller for the early part of his imprisonment. Les was promoted from sergeant to sergeant-major soon after his arrival in Java, so like Wooller, with ranking of an officer, was extremely lucky not to endure the terrifying hardships of lesser ranks. He secretly recorded his war experiences at great personal risk, including the hardships of life in Japanese prison camps, in a series of diaries which were published in 2012 in a book *From Java to Nagasaki*.

The men, who had joined up to provide air defence for Cardiff, Newport and Barry, had been sent to the Far East, as the Japanese bore down on Britain's so-called 'impregnable fortress' of Singapore. However, the Japanese swept through the jungle of the Malay Peninsula and took Singapore in seven days. The men of the 77th Heavy Anti-Aircraft Regiment had been diverted to Java (now Indonesia). They had been trained to fight the Germans in the deserts of the Middle East, but the

Japanese attack on Pearl Harbour on 7 December 1941, meant they were diverted to the Far East. Their troopship, part of a large convoy, arrived in Batavia (now Jakarta) on Java on 3 February 1942. Before they had docked in Java, Spence wrote omnisciently in his diary: "*It will be no picnic. I am afraid some of us will not see the end of next month.*"

The 77th's defence of Java got off to a terrible start as the Army tried to move many of them by train to defend the east of the island. In February 1942 Les Spence recorded, '*there was a head-on collision with a goods train loaded with bombs and petrol. It was terrible. I found poor old Ken dead*' (Battery Sergeant Ken Street had played 74 games for Cardiff from 1934-35 to the beginning of WW2)'... '*March 8, 1942 A day that will live in my memory. The Dutch army surrendered and we were left with the baby. We were ordered to fight on but later on the order was countermanded... I never thought I would live to see this day out.*' The following day, Spence noted: "*We've surrendered after being on this island for six weeks... So the war is over as far as we are concerned. Just prisoners of war.*"' There were terrible atrocities in Singapore. The Japanese bayoneted over 200 patients, doctors and nurses at one hospital, and are thought to have murdered up to 50,000 Singaporeans. Upon their own initiative Les Spence and Wooller took a jeep and tried to escape. They were bitter at the abject surrender by poor generals at both Singapore and Java.

A report in *walesonline*, 27 March 2013, tells us that his diaries: '*cover more than three years spent in captivity, culminating in witnessing the explosion of an atomic bomb in Nagasaki, Japan, in 1945, and his eventual release later that year... The diaries are a remarkable testament to courage and endurance in the face of hardship and cruelty. It explains how the prisoners learned to survive through bargaining for food, playing football and rugby, and maintaining a sense of discipline. Alongside Spence in the POW camps were a number of other leading Cardiff sporting figures, including Glamorgan cricketer and Welsh rugby international Wilf Wooller, Welsh international Ernie Curtis, who had been the youngest member of Cardiff City's 1927 FA Cup winning side, former Cardiff City and Wales centre half Billy James and Cardiff City goalkeeper John "Jackie" Pritchard. Perhaps the most dominant player, according to the diaries, was Lieutenant Wilfred Wooller. But the diaries also describe in shocking detail the journey endured by the prisoners in the hold of the so-called "hellship", taking them from Java to Japan via Singapore.*

For the first 18 months Spence and his comrades were kept in two prison camps on Java, and the diaries contain a daily account of battling the daily fears of starvation or disease. He wrote on May 28, 1942: "Another death occurred today. It's very, very serious this dysentery. I think we are in for a very rough time and many good people will die with this disease. I pray to God that I will come out safely." In September 1943 Spence and some members of the 77th were taken to Japan, where they spent the next two years in what the Japanese designated Camp 8 Kamo near the village of Inatsuki or Inatsukimachi, in Kyushu, southern Japan. The camp was mainly aimed at producing fuel for the Japanese war machine, and prisoners were required to work down a coal mine. In January 1944, Spence wrote: "I narrowly escaped death today when I was carrying a girder, struck by trucks and all came offline just in front of me. Severely shaken. I thank God for being still alive."

Spence's time in captivity was brought to an end by the detonation of an atomic bomb over Nagasaki, in August 1945, just 100 miles away from where the prisoners were being held. Spence wrote: "We hear from the guards that one bomb blew up Nagasaki. The huge cloud we saw must have been big oil wells catching fire. We must now take over the camp." On September 21, 1945, he wrote: "We left camp today. I left at 8am in charge of 215 English. The whole village turned out to see us off. I was the last man to leave the camp and the first to come in. We had uneventful train journey to Nagasaki and then we saw the result of the atomic bomb. It was simply astounding, nothing left standing for miles, everything flat and burnt out." The prisoners were taken by sea to San Francisco, where they then travelled east by train and boarded the Queen Mary in New York on November 13, 1945. As the luxury liner began its trip to Southampton, the soldiers were given letters from home, at which point Spence made the final entry in his diary. He wrote: "I received five letters. Pleased to see that (girlfriend) Babs is still waiting. I hope that she will accept my proposal. Lovely day, beautiful sunshine." After the war, the two were married, with Spence's friend and former fellow POW Wooller as his best man.' From Java to Nagasaki by Greg Lewis and Les Spence was published by Magic Rat Books and is available upon Kindle.

In other Japanese camps, there were far worse conditions and treatment. Sir Harold Atcherley was one of 1,600 Allied prisoners of war whom the Japanese sent from Singapore, to a camp called Sonkurai in April 1943, to build a three-span wooden trestle bridge for the infamous Burma-Thailand railway. By the time he returned to Singapore ten months later, only about 400 were still alive. Of those, only 182 survived until the war ended in 1945. 182 survivors out of over 1,600 fit men. After almost 70 years of never speaking about his ordeal, Sir Harold was persuaded, at the age of 95, to publish a war diary he had kept on scraps of paper. In *Prisoner of Japan – A Personal War Diary*, he wrote: 'Neither words nor pictures could ever convey the appalling stench of disease and death on such a scale.' More than 60,000 Allied PoWs worked as slave labourers on the Burma railway line in 1942-43 in brutal conditions. 13,000 POWs and 100,000 indigenous workers died building the line. In his 2012 book Atcherley remembered: *'we were part of the "forgotten war". ... Apart from the 40,000 British and Australians captured in Malaysia, 60,000*

126

Dutch were taken prisoner in the Dutch East Indies and a considerably larger number of Americans in the Pacific. ... All of us were subjected to inhumane and brutal treatment. The experiences I describe were therefore generally common to all. The death rate for Allied prisoners in Germany (excluding Russian prisoners) was about one per cent. For those held by the Japanese the rate was forty per cent. At Sonkurai camp on the Thailand/Burma border, the worst camp of the lot, **the death rate was ninety percent.**'

GWYN GLYNDWR WILLIAMS 20 May 1918 – 15 February 1997
Youngest Player to play for Cardiff (it is Gwyn or Jim Sullivan)
Youngest Player to play against New Zealand (at the time aged 17 years 5 months 6 days, certainly a pre-war record)
Joined the '*Best Rugby League club in the world*', Wigan - '*Wigan Welsh*', with its '*Welsh Galaxy*' (1938)
Cardiff Boys
Taff's Well RFC
Cardiff Athletic 1933-34 **aged 15**
Cardiff Athletic and Firsts (**aged 16**) 1934-35 to 1938-39
Wing Forward - 103 games, 12 tries
Cardiff RFC vs All Blacks 1935 aged 17 years 5 months
Barbarians aged 17, 1935 – possibly their youngest player (Gwyn or Jim Sullivan)
Wigan Rugby League 12 November 1938 - Wing, Centre, Loose Forward, Second Row 1938-39 - 32 games 4 tries
Wales Rugby League 1939
Welsh Guards XV
Wartime Internationals – 3 appearances for RL/RU combined teams
Wales – Wartime Service International 1942
British Army – 2 Services Internationals

'*The finest wing-forward I have ever played with*' – Haydn Tanner (1917-2009) of Cardiff and Wales. The truly great Tanner played for Swansea against Gwyn perhaps 16 times, before the war, when there were 4 fixtures a season, then played in the Welsh Guards XV, for the Welsh Services and in wartime internationals with Gwyn.
'*The finest wing-forward I've ever played against – he sorted me out without any bother!*' – Air Chief Marshal Sir George Augustus 'Gus' Walker, GCB, CBE, DSO, DFC, AFC (1912-1986), England fly-half 1939, who lost an arm in war, and played for Blackheath against Gwyn several times. (In 1935-37 and 1936-37 Cardiff scored 5 tries in each game against Walker's Blackheath team, winning 17-3 and 23-0.)
'*He would have played for Wales had he not turned League, there's no question of that*' - Bleddyn Williams.

'The best' of the Williams brothers at rugby – Bleddyn Williams

'The finest wing-forward' - Norman MacLeod 'Nim' Hall (1925-1972), England fly-half seventeen times 1947-1955, whom played against Gwyn during the war, England captain

Bleddyn Williams writes, in 'Rugger – My Life' that 'big Gwyn' was his 'veritable hero.' It appears that he never knew that Gwyn moved to Wigan to help pay Bleddyn's public school fees at Rydal. He writes of his pride seeing Gwyn play for Cardiff, and then: 'During the War, Gwyn served with the Welsh Guards, and while in the Training Battalion played with the great Haydn Tanner, who was later to be my captain in so many games for Wales. Tanner was captain of the famous Guards Rugby side, and like Gwyn he played regularly for the Welsh representative Services team. It was in North Africa where Gwyn's playing days ended. On notorious Long Stop Hill, where the Guards engaged the remnants of Rommel's Afrika Corps, and the Panzers showed that they had not lost the power to hit hard and ruthlessly, a sniper's bullet took Gwyn in the eye and passed out through the back of his head. That he survived is a miracle. Only many grave operations, and his perfect physique and immeasurable strength of will, brought him to a state of partial recovery. He endured all his sufferings with a smile, always eager to hear news of the game he would never play again. Happily, now (1956), though still not fully recovered, he stands among the "bob-bankers" on the Arms Park. It is a source of pleasure to me that such renowned players as Cliff Jones and Wilf Wooller, who were contemporaries of my brother, consider Gwyn one of the finest wing-forwards ever to play in Wales.' (It used to cost a shilling, or 'bob', to stand on the 'banked' terraces at the Arms Park for club games).

Gwyn's nickname as a boy was 'Fatty' Williams, in a time of slimmer human beings, and when the nickname 'fatty' was often used to mean bigger than one's peers. Certainly, Gwyn towered over his schoolmates, appearing like a full-grown man, aged just fourteen. His mother Nell was the daughter of Ted Roberts, and her young brother Roy Roberts joined the Taff's Well 3rd XV at the same time as the 14-year-old Gwyn. One day the Firsts were short of players, and three youngsters were called up from the 3rds, the strapping Gwyn, his great friend Iorwerth ('Iorrie') Jones and Vernon Harvey. Gwyn and Iorrie had taken boxing lessons at Melingriffith Boxing Club, Cardiff. (Melingriffith was the site of a major tinplate works, near the Radyr Weir of the Taff, north-west Cardiff). Taff's Well club captain Reg Field was unsure about the boys' safety but remarked that when they started playing, he was more worried about the health of the opposition. Aged 14, Gwyn became a regular for Taff's Well Firsts.

Gwyn appeared for Cardiff Athletic aged 15 in the 1933-34 season, according to Bleddyn, and he played for Cardiff Firsts aged 16, from 1934-35, gaining his cap in that season with the Athletic. Davies reports 'Two forwards made debuts in the back row, Eddie Watkins – hardly out of

128

Caerphilly Grammar School – and Gwyn Williams the first of the celebrated Taff's Well family of brothers who were to play for Cardiff and gain fame in the rugby world.' A local Cardiff boy, Jim Regan, also joined, playing 39 games as hooker in that season, and was instrumental in pointing out to Gwyn the advantages of turning 'professional'. Regan played 172 times before joining Huddersfield after 18 matches in the 1938-39 season. Gwyn made 103 First XV appearances, before heading North after 17 games in the 1938-39 season. In the 1935-36 season, Gwyn was in the Cardiff team that beat the Barbarians 7-3 in April 1936, after the Baa-Baas had won 22 consecutive games in South Wales in the previous six years. They had beaten Cardiff in their last 5 games from 1931. For 1935-36, Gwyn was awarded his First XV cap. 1936-37 saw Cardiff at the peak of their powers once more, drawing large crowds everywhere they played, and with Wilf Wooller, Eddie Watkins and Harry Rees playing in all three internationals. Cardiff easily beat the Baa-Baas 16-3, 3 tries to 1. Cardiff's outside half Tommy Stone and Horace Edwards were selected to play for Wales in Ireland, but a blizzard meant a postponed match, with Stone and Edwards dropped. The disappointed Stone turned professional with Barrow, after 317 games for his club. In 1936-37, in 32 consecutive appearances, Gwyn scored 5 tries, more than expected of a forward in those days, but Les Spence landed no less than 12.

A WELCOME
Mr. Harry Sunderland, the Wigan Rugby League club manager, and famous captain, Jim Sullivan, greet Gwyn Williams, a new arrival from Cardiff.

Gwyn on right, being greeted at Wigan by manager Harry Sunderland and the great Jim Sullivan

After 17 games in 1938-39, Gwyn headed North, his main reason being to help pay for Bleddyn Williams' school fees at Rydal. However, just look at who else Cardiff alone lost at this time, just before the war. Firstly, his friend Eddie Watkins (1916-1995) followed Gwyn from Cardiff to Wigan in 1939 after 21 matches. In one of only three games played in the 1938-39 season, Watkins is pictured alongside Jim Sullivan and five other Welsh players in the Wigan win against Hunslet. PC Edward Verdun 'Eddie' Watkins played 151 games for Cardiff between 1934-35 and 1938-39, scoring 10 tries. The lock gained eight caps for Wales, making his debut in the 1935 win against the All Blacks. Previously, Watkins had been chosen by Cardiff to face New Zealand, as Cardiff were hoping that a strong pack containing Watkins, Les Spence and Gwyn Williams would give the club an advantage in the forwards. An excited Bleddyn Williams remembers watching Gwyn play, but the Cardiff backs 'lost' the game in the first half. In March 1939 Watkins joined Wigan for a reported fee of £600, making his first appearance for the club alongside Gwyn Williams. In the War, Watkins played in three internationals during the war years for Wales against England and played in Services Internationals.

GLYN WILLIAMS, WIGAN
A new forward, from Cardiff; only 20, but stands 6ft. and weighs 14st. 4lb.

1938 Gwyn Williams, Wigan

Secondly, wing PC Arthur Bassett (1914-1999) had joined Cardiff, aged 21, in the 1935-36 season, and played 101 games. Cardiff's best wing, Bassett gained six caps for Wales, between 1934 and 1938. Leaving, like Gwyn, after 17 matches, he signed to play Rugby League for Halifax, moving to York in 1948. Bassett played for Great Britain twice in 1946, and three times for Wales between December 1939 and November 1946.

He scored a hat-trick of tries in Great Britain's victory over Australia at Brisbane in 1946, and was the brother of another policeman, the great Jack Bassett (1905-1989). Jack Bassett joined Cardiff at the same time as his brother, intending to play a few years in the 'Rags'. Full back Jack joined from Penarth, and had played for Wales fifteen times, nine times as captain, and toured with the British Lions to Australia and New Zealand. On that tour he was acclaimed as the *'greatest full back in world rugby'*, even outplaying New Zealand legend George Nepia. Bassett earned five Lions caps. *'He was seen as one of the most devastating tacklers in the game, and many opposing backs would throw the ball into touch rather than allow Bassett to hit them in full flow.'* In the season the brothers joined Cardiff, Arthur was the 1st XV's top try scorer with 27, and Jack was awarded his Athletic cap.

TURNS PRO TO REPAY PARENTS

BECAUSE his father, a former miner, has been unemployed for nearly six years, a young Welsh Rugby star has given up his chance of a Rugby Union cap, left his job as a Glamorgan policeman and signed professional forms for Wigan, Rugby League club.

He is twenty-one-year-old Gwynn Williams, brilliant Cardiff forward. Wigan have given him £400 for turning professional and guaranteed him a job.

But Williams's father doesn't at all like the idea of his son being a professional footballer.

Gwynn said it was time he did something to repay all that his parents had done for him and he made up his mind about turning professional when he had a peep at Jim Sullivan's bank book. Sullivan is the famous Wigan and Welsh international full back.

Third, James 'Jim' Regan was Cardiff's regular hooker and joined Huddersfield in 1939, playing alongside Gwyn Williams for the Wales rugby league team in April 1939. Scrums were still contested in rugby league at this time. Fourth, Alban Davies (the brother of the great Cliff Davies) had previously played for Monmouthshire and Cross Keys, and was thought to be a great prospect at Cardiff, being awarded his first team cap in 1938-39, but went with Regan to Huddersfield, signing on 2 January 1939. He played fullback for Wales rugby league in February 1943, kicking two goals, and again in March 1946. A programme note in the Huddersfield-Keighley game of 24 April 1939 reads that at the end of the season, Huddersfield had won 15 and drawn 1 out of 17 of their final matches, so were in a fine spell of form with Alban at fullback: '*Alban Davies, whose goalkicking has caused much discussion recently, has the best record for one match with eight v. Rochdale. He has registered no fewer than 12 goal hat-tricks in 18 matches. Next season should find him among the leading fullbacks of the rugby league.*' There were some wartime games and in 1945 Huddersfield won the Challenge Cup, beating Bradford Northern over two legs. Cardiff lost, alongside Gwyn, four international class players in just a few months. Gwyn, Jim Regan, Arthur Bassett, Eddie Watkins and Alban Davies all appeared in wartime internationals. Cardiff were to lose several men in the war, all playing colleagues of Gwyn – former player Maurice Turnbull, current player Ken Street and others being killed, and Wilf Wooller, Les Spence and others being captured and treated badly. Wilf and Les could no longer play rugby after ill treatment.

Wigan is the most successful club in the history of World Rugby League having won 22 League Championships (including 5 Super League Grand Finals), 19 Challenge Cups, 4 World Club Challenges and over 100 honours in total. Gwyn joined the truly great Wigan Rugby League team, following the example of many of his compatriots heading 'up North' in 1938/39, in order to provide a better life for their families in a professional rugby career. While qualified men like teachers and solicitors usually stayed in Wales, for those with fewer qualifications and opportunities there was little choice. In a faded newspaper cutting from Carey Collings, titled *A Welcome*, the photograph caption reads: '*Mr. Harry Sunderland, the Wigan Rugby League club manager, and famous captain, Jim Sullivan, greet Gwyn Williams, a new arrival from Cardiff.*' By a fortuitous encounter in a Penarth gym, this author discovered that after the war Gwyn was living in Energlyn, Caerphilly, before he retired to Swanage. Living in Energlyn Farm, his father asked why Gwyn had gone North. The truth was that Gwyn knew, by Wilf Wooller's machinations, that Bleddyn had been offered a place in Rydal Public School, near Conwy. Bleddyn entered Rydal in 1937, and in 1938 <u>Gwyn went professional to pay Bleddyn's school fees</u>, a fact that shows how remarkable a man he was. It seems that Bleddyn and the family did not know Gwyn's reason for heading North.

On 22 October 1938, Wigan won the Lancashire County Cup Final at Salford 10-7, but Gwyn only signed 3 weeks later, despite having been 'chased' by Wigan for some years. Bleddyn's school fees were the 'tipping point' in his decision to leave Wales. Aged 20, Gwyn stood six feet tall, but appeared bigger to contemporaries, and weighed a solid, muscular 14 stone 4 pounds. Gwyn is listed on *Wikipedia* as having played on the wing in that game, along with 7 other Welshmen in the team of thirteen players, but could not have played. Dennis 'Ted' Williamson was on the left wing, but when we see the make-up of this Wigan team (remember, 13 players and no substitutes), we can see why Gwyn joined. In the final the legendary Jim Sullivan played fullback, with Williamson and Jack Morley on the wings and Gwynne Davies and Ted Ward in the centre, apart from Williamson the famed all-Welsh back line which Gwyn was to join soon after. Gwyn played in the forwards or backs, he was that good. Gwyn's first match for Wigan was against Warrington away on 12th November 1938, Wigan lost 13 -7, and Gwyn played second row alongside fellow Welshman Trevor Thomas. Wigan had pursued Gwyn as early as 1937 and had 13 Welsh players on their books in 1938-39. They were known as 'Wigan Welsh' to other clubs. To be honest, to be working-class and having unemployment just around the corner, it is no wonder that so many Welsh players joined rugby league. In the other three home nations, rugby was very much an upper-class sport, probably until the 1970s. Even in the 1960s the Irish team was composed of 'professional men'.

However, in Wales, the rise of grammar schools allowed working class boys to gain a better education – and the county, then grammar, schools played rugby to the exclusion of soccer/football. Gwyn also played loose forward, the equivalent of number 8 in a modern pack, but with no wing-forwards in a 6-man pack of 3 front-rowers, 2 second-rowers and a loose forward. However, because of Jackie Bowen's expertise as a loose forward, Gwyn was shifted onto the wing – perhaps the first 'big' wing in both codes of rugby. We must note that in those days in rugby league, scrums were contested, so the loose forward often had to pick the ball up and drive forward. (It is a strange situation. Rugby Union evolved to the point where scrum-halves always 'feed' the ball into their second row, so the force of the forwards in not weakened by the hooker trying to gain the ball. It is totally illegal, but allowed in the interests of 'speeding the game up'. When this writer played hooker, the ball had to go in straight and both hookers 'struck' for the ball. A penalty was given for 'foot-up' if you struck for the ball too quickly, aiming to 'hook' it back into your second row. Thus, there were 7 forwards pushing against 7, and the only reset scrums were usually when mud caused forwards to slip. Over the course of almost 30 years of playing, I played every position except prop, second row and number 8, so am qualified as a 'jack of all trades' to have a reasonable opinion on most positions, even from a extremely lowly viewpoint).

Usually on the other wing to Gwyn was John 'Jack' Cuthbert Morley (1909-1972), who was a Welsh schoolboy international, and won 14 full caps for Wales when playing for Newport in rugby union. In his first season with Newport, Morley scored 29 tries, and by 1931, aged just 21, was the youngest player ever to captain the club. He captained Newport against the touring South Africans at Rodney Parade on 8 October 1931.

Morley was first capped for Wales against England on 19 January 1929 and scored a try from 40 yards out, breaking infield, cutting back inside and crossing wide, to touch down. He toured with the British Lions in South Africa in 1931, and played in all four matches of Wales's Championship winning 1932 campaign. In August 1932 he switched to rugby league with Wigan, and then won 5 caps for Wales RL, becoming the first player to tour Australia and New Zealand for both union and league British teams. In the seven years until 1939, Morley scored an amazing 223 times in 292 games and kicked 4 goals. Thus, Gwyn was regularly playing with two of the greatest players in history, Jim Sullivan and Morley, in the three outside backs (- full-back and wings).

In the centre were two other great Welsh 'escapees' from amateur rugby union. Edward 'Ted' H. Ward played rugby union for Amman United then Llanelli RFC, and then at club level for Wigan (two spells), Oldham and Cardiff RLFC. He won 13 caps for Wales in 1946-51 while at Wigan and Cardiff RL, and won caps for Great Britain while at Wigan in 1946, against Australia (twice) and New Zealand. He scored a goal in Wigan's 8-3 victory over Bradford Northern in the 1947–48 Challenge Cup Final at Wembley Stadium, London on 1 May 1948, in front of a crowd of 91,465. Ted Ward played 213 times for Wigan from 1939-1950, and in 1953, scoring 57 tries and 480 goals. With many cup and league honours, Ted Ward is one of fewer than 25 Welshmen to have scored more than 1,000-points in their rugby league career. Just 21 when war broke out, the right centre could have otherwise set many, many records.

Gwyn will have played rugby union for Cardiff alongside the other centre, Eiryn Gwynne 'Gwyn' Davies (1908-1992). Gwyn Davies played wing for Cardiff (1932-35) and played for Wales three times. After moving to Wigan, he won another 3 caps, all against England, and played on the 1936 Great Britain Lions tour of Australia and New Zealand. For Wigan, from 1930-39 he scored 127 tries in 300 games. He played left centre, and Gwyn Williams usually played on the left wing outside him. Gwyn's other outside backs were all Welsh, all formerly rugby union internationals and some British Lions – fullback Jim Sullivan, 'Jack' Morley, Ted Ward and 'Gwyn' Davies. In the all-Welsh three-quarter line, Gwyn Williams was a strapping wing, but could also play centre, loose forward or second row, during the era of contested scrums. His ideal position was probably wing forward, but there are no wing forwards in the 13-man code. For the two half-backs, there was an England international fly-half Jack Garvey, and scrum-half Hector Gee, who played for Australia and a British Empire XIII.

In the forwards, B.J. John ('Jack' or 'Jackie') Bowen was Wigan's loose forward. Llanelli's 'Jackie' Bowen (1915-2009) was on the brink of his first Welsh cap, playing for the Probables in the 1938 trial, but was approached while leaving the field, and offered an amazing ten-year

134

contract with Wigan. He waited a few days and was bitterly disappointed after being left out of the Wales side that met England the following week at Cardiff Arms Park, so, like Tommy Stone, signed professional forms. Bowen was the only change from the Probables side in the final trial. Often, not sometimes, selectors made wrong choices for Wales. For Wigan Jackie Bowen played from January 1939, alongside Gwyn in that season, until 1947, scoring 32 tries and kicking 8 goals. He also played for Wales in rugby league. The second rows were 'Ocker' Thomas and 'Ike' Jones, also Welsh rugby union converts. Merthyr Tydfil's William Trevor 'Ocker' Thomas played rugby union for Wales against England in 1930, while playing for Abertillery. For Wigan he made 112 appearances, scoring 9 tries from 1935-39. He also represented Wales in rugby league three times. Ivor 'Ike' Jones played from 1936 to 1945, ignoring the war years, with 146 appearances, 34 tries and kicking 3 goals. Gwyn Williams seems to have played with or against all the Welshmen in Wigan's team in rugby union, except 'Jim' Sullivan.

'Wigan Welsh' 1938 – Percy Moxey, Gwyn Williams,
Ike Jones, Jim Sullivan, Jack Bowen, Roy Francis

There was an All-English front row of prop George William Banks, 'Joe' Egan and Kennett 'Ken' Gee. Hooker Joseph 'Joe' Egan played for England and was vice-captain of the 1950 British Lions, and prop Ken Gee played for Great Britain, and England, 17 times and 18 times respectively. Thus Gwyn was at home in a team of 8 Welshmen, an Ozzie and 4 Englishmen, of which 11 were internationals. Wales was being sucked dry of its best players at this time. Indeed, Salford had six Welsh players in the 1938 cup final against Wigan, which Gwyn missed by just three weeks. For Salford there was the Welsh rugby union international Harold Thomas from Neath; Newport's Bert Day, who was in the Welsh team that won the Five Nations in 1931; Dai Davies; Billy Watkins from Cross Keys; Aberavon's Alan Edwards; and the rugby league true legend Augustus 'Gus' John Ferdinand Risman (born in Cardiff, educated in Barry, and signed on as a schoolboy). Risman played for 25 years, from 1929-1954, captaining the unbeaten British Lions in Australia, playing 18 times of Wales and 17 times for Great Britain. In his 791 first-class club appearances, not including internationals, he scored 201 tries and kicked 1611 goals. We see that over half, 14, of the 26 players in the RL Lancashire Cup Final were Welsh.

On 1 April 1939, Gwyn was playing in a cup semi-final against Salford at Rochdale, *'played in farcical conditions at the Rochdale ground after a crush in the crowd had led to railings at the front of the stand giving way. This led to thousands of fans crossing the dog track at the ground to stand at the edge of the pitch. The players and officials had to push through the edge of the crowds "six or seven deep" on the touchline to make it on to the field... An estimated 100 supporters climbed on to the railway stand roof and after a few minutes it partially gave way with a big crash. Many of the fans under the stand were injured as the stand came crashing down. Two players immediately left the field to help with the injured along with ambulance men and police.'* Two people died. Gwyn Williams won a cap for Wales while at Wigan, in April 1939, and scored a try when Wales beat England 17-9 at Llanelli.

Llanelli's Jack Bowen had joined Wigan shortly before Gwyn, and his ability at loose forward was the main reason why Gwyn usually played on the wing. A report of the cup final that Gwyn narrowly missed reads: *'In the loose it was a great battle. The man who took the eye most was Bowen, the Wigan loose forward, and well though his International opposite Feetham played, the honours easily went to the Wigan man, playing only his 13th game of Rugby League, and Bowen also effected a fine tackle of Edwards who was racing down the touchline.'* (- *Manchester Guardian*). A post-match commentator said, *'It's a long time since Wigan had such a fine trio of forwards in the loose as Trevor Thomas, Ike Jones and Jack Bowen'*, and the *Liverpool Echo* reported *'Bowen the ex-Llanelly loose forward, is very brainy, handles with the skill of a back, and knows when to part with the ball.'*

Having joined the Welsh Guards, Gwyn made his presence felt in the wartime internationals. A yellowed newspaper cutting reads: *'The Gentle Giant - Last week "Geevers" (G.V. Wynne Jones) wrote about the famous Welsh rugby family the Williamses. He has received this letter from Mr. Howard Hicks, the Stratford multi-millionaire, who played fly half for*

Pontypridd and is a patron of the club. "When I was well over the top I played in Belfast as fly half for the Army, in Northern Ireland against the British Army. About five minutes before kick-off a towering young man walked into my dressing-room to see me, and I discovered that Gwyn Williams was playing wing forward for the British Army. My heart dropped to see this very powerful young man and feel his hand enveloping my very small one. Although he smothered me half a dozen times in the game, he was as gentle as a mother with a babe. When we were dressed after the game he came to see me, as the gentleman that he was and, as a typical Welsh guardsman, stood rigidly to attention, saluted and said, 'I hope you enjoyed the game, sir.' "I looked right and left and whispered in his ear, 'Thank you very much, Gwyn.' He was one of the most likeable men I have ever met, and your article brought back many pleasant memories."'

Hartlepool Northern Daily Mail
Nov 3rd 1943

RUGBY STAR
WOUNDED

Gwyn Williams, the Welsh Rugby League and Services Rugby international forward, had a narrow escape from death during the fighting in Tunisia, when a bullet passed clean through his head. He is now in hospital in this country. Williams, a grand back row forward, played in Welsh football with Taffswell and Cardiff before joining the Wigan Rugby League club. He played for Wales in both war-time international matches with England in 1942 and once last season. He has also appeared for the Brigade of Guards, the Welsh Guards, and the Army.

Newspaper cutting about Gwyn getting shot in North Africa

Gwyn not only played for the British Army, but for the Welsh Guards, which like other Welsh regiments had great success in the Army Champions Cup before the War. There follows a list of finals involving Welsh teams (r.u.= runners up): 1907-08 - 1st Welch Regiment runners up; 1908-09 - 1st Welch Regiment winners; 1911-12 - 2nd Welch Regiment r.u.; 1912-13 - 2nd Welch Regiment r.u.; 1919-20 - 2nd Welch Regiment winners; 1920-21 - 2nd Welch Regiment winners; 1921-22 - 2nd Welch Regiment winners; 1922-23 - 1st Welsh Guards beat 2nd Welch Regiment; 1923-24 - 2nd Welch Regiment beat 1st Welsh Guards; 1924-25 - 1st South Wales Borderers winners; 1925-26 - 1st South Wales Borderers winners; 1926-27 - 1st South Wales Borderers winners; 1927-28 - 1st South Wales Borderers winners; 1928-29 - 1st Welsh Guards r.u.; 1931-32 - 1st Welsh Guards winners; 1933-34 - 1st Welsh Guards winners; 1934-35 - 1st Welch Regiment beat 2nd South Wales Borderers; 1936-37 - 1st Welch Regiment winners; 1937-38 - 1st Welsh Guards r.u.; 1938-39 - 1st Welch Regiment winners. Missing games in the First World War, in 16 out of 20 finals Welsh teams won or were runners-up. This says quite a lot about the condition of the game in Wales in these three decades. With the Depression of the 1920s and 1930s, many Welsh players joined the Army.

Serving in the Welsh Guards, Gwyn was penned in to play for the Army against the RAF side, containing brother Bleddyn. However, his regiment was being posted, and Gwyn declined the invitation, in order to stay with his 'mates' and head to North Africa, just a week before the game. A week later, Gwyn was almost killed by a sniper at the Battle of Longstop Hill (- see Bleddyn's account in this chapter). It appears that Gwyn was assumed dead from his terrible wound, and was heaved up onto a 'death cart' for burial in the Tunisian desert. Someone saw his body twitch on the cart, and he was taken down and treated, although no-one thought he could survive. It was touch and go whether his CO would bother to transport Gwyn with other wounded back on a hospital ship to Britain for treatment, but somehow he survived the repatriation. Even back in hospital, his surgeon was amazed that Gwyn had lived, and that he managed to pull through. *'All the regiments of the Brigade of Guards fought in the Tunisian campaign. Grenadiers, Coldstream, Scots, Irish, and Welsh were represented; every battalion saw hard fighting at one time or another... The much fought over Longstop Hill was captured in dramatic style by Guards regiments in April 1943, allowing the capture of Tunis... On April 9 a battalion of Welsh Guards carried out a brilliant assault on Saddleback Hill, with the aid of Sherman tanks, and then went on, supported by the Grenadiers, to storm the craggy hill of Rhorab. The whole operation fell short of complete success because the other troops were unable to force their way into Fondouk, but the Guards fulfilled their part of it to the letter, and enabled considerable loss to be inflicted on the retreating columns beyond Kairouan... The corps of which the Guards formed part was now ordered to ignore Tunis and break through eastward into the plain across the base of the Cap Bon peninsula. It was faced by a mountain barrier south of Hamman Lif, which it appeared certain the enemy would hold strongly, but when the Guards went in only the Welsh, in the centre, met with really stiff opposition, having hard fighting on the crest. The armour then forced its way through the narrow gap along the shore, and from that moment the campaign was virtually over.*

Huge masses of prisoners were collected, or marched in of their own accord at Grombalia, and the advance was continued with little or no opposition, to the sea at Hammamet. The Fifth Panzer Army was cut off from what was to have been its last refuge, the Cap Bon peninsula. These Guards battalions shared the task of holding its base with those from the Eighth Army, which had reached the neighbourhood of Grombalia after a long semi-circular flank march around the doomed German force. Later on, this force surrendered partly to the Eighth Army. On 11 May these Guards battalions brought their superb record in the Tunisian campaign to a fitting conclusion by occupying Bou Ficha, south of the Cape Bon Peninsula. This completed the encircling of the last resisting Axis forces... The Welsh Guards particularly distinguished themselves in these operations.' (The Times, Saturday, 26 June 1943 – 'The Guards in Tunisia –from Adversity to the Final Triumph'.)

From the Taff's Well history, '*A View from the Garth*', at the start of '*The Williams Clan*' entry, we read: '*GWYN 'FATTY' WILLIAMS' – Gwyn Williams, know to all locally as "Fatty", first played for Taff's Well in the early 1930s. A contemporary of Iorrie Jones and cousin Roy Roberts, Gwyn made his first appearance with Iorrie and Roy in the club 3rd XV. In the absence of a youth side, the third XV was the vehicle for "blooding" the youngsters. On one occasion when the First XV were depleted, Iorrie, Gwyn and Roy were taken as a "stop gap" into the senior team. Their ability so shocked Reg Field the captain, that they were immediately marked as First Team regulars. It must be remembered that Gwyn was then only 15 years old.*

Possessed of great physical strength, "Fatty" had been a schoolboy star, a man amongst boys. An excellent swimmer, athlete and boxer, he was one of those who come along only very occasionally. By 1935, Gwyn was on his way to the Arms Park and at the tender age of seventeen was in opposition against the mighty "All Blacks". At Cardiff, Gwyn became known as a really robust back row man, who really put half backs on their backs. After 105 First Team appearances, "Fatty" received a Northern League offer, which in those days of financial stringency, was impossible to reject. He joined Wigan and became an instant success.

In 1939 the war put a stop to many a career and Gwyn became one of its tragic casualties. Seriously wounded in action, he fought for his life. Given little hope of survival, he amazed his doctors by his will and strength. "Fatty" survived against all odds and now lives comfortably in Swanage, making occasional visits to his home village, where he is regarded by his contemporaries as something of a miracle. It is said that when "Fatty" Williams was made, they broke the mould.'

There is a photo of Gwyn in the *Manchester Evening News* in August

1939. His last game was on 29 August 1939, for Wigan against Dewsbury. He had played 36 games for the club. Bleddyn 'Keith' Bowen, Jack's son, remembers that *'Gwyn and Percy Moxey became great pals, going on holiday to the Norfolk Broads, where they ended up broke. Just as well then, that Percy by this time was living at Great Yarmouth where his parents were running a pub. Percy Moxey did not survive the crashing of his Wellington bomber over Birmingham. It collided with wires holding the Barrage balloons in place, on a practice night-time flight in 1942, 6 baled out, 3 survived but it seems Percy left it too late. He'd been married one month earlier and was living in Great Yarmouth where he'd also worked as a Policeman, a job he'd done in Glamorganshire.'* The *Pontypridd Observer*, 4 September 1943 reported: *'Wounded in Africa. Gwyn Williams, the well-known Welsh rugby international, who was seriously wounded on Active Service in North Africa, has now undergone an operation and is said to be making progress. His many friends wish him a speedy recovery.'* Also, the *Hartlepool Northern Daily Mail*, 3 November 1943 reported *'Rugby Star Wounded. Gwyn Williams, the Welsh Rugby League and Services International forward, had a narrow escape from death in Tunisia, when a bullet passed clean through his head. He is now in hospital in this country. Williams, a grand backrow forward, played in Welsh football with Taff's Well and Cardiff before joining the Wigan Rugby League Club. He played for Wales in both war-time international matches with England in 1942 and once last season. He has also appeared for the Brigade of Guards, the Welsh Guards, and the Army.'*

My brother Gwyn, a brilliant
wing-forward

R.A.F. days: happy hours
of duty—and football!

Don Llewelyn's father Trevor was a good friend of Gwyn, always saying *'Everyone liked Gwyn'*. In 1941 Gwyn had married Eunice M. Williams, whom he had met before the war at a dance in Caerphilly, where he was a PC. After recuperating from his injury Gwyn worked at County Hall, Cardiff, and moved to Energlyn, a new estate centred on Energlyn Farm, Caerphilly. It was to the owner of the farm that he confided in the late 1950s that he had headed North to pay for Bleddyn's school fees. Gwyn then moved to the seaside, to Swanage in Dorset, where the couple had a small bungalow, his sister Mair staying there for holidays. The Williams brothers were nothing if not versatile. Gwyn played second row, wing forward, loose forward, centre and wing. Brinley 'Bryn' was a centre but could play anywhere across the backs, as could Vaughan. Bleddyn was an outside half and centre. Lloyd could play scrum half, fly half or centre. Cenydd could play fly half, centre or wing. Elwyn played across the back row, but was versatile enough to play in the backs, and Tony played fly half, centre and sometimes wing for Cardiff.

FAMILY MEMORIES OF GWYN (All from *The Williams Family, Garth Domain* booklet, 1984)

Acknowledged by Bleddyn as 'the best' of the brothers to play rugby, this most versatile player was remembered with enormous affection by the family. After some games for the Athletic and many for Cardiff 1st XV, as a 'robust' backrow forward, he gained his senior cap in the 1935-36 season, playing 103 games for the First XV. Gwyn was a Caerphilly police officer when at Cardiff, but in 1938 he turned professional with Wigan, for whom he usually played on the wing. Unfortunately, after just 38 games for Wigan, and one Wales Rugby League cap, war broke out.

His career was tragically cut short by serious injury in the War, but after convalescing he used to watch both Taff's Well and Cardiff rugby clubs, sitting quietly in the club houses afterwards. In 2003-04 Gerald Edwards and Don Llewellyn interviewed his sisters Enid and Mair, and six of the brothers, for recollections of the great man, omitting only Cenydd, who was living in Lancashire. *'Gwyn, Bryn and Bleddyn were the first three Williams brothers to receive their grounding at Taff's Well School before going on to achieve considerable fame in the rugby world.'*

BRYN (BRINLEY) WILLIAMS RECALLS:

Bryn was the next oldest boy after Gwyn, so knew him well. *'Gwyn was playing for the Taff's Well senior side when he was 13 – for the seconds or thirds or whatever (they had four sides in those days). He was a big boy for his age. Then of course Trigg (his headmaster) got hold of this and he formed a schoolboys' side. He said it was ridiculous for Gwyn to be playing senior rugby.'* (There is a photograph of the school rugby team from 1932/33, with the 'giant' Gwyn in the centre of the middle row holding the match ball, Brinley (Bryn) in the back row, and the small Bleddyn sitting in front.) *'We both played for Cardiff Boys. Then Gwyn left school to work for a brewery in Cardiff. He was only seventeen when he played for Cardiff against the All Blacks in 1935! He then worked for a short time at a foundry workshop before joining the Police Force. He was in the force until he was about 19, and then he went north. There was nothing for them around here those days, so they used to go north.* (For a professional career in rugby league). *'I went up to Wigan to see Gwyn play. In his first game he played as a forward, but in the second he was at centre – he could play anywhere really.*

I remember Cled Williams telling me that when he was playing for Swinton against Wigan, he was standing near the line when Gwyn was coming at him. Cled thought "I'll get him" but it was no use, he had no chance – Gwyn hit him for six and scored the try. He was so strong you know.' (The Welshman Cledwyn Williams played at 12, wing, in the Lancashire County Cup Final, when Swinton beat Widnes over two legs in the 1939-40 season). *'He was playing in France when the war broke out. The war stopped the rugby of course and he came home. Called up at twenty, he joined the Welsh Guards. He went to North Africa in 1944 and landed there, as they were going to Italy. As it happened, I was in the Eighth Army and I didn't know he was coming out there because he was in a training battalion – training recruits, you know.*

He was wounded on "Longstop Hill" and had a bad time. I heard about it when I was in a rest camp. We had no leave then you know, just a couple of days in a rest camp. The Red Cross got messages home, but by the time the letters came to me (about three or four weeks later) and I had gone up there, he had already been put on a hospital ship. I had all the information from his commanding officer. My brother was hospitalised for some time because the bullet had gone through his head. He had shrapnel all in his body – and in one eye which he lost after a time. He was also paralysed so he was in a bad way. Gwyn wouldn't have known me anyway. I never saw any more of him until I got home, you see.' (Bleddyn thought that the injury was caused by a sniper's bullet, but Bryn spoke to Gwyn's CO, so it seems that Gwyn survived severe shrapnel wounds. A bullet would have killed him. Gwyn never spoke to the brothers about his injuries.)

I got home in August 1945 – I went out at the end of 1940 and came back in 45. By then Gwyn had recovered somewhat – not a lot, but his memory you know that was the trouble. It was Del Harris (Gwyn's Taff's Well teacher, who played rugby alongside Gwyn for Taff's Well) *who **taught him how to read and write again, because he'd lost all that**, you see. Del Harris was a wonderful man. Of course, he took over the schoolboy sides and a good coach he was too. Our Gwyn was a fine all-round athlete. He was a good swimmer. He competed in the Taff Swim when he was fourteen. Hundreds used to take part in that, and I think the boy came in 12th or* *something like that. He was a good boxer as well.'*

The Long-Distance Swimming Championship of Wales, known as '*The Taff Swim*', was held on the River Taff, which ran alongside Taff's Well, from 1924 to 1930. In 1931 it was moved to Cardiff's Roath Park Lake, because of the rebuilding of Cardiff Bridge, and the event ended in 1962. The A48 from West Wales to Cardiff crosses over Cardiff Bridge, just before the superb castle, and that was the starting point. It was open to all comers from any country, swimming downstream almost two miles to Clarence Bridge, down towards Cardiff docklands. Also known as the '*Evening Express Swim*', it attracted crowds of over 100,000 to 150,000 people. For young Gwyn to finish so well was an amazing achievement. The river was filthy beyond belief at this time, because of 52 coal mines in the Rhondda Valley, and the fact that Taff's Well was an important railway junction for coal trains heading down to Cardiff and Barry Docks. The Welsh Amateur Swimming Association promoted it as '*The Greatest Welsh Swimming Event of the Year, Sponsored and Organised by the (South Wales) Echo.*' Gwyn must have swum it at Roath Park on 4 June 1932, if he was fourteen, swimming two circular laps, around one and a half miles. Contestants seem to have been limited, as the 1932 programme shows just 12 female (all swimming club members) and 25 male entrants, of which 13 were swimming club members. The women started first, all swimming front crawl. Entries were low because of the clash with Olympic swimming trials in London.

'*Gwyn got married in the early part of 1941. I was home on embarkation leave to go abroad. They gave you a week, you see, and then you would go straight on the boat. I was due to go back on the day of the wedding (the Saturday), but Gwyn had asked me to be his best man. So on the Friday I sent a cable to my commanding officer requesting an extra day. I was given permission, on condition that I caught the next troop train, which I did. That was the last I saw of Gwyn then till after the war. In his time, he was to live at Energlyn in Caerphilly, and for a short spell at Station Terrace in Caerphilly. For most of his last years though he lived in Dorset where he had often spent holidays. He bought a bungalow there* (in Swanage) *and lived down that way for over thirty years. Yes, he had a hard time did Gwyn. But not only that of course, he lost a good bit of rugby didn't he. I remember when Haydn Tanner brought a side here to Taff's Well after the war and said that* **Gwyn was the finest wing-forward he had ever played with.***'*

ELWYN WILLIAMS RECALLS in 1984:

'*Concerning my memories of Gwyn, well we were kids you know, just after the war Gwyn would come home, beaming in his face and as strong as an ox. He would catch hold of each of us and our bones would be breaking. He was such an upright figure and a gentleman. And he had this little dog that used to walk with him, you know, and he used to walk from Caerphilly to Taff's Well regularly to see Iorrie Jones who was one of his pals.'* (Iorrie was a stalwart of Taff's Well rugby club in the 1930s alongside Fred Porter, Reg Field, Bob Lewis, Roy Roberts and the teacher, then headmaster Del Harris, who tremendously helped in Gwyn's recuperation. Iorrie was club captain 1945-49, a great man in the club's history.) *'And he'd go to the Taff's Well Inn to see Cassie. I would have liked to have seen him playing – he was such a big man. I mean he had arms – out there, like my legs. He was about six feet – but the sheer size of him! When he was playing at Cardiff I was told by people like Cliff Jones, who had played with him, how wonderful he was. He went north, you know, but as he was only about twenty-two to twenty-three when he was wounded, **the best of Gwyn wasn't seen.**'*

ENID WILLIAMS' THOUGHTS OF GWYN:
'Gwyn my eldest brother was an inspiration. He used to take me around with him – up into the woods for walks. He would put me on his shoulders to pick nuts and so on, and then he would take me to teach me to swim in the pool. As you know, he played for Cardiff against the New Zealand All Blacks in 1935 when he was seventeen, well he wanted me to go and see him play. My father said "there'll be too many people there and she'll be crushed" because I was only nine. Well, I went and there was a dog track there in those days, and Gwyn sat me on the rail so I wouldn't be amongst the crowd. Of course, I didn't know much about rugby and I told Gwyn there was one thing with which I was disappointed. I said, "you told me you were going to play all black players and they were not black at all – they were white.' He laughed you know – well he was eight years older than myself. He was a wonderful person; he was so kind and gentle – and to think that those terrible things happened to him.'

'MAIR WILLIAMS (THE YOUNGEST DAUGHTER)
'shares the family affection for the eldest brother: "I don't remember my oldest brothers and sisters living at home – there's too much of an age gap – but somehow I have a vague memory of Gwyn getting married. I must have been very young. I only just remember Enid and Joan at home. And my eldest sister is twenty years older than me. But I knew Gwyn of course, I was close to him as well. When he came home, he always used to come to me for dinner. Oh, Gwyn was lovely."'

I was lucky to speak to Mair and met her at her home. Mair married a local man, Brian Phillips, who worked at Forgemasters in Taff's Well. When Gwyn went to buy a cottage in Swanage, beautiful and quiet, he worked as a school caretaker. Mair's memory is that Gwyn was always immaculately turned out, with shiny black shoes – *'Once a Guardsman, always a Guardsman, I suppose'*. He married Eunice, who he met at a dance in Caerphilly where he was a PC. Eunice was a nurse in Caerphilly Miners' Hospital. After his injury, Gwyn worked at County Hall, Cardiff, then moved to Swanage where they had a small bungalow, Mair going there for holidays. Gwyn used to come back and stay at his mother's, until Nell Williams moved into a retirement home in Llantwit Fardre, then he stayed with brother Tony and then at a hotel in Cathedral Road, Cardiff. He used to be driven to Glynneath to meet his army friends.

Gwyn was always smiling and seemed content, and Mair used to love seeing him. His wife Eunice, as a former nurse, told Mair that he was often in real pain, and the only way she knew was that tears were running down his face. Mike Roberts, the son of Roy who played alongside Gwyn for Taff's Well and Cardiff, remembers his father telling him that Gwyn had to sometimes go into hospital to have pieces of shrapnel removed from his eye wound and body. Gwyn sometimes wore a patch and sometimes a glass eye. I asked Mair how her father, a coal tipper, could afford to bring up 12 children. Arthur Williams did not own his house – in general only the middle and upper classes could afford houses. If there was a small working-class family, one of the children might be lucky to be left the house in a will. The house in Moy Road was rented.

Mair told me that she, her mother and three sisters all sewed and knitted, which saved money, and her father Arthur Williams grew a lot of vegetables, supplemented by baskets of home-grown vegetables, brought by her grandfather Ted Roberts. She does not remember going hungry at all, just that her mother was always working, washing clothes by hand, heating a 'flat-iron' on the stove to iron clothes, etc. There was no bathroom, so she sometimes went to her grandfather's house for a bath, but there was no lock on the door. There was a tin bath in the kitchen, filled by water from a gas boiler, and it was emptied out into the yard. There was an outside toilet and gas lighting. There were three bedrooms, and a boxroom that Mair had. Her parents had a bedroom, and the youngest 5 boys shared the other two rooms. She remembers on match days her 'mam' making bacon and eggs for the boys' breakfasts, and the four youngest brothers cleaning their boots outside the kitchen. Enid was the sister who followed Cardiff the most, and knew all the statistics and players.

Arthur Lougher Williams's mother was a Lougher, one of Bryn's Christian names, which was supposed to be from a rich family. Roy Roberts was Nell Williams' younger brother. Mair's son Rhys played for Cardiff Under-11s, and Wales Under-20s but was injured. Her other son Gareth played for Cardiff Under-11s, Cardiff Youth and a couple of games for Bridgend but damaged his knees. He played for the District with Mark Fenwick, one of the three Fenwick brothers. Mair hardly knew the oldest children, for instance Bryn was away for 6 years during the war. She said that no-one who had fought ever mentioned the war. Bryn would never go on a plane again – it probably held too many memories. So although his wife went overseas on holidays, Bryn would never go. Mair hardly knew the first four children – Dilys was 19 years older, so had left home; Gwyn joined Wigan in 1938 and then was at war; Bryn left for war when Mair was 3 and did not return for 6 years; and Bleddyn, 12 years older, went off to Rydal for 3 years and then was also away in the war.

BLEDDYN ON GWYN, 1984:

'My brother Gwyn was a remarkably good rugby player; he was mainly a wing forward, but he was equally good at centre. He would have played for Wales had he not turned League, there's no question of that. I met several in my RAF days who had played against Gwyn and they were full of praise for him. The great England player Air Marshall Gus Walker, who had played against Gwyn, not only in the Services but also in games against Cardiff, said to me: "Your brother was the finest wing forward I've ever played against – he sorted me out without any bother!" Another great English outside half, Nim Hall, said exactly the same thing. Anyway, Gwyn went to Wigan and when I was at Rydal (the public school at Colwyn Bay), *he used to come over from there. Thirteen of that Wigan team were Welsh, including the legendary back Jim Sullivan.*

When I was at Heaton Park Manchester, waiting to go to America for my RAF training, I played on a number of rugby league grounds, including those of Salford and Wigan. At Wigan I met the chairman who had been club chairman when Gwyn was there. He it was, who wanted me to turn professional there and then. I declined the offer saying that I couldn't serve two bosses, and I wouldn't be allowed to turn professional in any case. But I made it clear that if I ever thought of going, I would choose Wigan. Gwyn of course was playing for The Guards, the British Army and the Welsh Services side. Strangely, when I joined the Services, I was selected to play with him at Gloucester – I'd only been in the RAF a few weeks. As it transpired, he went out to North Africa the week before, and consequently didn't play. They wanted to keep him in London to play rugby, but he said, "My regiment is going out, so I'm going with them". On the actual day I was playing in that game or near that day, Gwyn was shot by a sniper. He'd only been there a week.

There's another story about Gwyn involving me. I had found out from my mother that he had been brought over to a hospital in Oxford, so I decided to go down on the weekend. Anyway, the officer in charge (who knew I wanted to visit my brother) said to me "I understand Williams that you went to Rydal – well just because we went to the same school, means that you'll not get any favours from me, so you're not going." Well, I ignored him and went. I jumped on a train and went to see my brother who had horrendous injuries - shot in the head, a plate put in there, he was paralysed, he'd lost all his memory, didn't even know his wife. Incredibly, I was the first one he recognised – I felt pleased I had gone there, and my colleagues had covered for me in any case. It is amazing what some people are like, though. Sometimes it's just jealousy. When I was in London waiting to go to Cambridge that time, there was a corporal who knew I loved to play rugby, and when I was due to play for Rosslyn Park, he would keep me till the last minute scrubbing floors. Then I would have to dash away and get the Tube to arrive in time for the game.

I remember after I was commissioned as a pilot officer. I was home on leave and I was walking down St. Mary Street (Cardiff), *when who should be coming up the other way but Gwyn in his Oxford blue suit and a patch on his eye. That was when **Del Harris* the headmaster at Taff's Well school was teaching Gwyn to read and write again**. Anyway, Gwyn looked me up and down and he said "Our kid, you look wonderful – but get your bloody shoes cleaned!" Typical of the Guards – they polished everything! I saw him on and off during the war years. Of course, he worked at the City Hall for some time, but could only do menial jobs. My mother had a wonderful letter from one of the specialists who operated on him. The letter which came explained that although medicine played its part in Gwyn's recovery, what had really brought him through was his magnificent physique and strength and the will to live. He was very popular at the City Hall and when he retired, he moved to Swanage, Dorset. He lived until he was 78, which was quite remarkable considering his horrendous injuries, and the fact that he had by chance been seen to stir, amongst those who lost their lives and were on their way to burial in North Africa. His widow died only a few months ago.'*

*Del Harris was a marvellous teacher, then headmaster at Taff's Well School, beloved by all the Williams boys, and in his spare time coached the School XV. He played rugby for Taff's Well with Gwyn and Bryn Williams, plus Gwyn's uncle Roy Roberts. He also taught rugby to Bleddyn, Vaughan, Lloyd, Cenydd, Elwyn and Tony Williams. When Bleddyn helped Gwyn's recovery, Gwyn could not remember his wife, nor anything about his life except playing rugby as a youngster. Del Harris used to regularly visit Gwyn when he came home from hospital, helping him memorise his life, and teaching him to read, write and count from scratch. After school, and on weekends, Del spent over 18 months helping Gwyn's recuperation. A wonderful man.

THE ALLURE OF RUGBY LEAGUE by Keith Bowen

Jack Bowen's son Bleddyn, known as Keith, sent me the following from his fastidious research upon 'Wigan Welsh' and other RL players: 'There is a well-known book in Rugby League circles, called "They went North" by Robert Gate, published in two volumes. It details the many Welshmen who left their country and became professional Rugby League players in

England, from the start of the Northern Union as it was called, in 1895 to present day. Men who were induced to play the game they loved for money by switching codes from Rugby Union to Rugby League. A signing on fee and a decent weekly wage, especially if your team won, and Wigan tended to win the majority of games they played, my father was one of these players. Wales was a fertile ground for the rugby league clubs and Wigan were just one of many top-class sides that brought good players back from Wales to play a slightly different version of rugby. It wasn't without danger for both sides. The club usually made a hefty investment, the player gave up his amateur status, his Welsh lifestyle, language sometimes and quite often the chance of ever playing his beloved Union game ever again. This was because in those days the Rugby Union authorities permanently banned their players if they crossed the threshold and moved to the professional game. It reflected the fear perhaps in Union circles that their very best players may eventually be lost to them and their game. The other risk was that the player may find they could not fully adapt to this different game and the club may have wasted their money.

{25 JANUARY 1899 LLANDAFF SMITH? who did sign for Wigan

POACHING FOOTBALLERS IN SOUTH WALES.

A WIGAN AGENT'S EXPERIENCE.

The " Western Mail " (Cardiff) states :—After the Llanelly-Penarth match on Saturday afternoon a representative of the Wigan club intercepted Smith, of Penarth, and made overtures to him to leave Penarth, arranging to meet him at the Railway Hotel, where drinks were freely handed round. Coming to business, he offered Smith a sovereign to come into town with him that night. A cab was engaged, and instructions were given to the cabman to drive to Cardiff, via the beach. As soon as they got to the beach, however, another member of the Penarth team made his appearance, and the visitor from Wigan was hauled out, rushed down the boat club stage, and thrown into the water. He was then seized and rolled into the sand and mud. He was left to make the best of matters, and made his way to the Cardiff police station, where he complained that he had been robbed of a sovereign by two Penarth footballers, but was referred to the Penarth police, and nothing further has been heard of the matter.

1899 Llandaff Smith poaching

However, prior to the professionalisation of the game in 1995, it was a sad and depressing sight, from a Welsh point of view, to see the cream of the national side and even good club players disappearing to the north of England to play, what was to the union men, an alien game. Often these players would achieve fame and "fortune" (dubious at that time) in Rugby

148

League, yet this would go largely unnoticed in their home communities in Wales, and league players were even banned from attending rugby union clubhouses. My father testifies to that, as does Billy Boston and many others. Thankfully times have changed, and Billy is now welcomed and has been honoured in his own country, as well as in Wigan also. The exodus from Wales by "amateur" Rugby Union players started from 1895 (the game was never truly amateur) when the great split occurred between the Union game and the clubs in the north of England who broke away and introduced professionalism. It remained essentially the same 15-a- side game until 1905 when numbers were reduced to the 13-a- side game we know today, although the Northern Union only played games against one another.

To venture into the "Valleys" could be an intimidating experience for Rugby League scouts, after all they were trying to take away the best local talent and at the same time depriving local communities of their team's star players. The feeling of anger is understandable. However, in the 1920's and 1930's economic conditions in Wales were stressful and players often needed to improve their lot, and if signing professionally was the way out, then many were prepared to do just that. The fate of one such scout is documented in a local newspaper. It happened in January 1899 when a representative of the Wigan club intercepted Llandaff Smith of Penarth, and made overtures to him to leave Penarth, arranging to meet him at the Railway Hotel, where drinks were freely handed round. Smith was offered a sovereign to meet the scout that night, a cab was arranged and instructions to the driver were to go to Cardiff, via the beach. However, as soon as they got to the beach another member of the Penarth team arrived and the Wigan visitor was seized, and thrown in the water, then rolled in the sand. The visitor had to make his own way to the Cardiff police station to complain that he'd been robbed of a sovereign by two Penarth footballers, and the crime was referred to Penarth police, but nothing further was heard of the matter. It transpires that did not deter Llandaff Smith, who signed for Wigan, but only played a total of 8 games in the 1899 - 1900 season, before returning home. It could be looked on as if Smith took the money, played a few games and then he went home. I suppose we'll never know the full truth of the matter.

Wigan were frequent "raiders" into the Principality and I have compiled a list of Welsh players who signed for Wigan from 1895 to 1939 the outbreak of WW2. A total of 110 joined Wigan, one of whom was my father when there were no fewer than 16 Welsh born players on the books of the Central Park club in the 1938 - 1939 season. This represented 40% of the players Wigan had on their books. Welsh players continued to be signed after the war but on a smaller scale, as local players had successfully filled the gaps and produced great sides.

However, one of the greatest ever Welsh signings happened in 1953 when the fabulous Billy Boston was signed. He often brought me to my feet, along with thousands of other Wigan fans, as he got the ball and threatened the opponents' line, as often as not scoring a great try. He had everything, pace, guile, power and a great football brain, small wonder the good people of Wigan have honoured him with a statue in the town, to this genuinely modest great of the game. His greatness is now recognised in his own hometown of Cardiff, where along with other Cardiff Welshmen who went North and found fame, such as Gus Risman and Clive Sullivan, another statue of these three is to be erected in the Cardiff Bay area. An indication of how the prejudice of previous years has melted away since Rugby Union became a professional sport for the first time, allowing players to be paid to play for the first time in 1995, just 100 years after the Northern Union broke away and left to play professional Rugby League.

…Johnny Thomas was an early Welsh import, playing his first game on Christmas Eve 1904 and his last in April 1920, making a total of 435 first team appearances. At one time he was Landlord of one of the busiest pubs in Wigan, the Royal Oak, in Standishgate, later run by another later Welsh recruit, Wilf Hodder, before Thomas took over the running a Hotel in Morecambe, the hometown of his wife. Johnny was one of the first to welcome my father to Wigan. Johnny's career had ended some 18 years earlier, but he was not short of advice for my father, which went along the lines, *"Look after your money, Jack. I wish I had, I would have loved to have gone home as a successful sportsman who also excelled in business."* Alas it was not to be, Johnny without doubt, had a great and successful rugby career but his business acumen fell short of those wonderful accomplishments. Perhaps, unlike his exploits on the field, where he never took his eye off the ball, that perhaps wasn't the case when he ran the Royal Oak. Jim Sullivan always offered similar advice to all new recruits to the club. Tommy Thomas was another early Welsh recruit, he played just 35 games from 1906 to 1908, however, the Wigan club reluctantly took him to court for breach of contract, when after going home to Wales, he failed to return. It was a difficult situation, Wigan were trying to protect their investment, while Tommy was trying to protect his family. (I have articles giving details on his court case).

The main reason that Tommy wasn't able to remain at Wigan was because his Welsh wife Ellen, after moving up north with him could not settle due to "homesickness", she simply did not have the support network that she enjoyed at home in Wales. After becoming pregnant in the close season of 1907, she returned home while Tommy kept on commuting back and fore until early in 1908 when they lost the child at birth.

After the funeral Tommy never returned. Wigan did not take their action lightly but at Liverpool Crown Court Wigan were awarded £65 and costs. Tommy then signed for the Merthyr Rugby League team for £65 the exact sum of the judgement against him, it seems the Merthyr club paid the summons as a signing on fee. Tommy and his wife went on to have 12 children, four of whom were boys, and all of them went on to inherit their father's nickname "*Wigan*", as is the way in Wales, e.g. "*Jones the Milk*". Many Welsh signings played only 10 games or less, but also a lot of young Welshmen, after arriving at the club, went on to marry local girls. This, I think, was without doubt, a stabilising influence on their careers and encouraged their stay at the club. It ensured that despite setbacks, that any professional player will experience in their careers, they kept their faith in maintaining their stay at the club. They had a stable family base in Wigan itself because the wife had her relatives close to hand. Some of the Wigan Welsh who married locally were the legendary, Jim Sullivan (played 1921 - 1946), Gwyn Davies (1930 - 1940), Albert Davis (1933 - 1945), Frank Stephens (1925 - 1931), Johnny Thomas (1904 -1920) and Danny Hurcombe (1919 - 1926), as well as my father, Jack Bowen (1938 - 1948). There were undoubtedly many more over the years. I know that the players mentioned all had long careers at the club. In later years, after WW2, there was of course the brilliant Billy Boston (1953 - 1968) who also married a local girl. I also know that 4 of these 7 players went on to run public houses in the town after retirement, again many more players did the same.

No one at Wigan had a career as long as Jim Sullivan. He joined at the age of 17 from Cardiff RU one of the top Welsh clubs, where he was holding down the first team full back position at the tender age of 16, a child prodigy who lived up to his reputation in every respect. Jim had already represented the Barbarians. Some records he set are still standing, a prolific goal kicker, his sporting prowess was not limited to rugby. He was a Welsh baseball player and was seriously considering a professional career as a golfer. My father told me Jim was also almost unbeatable at snooker. He was a sporting phenomenon who played from 1921 until his last game in 1946. He had a commanding presence on the field, and all his colleagues, to a man, considered him the finest player of their generation. A strong and powerful presence, he continued as a very successful coach at Wigan and then at St Helens. A few incidents are worth relating. It's commonly known that Jim was probably the greatest ever goal kicker the game has known. Just how accurate was Jim? My father told me that during a training session Jim asked him to stand at the half-way line, positioned on the touchline. Jim took the football and from under the posts and out of hand, he kicked the ball repeatedly towards my father, time and time again, he repeated the kick. Almost on all occasions my father had to move but a step or two, either way, in order to catch the ball, such was Jim's accuracy from some 50 yards away.

During a match in those days, kicking for positional play, between full backs, was not uncommon. Jim was a master at this, his long kicking was unsurpassed. However, at times a high kick from the opposition full back was such that it enabled the opposing players to try and reach the ball, before Jim could collect it. At this point Jim would position himself and ensure the ball was going to be his, and to underline this fact he would use very loud and colourful language. The effect of this would be discourage the opposition, not only that but Jim's explosive language was so unnerving it also alarmed his own team-mates at times. If the opposition persisted and still attempted to catch the ball they would have to contend with a speciality of Jim's, his flailing sharp elbows, which underlined his determination. The rules were slightly different in those days as often one or more of the opposition players, who had been brave enough to try and wrest the ball from Jim, found themselves lying on the ground, while Jim prepared to kick again or link up with his players. Finally, as far as Jim is concerned, he was a leader, he had strong views and an imposing personality.'

JAMES 'JIM' SULLIVAN (2 December 1903 – 14 September 1977)
The youngest Cardiff player aged 16, (it seems to be either Jim Sullivan or Gwyn Williams)
'The greatest ever rugby player'
The **youngest Barbarian** 28 December 1920 vs Newport (aged 17 yrs 26 days)
Welsh trial aged 17
Cardiff 1919-20 to 1921-22, 38 appearances
Wigan 1921-1946 (aged 43) 774 games, 83 tries, 2,317 goals, 4,883 points, a **world record** (his records would have been higher but for war)
Captain-Coach of Wigan 1932-1946 – three league championships, two challenge cups
Wigan coach 1932-1952
St Helens Coach 1952-1961
Wigan Coach 1961, retired through ill-health
Three RL Lions tours, highest points scorer on all
60 International Test matches –25 for Great Britain - a record until recent times
World Record for most first-team appearances in Rugby League - 928

'the greatest Welshman ever to be signed' - Eddie Waring
'bestrode the Rugby League world like a colossus and was unquestionably the pre-eminent player of his era' – Robert Gate

Jim Sullivan knew Gwyn Williams and was instrumental in bringing Gwyn to Wigan. Sullivan was internationally the most famous player in rugby league, with claims to be the greatest ever rugby player, certainly of the inter-war years. He had played 38 times for Cardiff from 1919-20 to 1920-21 and will have known of Gwyn's prowess. Born in Elaine Street, Splott, and a product of St. Albans School, Cardiff, Jim Sullivan played for

Cardiff Firsts against Neath on 16 October 1920, aged just 16 years and 10 months.

Two months later he became the youngest Baa-Baa, playing against Newport aged 17 years and 26 days. An apprentice boilermaker, he was put on standby for Wales vs France on 26 February 1921. If chosen he would have been 17 years and 3 months old, a world record, but because of unemployment he signed for a record fee to join Wigan – the same as paid the previous year for Cardiff's international right-wing Wickham 'Wick' Powell. Words cannot describe his career. Also a Wales baseball player, he was holding down the full back position at Cardiff aged 16 and 17. When Sullivan signed for Wigan, he became known as the '*bargain of the century*', and a sporting phenomenon, he considered at one time becoming a professional golfer (he was that good) and according to Bleddyn Bowen's father, the RL star Jack, Jim was unbeatable at billiards and snooker.

Several rugby league clubs wanted him, and in June 1921 he signed professional forms for Wigan, then the best team in Britain. In December he played for Wales rugby league when they lost 21-16 to Australia. Sullivan toured with the Great Britain Lions three times (1924, 1928 and 1932) and was captain on the last occasion. He top-scored on all three tours, but refused a record fourth trip in 1936, for personal reasons. During the Second World War, he played infrequently for Wigan, as he chose to appear as a guest for a number of other clubs, including Dewsbury, Keighley and Bradford Northern.

Over 20 years, Sullivan made 60 appearances at representative level for England, Wales, Great Britain and Other Nationalities. He retired in 1946, after 774 appearances, scoring 83 tries, 2,317 goals and 4,883 points for one club, a record that may never be beaten. He scored another 174 for Dewsbury, 16 for Keighley and 10 for Bradford Northern. And remember, over 5 years of official fixtures were lost because of war. He scored 5,914 points when we include 31 guest appearances for other clubs and 51 representative matches and a world record 60 tests. In 37 games on tour for Great Britain 'Big Jim' accumulated 424 points. These figures are still unchallenged. With Wigan, he won three league Championships, two Challenge Cups and three Lancashire Cups. In his 25-year career, Sullivan made 928 first team appearances, a figure unmatched anywhere in the world. Jim Sullivan died in his hometown of Cardiff on 1 November 1977, becoming one of the inaugural inductees of the British Rugby League Hall of Fame in October 1988. His rugby league admirers included the former coach of Sullivan and rugby league commentator, Eddie Waring, who called Sullivan: '*the greatest Welshman ever to be signed.*'

Robert Gate, the eminent Rugby League historian said of Jim Sullivan: '*Throughout the 1920s and 1930s one man bestrode the Rugby League world like a colossus and was unquestionably the pre-eminent player of his era*'. Danny Davies, Cardiff Rugby Union outside-half and historian, wrote: *'had he remained an amateur he would most probably have become Cardiff's greatest of all full backs.'* And Gus Risman (Salford, Wales & Great Britain): *'Few men can ever have loved their sport more than Jim. he simply lived for it, and it was, perhaps, this passionate love for the game which made him such a remarkable player. So many fullbacks are either good in defence or in attack. Yet Jim Sullivan was simply brilliant at both.'* In 1946 he retired aged 43, but in 1944 when playing for a South Wales XV in a charity match, he clattered Bleddyn Williams, having been forewarned that Williams had a devastating side-step. Jim Sullivan then coached Wigan (1946-52) and St Helens (1952-59), both with the greatest success, before a spell with, before 3 years coaching Rochdale Hornets, returning to Wigan for a year but then retiring with ill health in 1961. That is a very truncated story of a fabulous player from Cardiff, and great personal friend of Gwyn.

1938 Lancashire cup

Jack Bowen of Llanelli joined Wigan a couple of months before Gwyn. He played in the 1938 Lancashire Cup Final, just 12 weeks after signing for Wigan, and according to his son, 'Dad was coming off the pitch at Rodney Parade, home to the Newport RU club, having played for the Probables team in the Final Welsh Trial, scoring a try in the process and surrounded by spectators who'd come onto the pitch at the end of the game. Two Directors, Tom Brown and Harry Platt were the two who came down to sign him in Llanelli, along with another Director Tom Hesketh and ex-Wigan Welsh player Wilf Hodder and formerly with Talywain RFC, Pontypool RFC and holder of 6 Welsh RU caps. Harry Platt was the one, who after the Welsh trial match ended, had wandered onto the pitch, mingling with some of the spectators. Out of the corner of his mouth and without a glance to dad, he rasped, *"Are you interested in League?"* and equally furtively my father answered curtly from the side of his mouth, *"Yes"* without a look. Harry was wearing a 'Humphrey Bogart 'style raincoat and trilby pulled well down to help cover his face, and with that he melted into the throng of spectators. It was a few months later when Harry, accompanied by fellow Directors Tom Brown (Landlord of the Park Hotel in Wigan centre), and fellow Director Wilf Hodder secured dad's signature. To celebrate, my grandmother, my father's mother, renowned for her culinary dishes, provided all with a slap-up meal. Tom Brown was so impressed with the meal that he never failed to regale my father with memories of it whenever they met. It could be a "dangerous" business for Rugby League scouts in those days and for my father. If it had come to light that he'd talked to RL officials he could have been stopped from playing RU. This was January and it was April when he signed for Wigan, he had to keep it quiet. I still have the contract but there is no sign of dad's signature on it.'…

'In the 1938 Final, Jim Sullivan had kicked all Wigan's points. Jim also had persuaded my father to play, but he had a broken small toe which was troubling him. Jim (ever the bluff "bully" or as some would have it, "leader") would have none of it – *"as soon as you start the game you won't notice it."* Dad played and according to reports had a good game, it was also reported that he tackled Alan Edwards (Salford's great Welsh winger) when he broke through. It would have been a certain try otherwise and would have changed the outcome. Wigan won 10 - 7. Jim kicked 5 goals. Jim was a colossus, if he was gathering a high kick, which was a frequent occurrence, he would shout expletives etc., that were so loud and alarming that it often put the wind up his own team mates never mind the opposition. As soon as he'd collected the ball, his arms and elbows would be flailing in all directions, any opposition player silly enough to be near him would soon regret it. In that final, the Salford winger Brown, a Wigan-born player came flying down the wing to be met by Jim who promptly knocked him head over heels into touch, without bending his back, no reprimand from the ref but on the second occasion Brown was slightly concussed, so the referee had a word. Jim had everything. 7 Welshmen played for Wigan in the final. Bowen, Sullivan, Ike Jones, Morley, Ward, Davies, Thomas. Jack Morley qualified as a Dentist after retirement and set up a practice, I believe in Newport.' *The Manchester Guardian* praised '*the Old Master'* Sullivan, in its headline for the unexpected win against Gus Risman's Salford, and commented '*the man who took the eye most was Jack Bowen, the Wigan loose forward, and well though his opposite number, Feetham, played, the honours easily went to the Wigan man.*' Because of his foot injury, Jack Bowen could not play loose forward for the next 10 weeks, so Gwyn Williams played there. When Bowen returned to the side, Gwyn moved to the wing, and there were 8 Welsh regular first-teamers in the 13-

man 'Wigan Welsh' side.

CHAPTER 16 - CARDIFF SEASON 1945 – 1946

THE FIRST FULL SEASON SINCE 1938-39 – '*A LEGEND WAS CREATED*' - CARDIFF'S BRILLIANT POST-WAR REVIVAL – AN ALMOST UNBEATEN SEASON - '*THE GREATEST RUGBY CLUB*': *HANSARD* – WILF WOOLLER

Bleddyn Williams P21 T30 90pts; **Bryn Williams** (Athletic); **Roy Roberts** P1 (Taff's Well); **Bill Tamplin** P33 C16 P4 44pts; Ray Bale P34 T3 9pts (Tongwynlais); Basil Evans P2 (Pentyrch)
The First XV appearances per season of the Williams brothers and the players from their local villages are denoted P (- played). There follows T (try), C (conversion), P (penalty) and D (dropped goal). Scores are try 3pts; conversion 2 points; penalty 3 points, and dropped goal 4 points until 1948, when it became 3 points)

'*ATOM BOMB Little did one realise that Cardiff were to burst upon the new era of peace like an atom bomb in the game. They were superb, and Dr. Jack Matthews an ideal leader, inspirer and controller. Then came Haydn Tanner and all the good players wanted to join Cardiff. It was so, because the war-time committee, "living on a shoestring" had kept the club alive and Cardiff had much more than a head start over their rivals. It was hard for the other clubs and many became envious because of the publicity the Club received. Critics went to watch Cardiff at the Arms Park, because the papers of the day wanted news and reports of their activities. People wanted to read about them.*' (It seems difficult to believe, but Cardiff reports featured in all the national press, such as the *Times, Daily Express, Sunday Telegraph, The People, Manchester Guardian, Daily Mail* etc.) '*Cardiff were the glamour boys of those first years of peace and the team gave many hours of pleasure to thousands, long before the advent of B.B.C. TV... **A LEGEND WAS CREATED** in those four years before the other great clubs recovered from the disaster of war... In the 100 years of life the club has won much and has beaten all three major touring teams in turn. It has produced great players and shared in great matches... The Club enjoys playing. Other clubs enjoy playing against the club and if they tried hard to beat Cardiff, then they are doing the right thing and paying Cardiff a compliment.*' – J.B.G. Thomas (Chief Rugby Writer, *Western Mail*), writing of Cardiff's immediate success and influence after the war, '*Cardiff's Centenary Year – Many Years of Fun*

P40: W32, L6, D2. Pts 661:233. <u>Tries 149-44</u>, Pens 18-19

8 May 1945 saw V-E Day, victory in Europe, when Germany officially surrendered. In that month, the Welsh Rugby Union had not resumed its normal activities, but Cardiff had available 35 players between its two teams, many of whom had played in war-time charity games and for their respective armed services. They included Bleddyn Williams, his cousin 'Bill' Tamplin, Les Manfield, Cliff Davies, Ray Bale, Billy Cleaver and Billy Darch. The club now began arranging fixtures upon an 'official' basis, captained by Bleddyn's greatest and inseparable friend, Dr. 'Jack' Matthews. As a Bridgend schoolboy, Matthews had been a Welsh sprint champion, and had joined Cardiff from Cardiff Medical School. A captain in the R.A.M.C., he had captained Cardiff 'Meds' in war time, when it defeated a Cardiff team 28-26, and he also captained army teams.

Danny Davies records: '*Jack Matthews was one of the strongest running centres of his time, his devastating tackling was I think, much feared by opponents. His speed and breaks through the centre made scores of tries for his co-centres and wings. Strong in personality, he was, with his colleagues, Bleddyn Williams, W. B. "Billy" Cleaver and later on, Rex Willis, destined to win the highest honours in the game... The brilliance of our centre Bleddyn Williams, to become one of the greatest centres of all time, the superb qualities of Billy Cleaver at outside half, who was a great reader of a game and one of the best tactical kickers of his day, formed the best mid-field triangle in Rugby football for some seasons. But there were also other players in Dr. Jack's XV who became great players; Maldwyn James a hooker of much craft and confidence; Lt. W. E. Tamplin one of the best post war leaders of a pack, strong in personality and an excellent kicker of goals; and Squadron Leader Les Manfield of the R.A.F., a great back row forward, already capped from Mountain Ash prior to the war, and set to gain many more with Cardiff.*

In addition we had our pre-war wing Graham Hale; Ray Bale our vice-captain, also capped for his club pre-war as a prop; at least three "medicals" now qualified, in Drs. Glyn Jones a wing, D. St. John Rees at full-back, and Hubert Jones another back row forward We also had George Tomkins and Gerry Blackmore, both forwards and now qualified mining officials; and the best 'nugget' of the props Cliff Davies the great-hearted character, the simple miner, beloved by all, who gained sixteen Welsh caps and a British Lions tour to New Zealand in 1950. Not to be forgotten was W. E. "Billy" Darch the diminutive and popular scrum half from the Rhondda. There were many heart-burnings when Billy Darch was superseded by Haydn Tanner who joined the club in January 1947. And so, "We were off!" Our team blended well and it was not long before our brilliant performances became the talk of the country, our "gates" were a godsend to the finances of the club, we were unbeaten until we met the "Kiwis" - the touring New Zealand Army team on Boxing Day and lost by a solitary try on a very heavy pitch, governed by much gruelling forward play. The New Zealand broadcaster Winston McCarthy described the match as a "Wales/New Zealand affair - where Rugby football is a religion supported by fervent singing"'.

In his biography, Bleddyn Williams pays tribute to the men who, unpaid, kept the Cardiff club going throughout the war years. *'Cardiff's strength was due entirely to the fact that the club had kept going throughout the war years, and the team formed the nucleus of players who had been regular performers despite war service. Many of the players went to great inconvenience to obtain leave to play, and often long distances had to be travelled. But I should certainly say that the results justified the means... Dr. Jack's leadership played a major role in our progress. Never have I met a more courageous player, who sacrificed everything for team unity, and who commanded such respect and admiration from his team that he almost never had to push his authority.* (Remember that there was no team manager, no coach, no team of physicians and analysts and all the paraphernalia of modern rugby). *Orders were given in a manner that inspired confidence, but generally the team pattern was so closely woven that tactics were virtually automatic; every man knowing exactly what was required of him and how to carry out his duty. This unequalled team coordination was the "secret" of Cardiff's sensational success. We were like a touring team, playing together regularly, completely intimate with each other's style of play and confident in each other's ability. We played attacking Rugby, as our points scoring clearly shows, and this policy not only brought crowds to the Arms Park, but carried us to the top of the popularity poll as Britain's No1 Rugby club of the year... That 1945-46 season was a year of vintage football. Some of the glories of the fabled "Golden Era" of Rugby were recaptured by the very spirit of adventure that marked every Cardiff game.'* Still in the RAF for part of the season, and playing in Victory Internationals and representative games, Bleddyn Williams only managed 21 appearances, compared to his cousin Bill Tamplin's 33, who was also involved in internationals. However, Bleddyn still touched down 30 times.

At last, with V-J Day (Victory over Japan, for younger readers) 2 September 1945, WWII was over. The fighting at least – but the country had the enormous task of reconstruction ahead. After eleven wins, Cardiff travelled to play a strong Coventry side on 17 November 1945, who had played 63 consecutive home games undefeated. The Cardiff centres Jack Matthews and Bleddyn Williams scored a try apiece and the wing Dr. Glyn Jones touched down twice, with two conversions by Maldwyn James. In front of a record crowd of around 15,000, Coventry scored a try, to make it

158

16-3 to the *'Blue and Blacks'*.

Eight VICTORY internationals began in 1945 when France were beaten 8-0 at Swansea. In 1946 Wales beat Ireland 6-4 at Cardiff and England 3-0 at Twickenham, then lost 25-13 to England at Cardiff; and lost 25-6 and 13-11 to Scotland at Swansea and Murrayfield; 12-0 to France in Paris and 11-3 to the 2nd New Zealand Expeditionary Forces ('The Kiwis') in a famous match at Cardiff. Lt. Cardiff unluckily also lost 3-0 to the Kiwis in the 1945 Boxing Day mud, but the Kiwis only lost two games on tour. Six weeks earlier, Wilf Wooller, now repatriated from being a Japanese P.O.W., kicked off in his service uniform for Cardiff against a strong New Zealand Services XV. The NZ Reserve XV played Northampton the same day. Cardiff won 14-3, 4 tries to a penalty. Cardiff supplied 13 players for the 'unofficial' Welsh international matches (where no caps were awarded) but remarkably won matches which clashed with those of the W.R.U. (The W.R.U had arranged their internationals after Cardiff's fixture list was completed - one might believe that Cardiff were not in the W.R.U.'s good books…)

Newport alone scored 36 of the 233 points against Cardiff, in 4 games. In a charity match, the Cardiff Past team were the highest points scorers in a single game against Cardiff present with 17, followed by Richmond with 13, and that score against a very make-shift Cardiff team. This was an astonishing season – because of war and then National Service, Cardiff had lost players, including their internationals Ken Street, Leslie Magnus 'Les' Spence and captain Wilf Wooller (except for a charity match and one game for Wilf, when Cardiff were short of players), and 13 others were chosen for Victory Internationals. However, Jack Matthews' team lost just 6 games in the season, and those only by a 15 points total: Kiwis 3-0; Cognac 19-18; Newport 7-3 and 6-3; Leicester 12-8; and Barbarians 10-9. And this in 40 matches, often missing players – it is an incredible record. In their two 3-3 draws, both away, Cardiff scored a try to a penalty in each, 5-3 wins in today's scoring. We can see that over 40 official games, Cardiff scored 3.4-1 on tries, but lost the penalty count 19-18. That is how rugby should be played, by outscoring the opposition upon tries.

And Bleddyn Williams was now in the same team as his uncle Roy Roberts and his first cousin Bill Tamplin, all of them returning after war service. After a 17-match unbeaten record, a possibly hungover team lost 3-0 on Boxing Day 1945 to the 'The Kiwis', a strong New Zealand Army team stuffed with internationals, but 6 weeks earlier had defeated *'a stronger New Zealand Services XV'* by 14-3. Dr. Jack Matthews recalled the defeat: *'This was my first season as captain (1945-46) and we had not been beaten till this meeting with the 'Kiwis'. The game was packed with thrills, our smaller pack playing a heroic game, and we three-quarters making every effort to score. We lost three points to nil – we might have drawn – but we failed with a penalty kick, a game and a kick I will always remember, and a capacity Arms Park crowd'* Of the former game, Davies writes: *'Cardiff's win over the New Zealanders was a splendid one, they were indeed a strong football unit, their Reserve XV taking on Northampton the same day.'* The Kiwis toured Europe, only losing twice in 33 games. On New Years' Eve, after a long journey by sea and coach, Cardiff beat Nantes 29-8, as part of a commitment to help the struggling game in France. On New Year's Day 1946 after four hours on a coach, Cardiff lost to Cognac, at Cognac, by a point 19-18. Their hosts for the evening before, and the morning of, the second game had been members of the Martell and Hennessey brandy families. Cardiff believed that the Cognac team were in attendance, also imbibing freely, but the actual Cognac XV did not attend. The Cardiff boys were very unused to strong spirits – they were simply not available during or after the war. Enough said.

1945-46 Cardiff beat Nantes

Against an excellent Newport team (fixtures had started in 1876), Cardiff won at home and away, 28-17 and 10-6, but also lost home and away, 7-3 and 6-3. They lost away at Leicester 12-8 after beating them at home 12-6. The two draws were at Bristol, 3-3 and at Pontypool by the same 3-3 score after a 25-0 home win. On the *bathrugbyheritage* website, we see that on 19 January 1946, their home match against Cardiff was *'cancelled due to heavy frost. Loss of gate money was a considerable blow, and emphasised the continued need for a public appeal for funds. The game was played upon 21 March: Home. Lost 3-11. The Cardiff side is worthy of note. A correspondent had enquired as to their occupations, and these are added, where known:- St. John Rees (Medical student), Selwyn Evans (Medical student), J Mahoney, W H Wilkins, Graham Hale (Bank Clerk), W B Cleaver (Colliery Manager – a miner before the war), W Darch, W G Jones (Collier), Tom Holley, Geo Tomkins (Assistant Colliery Manager), Cliff Davies (Collier), Ray Bale (Market Gardener), S Miller, Stan Bowes and Hubert Jones (Medical Student). The fabulous 'Billy' Cleaver and Cliff Davies were Cardiff's internationals. Cardiff's superior back play and support won the day, with a goal and two tries to Bath's solitary try by Pears. Astonishingly, Bath's Welsh born hooker, Donald Rees, won the strikes in a ratio of three to one.* (Don Rees joined Cardiff for the next season, playing 28 games before leaving to play rugby league in 1947-48).

Bath gained the ball from the tight 20 times to 6 in the first half, and 13 times to 5 in the second... The turning point came, when the Cardiff scrumhalf gave two dummies near the line, enabling Hubert Jones to go over near the posts, for 'Sinjon' Rees to convert. Tail-piece:- In these times of austerity, Cardiff came prepared – they brought their own lemons!' A later programme compares the abilities of the four Welshmen called Rees who played for Bath: *'Finally, there was the best of all the Rees clan - Don Rees, also in the Army, the best hooker seen in the Bath side for many years. Do you remember his feat at the Rec against Cardiff? He got the ball back 30 times to Cardiff's 11. He is now demobbed, and back in Wales, and the forecast is, for Victor Smith, that he will be in the Cardiff team and the Welsh side this season.'* The prop Stan Bowes had to play hooker in this game, and the point of this excerpt is to show that Cardiff had nowhere near their 'best' side, with men still in the forces, injured or unavailable. Even so, the team was always the greatest 'crowd-puller' in rugby – its record against Bath in 27 games from the first fixture in 1924 to 1975 (16 away) was won 24, drew 1 and lost 3, points for 366 – against 161; tries 79-36. Bath games were nearly always scheduled at Bath, for the day of the England-Wales international, so Cardiff were always missing their best players, sometimes up to ten men.

After a five-year break, Cardiff resumed its annual Barbarians match in April 1946, a series which began in 1891, losing 10-9. It is such a pity that traditional fixtures such as the Baa-Baas (who were founded in the season that they first played Cardiff), Leicester (played annually since 1885), Harlequins (first game 1882), Bristol (1888) and Gloucester (1892) have been lost. I well remember the Baa-Baas' annual Easter Tour, which kicked off at Penarth's ground on Good Friday, followed by Cardiff on Easter Saturday, Swansea on Easter Monday and Newport on the Tuesday. Living in Barry as a schoolboy, it was easy to get the train to see the three local games. Incidentally, in October 1966, the world's first floodlit rugby game was held at the old Arms Park, when Cardiff beat the Barbarians 12-

8. (Some of us remember the 452-yard greyhound racing track which encircled the pitch until 1977. Race distances were 300, 500, 525 and 700 yards).

Squadron Leader **Leslie 'Les' Manfield DFC** (1915-2006) lost 6 years of a great career because of the War. '*A Mountain Ash schoolboy with several schoolboy caps, he scored the winning try against England under-15s in 1930. A teacher took him by car to play, but he had to wear his elder brother's boots. The school staff, finding out, clubbed together and bought him a new pair of boots. His father, a railway signalman, had died and the family had to subsist on his mother's ten shillings a week widow's pension. Still only 15, he played for Mountain Ash Firsts against Aberavon. Les was head prefect for two years at the County School before taking a chemistry degree at Cardiff University and an MSc at Carnegie College in 1938. At Carnegie he was picked for Yorkshire and Otley. He gained no fewer than 19 wartime caps for Wales* (according to Baldwin), *all unofficial, RAF and Combined Services caps and played for the Barbarians. Les Manfield spent three years in the Middle East flying Wellingtons, being promoted to squadron leader. His plane was hit by flak twice whilst flying over Tobruk. While navigating an SOE operation to Crete his plane crash landed in the sea, after the engines failed.*

Manfield and three other crewmen survived at sea for two days before being picked up by a motor torpedo boat. On 4 April 1943, Manfield was awarded the Distinguished Flying Cross for his work in a Special Operations Unit. His 104 Squadron had 126 men killed or missing in action in a six-week period. Somehow, jerseys were made by servicemen, dying them red to meet England at El-Alamain in Egypt and Les skippered a side against England. The match kicked off in the heat on the afternoon of St David's Day in 1945, and Wales won 22-5. Around 15,000 servicemen watched the game with leeks planted on the goalposts, a Welsh flag waving and over 100 Welshmen forming a choir. Seven days later Les led a Wales XV to a 6-3 win over a Rest of the Empire XV at Alexandria. During the war he managed to play in charity games, in two Red Cross Internationals against England, in two Services internationals against England and a Red Cross game for Wales Services. At the war's end, he played in 7 Victory Internationals, and was always noted for his thinning hair.'

Les Manfield played for Cardiff 71 times from 1939-1949 in the second row, and at the time of his death aged 91, was the oldest man, at 34, to have played for Wales. He won his first senior caps in 1939 (winning against Ireland and Scotland). Les had been chosen for the English trials as his parents were English, but preferred to play for his place of birth, winning 7 full caps. His other 5 caps were against Australia (1947), and England, France, Ireland and Scotland (1948). **Les was one of only four men to play for Wales before and after the War**, along with hooker

'Bunner' Travers, scrumhalf Haydn Tanner, and fullback Howard Davies. Les played mainly for Cardiff, but also during his college days and after appeared for Penarth, Mountain Ash, London Welsh, Otley, Neath and Bridgend. His brother, fullback Ron, played a few matches for Cardiff in 1946-47 and just one in 1947-48 but could not displace Frank Trott and joined Pontypool. Les's son, John Manfield joined the club in 1971-72, playing 22 games up to 1973-74. The Cardiff, Wales and British Lion wing Haydn Morris also came from Mountain Ash, but Baldwin placed the prop John 'J.D.' Evans as the town's greatest player. Like Morris, Evans also joined Cardiff after playing for his hometown club, and was one of the inseparable *'three musketeers'* with Lloyd Williams and Peter Nyhan.

In this marvellous first post-war season, Cardiff's performances were such that they drew record crowds at home and away. In *Hansard* on 17 April 1946, it is recorded that James Callaghan, M.P. for Cardiff South, stated: *'I join in the congratulations which have been offered to the Chancellor of the Exchequer on this concession. In South Wales, particularly among the struggling Rugby clubs it is welcome as a valuable help. Speaking as one who has the honour to represent the City which has the finest Rugby Club in the four countries. Hon. members: No. (Opposition came from James Griffiths of Llanelly I understand). Mr. Callaghan: "I must appeal for your protection, Mr. Deputy Speaker. I repeat doubtless I shall be contradicted in later speeches if Hon. Members do not agree with me... that Cardiff Rugby Football Club is undoubtedly the finest Rugby football club. On their behalf, and on behalf of all those other Rugby clubs, particularly the smaller ones, in the South Wales area who have been struggling very hard, I welcome this as a valuable concession.'*

Dr. Jack Matthews scored two tries on the successful Cornish tour, also meeting his future wife. Invited a second year to the Middlesex Sevens, the team was: Dai Jones, Jack Matthews, Bleddyn Williams, W. B. Cleaver, Hubert Jones, Cliff Davies and George Tomkins. After beating Wasps and London Scottish, Cardiff sensationally beat the 'Kiwis' in the semi-final, the prop Cliff Davies running 40 yards to touch down for the only score in the game. Since 1939 Mary's Hospital had won the Middlesex Sevens Tournament 5 times and been once runners-up. Cardiff were exhausted from a much harder route to the final, but had opportunities to win. For no reason, Bleddyn Williams had a perfect try under the posts disallowed and the team lost 13-3.

In this season of 1945-46, under the heading *Sporting Prints – Bleddyn Williams,* there was an excellent and prescient newspaper article by J.B.G. Thomas: *'Bleddyn Williams, the Cardiff left-centre, has now firmly established himself now as one of the best of our young centre three-quarters. He has all the qualities and artistry that go to make an outstanding player. Upon him has fallen the mantle of the great Wooller as* the principal Welsh match-winner, an honour and responsibility which he carries proudly in his quiet and unassuming manner. Williams gained fame when young, and though given a great deal of praise which might have turned the head of many a similar player, he overcame these growing pains to blossom forth this season, at the age of 22, as a matured and brilliant centre three-quarter.

I first saw Williams play in December 1939, for a Public Schools XV, against the Cardiff High Schools. If the war did not last forever, he was certain to play for Wales. His outstanding asset, then as now, was his amazing side-step, for he seemed to shoot away to either side with the speed of a bullet for several yards, leaving would-be tacklers clutching at the air! This season his ability to side-step at speed is even more noticeable. Williams is very strongly built, weighing 13 stone and standing 5 foot 10 inches, which are perfect figures for a centre. When running at top speed he is very difficult to stop. He has a quick eye for the smallest opening in his opponent's defence, and with his clever running can soon make it into a tearing gap! Club defences have found it impossible to stop him breaking through this season, and Cardiff's large scores of 40 points v. Gloucester, 28 v. Newport and 27 v. the Wasps are a direct result of Williams' brilliant attacking powers in combination with his co-centre and outside-half, Matthews and Cleaver.' (These games were 40-9, 10-1 on tries; 28-17, 6-1 on tries; and 27-0, 7-0 on tries. 23 tries to 2.)

'The quality to be admired most in Williams is his unselfishness, for he endeavours to make openings and then feed his wings instead of trying to do it all himself – a characteristic of Gabe and Nicholls, which made Welsh rugby of the 1900s so beautiful to watch. This is praise indeed, but not too great for so promising a young player who might well be the fire of a renaissance of the true Welsh game. This season's International matches may well supply the answer. Born at Taff's Well, in February 1923, Williams played his first game for the local school at the age of eight! He continued doing so until he was 14, and gained a Welsh Schoolboys "cap" in 1937, before going up to Rydal. Here he was the mainstay of the school side, as was Wooller before him. His first Representative game was for South Wales against the British Army at the age of 19. Joining the RAF in December 1942, he was chosen for their representative XV, after two weeks' service. His first game for the Welsh Services came in March 1943, against England at Gloucester, and he helped in England's big defeat by scoring three tries. This fine effort was repeated in his second game for the Welsh Services. Last season he played for the Welsh Services, the R.A.F., the Barbarians, Great Britain and the British Empire, and this season Wales will build her back division around him in the hope that he will be the leader of a great Welsh revival.'

There was an unofficial game against the R.A.F. on 6 April 1946, where Flying Officer Bleddyn Williams played at 12, left centre, with number 2

Les Manfield (today's number 8) playing for the R.A.F. against their 'own' team of Cardiff. Cardiff had 9 internationals, numbered from Frank Trott, 1 at fullback, but the RAF numbered their fullback as 15 and the forwards as 1 to 8. The result is as yet undiscovered. There was another unofficial charity game on 1 May 1946, Cardiff Past vs. Cardiff Present, where Cardiff present squeezed home 5 tries to 4, 23-17. Roy Roberts, 'Wendy' Davies and captain Wilf Wooller played for Cardiff Past, Wilf scoring a try and a penalty; and Gwyn Porter, Hubert Johnson and A. Coombes also touching down, with a conversion by Ianto Jones. For Cardiff Present, Bleddyn swapped from left centre to outside half, scoring 3 tries. Dr. Glyn Jones and H.E. Jones also touched down, and Bill Tamplin knocked over 4 conversions. Cardiff Royal Infirmary benefited to the extent of £1,548, which included £1,482 which was Cardiff's share from the Middlesex Sevens. Wilf could only play twice after his return from Japanese imprisonment, in the Past vs. Present game, and previously against Richmond-Blackheath on 23 February 1946, to make up the numbers of a very depleted Cardiff side. He now concentrated upon cricket. To show the nature of how the team had been diminished during the war years, a record 14 players were awarded 1st XV caps in this year, playing 20 times. They were Gerald Blackmore, W. B. Cleaver, W. Darch, Cliff Davies, Maldwyn James, Dr. Glyn Jones, Hubert E. Jones, W. G. Jones, Les Manfield, D. St. John Rees, George Tomkins, Dr. Jack Matthews, Bleddyn Williams and his cousin W. E. Tamplin. Players and former players killed during the war were Pat Cox, C. R. (Cecil) Davies, Frank Gaccon, Ken Jones, Trevor Ransome, Howard Roblin, Ken Street (see under Wilf Wooller entry), V. Neil Taylor and Maurice Turnbull (see separate entry).

Readers may forgive me here, for noting the Cardiff High School Old Boy, Graham Hale – like so many others, his rugby career was affected by the war. His WRU Obituary reads in part: *'Officially, Harry Bowcott lived longer than any other Welsh international rugby union player, having reached the age of 97 years and eight months when he died. But, former Cardiff wing Graham Hale, who died on Monday, January 8 2018, outpassed that as he lived to be 97 years and 11 months. Hale will not be found among the official list of Wales players, but in 2013 the Welsh Rugby Union had awarded him a President's Cap in recognition of his appearance on the wing for Wales against the New Zealand 'Kiwis' in 1946.*

Hale joined Cardiff and made his debut in 1938-39 with war already looming. Speaking about the historic Middlesex Sevens victory in that year, Hale said: "We won our semi-final and we sat in the grandstand to watch London Scottish win the second semi. Wilf sat next to me and said: 'We must stop this blighter Logie Bruce-Lockhart running and we can win the final.' And so we did, winning by 11-6. We hurriedly raced to Paddington to get on the train to Cardiff, but there was no Cup and no Wilf. Then, as the train started we saw *Wilf hugging the Cup and loping down the platform to jump into our carriage. We got to Cardiff and went straight to the clubhouse, which was shut. Nobody had expected us to win, but very soon Wilf had the club open, and we were able to toast our success – never again achieved by a club from South Wales. The Cup was at that time called The Kinross-Arber Trophy."* Hale managed a try in the final and astonishingly dropped a goal in an earlier round, which was then worth four points. War then broke out and he joined up in the Welsh Guards but was taken prisoner by Rommel and Co at Benghazi in North Africa.

As with other POW's, Hale reckoned that Rommel saved their lives by refusing orders to shoot the prisoners, instead turning them over to Italian troops who took them back to Southern Italy and did not treat them particularly well. He was ill though and was among a band who were released to Britain. He said, *"I remember we even sailed up the Bristol Channel to Cardiff."* However, Hale was a fighter and as his strength came back, he played again for Cardiff and in March 1945 scored two tries in Cardiff's 22-11 win over a New Zealand Services side. His form was returning, and he forced his way into a Services International for Wales on the left wing, against France at Swansea on December 22, 1945 with Wales winning 8-0, thanks to two tries created by his left centre Bleddyn Williams, one scored by Dr Jack Matthews and one by a forward Selby Davies with a Maldwyn James conversion. Four days later on Boxing Day came one of the greatest games of the 2nd NZEF ('Kiwis') tour as they edged out Cardiff by 3-0 (a Jack Kearney try) at Cardiff Arms Park.

Only 10 days later Hale was in the Wales team to meet the 'Kiwis' again at the Arms Park. However, the New Zealanders won by 11-3 with just one try resulting. Hale played until the end of the 1946-47 season, but then retired, having lost his best years to war... He had been the last survivor of the 30 players of Wales-Kiwis and the oldest living Cardiff player.'

WILFRED WOOLLER 20 November 1912 - 10 March 1997
Rugby - Rydal School back row, Colwyn Bay RFC. Sale, Cambridge University – 3 Rugby 'Blues', Army, Cardiff, Barbarians, Wales.
Cricket - Cambridge University, MCC, Glamorgan 1938-1960
Glamorgan Cricket Captain 1947-1960, County Champions 1948, Glamorgan Secretary 1949-1962. Scored 1,000 runs in a season four times; 100 wickets twice; 1000 runs and 100 wickets double in 1955. Scored over 13,000 runs, took nearly 1,000 wickets and took 400 catches.
Cardiff RFC - centre – 71 games, 1936-37 – 1945-46 (one game), 38 tries, 30 drop goals (record), club points scored 512
Cambridge – 3 rugby blues, 2 cricket blues
Cardiff RFC Captain 1937-38, 1938-39

Soccer - Barry Town 1938; **Cardiff City centre-forward 1939** (as an amateur, or he would have been banned from rugby union, scored a hat-trick)
Squash - Wales
Hockey - Cardiff
Wales Rugby – 18 caps, 26 points: 1933 E, S, I, 1935 E, S, I, NZ, 1936 E, S, I, 1937 E, S, I, 1938 S, I, 1939 E, S, I
Chosen for British Lions 1938 but did not tour, as could not afford to lose job.
Chosen for Cricket Test Matches in 1948-49 and 1951-52 but could not because of business commitments.

'The Godfather of Glamorgan Cricket' – J.B.G. Thomas
'*The icon of a nation*' – 1997 Obituary
'The giant of Welsh rugby in the Thirties' - Danny Davies
(Wooller was) '*one of the greatest sportsmen Wales has ever produced, indeed there is any amount of evidence to suggest that he was the greatest of them all.*' Sir Tasker Watkins VC GBE DL Kt (1918-2007), President of the Welsh Rugby Union 1993-2004, Lord Justice of Appeal and Deputy Lord Chief Justice.

Tasker Watkins was the first Welsh member of the British Army to be awarded a VC during the Second World War. His citation read: '*On 16 August 1944 at Barfour, Normandy, France, Lieutenant Watkins' company came under murderous machine-gun fire while advancing through corn fields set with booby traps. The only officer left, Lieutenant Watkins led a bayonet charge with his 30 remaining men against 50 enemy infantry, practically wiping them out. Finally, at dusk, separated from the rest of the battalion, he ordered his men to scatter and after he had personally charged and silenced an enemy machine-gun post, he brought them back to safety. His superb leadership not only saved his men, but decisively influenced the course of the battle.*' Watkins' active service ended in October 1944 when he was badly wounded in the battle to liberate the Dutch city of 's Hertogenbosch. In a *Daily Telegraph* interview in 2001, he said, '*You must believe me when I say it was just another day in the life of a soldier. I did what needed doing to help colleagues and friends, just as others looked out for me during the fighting that summer... I didn't wake up the next day a better or braver person, just different. I'd seen more killing and death in 24 hours – indeed been part of that terrible process – than is right for anybody. From that point onwards I have tried to take a more caring view of my fellow human beings, and that, of course, always includes your opponent, whether it be in war, sport, or just life generally.*'

A native of Rhos-on-Sea in North Wales, Wilf Wooller first played cricket at Rydal School and at the local club, Colwyn Bay where he played alongside his father Roy and brothers Jack and Gordon. At school he played rugby in the back row, staying on for another year, to take Latin to get into Cambridge. He played for North Wales Schoolboys and for Sale, alongside the seasoned Welsh centre Claude Davey, who would from the following year captain Wales eight times. The pair were chosen together in the Possibles against Probables trial in early January, while Wilf was still a schoolboy, before the 1933 England game. Wooller strongly believed the selectors were *'mucking about'* with him, so in retaliation the hard-tackling Davey and the 6-foot 2-inch, 14 stone Wooller, a huge size for a centre back then, laid into their opposing centres with a vengeance. Cardiff's half-backs Harry Bowcott and Maurice Turnbull were also in the Possibles, with a point to prove, and they surprising won 15-6 at Swansea. The selectors, none of whom had seen Wooller play before the trial, were still unsure about both Wilf and the great Swansea fullback Viv Jenkins, and asked Wooller and Jenkins to play again, for Glamorgan against Monmouthshire five days later.

The Times reported that '*Wooller was the first to distinguish himself, his long, raking stride carrying him from his own 25 almost as far as his opponents… It was an impressive* (70-yards) *run… and ended in a great try.*' Wilf scored another try, Glamorgan easily won 23-8 and later that evening Wooller, Jenkins, Davey, Bowcott and Turnbull were selected to play at Twickenham on 26 January 1933. Wilf's father was driving him back home and had to stop for petrol, where the pump attendant told them the good news, from hearing a radio broadcast of the team. Even before playing for Wales, the newspapers were calling him '*another Gwyn Nicholls*', and *The Times* on the morning of the match reported: *So far, (Wooller) has exceeded all expectations. His passing is beautifully timed and balanced, even when he runs up to the man and takes the bump.*'

There had been nine successive defeats at Twickenham, but Barry man and Cardiff wing Ronnie Boon scored a try and drop goal in 1933, all of Wales' points, to win 7-3. He reminisced on 2 February 1983 in a *Times* interview on the fiftieth anniversary of the great game, that Wooller saved the match: '*Wilf however, who had had a good game was soon to prove what an exciting player he was. Wales were dominant now, but suddenly England gave us a terrible shock. The ball materialized with Elliot between the 25 and the halfway line and he broke clear with no one to stop him. Then out of the blue came Wilf Wooller, only 18 and playing his first game for Wales, who started to chase him. Imagine the scene the stands full of Englishmen on their feet cheering madly, and the banks behind the posts lined with stunned Welshmen seeing a great victory about to slip away from them. Elliot would have touched down under the crossbar. Then Wilf this tall young man with his long sprinter's strides imperceptibly at first, and then noticeably and with great increasing velocity, closed the gap and*

168

brought Elliot crashing down near the Welsh line. Wilf undoubtedly saved the game for us.'

Wilf played in the other two internationals, losses to Ireland and Scotland. In Cambridge from October 1933, his fly-half was the great Cliff Jones. Wilf had a brilliant performance in the 29-4 Cambridge win against Oxford in December 1934, when he dropped a goal from just inside his own half. He remarked *'That dropped goal pitched in the upper deck of Twickenham's North Stand.'* He had not been chosen for any Welsh trials or internationals in 1934, but his 'siege-gun' kicking brought him back into the selectors' favour. Also in that December, Idwal Rees withdrew from the final trial, Wilf replaced him and resumed his international career from January 1935 until the war, and was playing again outside Cliff Jones at Cardiff.

Paul Roos, the 1906 South Africa captain, said of the New Zealand defeat in 1935 to Wales: *'The All Blacks were playing Wales at Cardiff and were leading 3 - 0 at half-time. Cliff Jones, the Welsh captain, brought the tall and speedy Wooller from the wing, where he had been wasted in the first half, into the centre. It proved to be a magic change, for within seven minutes after the restart, the two of them had combined so magnificently that they had converted the debit of 0-3 against them into a credit balance of 10 - 3 in their favour. It all happened so quickly the crowd was simply left gasping.'* Later, with Wales losing 12-10, a man short and ten minutes left, Wooller made a carefully judged kick ahead that deceived the All Blacks and allowed Geoffrey Rees-Jones in for the winning score. *'The move was practically a carbon-copy of one involving the same players earlier in the match and which led to Wales's second try'.* The *Daily Telegraph* described Wooller's rugby talents as *'like the sacrificial car of Juggernaut, leaving a trail of prostrate figures in his wake.'*

He signed, as an amateur, for Barry Town in 1938, wishing to play soccer on weeknights and rugby at weekends. In 1938 he was invited to make the visit to South Africa with the British Isles rugby team, but Wooller could not afford to take unpaid leave for the duration of a major tour. In 1938 he made his Glamorgan Cricket debut against Yorkshire at The Arms Park. In 1939, he was Wales rugby captain, but he considered leading his guest side Cardiff to win the Middlesex Sevens of that year as a real rugby highlight. Years later he remembered, *'Six of us had never played sevens before'.* Wooller also played for Cardiff City at soccer in 1939, scoring a hat-trick at centre-forward. In his rugby prime, he was commissioned into the Royal Artillery, serving along with many Cardiff players with the 77th Heavy Anti-Aircraft Regiment, but played in many of the popular war-time charity internationals in 1939-40. In June 1939 he made his Glamorgan debut taking 5 wickets for 90 runs at Cardiff Arms Park, on the opening day of the Championship match against Yorkshire. He played cricket as part of his annual paid leave. He scored his maiden

169

century and took five wickets for 69 runs in the victory over the West Indies in 1939. Wilf's last international was in Paris in February 1940, when a British Army side smashed France 36-3 in Paris, and he scored three tries.

In 1942, he was captured by the Japanese at Java and imprisoned at Changi jail for the rest of the war. In *The Skipper*, Dr Andrew Hignell's biography, he described his time in camp, initially with Les Spence. As an officer, Wilf was treated better than many men, but for a while he worked on the Burma railway, watching his fellows starve and die and be brutally maimed around him. Wilf returned, a shadow of his former self: '*The experience left a deep mark; years later he was reported to have refused to use a Japanese-made pocket calculator.*' (It is strange that within two generations, we have forgotten war atrocities. My uncle Norman Thomas was captured in North Africa by the Italians, but was handed over to the Germans to slave for three years in a salt mine, against the Geneva Convention. This wrecked his health and personality. For years, my aunty did not know he was alive until he was repatriated, a coughing semi-skeleton. His friend Stan was imprisoned by the Japanese, and was allowed to stay in his local pub in St Martins, Shropshire until 4 in the morning, as on returning home he could not sleep, and always had to sleep with the light on. These men witnessed and suffered terrible cruelty. There was no compensation. We may forgive but must never forget.)

Wilf, with his 'iron will' survived, and with Les Spence returned to Cardiff, as the shadow of the giant centre who pummelled the All Blacks. After two post-war appearances for Cardiff, in a Past vs Present game for charity, and against Richmond-Blackheath because Cardiff could not scrape together a team, he never again played rugby. Around 850 POWs died during their internment in Changi during the Japanese occupation of Singapore, a relatively low rate, compared to the overall death rate of 27% for POWs in Japanese camps. Other camps were far worse, with many prisoners dying after being transferred from Changi to various labour camps outside Singapore, including those on the Burma Railway. In wartime Wilf had married Lady Gillian Windsor-Clive, but she was not there to meet him on his return, having met someone else. The marriage was soon dissolved, and his teammates rallied around him in some very dark days. Happily, he met Enid James and remarried in 1948, the start of a happy family life that greatly accelerated his physical recovery.

Wilf quickly established himself as an all-rounder with leadership potential at Glamorgan Cricket Club, becoming their assistant secretary in 1946 and captain in 1947. In that year he scored more than 1,000 runs for the first time, shared a record seventh-wicket partnership of 195 with Willie Jones against Lancashire, and took 79 wickets. In 1948 he led Glamorgan into their first county championship title. Wilf was a fearless short-leg fielder and in the 1950s often opened both the batting and bowling. In 1954, at the age of 41, he achieved the double, scoring 1,059 runs and taking 107 wickets. Captain for a decade, Wilf was twice prevented from playing Test cricket for England, in 1948-49 and 1951-52, owing to business commitments. He retired from first-class cricket in 1960, and as Glamorgan Secretary in 1977, having served as a Test selector from 1955 to 1961. To illustrate Wooller's will to win, he was a Test Selector when the MCC captain, Peter May, was in his prime. During a County Championship match with Surrey, Wooller was bowling and May left his crease, ready to run. Wooller did not release the ball, but instead 'stumped' May so he was declared out. (I cannot explain the arcane rules of cricket to readers, I am afraid, without adding another 100 pages to the book.) May was visibly shocked, but politely asked (- he was an amateur 'Gentleman' rather than a professional 'Player' – a cricketing distinction still prevalent in the 1950s) *'Isn't it customary to give the batsman a warning?'* Wooller happily answered *'Not in Swansea'* and May began to trudge back to the Pavilion. Wooller hated losing. Wilf also was a well-known broadcaster and commentator and became *'the backbone of the newspaper's sports pages,'* when asked to report on rugby and cricket for the *Sunday Telegraph*.

For Wilf, of all the great rugby players he played with or watched, he declared that Haydn Tanner was the nearest to perfection. Among post-war players, Cliff Morgan, Barry John and Gareth Edwards were among his 'greatest' and Rhys Williams of Llanelli was the most intelligent and hardest forward. As an example of his writing skills, his favourite match was the 1967 Wales-England game when the 18-year-old Keith Jarrett, playing out-of-position at full back, scored 19 points to deny England the Triple Crown. Wales easily won 34-21, with Jarrett being the youngest player to score points in an international. Wilf played five times in this fixture in the 1930s, for a grand total of 26 points in all, an average of 5 points a match – compared to a massive 55 in Jarrett's game. Wilf reported: *'This spectacle, to one who had fought England over dour 80-minute periods, was something one could not quite believe. The pace was as hot as the* (spring) *weather, and it never let up for an instant of the 80-odd packed minutes of movement. Spectators at this memorable contest will no doubt forget the score, if not the broad outlines of the game, but I doubt very much whether any single individual present will ever forget Jarrett's superb try in all its glorious technicolour. And the strangest thing of all is that happened in a game between England and Wales.'*

THE 'RAGS' ALMOST HAVE AN INVINCIBLE SEASON – CARDIFF LOSE CHANCE OF UNBEATEN SEASON OWING TO LOSS OF PLAYERS FOR SEVEN TRIALS AND INTERNATIONALS – *'THE MOST ATTRACTIVE SIDE TO WATCH'* – THE REMARKABLE TOM ROSSER – THE 'INDOMITABLES'

Bleddyn Williams P27 T12 = 36pts; **Bryn Williams** (Athletic); **Roy Roberts** P34 T5 C4 P1 = 26pts (Taff's Well); **Bill Tamplin** P30 C40 P12 D1 = 120pts (Risca); Basil Evans P5 Pentyrch; Ray Bale P24 (Tongwynlais)

P41, W31, L6, D4. Points 549-200. <u>Tries 122-32</u>, Pens 19-16

Without three Welsh trials and four international call-ups, Cardiff would have probably been unbeaten. Their losses coincided with losing their best players, and were 8-5, 10-3, 7-5, 8-6, 6-0 and 10-3 – 29 points difference over six games. Jack Matthews was elected captain again but was called up for National Service as a doctor with the R.A.M.C. and missed many games. He captained the Royal Army Medical Corps to win the Army Cup, receiving it from General Montgomery. In his absences, his vice-captain, international Les Manfield took over, always following Matthews' preference for open, flowing 'fifteen-man rugby' – this was decades before the term was misused for fifteen massive blokes bashing each other. Manfield had won 2 caps while at Mountain Ash in 1939, and gained another 4 when he moved to Cardiff. Haydn Tanner had won his first cap as a schoolboy, for Wales against the All Blacks in 1935 and brought with him 14 Welsh caps, when he moved to Cardiff from Swansea at the start of the season, in a move with his job. The Cardiff defence was tighter this season, with 12 fewer tries conceded, but 27 fewer tries were scored.

The open side wing forward PC Gwynfryn 'Gwyn' Evans, in his first season with Cardiff was be capped for Wales and played the next 10 games in the Five nations, and in the win against Australia, gaining 12 caps in all. He became a Chief-Superintendent, not bad for a 'beat' policeman. Old Penarthians RFC until recently displayed his shirts, donated by his son Jeff, a feared prop for the club in the 1960s and 70s. Gwynfryn was born in 1918, brought up in Clydach and played for Swansea RFC as an 18-year-old. He switched to football, where he excelled, when his employers, the South Wales Police, decreed that rugby was a *'barbaric activity'* and members of the Force were not allowed to play the sport. Gwynfryn later transferred to Cardiff City Police and following service with the Royal Engineers in the 2nd World War, joined Cardiff City Police and Cardiff

RFC for the 1946-47 season. Within six months, and despite being 29 years old, he was among 13 new caps selected by Wales to play against England at Cardiff Arms Park, in the first Five Nations International since for end of the war. Although managing to score a try, Gwyn ended up on the losing side with England winning 9 – 6. He kept his place for the rest of the season and the two following. He played 101 times for Cardiff in just three seasons, up to 1949-50, and retiring aged 32. Another great player whose best years were lost to war. Of the 13 new caps against England were Bleddyn, Jack Matthews, Billy Cleaver and Gwyn.

Full back Frank Trott, second row Bill Tamplin, hooker Maldwyn James and back row Sid Judd soon earned Welsh caps. Billy Cleaver was swapped between outside-half, fullback and centre. For the next few years, sometimes all the backs were Cardiff players except Newport's great wing, Ken Jones. Trott officially won his first cap against England in January 1948, but as the 29-year-old Penarth captain he had also played in a Victory International in February 1946, for which no caps were awarded. After the loss against Scotland, he was selected for the next game, where England were beaten at Twickenham. Frank Trott (March 1915-Jan 1987) was very under-rated. As Penarth captain aged 24, he had played in a Welsh trial before the war, during which he played for the British Army. Company Sergeant-Major Trott was chosen for the Barbarians in 1944 and 1945. At the relatively advanced age of 32, in 1948 he won his first cap for Wales, playing 8 times in 1948 and 1949, and 205 times for Cardiff from 1937-38 to 1952-53. From the age of 24 to 31 he had played hardly any rugby, serving in the war, but won seven Five Nations matches up till 1949, aged 33 – one wonders what his record could have been without 7 missing war years. In 1953 Frank retired from first-class rugby, aged 38, having played 205 times for Cardiff. The other newcomer to the Firsts, Sidney 'Sid' Judd, played for Cardiff High School, Cardiff Schools, Welsh Secondary Schools, Trinity College Carmarthen and Carmarthen Athletic. A student then schoolteacher during the war years, he was 18 when he joined Cardiff, going straight into the Firsts. In his 10 seasons he played 184 games, scoring 45 tries and appeared for the Barbarians. Judd was capped 10 times from 1953-55, when the Welsh backs were usually mainly Cardiff players and he was the only Cardiff forward. The famous and abrasive Jim Mills of Rugby League Fame, said on Twitter *'Sid Judd my teacher at Windsor Clive School, Cardiff, scored a try against the All Blacks, it was Sid who got me playing rugby. He also scored a try for Wales the following week to beat the All Blacks twice in a week. Great man.'*

There had been no Five Nations Championship in 1946, just unofficial internationals. In the final Welsh trial on 1 January 1947, no fewer than 7 of Cardiff's first team were playing for selection. Haydn Tanner captained the Probables, and Cardiff's Glyn Davies was outside-half. Cardiff's Billy

Cleaver was the Possibles outside-half, perhaps a unique occasion where one club supplied both players in probably the key position in rugby. England and Wales shared the Championship, each winning 3 and losing 1. Wales lost the first game at Twickenham 9-6, scoring 2 tries against a goal and a drop goal then worth 4 points. Bleddyn Williams was 'uncomfortable' at outside-half and was in future always picked at left centre. Wales then beat Scotland away 22-8 – 5 tries to 1. Apart from 2 tries from Newport wing Ken Jones, the other points were scored by Cardiff players - Bleddyn, Billy Cleaver and Les Williams with a try apiece, and Bill Tamplin with 2 conversions and a penalty. France were defeated away 3-0; and Ireland at home 6-0, in the championship scoring 37 against 17 points, and almost achieving a Grand Slam. England's points were 39-36, getting hammered by Ireland 22-0. In later years, Wales would have been awarded the Championship, but equal points for many years meant a shared title.

There were 3 Welsh trials and 4 internationals, with Cardiff 'losing' six or seven players each time. On these 7 dates, Cardiff's results were mixed, drawing with Bective Rangers 0-0 away (missing Haydn Tanner, Bleddyn Williams, Jack Matthews and Gwyn Evans in the final Welsh trial), but just losing to Bath 8-5, and Coventry 10-3. At home Cardiff had won 14-0, scoring two tries, with Bleddyn Williams outside half and Billy Cleaver left centre. Bleddyn's cousin and uncle, Bill Tamplin and Roy Roberts, played second row. Wasps, Richmond and Cambridge University were beaten, however. Winning 4, losing 2 and drawing 1 with half the team missing was a reasonable outcome. The other four losses were to Swansea 7-5 away, Neath 8-6 away, and Llanelli twice 6-0 and 10-3. The latter defeats had been postponed until 19 and 28 May, well after the normal end of season, because of bad weather, and the Cardiff team had suffered an accumulation of fixtures. The Arms Park pitch was probably the worse in Wales because of the amount of games played on it, by Cardiff, the Athletic, Cardiff Boys, Internationals, Trials and representative and charity games. Only 6 of 41 games were lost, by a total of 27 points, 4.5 per game. The 31 wins were won by an average of 11.3 points per game, and Cardiff scored almost 4 times as any tries as their opponents in the full season of 41 games.

On 28 October 1946, Bleddyn was still playing outside half for Cardiff, against Rosslyn Park, in a 26-8 victory, 8 tries (only one converted) against two tries (one converted). Ray Bale was wing forward, Bill Tamplin second row, but second row Roy Roberts was playing prop – he also was a fine number 8. Gloucester were beaten 20-8 (4 tries to a goal and a try) and then 12-11 away (goal, try, drop goal to a goal and 2 pens). From October 1936 to February 1952, Cardiff had beaten the mighty Gloucester in all 14 games, and then from November 1953 won 8 on the trot, with 2 being cancelled in February 1955 and 1956 because of frost and snow. The team

174

for the Gloucester match in this year was much more like a full Cardiff team: D. St. John Rees (full back) - Raymond Jones (left wing) - Dr. Jack Matthews (left centre and captain) - Billy Cleaver (right centre) - Gwyn Porter (right wing, he played 147 games from 1935-36 to 1947-48, a great career disrupted by war) - Bleddyn Williams (outside half instead of Cleaver, because the Welsh and Cardiff selectors were unsure as to positions, as both could play centre or fly-half) - Billy Darch (scrumhalf) - Stan Bowes (prop) - Don Rees (hooker, from Bath) - George Tomkins (prop, he retired this year, another man who lost his best years to the war, like Bleddyn and others in the team) - Bill Tamplin (2nd row, Bleddyn's cousin) - R.M. Glover (2nd row) - Hubert Jones (wing-forward, who finished this year, and had lost years to war, like Glover) - Les Manfield (number 8, usually a wing-forward, vice-captain, capped in 1939 against Scotland) - Roy Roberts (wing forward, usually a 2nd row, Bleddyn's uncle).

Upon Armistice Day, 11 November 1946, the Cardiff team flew to a game for the first time, two days after defeating Newport 11-0. Their plane, scheduled for 10 November for a return visit to Nantes, had been delayed by bad weather. The team had to fly from Pengam Airport outside Cardiff in a captured German Junkers JU-52 – basically an uninsulated metal can - in really uncomfortable and cold conditions. To clear Customs, the plane had to land at Bristol, but by then it was too late to fly, so they flew at 8am on Monday 11 November and won 22-5 in a packed ground. For part of the return journey, Bleddyn took over the controls, and his cousin Bill Tamplin pretended to be enraged. On 23 November, there was an 8-8 draw with London Welsh, with Bleddyn still outside half and acting captain, Cardiff scoring a goal and try against 2 drop goals. Swansea were beaten 13-8, 3 tries to 2 on 14 December, with Bleddyn outside half and Frank Trott right centre. Programmes show constant swapping of positions for forwards and backs over the years of this book. Frank Trott was a wonderful pre-war fullback for Penarth, but joined Cardiff in 1945. Fred Croster tells us, '*He had no hope of getting into the side as fullback, his rightful position, but was ready to play anywhere, most of his games were played as scrumhalf for either the Rags or the Firsts, just to be in the side. This was the spirit that prevailed.*' Frank soon had his First XV cap, playing 20 times in a season, and was to play for Wales.

That terrible frozen winter meant that many fixtures were cancelled or postponed, so the W.R.U. extended the season into May. Penarth had 35 fixtures, but 8 were cancelled and one abandoned against Aberavon, in the 'Big Freeze' of 1946. '*The congestion of fixtures in April and early May added to end of the season staleness and Llanelly* (sic) *accounted for the Blue and Blacks twice in a fortnight.*' '*The club was in much demand to tour and play additional and also charitable matches*', according to Davies. In April alone there was a charity match vs. Monmouthshire

175

Police, and fixtures against the Barbarians (5/4/47); Harlequins (7/4/47); Plymouth Albion (12/4/47); Devonport Services (14/4/47); Exeter (15/4/47); Llanelli (19/4/47); Coventry 22/4/47); Pontypool (26/4/47) and Llanelli again 28/4/47. Plus there was a charity game against Monmouthshire Police. Eleven known games in 31 days, plus other games in May against Penarth, Bridgend (– to help its finances) and another for the Sker Disaster Appeal.

Cardiff was known everywhere as *'the most attractive team to watch'*. In April Sergeant Bill Tamplin's Cardiff XV played the Monmouthshire Police for charity, and another end-of-season unofficial game was played at Bridgend, to help that club's precarious finances in the immediate post-war years. Gate receipts for the game against Penarth on 3 May were donated to the *'Western Mail'* appeal for dependants of the eight crew of the Mumbles lifeboat who died on 23 April attempting to save the SS *Samtampa, 'which was blown on to the rocky beach at Sker Point in a howling gale with the most cruel loss of the whole of her crew'*. The former Liberty ship unable to proceed to Newport in the face of a gale gusting up to hurricane force, huge waves and adverse currents. The captain decided to hove-to in the Bristol Channel to wait for better weather, but the anchor cables were unable to hold the ship in such adverse conditions. The vessel broke into three sections in just 80 minutes on Sker Rocks, near Porthcawl. Witnesses described the scene as a 'seething cauldron of fury.' The *Samtampa's* lighter bow and stern sections were thrown up onto a rock plateau 25 feet above the beach. All 39 crew died, not from drowning when the ship broke up, but by suffocation from leaking fuel oil fumes. In a hopeless task, the Mumbles lifeboat had been launched, much too late to save the men, and all her 8 crew also died when their boat capsized, in giant seas alongside the *Samtampa*.

Try scoring was shared via many team changes, with Howell Loveluck leading with 14, Billy Cleaver 12, Bleddyn Williams 12, Gwyn Porter 11, Hubert Jones 7, Cliff Davies 6, and five each came from Gwyn Martin, Dr. Jack Matthews and Bleddyn's uncle Roy Roberts. 77 tries came from these 9 men, with another 45 being shared around. Bill Tamplin kicked 52 penalties and conversions, and new 1st XV caps were given to Stan Bowes, Gwyn Evans, Howell Loveluck, Don Rees and Frank Trott. Cardiff scored around four times as many tries as their opponents, but successful penalties were almost identical. T. Lyn Williams, a centre and outside half first capped for Cardiff Firsts as far back as 1936-37 – another who lost years of rugby - was captain of the 'Rags'. They had a magnificent season, and although only 22 matches were played because of the weather, 19 were won and 2 drawn. The only loss was to Maesteg away, 16-14, 4 tries apiece with Cardiff missing three conversions. T. Lyn Williams was rewarded with the captaincy again in the following season, when he also played his last game for the Firsts. The Rags could have had an Invincible season, with many youngsters coming in, a great omen for the First Team's future.

THE REMARKABLE TOM ROSSER - TOM HYWEL LEWIS ROSSER 19 September 1918 - 14 August 2014

I first came across this forgotten war hero, and friend of Cardiff's Bleddyn Williams, Billy Cleaver and D. St John Rees, in an article *Wartime Years - Keeping the Ball in Play*, the reminiscences of Dr Jack Matthews. '*Jack Matthews captained Cardiff, Wales and also the British Lions in one of their 1950 tour games in New Zealand. He played in all four Tests on that trip, won 17 Welsh caps and made 180 appearances at centre for Cardiff RFC. Here he recalls his war efforts on behalf of the Accies.* "*It is true to say that I did my best to help Welsh Academicals keep the ball alive during the war years while a student at Cardiff Medical College. I had actually joined the RAF as a fighter pilot for the Battle of Britain, but when the War Office discovered that I was a medical student they demobbed me and sent me back to Cardiff to resume my studies (though they caught up with me again later). As with the miners and steelworkers my progress as a would-be doctor was deemed essential to the War Effort. Thus the "Meds" had enough young personnel, fit and eager for games of Rugby, to put a team together most weekends. On one occasion we played a wartime Cardiff XV and won by 28 points to 26.*

Up at Mountain Ash, Jimmy Austin was determined not to let the Welsh Academicals wither away through inactivity, and valued the players whom I could persuade to turn out in the red jerseys provided by the club (the rest of our kit we bought ourselves). They included St John Rees, later Cardiff RFC's full back; **Tom Rosser,** *who became a cardiac surgeon; Roger Seal, an old Llandoverian and later a top pathologist in Cardiff; not to mention the late Peter Williams, father of JPR and his brothers. From the mining community there were students from the prestigious Cardiff School of Mining like Billy Cleaver, Gerry Blackmore and George Tomkins, as well as colliers Maldwyn James and Cliff Davies, who both played post-War International Rugby in the Wales front row. On the whole, 'Accies' fixtures were few and far between. However, when they came they were often big challenges: for instance an 'Accies' side which I captained took on a New Zealand Army XV in 1945. I can't remember the result – fifty-five years ago, but I do recall that it was tough, and that several of our opponents went on to become All Blacks*'.

This led me to a *Walesonline* obituary about this very remarkable man: **The remarkable doctor who performed Wales' first open heart surgery, played rugby with the greats and ran clinics among Borneo's head-hunters** - *Tributes to miner's son Tom Rosser, who became known for his pioneering medical work, and even established a flock of hospital sheep to help advance ground-breaking surgical procedures. T.H.L. "Tom" Rosser*

177

carried out Wales' first open heart surgery, ran medical clinics among Borneo's head-hunters, and was also a first-class scrum half regularly playing with some of rugby's greats. Miner's son Tom, who has died at the age of 95, was the youngest in a family of four and the only boy. Growing up in Llantwit Fardre, he won a scholarship to Pontypridd Grammar School where he excelled both in the classroom and on the rugby pitch. (Working-class boys in these days generally had to gain a scholarship to get into grammar schools, where rugby was played, and there was a far better opportunity of entering a profession.) *The early death of his father, a miner turned insurance agent, initially dashed his hopes of going into medicine due to limited family finances. But joint efforts from his mother and the school headmaster secured a county scholarship for him to study medicine in Cardiff in 1938. He lived at home and travelled to the Welsh National School of Medicine for lectures, spending his evenings studying. During the Blitz he was kept busy treating casualties, fire watching and helping to evacuate the burning Royal Infirmary. He was Cardiff Medicals rugby captain 1940-41.*

He played rugby and gained a place in the Welsh Academicals First XV in his first year where he played alongside fellow student Jack "Dr Jack" Mathews, a lifelong friend and later Captain of Cardiff, Wales and British and Irish Lions. Tom turned out for Cardiff and Pontypridd in the holiday, forming a friendship with Bleddyn "Prince of Centres" Williams, later another Wales, Lions and Cardiff skipper. He qualified in 1944 becoming a house surgeon at Morriston Hospital where he gained experience treating war casualties returning from D-Day. In 1945 he entered the army as a doctor in the Royal Army Medical Corps, where he treated released prisoners of war from Italy and Germany. Later that year he was posted abroad and, while on secondment as Medical Officer to the 9th Australian division, joined in the invasion of Borneo including Brunei, Sarawak and Sabah. Tom Rosser pursued his career when cardiac surgery was an emerging specialty. He worked towards modernising surgical techniques, including open heart surgery at Sully Hospital and later at the University Hospital of Wales.

Tom, the son of a miner, had gained a scholarship to Cardiff medical school, followed by National Service with the Australian 9th division in Borneo, where he treated prisoners of war and indigenous people, travelling by dug-out canoe around jungles. At the end of the war, he worked as a member of the Sarawak medical services as MO in charge of the 4th division, an area the size of Wales. He made journeys by longboat and foot to take treatments to the native tribes of Borneo. It was when he returned to Wales that he started surgical training at Morriston Hospital, becoming one of the first to pass the primary and fellowship examinations of the Royal College of Surgeons at their first attempt. In 1951 his interest in thoracic surgery led to his appointment as Senior Surgical Registrar at

Sully Hospital, a purpose-built centre for treating tuberculosis, heart and lung cases in the Vale of Glamorgan. He spent time as a senior registrar at the Brompton Hospital the following year, where he came into contact with surgeons who shared his view that techniques had remained stagnant for too long.

Later Tom, who was keen that Wales should not lag behind, was to perform Wales' first open heart operation. To develop new techniques, he set up a flock of sheep at Sully hospital for experimental surgery and collected blood from a Cardiff abattoir so he could explore procedures for lung transplantation, bypass attempts, valve replacements and transfusions. He was a member of "Pete's Club" (later the Cardiothoracic Surgery) where he shared techniques with other top surgeons. In the early 1970s cardiac surgery was transferred from Sully to the new University Hospital of Wales in Cardiff, where Tom continued to practice heart surgery until his retirement in 1979. Later, with his wife Barbara who had been a physiotherapist at Sully Hospital and who he had married in 1956, he moved to Solva in Pembrokeshire. During their time in West Wales, the couple had to cope with the tragic loss of their son Michael, a newly qualified doctor, in a motoring accident. Tom is survived by his wife Barbara and their daughter Sally, a GP in Wiltshire.' What a man – and virtually forgotten.

The Indomitables

In 1946, the Great Britain Rugby League team scrounged a lift to Australasia on the aircraft carrier *Indomitable*, taking 4 weeks to arrive for a 6-month tour, and went down in history as '*The Indomitables*'. All commercial transport was being used to transport troops back home, and to carry foodstuffs and materials into battered Britain. Some of the players had just been demobbed, and the tourists played 20 games in Australia, including 3 Tests, and 7 matches in New Zealand, including 1 Test. All available merchant ships had been requisitioned moving troops and food and supplies in the war's aftermath.

Cardiff-born 35-year-old stand-off, centre and fullback 'Gus' Risman was captain, and said '*By the time we arrived in Melbourne we must have been the most unfit rugby league side to ever arrive in that famous city,*' as their only training was throwing a ball about on the flight deck, not being able to kick it. For the train journey to Sidney, a compartment had been reserved, but only had room for 13 players. Risman said '*There were 26 of us and a couple of managers. There was nothing for it but to pile into the cramped space, 28 people in the space reserved for 13 and when we arrived in Sydney we were still wearing the same clothes we had worn when we had left Fremantle. We had been transformed from the fittest to the unfittest and then the most disreputable looking side, all in the space of the week.*' 'The *Indomitables'* were the only side to go unbeaten in a Test Series against Australia. GB unluckily drew the 'brutal' first test 8-8 at Sydney after the Bradford centre Jack Kitching was mistakenly sent off towards the end of the first half. Eddie Waring, the journalist and future Rugby League commentator on BBC TV, sailed with the 1946 Lions, and at the time: '*Kitching tackled Jorgenson and... Kitching felt a sharp pain in his side. He pushed Jorgenson off, got up, and immediately put his hand on his side. Referee McMahon thought he had hit Jorgenson, and... he had to walk*' which gave '*England an uphill battle with 12 men in the first Test.*' Former Cardiff player Frank Whitcombe scored one of the tourists' two tries, converted by Risman.

Incidentally, this 'English' squad of 26 had 11 Welsh players: Cilfynydd's Joe Jones; Kenfig Hill and Cardiff's Arthur Bassett; Cardiff's Gus Risman; Garnant's Ted Ward; Penclawdd's Willie Davies; Treherbert's Dai Jenkins; Cardiff's Frank Whitcombe; Llanelli's Fred Hughes; Neath's Douglas Versailles Phillips (born on the day the Treaty of Versailles was signed); Newport's Trevor Foster MBE; and Pontycymmer's Isaac 'Ike' Owens. For the Second Test, Gus Risman switched from fullback to replace Kitching, and Arthur Bassett, now 32 after missing the war years, came into the team on the wing. The GB team was fuming because of the referee mishandling the First Test and were determined to win. 65,000 spectators crammed into the Brisbane Exhibition Ground. Arthur Bassett took his chance and scored 3 of the 4 tries in a 14-5 win, where the hooker Joe Egan was sent off towards the end. (Egan played alongside Gwyn Williams at Wigan). Egan hit Australian second-rower Arthur Clues, who had not been penalised for a particularly vicious tackle on Wigan centre Ted Ward (another of Gwyn Williams' Wigan team-mates, who had played for Llanelli. Dai Jenkins, a former Cardiff scrumhalf who played there with Gwyn in 1934-35 was also on the tour). Leaving the pitch Egan was heard to say, '*If the referee won't do his job, then someone has to*'.

GB had already retained the Ashes, and in the deciding Third Test at Sydney, Arthur Bassett scored 2 of the 4 tries in a comfortable 20-7 win, 17 points coming from Welsh players, and 31 of the 42 points scored in the 3 Tests. Arthur Clues was sent-off for attempting a dangerous swinging arm tackle on Britain's best player and captain Gus Risman. Thanks to Risman's quick reaction, Clues missed but the referee had to send Clues off. And massive forwards hitting smaller backs is never right. Apart from Bassett's two tries, Ike Owens scored one, Gus Risman converted three, and Ted Ward kicked a goal. With just 26 players, instead of the customary touring squad of 30, GB won 21 of 27 games, becoming the only team to go unbeaten in a Test series in Australia.

The New Zealand test was lost 13-8 by the exhausted tourists, having travelled thousands of miles in uncomfortable conditions, but these last

180

games there were marred with heavy, rain-soaked pitches. Of the Kiwi Test, Eddie Waring wrote: '*It was not possible* (to play rugby) *on a ground, inches deep in mud. It was the first time I had seen seagulls at a football match, but there they were, with the teams in one half of the field and the gulls in the other*'. Egan's former target Arthur Clues moved to rugby league in Britain, playing for Leeds in the 1946–47 Challenge Cup Final. Yet again Clues showed that he had little clue about playing proper rugby, swinging a boot at the head of Bradford Northern's little Welsh scrumhalf Gwylfa Jones at a scrum, just missing. At once, Frank Whitcombe, the former Cardiff player, body-charged Clues unconscious, and as he lay on the ground, walked off the pitch. When Clues came around, the referee also sent him off. Some people should not play rugby. Only playing in 2 of the 3 tests, Bassett was top scorer with 5 tries.

Leaving Halifax for York in 1948, Arthur Bassett had scored 66 tries in 110 appearances. Bassett had scored 99 tries in 101 games for Cardiff. Like Billy Boston, Gus Risman never played for Cardiff but may be '*the finest player the city has ever produced*'. Aged 18 he joined Salford rugby league club in 1929, and was still playing professional rugby aged 43, in 1954. An outside-half, Gus briefly returned to union during the war partnering Bleddyn Williams in the centre. Bleddyn said Risman was 'the best' he'd ever played with. In December 2020 Risman was named as one of three Welsh rugby league players to be honoured with a new statue in Cardiff Bay, the other two being Billy Boston and Clive Sullivan, all Cardiff-born and bred. Despite Cardiff's serious losses to rugby league, W. R. 'Billy' Davies from Kenfig Hill joined, to replace fly-half Cliff Jones, who was often not available. Davies played 31 games, scoring 4 tries, then 'went North' to Wigan.

At times there were 9 Welshmen in Wigan's team of 13 and a total of 17 on their books in 1938 -1939. They were known as 'Wigan Welsh'. Gwyn Williams must have felt 'at home' there. Willie Davies' brother was a miner, the famous prop Cliff, who joined Cardiff in 1945-46, playing 190 times for Cardiff, 16 times for Wales and was a Lion in New Zealand in 1950.

CHAPTER 18 - CARDIFF SEASON 1947-48

CARDIFF'S GREATEST SEASON – THE SECOND 'GOLDEN ERA' - BLEDDYN WILLIAMS SETS THE TRY RECORD WITH 41 - TEN PLAYERS CHOSEN FOR WALES - A THIRD QUADRUPLE AGAINST NEWPORT – AMAZING CLUB TRY RECORD - AUSTRALIA BEATEN – CARDIFF TERMED *'THE AUTOMATIC SCORING MACHINE'* – *'THEIR STYLE OF TEAM-WORK PLAY WAS UNEQUALLED SINCE THE "GOLDEN DAYS" OF WELSH RUGBY AT THE BEGINNING OF THE CENTURY'*

Bleddyn Williams P30 T41 = 123pts; **Bryn Williams** (Athletic); **Roy Roberts** P38 T2 C30 = 66pts (Taff's Well); **Bill Tamplin** P24 T1 C41 P14= 127pts; Doug Jones* P29 T22 = 66pts (Taff's Well); Ray Bale P9 (Tongwynlais)

(* The Taff's Well wing Douglas H. Jones scored a try when Cardiff defeated Australia, but left to play for Aberavon, Swansea and Maesteg, only playing one more game for Cardiff, a season later. This was his debut season and he scored 4 tries in one Harlequins game, a season in which Quins were beaten 29-8 and 31-5, 13 tries to 3. In the 29-8 morning victory, 9 Cardiff players that afternoon were in the Welsh team than defeated Australia, Bill Tamplin kicking 2 penalties to win 6-0. That Harlequins 'away' game was played at Penarth, as the RFU was holding its final trial at Twickenham.)

Pl 41, W 39, L2, D 0. Points 803-161 Tries 182-22, Pens 23-13

Davies compared this season to the two other 'great' seasons:
1885-86 Pl 27, W 26, L 1, D 0. Points 533-18. Tries 133-4 (four - not a misprint!)
1905-06 Pl 32, W 29, L 1, D 2. Points 513-86. Tries 118-20
1947-48 Pl 41, W 39, L 2, D 0. Points 801-161. Tries 182-22, Pens 23-13

In 1947-48, **Cardiff outscored their opponents by over eight tries to one!** At top level rugby this has never happened over the course of a season. Their two narrow losses were when up to 10 of the First Team were playing for Wales or in International Trials. And pitches, especially at home on the Arms Park, were terrible for three to four months of the season. Their match average was 4.4 to 0.5 on tries, and 0.6-0.3 points on penalties. The team scored 98 tries, converted another 84, dropped 5 goals and kicked 23 penalties, 803 points in the scoring of the day, but with modern scoring 1,162 points, 28 points per game. With modern scoring, Cardiff's opponents scored 12 goals (converted tries), 10 tries, 8 dropped goals and 13 penalties, 197 points, or 4.8 points a game. **In today's**

scoring the average result would be **Cardiff 28 – Opponents 5**.
Interestingly, Bleddyn always played left centre, and Jack Matthews right
centre, although some teams preferred today's specialisation of inside and
outside centre, often one big and one very big (not a misprint). Their wings
were very lucky men, as both centres held to the credo of putting their
wing over the line to score tries. Neither centre ever played for personal
glory. Incidentally, as a rule, more tries were scored by the left wing, as
most players were better at passing off their right hand, to their left. With
virtually infinity times the coaching and training, today's top professional
players are probably more adept at passing both ways, however. (The
strangest occurrence in modern rugby however, is that you see players with
hands like dinner-plates, especially forwards, dropping the better modern
ball).

1947-48 Cardiff supplied 11 players this season

Bleddyn Williams scored his Cardiff record of 41 tries, followed by Les
Williams 34, D.H. Jones 22, Jack Matthews 12, Billy Cleaver 12, H.
Loveluck 7, Cliff Davies 6, Elvet Jones 5, H. Thomas and Dai Jones 5,
Gwyn Evans and Ian McJennett 4 each. Bleddyn always preferred to put
his wing (Les Williams) over for the try, remember, so they scored 75
between them, 41% of Cardiff's tries. 152 of the 182 tries were scored by
11 players. It was only in the very last game, that his teammates convinced
Bleddyn to go for the try-scoring record and went all-out to help him.
Bleddyn's left wing partner Les Williams was to score 47 tries in 51

matches between 1947 and 1949, before the Welsh international 'went North'.

Haydn Tanner was captain, with Bleddyn Williams vice-captain. Tanner was considered the greatest scrumhalf of the day, leading Cardiff and the Barbarians against the touring Australians, and captaining Wales four times. Almost as good as Tanner was the young Llandaff player Rex Willis, making his Firsts debut. Because of the Athletic's previous wonderful season, Cardiff had a choice from around 42 excellent players for their two teams. Early in the season, a visiting combined Stade Nantais/U.S. Cognac XV had been beaten 18-0 (3 converted tries, 1 try), with Bleddyn scoring all three tries. Before the game, Wilf Wooller made his final appearance on a rugby field, when Cardiff played Nantes for the 'Veterans Championship of the World'. The imposing Wooller was still regarded as a dangerous player by the French, with their small international centre Henri Behoteguy often tackling him before the ball was on its way. Cardiff's Veterans won 29-8.

Bleddyn and Billy Cleaver are either side of captain Haydn Tanner. Roy Roberts and Bill Tamplin are the second and third players from the right, standing

On 27 September 1947, a week after the Nantes/Cognac game, 40,000 spectators saw Cardiff beat Australia 11-3 (converted try, try, drop goal and penalty to penalty), in a great game. Bill Tamplin remembered, *'I think the most famous match in which I played for Cardiff was that against the Australian Touring Team, on 27th September 1947, in which we did what I* should imagine very Welshman wanted us to do. *It is very difficult to remember any difficult individual effort on that day, because each and every one of the team played like men possessed. The one thing I shall never forget is the look on Cliff Davies' face when, in the closing minutes of the game he hurled himself across the Australian goal-line with two or three Australians hanging on to him, and then getting up and saying, "How's that Tanner, just to make sure!"'* Haydn Tanner recalled the same contest – *'The Cardiff v. Australia game in the 1947-48 season will always stand out in my mind as THE match as far as the Cardiff XV is concerned. First it was against a touring XV which is always an occasion; secondly, we were the first team to defeat them on their tour; and thirdly, it was during this game that the Cardiff XV really settled down into the brilliant combination that established a new record by scoring over 800 points in one season.'* Australia beat England, Scotland and Ireland, only losing to Wales and France. And Cardiff, as always.

Unfortunately, Australia were down to 14 men for over half the game, when a forward was injured and went off, but Australia's captain was generous in his praise of *'the best team'*. The *Daily Telegraph* reported that both defences were so good that the only way to make ground was the kick ahead, and Billy Cleaver played the kicking game to perfection. Cleaver played fullback in this game, instead of his normal fly half position for Cardiff, where for Wales he played three times outside scrumhalf Haydn Tanner. Cleaver then played outside Rex Willis in the 1950 Grand Slam team. Billy Cleaver played the rest of his 14 internationals in the centre, but was again fullback for the Lions in 3 tests on tour against New Zealand. An exciting player, with a shock of curly blond hair, he was a Treorchy coal miner during the war years, and debuted for Cardiff in its first match after WW2. He retired in 1951 after 141 games for the club. William Benjamin Cleaver was born in 1921, and with mining being a protected industry, served the war effort down the pit, but later graduated from university and became a manager in the coal industry. A Barbarian, Cleaver played in the first Welsh international after the war, in 1947, at the age of 26. (Yet another star, some of whose best playing years, aged 18 to 25, were 'lost'.) A wonderfully intelligent playmaker, Cleaver became secretary of the Contemporary Arts Society for Wales and vice-chairman of the Welsh Arts Council.

The team scored 13 tries in the two Harlequins fixtures, against just 3, winning 29-8 and 31-5. Gloucester were defeated 11-1 on tries, 12-6 and 33-3. The December Coventry game was cancelled owing to frost, but at home Cardiff won 33-8, scoring 9-1 on tries. It was not a good year for English clubs. Bristol lost 29-6 and 16-0, 11-1 on tries. Even Leicester were routed by 13-1 on tries, a modern-day score of 64-5, and Bleddyn wrote: *'It was this season that Cardiff scored a 50 point to 5 victory over Leicester at the Arms Park; I scored four tries in our first meeting with*

Newport, and figured at out-half in place of injured Bill Cleaver at Neath, where Cardiff won 6-5 after I had first cut through to send Les Williams over, and then punted to the corner, and followed up to score as Gwyn Evans tapped the ball back inside to me. Towards the end of the season Cardiff defeated Pontypool 30-3 in a match of fisticuffs. Tempers boiled over and blows were struck. Dr. Jack figured in one such incident, but he also scored four tries! That was the only unpleasant match we had, and throughout the season we maintained our attacking policy, often starting moves from our own "25" – and once or twice from behind our touchline.'

Cardiff beat Wasps away by 7-1 on tries, and at home by 5 tries to 0. (Wasps were and are a first-class side, and in the 44 games against Cardiff between when fixtures began in 1945-46, and when this book stops featuring Cardiff, in 1974-75, the record is as follows: Played 44 – Cardiff won 39, lost 3, drew 2. Cardiff points 721-225; tries 160-39. It is an amazing record.) Even Swansea shipped 6 tries at Cardiff, and on the annual tour the clubs Plymouth Albion and Penzance lost the try count 11-0 and 8-0 respectively. In the 72nd year of four matches in a season, for the third time in history Cardiff beat Newport in every game. The second match at Rodney Parade drew a crowd of 22,000, a record attendance for a club match at the ground. The only close match was the third match at Rodney Parade when Cardiff narrowly won 8-5. The scores were Cardiff H 29-0, A 12-0, A 8-5, H 19-3. In the four Newport games, Cardiff won their Grand Slam with a try count 13-1. In the last game Bleddyn was unusually playing right centre. Newport had a very good side at this time, it is just that Cardiff were unstoppable, even in dire playing conditions and missing their best players, being able to win.

Bath rugby club reported on its 3-0 away loss to Cardiff on 17 January 1948: '*Cardiff fielded just three of their normal side. They had a record of ten players on duty at Twickenham. (Frank Trott, Les Williams, Billy Cleaver, Bleddyn Williams, Haydn Tanner, Cliff Davies, Maldwyn James, W E Tamplin, Les Mansfield and Gwyn Evans!) In the early stages, both sides tried to play an open game, but incessant rain gradually made handling impossible, and players became almost unrecognisable under a layer of all-pervading Arms Park mud. Cardiff had the better of the scrums throughout and amidst the scramble Cardiff's determination was rewarded with a try by Loveluck.'* The Reverend Howard Loveluck played the first of his 37 games for the team before the war, retiring from rugby in 1949-50. In all 28 games against Bath, from 1932 to 1975, Cardiff won 24, drew 3 and lost only 1 when missing their best players.

The cream of English clubs were literally hammered in this season (there were no Northampton fixtures): Harlequins 29-8 and 31-5 (13-3 try count); Gloucester 12-6 and 33-3 (11-1); Coventry (only 1 game) 33-8 (9-1); Bristol 29-6 and 16-0 (11-1); Leicester 50-5 and 8-4 (13-1); and Wasps 23-7 and 20-4 (12-1). Cardiff averaged 6 tries per game against 1, in these 11 fixtures. Played 11 – Points for 284 – Points against 56 – Tries for 69 – Tries against 8. The reader may search for a suitable adjective for these results. 'Remarkable' cannot suffice. 'Astounding' will serve.

Cardiff were constantly under strength because of losing up to 10 players at a time for international trials, internationals, work commitments and injuries, losing only two games for these reasons. (International trials were held at Cardiff, usually the Final Trial of three, but also at other grounds across South Wales). In over half their matches, however, they scored four tries or more. Of the 24 tries conceded, 3 were in the 'reserve team' loss at Penarth. No other team scored 3 tries, and the only clubs to score 2 were when Cardiff were running the ball from all over the pitch, when Cardiff defeated Devonport Services (7-2 on tries), Cardiff and District (7-2) and Harlequins (6-2). No other team scored more than one try. The only other loss was another severely weakened team away at Pontypool in September 1947. Cardiff scored a converted try, two tries and a penalty, to a try and three drop goals, losing 17-14. In modern scoring, with a try being worth 5 points and a drop goal being 3 instead of 4, Cardiff would have won 20-14. A form of revenge was achieved against Pontypool in the return fixture in April 1948, with Cardiff's full team scoring 8 tries to 1, winning 30-3, in modern scoring 46-5. Jack Matthews ran in for 4 tries. The backs were: Frank Trott, Les Williams, Bleddyn, Dr. Jack, D.H. Jones, Billy Cleaver, Haydn Tanner. Forwards: W.G. Jones, Maldwyn James, Ray Bale, R.M. Glover, Bill Tamplin, Elvet Jones, Roy Roberts (No 8), Gwyn Evans. For Cardiff, Roberts played Number 8, wing forward, second row or prop and shared the kicking with Tamplin. With a full team, Cardiff never looked like being beaten. The remarkable Stan 'Buttons' Bowes could play wing forward and second row as well as his preferred position of prop. Bleddyn began playing rugby at scrumhalf, but was adept at outside half and centre. All the Williams brothers could play in multiple positions at the top level.

Record gates were seen at home and away, when Cardiff's stars were known to be playing, for example at Newport and Bristol. Gates had to be closed before kick-off at Newport, and 30,000 squeezed into the Arms Park to see the Barbarians easily beaten in March 1948, 14-3 (2 converted tries, a try and a penalty to a penalty). Cardiff had to rearrange an away match against Harlequins, to play it at Penarth, on the morning of Saturday 20 December, scoring 6 tries in their 29-8 win, although missing 9 men playing for Wales against Australia that afternoon. The 'full' team later played 'Quins' at home, scoring 7 tries and winning 31-5.

There would have been 10 Cardiff players against Australia, on 20 December 1947, but Haydn Tanner was unfit, and Cleaver was switched from outside half to fullback. Cardiff No.8 Les Manfield was reported to be the best forward on the field. Bill Tamplin was captain and kicked 2 penalties, one from 40 years on the touchline, for Wales to win 6-0. Cardiff also had 9 players playing away against Ireland on 13 March, losing 6-3 to the eventual Grand Slam winners. Upon this day Penarth beat Cardiff 15-6, only the second loss of the season. Cardiff scored 2 tries against 3 converted tries, both teams playing most of the game with 14 men because of injury. Davies writes: '*The defeat at Penarth came on the same day that Wales were playing Ireland at Belfast – a game that included nine Cardiff players.*' The full Cardiff team met Penarth again on 4 April 1948, scoring 5 tries to none and winning 29-3, in today's scoring 36-3. It was the only game of the season where Cardiff kicked 3 penalty goals, probably 'rubbing it in' to avenge their earlier loss. They kicked 2 penalties apiece against Gloucester, Swansea and Llanelli, and a single penalty in just 14 of their other 23 games – a statistic unheard of today, of course.

Cardiff supplied 11 players to the 1947–48 Wales sides, skippered by scrum half Haydn Tanner. Standing: W. Les T. Williams, C.Davies, G.Evans, L.Manfield, R.F.Trott, D.M.James. Seated: W.B.Cleaver, H.Tanner (capt.), B.L.Williams, Dr J. Mathews. Inset: W.E.Tamplin.

The Welsh team had begun the Five Nations Championship by drawing 3-3 at Twickenham in January, then easily beat Scotland 14-0 at home, but lost the next home game to France 11-3. After losing 6-3 away to Ireland, only England's results prevented Wales from receiving the 'Wooden Spoon'. In 4th place, Wales finished on 3 points, with 20 points for and 23 against – a most unusual occurrence. In a team packed with the best players from the best club in Europe, one would have hoped for better. I blame it upon leaving out Roy Roberts, Tamplin's partner in the 'engine room' of the Cardiff scrum. (Another point to note is that the French game was riddled with professionalism at this time.) Eleven of Cardiff's players were capped for Wales when fit: Cliff Davies, W. B. 'Billy' Cleaver, Gwyn Evans, Maldwyn James, Les Manfield, Jack Matthews, R. F. 'Frank' Trott, Les Williams, Bleddyn Williams, Haydn Tanner and Cardiff's pack leader W. E. 'Bill' Tamplin. Against Australia and Ireland there were 9 Cardiff players, and **against England, Scotland and France, 10 played**.

188

Billy Cleaver reminisced: '*In March 1948, the Welsh XV, at that time nick-named by many cynics in the West "The Cardiff 2nd Team", gave an ignominious display against France at St. Helen's. The following Saturday, the entry of the Cardiff team on to Stradey Park to play Llanelli was greeted by caustic comments and ripe remarks. That day the team played magnificently, and the shouts of derision soon changed to shouts of acclaim. Apart from personal satisfaction and redemption, it proved to me that good rugby anywhere will overcome any prejudices.*' (The game was actually upon 21 February). Cardiff won at Llanelli 14-0, scoring 4 tries, one converted, a score today of 22-0. In the following season Cardiff won both games 9-8 (H) and 3-0 (A), scoring 3 tries to 1. Eleven Cardiff doubles against Llanelli were achieved in this post-war period, when 4 fixtures per season had been reduced to 2, in 1947-48, 1948-49,1954-55, 1955-56, 1959-60, 1960-61, 1961-62, 1963-64, 1966-67, 1968-69, and 1971-72; Llanelli scored doubles in 1958-59, 1967-68 and 1973-74. Cardiff played against Captain Geoffrey Crawshay's Rest of Wales XV on 28 April 1948, to pay for the Gwyn Nicholls Memorial Gates, which now adorn the Quay Street entrance to the Cardiff Arms Park. The only scores were from Bleddyn Williams, two unconverted tries.

Cardiff won 3 games at Easter weekend 1948, including against the Barbarians 13-3, and on the following weekend on the Devon/Cornwall tour had an aggregate score of 78-0. Cardiff had beaten Newport 3 times in the season, 29-0 (including 6 tries) at home, 12-0 (4 tries) away, 8-5 away (a try apiece), and were hoping to win all four of their local Derbies. Newport had never achieved the feat, since the 4 games a season was established in 1888-89, and Cardiff had last won all 4 in 1905-06. Four days after the Cornish tour, on 10 April, the Arms Park was filled to capacity, and Cardiff won easily 19-3 (converted try, two tries and drop goal to a penalty). In the previous season, Cardiff had won 3 and drawn one and were unbeaten for 15 matches, until 1 April, 1950 against the '*Black and Ambers*'. Newport have had sequences of 4,5,5,5,4 and 4 wins against Cardiff from 1876 up to 1975, but never 4 in a season. Cardiff had sequences of 4,8,4,6,5,4,4,5,7,4,6 and 5 wins in the same period, but 'slams' of 4 wins in a season were rare indeed. It was Cardiff's third 'Slam'. Newport attracted players from the town and the Gwent Valleys, whereas Cardiff had a far higher population, plus Penarth and the Rhondda and Cynon Valleys which supplied great players. Access from the Valleys was easy by train for players and supporters. Also, Cardiff always had the prestige of being the 'best' even in, for them, poor seasons, and to play for Cardiff meant that one was in the forefront of the Welsh selectors' eyes.

Australia's last tour match was an inaugural game against the Barbarians. Cardiff supplied five players to the 'Baa-baas', Haydn Tanner (captain), R. F. Trott, W. E. Tamplin, W. B. Cleaver and Bleddyn Williams, and Australia lost 9-6. Tamplin, Cleaver and Bleddyn also had won for Cardiff and Wales against the tourists, who only lost 6 games out of 39. None of the four home nations could score a try against them, but Cardiff scored two and France three. Apart from the Barbarians, Wales and Cardiff, the tourists only lost to France 13-6, Lancashire and Cheshire 9-8, and London Counties 14-8. The last match of Cardiff's season was Gloucester at Cardiff on 28 April. The individual Cardiff try-scoring record of 40 had been set by T. W. Pearson in 1892-93. Danny Davies had been club captain in 1925-26, played 192 games at fly half, and was now the club's official statistician, later to be a Lions assistant manager and President of the WRU – a great man. He waited until a few days before the game, before telling the players that Bleddyn had already scored 37 tries in 1947-48, so only needed 3 more to equal the 55-year record.

The players were enthused, and as Davies reports: *'so they had one main object in view – "we've got to help Bleddyn get the record" ... The team played splendidly and attacked from all angles and opportunities, they ran and looked for Bleddyn to pass to, when some of them could have easily scored themselves. Gloucester were over-run, nine tries in all were scored and Bleddyn got four to beat Pearson's record, a great night for Bleddyn, his team and the club. The record of 41 tries in one season stands today.'* Bleddyn said *'It was a wonderful end to a wonderful season for all of us'* – a record achieved not by grinding down the opposition and using 23 over-sized professionals, as today, but by just 15 fit, unpaid men enjoying throwing the ball around – and knowledgeable crowds flocking to be entertained. Today's game is *'brutal'*, an aspiration of England coach Eddie Jones for his team over the first seven years of his tenure.

In his biography, Bleddyn records that he had no idea the record was at stake: *'Casually, Danny Davies, the club statistician, mentioned to me as I trotted out of the dressing-room, "Score three tries today, Bleddyn, and you'll be the record club try-scorer." The word had spread like bushfire throughout the team; every player knew, and so did the 20,000 Arms Park crowd. I scored only one first half try, and it looked far from certain that I would make the target. Indeed, Gloucester had startled us by scoring first! In the second half, as soon as a Cardiff player received the ball he would look around for me. "Give it to Bleddyn" seemed to be on everyone's mind. And I never felt so tired in all my life! I chased everywhere, and when I eventually plumped the ball down for try No. 3, I felt I should stay on the ground and let them carry me off. Exhaustion does not adequately describe my feelings. A record-breaker! Forty-one tries! It hammered in my head to the rhythm of the train wheels on my way home to Bristol, where I was living at the time. It was not until Violet read it in the newspapers that she knew. Never have I known a wife so furious. "Why didn't you tell me?" And it required a persuasive explanation to convince her that I did not even know myself until a minute before the kick-off!'*

Unusually, Roy Roberts played number 8, instead of second row alongside Bill Tamplin in Bleddyn's milestone game, and his son Mike loaned me the Cardiff - Gloucester match programme. There are adverts for the two great Cardiff department stores, now sadly gone, David Morgan (telephone 6200) and Howells, adjoining each other in St Mary Street; one for the Angel Hotel with its 'American' and other bars; an ad for ex-player W. Wooller & Co Hire Purchase and Insurance Brokers; and one for *'for keeping muscles suppled and toning them up... there's nothing more effective than... Elliman Athletic Rub'*. The advertisement for Welsh Sports in Castle Arcade offered *Rugby Cases; Bladders* (these two together with a lace, made a leather ball for younger readers); *Hose* (socks); *Boots* (only black, with ankle protection, i.e. proper rugby boots, not the white, yellow, forget-me-not blue or pink ballet slippers we witness today); *Scrum Caps* (only in brown leather, of course); *Boot Studs* (at this time they were nailed in, using longer studs for muddy pitches); *Jerseys; Shirts* (even this decrepit old fool is not sure of the difference between the two); *Anklets; Knee Supports* (crepe bandage strappings, modern materials like neoprene did not exist); *Crepe Bandages etc., etc.* (Crepe was a white or cream, slightly 'stretchy' wool fabric material.)

It is worth repeating the *'Notes and Comments'* from Roy Robert's faded blue and black programme of this Gloucester end-of-season game: *'All good things come to an end! This rugby season has been an enjoyable one for Cardiff rugby followers, and although not perhaps from mere statistics an all-time record, since in 1905-06, only one match was lost – that against New Zealand. However, this season's matches have produced a host of new records, and first and foremost comes the huge tally of points. Before today's game begins, Cardiff will be 30 short of 800, and it will be up to Gloucester to try and succeed where others have failed. Today's match is the 41st on the Cardiff fixture list and is a rearranged fixture from February 21, when the ground was too hard to play. Gloucester have had a splendid season, and their outside-half W.E. Jones – unfortunately engaged in a lighter battle on the adjoining cricket field and consequently not available for today's match – has scored well over 200 points to create a personal record. His magnificent kicking has won match after match, and he is quite the best kicker in the game today. They have a splendid pack of forwards and promise to make a grand game of it and not fall into the error made by Pontypool on Saturday. All was going well until a Pontypool forward lost his head, and then trouble – real trouble – started. After the match apologies were made but too late for 25,000 spectators had seen unpleasantness that could have been avoided so easily.'* Cardiff had won at Gloucester 12-6, by 2 tries and 2 penalties to 2 penalties. In this home game, Cardiff scored 9 tries, 3 converted, to 1 try, to beat Gloucester, one of England's top teams, 33-3, in modern scoring 51-5. Just four days before, Cardiff had played Pontypool at the Arms Park. After their home win against a weakened Cardiff team, Pontypool were desperate for a double against Cardiff, and there had been some rough play, but Cardiff won their home game 30-3, with 8 tries, three converted, against a try – in modern scoring 46-5. In the 13 previous 'Ponty' games, Cardiff had won 11, with 2 drawn, and in the next 18 games, Cardiff won 17 with 1 drawn. (In 121 games against Pontypool, from 1908 to 1974, Cardiff won 83, lost 25 and drew 13, with 281 tries against 135, but Pontypool shaded Cardiff on penalties, like many other teams, 60-58. Just four days later, Cardiff also thrashed Gloucester.

The programme continues: '*The Cardiff Club, 1947-48 - An Appreciation*' by J.B.G. Thomas: '*This season has been a splendid one, and followers of the game will discuss for many years whether it is a better one than that enjoyed in the 1905-06 season. It is difficult to compare any two seasons so far apart, but it is correct to say that the present-day side is a very fine collection of individual players welded together into a first-class combination. Under the inspiring leadership of Haydn Tanner, they have upheld the traditions of the Club and produced much brilliant rugby to delight crowds at home and away. At all times they have played the open theoretical game and brought much pleasure both to themselves and to their opponents. It is only on rare occasions that their opponents have attempted to frustrate the very excellent spirit. Looking back over the season, it is a good thing that the first match was lost, since it left the team with no unbeatable record to defend.* (A very weakened team just lost to Pontypool away). *They were free to play the game in the spirit they enjoy so much. It is to their great credit that never once at the Arms Park have they closed the game up, in order to preserve their ground record. Throughout, the forwards have done sterling work and achieved one great feat in holding and getting on top of the Australian touring pack to lay the foundations of that side's first defeat. In most games they have got on top to enable the backs to score points and win matches.*

Well led by Tamplin and Roberts, they always held together as a unit in the midst of difficulties. Maldwyn James won most of the hooking duels and had splendid assistance from W.G. Jones, Cliff Davies, Bale and Bowes. In the second row Tamplin, Roberts, Carter and Glover have pushed hard and jumped well in the line-outs. The back row have set a high standard of intelligence and enthusiasm with Elvet Jones unlucky in not getting a "cap". At half back, Tanner and Cleaver have generally dominated the opposition, to cover and kick in defence and make a continuous series of openings for a remarkably powerful three-quarter line. J. Matthews and Bleddyn Williams have been the outstanding pair of club centres in the four countries, and reached their best form last Saturday. They have fed their wings with accuracy and regularity, for them to score over fifty tries between them.

Finally, the modest Frank Trott at full back – reliable and accurate –

well deserving of his honour of playing for Wales. Yes, it has been a grand season and much of the credit must go to the Athletic XV – the "Rags" – who have supplied the all-important reserves to fill the "gaps" when the leading players have been away. It proves the old maxim that the strength of a successful club must lay in its reserves. Cardiff's Record to Date - P.40, W.38, D 0, L.2, Points for 770, Against 158. How the Points were Scored – For C.G.81, T.19, D.G.5, P.G.23, Total 770. Against – C.G.12, T9, D.G.8, P.G.13, Points 158.' Most of Cardiff's tries were scored under or near the posts, accounting for the high percentage of conversions (81%), as a result of attacking from distance, a tad different to today's trench warfare and long-term sieges of the try line.

We should here mention Richard 'Frank' Trott, who won 8 Welsh caps at fullback from 1947 to 1948. Born in 1915, he missed the playing years of 1939 to 1946 because of the War, when he was aged 24 to 31. Joining from Penarth, where he was captain, Frank had first played for Cardiff in 1937-38, retiring after 205 appearances in 1952-53, and becoming the club's Honorary Secretary for many years. Frank was a Cardiff boy, as was his cousin Frank William Whitcombe, *'The Big Man'*, who played for Cardiff Athletic in 1931, and then London Welsh as a prop, before heading North in 1935 for a stellar career in Rugby League. From Grangetown, and one of ten children, Whitcombe was given 2 new suits and £100 when he went professional, and had to pay £90 to buy himself out of the Army. He would have walked into the Welsh Rugby Union team, and Bradford Northern paid a **world record transfer fee** of £850 in 1938, calling him *'the best in the game'* (- scrums were contested at this time in league). Like Frank Trott, his career was upset by war, but he won the Lance Todd Trophy as best player in the Challenge Cup Final at Wembley in both 1946-47 and in 1947-48. After the second game, he was the first player to be awarded The Lance Todd Trophy while on the losing team, as well as the **first forward and the oldest player**. Bradford Northern's 12–0 victory over Halifax in the 1948-49 Challenge Cup Final, their third in succession, was the first Challenge Cup Final to be sold out with 95,050 spectators. Just 29 days short of his 35th birthday, he again became the oldest as well as the heaviest player to play in a Challenge Cup final.

No one in Wales remembers Whitfield, but regarding the 1947 Final, his teammate Trevor Foster in his biography recalled *'On our bus journey to the stadium we were caught up in a traffic jam and running late. The driver was in a state of panic, it could have been something to do with him not being sure of the route through London. Much to our amusement the great character, Frank Whitcombe, took over the driver's seat and proceeded to bypass all traffic in front and put his foot on the pedals. We sailed through the centre of the big city. Past the Palace of Westminster with motorists bellowing and waving fists at our bus. Frank, with a huge smile sailed away to get us to Wembley bang on time'.* Foster also remembered an incident after Bradford Northern's 8–4 victory over Leeds, in the 1946–47 Challenge Cup Final. (Northern also beat Leeds 11-9 in a fierce Yorkshire Cup tie win). The Australian international Arthur Clues kicked out violently at Northern's Welsh scrumhalf Gwylfa Jones at a scrum, missing his head by inches. *'Immediately Whitcombe stood up from the scrum and confronted his reckless action. He ran towards Arthur with both fists clenched. Whitcombe drove the full force of his 18-stone frame into Arthur Clues' chest and pole-axed him.*

Clues could not get his breath and for ten minutes received emergency medical attention in front of the 17,000 Odsal crowd. Before the referee could send Whitcombe off, Whitcombe was already walking towards the changing rooms, knowing what was coming. Arthur Clues was carried off on a stretcher and also sent off. In time-honoured tradition the two men shook hands after the game, to show their mutual respect for each other. Clues later confessed that no one had ever hit him so hard. Whitcombe received a 9-week ban for his actions. Whitcombe and Clues became great friends when their playing days were over. They used to spend a lot of time in Whitcombe's public house, The Kings Head in Bradford. Whitcombe took on the role of self-appointed 'minder' for Bradford Northern's slightly built, mercurial Welsh stand-off Willie Davies when he was targeted by opposing teams.' What a loss to Welsh Rugby Union. One hesitates to call the Australian Clues a thug, but he appeared earlier in this book in that role.

A Taff's Well player, who had played for Cardiff during the war, but only for the 'Rags' after, being kept out of the First team by Billy Cleaver, was Jack Russell, who now joined Penarth for this season. A fly-half, he helped give *'a sense and purpose to the Penarth team effort'*, and his talent was soon recognised. The revitalised Penarth beat Aberavon, just lost at Maesteg 13-11 and 8-5 at Pontypool, and drew with Neath 9-9, although missing up to four first-teamers for these games, playing for their counties or other representative teams. With 14 men after an early injury, Penarth beat Birmingham 11-3, but mounting injuries, including one to Jack Russell, left the team depleted before a 'bruising' 3-0 defeat to Ebbw Vale. The team needed to appeal for 'clothing coupons' in these days of rationing, to buy shirts for their teams. However, at the end of January 1948, Jack Russell had left Penarth for Hunslet Rugby League, joining two other recent Penarth players, Delgado and Slamin. Even so, it was a good season for Penarth, finishing above Abertillery, Llanelli and Cross Keys in the unofficial table, and beating the merit table leaders Cardiff (who were without nine of their internationals playing against Ireland). Ray Roberts scored one of Penarth's three converted tries against his cousin Roy Robert's team's two tries. Ray joined Roy at Cardiff for the next season, 1948-49, but only played five times for the Firsts, becoming a fixture for the 'Rags'. Penarth hooker Ray Roberts from Taff's Well was one of

Penarth's recognised kickers. Ray Roberts was so good that he was selected for the first Welsh Trial in 1950-51, having left Cardiff after 5 games in that season, not being able to oust Geoff Beckingham from hooker.

Jack Russell, well known to the Williams brothers, has a small display cabinet in Taff's Well clubhouse, added after the fire that burnt the treasured Bleddyn Williams and other collections. It reads: *JACK RUSSELL – JOHN MARTYN RUSSELL (JACK) Born 29.10.23. Playing Record. Taff's Well School - Cardiff Schoolboys - Taff's Well RFC – Penarth RFC – Cardiff RFC – Royal Inniskilling Dragoon Guards – British Occupation Army of the Rhine (B.O.A.R.) – Combined Services – Welsh Triallist - Hunslet RLFC – Cardiff Rugby League (Capt.)'* A January 1948 newspaper cutting reads: '*Hunslet sign Welsh Fly-Half – Hunslet R.L. scouts have returned from South Wales with the signature of a stand-off, John Martin Russell, 24, 5ft 9in, 11st 8lb, who has played with Penarth since he was demobilised last September. He is travelling North on Friday... the Hunslet coaches can talk to him about the differences between Rugby Union football, in which Russell has played so well, and the Rugby League game, for which he has, Hunslet scouts say, the highest promise. Russell, who is said to be fast and elusive, had two years with Cardiff before he went into the Royal Armoured Corps – he is a toolmaker – and while with Cardiff played alongside Bleddyn Williams and Cleaver. He played in the British Army of the Rhine in representative football* (rugby) *against the Central Mediterranean Forces and the Army of the United Kingdom, and with a representative side he had a six-week tour of Italy. Partnered R. Williams. He played in representative schools football, then he partnered Dickie Williams, the Leeds stand-off half, in the centre – and he is a young man on whom more than one Rugby League club has looked upon hopefully. Hunslet had heard of him when they sent their scouts to South Wales the other week, but that afternoon they were first of all interested in a Penarth wing-man. They were, however, so impressed with Russell's work, that they had another deputation to South Wales on Saturday, and after the game they signed him. He is eligible for cup-ties. Hunslet interest in South Wales is not ended...*'

An adjacent article is full of Welsh names playing in the league game. 'Jack' Russell was annoyed that he could not break through into the Cardiff First team after the war, being kept out by international Billy Cleaver, and was not content playing for the 'Rags'. At Taff's Well, he had been offered money to play for Senghenydd, but refused, and the current joke at that time was that at Llanelli the car park money was for the players. Like all RL players, Jack was supposed to have a job, but was not needed much at Jowett Javelin cars, where he earned £4 a week, plus his £9 a week for rugby. (The Jowett Javelin was an executive car which was produced from 1947 to 1953 by Jowett Cars Ltd of Idle, near Bradford in

England. Hunslet is in central Leeds.) Russell's move to Hunslet may have influenced international Les Williams to also leave Cardiff for that club. From 1940s pen pictures on the *Hunslet Heroes* website we read '*John Russell. Born Wales. Height 5 ft 8 in, Weight 11 st 8lbs. Age 24. Signed from Penarth, just in time for Cup-ties. Received his baptism in Rugby League in replayed First Round at Widnes, came through with flying colours and has settled in like a duck takes to water since then. Will develop into a great attacking player. Is sound defender, good handler and uses both feet well.*'

After 42 games, Cardiff easily topped the Welsh Unofficial Table, with the most difficult fixture list of all British teams. All teams aspired to improve their fixture lists, and games against prestigious Cardiff were eagerly sought. Apart from games against visiting international teams, the Barbarians and representative teams, the best English sides were always played. Dublin's Bective Rangers, Ireland's best team, was played regularly from 1956-57 until 1974-75, with Cardiff winning 16, drawing 3 and losing only 2. Edinburgh's Watsonians, the team of Scottish internationals Gavin and Scott Hastings, was a regular fixture from 1896 to 1973, and Cardiff won 34, lost 2 and drew 1 of 37 games. In the 100 years covered in this book, from 1876 to 1975, Cardiff has played against premier clubs Aberavon 85 times, Barbarians 91, Bath 28, Blackheath 98, Bridgend 95, Bristol 142, Coventry 85, Gloucester 157, Harlequins 91, Leicester 72, Llanelli 184, London Welsh 78, Moseley 65, Neath 156, Newport 328, Northampton 47, Penarth 126, Pontypool 121, Swansea 227 and Wasps 44. Against the England-based senior clubs – Bath, Blackheath, Bristol, Coventry, Gloucester, Harlequins, Leicester, London Welsh, Moseley, Northampton and Wasps – there were 971 matches, Cardiff winning 682 (70%), losing 221 (23%) and drawing 68 (7%). Amazingly, almost half the draws were against two of the eleven clubs: Gloucester 18 and Leicester 14.

There were just four new First XV caps in 1947-48. They were forward Elvet Jones, Welsh international Haydn Tanner who joined from Llanelli, D. H. Jones and Llanelli's wing Les Williams. In his first season, Elvet Jones played in 39 of 41 games, followed by W. G. Jones and Roy Roberts with 38. Les Williams played 35 times, and Haydn Tanner 33. Along with Trott, Tanner and other Cardiff players, Bleddyn Williams (30 games) and Billy Cleaver (29 games) had to fit in Cardiff games around Trials and Internationals. Club games were usually not cancelled for internationals, just shifted to the Saturday morning or the Friday before the game. Internationals were always played upon Saturday afternoon, unlike today's potpourri of fixture timings. T. Lyn Williams again captained the Rags, and their record was also outstanding: P31, W26, L3, D2, with points 453-124. One final note from Thau's marvellous history of Penarth RFC, about Cardiff in this season: '*Their style of team-work play was unequalled since* the *"Golden Days" of Welsh rugby at the beginning of the century.'* I make another digression here, to point out Cardiff RFC's unique record, not just having beaten every major touring team, but being unbeaten by Australia in six games, scoring 15 tries to 7. That record will always stand. And we must remember, all touring teams have <u>always</u> treated Cardiff as an 'international' fixture in the period of this book, always playing their First XVs.

28 December 1908 – Cardiff 24, Australia 8
Cardiff - 5 tries - Rhys Gabe, W.L. Morgan, Louis Dyke, J.L. Williams (2); 1 conversion (Percy Bush); 1 drop goal (Bush); 1 penalty (Bush). Australia - 1 converted try, 1 try
This was easily the biggest Australian defeat of the tour, Wales only winning 9-6, 2 tries and a conversion to 2 tries. Australia won the only other international, against England, 9-3, 3 tries to 1. (In 40 matches, Australia only lost 5 games, to Cardiff, Wales, Llanelli, Swansea and Midlands Combined, which shows the strength of Welsh rugby in this first 'Golden Age'.)

27 September 1947 - Cardiff 11, Australia 3
Cardiff: Frank Trott; Doug Jones, Jack Matthews, Bleddyn Williams, Les Williams; Billy Cleaver, Haydn Tanner (capt); Cliff Davies, Maldwyn James, WG Jones, Roy Roberts, Bill Tamplin, Elvet Jones, Gwyn Evans, Les Manfield

Scorers: Try: Doug Jones, Cliff Jones; Con: Tamplin; Pen: Tamplin. Australia - Scorer: Pen: Allan (Australia beat ALL the Home Nations, except Wales).

14 December 1957 - Cardiff 14, Australia 11

Cardiff: Alun Priday; Glyn John, Gordon Wells, Alan Barter, Howard Nicholls; Cliff Morgan, Rex Willis; Colin Howe, Geoff Beckingham, John Evans, Roddy Evans, Eddie Thomas (capt), Dai Hayward, CD Williams, Kingsley Jones

Scorers: Wells 2, John; Con: Priday; Pen: Priday. Australia - Scorers: Try: R Harvey, Shehadie; Con: R Harvey; Pen: Lenehan. (Australia beat ALL the Home Nations and France).

5 November 1966 - Cardiff 14, Australia 8

Cardiff: Ray Cheney; Keri Jones, Ken Jones, Gerald Davies, Maurice Richards; Phil Morgan, Billy Hullin; John O'Shea, Billy Thomas, Howard Norris, Keith Rowlands (capt), Lyn Baxter, John Hickey, Clive Evans, Tony Pender.

Scorers: Tries: Hullin, Ken Jones; Con: Cheney; Pen: Cheney; DG: Hullin. Australia - Scorers: Try: Boyce; Con: Lenehan; DG: Hawthorne (Australia gave England its heaviest defeat in 16 years, 23-12, scoring 5 tries to 2, beat Wales 14-11, but lost to the other Home Nations and France).

1 November 1975 - Cardiff 14, Australia 9

Cardiff: John Davies; Gerald Davies (capt), Paul Evans, Alex Finlayson, Lyn Jones; Gareth Davies, Brynmor Williams; Barry Nelmes, Alan Phillips, Mike Knill, Ian Robinson, Mark McJennett, Trevor Worgan, Stuart Lane (repl. Bob Dudley-Jones 63), Roger Lane.

Scorers: Tries: Jones, Gareth Davies; Pens: Gareth Davies 2. Australia - Scorers: Pens: McLean 3 (Australia were hammered 28-3 by Wales, losing also to Scotland and England, but beat Ireland 20-10).

24 October 1984 - Cardiff 16, Australia 12

Cardiff: Paul 'Pablo' Rees; Adrian Hadley, Mark Ring, Alun Donovan, Mike Carrington; Gareth Davies, Steve Cannon; Jeff Whitefoot, Alan Phillips (capt), Ian Eidman, Kevin Edwards, Rob Norster, Owen Golding, Gareth Roberts (repl. Bob Lakin), John Scott.

Scorers: Try: Hadley, penalty try; Con: Davies; Pen: Davies; DG: Davies. Australia - Scorers: Try: Black, Slack; Cons: Black 2.

(This was a superb Cardiff side and they were dominant in this game, scoring 2 tries to 1. However, this Australian side completed a 'Grand Slam', beating England 19-3, Scotland 37-12, Wales 28-9 and Ireland 16-9 – a total of 100-33 on points, averaging 25-8 per game. The only try scored against them was by David 'Dai' Bishop for Wales. So Cardiff scored twice as many tries as the four Home Nations. Australia have not played Cardiff RFC since, leaving the club with a **perfect record** of six wins from six games against the Wallabies. Cardiff were never once outscored on tries by Australia, counting the penalty try in 1984 as a try, the try count being 15-7. The regional team Cardiff Blues lost to Australia 31-3 in 2009, which to some of us shows the former strength of traditional – and profitable - Welsh club rugby over the regional imposition.)

CHAPTER 19 - CARDIFF SEASON 1948-1949

BLEDDYN'S SECRET – A CARDIFF PROFESSIONAL PLAYS FOR WALES – *'CARDIFF STILL SUPREME'* – *'THE GREAT CLUB TEAM OF THE UNITED KINGDOM'* - ROY ROBERTS CHANGES CLUBS

Bleddyn Williams P32 T25 = 75pts; **Bryn Williams** (Cardiff Athletic); **Bill Tamplin** P25 C41 P14 = 72pts (Risca); **Roy Roberts** P24 T4 C17 P6 = 64pts (Taff's Well); **Ray Roberts** P5 (Roy's hooker cousin, Taff's Well); Ray Bale P1 (Tongwynlais)

P44, W38, L3, D3. Points 630-213. Tries <u>146-33</u>, Pens 22-19

On 2 September 1948, Brice Jenkins, Cardiff's Honorary Secretary in succession to R.A. Cornish, sent a letter to Barry hooker Geoff Beckingham: *'Dear Sir, Following your recent Trial Game with this Club, my Committee would be glad if you would avail yourself of the facilities offered for training on our Ground. Training takes place on Tuesdays and Thursdays from 3.30p.m. to 8p.m. Should you need Training Kit the Head Groundsman will meet your needs. Until you are more acquainted with the Staff and Officials of this Club, you should produce this letter if necessary. Yours faithfully, B.H. Jenkins'* A following letter on 28 October was addressed *'Dear Beckingham, As a playing member of the Cardiff Rugby Club you have been accepted for membership of the Cardiff Athletic Club for Season 1948-1949. I shall therefore, be glad to receive your annual subscription of £1. 1. 0. As soon as convenient. Yours sincerely, BH Jenkins.'* Geoff Beckingham had obviously made it from 'faithfully' to 'sincerely', in the letter asking for a guinea. With Don Rees having moved to Neath, Cardiff's search for a new hooker was over, with Beckingham and John Phillips joining the club. (Rees later moved to Hunslet Rugby League). In the next page of his scrapbook, Geoff has pasted something rather different from more modern rugby songs:

To the Club that stands in Cardiff where the Rugby's played so well
To the dear old cocktail bar that we love so well,
Where the Blue and Blacks assemble with their glasses raised on high,
And the magic of their drinking casts a spell.
Yes, the magic of their drinking, of the beer we love so well,
The Committee knocking whiskies back like hell,
Your expenses are forthcoming – that's all old Brice will say,
So that the boys can tell old "Geevers" Brice won't pay.
Chorus
We're just a few of the boys who have played today, Oh! Oh! Oh!
We're just a few of the boys who have had their day, Oh! Oh! Oh!
Gentleman players all on the spree,
Doomed to the "Rags" for eternity
Rex have mercy on such as we, Ta! Ta! Ta!

In November 1948, the beginning of an article in *Rugger* (*Rugby World's* precursor) reads '*CARDIFF STILL SUPREME – No Signs of "Anno Domini" – out of the first two months of Welsh Rugby – one dominating fact emerges – Cardiff is still the greatest side in Wales. Indeed, it is the great club team of the United Kingdom.* **Tanner, Cleaver, Dr. Jack Matthews, Bleddyn Williams, Les Williams** *and* **Trott** *are playing brilliant rugby. The forwards have not been doing so well, although forwards* **Ewart Tamplin** *and* **Gwyn Evans*** *(both policemen by the way, seem as "Peter Pannish" as their backs. One cause of the forward weakness is due to the club not being able to find a good hooker, the ironical touch being that this season's Neath hooker is* **Don Rees**, *who was with the* **Cardiff** *club last year; moreover Rees is doing splendidly for his new club.* **Cardiff** *is also blessed with two top-notch right wings, and the big problem each week is to decide whether* **Russell Burns** *or* **T. Cook** *shall have the job'.* (*The article wrongly states Gwyn Williams.) At the time, Cardiff, over 53 days, had won their first ten matches: Cardiff & District 49-6 (H); Coventry 12-11 (A); Northampton 27-12 (A); Devonport Services 38-14 (H); Llanelli – then spelt Llanelly 3-0 (A); Neath 32-8 (H); Newport 9-0 (A); Gloucester 20-6 (H); Swansea 11-3 (A) and Rosslyn Park 24-0 (H).

Rugger, November 1948 reported '*Neath, who promised to be the team of the year, started off as they intended, making mincemeat of every other club. They astonished the crowds with their pre-Cardiff displays, but immediately they went to the Arms Park they "flopped" – and "flopped" pretty badly. Their defeat by a* **Cardiff side which would have beaten any other club side in the world on that day**, *was their heaviest for more than 40 years. Scoring only 8 points themselves, they had 32 points piled against them by the Cardiff scoring machine...*' Cardiff scored 8 tries to 2, winning 32-8 on 25 September, (in today's scoring, 48-12), but later at the Gnoll in April only scored 3 tries to 1 to win 11-5. The 9 October 1948 home game was won 20-6 against Gloucester, with Cardiff scoring 4 tries, a goal and a penalty to two penalties, and Cardiff had 11 internationals on the pitch. The programme thanked Gloucester for 'contributing' to the last game of the previous season, where Bleddyn had broken the try scoring record of 41 in a season and the club had reached a record 803 points. *'Cardiff had a hard game last week, but despite a good beating in the set scrums, produced team-work good enough to bring them a nine-point victory. The search for a hooker continues... The pack lack power in the set scrums, but all the forwards show their usual enthusiasm in the loose, and none did better than Elvet Jones and Gwyn Evans against Newport. They harassed the Newport midfield backs out of the game... The backs, however, particularly Haydn Tanner and Billy Cleaver, the now established half-back firm, were bang in form, and tackled man after man with amazing regularity. Only once did a Newport player cut through, and when faced by Frank Trott, his inside pass was dropped... This week a popular member of the two clubs, Ivor Williams, the wing forward who toured South Africa with the British Team in 1938, left the Cardiff area for London'*. Ivor left with his job, and then played for London Welsh. In this game Bleddyn partnered Jack Matthews in the centre, although St. John Rees was in the programme to play left centre, and Bleddyn's uncle Roy Roberts and cousin Bill Tamplin formed the second row.

Cardiff had an undefeated away season, and *'Cardiff Backs in Invincible Form at Bristol'* was a headline for the 30 October 1948 game. Bristol had beaten Swansea and Llanelli, and unbeaten Cardiff attracted a Bristol crowd of 12,000. Billy Cleaver scored two tries and Jack Matthews one, all converted by Roy Roberts, who also scored a penalty, to Bristol's penalty – an 18-3 win. On 20 November, unbeaten Cardiff could not score a try against Leicester away, Bleddyn's uncle Roy Roberts kicking two penalties to win 6-0. Roy seemed to be sharing the kicking duties with his partner in the second row, Bleddyn's cousin Bill Tamplin. In the home game vs. Leicester, in January, Cardiff scored 6 tries (2 converted) against 2 penalties to win 22-6.

At long last, the Luftwaffe damage to the North Stand was repaired, in time for the Newport game on 5 March 1949, won by Billy Cleaver's try, converted by Bill Tamplin, for a 5-0 win. In *Rugger*, December 1948 we read: *'Cardiff remains Cardiff, playing its usual superb rugby and looking forward to supplying the entire back divisions for this year's Welsh side. The Cardiffians were, of course, very lucky to have beaten Newport at Arms Park, the Newport forwards completely outplaying the home eight. Unfortunately, there was bad feeling on both sides, and it is rarely that the public reads a "Fisticuffs at the Arms Park" headline. A goal to a try was the result of this game, a game which was described as being the closest seen at Cardiff for some years.'* In the previous season Cardiff had achieved the 'Grand Slam' winning all four games against Newport. In this

201

season the Cardiff scores were: 9-0 (A); 5-3 (H); 3-3 (A); and 5-0 (H), 5 tries to 1 over the season. Cardiff scored a try against a penalty in the drawn third game – in today's scoring winning 5-3 and achieving a 'slam'.

In his final year of just three seasons, Haydn Tanner was again captain with Bleddyn again vice-captain. Haydn wished to become a rugby commentator for 'The Daily Graphic', which was classed as being a 'professional' – and was not allowed in strictly amateur rugby union. A few of the 'old guard' had retired, including hooker Maldwyn James, Les Manfield, W. G. Jones and Ray Bale. However, the excellent international William Leslie Thomas 'Les' Williams (1922-2006) had joined in 1947-48, scoring 47 tries in 51 matches. Les Williams served in the Royal Navy in the war, playing for the Navy and Combined Services. He made his debut for Llanelli in October 1945 and was their leading try-scorer with 15 touchdowns. Upon 5 January 1946 he had played in an uncapped game for Wales, partnering Bleddyn Williams at centre in the 11-3 loss. He won his first four full caps with Llanelli. In 1947 Les Williams had played in the 9-6 loss to England, but was on the winning team in the next three games, so Wales shared the Five Nations with England. He played for Wales three times when at Cardiff and had been in the Cardiff team that beat Australia.

His last game for Cardiff was at Bristol on 8 January 1949. Bleddyn takes up the intriguing story, as told to *Walesonline: 'Les was lodging with me in Bristol, where I was living and he was teaching at the time, and he actually signed for Hunslet in my front room. I wasn't with him at the time, but I think I was the only one who knew that the game against England would be his last rugby union match. In those days, when rugby league was very much the enemy of union, I could have been professionalised for knowing about what was happening. Les was ideally suited to rugby league - he was fast, had good hands and was a deadly tackler. He was a great finisher and he took his two tries against England very well. He was a loss to Welsh rugby.'* Les Williams was on the wing outside Bleddyn and Jack Matthews, as Wales beat England 9-3 in Cardiff on 15 January 1949, <u>two days after signing for Hunslet</u>. Les Williams scored two of Wales' three tries, to an England drop goal, but had secretly signed to play rugby league for Hunslet on 13 January. Bleddyn kept quiet about his knowledge of the affair until years later. *Rugger*, February 1949 comments, *'So the Rugby League has captured another Welsh star, Les Williams, after his grand game against England, not by any means the first. No one can blame him... by far the greatest onslaught by Rugby League scouts is reserved for Wales.'* There had been major criticism in the press and among the rugby public about Les Williams' selection for Wales, as he could not even get a regular place in the Cardiff team at the time, Cardiff having a surfeit of excellent wings such as Terry Cook, who had displaced him, and was to take his place in the Welsh team.

A full page in *Rugger* February 1949 was devoted to *'Les Williams'*

Farewell', reckoning that Hunslet had offered him £2,000 plus a job and a house – '*The job is important because he had to resign his school-teaching position at Bristol, while the house is a godsend to a married man with a wife and baby son… it was only the sheer brilliance of outside-half Glyn Davies which robbed Williams of the honour of being described as hero of the match.* **His selection for the English game did not surprise Welshmen – it hit them for a glorious six (if that phrase may be applied to Rugby). They were stunned, dazed, bewildered, and then indignant, that the "Big Five" had selected a man who had even been uncertain of a regular place in the Cardiff side.**' (Emboldened text as in the magazine). Indeed, his crash tackle in the opening minutes, upon the English flyer Jack Gregory, set the tone for the match.

Bleddyn's wing Les Williams scored 2 of the 3 Welsh tries
In a historic win at Twickenham in January 1949

Les actually went north for £1,450 (plus a house) and scored 116 tries in 236 games for Hunslet between 1949 and 1956. He skippered the club in the 1950-51 season and won 15 caps for the Welsh rugby league side, scoring 5 tries. He was asked to join the 1950 British Lions Rugby League tour to Australia, but declined the invitation because he was taking a PE course at Carnegie College in Leeds. He would have needed to take an extra year of study if he had taken so much time off. When he retired in 1956, aged 34, he turned to athletics, becoming a world record holder in the veterans' over-60 category, at 60 and 200 metres, as well as the British record holder in the triple jump. This seems to be a unique instance of a Rugby League player playing Rugby Union for Wales in an official international. There are, of course, cross-code changes now. The Hunslet RLFC website has a list of players 'from the valleys', and under William Leslie Thomas Williams we read: '*The big prize of this season was the surprise signing of Les Williams from Cardiff RU. He had played for Wales v England at Rugby Union the previous week, scoring a couple of tries. He had played 51 games for Cardiff, scoring 47 tries. He was signed as a winger but could operate just as easily at centre. He played 15 times for Wales at League, scoring five tries. He was very unlucky in 1950 when he was selected to tour Australia but couldn't get time off from work, and had to drop out. He retired on 31 December 1955 after a game at Featherstone, at the age of 33, having totalled 227 appearances, scoring 110 tries and one goal. He had accepted an appointment at a school in Cornwall. In later life he became a champion at sports for older people, being tremendously fit. A massive SUCCESS.*'

Llandaff's Rex Willis (1924-2000) replaced Haydn Tanner 10 times when Tanner was unavailable, and showed wonderful form, later becoming a Barbarian and British Lion, and winning 21 Welsh caps. Cardiff did not lose to any Welsh clubs, drawing in poor conditions away at Newport 3-3, to a capacity crowd, and home against Swansea 0-0. Cardiff's post-war unbeaten home record had lasted since 19 April 1947, when Llanelli won by a try and a drop goal (7) to two tries (6), a score that today would have been recorded as 10-8 to Cardiff. However, on 11 December 1948 another unbeaten home record came to an end after 18 months, with a winning try by Cambridge University in the last few minutes, the final score being 8-6. The students' team included current Cardiff and Welsh fly-half Glyn Davies, two future England internationals and two famous future Welsh caps, R.C.C. 'Clem' Thomas and John Gwilliam.

On 15 January 1949, Bath RFC reported its home loss, 9-6 to Cardiff: '*The teams were level at 3-3 at half time. Wilfred Williams had dropped a goal for Bath and Burn had scored a try for Cardiff. Bath changed into white jerseys at half time. Dai Jones put Cardiff in the lead with an unconverted try, but Bath revived strongly for Arthur Burcombe to touch down. Cardiff were not to be outdone and their speedy backs, well supported by the forwards, led to W. Jones putting them in a winning position. Right on the end Roberts* (Bleddyn's uncle) *missed a penalty goal for Cardiff just in front of the posts, and this ended a grand game with Bath going down with flying colours in what was a close affair.*' Upon Easter Saturday 1949, missing Tanner, Matthews and Tamplin, Cardiff were just beaten by the Barbarians 6-5, before 30,000 spectators. Just four days later, owing to injuries and commitments, a '*very weak*' Cardiff side lost at home to Northampton 15-8, with each team scoring two tries. (Cardiff had won away in September 1948, scoring 5 tries to 1 in a 27-12 rout). With the Cambridge loss, there were just three losses all season, in 44 games, by a total of 10 points – it was a major achievement for a team constantly raided for players. Yet again, it could so easily have been an unbeaten season.

In the First Welsh Trial, Cardiff had supplied all the Probables backs except Newport wing Ken Jones, six out of seven, and C.D. Williams and Elvet Jones were in the Probables forwards, to win 9-6. New hooker John Phillips and wing Terry Cook were in the Possibles, giving Cardiff 10 of the 30 men on the field, while the Cardiff First XV was also playing. Tries were scored by Cardiff's Russell Burn, C.D. 'Seedy' Williams and Elvet Jones, against tries by Cardiff's Terry Cook and John Phillips, giving Cardiff 4 of the 5 tries in the game. On 4 December 1948 Cardiff played at Blackheath, with Tanner injured and six players involved in the Second Welsh trial, but Cardiff still won 8-3. Seven Cardiff players were also missing from Firsts to play in the Third Trial.

In *Rugger*, January 1949, the leading article reads '*The fantastical situation which arose just before Christmas, when Wales selected the London Hospital player, Gwyn Rowlands, for their final trial after he had already had two trials for England and then been discarded by the Rugby Union selectors, is without parallel... What are we to think of these strange capers buy international selectors?... What would happen if some of the other sports would carry on in this way, I shudder to think... The whole business is ludicrous, it makes Rugby a laughingstock...*' and so on. Dr. Gwyn had two trials for Wales and played for London Welsh, but during National Service he was stationed at St Athan, so joined Cardiff in 1951. He established himself as a goal-kicking wing and went on to top 100 points in a season twice, very rare at that time, finishing with a career record of 66 tries in 99 matches for the Blue & Blacks, and the vice-captaincy in 1955-56. Gwyn's presence was crucial for Cardiff and Wales against the 1953 New Zealanders, when he won his first cap – England's loss – Wales's gain.

Playfair Rugby Annual 1949-50 reports that: '*Wales, as usual since the war, fell back upon a capable Cardiff nucleus.*' England were beaten by 3 tries to a drop goal, 9-3, with 6 Cardiff backs - Frank Trott, Jack Matthews, Bleddyn Williams, Les Williams, Glyn Davies (who had just left Cardiff for Cambridge), Haydn Tanner (captain) and the great and speedy Newport wing Ken Jones. Cardiff's Gwyn Evans was wing-forward. As noted previously, Les Williams scored two tries and Bryn Meredith one. *Rugger*, February 1949, begins with the headline and text: '*Wales Put Fresh Heart Into The Game. Every so often something happens in the world of rugby which restores one's faith in the game... Now it is Wales who have provided the neat, much needed tonic. The Wales and England match deserves to rank as a classic... Wales have not produced a better game, or exhibition of football, since the war. It was all most heartening... Wales played only as a Wales team can when it knows it is going places. Welsh back play is still the greatest thing in rugby anywhere...'* **Of the 9 backs awarded Welsh caps in 1948-49, 8 were Cardiff players**. When you think that there are only 7 backs in a team, it gives some indication of Cardiff's strength.

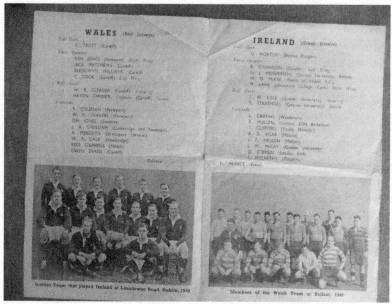

6 Cardiff backs and a forward play against Ireland, March 1949

The *Playfair Rugby Annual* of 1949-50 informs us that *'for reasons connected with dyeing and laundering rather than high taste or policy, Wales appeared last season* (1948-49) *in white shorts instead of the traditional dark blue. A brilliant victory over England seemed to have set the seal of the success upon the experiment, but...'* The rather negative conjunction 'but' was prescient. *Playfair* had some wonderful advertisements – a full page ad with a man using two – yes two – brushes either side of a parting claims. *'There's no fear of Dry Hair and Dandruff when you ... BRYLCREEM your hair.'* One assumes that dandruff, instead of falling, sticks to one's hair… After the England win, Wales then lost 6-5 at Murrayfield, with the same Cardiff players but their teammate Terry Cook had replaced Les Williams after his very unexpected defection to league. Bleddyn scored a try, converted by Frank Trott, and the game could have been won. The same Cardiff nucleus lost against Ireland at Swansea 5-0, with teammate Billy Cleaver replacing Glyn Davies, but Bleddyn firmly believed that the Irish try was offside. For the first and only time, Bleddyn was selected as right centre for the French match, but the previous Sunday played in a charity game at Clifton, Bristol to fulfil a commitment

206

made many months before. He wrote: '*International players are forbidden to play within seven days of an International game, and I pondered the risk I was taking. But I had promised... So it came about that I missed my first International match for Wales, for in the charity game I strained a muscle in the very last minute. I was grateful to the Press for their promise of silence on the matter, and hoped I might be fit for the French game. It was not to be, and in fact, I did not play again for Wales for two years, though selected for the first match of the 1949-50 season – and as captain, too. Injury robbed me of my chance, and at one time I despaired of ever regaining a place among the scarlet-jerseyed backs of Wales.*' In Paris Wales lost again, 5-3, Ken Jones missing the conversion to draw the match. In the French game, Trott, Matthews, Glyn Davies, Haydn Tanner were the Cardiff backs playing and teammate Cliff Davies was propping. Wales won their matches on tries 5-4, incredible for a team that only won one of four games, and being beaten in 3 games by a total of 8 points. Wales had the Wooden Spoon scoring 17 points and only conceding 19.

1948-49 The much-loved Cornish tour, Rex Willis kneeling.
Standing from right Bleddyn, Jack and Sid Judd

Nine Cardiff players were capped for Wales in the season. Bleddyn Williams topped the Cardiff try scoring list again with 25 tries, followed by wing Terry Cook 23 (Cardiff's only new Welsh cap this year), wing Russell Burn 20, wing Les Williams 13 (for a part-season) and Jack Matthews 10. Goal kicking was shared, generally between Bleddyn's cousin Bill Tamplin (31 goals), and Bleddyn's uncle Roy Roberts (25), both second-rows. Len Evans captained the *Rags* to another very good season of: P38, W28, L8, D2, points 636-222. With the First XV rebuilding, and giving the Firsts players to cover injuries, trial and international dates, Evans had to use no fewer than 80 players. There were

11 new Athletic XV caps included Barry's Geoff Beckingham (soon to be the regular First XV hooker), K. E. Brookes, Peter Goodfellow, Gower Jenkins, Dai Jones, Sid Judd (a wonderful servant to Cardiff and Wales), Victor Keitch, K. C. Lloyd, and J. B. Neagle. Davies missed out Roy Roberts' cousin the hooker Ray Roberts, who played 5 times for the Firsts, and was awarded his Athletic cap before returning to Penarth for regular first team games. Roy Roberts left for Pontypridd and eventual captaincy there, and his second-row partner, Bleddyn's cousin Bill Tamplin retired. Haydn Tanner retired but his successor was the talented local boy, Rex Willis.

The WRU asked clubs to start youth sections, and Cardiff's first side in 1949-50 was named the Cardiff Juniors, which the four youngest Williams brothers began playing for, when of age. One young Tonyrefail County schoolboy fly-half was being reported as having 'great potential'. Cliff Morgan captained Welsh Secondary Schools against Yorkshire Secondary/Grammar Schools, and was soon to join Cardiff and have a glittering career. To end the season, upon 28 April 1949, Cardiff played Captain Geoffrey Crawshay's 'Rest of Wales' team, in aid of the Gwyn Nicholls' Memorial Fund. Roy Roberts' Souvenir Programme lists Nicholl's 24 appearances for Wales, including against New Zealand and South Africa in 1905 and 1906. *'E. Gwyn Nicholls (1874-1939) played for the Cardiff Rugby Club as full-back and centre-threequarter from 1884 to 1907. Captained the Club in seasons 1898-1899 to 1900-1901... Today's match is a historic one. The Cardiff Club meets, for the first time on record, the Rest of Wales; in a friendly way it will be a grand challenge match. Yet more important it will be a Memorial Match to a really great player – one of the greatest players and gentlemen ever to play rugby football. Down through the years, the Cardiff Club have stood firm for the highest ideals in sport. This season's team, so ably led by Haydn Tanner, have endeavoured to follow in the spirit fostered by Gwyn Nicholls and his men in the four years he was captain of the Club. It is fitting that Haydn Tanner and his men should play an important part in today's game for they have brought new honours to the Club in the last two years. Gwyn Nicholls, had he lived, would have been the first to have showered praise upon them for their displays.'*

There was also an appreciation of Gwyn Nicholls by his co-centre for Cardiff and Wales, the legendary Rhys Thomas 'Rusty' Gabe (1880-1967). I knew his grand-daughter, the late Marian Gabe, 100 years old and a friend and neighbour of my 98-year-old mother, and discovered that he was christened Gape, not Gabe. Rhys Gabe also had 24 caps, forming a 'devastating' centre partnership with Nicholls, and wrote in the programme: *'The younger generation might ask "Why commemorate this old rugby player out of all the old players who have distinguished themselves in Welsh football, and whose names have also been household* words in Rugby homes?" The answer is, that Gwyn possessed that little extra something which put him upon a pedestal above the others, and which made him, in my opinion, the best-ever centre three-quarter that played for Wales. To me he was the Prince of Threequarters. To know and appreciate his sterling qualities, one had to play along-side him. The on-looker saw a great deal, but only part of his activities. A colleague had the opportunity of seeing from the inside his true merit. I attribute the small measure of my early success directly to his acknowledged greatness, for he demanded such anxious watchfulness from his opponents that his colleagues were afforded much more scope and freedom. I found a difference when he was not at my side.

Off the field, "G.N" was outstanding as a personality and a gentleman. To associate with him was indeed an honour and a tonic. He was my hero long before I met him. As I came to know him more intimately – I played 12 times as his co-centre for Wales – my affection for him continued to increase, if that were possible.

"His life was gentle, and the elements
So mix'd in him that Nature might stand up
And say to all the world, 'This was a man'."

In repeating that quotation from Shakespeare's Julius Caesar, I can think of no better way to pay my tribute to his manliness, his football skill, his endearing temperament and his outstanding good nature. Gwyn died in the Spring of 1939, and had the war not broken out, the memorial would have been erected that year. But the project had to be suspended because of other matters more pressing to be attended to. Today the Gwyn Nicholls' Memorial Fund Committee hope to fulfil their ambition and notch the total required to purchase and erect the Memorial Gates at the Quay Street/Westgate Street Entrance to the famous Arms Park.' Bleddyn Williams and Bill Tamplin played, with Bleddyn scoring two tries to win the game. The gates were later moved along Westgate Street to Cardiff's new ground because of the new National Stadium and then the replacement Millennium (now Principality) Stadium rebuilding.

J.B.G. Thomas reported of this year in *Playfair Rugby Annual* 1949-50: 'Cardiff again headed the Welsh Rugby Club Table, though it was not their year completely, as in the previous season. Their record in figures was almost as good, and instead of an unbeaten home record they were not beaten away, although engaged in one hard match against Oxford University which ended in a pointless draw. In the face of much stiffer opposition at home, they never really touched the form which made them such an automatic scoring machine in 1947-48. They remained unbeaten by a Welsh club, and suffered only three defeats – by Cambridge University, the Barbarians and Northampton. In the first match they missed several scoring chances and were beaten in the last minute by a sensational Cambridge breakaway; in the second they were without

Tanner and Matthews; and in the third they played virtually a second XV... Trailing Cardiff throughout the season were two Monmouthshire clubs, Newbridge and Newport, who showed splendid form... Their (Newbridge) *ambition is to play Cardiff in an official fixture, but like many other Welsh clubs they must wait their turn... Newport enjoyed their most successful season for 25 years and played excellent football, with many large victories. This season, Newport will present even stiffer opposition to their close rivals, Cardiff, and might even beat them for the first time since 1946!'* (Newbridge did not have a fixture with Cardiff until 1963-64, with alternate years playing home and away. Their sequence of results was that Newbridge only won one game in 9 - D D W L W W W W W until 1973-74, and they were always fine hard-fought games, with a try count of 22-13. They were the only other Welsh first-class side to play in Blue and Back hoops.)

Gwyn Nicholls programme

There is an interesting note in *Rugger*, Sept-Oct 1948: '*The August trials did, or course, provide what the clubs call "a wealth of talent," but these claims must, naturally, be taken with a grain of salt until the real "battles" start. Many triallists go up like the proverbial rocket, only to come down like the stick when they find themselves up against the cream of first-class Welsh Rugby. It may be all right to show brilliance against the "Colours," but it is another thing altogether to do it against Cardiff.*' (Often in club trials the select team would play in their club colours while the men trying to get into the squad would wear any differently coloured jerseys, usually from their existing club.) The writer came strongly against the idea of stopping internationals at Swansea, '*which would have been a body blow to thousands of West Wales fans. Cardiffians have done everything but carry sandwich boards in their almost fanatical attempt to get all internationals staged at the Arms Park. It is a selfish, unforgiveable attitude by men who wish to dominate Welsh Rugby... despite its threats, the Welsh Union knows it will be a sorry day should it ever decide to play all internationals at the Arms Park.*'

We are parochial in Wales, as much as any other nation, to be honest. Players today can reach over 100 caps, but after the 1948-49 season the record cap holders were as follows: England: W. Wakefield 31; R. Cove-Smith 29, A.T. Voyce and J.S. Tucker 27 – Scotland: J. MacD Bannerman 37, I.S. Smith 32, W.M. Simmers 28 – Ireland: G.V. Stephenson 42, E. O'D. Davy 34, W.E. Crawford and J.D. Clinch and G.T. Hamlet 30 – Wales: R.M. Owen 35, W.J. Bancroft 33, W.J. Trew 29. In 2020, the Home Nations leading caps are Alun Wyn Jones 153 (inc. 9 Lions caps) - the world record; Ireland's Brian O'Driscoll 141 (inc. 8 Lions); England's Jason Leonard 119 (inc. 5 Lions) and Scotland's Ross Ford 110. Of the other Six Nations teams, Sergio Parisse of Italy had 142 caps and France's Phillipe Sella 111. 'Alun Wyn' has over four times as many Welsh caps as the record-holder in 1948-49, despite missing some caps through injury. New Zealand captain Richie McCaw gained 148 caps. There follows a brief biography of Roy Roberts, the uncle of the Williams brothers, who played with Gwyn, Bryn, Vaughan and Bleddyn.

LESLIE* ROYDON 'ROY' ROBERTS MM 3 June 1917 - 2 November 1988

* he was Christened Roydon Leslie, born at 11 Moy Road, Taff's Well.
Married Emma Millicent 'Millie' Arnold, children Michael and Gillian
Taff's Well RFC (with his nephew Gwyn Williams)
Cardiff RFC (with Gwyn Williams pre-war; Bleddyn Williams and Bill Tamplin post-war)
1940-46 Welsh Guards Regimental Brigade, Divisional sides and the Army XV, captained the Battalion side, seasons 1943-44 and 1945-46, plus some wartime matches for Cardiff and representative sides
Cardiff 1936-37 to 1938-39, 1945-46 to 1948-49 - second row, flanker, number 8. 150 games, 14 tries
Pontypridd 1949-1952, captain (with Des Jones) 1950-51

'*Roy certainly should have played for Wales*' – Dr. Jack Matthews
Roy Roberts was '*the best forward never to play for Wales*' – Don Llewellyn

211

Roy was the younger brother of Nell Roberts, the Williams boys' mother, and the son of Ted Roberts, a driving force in Taff's Well RFC. His sister Nell was born in September 1898, and Roy almost 19 years later in June 1917. Nell married Arthur Williams, and her second child Gwyn Williams was born in May 1918, so was less than a year younger than his uncle Roy Roberts. However, Gwyn played for Cardiff a year before his uncle. Roy played alongside Gwyn Williams for both Taff's Well and Cardiff. Roy Roberts was awarded his Cardiff first team cap in his second season, 1937-38, and also in that year scored seven tries for the 'Rags'. The 'Cardiff RFC Season Review 1939 – 1945' notes the outbreak of war, and 'the prospects for another successful season were excellent, Cliff Jones was now available after his studies, and top newcomers were Les Manfield - already Welsh capped from Mountain Ash - Howell Loveluck from Bridgend, Roy Roberts another grand forward...' Roberts took part in some unofficial wartime matches for Cardiff, and in 1945-46 scored five tries, excellent for a forward in those muddy days. His fellow kicker and second row forward Bill Tamplin scored 7 tries in 250 games, but the more mobile Roy touched down 14 times in just 203 games, of which 53 were before the war. Roy played for Cardiff until 1949, but injured, joined Pontypridd. His captaincy there was cut short by a serious leg injury, and aged 34 he was advised to retire.

Immediately war started, Roy enlisted in the Second Battalion Welsh Guards, originally an infantry unit but later converted to an armoured role, becoming the divisional scouting and reconnaissance unit of the Guards Armoured Division. Towards the end of May 1940, the German Army was sweeping through France towards the coast. The British Expeditionary Force (BEF) was in heavy retreat and desperately planned evacuations from Calais, Boulogne and Dunkirk. Unfortunately, the speed of the German blitzkrieg ('lightning advance') meant that Dunkirk quickly became the only realistic evacuation point. The defence of Boulogne and Calais was then intended to slow the German assault upon the Dunkirk evacuation pocket, with the Germans attacking those two ports to prevent soldiers escaping. The British generals kept up this pretence, weakening the attack on Dunkirk, and giving the BEF extra time to evacuate troops from there. Roy Roberts was with the 20th Guards Brigade, having arrived at Boulogne from training camps in Surrey. Realistically Calais and Boulogne were not optimal places for evacuation, but their spirited defence meant that the Germans thought that they would be used. In reality they were sacrificed so that Dunkirk could be successful. At Boulogne the 2nd Panzer Division bombarded the port, but many troops managed to be taken off by destroyers and other vessels under intense artillery bombardment and air attacks. Roy made it on the last ship to manage to leave, under heavy attack.

Around 300 Welsh Guards remained, holding out in Boulogne for another 36 hours, until they ran out of ammunition and surrendered. That same day, 23 May 1940, Calais was attacked by the 1st and 10th Panzer divisions, but against incredible odds, British troops held off the German advance. By the night of 26 May, they were running out of men and supplies, and the Germans advanced through the town in hand-to-hand fighting, capturing the few remaining British defenders. At Calais the 3rd Royal Tank Regiment had landed with 40 tanks to drive towards Boulogne, to relieve the terrible pressure there, but the allies could make little progress against the more powerful 1st and 10th Panzer Divisions. From Calais, only the wounded were allowed to be evacuated and around 4,000 men were captured. However, that initial defence of Boulogne and the four-day defence of Calais gave the Allies time to start their successful evacuation from Dunkirk.

Roy Roberts with his crews in front of captured German munitions

After fighting in Belgium with the Second Battalion Welsh Guards, Roy had been one of 340,000 British and French troops evacuated from Boulogne and Dunkirk between 26 May and 4 June 1940. The British Army desperately needed to re-equip. At incredible risk, and with British losses, 123,000 French troops were taken to Britain, but nearly all chose to be repatriated to France in the next few days, rather keep on fighting. This is hardly mentioned in history books, and one suspects never in France. Colonel Charles de Gaulle had been promoted to Brigadier-General on 1 June 1940. Major-General Sir Edward Spears, KBE, CB, MC was noted for his role as a liaison officer between British and French forces in two world wars. Winston Churchill wrote that Spears personally rescued de

213

Gaulle from France just before the German conquest, literally pulling the Frenchman into his plane, when it was taking off from Bordeaux for Britain on 17 June. Spears himself wrote that he had to almost force the 'reluctant' de Gaulle to leave and had to bundle him into the plane. Hardly any of the Dunkirk refugees had remained with the little-known colonel, and of the meagre 1,300 Frenchmen at his disposal in Britain, the vast majority had recently been evacuated by British ships from Narvik, following the Norwegian Campaign.

Britain was fighting alone, despite persistent propagandising the myth of the 'Free French' Army. In June 1940, Marshall Pétain and his generals told Churchill that *'in three weeks, England will have her neck wrung like a chicken.'* The French armed element grew throughout the war, however. Mainly coming from Tahiti, there were 550 volunteers in April 1941. The Free French forces also came to include 5,000 <u>non-French</u> Europeans, mainly serving in units of the Foreign Legion. They were joined by 350 escaped Spanish Republicans, Spanish Civil War veterans, and over 20,000 troops from Morocco, Algeria and other Spanish colonies. Indeed, the Free French Army had very, very few soldiers from the 'professional' French Army that fought in Europe.

After some bleak years for Britain, on D-Day plus 2, 8 June 1944, the Welsh Guards took part in the invasion of Europe by 156,000 British, American and Canadian forces. Roy Roberts, and the 2nd Battalion Welsh Guards Armoured Division landed in France on 29 June 1944 with tanks and artillery, once the bridgehead was secure, and then fought its way across Northwest Europe. Roberts participated in many of the Normandy breakout battles, and then in *Operation Market Garden* - the advance on and subsequent crossing of the Rhine, and the drive into Germany itself. (Indeed, Bleddyn Williams could have flown his glider, full of troops and equipment, in the skies above Roy.) By the end of June 1944, around a million Allied troops were in France, and upon 26 June the port of Cherbourg was taken, and on 25 August Paris was liberated. The 1st and 2nd Battalions of the Welsh Guards formed part of the Guards Armoured Division, 1st Battalion serving as infantry and Roberts' 2nd Battalion as an armoured unit. The two battalions fought their way through northern France, Belgium and Holland.

The 1st Battalion, being infantry, was assigned to the 32nd Guards Brigade, and the 2nd Battalion being armoured, became part of the 6th Guards Armoured Brigade. The two battalions worked closely, being the first troops to re-enter Brussels on 3 September 1944 after an advance of 100 miles in one day in what was described as *'an armoured dash unequalled for speed in this or any other wa*r.' It was led by Major-General Sir Allan Henry Adair, the divisional commander. When the Welsh Guards liberated Brussels, Roy Roberts was **one of the first ten soldiers welcomed by the citizens**. On 16 December 1944, the Battle of the Bulge, the last German offensive on the Western Front, began, with a quarter of a million German troops across Luxembourg being ordered to push back the Allies. The Germans advanced 50 miles into Allied lines creating the 'bulge.' But on 16 January 1945 they were repelled and began a bitterly-fought, slow retreat. In Belgium, on 16 February 1945, Roy won his Military Medal.

The official citation for Roy's medal reads: '*2735883 Cpl (L/Sgt) ROYDEN ROBERTS WELSH GUARDS Citation For MILITARY MEDAL*

In the neighbourhood of HOMMERSON on 16 Feb 1945, this L/Sgt was acting as a Tank Commander in a squadron of Tanks which were supporting a Battalion of Infantry in an attack on a section of the Siegfried Line. During this attack, owing to treacherous and deep conditions underfoot, many Tanks got bogged.

This L/Sgt's Tank was one of the few which were still operational just before the objective was reached. His troop now only composed of two Tanks. Enemy resistance at this point was extremely strong, and the entire front was being subjected to very intense enemy bombardment.

L/Sgt ROBERTS quickly appreciated the situation, and after informing his Troop Leader, manoeuvred his Tank into position to support a third Company of Infantry, all of whose supporting Tanks had been bogged. He gave the greatest assistance with his own Tank, and was successful in putting down such a weight of fire that the Infantry were able to go forward to their objective.

Immediately after they had consolidated, L/Sgt ROBERTS returned to where his Troop Leader was supporting the Left Hand company. On his way, his own Tank became entirely bogged, and owing to the distance from the Company, fire from his own Tank would have given no assistance to the Infantry.

L/Sgt ROBERTS displaying the greatest initiative, and complete disregard for danger, dismounted from the Tank, and taking a Bren gun with him, advanced upon his feet across an area upon which a hail of enemy fire was descending. On arrival in the Company area which he was supposed to have been supporting with his Tank, he took up a position on his own with his machine-gun, and went in with the Infantry himself, firing his gun from the hip in the closing stages.

Throughout the whole of this action, the N.C.O. had revealed initiative of the very highest order, and disregarding his own safety in the face of some of the heaviest artillery fire any soldier has had to face during this War, had succeeded in assisting one Company onto the objective in his Tank, and, on his own feet, helping another action which was part of the Left hand Company, onto their objective as well.

His calmness and complete contempt for danger made a profound impression, not only upon the crew of his Tank, but also upon the Infantry in whose close support he was acting.'

215

Then, in March 1945 US troops crossed the Rhine and Germany troops retreated more. Upon 15 April British troops liberated Bergen-Belsen concentration camp, with Roy telling his son Michael that he arrived there 2-3 days later, but never spoke about its horrors. Men of that generation kept their experiences to themselves – there was no such thing as counselling for soldiers. On 28 April, Roy Roberts was one of the first men to free Milag Nord Prisoner of War Camp in Germany. Hitler committed suicide on 30 April, and after six years of war, 8 May 1945 saw the final victory in Europe (VE-Day). WW2 ended when Japan surrendered on 15 August (VJ-Day). Little of this is taught in schools, unfortunately, of the saving of European democracy. And Europeans in particular seem to care little that without British help in two World Wars, their lives would be very different, and almost certainly worse. Without Britain, post-World War I Europe would have been Prussian-controlled. And after World War Two they would have been speaking German or Russian.

*Roy Roberts around the time he
received his Military Medal*

Roy's daughter Gillian and her husband, many years later, took Roy on a tour of battlefields around Arnhem, but again, he never spoke of his experiences there. In the Cardiff-Neath programme (*'the visitors from Castell-Nedd'*) of 27 January 1947 we read: *'Roy Roberts, today's "Players' Gallery" subject, is an uncle of Bleddyn Williams and a cousin of W.E. Tamplin (actually an uncle), and who can dispute that these three players are not suffering from rugby blood pressure!! Further, that second row in the Cardiff pack consists of Roberts and Tamplin, and its success is undoubtedly due to the plan of campaign which the "cousinly talks" hit upon, remembering that the ubiquitous Bleddyn would be somewhere behind to finally receive that elusive oval passed back through the avenue by that good hooker Don Rees. Roy learnt his rugby at the Taff's Well School, thence to Caerphilly Secondary School, played for 1ˢᵗ XV during his last two years. After playing for Taff's Well for a while, Roy moved to*

Cardiff and his outstanding abilities got him into the Cardiff team in 1936-37 and won him his Cardiff "Cap" the following season at the age of 19 – good going indeed.

Roy joined the Welsh Guards on the outbreak of hostilities, was in France in 1940 and after Dunkirk remained in this country until 1944. He played for the Regimental Brigade, Divisional sides and the Army XV, and captained the Battalion side, seasons 1943-44 and 1945-46, scoring over 100 points in the two seasons, mainly by his goal kicking. He landed on Normandy beaches on D+2 day and was among the first ten Allied soldiers to enter Brussels after advancing 600 miles in 9 days!

Roy won the Military Medal while liberating a P.O.W camp at Kirktimke, Germany, where incidentally there were a large number of Cardiff men, and that was a grand climax to an excellent military record. Roy was demobbed in March 1946, and when he played in the Past v Present match to help the Infirmary, he intended that to be his last game. He was persuaded to continue, and his fine physique – weight 14st. 7lbs. and 6ft. 1in. height, and experience found him once more in the Cardiff pack, doing great work in the second row, and occasionally in the back row, besides kicking goals at intervals. A very conscientious and consistent front-ranker, he has helped solidify Cardiff's scrum this season, and he will be missed through sustaining a nasty injury at Bath last Saturday. Our sympathy goes out to him, with sincere wishes for a speedy recovery, for Cardiff can ill afford to lose forwards like him.'

Also referring to Roy's war record, a faded newspaper cutting loaned to me by Carey Collings, former Taff's Well scrumhalf, who knew all the Williams family, is headlined '*GALLANTRY IN N.W. EUROPE Cardiff Rugby Player's M.M.* - Sergt. Roy Roberts, Welsh Guards, who, as stated in our issue of Tuesday, has been awarded the Military Medal for distinguished and gallant services in North-West Europe, is the youngest son of Mr. and the late Mrs. Edward Roberts, of Bryncoch, Taff's Well, and uncle of Gwyn, Bryn and Bleddyn Williams, the well-known Rugby footballers. A keen Rugby player himself, Roy, who is 28 years of age, played for Cardiff for several years before joining the Welsh Guards early in 1940. He recently played for the British Army at Brussels. His wife and two children reside at Anchor Street, Taff's Well.' To check upon this hardly known hero, there is virtually nothing upon the Internet, but the author was lucky to find the following in the '*Supplement to the London Gazette*' 24 May 1945. Military Medal recipients included: '*No.2735833 Sergeant (acting) Roydon Leslie Roberts, Welsh Guards (Cardiff).*' It was thought by some in Taff's Well that he gained his medal by rescuing men from a burning tank, but that may well have been another action involving Roy. Just as after WW1, returning men were very reluctant to talk about the war, except the happier times reminiscing with old comrades. Those generations just 'bottled things up' and got on with life. They had to work to raise their families – there were none of the benefits that today's unemployed have, and no cheap housing (- nearly all the working classes rented properties, or lived with parents until they inherited the house). Probably a majority who saw action and death would be diagnosed with PTSD (Post-Traumatic Stress Disorder) today, but they had to get on with life. (An old man I knew, in his later 80's, Cardiff's last cooper, suppressed all memory of WW1, but in his last days began falling out of bed, screaming *'Let Me Out! Let Me Out!'* It turned out, and his family never knew, that he had been buried in the trenches, and was lucky to be dug out when the action finished.)

CHAPTER 20 - CARDIFF SEASON 1949 – 1950

BLEDDYN CAPTAINS CARDIFF AND IS SELECTED FOR LIONS – BLEDDYN AND BRYN PLAY TOGETHER - CLIFF MORGAN'S DEBUT – *'THE GREATEST CROWD DRAWING CLUB IN THE GAME'* - WALES WIN THE GRAND SLAM - THE WORLD'S GREATEST AIR DISASTER – <u>BRINLEY 'BRYN' WILLIAMS PLAYER PROFILE AND REMINISCENCES</u>

Bleddyn Williams P24 T23 = 69pts; **Bryn Williams** P2 T2 (= 6pts) plus Athletic; **Bill Tamplin** P38 T4 C30 P22 D1 = 141 pts (Risca); Doug Jones (Taff's Well) P1 T1 = 3pts); Basil Evans P1 (Pentyrch)

P47, W29, L10, D8. Points 523-243. Tries 121-38 Pens 25-26

Rugger, October 1949, comments: *'The Clubs in Wales were circularised early in the month, as at the end of last season, to lay special emphasis on open and brighter play, and invited to curb the activities of the wing forward as much as possible. There was a genuine desire for an improved standard of play and of the leading Clubs,* **Cardiff**, **Swansea**, **Aberavon** *and* **Newport** *were quick to answer the Union's appeal. In their first three matches Cardiff ran up a total of 91 points, with their new captain* **Bleddyn Williams** *playing as well as he has ever done. If he maintains this good form, he will captain Wales in the International series, and quite possibly the British Team (the Lions) in 1950. The young Cardiff pack looks sound enough to give* **the best Club back division in the four Islands** *all the chances they need.'* (One is unsure of the geography of the *'four Islands'*).

As stated, Bleddyn was captain, with vice-captain Frank Trott taking over in 1950 when Bleddyn was injured. Bleddyn played 22 games up to the Final Trial on 7 January, when he injured his knee badly, and only played another 2 games at the season's end. However, his very late recovery allowed his selection for the British Lions tour to New Zealand and Australia. *Rugger*, October 1949, reports that *'Haydn Tanner's decision to retire altogether from the game is an incalculable loss to Welsh rugby'* in a page and a half eulogy to the player. *'The opinion in Wales? He is regarded by some as the greatest inside-half of all time but by everybody as a truly great player.'* Cardiff captain for the previous two seasons, Tanner had been an 18-year-old schoolboy when he played for Swansea, beating the All Blacks in 1934-35, partnering his schoolboy cousin and next-door neighbour Willie Davies. His first cap was that year when he inspired Wales to also beat New Zealand 13-12, and he played for Wales 25 times in succession except for the Australia game in 1947, when he was injured. A British Lion in 1938, Captain Tanner played for the Welsh Services, Welsh Guards and the Army in the War, and captained the Barbarians, scoring the winning try against Australia in January 1948. Luckily Llandaff North's Rex Willis succeeded seamlessly for Cardiff and Wales. The outside half (also called fly half, stand-off and now more prosaically No. 10) Cliff Morgan made his first appearance on 22 October 1949, in an away draw at Cambridge University.

Karl Mullen and Jack Matthews help me off the field at Sydney after a kick in the back. Lions finally beat New South Wales with thirteen men!

Bleddyn is helped off the field by Karl Mullen and Jack Matthews, after a kick in the back against New South Wales in Sydney. The Lions still won 20-13, with 13 men, on 3 June 1950.

His great partnership with Rex Willis, from this season until 1957-58 was possibly Cardiff's most successful in its history, until that of Barry John and Gareth Edwards 1967-68 to 1971-72, who established the best half-back pairing that this author has ever witnessed. For Wales, Edwards and Phil Bennett of Llanelli was probably as good, but as Edwards and John played together for Cardiff, they had a tremendous understanding of each other's game. I cannot remember Barry John ever in any trouble in a game, against any opposition. And somehow he had that ability, like Michael Laudrup in his pomp for Real Madrid, Johan Cruyff and other great team players, of always finding time and space in a game. I remember Barry saying that when he wanted to run past any player, he would be watching which way their feet were placed, before deciding on which way to go past him. He scored a try on tour against New Zealand Students, I think, when he seemed to saunter through four players who all fell over. Magic.

Cliff Morgan was to gain 29 Welsh international caps, becoming the star of the 1955 British Lions tour and captaining the Barbarians on two Canadian tours. Danny Davies was Assistant Manager on the Lions Tour and wrote about Cliff on tour: *'off the field he was the joker, the story-teller (he could stretch them), strong singer and choirmaster, creating much enjoyment in which I happily shared. I think I should record here that Cliff, and another great outside half of the past, Percy F. Bush share a most unique Cardiff distinction, in that both appeared in winning teams against New Zealand, Australia and South Africa, namely P. F. Bush 1905-06 for Wales v. New Zealand, Cliff Morgan 1953-54 for Cardiff v. N.Z.- P. F. Bush 1908-09 for Cardiff v. Australia, Cliff Morgan 1957-58 for Cardiff v. Australia. - P. F. Bush 1906-07 for Cardiff v. South Africa, Cliff Morgan 1955 for Br. Lions v. S. Africa.'* Regarded by all and sundry as *'a lovely man'*, Cliff became a major figure at the BBC.

Yet again Cardiff's year was somewhat spoiled, not just by Bleddyn's injury and other events, but as usual by 3 Welsh trials and 4 internationals. Bleddyn was appointed captain of Wales, to play England away in the first game of the Five Nations, but his knee damage kept him out of the tournament. Cardiff won 3 of 4 games against Newport, and against Welsh clubs only lost to Swansea twice and Newport once. Cardiff lost to Coventry (H and A), Northampton (A), Wasps (A), Cheltenham (A), Barbarians (H) and Penzance-Newlyn (A). None of the five British Lions from Cardiff were available after 25 March, missing the Barbarians and Penzance games, both lost, and of the remaining matches Cardiff won 4, lost 4 and drew 2, these statistics spoiling what had been a fair season. *Playfair Rugby Football Annual* reported on the Cardiff – Barbarians game in front of 40,000 spectators where Cardiff were missing Tanner, Matthews, Tamplin and others, where the Baa-Baas snatched the lead with 20 minutes to go, when *'Cardiff had shot their bolt physically in this their fortieth match of the season and they were weakening fast, especially in the scrummage.'* The Baa-Baas had 34 men on tour, playing their second team the previous day at Penarth, and their freshened first team scored two tries to win 8-6. From Cardiff, Bleddyn, Haydn Tanner, Gwyn Evans and Glyn

220

Davies played for the Barbarians to defeat the East Midlands, Bleddyn scoring two tries in the 22-9 game.

Cardiff and Wales full-back and 1950 Barbarian Frank Trott surprisingly gave his favourite memory as the loss to the Baa-Baas on 8 April 1950: '*The five brilliant Cardiff Tourists had left on the first stage of their journey to New Zealand. The team on paper was weak and the Barbarians very strong. But a Cardiff side is always able to produce that something extra. The Baa-Baas with a gale behind them and the genius Lewis Jones as spearhead had a lead of 8 points at half-time. Then Cardiff took over and had the Internationals so rattled that one saw the strange spectacle of place-kicks to touch being taken. A Tamplin special and a brilliant Terry Cook try almost levelled the scores. The last ten minutes were some of the most exciting I have ever experienced. The final score was 8-6 to the Baa-Baas, but what a moral victory for the Blue and Blacks!*'

Cardiff drew record gates at home and away, for instance at the Arms Park on 15 October, when 35,000 saw an excellent 'All Whites' side win 18:12 (- 3 tries apiece, a penalty to Cardiff and a drop-goal to Swansea, but Swansea converted all 3 tries for the 6-point margin.) Swansea's programme of 28 January for the return match stated: '*Welcome to Cardiff the greatest crowd drawing club in the game*'. On 10 December, Gloucester's programme notes called Cardiff '*the champion post-war team of the Rugby world*'. Although playing in only 24 games Bleddyn was top scorer with 23 tries (and 5 for the Rags). Wings Terry Cook and Russell Burn scored 21 and 17, fed by Dr. Jack and Bleddyn. J. D. Nelson, an excellent back row forward scored 8. First team caps were given to Cliff Morgan, Paul Ash, Malcolm Collins, Peter Goodfellow, the prop Gower Jenkins and flanker/No.8 Sid Judd. Goodfellow was a former Captain in the Gurkha regiment, a hard man, who became a Cardiff rugby institution, playing in the back five of the scrum from the end of the war to the early 60s.

On 21 January 1950, when Bath were easily beaten at the Arms Park, Cardiff were without the injured Bleddyn, their half-backs Billy Cleaver and Rex Willis, centre Dr. Jack Matthews (four of their seven first-choice backs), and the great prop Cliff Davies, all playing against England. Bath RFC reports its game vs Cardiff which it lost away 18-8: '*Cardiff built on a first half lead of nine points to three, to run out comfortable winners by 5 tries and a penalty to Bath's goal and a penalty. Bath's demise was witnessed by a handful of spectators, as the overriding interest was focussed on the Wales v England encounter at Twickenham. The game was punctuated by announcements as to the big match progress. Sullivan kicked a first half penalty. Play was of an exciting nature with attack and counterattack. After 18 minutes of the second half, O'Shaughnessy ran brilliantly to touch down under the bar, for Sullivan to convert. The Bath forwards had a magnificent afternoon, but there was not the same thrust amongst the three-quarters. The Cardiff backs were brimming with talent and their efforts were reflected in the score-sheet.'* Cardiff beat Bath away 10-8 in March. Unusually, in their 27 Bath fixtures from 1924 to 1975, Cardiff played 16 away and only 11 at home, their only 3 losses being in 1927, 1928 and 1947 and the only draw in 1925, all away. Cardiff's last 15 games vs Bath, an excellent side, were all won, 9 of them away.

1949-50 Bleddyn is captain, flanked on his left by Dr. Jack Matthews and Frank Trott

Wales, for the season without their injured captain Bleddyn, won at Twickenham against England 11-5, where Rex Willis made his debut to gain the first of his 21 international caps. Cardiff's Cliff Davies scored a try, from an opening created by Llanelli's Lewis Jones from the halfway line. It was also the 18-year-old Jones' first game, managing to get leave from National Service in the Royal Navy. Lewis Jones was a real phenomenon, who could play fullback, centre or wing. He joined the 1950 British Lions as a replacement, playing in 3 tests against New Zealand, scoring 63 points in 7 games, and 16 points against Australia. He played 10 times for Wales before joining Leeds rugby league for £6,000 in November 1952. He broke all sorts of scoring records, and often played fly half, but rugby league historian Robert Gate called him *'arguably the most devastating attacking back Wales has ever produced.'* Yet another man one wishes had not 'gone North'.

Wales beat Scotland at St. Helen's, Swansea 12-0. Then, on 11 March Wales defeated Ireland at Ravenhill, Belfast 6-3 to win the **Triple Crown, after a gap of 39 years**. Davies records: *'I remember well the last few* minutes of the game, the Irish forwards seemingly berserk in their pounding efforts to save the game, and the courage of Rex Willis going down to the ball to stop them, as he did successfully. The next day, Sunday 12th March in the early evening a large crowd gathered at the Cardiff Central Railway Station, to meet the victorious Welsh players and officials, of whom I was one. Led by St. Albans Military Band, the Cardiff players were transported to our clubhouse, where the tremendous enthusiasm was suddenly and tragically dimmed by the shocking news which came through, that a large Tudor V aircraft with more than 80 Welsh supporters on board had crashed nearby at Llandow airport. They had been returning happily from Dublin laden with gifts and souvenirs., etc., of the Welsh victory. There were but three survivors, and amongst those who died was the secretary of the Cardiff Supporters Club, who had organised the trip in the charter aircraft. Many were the touching enquiries which came to our club from all parts, concerning those who may have been in the aircraft. It was a never-to-be-forgotten sequel to the winning of the Triple Crown by Wales for the eighth time.'

On 12 March, Llandow had been the **world's worst air disaster**, with 80 deaths and only three survivors, one of whom, Handel Rogers of Llanelli, became President of the Welsh Rugby Union in 1976. Two weeks after the disaster, five uniformed buglers played the '*Last Post*' to a tearful Arms Park crowd, before the French international. Only an old, hidden, tiny plaque on a road between Llantwit Major and Cowbridge commemorates what was the world's greatest air disaster. An Appeal Fund for the Llandow victims raised £40,000. Against this sombre background, Wales hammered France 21-0 to win the Grand Slam. This was a strange championship – to be honest it may be the most unpredictable contest in the world. Wales scored 50 points to 8, +42. Scotland won 2 and lost 2 to finish second with points of 21-49, -28! Then came Ireland and France, both winning, drawing 1 and losing 2: 27-12 and 14-35; +15 and -19 points respectively. England with 1 win, scored 22-30 on points, -8. Wales scored 10 tries to 1, a fair old season. If fit, Bleddyn would have played in this glorious tournament, but Jack Matthews, Billy Cleaver, Rex Willis and Cliff Davies had played in all games to win the Triple Crown, and sealed the '**Grand Slam**' when France were beaten. It was the first time since 1911 that Wales had won all four championship games, and the first time since 1936 that Wales took the championship outright.

In this season, someone termed the Cardiff Athletic XV '*the bundle of rags*', possibly owing to mismatched shorts and socks on some occasions, and the epithet was adopted and has stuck for 72 years. To play for the 'Rags' became a real achievement in Welsh rugby. For youngsters with ambition and talent, it was a showcase for them to be considered for the Firsts. Former First team players, like Elwyn and Tony Williams often loved finishing their careers with a few seasons not at the very top level, enjoying their rugby and imparting knowledge to younger, up and coming players. And they were always available to 'step up' back to the Firsts as cover for absences. Firsts with injuries, like Bleddyn, eased themselves back into contention by playing for the Rags, and any player always felt that they had the opportunity of playing at some time for the Firsts. Players were in this season constantly being gifted to the Firsts. Cliff Morgan gained his First Team cap but also kicked 7 goals and scored one try for the Rags. Malcolm Davies was the Athletic top scorer with 13 tries, then Bleddyn with 5 in 5 games, coming back from his knee injury. They were captained by Rev. Howell Loveluck, and the season's results were fairly average: P33, W19, L10, D4 with points 258 to 141.

Perhaps indicative of the strength of Cardiff's 44-game fixture list in this year is the names of the 10 teams (15 games), that they did not play, that were in Llanelli's 40 fixtures this season -Torquay, Paignton, Felinfoel, Aberavon (4 games), U.A.U., Bridgend (2), Abertillery (2), R.A.F., Cross Keys and Waterloo. Cardiff's one regular 'weak' opposition was the Scottish side Watsonians, an old-established game, where from 1896-1973 Cardiff won 34, lost 2 and drew 1 of 37 matches. Then there was the regular April tour of Penzance and Newlyn, and Falmouth. The players really wanted to go on this 'tour', as it was a holiday for them, quite possibly the only one away from home in the year. In these latter games, from 1946 to the end of fixtures in 1971, the record against Penzance and Newlyn was P18; W15; L2, D1. Against Falmouth from 1931 till the fixtures ended in 1952, Cardiff won 13 and drew 1 of 14 games. The games were played on successive days, and the Cardiff team was a mix of Firsts and Rags, generally out for a good time away from home for 3 or 4 days. Apart from these three 'easy' games, there was the traditional warm-up against Cardiff & District, where local 'star' players tried their utmost to catch the eye of Cardiff selectors. If they 'showed up' well, they would be invited to Cardiff trials. Firsts and Athletic players also played in these trials, a form of training before the real season. Between 1882 and the fixtures ending in 1966, Cardiff won all 67 games. Cardiff played four more games than Llanelli, which make up their 'easy-ish' games – Cardiff and District, Watsonians, Penzance and Newlyn, and Falmouth. All were discontinued to make room for stronger teams wishing to play Cardiff.

Professional rugby league was making real inroads after the war, with clubs setting up in Wales at Cardiff, Bridgend, Llanelli, Neath, Ystradgynlais, etc. To try and halt its progress, the WRU wrote to clubs, resulting that the management committee of Cardiff Athletic Club (in effect Cardiff RFC) passed the resolution: '*That no person who is, or has been, engaged in the playing, administration, promoting, or fostering of Rugby League Football, or other Professional Rugby shall be admitted to the club either as a member or as a visitor.*' As had happened four decades earlier, rugby league thankfully failed to take hold in Wales, but Wales still

224

was the favourite hunting-ground for scouts from North of England RL clubs. This rather spiteful edict remained in force across much of Wales for decades, with vindictive effects upon those who found League was not to their liking and wished to return to Union. Much the same *fatwah* was pronounced upon those who wrote a book, reported or commented upon rugby. They were refused entry to clubhouses, but much worse, not allowed to coach at any level or contribute their expertise to Union clubs.

Incidentally, the 1949-50 *Playfair Rugby Football Annual* has on page 223 the title *'The Laws of Rugby Football'* and under that heading is a plan of a rugby field – measured in yards, of course – the '25' will always be the '25' to some of us. On page 224 on this little book is Part I - *Definitions, and Glossary of Terms*. Page 225 sees *Part II – Preliminary*, and halfway down page 226 there is *Part III – The Play in Detail*. There are just a few words completing the 'laws' on page 232. Thus we have 'The Laws' of rugby union covered from p224 to p231 – in just EIGHT PAGES. If one cares to check the web, there are now 190 – for emphasis ONE HUNDRED AND NINETY PAGES - of so-called 'laws', an absurd nomenclature by any standard. In the England-Italy match in 2017, the English players had to have the rules - I refuse use the term 'laws' - explained to them. Spectators do not know what is happening much of the time, which makes it now a difficult game to attract people to watch or play. If a scrum wheels, it is either reset or there is a full or indirect penalty to one of the sides, the awarding of which seems to be a lottery. The same goes for collapsed scrums, they are either reset, or a side seemingly chosen at random is penalised. We could here talk about every other area of the breakdown in rugby, but it would take two volumes of impenetrable, obfuscatory obscurantism – you get the picture. Basil Evans returned from mainly playing for Cardiff Athletic, to play for his home club of Pentyrch. Under the heading *'Gentleman Wing Forward'* there is an old newspaper cutting reading: *'Two players from district club, Pentyrch, have given Cardiff valuable service this season. But with cheery Basil Evans it is a case in contrast. When only 17 Basil played in war-time games for Cardiff, and during service in the Royal Navy played in the Navy Representative XV. While at Caerleon College he became vice-captain of the First XV and also played for London Welsh during vacations. A back injury kept this friendly 6ft. 1in. schoolmaster out of football for 18 months, although he appeared for Cardiff Athletic last season. Now aged 25, and weighing 13st 10lb., he is described by club secretary E.P. Evans as "a thorough gentleman and a grand clubman".'*

BRINLEY 'BRYN' EDWARD LOUGHER WILLIAMS 20 December 1920 (registered) March 1921 – 7 April 2011. 1944 - Married Elizabeth Phillips
Taff's Well centre, outside-half 1936-38

Cardiff Athletic 1938-39 left centre, outside-half, wing
Cilfynydd 1940 outside-half
1940-46 played for Army, serving in North Africa vs Rommel, then in Iraq, Lebanon, etc.
Cardiff - charity matches
Cardiff Athletic 1946-1950
Cross Keys 1947-49 centre
Cardiff First XV 2 games 2 tries 1949-50, and Cardiff Athletic 1949-51
Taff's Well 1951- 69 centre and full-back (played until age 48)

The Taff's Well player Ted Roberts was the father of Nell, who married Arthur Williams, who were the parents of the Williams brothers and sisters. Her younger brother Roy Roberts was the thus the uncle of the eight Williams brothers who played for Cardiff, playing many times alongside the eldest brother Gwyn, and also sometimes with Brinley (usually known as Bryn) and Bleddyn Williams. Bryn, like his brothers Gwyn and Bleddyn, their uncle Roy Roberts and cousin Bill Tamplin, was involved in World War 2, in Bryn's case spending five years in the Middle East and six years away from home. Brother Bleddyn made his debut for Cardiff, alongside Bryn, in a Cardiff Athletic game in 1938-39 against Ebbw Vale. In that season, Bryn played 10 games for the 'Rags' and Bleddyn 4. Bryn recounted in 1984 to Gerald Edwards and Don Llewellyn: *'Well I went to Cardiff when I was 18. Tony was telling me some time ago, that he went into the Players' Room at the Cardiff club, and he said my photograph is on the wall there. It's from 1938. That was the year that Cardiff won for the first time the Twickenham "Sevens" and I remember training with them on the cricket pitch, because at that time the Arms Park pitch still used to churn up. I played there till the war broke out at outside-half or centre.*

I was at the club the week after war had broken out on the Sunday and of course, men like Wilf Wooller and Les Spence, who had been in the Territorial Army, had already gone. Most clubs immediately suspended their activities and their players, so it was going to be difficult to get a game of rugby. When I was invited to play for Cilfynydd, I agreed. In those days, mind, Cilfynydd played first-class clubs. It was a colliery side really, you know – it was the colliery manager in fact who was running it. They tried to persuade me to work underground, and I said, "no bloody way" – I liked the fresh air too much.' (Miners like Billy Cleaver were classed as a restricted occupation so were exempted from joining the armed forces). *'So I played there at outside half. When I took Bleddyn there to play for Cilfynydd, when he was still a pupil at Rydal School, I moved to centre so he could play outside-half. He played a few times for us. He was in the Cilfynydd side that beat Pontypridd 33-8. He also played in that charity game against Aber and Senghennydd.*

226

After the war I returned to play for the RAGS and I can tell you there were some great players there... Cliff Morgan was one. Then I played a few games for the Firsts. Mind I did an extra year in the army at home. I was in it six years altogether by the time I got demobbed and everything, and you would be kept moving from place to place, you know. I was an infantry trainer for a while, and a machine-gun operator, which I had been myself. I was instructing the new boys coming in. Yes, there was a good crowd of lads down at the Cardiff club. It was a good club to play for – but I went to Cross Keys then for a change.' (Cross Keys was then an excellent club which played Cardiff nineteen times between 1920-21 and 1967-68, and Cardiff had an all-international back line, so it was difficult to get first team games. Of Bryn's preferred positions, the outside half and centres were always Cardiff current internationals). *'The first game I had for Cardiff, after going back there was against Newport. After a while I went back to play for Taff's Well – back home. I was still playing in the 1960s. I played in the centre when I was forty, and when I finished altogether, I was 48! I was playing fullback by then.*

Do you know, when I was abroad, I played soccer too! We were at Tobruk and we had a quiet moment. It happened sometimes you know – the guns stopped firing. We were playing football with two petrol cans as goalposts. They'd seen me playing a bit of rugby in Cairo and they said I should now play some soccer. So, I said "alright" and became the goalkeeper. Then when I went on leave to Cairo, I played a bit of soccer down there too. I played with Tom Finney. In the Tank Corps he was – well, in the cookhouse; he never moved from base. I played with Tom and against him.' (Sir Thomas Finney CBE, 1922-2014, was one of the greatest ever footballers, scoring 187 goals in 433 appearances for Preston North End, and 30 goals in 76 games for England between 1946 and 1958).

'I have to say that Del Harris did a wonderful job with Taff's Well Schoolboys. Bleddyn was two years behind me, and we both played rugby for Taff's Well Schoolboys. They had remarkable success. Bleddyn was still attending Rydal when I went to the Army. I was twenty and he was 17 going on 18. When he finished with Cilfynydd, he joined Cardiff in about 1942, but there wasn't much rugby going on just then. Then he went to the RAF and would be in it for some time. I was away for so long, that I didn't hear about Bleddyn so much, until I came back, of course. I knew he played for the Combined Services. Then as you know he went on to captain both Cardiff and Wales in those magnificent victories against the All Blacks.'

From the Taff's Well RFC history: *'BRINLEY "BRYN" – Bryn Williams played for Taff's Well before and after the war and was renowned for his crunching tackles. During this time, he made continual excursions to Cardiff to play for the "Blue and Blacks" senior teams. At Taff's Well Bryn was later a respected committee man and vice chairman. He still lives in the village, where he takes an interest in the playing fortunes of Taff's Well R.F.C. In his playing days for Taff's Well, Bryn was a regular and consistent goal kicker and smooth link at outside-half or centre.'* Bryn played alongside 16-year-old Bleddyn in 1938-39 for Cardiff Athletic, and also with him in 1949-50 for the Firsts. Bryn was a stalwart of the excellent Taff's Well side during the 1950s, and in 1960 helped form the youth team.

CHAPTER 21 - CARDIFF SEASON 1950 – 1951

'THE MOST SOUGHT-AFTER TEAM IN THE BRITISH ISLES' - 'W. E. TAMPLIN'S YEAR' - WORLD RECORD CLUB GATE OF 48,500 -

BLEDDYN REFUSES TO GO NORTH – CARDIFF'S 75TH ANNIVERSARY, FIVE CARDIFF LIONS

Bleddyn Williams P22 T5 = 15pts (TW); **Bill Tamplin** P39 C35 P22 D1 = 139pts (Risca); John Llewellyn P5 (Taff's Well); Derek Murphy P36 T12 = 36pts (Pentyrch); Glyn 'Faldau' Williams P16 T3 = 9pts (Pentyrch)

P45, W34, L6, D5. Points 480-192. Tries 97-32, Pens 29-20

Missing their five British Lions for the first 13 games, this was a reasonable season for Cardiff. Back-row Glyn 'Faldau' Williams joined, along with future international Derek Williams, both from Pentyrch RFC. Both were aged 23, with Murphy an NCB clerk and 'Faldau' a corn and seed salesman. It was reported *'both gained Cardiff "colours" in their first season direct from a district club – a feat recognised as meriting a "cap".'* Billy Cleaver was elected captain, but just before the season started, he told the committee that he would retire at the end of the 1950 British Lions tour. Perhaps he wished to end at the peak of his career, or wanted to make way for the young and talented Cliff Morgan – such an occurrence often happened when rugby was amateur. The British Lions tour lasted around 6 months, as usual, from mid-April, with the first match on 10 May, returning home at the end of October. It was the first British touring side since 1938, with a name change from British Isles to British Lions, and new shirts – red – say no more. They were given an allowance of five shillings each a day and free cigarettes. Because of the previous season's Grand Slam, of the 31 players selected, 13 were Welsh, but 14 played – Lewis Jones joined as a replacement. There were 5 Lions from Cardiff (Billy Cleaver, Bleddyn, Jack Matthews, Rex Willis and Cliff Davies); 3 Newport (Ken Jones, Bob Evans, Malcolm Thomas) and 2 Neath (Rees

228

Stephens and Roy John). The other Welsh international selections were Lewis Jones (Llanelli), Don Hayward (Newbridge) John Robins (Birkenhead Park) and Dai Davies (Somerset Police). With 9 Irish and 5 Scots, there were only 3 English players, and two of those, Ivor Preece and Vic Roberts, certainly had a Welsh pedigree somewhere along the line.

The WRU website tells us that it took the 2021 British & Irish Lions 11 hours to fly from London to Johannesburg, staying for five weeks and playing eight matches, including three Tests. However, the 1950 Lions played 29 matches, including six Tests – four in New Zealand and two in Australia. They also played an extra game in Ceylon on their way home.

1950-51 Cardiff's British 'Lions' Rex Willis, Jack Matthews, Bleddyn Williams, Billy Cleaver, Cliff Davies

On 30 March, the players gathered at the Mayfair Hotel, London - five days after Wales had beaten France to clinch the Grand Slam in Cardiff. There was still a full month of the club season to run. '*The players were guests at the annual dinner of the New Zealand Society at the Savoy Hotel on their first night together and then travelled to Twickenham the next day to get kitted out and photographed. As well as playing kit, they were issued with a tour blazer and tie, but had to provide their own trousers. They were also forbidden to swap playing jerseys.*

They left Euston Station for Liverpool on the morning on 1 April, where the boarded SS Ceramic 2. Ahead of them was four weeks at sea as they headed to New Zealand. They kicked-off with a six course, gourmet dinner, but then hit choppy waters and were hit by the ravages of seas-sickness. All that is, except the Irishman Tom Clifford. He vowed to eat his way through the whole menu on the Sunday night. He just about managed it, getting through the following: Hors d'Ouvres (various), Creme de Tomato, Fillets of Tartare, Sweetcorn en Corotte, Lamb Cutlets Parisienne, Braised York Ham Oporto, French Beans, Boiled and Roast Potatoes, Roast Norfolk Turkey with Cranberry Jelly, Rolled Ox Tongue with Leg of Pork and Apple Sauce, Salad with Mayonnaise Dressing, Plum Pudding with Cranberry Sauce, Peach melba, Dessert Fruit, Coffee, Fromage.

After 11 days at sea the players got the chance to get onto dry land when the Ceramic docked at Curacao in the Dutch West Indies. Two days later they reached the Panama Canal and had another stop off in Panama City. They crossed the Equator on 17 April and the international dateline on what should have been Monday, 1 May. They finally arrived in Wellington Harbour on Tuesday, 2 May. There was a civic reception, the Prime Minister welcomed them, but then it was back on board the Matai to cross the Cook Straits to head to Nelson. They had eight days to prepare for their first game, against Nelson-Marlborough-Golden Bay-Motueka at Trafalgar Park. They won 24-3 and triumphed in 17 and drew another of their 23 games in New Zealand. They drew the first Test and lost the other three – two by three points and one by eight. In Australia, they beat the Wallabies 19-6 and 24-3, but lost their final match against New South Wales. It meant they ended with 22 wins and a draw from their 29 games, including two wins and a draw in their six Tests. It was an eventful tour for Jack Matthews. He celebrated his 30th birthday by captaining the Lions in their 27-3 win over Poverty Bay-East Coast-Bay of Plenty on 21 June, scoring two of his six tour tries. He played in 20 matches and started in all six Tests.

Nothing was going to stop Dr Jack going on tour and he had to engage a locum to take over his general practice in Llandaff. He reckoned the tour cost him £5,000 – the players received 50 shillings, or £2.50 in today's money, allowance per week – and by the time he came home his son, Peter, was two months old and had yet to meet his father. The players had been away from home since 30 March, they began their homeward journey on SS Strathnavar from Melbourne on Tuesday, 5 September. They still had 32 days to go before arriving home. They sailed home via the southern coast of Australia, the Indian Ocean, the Arabian and Red Seas, the Suez Canal and the Mediterranean. They stopped off at Adelaide, Freemantle, Bombay, Aden and Marseilles. There was also time for one more match at Colombo against Ceylon in an unofficial fixture. They reached Brixham on Saturday, 7 October and disembarked at Tilbury the next day. The Cardiff players had a few games for the 'Rags' before re-joining the Firsts, after over a month at sea.'

There were 30 games and an immense amount of travelling between 10 May and 18 September 1950. After a 9-9 draw with New Zealand, the

Lions narrowly lost 8-0, 6-3 and 11-8, all games that they thought they could have won. The Australian Tests were won 19-6 and 24-3. On 19 August 1950, a Lions record of 10 Welshmen beat Australia 19-6, with Lewis Jones, Jack Matthews, Bleddyn Williams (c), Malcolm Thomas, Rex Willis, Dai Davies, John Robins, Rees Stephens, Bob Evans and Roy John. The tour 'replacement' Lewis Jones became the only Lion to score a test match 'full house' of two conversions, two penalties, a drop goal and a try. Bleddyn Williams scored the other try. *The Western Mail* on 20 August led with the headline *'Great Performance from Lewis Jones.'* *'This young player took nearly all the honours of a match watched by 20,000 people, his highlight being a drop goal from fully 50 yards'*. *'The whole British team played well. Not only did they possess greater skill than their opponents, but they held a marked advantage in pace.'* Rugby historian Peter Stead told *The Western Mail* *'Like Lewis Jones, I was a pupil at Gowerton Grammar School and he was considered a hero there in my formative years. He was the greatest player of his generation, a revolutionary and a huge loss to Wales when he later went to northern England to play rugby league. In fact, he has been held in such high esteem since that every Welshman who has headed north after him, has been sent to speak with Lewis Jones for advice as a first port of call.'*

In 1950, 18-year-old Lewis Jones was a conscript in the Royal Navy, and had been plucked from the relative obscurity of Devonport Services by the Wales selectors, following the unexpected retirement of the 34-year-old Frank Trott. Lewis Jones remembered, *'Cliff Morgan reminded me recently of the letter we received from the selectors. It read something like this: "You have been selected for Wales versus England at Twickenham on 21st January 1950. Would you make sure you are at the ground two hours before the kick-off. Shirts, shorts and socks will be supplied. Shorts and socks must be returned after the match... That year, 1950, was wonderful. When George Norton, the Ireland full back, broke his arm I was called up to replace him.'* The Lions had sailed to New Zealand and Lewis Jones was the first player ever to be flown out to a tour. *'When I arrived at London Airport I looked out at the plane, it was a monster, a Boeing Stratocruiser. No doubt, by today's standards it would be dwarfed by the Jumbos and so on, but to me it was huge. These days it's a journey that means 24 hours flying time to New Zealand. Back then it was somewhat different. It took four and a half days, with four or five changes of planes to fly there. We landed in Gisburn on the east coast and my first game was the following day.'*

Peter Stead said: *'That Lions side in 1950 boasted some of the best players ever to have played for Wales. Before their deaths, Dr Jack Matthews and Bleddyn Williams would meet almost daily in the Cardiff clubhouse for a drink, they looked exactly the same as they did in their playing days and would regale drinkers with great rugby tales. Bleddyn's career came just before televised rugby, and he would have been an absolute star had he played a few years later. The great Cardiff scrumhalf Rex Willis was also a familiar face around the city until his death. These were legends of the game, like tomorrow's players could be. As proud as we are of our national identity in Wales, we have always been great supporters of the Lions. We have always regarded it as the pinnacle of sport, something to celebrate, a great honour and source of pride. But we have had to wait a long time to see as many Welshmen on the field, and so it is a great day for Wales.'*

History repeats itself. In 2013, the Lions fullback, like Lewis Jones, was also from Gorseinon, the brilliant Leigh Halfpenny, who played in all 3 tests against Australia and was named *'Player of the Series'*. The Lions won two and lost one. There were 15 Welshmen, 10 Irish, 9 English and 3 Scots players selected, with the youngest ever Lions captain, Cardiff's 24-year-old Sam Warburton. 8 Welshmen and 2 replacements played in the first test, won 25-23, the first time 10 Welshmen had been in a Lions Test together since 1950. With 3 penalties and 2 conversions, Halfpenny won the match, and the only two tries were also Welsh, by North and Cuthbert. In the next test, Leigh scored all the Lions points with 5 penalties in a 16-15 loss. Obviously to some of us, there were only 7 Welshmen starting the game, with 2 coming off the bench, which resulted for the marginal loss. Coach Warren Gatland had the selection correct in the 3rd and deciding test, replicating the 1950 fixture with 10 Welshmen starting and one coming in off the bench. The Irish press was incandescent with rage when the truly great Brian O'Driscoll was replaced - Cardiff's Jamie Roberts was drafted in, with one of the world's greatest centres, Jonathan Davies, being shifted into O'Driscoll's berth.

Roberts and George North scored 2 of the Lions' 4 tries, with Leigh Halfpenny converting 3 and kicking all 5 attempted penalties for a total of 21 points. This 'Welsh' Lions team easily won 41 - 16. For those non-Welsh readers thinking that there is a bare smidgeon of partiality creeping into this narrative – you are misled. However, there is a great deal of preference – an arcane distinction, favouring this author. One has only ever supported Cardiff Rugby and Cardiff City football clubs, Wales at rugby and footy, then other Welsh clubs, and finally British teams. We all know Manchester United supporters who have never been to Manchester. I was in university there, when Best, Law and Charlton were in their pomp, but saved my sparse grant for beer. One's local team comes first – always. Anyway, statistically speaking, if a Lions team picks 10 Welshmen to start a Test Match, they always win.

Back to what was called *'W.E. Tamplin's Year'* by Danny Davies. In Billy Cleaver's place, the pack leader Bill Tamplin was Cardiff captain, and chose his cousin Bleddyn as vice-captain, despite Bleddyn being unavailable for around 20 matches with the Lions and on Wales duties.

Tamplin had previously played for Pontypool, then was a lieutenant in the Army during wartime, but *'Bill Tamp'* had joined Cardiff upon demobilisation. An acknowledged great leader of men, he was an inspiring captain, one of the best goal kickers in rugby and could happily play second row or lock (today's No. 8). Cardiff's five Lions were not available until the home game vs. Bridgend on 4 November, and the excellent wings Terry Cook and Russell Burn had left for Rugby League, for a tax-free signing-on fee, a decent job and to be paid for playing rugby. John Llewellyn of Taff's Well played 152 times for Cardiff from 1950-51 to 1956-57, while flanker Charles Derek 'CD' Williams appeared no less than 248 times between 1945-46 and 1958-59. C.D. Williams had scored a try for the Probables in a Welsh Trial in 1948, and it had been a long wait to win his first cap, aged 30 in 1955. In the following year he scored the try against France that won the Five Nations Championship, his only two caps. His problem was that Cardiff were filling the backs places in the Welsh team, and to 'balance' geographical interests, the 'Big Five' were usually unwilling to pick Cardiff forwards.

There was a French referee for the London Welsh game at the Arms Park, the first French official at the ground, and he presented special medals to Bleddyn and Jack, for being picked for the Lions, and upon becoming life members of Nantes Rugby Club. When France played Wales at Stade Colombes on 7 April 1951, the French Minister of Sport presented Danny Davies with a gold medal of *'Education, Physique et Sport'* honouring his efforts for fostering Anglo-French rugby, the first time it was awarded to a foreign national. The wing Terry Cook had joined Cardiff from Pontypool at the start of the 1948-49 season, scoring 9 tries in his first 5 games, and 24 tries in 27 games that season, including 3 hat-tricks against Devonport Services, Wasps and Leicester, and 4 tries against Rosslyn Park. He then scored 20 tries in the 1949-50 season, ending his Cardiff career with 44 tries in 71 matches, and scored two tries in the win against England. While Cook went North to Hunslet, his wing partner Russell Burn, who had scored 38 tries in 62 games in tandem with Cook over two seasons, joined Swinton RL.

Fortunately, the excellent wings Haydn Morris, a future Lion from Mountain Ash and Pentyrch's Derek 'Spud' Murphy replaced them. Murphy played 162 times between 1950-51 and 1957-58, scoring 77 tries. Haydn Morris made 129 appearances on the left wing, between 1950-51 and 1955-56, scoring 101 tries. He scored 18 tries in 25 games in his first season and was selected for Wales away against France in April 1951, in the 8-3 loss. Haydn was an International and a Lions cap in his first season in first-class rugby – how many players can claim that? His left centre, of course, was Bleddyn Williams, and it was usually 'his' wing that topped the try scoring table. Haydn won two more caps in 1955 against Ireland and France, scoring a try in each match. He was selected for the 1955

British Lions tour to South Africa, scoring nine tries in eight appearances, which must be some sort of record, but then was injured and out for the rest of the tour. (How the Lions managed to draw the series 2-2 is a mystery to this day). I knew Haydn when he was teaching me maths and coaching rugby at Barry County-Grammar School, along with Cardiff's Geoff Beckingham joining in some rugby sessions – Haydn's favourite exhortation was – '*Cool head, boy, cool head.*' He also admitted that when he joined Cardiff he checked inside his boot for '*boot money*', usually a ten-shilling note that he got at Mountain Ash, and was told in no uncertain terms that Cardiff '*was not that sort of club*'.

Cardiff scored fewer points this year, as the season was one of the wettest on record, and many of us remember the Arms Park in its quagmire days, when the only dry bit was the dog-track around the pitch (until 1977). Games were played on it by Wales, Cardiff, Cardiff Athletic, Cardiff Boys and various representative county, schools and police teams, perhaps up to 60 games in around 30 weeks. One pitied the groundsmen. Other Welsh venues suffered. The Penarth pitch, for one, became unplayable and their game at Cardiff in January was cancelled, because of the 'wet state of the ground'. Cardiff's brand of running rugby was impossible in months of almost monsoon conditions. However, Cardiff only lost to four clubs, away to Coventry, Oxford University and Bristol, and being beaten by a great Newport team 3 times. Cardiff lost the first two games 8-3 (H) and 8-6 (A), and the third match at Cardiff on 17 February was a pulsating affair, Cardiff losing 8-3 in front of a world record crowd for a club match of 48,500, with gate takings almost £2,600. It seemed that Newport had emptied its population to see their team try to make history.

A friend recalls Bleddyn sheltering behind a post in this game, and Danny Davies remembers: '*The February 1951 match was played under bitterly cold conditions, and in the second half, a cold and biting hailstorm descended upon the players, who were forced to bend down in the cold to let the biting hailstones fall on their backs. The match was temporarily halted, and, as one of the touch-judges on the occasion, I was, in other vernacular terms, frozen stiff. There was a pleasant sequel to the match as the Welsh Rugby Union sent letters to both clubs expressing its thanks and admiration for the sporting spirit in which the match was played, a fine example to all clubs exemplifying the splendid relationships between two of the world's greatest Rugby clubs. But television was not far away!*' In the fourth local derby at Newport, a penalty goal by 'Bill Tamp' saved Cardiff's record, with a 3-3 draw, of never being beaten 4 times in a season by its neighbours. Cardiff could not score a try against their neighbours, but Newport managed 5 in the four games. Apart from injuries, Cardiff were missing their five Lions on tour until 4 November. A very fine Newport side nearly achieved an unbeaten season, only losing to Harlequins and Exeter away.

234

Pontypool's ground record was taken again, and the Barbarians easily defeated at Easter 13-3 (2 converted tries and a penalty to a penalty). Cardiff did not lose a match from 17 February to the end of the season. Haydn Morris scored 18 tries, Gareth Griffiths and Derek Murphy 11, Alun Thomas and Bleddyn Williams 6 each and the forward Malcolm Collins 5. Tamplin scored a total of 65 goals from conversions, penalties, a drop-goal, and a goal from mark, equalling 139 points. First XV caps were awarded to: Derek Murphy (36 appearances), Haydn Morris (25), C. D. Williams (24), W. E. Davies (23), Hughie Greenslade (23) and outside half/centre Gwyn Llewellyn (23). Added to their previous games for the Firsts, Des O'Brien (17 games), Alun Thomas (15), and wing Glyn Williams (16) were also capped. Pentyrch's wing-forward Glyn 'Faldau' Williams only played 16 times for Cardiff, just in this season, but his performances in Mallett Cup finals meant that he travelled as a Wales Reserve. He moved on, to play for Bridgend.

The monthly magazine *'Rugger'* has a table of First-Class Clubs compiled by Brigadier M.C.T. Gompertz for the season 1950-51. The qualification for inclusion is 14 fixtures with other clubs in the table, and Newport had a wonderful season, going from 7th in the previous season to top the table. Cardiff, as always, had fixtures against 18 of the top 20 clubs – the toughest fixture list of any club, losing 3 games and drawing one against a superb Newport side. Cardiff did not play Bedford (2nd), London Irish (14th) or Richmond (20th). Bedford, who came second, had <u>no</u> fixtures against Welsh clubs. Gompertz makes the point that *'it is an "event" for an English club to beat a Welsh club:* **for a Welsh club to beat an English club is not an event at all.** *The five Welsh clubs in the table played 55 matches against English clubs, excluding for obvious reasons the London Welsh. Forty-six were won by Welsh clubs, eight by English clubs, one was drawn. The points margin was 690 to 237 in favour of the Welsh, and of the twenty-five visits of English clubs,* **not a single win or draw** *went on the record. So, the final word must go to the* **chief slaughterers – Cardiff and Swansea.** *They have not been mentioned earlier, because one takes them for granted and it is not "news" at all to find them so regularly in the first four.'*

	P	W	L	D	For	Agst	%	1949-50	1950-51
Newport	26	24	1	1	363	94	94.23	7	1
Bedford	19	14	3	2	183	64	78.97	9	2
Cardiff	27	19	6	2	265	138	74.07	3	3
Swansea	20	12	5	3	193	106	67.50	3	4
Bath	23	14	6	3	190	180	67.39	24	5

This top 5 were followed by Harlequins, Coventry, Neath, Gloucester and Leicester (tied 9th), Oxford University, Northampton, Wasps, London Irish,

Cambridge University, Bristol. Blackheath, Llanelli, London Welsh and Richmond. Cardiff, always missing their best players – the usual excuse – lost to Newport 8-3, 8-6, 8-3 and drew 3-3, by a total of 12 points in 4 matches, otherwise they would have headed the table. (The following year, Cardiff would yet again score a 'quadruple' over their greatest rivals). However, Cardiff beat Swansea 11-6 and 19-6, 8 tries to 3. Bath were beaten away, 25-11, 6 tries to 2. Sixth in the table were Harlequins, beaten by a try, 3-0. Seventh were Coventry, who beat Cardiff at Coventry by a try and a penalty 6-0, while Cardiff beat them at home 11-0, scoring two tries. Eighth were Neath, with Cardiff scoring the only try of the game winning 6-3 at home, and at the Gnoll scoring the only two tries but drawing 6-6. Gloucester was joint ninth, and Cardiff won at home 16-9, 4 tries to 2; and won away 6-3, scoring the only try. At Leicester, joint ninth, Cardiff won 3-0 away with a try, and at home scored the only 3 tries winning 17-6. There was no tenth place, and eleventh-placed Oxford won 11-6 at home, outscoring Cardiff by 2 tries to 1. At number 12, Northampton were beaten 6-0 away and 8-3 at home, Cardiff scoring 2 tries to 1.

Bleddyn Williams, Cardiff, scoring his third and much-discussed try for Cardiff against Llanelly.

1950-51 Bleddyn scores his third try against Llanelli

Wasps were in thirteenth position and Cardiff beat them 8-3 away, a try apiece, and 14-13 at home, each side scoring 3 tries. There was no fixture against London Irish, in fourteenth place, and fifteenth-placed Cambridge conceded 2 tries to lose 6-0. Cardiff lost 3-0 at Bristol but won at home 14-

10, unusually conceding the try count 3-1 to the always attractive sixteenth-placed team. In seventeenth position, Blackheath were defeated away 17-12, 4 tries to 1. Cardiff drew 0-0 away with Llanelli (18th) but outscored them on tries 5-2 to win 27-6 at home. In nineteenth place, London Welsh were beaten 26-0 at Cardiff, with the home team scoring 6 tries. Richmond were in 20th place, but Cardiff had halted fixtures in 1947-48 after winning eight successive games. Thus, apart from the four close games against Newport, Cardiff played 24 games against 16 of the top 20 first-class clubs, winning 19, drawing 2 and losing 3 (by a total of 14 points), scoring 54 tries against 21, with a points score of 255 against 117. At home, Cardiff defeated an excellent Pontypool team 3-0 in September 1950, with the only try of the match. Then, on 28 April 1951 Cardiff took Pontypool's unbeaten home record, in Ponty's last official match of the season 11-6. Between September 1959 and October 1972, against Pontypool Cardiff won 24, drew 2 and lost 3 matches, with all draws and losses being away from home. To be honest, there was some very variable refereeing throughout the post-war years, surprisingly always favouring the home team, until, probably, the 1990s, with professional refereeing. Professionalism in the 21st century should have brought very high standards of refereeing at the top echelon, but certain international referees are still not fit for purpose. A certain Georgian in the first Test of South Africa vs. Wales in 2022 springs to mind.

Cardiff were now in demand to play everywhere, and upon 30 December 1950 played against Northumberland, where both sides scored two tries, but Cardiff missed the conversions to lose 10-6. In the *Rugger Annual* for 1950-51, we read: '*Steam Roller on Pitch. The Northumberland-Cardiff match in December last season afforded an unusual sight for, before the kick-off, a steam roller "invaded" the pitch to flatten protruding icy tufts. Originally scheduled for the County Ground at Gosforth, the match had to be switched mid-week to Percy Park's North Shields ground. Unfortunately, the frost struck through straw which was laid overnight. In effect, the match was only token rugby for tackling was barred. In this game, Northeast supporters saw Cliff Morgan for the first time – and no one was surprised when he went on to get his Welsh "cap".*'

Bath RFC reported its home loss to Cardiff on 20 January 1951, when Cardiff were again hurt by international calls for the England game at Swansea, when Jack Matthews and Malcolm Thomas shared four of Wales five tries: '*Cardiff fielded Internationals Frank Trott, Bill Tamplin and Des O'Brien (Ireland). They submerged Bath with 2 goals, 4 tries and a drop goal to a goal, a try and a penalty. Bath experienced a devastating opening spell in which Cardiff touched down twice within twelve minutes. Glyn John was notable for one of his unorthodox breaks-through and by way of compensation in the 17th minute Sullivan landed a penalty goal from in front of the posts. Cardiff piled on the points... but Bath struck back in blood-warming fashion. Amid terrific cheers the Cardiff line fell at last, and it was Addenbrooke who was responsible for a try that will live long in the memory. Three times they tried to tackle him and once to hurl him into touch, but an amazing fast, and determined run took him in at the corner to help redeem the ineffectiveness of the backs today. Next, Trevor Lewis stormed over for Sullivan to convert. Although Bath lost, it was somehow fitting that their Welsh contingent of Addenbrooke, John and Trevor Lewis, should have particularly good games.'* Cardiff scored 6 tries to 2 at Bath, in a 25-11 win.

As regards the season for Cardiff Athletic XV, the veteran prop Stan Bowes, with the club since 1938-39 except for wartime service as a Petty Officer in the Royal Navy, was captain. A 'larger than life character' who this author remembers playing and then many times 'running the line' for Cardiff after he retired, Stan was noted for habitually referring to Newport as those *'Black and Amber bastards'*. Stan once reportedly almost pulled out of a game at Llandovery, because the team he had been selected to play for were wearing Black and Amber. He refused to have Newport colours next to his skin and would not put the shirt on until somebody found him a Cardiff shirt to wear underneath the *'Black and Amber rag'*. He anchored the Cardiff scrum from 1938-39 to 1955-56 – an incredible man, and the heart and soul of all social activity at the club. At Blackwood on 28 October 1950, the British Lions Cliff Davies, Jack Matthews, Bleddyn Williams and Rex Willis played for the Rags after returning from the tour, limbering up before a Firsts game against Bridgend the following Saturday. How many other reserve teams could turn out four current British Lions? The Rags Played 31, Won 23, Lost 7 and Drew 1, with points 351-156.

Cliff Morgan was awarded his first Welsh cap, against Ireland, and Haydn Morris his first against France. Three other Cardiff players played in all of Wales's games - Jack Matthews, Cliff Davies and Rex Willis. Bleddyn only played once, because of injury. In the Five Nations, after the Grand Slam season hopes were again high. In the first game Wales hammered England at Swansea 23-5, but in the second game, away at Scotland, were unaccountably thrashed 19-0. It was Scotland's only win. It was a freak result, and nearly every year the Nations Championship springs incredible surprises. (Think Wales-Italy 2022). At home, a 3-3 draw prevented Ireland getting a Grand Slam, and a loss away in Paris 8-3 ended a year that began with great promise. Wales finished 3rd, above Scotland with England taking the Wooden Spoon. Amazingly, after 3 wins and a draw to win the 5 Nations, Ireland's point difference was just 5, with wins over France 9-8, Scotland 6-5 and England 3-0 – a penalty. Against England, Wales had scored 5 tries (4 converted by Lewis Jones) to one, in their 23-5 victory, in modern scoring 36-5. One wonders what would have happened if Bleddyn had been able to play in all games, as he only played in the 3-3 draw with Ireland, Lewis Jones partnering Dr. Jack in the other matches.

In the *Rugger Annual Number 1950-51*, rugby correspondent H.L.V. Day, of Leicester, the Army and England, wrote: '*After the 23 points to 5 defeat at Swansea, there was an immoderate use of superlatives at the Welsh fifteen, though why I could not possibly fathom. Wales certainly gave a lesson in teamwork, but at least three tries were presented to them by atrocious defence in the centre. I never expected L.F.L. Oakley, usually a magnificent defender who follows in the true tradition of Hasting Dasent's famous exhortation "crash into him", to be afflicted with the pernicious virus of shadow tackling. Lewis Jones and Matthews simply waltzed through between Oakley and Boobyer and proved conclusively, that to allow fast backs to get under way, must be more dangerous than flattening them early in their run.*'

In the *South Wales Football Echo & Express*, 18 November 1950, a headline reads '*Bleddyn to try for outside half berth in Welsh XV? Cardiff fans no doubt heaved a great sigh of relief on Thursday when it was announced that Bleddyn Williams had rejected all offers to turn professional and had denied that he was negotiating with a rugby league club. The loss of Williams, so soon after Billy Cleaver's decision to retire from the game, would indeed have been a blow to the Cardiff playing strength. It was reported that Leeds had offered him £6,000 and that he was giving the offer very serious consideration.*' Bleddyn was 3 months short of his 28th birthday – it must have been an extremely tempting offer, as one injury could have halted his career in an instant. It would have been a **world record fee**, with the new record being set in 1950 of Joe Egan moving from Wigan to Leigh for £5,000. That lasted until the wonderful Lewis Jones was paid £6,000, to move from Llanelli to Leeds in 1952. The five-figure mark was broken in 1959 with Ike Southward moving to Oldham in 1959 for £10,650. However, the transfers of Joe Egan and Ike Southward were between clubs. In the case of Bleddyn and Lewis Jones, as amateur players they would have received the fee themselves. One must recount Danny Davies' conversation with Bleddyn this year: '*In our coach on the way to Newport for the match with Cardiff on 11 November, Bleddyn Williams joined me, and we discussed the offer of £6,000 made to him to turn professional with the Rugby League, a most tempting sum at that time. Apart from saying that the Cardiff Club would miss him greatly, and that the choice was strictly his to make, I expressed the view that in the long term there were important occupational and professional prizes to be gained as an amateur, broadcasting and writing for an example. We are, I suppose, very glad that he stayed with his own amateur club Cardiff, he went on to win further honours; in 1953-54 he captained the club and, triumphantly, led his club to defeat the All Blacks. Glory indeed.*'

The Football Echo article continued: '*He has said, however, that he is *very happy playing the Union code and that his main concern is to regain his place in the Wales team. On this latter subject there are many theories going the rounds at the moment, not the least that Bleddyn will try to win a new cap at outside half. It was rumoured that before the Newport-Cardiff clash, that Bleddyn was to ask the Cardiff selection committee to play him in that position at Rodney Parade.'* (The club selection committee was always former players, who nearly always chose the 'best' team, while also trying to keep the Rags players committed to the club. There was no partisan 'horse-trading', as among the 'Big Five' national selectors, who wished players from their own regions and clubs to play.) *'He did not, however, make the request, and Gwyn Llewellyn partners Rex Willis'.* Gwyn only played 21 games for Cardiff Firsts, all in 1950-51, with Cliff Morgan being unavailable. Glyn Davies played outside half against England. *'Against Leicester today, however, Llewellyn and Williams switched positions, and if Bleddyn really settles at stand-off it is quite likely he will remain there, at least until the return of Cliff Morgan. Whether Bleddyn is to make a serious bid to take over from Cleaver both in the Cardiff and Welsh XV's however, remains to be seen, and Cardiff supporters will no doubt follow the trend of events with the utmost interest.'* Cardiff beat Leicester 17-6, 3 tries to nil.

It would be remiss of me to forego an opportunity of explaining that crowds in former days were far, far more knowledgeable than those of today. We must add the caveat, of course, that rugby was much simpler to understand. In the *Football Echo* of 18 November 1950, it mentions that Scotland were going to adopt the Welsh method of ticket allocation for international matches – to affiliated clubs only. Schools could also receive tickets for their rugby teams. In Wales, if you played rugby, you either had a ticket, or an excellent chance of a ticket – and very few ended up in the hands of touts – players wanted to see the games. It was a day out for rugby men and boys from across the nation. However, over the years, the allocation of tickets to players via clubs has nose-dived, as the WRU seeks to make money. Within the clubs, tickets are often sold on to help club finances.

It does not help that many former rugby players, still rugby club members, do not find modern rugby entertaining, and do not wish for tickets. Watching a game, one used to be surrounded by similar people, some of whom would have had a drink before the game, and almost all of whom would find a hostelry after the match. There were no constant interruptions of people with little interest in the game, heading back and fore to the bars and toilets, checking their phones, buying large cokes and topping up with vodka from their handbags (mainly ladies, this activity), chatting to each other and not watching every minute of the game. For some reason in the new stadium, people stand up to watch a try being scored, or when the game moves into a corner of the pitch, although it is

240

simultaneously being displayed on large screens. Also, the absurdity of keeping the roof open in cold weather – the wind comes howling through the multiple entrances – one can shiver if seated near the entrances, despite being wrapped up. Ah well, mustn't grumble – but I know 'well-padded' men and women who have left the ground at half-time to watch the game in their hotel. And I know many others disaffected by the regionalisation of Welsh rugby, who simply will not head to Cardiff for an international. In the 1950s, 60s and 70s, probably a majority of international spectators had played the game at some level. Now one wonders whether if any have. And don't get me started on 'Mexican Waves' and '*Oggy* bloody *Oggy*'.

DAI MILLWARD

In the display cabinet at Taff's Well R.F.C. there is a photo of Dai Millward, as captain of the rugby youth team in 1913. Next to it is this text from Peter Thomas' history of the club: '*On the main road in Taff's Well stands the house Taf Olwg, where lived the man who was destined to become "Mr Taff's Well", and one of the true characters of rugby football itself. In 1908 he had helped form and had played for Glanyllyn Juniors, who started their activities with a Christmas Day game against Garth. He agreed to come along to the meeting at Harry Field's for 20 minutes or so. He was appointed Secretary and that 20 minutes turned into 40 years! Dai, a gentle, quiet man, unless you said something derogatory about Taff's Well, was also a well-known referee and refereed for more years than anyone before or since. He was a founder member of the Referees Society. On retiring from his main occupation as an accountant in Cardiff, he was appointed to the staff of the W.R.U. and earned immortality as one of the most meticulous officials in the history of the Union.*

Dai Millward had a dream. He wanted to create a rugby club in Taff's Well that would have such firm foundations that nothing could threaten its continued existence. He had a vision of Taff's Well R.F.C. as respected members of the W.R.U., playing attractive and sporting rugby. Throughout our history men have emerged that have been larger than life characters – Fred Harris, Fred Porter, Ted Roberts, Tony Bonetto, Elwyn Williams (one of the Williams brothers), Iorrie Jones. The list is impressive. Yet it was this diminutive, dapper little man (Dai Millward) *who bestrides the history of Taff's well R.F.C. like a giant.*'

'Dai' Millward was instrumental more than any other man in the good fortunes of the club. Upon 18 November 1950, there was a tribute to the man behind Taff's Well, and '*a great support to the Williams brothers*', Dai Millward, in the *Football Echo*: '*The outstanding impression of Mr. D. Millward, of Taff's Well, during his long experience as a referee has been that players and committee members used to look upon the whistler not as a person helping in the game, but with indifference. He feels, however, that this attitude has changed in recent years thanks to a better understanding*

241

of the game and assisted by some "welcome directives from the W.R.U."
Mr. Millward, who was born in Glanyllyn, Taff's Well, and despite being a
little thin on top he is quite fit for his 56 years and able to keep up with the
fastest of play – a legacy probably of his younger days when he did a fair
amount of professional sprinting. From a very early age, rugby became his
favourite sport and he played for the local junior team when 15. Later he
was secretary of the juniors and then graduated to the secretaryship of the
present Taff's Well XV – a position he still holds.

As a player, however, he modestly states, his only useful feature was an
ability to run quickly, an advantage that saved him on numerous occasions
from the impact of heavy opponents upon his 8st. frame. When not engaged
upon his rugger activities, Mr. Millward is an accountant... He is, he says,
very keen upon strict administration, a fact which Taff's Well members
should know only too well. With a good grounding in refereeing in the
Cardiff and District Rugby Union, he sat and passed the W.R.U. exam in
1929, although he might not have done so, had not Taff's Well been with a
home ground that season.... he claims to have visited every ground from
Cardiff to Treherbert and from Newport to Brynmawr. Coming from a club
which has always been strictly non-competitive, he found the stern
Glamorgan and Monmouthshire League tussles quite a handful at first...
he has also had his fair share of games between first class Welsh clubs and
between Mon. County and Gloucestershire... English public schools have
come under his control... "I well remember", says Mr. Millward,
"refereeing a game at Downside College (where the Turnbulls learned
their rugby) against another famous school when the visiting captain gave
one of his side a dressing down for kicking into touch, although his side
were 30 points down."

On one occasion, while leaving the field in company with members of a
club committee, one of whom was landlord of a local pub, one home fan
called upon the publican to "drown him in your barrels as there's no river
near." A Welsh-speaking Welshman, he has also caused some electrical
reactions in West Wales. When asked for reasons for penalty awards, he
replied in the Welsh tongue, that certain rather ungentlemanly orders
issued by the home captain in Welsh, had been understood by him...'

THE GREATEST CLUB CROWD IN HISTORY

Newport-Cardiff clashes used to be 'something else' – wonderful affairs,
the most important games of the season except for touring teams, often
drawing even more crowds than the Barbarians. And one must remember
that the weather and pitch was better on Easter Saturday for the Baa-Baas'
visit. A wonderful atmosphere, near-capacity crowds in Wales' national
ground for the 2 home fixtures of the 4 Newport games, with good-natured
supporters enjoying the games. At other grounds there was far more

hostility towards Cardiff – mentioning no names – probably owing to resentment of Cardiff's 'glamour boys', playing in the 'big city'. No doubt, anyone who managed a regular place in Cardiff's team was in with a shout for a Welsh cap, when so few were awarded in those days. The best players often gravitated towards the capital city to improve their chances of being selected for Wales. Players loyal to unfashionable clubs such as Cross Keys, Maesteg and Abertillery often found it extremely difficult to be selected for the full Welsh team, which made the three Probables vs. Possibles game intense affairs. Their players really had to really make a very strong case for selection.

And, of course, there was no national coach, nor any structured training for those chosen for Wales. They were decided by 'the Selectors' – five senior men known as *'The Big Five'*, usually from different club backgrounds, ostensibly to try to prevent any bias towards Llanelli or Swansea or whatever. They often got things wrong – of course – sometimes glaringly so. There often also seemed to be a trading off – no, I shall rephrase that – there often was a trading off - *'you can have him and him, then I can have him and him and him, and he can have him,'* and so on. While writing this as a Cardiff supporter for almost seven decades, sometimes Cardiff players have been chosen over, to my mind, better players from less fashionable clubs, or those playing in England. However, on the other hand there is no doubt whatsoever in my opinion that Elwyn Williams should have had at least five seasons playing for Wales in the early 1960s – and for the British Lions. He was a player before his time, with a mission of keeping the ball in play, who could play across the back row, preferably open side, but was also comfortable playing centre in the backs – Justin Tipuric among today's wing forwards is in a similar mould.

The world club record attendance of 48,500 (gate receipts £2,587), for the 8-3 loss to Newport, stood until the modern era of rugby, from the 1980's onwards with leagues, cups and then professional rugby. The Cardiff programme for the great game between Cardiff and Newport, which filled the national stadium, is found on *'The History of Newport RFC'* website, taken from the Cardiff programme: *'TO-DAY'S BIG CLASH! The great day has arrived! Newport, our great and friendly rivals, visit the Arms Park unbeaten. The glove is down and we do battle with them for the honour of being the leading club side in Wales! It should be a great game - it will be a great occasion! We expect a record club gate, in fact, a world record for any club match. This will be an honour in itself, for Welsh Rugby and for the two clubs. There is a great history around the rivalry of Cardiff and Newport, and it first started in April 1875. The two clubs fought a draw in their first meeting and since that day have met on 240 occasions. Cardiff have won 106 games to Newport's 95, with 39 games drawn. The last three games have been won by Newport. The Newport club this season have won 23 matches in a row and have fulfilled the promise they showed at the end of last season, when they won their last ten matches.*

They are a magnificent team, sound in every department, with every member of the side playing not for himself but for the club. It has made no difference whether Ken Jones, Bob Evans or Roy Burnett has led the side, the spirit has been the same. Everyone all out for Newport from the first to last whistle.

To-day they meet a side blessed with the same team spirit. Bill Tamplin and his merry men will play rugger as it should be played to combat the match-winning brilliance of Newport. The result might be stalemate or a magnificent game of open rugby. Win or lose, we are sure that Newport will give of their best. The referee to-day will be Mr. Ivor David, of Neath, who substitutes at the last moment for Mr. Harold Phillips, also of Neath... It is anticipated that several of the Welsh Selectors will be present to-day, for the match will serve as an extra trial. Many of the players on both sides are under review and we wish them well. On with the game!' Modern programme writers, please take note – albeit some rugby and football clubs are abandoning programmes for digital information, hardly collectable, but that is progress (of some description).

The Times of 19 February 1951 reported the game: *'NEWPORT WIN AGAIN - Newport go on from strength to strength. On Saturday they gained their third victory of the season over Cardiff, scoring a goal and a try (8 points) to a penalty goal (3 points), this being their thirty-fourth win in successive matches - including nine at the end of last season. Their visit resulted in a new record being established, for the crowd of nearly 45,000 at Cardiff Arms Park was the* **greatest ever to watch a club fixture in Great Britain***, exceeding the 36,000 at the Cardiff v. Swansea match on the same ground in 1949. The all-round strength of the Newport side was never more exemplified than in this game. With the wind and sun at their backs in the first half Cardiff gained an interval lead of three points with a penalty goal by W. E. Tamplin, but the powerful Newport forwards gradually gained the mastery. They paved the way for clever play by their backs, and in the second half T. Sterry and J. Lane obtained tries, the second of which B. Edwards converted. Sound defence checked all efforts by Cardiff to wipe out the deficit.'* Newport had won 8-3 (A), 8-6 (H), then this game in February 8-3. Newport had a chance of their first quadruple, so Rodney Parade was packed to the rafters for the fourth game on 7 March 1951. Cardiff could not let their record of never losing four games in a row in one season to Newport, and the game ended 3-3, a penalty apiece. Supporters packed the trains back to Cardiff, having seen a titanic struggle. *'I was there'*, in the words of Max Boyce, in the 1968-69 season, when Newport won 11-6, 9-6 and 6-3. At the Arms Park, Cardiff held on again against a better team, to draw 9-9. Barry John only played 14 times that season, but he was there for the vital final match, drawn 9-9, to again stop the season 'Grand Slam'. I always remember Cardiff being pinned on their line for ages, and a mate saying, 'Bloody Hell, Barry John's tackling.' No one wanted to be in a Cardiff team beaten four times in a season by Newport. Under-resourced, then as now, Newport have been, and are, a great club with great supporters. As a youngster, I disliked them because they were a difficult team to beat, and the colour yellow because of their shirts. I have now grown up. Almost. And Cambridge Blue and Black are still the best colours. My neighbour just bought a black BMW electric car, but insisted on blue detailing, as a Cardiff City 'Bluebirds' supporter. I remarked that instead of buying the car, he could have bought Cardiff a centre-forward.

CHAPTER 22 - CARDIFF SEASON 1951 – 1952

CARDIFF'S 75th ANNIVERSARY GAME WITH THE LIONS - THE 4th SPRINGBOKS ARE LUCKY TO WIN - NEWPORT AGAIN BEATEN FOUR TIMES – WALES GRAND SLAM

Bleddyn Williams P22 T11 = 33pts; **Bill Tamplin** P32 C26 P22 = 118 pts (Risca); John Llewellyn P32 C2 = 4pts (Taff's Well); Derek Murphy P33 T9 = 27pts (Pentyrch)

P46 W34, L9, D3. Points 465-235. Tries 106:41 Pens 25:26

In his *Review of the Welsh Season*, in *Rugger Annual Number 1950-51*, J.B.G. Thomas writes that in Wales the weather was particularly bad, with many fixtures cancelled or postponed – *'Even so Cardiff and Newport managed to attract a world record crowd of 48,000 to one of their meetings at the Arms Park in February. This really was the climax to a magnificent season enjoyed by Newport. They finished not only unofficial champions of Wales, but champions of the British Isles and were worthy of the honour and praise bestowed upon them... the great rivalry between Cardiff and Newport reached new heights last season for the two clubs played some remarkably good football against each other...* (Newport) *had a big "camp" following and only twice did they disappoint their supporters – against the Harlequins and Exeter'.* (Cardiff scaped home 3-0 against Quins, but only had 7 fixtures against Exeter between 1890 and 1970, winning all and scoring 156 points to 32, 35-8 on tries.) *'It was Newport's year, and this new season will find them meeting greater resistance than ever from Cardiff.*

Cardiff's 75th Anniversary

Cardiff might well prove to be the team of the year, because they celebrate their 75th Anniversary (in 1951-52). *Their long history is full of glamorous occasions and dotted with brilliant players and combinations. From F.E. Hancock down to Haydn Tanner, they have always played open rugby and* **no side has ever proved more attractive**. *Last season Newport were their equal, but though effective as a winning combination, Newport could not bring off the coveted record of 4 wins in a season against Cardiff! Cardiff got away to a bad start, but recovered particularly during the latter half of the season, to finish second in the Championship Table to Newport. Indeed, they went through their last 15 battles without defeat, and it remains to be seen which of the two great teams will survive their first meeting of the season in October! For rugger followers at the Cardiff Arms Park this season there will be a feast of good things – three visits from the Springboks, two from the Barbarians, one from the British lions and two from Newport. What more could one want to celebrate a 75th Anniversary?'*

Messages were sent on Cardiff's 75th Anniversary from all over the world. Stade Nantais Université Club wrote: '*For its technical value on the field of play and for the grand spirit and hearty friendship of its players during its 75 years of history, the Rugby world owes much to the Cardiff Rugby Club. As for my own club during its best seasons, it owes much to the Cardiff Club for the Percy Bush days and for its help towards the recovery of our prestige after the ravages of the last war. Felicitations! Vive Cardiff!*' … '*Bristol RFC send their greetings to one of the greatest – if not the greatest – Rugby Club in the British Isles. Your achievements over three-quarters of a century, will forever be written large in the history of our game, not only for the innumerable brilliant players that have worn the Cardiff jersey, but also for that indefinable rugger spirit, on and off the field, that has always been associated with and fostered by the Cardiff Club. May your greatness never be undimmed.*'

Cardiff's 75th anniversary saw Dr. Jack Matthews' third term as captain. To celebrate, a match was arranged with the 1950 British Lions on 22 September 1951, with a capacity crowd of 45,000 spectators. A 44-page souvenir programme featured contributions from past and present rugby greats from all over the world, and the game itself was '*a magnificent one of exhilarating Rugby football and helped to make the occasion a memorable anniversary, a pleasure to players and spectators alike. The Lions won the game by one goal, one penalty goal and two tries to Cardiff's four tries - scored by Derek Murphy (2), Bleddyn Williams and Sid Judd, Judd's try was under the posts and sensationally the goal kick failed. It was Lewis Jones's kicks which won the match for the Lions.*' As usual, Cardiff scored more tries. Cardiff's team differs from the programme, but they had twelve internationals playing. The team was

Frank Trott, Haydn Morris, Bleddyn Williams, Jack Matthews and Derek Murphy; Cliff Morgan and Rex Willis; Cliff Davies, Geoff Beckingham, J. R. Phillips; W. E. Tamplin and Malcolm Collins; Peter Goodfellow, Sid Judd and C. D. Williams.

Probably uniquely, Cardiff had two international captains playing in this season, Dr. Jack Matthews, and Des O'Brien of Ireland. The season's results were adversely affected again, not just by trials and internationals, but by some bad injuries. Bleddyn Williams, Cliff Morgan, Rex Willis and Alun Thomas played for Wales, but Rex Willis suffered a fractured jaw against Scotland, refusing to leave the field (- remember, there were no substitutes). He had ongoing treatment at Chepstow Hospital, and could only play one more match that season, against Penzance on 21 April. There is a lovely account in the Penarth RFC history of their game against Cardiff in this year – with Cardiff full of 'Rags' players. *'In the third match of the new season against a star-studded Cardiff team, the new Penarth team surprised both the pundits and their opponents, with their drive and determination. The difference in a fiercely, yet fairly contested battle was made by the impeccable display of the new Cardiff full-back, John Llewellyn, formerly of Penarth, deputising for the former Penarth guardian, Frank Trott, and the remarkable C. Derek Williams, displaying the pace and ball sense that took him all the way to the Wales back row. Also, there was Rex Willis in a rare partnership with Bleddyn Williams playing at outside-half. Llewellyn's opposite number Kevin Bush, who had an equally outstanding game, was seen from time to time to applaud his opponent for the length and accuracy of his kicks. With the young Penarth pack marshalled by the live-wire Jack Cavanna, playing at scrumhalf, they were able to match their famous opponents punch for punch, rush for rush, and kick for kick all the way, though in the end Cardiff prevailed by a converted try to nought (5-0) in an exciting encounter.'*

Newport had almost achieved the quadruple over Cardiff in the previous season, but against all odds, 'Doctor Jack' inspired defeats of Newport <u>four times in this season</u>, following the example of Selwyn Biggs, 1897-98; Percy Bush 1905-06, and Haydn Tanner 1947-48. *'Tamplin's boot was again in successful evidence against the Usksiders.'* The wins were tight, 11-6, 6-5, 6-3 and 11-6, but Cardiff scored 7 tries to 4. Davies writes: *'One of our victories gave our skipper much pleasure. It was that over the Barbarians when he played 'a stormer' without six of his leading players.* (6-3 to Cardiff, 2 tries to a penalty). *His play against the British Lions with Bleddyn Williams was quite superb. Another outstanding match was that with South Africa on 20th October, an exciting one which we should have won and very nearly did win. On the run of the play the tourists were perhaps a little fortunate, there were two incidents which had decisive effects. One relates to Jack Matthews who charged down a kick by the Springbok scrum half J. Oelofse on his line, to fall on the ball and score what he claimed to be a try. The referee ruled it was a "knock on", but under the new law for the season it was not a knock on "if a player is in the act of charging a kick down".* (Some referees deserve swear-words as adjectives). *The score - if allowed, may well have sealed the doom of the Springboks who came strong in the very late stages and scored a very tactical try. Near Cardiff's twenty-five the Springboks heeled from a scrum, roughly midfield and J. D. Brewis kicked sharply towards the left corner flag. The position to me as the touch judge on the opposite side of the field did not appear to be dangerous, but the South African left wing J. K. Ochse had taken off like a bomb to follow up the kick and Alun Thomas had to turn and chase him. Frank Trott from a position in front of our posts could now be seen trying desperately to cut off Ochse, but he lacked speed and the South African scored the try and ensured victory for his side (11-9) to the immense relief of his team and management officials. It has been stated that the hon. manager got through fifty cigarettes during the match, but he, Dr. Danie Craven and the captain Basil Kenyon acknowledged that the Springboks were a trifle lucky. Later in the season the visitors presented the club with a Springbok head as a sporting gesture to the best losers on tour.'*

The chapter heading of 'lucky' Springboks is justified. Let captain Dr. Jack explain: '*I charged down a clearance kick by Brewis, picked the ball up and cross the line for the try. There was nothing wrong with it – even the Springboks lined up for the conversion. But to my amazement the referee, Cyril Johnson from Caerleon, ruled the charge-down a knock-on and disallowed the score. At half-time I reminded him that the law about charge-downs had changed and that what I had done did not constitute a knock-on. What was doubly infuriating was that in the second half exactly the same thing happened in reverse, when their scrum-half charged down a kick by Cliff <u>and the try was awarded</u>.*' Cliff Morgan was criticised for kicking too much in the game, and admitted as much, but was to gain revenge in South Africa in 1955. Top try scorer was again Haydn Morris with 25, followed by 11 from Bleddyn Williams, 9 by C. D. Williams and 7 each from Jack Matthews and Sid Judd. Left wing is the most likely wing for scoring tries as most centres more easily pass that way, and the left-wing Haydn Morris usually had Bleddyn inside him. As mentioned previously, it was always Bleddyn's intention to free his wing rather than go for glory himself. This author remembers the change from left and right centre to inside and outside, and consequent specialisation, but would still prefer to see the old centre-wing partnerships. Bill Tamplin kicked 48 goals. New 1st XV caps were the prop J. D. Evans, soon to be joined by prop Colin Howe in a great pairing. Centre/wing Gareth Griffiths and J. E. G. Llewellyn at full-back also gained Cardiff caps.

For the game at Bath on 19 January 1952, the Cardiff team was J Llewellyn, D Murphy, Dr. J Matthews, G Griffiths, H Morris, P Ash, B

Mark, C Davies, G Beckingham, J D Evans, W E Tamplin, M Collins, C D O'Brien and S Judd. There was a superb back line and pack, but the half-backs were Paul Ash, who only played 32 games in 7 seasons, and inside him Brian Mark, who generally played for the Athletic, gaining 95 Firsts appearances from 1949-50 to 1957-58. Yet again, the Bath fixture had been arranged upon the date that Wales played England, so Cardiff were missing their great half-backs Cliff Morgan and Rex Willis. Cardiff came up against a strong Bath team who were determined to break their losing streak. The Bath Heritage Rugby site records that on 19 January 1952: '*A sparkling try in the first five minutes gave Cardiff an edge, which they kept to the end of an extremely hard-fought game. Forwards and backs had joined in a passing movement, with frequent changes in direction, and prop Cliff Davies was eventually free to touch down. Bill Tamplin converted with a well-taken kick. Bath backs made a number of forays but were cut down by stout defence. In turn, Tim Thorne brought off a thumping tackle when Cardiff's Murphy looked certain to score. Welshman Trevor Lewis was in the van of Bath's fight back and Cardiff were contained for long periods. Bath forwards were good in the mauls and often came out on top. This was a stirring game, full of excitement. Lewis again featured in fierce and spectacular rushes which took them to the Cardiff line. There had been a few near misses with Porter's penalty attempts, but in terms of team effort, perhaps a draw would have been a fairer result. How Cardiff held out was one of the surprises of the season, for they took a tremendous battering and yet kept their line inviolate. Bath's last victory at Cardiff had been on January 18th 1947.*' Cardiff had scored 6 tries in the previous match, but only won 5-0, one of 15 consecutive wins in the annual fixture from 1948-1975. Even before an 8-5 away loss in 1947, Cardiff had won 5 consecutive matches – and Bath were one of England's finest teams.

A week after the Bath game, on 26 January 1952, Cardiff scored the only try of the game to win 5-3 at Swansea. Cardiff, missing four internationals, were subjected to shouts of '*Play the Game!*' as Alun Thomas, playing outside-half, repeatedly kicked to touch in the cold conditions. Swansea scored first with a penalty, and '*Tamplin had a chance to equalise with a penalty kick from a favourable position, but he sliced the ball. The fact that it was placed on a patch of snow probably contributed to the result*'. On 23 February 1952, the *Observer's* headline was '*Cardiff's first defeat for four months*', with V. Hinam playing scrumhalf – he only played three times, all in this season. Gloucester scored two tries in a deserved win 14-0, after 15 successive losses. From November 1953 to November 1957, Cardiff won another 8 matches against Gloucester 'on the bounce', with two games cancelled because of frost and snow in February 1955 and 1956. Against one of England's senior clubs, from 1882 to 1975, Cardiff won 104, lost 35 and drew 18 of 104 fixtures, scoring 1661 points to 781. More importantly, Cardiff scored 395 tries to 146 but lost on penalties 58-45. In April Cardiff, missing *'four of their international midfield players'*, and with Jack Matthews having to play fly-half, easily beat the Baa-Baas, who were fielding 12 internationals, by two tries to a dropped goal, 6-3.

1951-52 Bleddyn scores the only try of the match versus South Africa

In the Five Nations, Wales won at Twickenham 8-6, then beat Scotland 11-0, won away in Ireland 14-3 (3 tries, a conversion and a penalty against a penalty), and narrowly sealed the **Grand Slam** at Swansea by beating France 9-5, with a points total of 42-14. Rex Willis, on 3 May 1952, was awarded *'Pluckiest Player of the Year'* by the *South Wales Football Echo and Express* – as he *'played to the bitter end of the Scotland-Wales game at the Arms Park with a badly fractured jaw.'* Cliff Morgan was hurt before the French match, being replaced by Cardiff's Alun Thomas, who dropped a goal to secure the Welsh win. This situation of Cardiff having two concurrent fly-halves playing for Wales was replicated by scrum-half Gareth Edwards and the vastly underestimated Brynmor Williams in later years. Indeed, Brynmor was first-choice scrumhalf in tests for the British Lions even **before** he won his first Welsh cap. A wonderful player and a great man. Most appearances in the season were Sid Judd and Malcolm Collins with 43, followed by Jack Matthews and Cliff Davies with 39, hooker Geoff Beckingham with 38 and C. D. Williams with 36. Rex Willis, owing to his fractured jaw was only able to play in 23 games, and Bleddyn Williams and Cliff Morgan only featured 22 times, Alun Thomas 23, and Haydn Morris in 29 games. Frank Trott was only available for 14 fixtures, but John Llewellyn, a Taff's Well boy, very capably stepped up from the Rags to replace him.

Stan Bowes captained the Athletic again, playing in every match. He had played for Cardiff since 1937-38, except for war service. The record was P31, W23, L6, D2, points 344-173. Alun Priday, later to play twice for Wales, was their main goal kicker with a total of 29. The full-back received his Rags cap and was to soon serve Cardiff Firsts from 1952-53 until 1965-65, with 410 appearances over 14 seasons. Fourteen years at the pinnacle of rugby – in today's game one is lucky to go 14 months before injury. He would have played even longer but for a disgraceful punch, and is included in the local players because he started his rugby career with Tongwynlais, although he was born in Whitchurch, Cardiff. In researching this book, broken jaws seem a fairly common occurrence among Cardiff players.

And remember these men were all amateurs, often losing money through not being employed when touring. Bleddyn Williams claimed that touring with the Lions cost him at least £200 (perhaps £15,000 today). Some could not afford to tour, so had to refuse the honour. The great Delme Thomas was selected for the first of his three Lions tours in 1966, before he had played for Wales: *'The first thing I had to do was ask work if I could go. I was very lucky with my job working with the electricity board - they let me go and I was getting paid. A lot of the boys weren't getting paid when we were out there, only the 50p a day we got for expenses.'* Neath's Captain Walter Enoch Rees (1863-1949) did not play rugby, but was Neath RFC secretary from 1888, and then for 52 years he was Secretary of the WRU (1916-1948), acting as a major influence in Welsh rugby. He would regularly walk into the changing room before an international, to lay the law down on expense claims. The Cardiff and Wales star Ronnie Boon was interviewed by *The Times* in 1983, about the first Welsh victory at Twickenham in 1933: *'Fifteen minutes before the game was due to start, Walter Rees, secretary of the Welsh Rugby Union and a great and dominant character in Welsh rugby came into the dressing room and said, "Now boys I want you to remember this I don't want to see you charging for taxis to Cardiff when you put your expenses in." Wages were low and there was a lot of unemployment in those days. For boys who worked in industry, charging taxi fares when they had taken buses to Cardiff from their homes was the only way they could make half-a-crown or so to help their families and give them an extra pint or two. Who could blame them? I still smile when I think of Walter worrying about expenses at such a moment.'* Fast forward to 1952, with the Welsh Grand Slam captain John Gwilliam writing: *'No doubt the post of secretary has changed a lot in recent years. I look back with amusement at dear old Walter Rees who was in charge when I started playing after the war. It was said that he did everything from the front room of his house in Neath. He certainly frightened us as young players, queueing at his table for expenses at trial matches etc. He was quite capable of refusing anyone who claimed for more than a cheap day return.'* Even in Barry John's day, his expenses were minutely inspected.

251

CARDIFF vs THE BRITISH LIONS

Mike Roberts loaned me his father Roy's souvenir programme for the 75th Anniversary of Cardiff RFC, playing the 1950 British Touring Team (later called the British Lions) at the Arms Park on 22 September 1951. The Lions were all internationals, with Ireland star Jackie Kyle at fly-half, and six brilliant Welsh internationals - Lewis Jones, John Robins, Don Hayward, Rhys John, Rees Stephens and D.M. Davies. Of the 31chosen tourists in 1950, 14 were Welsh (plus Lewis Jones, who was flown out to join); 9 Irish; 5 were Scottish and 3 English – of whom Preece and Roberts were qualified to play for Wales. From Roy Roberts' Souvenir Programme (cost – one shilling) we read some of the glowing tributes to Cardiff R.F.C. Sir David Rocyn Jones, President of the WRU, wrote: '*It gives me very great pleasure on behalf of the general committee of the Rugby Union and myself to congratulate the great Cardiff club on their 75th anniversary. One of the founders of the amateur handling code, their fame has spread to the far corners of the earth. They have been 75 glorious years and we look to them in the future to uphold the great traditions of the game.*'

75th Anniversary Cardiff 12 British Isles Touring Team (Lions) 14. Cardiff scored 4 tries to 2 and missed a conversion in front of the posts

Colonel F.D. Prentice, Secretary of the Rugby Football Union, echoed Jones' feelings: '*... I have many happy memories of visiting the Cardiff Ground during my playing days. The visit of the British Lions to play* *during your Anniversary Celebrations also brings back the happiest memories of the 1930 British Tour to New Zealand and Australia, when I had the great pleasure of having in my team such splendid Welsh players, including four from the Cardiff Club…'* A letter from the New Zealand Rugby Union reads: *'The New Zealand Rugby Football Union sends its heartiest congratulations and best wishes for a successful celebration. New Zealand's memories of Cardiff are of great struggles with Welsh International and Club teams on every occasion in which an All Black team has toured your land. In two years' time our representatives will be with you again, and we know that. as always, our hardest matches will be at Cardiff. The Lions, with a preponderance of Welshmen* (14 out of 31), *delighted thousands of New Zealanders last year. It is hoped that the 1953 All Blacks will thrill the Cardiff crowds as New Zealand was thrilled in 1950 by your men.* (Spoiler alert, their only two losses were to be against Cardiff and Wales). *Our greetings to you, after three-quarters of a century's service to rugby.'*

And from the South African Rugby Football Board, *'It is with real pleasure that I offer the Cardiff Rugby Football Club on behalf of the S.S.R.F. Board hearty congratulations on the celebration of its 75th Anniversary. The fine traditions, the splendid achievements and the great contribution which your Club has made to our game are familiar to us in South Africa. Our touring team will be playing at Cardiff Arms Park three times, during their coming visit to Great Britain and are looking forward to meeting old friends and making new ones. We wish the club continued prosperity and many more successes – but not necessarily such a one as they achieved when they beat our team 17-0 in 1906 – when Gwyn Nicholls was in such brilliant form.'* (They played Cardiff at Pontypool according to Wikipedia, but at the Arms Park in reality, and very luckily won 11-9, presenting Cardiff with a Springbok head for being the best loser on the tour. They also beat Wales 6-3. New Zealand only lost to London Counties 11-9, and beat Scotland 44-0; Ireland 17-5, England 8-3, France 25-3 and the Barbarians at Cardiff 17-3).

Surgeon-Captain L.B. Osborne R.N. was the honorary manager of the British 1950 tour of New Zealand and Australia, and wrote *'from Korean waters'*, *'Many, many congratulations to the Cardiff Club, on this, their 75th Anniversary, and may they long continue to give to the rugby world the inspiration of their open and adventurous style of play…'* There were also fulsome tributes from the rugby clubs of Neath, Penarth, Bridgend, New South Wales, Harlequins, Gloucester, Blackheath, and Captain Geoffrey Crawshay. Coventry RFC expressed *'Greetings and congratulations from 77 years old. May your efforts continue to be successful, except, of course, against Coventry R.F.C.! From one of your friendliest rivals in innumerable enjoyable and spectacular games.'* Their paeon of praise was repeated by Swansea – *'To Cardiff Rugby Club,*

*"**Makers of Rugby History**" – Greetings and Congratulations from your friendly rivals in the "West" over the past seventy-five years. What visions are conjured up by epic games with such illustrious names, to mention but a few – Nicholls, Winfield, Bush and Gabe. That you may go from victory to victory (except two) is the sincere wish of our Club, and all sportsmen of Swansea, on this your 75ᵗʰ birthday.'*

Llanelli commented *'Your Club was well established, has grown in strength and produced administrators and footballers of repute, the name of Cardiff R.F.C. stands high in the affection of Rugby followers all over the World, and we in Llanelli join with them in expressing the hope that they will continue to earn the deserved reputation for skilful Rugby, Sportsmanship and good Fellowship.'* Pontypool congratulated Cardiff *'on their great and glorious achievements over the last 75 years... Many Clubs, including Pontypool, will always be grateful for the kind way we have been treated by this grand Club; the standard of open Rugby played by them symbolises all that is best in our great game.'*

Aberavon RFC wrote: *'We look back with admiration upon the excellent record of the Cardiff Rugby Club. Its record for a long period has been a glorious one and in keeping with the dignity of the City of Cardiff. The record of playing successes has been outstanding, but of more importance still is the reputation the Club has built up in playing that open type of Rugby which has become associated with the Cardiff Club, together with the sporting qualities of its players. This reputation has spread far beyond the confines of our little Country, and the names of many of your players are known and will never be forgotten throughout the Rugby world. May the tradition created by these players last for all time...'* One final letter from those whom the irrepressible Stan Bowes always called *'those Black and Amber bastards'*, Newport R.F.C.: *'It is a great pleasure and privilege for the Newport Club to be able to offer to our greatest friends and hereditary foes at Cardiff our sincere congratulations on their completion of 75 years of distinguished service to Welsh and International Football. It is Newport's wish that the future will be as happy for Cardiff, for their opponents, and for Welsh Rugger, as the 75 years that have just passed.'*

Cardiff scored four tries, by Bleddyn Williams, Sid Judd and Pentyrch's Derek Murphy bagged two. None were converted, although Sid Judd went over between the posts. The Lions scored three tries, with one converted and a penalty goal, with Cardiff not taking penalty kicks at goal, and missing all four conversions, one from under the posts. Lewis Jones' successful kicks won the match 13-12.

LLOYD WILLIAMS PLAYS FOR CARDIFF and VAUGHAN WILLIAMS FOR CARDIFF ATHLETIC – '*A REAL HOODOO SEASON FOR INJURIES*' -THE 1952-53 SEASON IN DEPTH - COUSIN BILL TAMPLIN RETIRES

Bleddyn Williams P26 T6 = 18pts; **Lloyd Williams** P7 T1 = 3pts; **Vaughan Williams** (Athletic); **Bill Tamplin** P30 T2 C38 P16 = 130pts (Risca); John Llewellyn P39 C9 P5 = 43pts (Taff's Well); Alun Priday P2 (Tongwynlais); Derek Murphy P2 T1 = 3pts (Pentyrch)

P48, W37, L8, D3. Points 636-240. Tries 141-45, Pens 25-18

Bleddyn Williams selected and captained a 'star-studded' International XV for an exhibition match with Penarth at the start of the season. Eight Wales internationals took part, mainly from Cardiff. The team included Frank Trott, Alun Thomas, Lewis Jones, Haydn Morris, Cliff Morgan, Cliff Davies, Emlyn Davies, Ben Edwards and South Africa's Tony Davies, at that time playing for Aberavon. Chris Thau tells us: '*Penarth were submerged 28-3, with Haydn Morris scoring five tries. This was Cliff Davies' farewell first-class match and Bleddyn Williams had to leave the field with an injured knee... A week later, Penarth gave Cardiff a fright, before going down 25-8 (6 tries to 2) at the Arms Park.*' That game was on 10 September, but at Penarth on 14 March 1953, the home side scored a try to Cardiff's 2 in a 6-6 draw. From 1887 until the 1969-70 season, the teams met twice a year, then once for a few seasons before Penarth was omitted from the fixture list. Of the 126 fixtures until 1974-75, Cardiff won 108, lost 8 and drew 10, scoring 1874 points to 420, 430 tries to 76.

The world-class Rex Willis, born around two miles north of the Arms Park in the Cathedral City of Llandaff, was chosen captain and nominated No.8 Sid Judd as his deputy. Davies writes: '*Many judges rated his ability higher than that of Haydn Tanner whom he had studied, and subsequently superseded. His passes were not so lengthy as Tanner's but his service from the scrum was excellent and accurate, chest high always, to enable his partner to run on to the pass at speed and gain many attacking advantages. Unselfish to a degree, his individual breaks from a scrum were rare, but nearly always successful for the openings which were created. He would never give a pass from a scrum from a slovenly heel or when harried by opponents, and never allowed his outside half to take a hiding; he was most successful in preventing the opposing scrum half from getting a good pass away. Rex was the personification of courage, and most probably the best scrum half of his kind in the club's long history. A grand sportsman, he was a credit to his club, gaining all the highest honours from club, country, Barbarians and the British Lions, and served the committee for some years after retirement'.*

Davies called this '*a real hoodoo season'* for injuries, with Rex Willis again the player who suffered most. In the club's August trials, he damaged his shoulder badly, so his first game was not until Boxing Day against Wasps. Against Scotland on 7 February, again the same shoulder was injured, keeping him out of the remaining two internationals. Against Cheltenham in April, yet another injury meant that the captain only played 12 club games in the season. Sid Judd took over as captain, and Brian Mark played scrum half in 25 games. '*Cliff Morgan, Bleddyn Williams, Alun Thomas and others were all injured from time to time, and we had lost through retirement Frank Trott, Dr. Jack Matthews, Des O'Brien and our grand prop, the great character Cliff Davies, beloved by all whom he played with or against; a man of humble birth from Kenfig Hill, who had served the club from its war-time period and gained all of Rugby football's highest honours.'* Welsh Rugby, November 1971 belatedly noted: '*Sad Loss – It was with deep sadness during the season that we learned of the death of Cliff Davies, without doubt the greatest rugby character of his era, respected with affection wherever the game was played. The Old Players formed a special sub-committee with Dr. Jack as chairman to ensure that his dependants would not want.'* In October 1967, Cardiff had beaten a British Isles XV 13-9 in a spectacular game, to raise money for Cliff's family. Kenfig Hill's Clifton Davies had passed away on 28 January 1967, aged just 48. Capped for Wales 16 times, a Barbarian, the prop was selected for the 1950 Lions tour of Australasia. After the war, Jack Mathews had persuaded Cliff to join Cardiff, and he was 28 when he first played for Wales in 1947, the first post-war international season. His try against England at 'Twickers' enabled Wales to win their 1950 Grand Slam. In October 1951, Cardiff were very unlucky to lose to the Springboks 11-9, owing to the referee not knowing that the law had changed to allow Jack Matthews' charge-down of a kick and his try. How shall I phrase this? The idiot referee, gave a knock on. The crowd and players knew more about the 'laws' of the game than he did. Cardiff lost 11–9 to a fluke try. Which brings us back to Cliff, who had a fine game. A collier, he had no time after finishing his shift to have a shave. He thus used his stubble against the South African prop, Jaap Bekker in the scrum. Bekker warned Cliff to stop, or he would bite him. Which at the next scrum he did, biting a piece out of Davies' ear which caused a heavy bleed. Cardiff was a truly amateur team, but its players were helped in seeking jobs, and in the case of bereavement, the club always rallied around, often with a benefit match, e.g. for the great Sid Judd later in this book.

Despite player losses, young incomers Gareth Griffiths, Gwyn Rowlands and David James showed great promise. Alan Barter (a Cambridge Blue) and for our specific interest, Lloyd Williams, made their first team debuts.

Lloyd was considered big for a scrumhalf, and like brothers Bleddyn, Bryn, Vaughan, Cenydd and Tony, could play centre or fly half. Despite injuries, Cardiff won its first 14 games, then lost on 1 November 1952 to an Oxford University XV, which included 7 South Africans, 5 of whom made for a strong pack. A weakened Cardiff side lost by 2 penalties to a try, missing several penalty goal attempts. (The following season, with an almost full team, Cardiff scored 8 tries against Oxford University, winning 30-0.) After 14 wins, then came a terrible month, which Davies calls '*black November*', with losses to Oxford 6-3 (A), Northampton 11-6 (A), Llanelli 5-0 (A) and a strong Neath team 8-0 (A). Other away losses were to be at Aberavon 11-9, two tries apiece, Newport 6-0 (2 penalties), Gloucester 14-9 and Birkenhead Park 6-0. We can see that an injury-struck Cardiff side only lost 8 games all season, all narrowly, and **all away**. The website Bath Rugby Heritage reported on their home game vs Cardiff on 17 January 1953, losing 16-3: '*Briefly ignoring the general run of play, Bath's Peter Hall concentrated on downing his former schoolmate, Cardiff centre Alan Barter and finally caught him in possession – but only once! The whole of Bath's back row had similar trouble with Cliff Morgan, who enjoyed a comparatively quiet game, until he decided to 'Go' – and as was usually the case – no one could lay a hand on him! Ten of Cardiff's points came from kicks, but with two electrifying tries from Haydn Morris. The Bath pack did well to hold the Cardiff eight, and John Dingle scored Bath's try. A good game, with some brilliant passages of play.*' As usually was the case, Bath played their home games against Cardiff on the day of the England-Wales game. Bleddyn and Gareth Griffiths were centres for Wales, and Geoff Beckingham won his first cap, as did No.8 Sid Judd, playing blind-side wing-forward.

In these days, the Five Nations fixture list was 'sensible' instead of truncated to suit TV. The England loss was 8-3 (A) on 17 January 1953; Scotland at home was won 12-0 (3 tries) on 7 February; Ireland at St. Helen's, Swansea was won 5-3, a goal to a try; and at Stade Colombes Wales beat France 6-0 (2 tries to a penalty) on 28 March. Other internationals were played on the other weeks over these two months. With a different selection for the England game, Wales would have won a Grand Slam, winning the difficult away games at England, Ireland and France. Because Willis was injured, the selectors dropped Cliff Morgan and played the Newport half-backs. As well as the injuries, Cardiff again lost players to Wales. Bleddyn played in all 4 internationals, captaining and winning 3 times in the games after the English defeat, but Rex Willis only appeared against Scotland when he was injured in the second half, curtailing his season. He went off, and Cliff Morgan played scrum-half to Bleddyn at fly-half, and wing-forward Clem Thomas moved to the wing. Bleddyn scored 2 tries and Ken Jones one in the 12-0 win, where they had lost 19-0 in their last visit. The backs included Cardiff centres Bleddyn and Alun

Thomas, Gareth Griffiths on the wing, Cliff Morgan and Willis, with Beckingham and Sid Judd in the pack. For Ireland, Beckingham was dropped (wrongly) and Willis unfit for the win, with Maesteg's Trevor Lloyd partnering Cliff Morgan. Against France, Gareth Griffiths scored the two tries.

Cliff Morgan and Alun Thomas played three times for Wales. Three men gained their first Welsh caps, the hooker Geoff Beckingham, Gareth Griffiths and Sid Judd. Beckingham played for Wales only three times, kept out for years initially by Penygraig's British Lions' Test player 'Dai' Maldwyn Davies, then with Somerset Police and then by Newport's British Lions' Test player Bryn Meredith. As I met Geoff a few times, I add this note from the Cardiff rugby website: '*Beckingham played 331 games for the Blue & Blacks and won three caps for Wales against England and Scotland in 1953 and France five years later. He was also an international reserve for several seasons to the Newport and British Isles' hooker, Bryn Meredith. His finest hour came in November 1953 when he was the unsung hero of his club's legendary 8-3 victory over the All Blacks. The match is remembered for two textbook tries by the Cardiff backs, spearheaded by Cliff Morgan and Bleddyn Williams, in the opening 20 minutes. On both occasions it was Beckingham's clean striking in the scrums that set up swift ball for the backs to exploit. Equally crucial was his skill at the final three scrums of the game as the All Blacks camped on Cardiff's line and threatened to snatch a draw. Against all odds the hooker stole their put-in at the third of those scrums and Cliff Morgan cleared to the safety of touch as the final whistle was blown. Beckingham, who also played in the Cardiff team that beat the Wallabies in 1957, was a proud son of Barry where he worked as a municipal gardener. He put his fitness down to the fact there was only one lawn mower for all of the town's parks and he was pushing it for 15 hours a day in the height of summer.*'

The 1955 British Lion Gareth Griffiths was another real asset. As a wing and centre, he played 140 times for the Blue and Blacks from 1949-1960, scoring 74 tries. He won 12 Wales caps and was among the players who beat New Zealand twice in 1953, for club and country. His obituary is later in this section. The flanker Sid Judd won 10 caps for Wales and scored one of Wales' two tries in their 1953 victory over New Zealand. A Barbarian in the 1951-52 season, he had first joined Cardiff in 1946, and in ten seasons he played 184 times for the Firsts, scoring 45 tries. Top scorers were Haydn Morris with 26 tries (5 against Plymouth Albion and 4 against the combined Cognac/Nantes XV); Dr. Gwyn Rowlands 16 (plus 16 goals); Gareth Griffiths 13 (3 against Cambridge University), Cliff Morgan 13 and the newcomer C. L. 'Cowboy' Davies scored 8. Davies writes: '*Tamplin the Great' kicked 54 goals and scored a try against Moseley to amass a total of 128 points. Cliff Morgan, Gareth Griffiths and Alun Thomas certainly enhanced their reputations and new cap awards went to C. L.*

Davies, Dafydd James, Dr. Gwyn Rowlands and Eddie Thomas'. Cardiff beat Moseley 16-6, with the relative closeness of the scores having something to do with the fact that nine Cardiff players, including Cliff Morgan, were involved in that day's final Welsh trial. In 1952–53, Cardiff won the unofficial Welsh championship again, helped by the rise of their prodigiously talented outside-half Cliff Morgan, but the best was yet to come.

The veteran prop Stan Bowes captained the Athletic for the third year running. However, he was playing so well that he was asked to play for the Firsts 25 times. The Athletic season's results were: P36, W26, L9, D1, points 388-132. No fewer than 64 players were called upon, with Dr. Jack coming from retirement to captain the Rags 6 times when Stan Bowes was playing for the Firsts. From Llandaff, former Petty Officer Stan Bowes used the term *'those Black and Amber Bastards'* repeatedly and good-humouredly about the neighbouring Newport club, and made 184 appearances for Cardiff Firsts between 1938-39 and 1955-56. Bryn Mapstone scored 7 tries and kicked 23 goals, and Alun Priday kicked 17 and scored a try. Cardiff Juniors (the Youth team) had become a nursery, with Mapstone, Priday and Bleddyn's brother Lloyd moving up to Senior level. The promising W. Gerard McCarthy died on National Service in an incident at Brecon, one of the sporting McCarthy family which provided five brothers to play in the backs for Cardiff. What is it about brothers playing for Cardiff? Does any other great team in any 'real' sport have such a record? Eight Williams (of eight), six or seven (of eight) Turnbulls, five McCarthys, four Griffiths and so on. Brief pen pictures of brothers playing for Cardiff are given elsewhere in this book.

There were four 'tours': to Ireland; to the Midlands to play Coventry and Leicester; to the northwest against Birkenhead Park and Sale; and to the southwest against Devonport Services, St. Ives and Penzance/Newlyn. On 26 September 1952, on the evening before Cardiff's home game against a Cognac-Nantes XV, won by Cardiff 36-11, Cardiff Veterans played their French equivalents for what the French termed the *'Championnat du Monde.'* Cardiff easily won 20-3, perhaps by supplying their opponents with an over-abundance of Brains SA on the day, in retaliation for the overdose of brandy they had suffered a few years previously. The Noilly Prat Cup was thus retained, by a Cardiff team which included Les Spence, Doc Drummond and Harry Rees (a former Taff's Well player), all 44 years old. Other 'oldies' retaining the 'World Championship' were Edgar Welch, Les Manfield, Tom Holley (the Cardiff masseur in these years), Wilf Wooller, Maldwyn James, Lyn Williams, Gwynne Porter, Haydn Wilkins, Gwyn Davies, 'Wendy' Davies, Gwyn Evans and Billy Cleaver – Cleaver was the baby aged 31. To be fair, the French captain was 57 and his brother 54.

THE 1952-53 SEASON IN DEPTH

I hope the reader will forgive me for this discursion into a particular season, but I knew Geoff Beckingham from when he came to help Haydn Morris in rugby training at Barry Grammar School. I was loaned Beckingham's scrapbooks from Dai Richards at *Rugby Relics* (see book sources), and this particular season shows the strains upon Cardiff, when its best players were involved in three Welsh trials, four Internationals and several charity games, as well as training and 48 club matches. And they all held down full-time jobs, some having to work overtime in order to take time off, if Cardiff were on tour or Wales was playing away. I have taken all of this chapter from Geoff's scrapbook for the year 1952-53, specifically because it shows the shortcomings of the 'Big Five' selectors. (Cardiff supporters were not alone in complaining about teams chosen for internationals, by the way.) As the Cardiff ethos, *'the Cardiff Way'*, was to get the ball to the backs at all costs, and try and put the wings free in all games, its backs had many more opportunities than most other teams to 'know' each other and think about keeping the ball in play. As a result, Cardiff often had 4 to 6 of their backs playing for Wales. Players were selected from places like Cross Keys, Abertillery, Bridgend, Aberavon, etc., as well as 'the Big Four' of Cardiff, Newport, Llanelli and Swansea, and each selector seemed to represent a different region of Welsh rugby. There were sometimes, if not often, trade-offs, not based upon excellence but upon a 'rightful share' of regional members in the Welsh team. When Cardiff were constantly supplying most of the backs, it was very, very difficult as a Cardiff forward to be selected for Wales. Geoff Beckingham's case is instructive – a great player, often Welsh reserve, but with only three Welsh caps although he was excellent around the field ('in the loose') and the outstanding hooker of his day. Also, this is the year when Cardiff Youth player Lloyd Williams made his first appearances for Cardiff Firsts, and was the precursor to the fabulous 1953-54 season under Bleddyn's captaincy. One can see all the signs of a truly great team pulling together, in Geoff's newspaper cuttings.

A 30 August 1952 cutting from Geoff Beckingham's scrapbooks is headlined *'Rex Willis and Co. Should Have Few Worries…The forebodings and fears expressed by many Cardiff club followers as to the thin time ahead for the club, and which was deepened by the news of the retirement of Cliff Davies, Frank Trott, Jack Matthews and Des O'Brien, were somewhat allayed by the obvious wealth of talent on show at this week's practice and trial games. In fact, there were so many youngsters keen to wear the famous blue-and-black colours that Rex Willis, this year's skipper, vice-captain Sid Judd and the members of the selection committee were forced to stage an additional trial game and to postpone the final trial itself until this afternoon.'* Players noted as *'showing up well'* were

Gordon Wells, Gareth Griffiths and Alan Barter, while '*Cardiff have such brilliant prospects as Brian Mark, Lloyd Williams and V. Hinam*' to succeed Rex Willis. In the final trial, Cardiff beat 'The Rest' 21-8, with Haydn Morris scoring four tries. '*The trouble is that the reputation enjoyed by the Cardiff club is so high that a half dozen defeats in a season is considered to be indicative of a serious decline, and few people realize that last season's 75th anniversary year came within inches of being* **one of the greatest years in the club's history**. "*Doubles*" *by Neath and Aberavon apart, it must be remembered that four wins against Newport, the defeat of the Barbarians, the "near things" against the star-studded Springboks and British Lions sides were feats that will be remembered for years. Yes! Jack Matthews and Cliff Davies and the rest can look back upon their last season in rugby football with pride, and as they retire from the scene it would be an opportune moment to pay tribute to their wonderful services to the club.*' It should be again emphasised that First Team Cardiff players were not excused trials, so on top of their, perhaps, 40 club games there could be two or three club trials and three or four charity games as well. Indeed, on 1 September, Cardiff players Bleddyn Williams, Frank Trott, Alun Thomas, Cliff Morgan, Haydn Morris, Brian Marks, Cliff Davies, Geoff Beckingham and Sid Judd had played for the Bleddyn Williams International XV against Penarth.

In the traditional first game of the season, on 3 September against Cardiff and District, the club won 22-9. J.B.G. Thomas wrote that Cardiff '*won comfortably through the imp-like genius of Cliff Morgan*' but '*it is obvious that they will miss Bleddyn Williams and Rex Willis through the month of September. **Splendid Centre**. The District XV had a splendid centre in W. Boston, who should be in the Cardiff Athletic XV. He had no chance in attack, but kicked and defended excellently.*' This was the marvellous 'Billy' Boston, along with Jim Sullivan and 'Gus' Risman, probably the greatest loss to Rugby League from Welsh rugby union. '*Observer*' wrote of the game, in the only bold text in his report, '***Outstanding for the District was the redoubtable Billy Boston, their skipper, who set the pattern for the game with some whole-hearted covering and tackling which inspired his side to great deeds in defence.***'

20,000 people watched the first game of the season, on 6 September, J.B.G. Thomas writing, '*the warmly-favoured Neath were outplayed by Cardiff in a hard and fast game by three goals, a penalty, and a try to a dropped goal*'. Cardiff's young pack had been expected to take a hammering, and Cliff Morgan was the 'man of the match.' Bleddyn Williams, Rex Willis and Alun Thomas were unavailable through injury. At the last minute, Dr. Gwyn Rowlands was drafted in to play on the wing, replacing Thomas. (Alun Thomas was equally adept at outside half and centre). The previous day Thomas had joined the RAF as a flight-lieutenant surgeon, and scored '*a splendid try*' in that game. September

10th saw Cardiff down Penarth, scoring six tries, 25-8. September 13th saw 14,000 watching Cardiff beat Plymouth 47-0, Haydn Morris scoring 5 of the 11 tries. The Cardiff legend Rhys Gabe reported upon the game. Then it was off on the East Midlands annual tour, playing Coventry on 20 September winning 13-3. On 22 September, away at Leicester, Cardiff had scored a try and a penalty to two penalties and with a minute to go there was a scrum on their five-yard line. '*The ball came out on the Cardiff side and Bleddyn Williams set his line going with the result that the three-quarters raced the whole length of the field for Rowlands to ground the ball in the corner.*' Tamplin missed the conversion and the full-time whistle was blown for a Cardiff win 9-6.

On 29 September Cardiff ran in 8 tries to beat a Combined Team of Stade Nantais, U.C. & U.S. Cognacaise. In front of Cardiff's Lord Mayor, the French Consul and '*scores of bereted Bretons, 30,000 Welshmen and American sailors, Cardiff ran riot against a combined NANTES-COGNAC XV to win by 36pts to 11... they had no answer to the devastating running of the Cardiff backs. After the game one of the French three-quarters (who had no English) could only wave his arms and mutter "Bleddyn Williams, Alun Thomas, Haydn Morris, Cliff Morgan!" He named the stars of the game. But it would be impossible to fault a man on the Cardiff side. They were all good; Geoff Beckingham for his smooth hooking, Bill Tamplin for his superb kicking and, not least of all, 18-year-old* **Lloyd Williams** *(brother of Bleddyn) who emerged with credit from his first big ordeal.*' Haydn Morris scored four tries again, and *Observer* reported that '*In a 40-yard run, BLEDDYN WILLIAMS beat man after man with his celebrated jink before scoring under the posts.*' After three August trials, on 1 September, nine of Cardiff Firsts played for Bleddyn's International XV against Penarth, then Cardiff played Cardiff and District on 3 September (22-9); Neath on 6 September (21-3); Penarth on 10 September (25-8); followed by Plymouth on the 13th (47-0); Coventry on the 20th (13-3); Leicester on 22 September (9-6); and on 29 September Nantes-Cognac (54-11).

Eight games in 29 days saw dozens of tries scored. Nothing says so much for modern-day rugby as the lack of really serious injuries in this era of rugby. As of January 2021, the Welsh first-choice internationals Ellis Jenkins and Gareth Anscombe have been out of the game for over two years with injury. After the first Six Nations International against Ireland, 6 players could not play, and 21 Welsh squad members were unavailable through injury. In the second game against Scotland the five first-choice blind-side wing forwards were all unavailable. The 2019 World Cup semi-final had been narrowly lost to South Africa, via what a renowned English referee called poor refereeing, with Wales fielding virtually a patched-up reserve team. Will no one address the brutality of the modern game, which combined with over-training, is wrecking players' health? We desperately need a return to older rules with a straight input of the scrum ball that both hookers must try to strike; the end to the practice of 'clearing out' players; substitutes only for assessed injuries and in the event of any hits to the head; and a weight limit on teams. When international three-quarters average 6 foot 2 inches and over 16 stone, the game is becoming more like American football every day. (This was written before the July 2022 court cases involving premature dementia and other illnesses resulting from knocks to the head – many owing to crash tackles and the 'clear-out' rules over recent years).

One should mention here that Lloyd Williams, although happy to play outside-half if required, had Rex Willis as the incumbent scrumhalf, with at this time Brian Mark usually substituting in Willis's absence. Rex Willis played 208 games from 1947-48 to 1957-58, and Brian Mark appeared in 94 games from 1949-50 to 1957-58. Lloyd played in 310 games between 1952-53 to 1963-64. From his first games in this season of 1952-53, until 1958-59 he was faced with two others competing for 'his' position. Thus, including this season, for his first four years he only played 43 times, until 1956-57 when he was at last the regular scrumhalf, with 37 out of 50 official matches. There was a dip to 21 games in 1957-58, when Lloyd, Cliff Morgan, Alun Priday, 'Roddy' Evans and Howard Nicholls won their first Wales caps, playing alongside Cardiff's Cliff Morgan and Gordon Wells. In that season, brother Cenydd achieved his Cardiff cap. For the remaining six years of his 12 years with Cardiff, Lloyd played 36, 33, 32, 34, 34 and 38 official games.

Soon after Lloyd's excellent performance in his first big game against Nantes-Cognac, *Observer* gave us the headline '*Pontypool Beaten 8-3 in Dour Match at Cardiff*.' On 11 October 1952, '*Cardiff retained their unbeaten record and inflicted the first defeat of the season on Pontypool by eight points to three in a dour battle characterised by hectic forward play at Arms Park today*.' The Pontypool forwards pressed strongly, Cliff Morgan had to leave the field for treatment for ten minutes and the home team was under '*relentless attacking*' pressure for the whole match. It seems that Lloyd Williams took a bit of a hammering. At fullback, Taff's Well's John Llewellyn had a superb game, but '*Cliff Morgan was receiving a terribly erratic service from Lloyd Williams*', which did not allow him to release the backs. '*Cardiff have seldom appeared more ineffective, the root of the trouble being at half-back where Morgan had a thoroughly unhappy afternoon juggling with a woefully erratic service from young Lloyd Williams, who had little opportunity of settling down in this "needle" atmosphere*.' Bleddyn was playing at Penzance on that day, but Ewart 'Bill' Tamplin was '*outstanding*' in the pack, and will have commiserated with his cousin Lloyd after the game. Another report reads: '***Cardiff Hold Grimly to that Record***. *Morgan's Wonder Run. Star centre Bleddyn Williams and vice-captain Sid Judd absent… outside-half Cliff Morgan and* *partner Lloyd Williams limping throughout the second half... yet Cardiff held grimly to their 100 per cent record at Arms Park on Saturday, and shattered Pontypool's. It was a relentless match, with all the scoring in the first 12 minutes. First a 40-yard penalty goal from Cardiff's Ewart Tamplin. Then a John Jones try to equalise... and a wonder run by Cliff Morgan to scheme a Gwyn Rowlands try which Tamplin converted. That made it 8-3 for Cardiff... pictures show the tough story.'*

There was then an unofficial charity match to celebrate Pontypridd's 75th anniversary, before Haydn Morris scored two tries in the 8-0 win over Gloucester on 18 October, with Brian Mark, back from injury, playing scrumhalf. On 27 October, the Cardiff pack laid the foundation for a 12-6 win against Llanelli at Stradey Park, in what was billed '*the club match of the season.*' Cardiff scored 4 unconverted tries to a penalty and a dropped goal. Three days later, Cardiff Firsts played at Mountain Ash in another unofficial fixture, for that club's 75th anniversary. Mountain Ash had regular fixtures with the 'Rags', and also supplied the remarkable trio of Haydn Morris, Colin Howe and J.D. Evans to Cardiff. Absentees in the first Welsh trial at Pontypridd on 1 November - and injuries to Cliff Morgan, Rex Willis, Gordon Wells, Colin Bosley and others - finally ended the unbeaten run, with losses to Oxford on 1 November and Northampton on 3 November. Sid Judd, Cardiff's number 8, was too good to leave out of the Welsh team, which would mean displacing pack leader John Gwilliam, so the selectors moronically chose him as a prop for the Reds (Probables) in the first Welsh Trial, with clubmate C.D. Williams as flanker. In the Whites (Possibles), Gwyn Rowlands and Geoff Beckingham won 16-8 but Beckingham was injured.

Rex Willis and Cliff Morgan were still out with long-term injuries, and Alun Thomas and Haydn Morris also missed the Oxford loss, where Cardiff scored a try against two penalties to lose 6-3. The depleted team then lost 11-6 away at Northampton, whereas the full team a year previously had won away 20-0, scoring 6 tries, only 1 converted. Two away defeats in three days were followed by an easy win, again without Cliff Morgan, at Newport 14-0, and victory at Wasps 16-5 on 15 November – '*a great game deservedly won by Cardiff who proved that class must tell in the end.*' However, on 29 November in '*atrocious conditions*' at the Gnoll, Rees Stephens inspired the Neath team to win 8-0. Neath '*quickly realised that forward rushes were the solution to the driving sleet and slippery ball, whereas Cardiff forwards persisted in giving the ball to their backs.*' Sometimes '*the Cardiff Way*' needed to be tempered with pragmatism.

In the second Welsh Trial at Neath on 13 December, Geoff Beckingham yet again out-hooked the incumbent Bryn Meredith, as in trials and club games over the years – his meagre return of just three Welsh caps is saddening. *Observer* called Geoff '*the best hooker in Wales today*', and along with him in the Whites pack in the trial, were Cardiff forwards Malcolm Collins ('*the second-row line-out ace*') and Sid Judd, playing wing forward rather than his preferred number 8. Bleddyn was also in the Whites (the 'Possibles') as captain, along with Haydn Morris who was strangely placed on the right wing instead of his favoured left outside Bleddyn. In the Reds, Alun Thomas was centre to Dr. Gwyn Rowlands on the left wing instead of his preferred club position of right wing. *Observer* presciently wrote '*the "White" side, skippered by Cardiff centre Bleddyn Williams, might well cause the greatest upset of recent times. Its youthful (and zestful) pack might well give the star-studded "Red" eight an almighty going over.*' Tudor James wrote that the Possibles pack decided the game, winning 14-8.

Observer wrote: '*The Cardiff forwards Geoff Beckingham* (who again out-hooked Bryn Meredith), *Sid Judd and Malcolm Collins played magnificently in a tearaway Possibles pack and enhanced their already sound reputations and their chances for gaining caps this season.*' While the Second Trial was being played, Gareth Griffiths put on an '*amazing*' performance as Cardiff beat Cambridge University, with '*a display reminiscent of Bleddyn Williams (side-step and all!) at his best.*' Cardiff won away 14-5, 4 tries to 1. On Boxing Day, Wasps were easily defeated 27-0, by 3 goals, 3 tries and a drop goal. The following day Cardiff hosted Scotland's Watsonians, with most players playing on successive days. The two previous games had been won 6-0 then 3-0, but this Cardiff team played with verve to score 7 tries and win 29-3.

At this time, *Observer* wrote an article entitled '***Cardiff's Bill Tamplin is "Forgotten Man***" - *Just how much the Cardiff club has suffered this season by the unprecedented spate of injuries to key players and the temporary loss of up-and-coming youngsters to the Forces may be assessed during the Christmas rugby programme when "invalids" and National Service men on leave will be available. Rex Willis understandably is leaving nothing to chance and is making a gradual comeback with the Athletic side. Cliff Morgan, "itching" to get his damaged ankle out of plaster, can be expected to follow his skipper's example by having a sound work-out with the "Rags" before returning to the slam-bang buffeting of club and international rugger. Other notable absentees, Gordon Wells injured in the Pontypridd anniversary game and Colin Bosley (suffering from a fractured jaw), are making satisfactory progress. **Belated Tribute** – The choice of three Cardiff forwards for the second Welsh trial is a well-merited (although somewhat belated) tribute to the excellence of the Cardiff pack. Geoff Beckingham, Malcolm Collins and Sid Judd are on the threshold of international honours, while many sound critics are of the opinion that it will not be long before the qualities of such players as Gower Jenkins, J.D. Evans and Derek Williams will be recognised. But, strangely enough, the one man who towers head and shoulders over them* *all in all phases of forward play (and the players involved would be the first to admit it!) continues to be neglected.*

Bill Tamplin (and let us ignore the "Too old" label) is unquestionably the most respected forward now playing in Welsh rugby, as most present-day forwards, whether from east Wales or west Wales, would hasten to agree. Unerring Kicker – Wherever I go I hear the same spontaneous tributes to Wales's "Forgotten Man" – the forward who is playing as well this season as ever he did in gaining his seven Welsh "caps" in 1947-48, and that is saying something. Any member of the British Isles touring team which visited Australia and New Zealand will tell you quite frankly that with "Tamp" in the side we would not have lost a Test! His kicking is as unerring as ever and not that Wales are likely to miss the peculiar talents of Lewis Jones, there are many people (current internationals amongst them!) who feel that the Magor policeman would not let Wales down this season, should the occasion arise!'

Upon 3 January 1953, the day of the Final Trial, the *South Wales Football Echo and Express* reported '**Brighter Outlook with Return of Key Players** *– After one of the most unlucky starts to a season on record, caused by an unprecedented amount of injuries to key players, Cardiff's future is filled with happy auguries as one by one the invalids return to active service (writes Observer). The reunion of the international halfbacks Cliff Morgan and Rex Willis against the Watsonians proved that neither player has lost his touch and both Cardiff and Wales should benefit from the zest and enthusiasm of this talented pair...The continued "cold shoulder" given by the Welsh selectors to Sid Judd and Geoff Beckingham has raised the ire not only of Cardiff supporters but of rugby fans in West and East Wales as well! "The best forward to play at Stradey for a long time" is one Llanelly tribute to the tearaway Judd, while tributes to the quiet efficiency of hooker Beckingham come from all sides.'*

Haydn Morris had badly injured his shoulder in the second trial and was out for some weeks. With the Probables team being beaten twice, and Cliff Morgan and Rex Willis at last available, the 'Big Five' had some thinking to do, before the Final Trial at the Arms Park on 3 January 1953. Willis and Morgan went straight into the Reds team, with Gwyn Rowlands on the wing and Alun Thomas inside him, while lineout specialist Malcolm Collins was promoted into the pack, with Rees Stephens captain, replacing John Gwilliam at number 8, who became Whites captain. Bleddyn, Geoff Beckingham and Sid Judd at wing forward stayed in the Whites team, and Gareth Griffiths was a late Whites replacement. Bryn Meredith, after his display against Beckingham in the previous trial, was dropped from the Reds but replaced by 'Dai' Maldwyn Davies of Somerset Police. Nine Cardiff players thus took part, and yet again Beckingham won the hooking duel. Terry Davies scored a penalty for the Possibles, and the *'quick-breaking Possibles forwards, Johnson and Judd combined for Johnson to*

266

touch down' after the pair *'had completely demoralised the Probables defence'* Davies converted, and *'a minute later the Possibles went further ahead when Judd brushed of some shadow tackling to get away down the field with Beckingham in support, and when the latter passed to Gareth Griffiths the winger scored more or less as he liked. Terry Davies converted. The Probables were completely disorganised, and Judd scored an unconverted try in the corner. The Possibles were 16 points up in 22 minutes'*, in front of a huge crowd. *'The Possibles pack completely dominated the exchanges in tight and loose with W.O. Williams, Beckingham, S. Judd and Dil Johnson showing up strongly.'*

The brilliant Newport fly-half Roy Burnett unluckily knocked on with a certain Possibles try under the posts in front of him, to save Red blushes, and then Robins kicked a penalty to reduce the deficit to 16-3 at half time. The 'Big Five' only had five minutes to rearrange the sides. One only wishes one had been there for this exciting game. Six Reds players, including Willis in his first First-class game for months, were transferred to the Whites, while their replacements included Bleddyn and Sid Judd but not Beckingham. The Probables looked better, with Cliff Morgan, Bleddyn, Alun Thomas and Gwyn Rowlands combining well, but for the Whites Gareth Griffiths almost scored a try and fullback Terry Davies was having a superb game. Huins then scored from close range for the Reds, and Cliff, Bleddyn and Alun combined for Gwyn Rowlands to score shortly after – 16-9. Davies then hit a penalty and Gareth Griffiths touched down. The Possibles led 22-9 – 4 tries to 2. The Neath wing Keith Maddocks then scored *'the best try of the game. Receiving the ball near his own 25, he cut into the centre, feinted to pass to Peter Evans, sold an outsize in dummies to the Probables defence, and streaked away on a sensational 70-year run, which ended in a try under the posts, which Terry Davies converted.'* The Big Five's Probables selection had been easily beaten 16-8, 14-8 and 27-9. Beckingham had been the best hooker and on the winning team in each trial, and although travelling Welsh reserve in the previous season, had never appeared in the Probables side. The failure to switch him to the Reds at half-time was criticised in all the Welsh press.

Reg Pelling, in the *News Chronicle* 5 January 1953, placed three players as *'first in the queue'* for their first caps against England. *'First I would place in the headgear queue I would place a modest 20-year-old youth who could settle down to be Welsh full-back for years to come.* **Terry Davies** *is the name. A pit boy from Binea, a village near Llanelly, Terry was playing for Swansea at the age of 18 and is now a Royal Commando doing National Service, He tackles like a lion, kicks strongly (both feet) and fills the goal-kicking gap left by Lewis Jones's departure. Fifteen of the Possibles' 27 points came from his goal-kicking. Physique query: ideal, he stands 5ft. 11in.; weighs 12st. 12lb. Next in line:-* **Sid Judd***, Cardiff schoolmaster, and as a blind-side wing forward the nearest approach we* *have found to Ray Cale. Judd is 22, stands 6ft. 2in., scales 15st. He has* been **the outstanding forward in Wales** *this season and must go into the team against England. Get a cap ready, too, for the Barry gardener,* **Geoffrey Beckingham**, *who, as I have stressed before, has proved unmistakeably that he is* **the best hooker in Wales**. *With a wonderful variety of prop men in all three matches, his striking has been far superior to that of any of the hookers matched against him. He is 28, 5ft. 10in. tall, and weighs 13½ stone.'*

Sid and Geoff were finally chosen, but the Wales – England game on 17 January was a massive disappointment, an 8-3 loss in Cardiff, with the selectors sticking to some men from the Reds pack that had underperformed in the three trials. **Wales missed 14 penalties** and Beckingham out-hooked England's South African hooker Labuschagne. *Observer* headlined a long article '*Too Much "Dead Wood" in Beaten XV'.* He advocated the removal from the pack of the older and less mobile Gwilliam, Rees Stephens and possibly Roy John. Cliff Morgan and Rex Willis had been omitted although now fit, along with C.D. (Derek) Williams, the Cardiff flanker and Alun Thomas and Malcolm Collins of Cardiff. Cardiff's Gareth Griffiths had played well, and '*Bleddyn Williams may be moved to partner Ken Jones, and his ability to give a pass might avoid a repetition of that tragic blunder which robbed Wales of a possible draw last Saturday.*' '*Good Front Row… The front row trio, John Robins, Geoff Beckingham and W.O. Williams emerged from the recent international ordeal with reputations intact, and I shall be surprised, indeed, if the selectors upset this hard-grafting, low-shoving unit… Beckingham, who hooked and grafted superbly in his first international, is there to stay.*' Somehow, Geoff only played twice more for Wales despite constant superb seasons for Cardiff and excellent performances in Welsh Trials.

(Lack of players owing to international and representative calls can be even worse today for top clubs. Small crowds for the four Welsh regions these days means that the WRU has to subsidise their expenses, mainly wage bills, leaving less to support the smaller clubs. *Cardiff Rugby Life* website reported on 16 February 2021, that the difficulties of putting out a first team is not only affected by more long-term injuries in the modern game, but that the increasing number of international breaks disrupting the club season. '*Our season so far has taken in 13 games across the league and Europe, seven outside the international window and six inside it, the crucial difference of course being the availability of top talent like Rhys Carre, Dillon Lewis, Seb Davies, Cory Hill, Tomos Williams and Josh Adams. In the seven games outside the international window we have six wins from the seven games, whereas during the international window we have just one win from the six games, exposing our lack of quality depth when comparing Cardiff to the likes of Munster, Leinster, Ulster, Glasgow and Edinburgh.'*)

On 25 January 1953, the *News of the World* reported: '*A Welsh Problem No Longer – Morgan, Willis – "Musts" – Cardiff 17 pts., Swansea nil - Wales half-back problem solved itself at Cardiff Arms Park, where two members of the "Big Five" were among 20,000 who saw Swansea outplayed. If the Cardiff pair, Rex Willis and Cliff Morgan do not suffer some unfortunate injury in the meantime, they are "musts" for Wales against Scotland on Feb. 7... Aided by the hooking of Geoff Beckingham and the line-out tactics of Malcolm Collins, Sid Judd and Bill Tamplin, Willis and Morgan completely baffled the Swansea defence at times.'* In the *South Wales Echo, Observer* reported **Cardiff Reach Great Heights** - *Cardiff displayed some of the best football of recent months, honours going to a magnificent pack and a lively back division... Malcolm Collins, probably the best line-out forward in Wales this season (Roy John included) showed up well in the lines-out and the loose, while his 17 st. would make all the difference to team-mate Geoff Beckingham, who seems fated to hook against the shove in this season's international series.'*

However, the relatively light Neath second-row of Roy John and Rees Stephens was then selected for the Scottish game, and *Observer* on 31 January pointed out that *'Geoff Beckingham, grand hooker that he is, will have again to work "might and main" against the shove...'* Terry Davies was announced fit to play full-back*, 'now happily recovered from a somewhat unnecessary "roughing" in the Wales-England game.'* On 1 February, Cardiff fielded 8 internationals at Aberavon, 7 of whom were to play against Scotland the following Saturday, and lost 11-9, with Tamplin failing with a conversion in front of the posts. Two tries and a penalty apiece were scored. Cardiff had beaten them 3-1 on tries, 13-5 in November. To be fair to this Cardiff result, when half of the team were playing for their country a week later, their internationals did tend to 'ease off', fearing injury. There were no two-week camps at a hotel with masseurs and ice baths in those days. Often internationals played for their clubs on the Wednesday before the big game.

In the Scottish international on 7 February, in front of 70,000 people at Murrayfield, Bleddyn scored two tries, his wing Ken Jones one, and Terry Davies kicked a penalty for an easy 12-0 win. Cardiff players were Bleddyn, Alun Thomas, Gareth Griffiths, Cliff Morgan, Rex Willis, Beckingham and Judd. For an unfathomable reason, Beckingham was the only Cardiff player dropped from these seven, replaced by Dai Davies for the Ireland game at Swansea. It was won 5-3, with Gareth Griffiths scoring a try, converted by Terry Davies. Beckingham was widely regarded as better than the two hookers who now took over Wales duties, Bryn Meredith and 'Dai' Maldwyn Davies, and was very often a travelling reserve. With any non-'Big Five' Welshman picking the team against England, there would have probably been a Triple Crown and Grand Slam.

France were beaten 6-3 on 14 March, for Wales to finish runners-up to England with 6 points to England's 7, the latter having drawn with Ireland.

On 14 February Cardiff outscored London Welsh 4–1 on tries, 12-3, with a newspaper headline '***Beckingham gave Cardiff the ball***... *Beckingham heeled constantly from the scrum in the second half, giving Cardiff a monopoly of the attack...*' After two wins against Newport 9-3 and 14-0, on 21 February Cardiff lost to two penalties, 6-0, in a terrific game at Rodney Parade. Vivian Jenkins wrote that '*Judd, Beckingham, Collins and Bowes never gave up the struggle... Cardiff's colours are blue and black and for several days their bodies will be similarly tinged following this battle between the two giants of Welsh Rugby – Cardiff with seven internationals and Newport with four. **It was amazing, and most praiseworthy, that in such fierce and intense forward struggle not one untoward incident took place throughout.***' Brian Marks' service to Cliff Morgan was erratic – Rex Willis's injuries meant that he had only played in the part of the Scotland game – and Newport, like Cardiff, used to play incredibly hard to avoid a four-game 'whitewash'. The final game was drawn 5-5. To be honest, Cardiff-Newport games were always the most intense – and this writer remembers hard games in the mud, but never any overt dirty play. The committees of both clubs, in the course of their history, have disavowed foul play. There were three teams, however, who often seemed to specialise in aggression against Cardiff – but not Llanelli, Swansea or Newport – the other three of the 'Big Four' Welsh clubs.

After just two internationals, Beckingham gained just one more cap in March 1958, against France, at the end of his career of 331 games for Cardiff – perhaps the Big Five had a brainwave between them. However, stranger things have happened in Welsh selection policies. Geoff also helped coach Barry and Penarth, and Barri Hurford, secretary of the Welsh Rugby Writers Association, wrote: '*At the time of the 1953 triumph Geoff was a gardener with the Barry Parks department. He had a lifetime hatred of neckties and steadfastly refused to wear one. There are some who say that he would have gained more than three Welsh international caps if he had been able to conform to this sartorial requirement. At his Barry funeral, attended by more than 300 friends and relations, there was - at the request of the family - **not a tie in sight**, not even around the necks of the pallbearers or funeral directors.*'

On 21 March Cardiff beat Coventry 19-6, 4-2 on tries, and on 28 March Sale were beaten 14-3, 3-1 on tries. Short of players, Jack Matthews had returned to play after retiring from the First XV and playing for the Athletic. On this day, Bleddyn was captaining Wales to beat France, alongside Sid Judd, Gareth Griffiths, Alun Thomas and Cliff Morgan. Rex Willis, John Llewellyn, Malcolm Collins and other first-teamers also were missing. We see the headline '***Tamplin in Kicking Form for Cardiff*** *– Although weakened by international calls and injuries, Cardiff gained a* *well-deserved 14-3 win after a shaky start. Tamplin scored eight points – two penalty goals and a conversion...'* Bryn Mapstone, related to the Taff's Well rugby family, and Haydn Morris touched down. (Cardiff only played Sale four times, between 1951 and 1954, winning all games with 76-6 points aggregate, and 20-1 on tries).

Brian Marks played scrumhalf 25 times this season, as 'world-class' captain, Barbarian and Lion Rex Willis was still out with recurring shoulder injuries, playing only 12 times. Cliff, Bleddyn, Alun Thomas and others also missed many games. Upon 4 April Lloyd Williams was chosen against the Barbarians. He had been playing regularly in the Athletic, and played 7 times for Cardiff this season, followed by 10, 11 and 15 appearances, until in 1956-57 he played 37 times, and was the first-choice scrum half until he retired at the end of 1963-64. Other players would have gone to play first team rugby at another club, but Cardiff was the closest top-class team to Taff's Well, the club most associated with the village, and his four older brothers had all played for the team. (I am not forgetting Pontypridd, but Cardiff had not played them since 1931, then having regular fixtures in the 1970s. Between 1878 and 1974, of 33 fixtures, Cardiff won 26, lost 5 and drew 2, points 423-118, tries 100-24, but Pontypridd scored 10 pens to Cardiff's 7).

Lloyd was ready, playing well as Cardiff beat the Baa-Baas 14-0, with three tries and a penalty. After ten minutes, Alun Thomas had gone off with a suspected fractured collar bone, and Cardiff were down to 14 men, so Gareth Griffiths moved from wing to centre, scoring two tries. Derek (CD) Williams scored the other try, and along with Judd played all over the field. *'"Open Rugby" is the Barbarians cry, and in that style, Cardiff, who have the same ideal, beat them. They threw the ball about as freely as did the visitors, because hooker Beckingham saw to it that they had as many chances, even though their pack was nearly always a man short.'* The report ends, *'Lloyd Williams, Cardiff's 20-year-old scrum half did well. He made sure that brother Bleddyn, Cliff Morgan, and Griffiths had plenty of chances to upset the Barbarians' defence.'*

A report from the away win at Penzance and Newlyn 'Pirates' on 14 April states: *'G. Beckingham hooked the ball from nearly every set scrum, and M. Collins almost completely dominated the line-outs.'* Cardiff made hard work of it, scoring two tries to a penalty and wining 8-3, but it was a game they expected to win, and their annual tour of the West Country involved a certain amount of alcohol. There was a cracking match at Pontypool on 18 April 1953, *'a match packed with thrills'* where *'the visitors pulled the game out of the fire in the closing minutes'* to win 16-15. Beckingham was injured and left the field for six minutes. *'This was the match of the season. It had everything – drama, excitement and thrills to the very last moment and Cardiff, who had trailed behind all through the game, had Cliff Morgan and Gareth Griffiths to thank for this narrow one-*

point victory.' It was Pontypool's biggest crowd of the season. In 19 games against between April 1948 and September 1957, Cardiff won 18 and drew one, scoring 65 tries to 18 – they did not want to be remembered as the team that lost to Pontypool. These are the main cuttings for the season 1952-52 from Beckingham's scrapbook. Geoff's importance to Cardiff is shown in his number of appearances. From 1948-49 to 1950-51, he played 12, 17 and 24 games. From then on, he was indispensable. From 1951-52 to 1957-58 and retirement after a belated third Welsh cap, he played 38, 35, 37, 42, 40, 43 and 39 times, 327 times for the best team in the world, but winning only three caps – because Cardiff's backs were so good, and his closest rival, Bryn Meredith of Newport, was excellent hooker and a British Lion.

Bill Tamplin was not alarmed by the Wallabies' record.
'We'll take 'em on,' he growled, 'and we'll beat 'em.'

WILLIAM EWART 'BILL' TAMPLIN 10 May 1917 - 20 October 1989
'The King of Kickers'
Pontypool second row 1939
Newport 1939-40
Lieutenant, Welch Regiment, was years
Services and Victory Internationals
Cardiff - 252 appearances 1945-46 to 1952-53, **Captain 1950-51**

Cardiff - 7 Tries, 247 Conversions, 122 Pens, 3 Drop Goals = 891 Points
Barbarians 1947-48
Wales 7 appearances 1947 and 1948 – 6 pens 3 conversions = 24 points
In 1947, as **Captain of Wales**, he scored the two penalties to beat Australia
6-0

'Bill', the second cousin on their mother's side of the Williams brothers,
was born at 12 Dixon's Place, Risca. He first played second-row for
Abergavenny, then for Pontypool in 1939, joining Newport in 1939-40,
and then Cardiff when rugby began after the war. (Second-row for many
has been renamed 'lock', whereas lock used to be what is now the 'number
8'). Like his relative Roy Roberts, Tamplin's best years were lost to WW2.
In the *Supplement to the London Gazette* of 30 November 1943, we see
under *'Welch R'* (Welch Regiment) – *'25th September 1943; 14320578
William Ewart Tamplin (293567)'* named alongside Donald Gordon
Bowen and Frank Graham Jenkins, being granted an emergency
commission as a Second Lieutenant, probably during advance of the Eighth
Army through Italy, which sustained very heavy casualties. His promotion
seems to have been made permanent in 1944. Bill Tamplin played for
Wales against England in the uncapped 1945-46 Victory Internationals.

A Police Sergeant at Magor, Monmouthshire, Bill Tamplin was a regular
in Cardiff's team when fixtures restarted after the war, and played for the
Barbarians in 1947-48. His international debut had been Scotland v Wales
at Murrayfield, 1 Feb 1947, and his last international was Wales v France
at Swansea, 21 Feb 1948. 'Bill' Tamplin was picked for three games in the
1947 Five Nations, missing the first match against England, but scoring on
his debut against Scotland with two conversions and a penalty. In the next
match he kicked the only score of the 3-0 win over France. Tamplin also
converted a try in the win over Ireland. In December 1947, the 30-year-old
Tamplin captained Wales against the touring Australians, and scored all the
points in a 6-0 victory with two penalty kicks. He was known as *'the king
of kickers'* in the press, being able to convert a heavy ball over prodigious
distances. Bill Tamplin kept his place for three matches in 1948, drawing
with England and beating Scotland but was dropped after the poor home
defeat to France.

Two of his brothers, Tom and Ewart, also played first class rugby but
they never represented their country. Bill last played for Cardiff, aged 35,
against Neath in 1952. He was lucky in being a serving police officer, and
thence able to take time off to play in some weekday and away matches.
From 1946-47 to 1952-53, he scored more than 5 penalties and/or
conversions in a match ten times, against Cambridge University, Newport,
Swansea, Leicester, Penarth, Devonport Services, Cardiff and District,
Bridgend, Plymouth and Cognac-Nantes. In 1948-49, *'the goal kicking was
shared, mostly by W. E. Tamplin with 31 goals, Roy Roberts 25, and R. F.*

Trott.' Roberts would have probably played for Wales, but for the war.

On 17 February 1951, a two-pence programme gave the details of Cardiff, captained by Tamplin, playing at the Arms Park against a Newport side which was unbeaten in 33 games, including 23 in that season. They had already beaten Cardiff twice, and Newport were a formidable side. There was a world record club attendance of 48,500 (gate receipts £2,587), a figure unbeaten until the modern era, and surpassing the previous record of 36,000 for Cardiff-Swansea in 1949. The programme notes that the rivalry began in April 1875, and of the 240 games, Cardiff had won 106, Newport 95, with 39 matches drawn. Newport won 8-3 (2 tries, 1 conversion, against a penalty by Tamplin. Cardiff had an international back line of Frank Trott, Haydn Morris, Bleddyn Williams, Jack Matthews, Derek Murphy, Cliff Morgan and Rex Willis. Cardiff avoided the unthinkable whitewash in a hard-fought game on 3rd March, each side converting a penalty at Rodney Parade. However, the following year Cardiff came back with a vengeance, winning all four games. Bill's record for Cardiff is as follows:

TEST SUMMARY

SEASON	P	W	D	L	TRY	CON	PEN	DG	PTS
1945-1946	33	26	2	5	0	16	4	0	44
1946-1947	30	24	3	3	0	40	12	1	120
1947-1948	24	23	0	1	1	41	14	0	127
1948-1949	25	23	1	1	0	21	10	0	72
1949-1950	38	28	3	7	4	30	22	1	141
1950-1951	39	30	4	5	0	35	22	1	139
1951-1952	32	24	2	6	0	26	22	0	118
1952-1953	30	23	2	5	2	38	16	0	130
TOTAL	251	201	17	33	7	247	122	3	891

WILLIAM JOHN 'BILLY' BOSTON MBE (born 6 August 1934)
'THE ONE THAT GOT AWAY'
Cardiff Boys

Wales Youth

Neath Rugby Union, several games when aged under 17

Pontypridd 1 game, 1 try 1952

Cardiff and District vs Cardiff 1952

Wigan 1953-1968 – Stand-off, Centre, Wing - Played 486 games (+2 substitute appearances = 488) – **478 tries** (a record) and 7 goals = 1,448 points

Blackpool Boro 1969-70 Played 11 – 5 tries – 15 points

Points scored in RL club rugby – 1463, a record, in **499 appearances with 483 tries** and 7 goals

64 Internationals – 89 Tries = 267 points

Great Britain XIII 1954-1962 Played 31, Tries 24 = 72 points
Great Britain Touring XIII Played 27, Tries 53 = 159 points
Also played 6 internationals for Welsh XIII, Other Nationalities (2),
English XIII, British XIII and GB vs France 12 tries = 36 points
Total first team games inc. 64 internationals: P563, T572

*'probably the most magnetic crowd puller in the history of British Rugby
League'* - Vince Karalius, rugby league legend

There is no player in British history who can approach Boston's try-scoring
ability. Playing at top level, in 563 appearances, he scored 572 tries. But let
us begin at the beginning. Two boys who lived a few doors away from
each other, in Angelina Street, played for Cardiff Schoolboys rugby team
in the late 1940s. The boy from number 4 was Joe Erskine, who became
British and Empire heavyweight boxing champion, beating three world
title contenders in George Chuvalo, Willie Pastrano and Henry Cooper.
The boy from number 7, Billy Boston, was greatest try-scorer in rugby
history. In December 2020 Billy Boston was named as one of three
Cardiff-born rugby league players to be honoured with a new statue in
Cardiff Bay, the other two being Gus Risman and Clive Sullivan. I
remember vividly Billy thundering up the wing for Wigan, the best team of
the day, tacklers bouncing off him, when rugby league was regularly
shown upon BBC TV on Saturday afternoons. The commentator Eddie
Waring used to go into raptures whenever Billy had the ball. From
Butetown, in Cardiff Docks area, Billy began playing as a teenager for the
multiracial docks team CIACs (pronounced kayaks) and Cardiff Boys.

In 1950 he played for Neath and in 1951-52 was a huge factor in the
CIACs' 'Invincible' season, winning all 32 games. The CIACs call
themselves the 'Grangetown, Butetown, the Docks and Cardiff Bay Rugby
Club, and just celebrated 75 years since their foundation in 1946 in Tiger
Bay, near Cardiff Docks. The team won 50 competitions in its first 50
years, and Billy was the star player in their 'Invincible' season. *'Their
name Cardiff Internationals "came up because there were so many
different nationalities,"* explained Philip John, club captain for a record 10
years. *"But sometimes the opposition thought we were actually
international players from the Cardiff City team."* The misunderstanding
resulted in some hard games against teams with genuine internationals,
though the CIACS always did themselves proud. In the showers after one
such game the Irish stand-off was heard to say that the two CIAC forwards
had given him a harder game than any full international.'

Billy played a game in 1952 for Pontypridd, but was desperate to play for
Cardiff. In 1952, he was described as *'outstanding'* playing for Cardiff and
District against Cardiff but was overlooked by Cardiff. Cardiff had three
international wings at the time, and others joining, which is the most

charitable take as to why Billy never joined. He had a Sierra Leone father and an Irish mother, and dreamed of playing for Cardiff and Wales. Billy was being constantly being scouted by rugby league clubs, but had always refused, but when on National Service he was approached again by Wigan. He was home on leave, when the club's chairman and vice-chairman came to the family home, where Billy was the middle of eleven siblings, and offered £1,000. His mum rejected the offer, and the Wigan officials spread £1,500 in white five-pound notes across the kitchen table. Billy said no, and his mother asked for a few moments alone with him, saying, as he told Peter Jackson a few years ago. *'Billy's mother said, "Don't worry son, I'll get rid of them for you. I'll ask them for so much that they'll go home." They returned to their tiny front room, and told the Wigan pair, "Right pay him £3,000 and he'll sign." Billy thought "That's a really smart way of getting rid of them. Three grand? Nobody's worth that much." However, before leaving for Cardiff, the Wigan men had withdrawn £3,000 in cash from the club's bank account. They talked quietly to each other for less than a minute and answered: "OK, Mrs Boston we will pay you three thousand pounds. All Billy has to do is sign this contract." Still wanting to play for Cardiff and Wales, Billy refused to sign until his mother reminded him that Wigan had come up with the money, now they had to keep their word. Billy signed and years later told Peter Jackson that he cried that night, and couldn't sleep, as his Cardiff and Wales ambitions had been shattered.'*

Boston could only believe that Cardiff did not want a non-white player, an 18-year-old who had *'all the tricks of his trade. He could beat opponents any and every way - body swerve, side-step, hand-off or just sheer pace because most didn't see him for dust.'* Jackson continued: *'The late Great Britain test captain Vince Karalius, one of the hardest men to play the game, described Boston "probably the most magnetic crowd puller in the history of British Rugby League." Another called him the Oscar Peterson of 50s rugby, a striking comparison with the virtuoso jazz pianist given that Billy led most opponents a merry dance... In 15 years at Wigan until the late 1960s, he left records that will never be broken, not least 478 tries in 487 matches for the club. And even when he was winning Challenge Cup finals at Wembley, with Billy it was all about the team, never about himself. They loved him so much in Wigan that they stumped up £90,000 to put a bronze statue of him up in the town.'*

A 'living legend', Billy played 58 games for Great Britain, becoming the first player to score four tries in a game against New Zealand. He was also the first non-white player to be selected to tour Australia and New Zealand, in 1954, setting a new record of 36 tries in 18 games. Boston also scored 22 tries in the 1962 tour, and twice equalled the then Wigan club record of seven tries in a game. He played left centre when Wigan beat Workington in the 1958 Challenge Cup Final at Wembley Stadium, in front of a crowd

276

of 66,109, and then on the right wing, scoring two-tries in the victory over Hull F.C. in the following 1959 Final in front of a crowd of 79,811. He was on the right wing again when Wigan beat Hunslet in 1965, in front of a Wembley crowd of 89,016. Boston was a remarkable loss to Rugby Union. It was not until 1986 that Pontypool flanker Mark Brown and the Bridgend wing, Glen Webbe, became the first black players to represent Wales. However, in 1935 George Bennett had been the first black man to play for the Welsh Rugby League side.

From the *iloverugbyleague* website we read: '*A true icon of the sport, especially in Wigan,* **Billy Boston's** *career followed a typical trajectory for a Welshman from his background. A native of Tiger Bay, Cardiff. His mother had Irish roots, while his father was a sailor from Sierra Leone. Always big for a three-quarter, he weighed 15 pounds when he was born. Frustration with a lack of progress in rugby union saw him come North. He said: "I was disappointed that Cardiff never showed any interest in me and I think that was because of my colour. They certainly wouldn't let me into their clubhouse after I turned professional. I don't think I would ever have been picked for Wales at union." Union's loss was league's massive gain, however, when Boston signed for Wigan in 1953. He would go on to win 31 caps for Great Britain, scoring 24 tries. He also played two games for the Other Nationalities, and one game for a Welsh XIII. He would leave Wigan in 1968 and play one season for Blackpool Borough before his retirement in 1970.*' What a terrible loss for rugby union, but a stellar career in rugby league for a wonderful man.

The same site also tells us '*Butetown's* **Colin Dixon** *was a scrumhalf and a centre, before finally blossoming in the second row as his strength and power grew. Like fellow Welsh league greats Gus Risman and Billy Boston, he was a product of South Church Street School in his hometown. Another victim of the unspoken racial prejudice which prevented many black and ethnic minority Welshman from winning caps in rugby union in the 1960s, Dixon thrived in the grittier surroundings of rugby league. He would go on to be a* **world record signing***, at £12,000 plus a player worth £3,000, when he joined Salford in 1968. A bruising forward, he was a part of the 1972 World Cup winning Great Britain side, and played 245 games for Halifax, 418 for Salford, and 25 for Hull KR. With 16 caps for Wales, and 14 for GB, Dixon is one of Welsh rugby league's true heroes. He died in 1993 of a stroke, at the tragically young age of 49*'.

… '*Boston's status in Wigan is matched by that of* **Clive Sullivan** *in the city of Hull, where the main route into the town, the A63, is named Clive Sullivan Way after the great winger. Born in Cardiff, Sullivan's childhood operations on knees, feet and shoulders made it seem unlikely he would ever play rugby. In the army in 1961, however, he played a game of rugby union, and showed his immense talent. He signed for Hull FC in 1961, but his career did not really blossom until he left the Army in 1964. He scored*

250 tries for the Airlie Birds (Hull rugby league) *in 352 games, before joining Hull KR in 1974. He would repeat his amazing feats with the Robins, notching 118 tries in 213 games. Sullivan was **the first black captain of any British national team**, and remains the only Welsh skipper to ever lift a World Cup in any sport, when he helped GB to win the World Cup in 1972, scoring a memorable try in the decisive match against Australia. His 17 caps and 13 tries for GB are complemented by 15 caps for Wales, for whom he scored seven tries. He died in 1985 of cancer, aged just 42'* Another great loss for the Union game.

... *'**Jim Mills** - One of the game's real hardmen, 'Big Jim', famously had his 'eyes of blue' to accompany his 18 stone miner's build. This Aberdare native is an icon in Widnes. Mills began his rugby career playing RU in Cardiff, before joining Halifax in 1965. He would move to Widnes in 1968, and it was there that he would establish himself as one of rugby league's most fearsome forwards. He would win six test caps for Great Britain and play five times for Wales. Although his stamp on the head of Kiwi John Greengrass at Swansea in 1975 is remembered by some, his brutal effectiveness and rough-hewn charisma is recalled with affection by far more, especially by fans who wear black and white. Mills has also managed the Wales national team.'* I watched and admired these great players Billy Boston, Colin Dixon, Clive Sullivan and Jim Mills many times, on Saturday afternoon BBC television as a youngster. Along with Jim Sullivan and Gus Risman – these were world-class players in their time, a massive loss to Union. Playing Rugby League did not mean that it was fully professional – players also had full-time jobs which their clubs found for them, but they were allowed time off for games and given match fees which virtually doubled their incomes. And unless they were switching RL clubs, the signing-on fee was in their pockets, almost always enough to buy a house for good players from Union.

CHAPTER 24 - CARDIFF SEASON 1953 – 1954

BLEDDYN CAPTAINS CARDIFF AND WALES TO VICTORY OVER NEW ZEALAND - HIS PROPHECY TO EAMONN ANDREWS – DR. JACK MATTHEWS - GARETH GRIFFITHS

Bleddyn Williams P39 T17 = 51pts; **Lloyd Williams** P10; John Llewellyn P37 C16 P14 = 74pts (Taff's Well); Alun Priday P12 C7 P2 = 20pts (Tongwynlais); Derek Murphy P18 T8 = 24pts (Pentyrch)

P49, W37, L9, D3. Points 616-284. Tries 138-44, Pens 29-25

'Between ourselves, we consider that our matches against Wales and England are secondary affairs. Our primary aim is to beat Cardiff.' Bob Stuart, New Zealand captain, speech to Cardiff Rotary Club 16 November 1953 five days before the match

'Cardiff's victory against the All Blacks on Saturday was like a symphony on a football field, a masterpiece of design, an anthem of courage. These international matches are somehow above and beyond the game of rugby – they are battles of the giants and Cardiff Arms Park is the Olympus. It is no exaggeration to say that it is the game of rugby more than anything else – including coal – which over the years has put Cardiff on the map of the English-speaking world.' – South Wales Echo 23 November 1953

MCMLIII was indeed an eventful year. I am reliably informed that there was, indeed, *'fear in the air'*, but all we seven-year-olds used to want to do, was get out of the house and play. (For the benefit of the younger reader, very few people had a car, a fridge or a 'telly', let alone books in the house – libraries were used by many children. Without central heating or double glazing, it was often warmer to play outside anyway.) Back to '53. The USA developed and tested the Hydrogen Bomb. In the ongoing 'Cold War', so did Russia. The USA elected as President a former general, Dwight David 'Ike' Eisenhower, a man with no political experience. History always repeats itself. DNA and the vaccine for Polio were discovered. Stalin died. Hooray! A New Zealander and a Nepalese were the first to climb a very high mountain named after a Welshman. The King died and was replaced by Queen Elizabeth Alexandra Mary Windsor, with celebrations and street parties across the land. The Korean War ended, and a very unusual era of peace (save for the *Mau Mau* Uprising), ensured that this writer's generation was the first in centuries never having to kill unknown people from unknown countries. England was smashed 6-3 at soccer at Wembley by Hungary in 1953 – sending shockwaves through the nation. Worse was to come – in Budapest the following year England lost 7-1. The USA and UK conspired for economic reasons, to overthrow Mohammad Mosaddegh's democratic Persian government and make the Shah all-powerful. It was a most interesting year. The rationing of sugar ended, but I had to wait until 1954 for restrictions on meat and bacon to be lifted – later than on the Continent, thanks to our American friends who poured food and resources into it. All kids were lean in those days. Lots of other important things happened, but for Cardiff and Wales supporters there were two other world events, upon 21 November and 19 December 1953. Of which more later.

Bleddyn, *'the greatest centre three-quarter of his time'*, was captain, with pack leader Sid Judd again vice-captain. Bleddyn's cousin Bill Tamplin had retired after 242 games from 1945-46 to 1952-53. He was 36 and had lost 6 years of rugby owing to war, otherwise would have played over 300 games for the club. Up to ten Cardiff players were to be involved in internationals and even more in trials, accounting for the high number of club losses. This accounts for a bad away defeat to Dublin's Bective Rangers, perhaps then Ireland's top team, which won the Leinster Cup in 1955, 1956 and 1962, but in the following fixtures until 1975, Cardiff won 11 and drew 2, scoring 42 tries to 13. Indeed, there were 10 players involved in when Wales beat France 19-13 upon 10 April. (This includes reserves, who had to be ready to play, but only did so if a doctor reported a selected player to be ill upon the morning of kick-off). Upon the previous Wednesday, without these players, Cardiff had beaten Swansea 13-10.

Wales, France and England all won 3 games and lost 1, and Wales headed the Championship on points difference. Today, they would have won the Championship, but in those days it was shared between teams on equal points. The loss was 9-6 to England at Twickenham, Bleddyn being unavailable because of his leg injury picked up against New Zealand in December. Fullback Gerwyn Williams dislocated his shoulder trying to stop England's first try, had it treated at half-time and returned as a passenger. He never played rugby again. Rex Willis was injured, forcing Cliff Morgan to play scrum-half and Cardiff's wing Gwyn Rowlands shifted to fullback while the badly injured Gerwyn Williams moved to the wing. Gwyn scored a try and kicked a penalty in the 9-6 loss, with forwards Roy John, John Gwilliam and Dai Davies never being picked for Wales again. Injuries in this game cost Wales a Grand Slam. Ireland were beaten in Dublin 12-9, and Scotland were defeated at Swansea 15-3 with Wales scoring 4 tries. France were beaten at the Arms Park 19-13. Because of ongoing injuries, Bleddyn only played in the final Scotland game.

Despite often not being able to play its best team, the Cardiff side knitted together and only lost one match in its last 19. The first game against Newport, on 14 November 1953 was reported by Dave Phillips as *'Forwards Battle At Arms Park – Backs Subdued by Keen Tackling'*. Derek 'C.D.' Williams scored two tries and Eddie Thomas one, to Newport's try by Wills. Newport were unchanged, but Cardiff were without any first team centres except Bleddyn Williams. The injured Rex Willis and Haydn Morris were omitted, and Sid Judd was forced to move into the second row. There was a crowd of nearly 40,000 – today the equivalent fixture is lucky to get 7,000. *'Cardiff surprisingly overcame their staunch rivals after a fierce and hard-fought encounter. Newport were without their injured captain, Ken Jones, and four other key players, absent on trial duty at Swansea. But Cardiff were the worse sufferers in thus respect. No fewer than nine of their regular players were seeking inclusion in the Welsh team to meet the All Blacks.* (And there were 4 injured players). *Cardiff undoubtedly owed their victory to the sterling performance of their young, virile pack, ably led by veteran Stan Bowes. They packed far lower and tighter than their opponents and as a result Geoff Beckingham had a field day.'* Cardiff won 15-6, then 5-3 at Rodney Parade. The third game, on 6 March 1954 in front of a crowded Arms Park saw just a try apiece, ending Cardiff hopes of another quadruple. On 17 March there was another terrific game, Cardiff scoring 3 tries to 2 at Rodney Parade, to win 13-9.

Just a week after that bitterly contested first game at Newport, Cardiff faced New Zealand on 21 November 1953. In the team photo before the game, the six-foot second row Edwin 'Eddie' Thomas stood on tiptoe, to try and match his fellow second-row, the 6 foot 2 inch Malcolm Collins, standing alongside him. Eddie duly earned the nickname 'Toesy' Thomas. The unbeaten New Zealand rugby team, then known as the *Kiwis*, had a full week to prepare for this *'sixth international'*, the game that all touring nations wish to play, against Cardiff. Cardiff was their 7th game, having beaten Llanelli 17-3 a week earlier and racking up 99 points against 19 in those matches. In the weeks leading up to the Cardiff-New Zealand game, preparations did not look good. The *Football Echo* reported: *'Haydn Morris, the speedy left-wing has been forbidden to play for a period on medical advice, while internationals Bleddyn Williams, Sid Judd and Geoff Beckingham are others who have been "in the Wars" recently. The Cardiff skipper sustained a badly bruised hand in getting the first of his two fine tries against Bristol last Saturday and it is hoped that the damage can be rectified in time for the "All Blacks" tussle.* **Worthy of Trial** *Another stalwart, who has been out of action for the last week or so, is John Llewellyn who injured a shoulder against Llanelly, but hopes to be fit and well in plenty of time for the tourists' visit. A player who must have caught the eyes of the W.R.U. selectors at Bristol last week was Derek Williams, the former Oxford "double blue" who is running into his peak form at this time.'*

Roy Roberts' match programme of 21 November 1953 notes *'The brilliant handling and running of the post-war Cardiff back divisions has gained the admiration of Touring sides. The "Wallabies" in 1947 fell before it and the mighty "Springboks" in 1951 were fortunate to escape defeat, in an exciting match. Indeed, so lucky did they regard themselves, that they presented the Cardiff Club with a "Springbok" head which now holds a place of honour in the Cardiff Club Museum. Thus, the Fourth "All-Blacks" will enter the field today, knowing full well the great traditions and spirit that fosters successive Cardiff Teams. They themselves have great traditions. Rugby Football is the national Game of New Zealand. Victory on the field of play is important, and so is the comradeship after the final whistle. The Cardiff Club have always been great hosts, and the full hospitality of the Club and the great crowd present will be extended to the visitors today. May the match be worthy of the great occasion. Let the trumpets sound and the great Game of Rugby Football be honoured by great deeds. Welcome to Cardiff, "All Blacks!"'* They don't write programme notes like that anymore … There follows '*Memories of the Past*'.

1905

Dave Gallaher's First "All Blacks" of 1905 were one of the greatest ever of New Zealand combinations. They swept through the four Home Countries in a riot of scoring, and it was not until they came to Wales that they experienced stern opposition. The first match in the Principality was lost by a try to nil against Wales, and this was the only defeat they sustained on tour. However, Welshmen felt they were lucky to win against Cardiff at the Arms Park on Boxing Day, 1905. They won by two goals (10 pts.) to a goal and a try (8pts.) Gwyn Nicholls and Ralph Thomas scored tries for Cardiff, one of which Winfield converted. New Zealand's tries were obtained by Thompson and Nicholson, but the second was scored as the result of a regrettable error by the Cardiff captain, Percy Bush. The ball was kicked into the in-goal area and Bush had plenty of time to clear. However, he mis-kicked and the "All Blacks" forwards scored a try. Percy Bush still regrets this error, for had Cardiff won it would have crowned a wonderful season under his captaincy. (Lost 10-8)

1924

The Second "All Blacks", under the captaincy of C.G. Porter, were a magnificent side. They did even better than the First "All Blacks", for they remained undefeated. However, there were several matches in which they experienced a hard time, and one of these was the game at the Arms Park on November 22, 1924. They won by two goals, a penalty goal and a try (16pts.) to a goal and a penalty goal (8pts.) At half-time they led by 11 points to nil, but were fortunate to have gained such a commanding lead over the Welsh club. In the second half, Cardiff fought back magnificently. First Dr. Tom Wallace kicked a penalty goal and then W.J. "Billy" Delahay crossed for a try between the posts for Delahay to convert. Throughout this half it was a ding-dong struggle, and although the "All Blacks" scored again, they had to defend desperately before the end came, with Cardiff sharing a great deal of the honours. (Lost 16-8)

1935

The Third "All Blacks", under J.E. Manchester, were a happy band of players, and although they lost three matches to Swansea, Wales and England, they gained a big victory over Cardiff in a delightful game of Rugby. At half-time they led by 15 points to nil; but in the second half, each side scored five points and the final score was 20 points to five. The New Zealanders said they were delighted naturally to win at Cardiff, but appreciated the reception from the crowd and the approach of the home team to the open game. Caughey (2), Mitchell and Reid scored tries for New Zealand and Gilbert converted two and dropped a goal. Vic Osmond scored a try for Cardiff which Ronny Boon converted. Cardiff's captain was Tommy Stone.' Bleddyn's 17-year-old brother Gwyn played wing forward in this game, on 26 October. (Lost 20-5)

According to Danny Davies, his great friend Bleddyn *'had long planned tactics to defeat the All Blacks, he had gained much knowledge from his tour to New Zealand in 1950 with the British Lions. Simply, it was to run at "em", make their pack run about the field and tire them. To his own forwards he said, "give me two-fifths possession of the ball and we'll win". He had a grand XV to lead although his own pack was much lighter than that of the All Blacks, but he also knew that the atmosphere of the Cardiff Arms Park was worth a couple of points to the home team, and could be unsettling for a while to the visitors.'* A couple of days before the game, the famous broadcaster Eamonn Andrews visited the club for research about the game. He was taken into a committee room, and asked Bleddyn about Cardiff's chances. Bleddyn pointed out a blank space on a wall and replied *'That is where we are going to hang a photograph of the Cardiff team that beat the All Blacks'*

The team was as follows – I have added age, height and weight for modern comparison: fullback John Edward Leighton Llewellyn 26, 5'11", 12st 0lb (formerly a wing, full-back John was from Taff's Well and first played for Pentyrch, Taff's Well's traditional opponents) – right wing Dr. Gwyn Rowlands 24, 5'11", 12st 8lb – right centre Alun Gruffydd Thomas 27, 5'10", 11st 10lb – left centre Bleddyn Llewellyn Williams 30, 5'10", 13st 8lb – left wing Gareth Meredith Griffiths 21, 6'0", 12st 10lb – outside half Clifford Isaac Morgan 23, 5'7", 12st 0lb – scrumhalf William Rex Willis 29, 5'9", 12st 7lb - tight-head prop Arthur David Stanley Bowes – 36, 5'10", 14st 7lb – hooker Geoffrey Thomas Beckingham 29, 5'10", 13st 10lb – loose-head prop John Davies Evans 27, 5'11", 15st 2lb – second row Malcolm Collins 25, 6'2", 16st 7lb – second row Edwin Thomas 30, 6'0", 14st 1lb – open-side wing forward Charles Derek Williams 28, 5'11", 13st 0lb – number 8 Sidney Judd 25, 6'2", 14st 12lb – blind-side wing forward John Daniel Nelson 28, 6'1", 13st 7lb.

There were 56,000 inside the Arms Park, and several thousand outside the ground on 21 November 1953. On the Cardiff RFC website we read: *'Bleddyn instructed his team to run at every opportunity, even from the deepest defence. Thus, after six minutes Cliff Morgan broke from the scrum in his own 25 with the captain's words still ringing in his head: "We have got to try things... if we fail, we fail, but we have got to be different"'.* *'Cardiff scored first. Cliff Morgan received the ball from Rex Willis, put in a short punt ahead, raced up and caught the ball on the rebound from one of the defenders. He passed it to Alun. Thomas, who, after making some ground passed it to Gwyn Rowlands who cross-kicked towards the posts. Sid Judd, dashing up at full speed caught the ball and crashed over for a try underneath a group of All Black defenders. Gwyn Rowlands converted.*

283

The try was followed by a magnificent penalty goal from R. A. Jarden, from a range of 45 yards. With the score at five points to three in Cardiff's favour, the Cardiff pack was going great guns against its heavier opponents and our side doing the pressing, the excitement was intense.

Within minutes Bleddyn carried on another audacious Morgan break-out from defence, and put in a perfect short punt. The ball was gathered by Alun Thomas who raced up to Bob Scott the full-back, before giving a long pass to Gwyn Rowlands who ran thirty yards and scored in the corner. The kick for goal failed. There was no more scoring in the second half and Cardiff were worthy winners by eight paints to three, thus completing a wonderful record of having defeated all three Commonwealth countries - South Africa 1906-07, Australia in 1908 and 1947, and now New Zealand in 1953. Dave Phillips in the "South Wales Echo" wrote "For 80 minutes we saw the traditional skill and fire of what has rightly been termed "The greatest Rugby Club in the World", countered by the all-action enthusiasm of a determined All Black side who tried everything in their power to whittle down Cardiff's half-time lead of five points in a storming grand-stand finish."'

J. B. G. Thomas in the *Western Mail* wrote, '*What a game it was! How magnificent the players performed. The blood raced through their veins as they bent to their tasks in attack and defence. The voice was raised to cheer as Bleddyn Williams, and his fellows split open the New Zealand's defence like a destroyer's bow ripping through the flimsy hull of a crippled submarine. The Rugby triumph which had eluded Cardiff since 1905 was achieved in a match full of excitement and glory accompanying a great sporting occasion.*' G.V. (Geevers) Wynne Jones headlined his report, '*It Was A Glorious Day For Wales – Cardiff backs inspired downfall of All Blacks... where a record crowd of more than 60,000 saw the club side, thanks to their brilliant backs, inflict on the All Blacks their first defeat of the tour... The mighty Bleddyn Williams has schooled himself into a state of peak fitness, and any doubts that he would be left out of the Welsh team have been completely dispelled... Outstanding was Stan Bowes'* (- the prop who first played for Cardiff in 1936 and served in the Royal Navy throughout the war).

And in a leading article in the *Western Mail* on 23 November 1953, we read: '*We do not think that the passing of the years will ever dim for us the gleam and glory of the historic encounter at the Cardiff Arms Park on Saturday, or tarnish the memory of Cliff Morgan's darting and swooping across the turf and skimming past every obstacle like a swift at play. There was greatness in that clash of bone and sinew wherein the impenetrable object that was the Cardiff pack successfully withstood the supposedly irresistible force of the New Zealand "terrible eight". The Cardiff team had played magnificently and towards the end of the game appeared stronger and fresher than their opponents.*' A cartoon the day after had a note in the corner saying: '*Advice After Saturday's Game – Anyone who can't hold his breath for the last ten minutes should get rid of his international ticket!*' And another newspaper report eulogised the team: '*Cardiff's victory against the All Blacks on Saturday was like a symphony on a football field, a masterpiece of design, an anthem of courage...*' They don't write them like that anymore – but then again, the steroidal modern game is far too brutal to deserve much praise. New Zealand in the last few minutes had the put-in on the Cardiff line three times, with a much heavier pack. Beckingham amazingly struck against the head each time, with Cliff Morgan having just enough breathing space to kick the ball out of play after the third scrum, for the referee to whistle full-time.

The former Welsh international and British Lion Vivian Jenkins' headline was **History Knows No Greater Rugby Feat** *– I have seen one of the classic games of British rugby history... Giving away a stone a man, the Blue and Black forwards hurled themselves into their heavier opponents... Cardiff were worthy of the title often conferred upon them – **the greatest rugby club in the world**. Cliff Morgan was a scintillating star, here, there and everywhere. And so were his fellows Bleddyn Williams, Thomas, Griffiths and the rest. Judd led a pack of forwards who should be proud of themselves until their dying day...*' Bleddyn was chaired off the pitch, and in the evening dinner the New Zealand manager J.N. Millard said. '*We were beaten by a better team, but are pleased to have given pleasure to 56,000 people.*'

In his first column as a rugby critic for *The People*, and thus no longer able to play rugby union, Bleddyn reminisced about the game, '*Who,* among those fortunate enough to be there, will ever forget the game's dying minutes, when, with the All Blacks pounding the Cardiff line, the crowd stood with bated breath awaiting the "no side" whistle? John Llewellyn, the Cardiff full-back, stood like a rock. He fielded all the high kicks aimed at him, as cool as the River Taff itself. Geoff Beckingham reached the heights as a hooker **when he heeled the ball against the loose head in the last three scrums**. If he had lost just one, it would have meant a draw. Then, the final whistle. The great roar from the crowd. My own feeling of elation and relief. The spectators, too exhausted to move, stayed on long after normal departure time. And my team carried me shoulder-high off the field. I shall never forget it. How magnificently the Cardiff pack - the whole side, indeed – had risen to the occasion. And yet we only had one combined practice together – on the Thursday before the game. The greatest satisfaction I personally got out of the game – apart from the honour of captaining the winning side, was the tactical success we achieved. We had planned to score early – before the All Blacks had settled down. And we did so. We were up 8 points to 3 within 20 minutes.

I'll always remember our first try. The ball went from the scrum to Rex Willis and on to Cliff Morgan. He short-punted over his opponent's head; caught it before it bounced; and then handed on to Alun Thomas, who, in turn, passed to Gwyn Rowlands. Gwyn made ground and, when challenged by Bob Scott, cross-kicked for the ball to land near the All Blacks' posts. A loose melee developed. Then Sid Judd gathered and dived over for a try. Gwyn Rowlands converted to give us a five-point lead. The All Blacks pegged us back when Ron Jarden kicked a magnificent penalty goal when a Cardiff forward had got offside. Then came our second try. From a set scrum the ball travelled from Willis to Morgan and on to me. I saw that Alun Thomas was covered so put in a short punt. Alun rounded his man, collected the ball, drew Bob Scott and passed to Gwyn Rowlands. And Gwyn ran 30 yards to score in the corner. Great players; great games; great days. I'll never forget them!'

In 'Taming the Tourists' we read of the excitement: 'The superior fitness of the touring team had overwhelmed Llanelli in the final twenty minutes. Would Cardiff suffer the same fate?... C.D. Williams was momentarily injured but played on after treatment and with little time left it was the extraordinary Bowes who led another foot rush. Llewellyn almost succeeded with an ambitious penalty attempt from halfway as the game entered its final few minutes. The singing had now reached a crescendo and out on the pitch it was mayhem. Scott had abandoned all pretence of being a full-back, lining up and running with his three-quarters. A high kick by him to the posts could have led to a replay of Jud's early score but this time it was Morgan to the rescue, collecting the ball under the noses of the opposition pack and clearing to touch. A converted try would still secure the draw and rescue the tourists' unbeaten record and at the last *breath they secured two attacking scrums on the home line.*

At such moments heroes are made and games won or lost. It was a situation made for Geoff Beckingham and his pals. "We knew that the All Blacks needed to score a try and convert it if they were going to pip us," he said, "and the word from one of the seagulls in the back row – that's what I called them – was that we should concede a penalty. But I was still thinking positively. Then John Nelson was whispering in my ear, going on about how we needed this ball. I told him to go back to the back row where he belonged. Stanley, JD and myself knew what to do. The All Blacks had the crucial put-in but I had noticed during the game that their scrumhalf, Vince Bevan, has a habit of spinning the ball in his hand then tapping the seam with his finger a moment before he fed it into the scrum. So the moment he did that I struck for the ball and won the ball on the tight-head. The heel shot back to Rex and then Cliff and he cleared to touch. The pixies had done their job again!"'

CARDIFF RUGBY FOOTBALL TEAM
THAT BEAT NEW ZEALAND RUGBY FOOTBALL TEAM
at Cardiff Arms Park, 21st November, 1953

Back Row: G. GRIFFITHS, J. E. LLEWELLYN, E. THOMAS, M. COLLINS, J. D. NELSON, J. D. EVANS

Front Row: C. D. WILLIAMS, A. D. S. BOWES, R. WILLIS, S. JUDD, B. L. WILLIAMS *(Captain)*, C. MORGAN, A. THOMAS, G. ROWLANDS, G. BECKINGHAM.

1953-54 Cardiff 8 New Zealand 3

Barry's Geoffrey Thomas 'Geoff' Beckingham was held in great regard by all his team-mates, providing fast scrum heels which allowed the backs to create Cardiff's two tries. Vitally, he hooked balls against the head when the Cardiff skipper decided to play defensive, no-risk rugby in the second half, something that both Cliff Morgan and Bleddyn always regretted. All match reports note the contributions made by the Cardiff front row, the *'pixies'*, in loose play throughout the game. Geoff had won his first two Welsh caps on merit earlier in 1953, against England and Scotland, but only won his third in 1958 at his career's end, as an eleventh-hour replacement for the great Bryn Meredith against France. Geoff played against all three Southern Hemisphere touring teams, with a total of 331 games joining his prop JD Evans in the top ten appearances for Cardiff, along with Lloyd, Elwyn and Tony Williams.

In two separate reports, the much lighter Cardiff pack were called 'terriers'. Dave Phillips in the *South Wales Echo* reported: *'For 80 minutes we saw the traditional skill and fire of what has rightly been termed the greatest rugby club in the world, countered by the all-action enthusiasm of a determined All Blacks side who tried everything in their power to whittle down Cardiff's half-time lead of five points in a storming grandstand finish. Maligned and under-estimated before the game as a suspect pack, the Cardiff eight, well led by international Sid Judd, played the terriers against a larger and heavier eight and seemed to increase in spirit and fervour towards the end rather than wilt as had been forecast.'* Terry McLean, the official correspondent of the New Zealand Press Association, was attached to the All Blacks for the tour, and reported to The Wellington Evening Post: *'One must pay proper and adequate tribute to the terrier-like qualities of the Cardiff forwards, who were only contained in the last few minutes, and to the elegance and speed of the Cardiff backs. Rowlands, Morgan, Willis, Bowes, Beckingham, Evans and Judd were the stars in what, to judge from the stupendous roar at the last whistle, will go down in history as one of the great achievements of Cardiff's long and illustrious rugby history.'* This must be a first in rugby reporting – the *'stars'* were the fullback, both halfbacks and the entire front row. McLean also wrote in the *Christchurch Star* that *'Cardiff used every opportunity to swing the play away from the All Black forwards, either by fast running or long kicking. This often resulted in breaks of up to seventy yards. The All Blacks pattern, on the other hand, was to keep the ball among or close to the forwards, and Bevan's many breaks from the scrum usually ended in turning the ball back towards the pack. This was punishing but not winning rugby.'*

A letter from the liaison officer for the New Zealand Tour to Cardiff RFC reads in part: *'May I, on behalf of the Four Home Rugby Unions, thank you and the officials of the Cardiff Club for the grand welcome and Game you gave to the All-Blacks Team on Saturday last. I think you will know by now that although our boys were beaten, they thoroughly enjoyed the Game, and greatly appreciated the manner in which the victory of the Cardiff side was gained. I am sure we shall not meet a side playing a better brand of Rugby Football during the whole Tour, and certainly not a side with as great a Team spirit…'*

A week later, Cardiff crushed a depleted Gloucester at Kingsholm 19-3 on 28 November. Gloucester were captained by the Welsh forward John Gwilliam, but had a man out injured and another five playing county rugby. *'The crowd of 9,000 gave the visitors a big ovation in tribute to last week's magnificent performance against the New Zealanders.*' Gwyn Rowlands converted 2 of 3 tries and kicked two penalties to Gloucester's dropped goal – '*Cardiff delighted the Gloucester spectators by their brilliant play, particularly behind the scrum, where Willis and Morgan gave the three-quarters many attacking chances. The three-quarters were in good form and yards faster than anything Gloucester had. Gloucester were not disgraced. It took the Cardiff giant-killers to capture their home record.*' The next game was lost 18-9 against Combined Services, where '*Touch-judge Gwyn Rowlands could have played for either side but preferred to rest in view of Saturday's final Welsh trial.*' Cardiff fielded 6 reserves, and scored 3 tries, missing all their kicks which could have won the game. Combined Services also scored 3 tries, all converted, and all interceptions as Cardiff threw the ball about. Worryingly, Peter Moss reported that '*near the end Swan prevented a score by Bleddyn Williams when the Welsh captain received the ball, going at full speed, only 20 yards out. But to outpace Williams is not such a feat these days.*'

The Saturday before Wales were to play the All Blacks in their 13th Tour match, '*Full of fire in the highest Welsh tradition, Cardiff were much too good for the Harlequins at Twickenham. On paper they won by a goal, a penalty goal and a try, but on the field their superiority was even greater.*' Cardiff won 11-0, playing with 14 men for much of the match after Dafydd James was injured. Sid Judd and Gareth Griffiths scored tries. In a separate report, Roy McKelvie wrote: '**Cardiff show wealth of pack talent** – *There is some indignation among the Cardiff team that **none** of their forwards, who more than held the All Blacks, is included in the Welsh side to meet New Zealand next Saturday. Those who saw Cardiff beat the Harlequins at Twickenham by a goal, a try and a penalty goal will understand. A country which can leave out such a forward as S. Judd and forgo such a useful hooker as Geoff Beckingham are either **suffering from rugby politics** or are uncommonly wealthy in players. Judd, outstanding among the forwards, scored a splendid try when his side were a man short (D. James having left the field) and Beckingham out-hooked N. Labuschagne, who played for England once last season.*

The contrast. *In view of Harlequins' good record this year, their forward play was unimpressive… A joy to the crowd was the play of the Cardiff back division, especially when Gareth Griffiths came from the wing to join Bleddyn Williams in the centre in the second half.* (Forward John Nelson had gone on the wing as Dafydd James had left the field, injured). *Then he scored a try converted by J. Llewellyn, who also kicked the penalty goal. Cardiff never seemed flat out, otherwise they might have won more easily. But after playing about behind the scrums in the first half, they got down to more serious business in the second. One saw how well Rex Willis can nurse Cliff Morgan, delaying his passes to draw the defence. Admirable, too, was the switching of the point of attack by Morgan, Williams and*

Griffiths, who used every trick, from the diagonal punt to the dummy scissors with which to confuse an alert defence.' Somewhat luckily, a player dropped out, and Sid Judd – but not Beckingham -was next week playing for Wales.

There is a lovely anecdote about a Harlequins game, recorded by Alan Evans in *Taming the Tourists*. Cardiff had a relatively small front row with Colin Howe and J.D. Evans propping. Geoff Beckingham related that *'we would lack bulk as a unit but would have the scrummaging technique to come out on top. We would be shorter than them as well but we had short fat hairy legs and they would have to come down to us as we would be packing low and hard.'* He was hooking against Labuschagne, the England hooker, a South African at Quins' home pitch of Twickenham: *'He was another tall hooker, well over six feet, and ripe for the treatment. Again we scrummaged very low so he and his props were really struggling. Late in the game I even "hooked" the ball back with m head. As it happens Bleddyn Williams who was out in the centre spotted what I'd done. We won the game and as we were coming off the field he came over to give me a ticking off for illegal tactics. My props, 'JD' and Stanley agreed. Bleddyn shook his head and said "That's the trouble with you flaming forwards, you always stick together – but don't do it again!" I muttered "not until next time" ... he wasn't amused.'*

Four weeks after Cardiff beat them, NZ had another fixture-less week before the match with Wales. And a good-looking 5-foot 10-inch, well-built boy from Taff's Well captained Wales, as he had Cardiff, against them. A packed Arms Park saw a Wales team containing five of Cardiff's backs, with Sid Judd playing flanker and scoring a try, something he did every fourth game on average. The team was: Gerwyn Williams (London Welsh), Ken Jones (Newport), Gareth Griffiths (Cardiff), Bleddyn Williams (Cardiff, captain), Gwyn Rowlands (Cardiff, his first cap), Cliff Morgan (Cardiff), Rex Willis (Cardiff), Billy Williams (Swansea), Dai Davies (Somerset Police), Courtenay Meredith (Neath), Rhys John (Neath), Rees Stephens (Neath), Sid Judd (Cardiff), John Gwilliam (Gloucester) and Clem Thomas (Swansea).

Gwyn Rowlands for Wales, and Jarden for NZ scored a penalty each, 3-3, and then Bill Clark had his New Zealand try converted by Jarden – 8-5. Ten minutes into the second half Gareth Griffiths went off with a dislocated shoulder, but somehow returned to play (no pain-killing injections, then!), against medical advice. He was not to play for months after. Bleddyn had torn his thigh ligaments, *'yet played on in pain and disguising his lack of mobility'*, causing him also to be unavailable to Wales and Cardiff for two months. With 15 minutes to go, Wales were losing 8-5, but Cardiff's Sid Judd plunged over to touch down and level the scores at 8-8. Soon after, the other wing forward Clem Thomas was hemmed in on the wing and caught the All Blacks flat-footed, when he launched a diagonal kick into the New Zealand 25. Wing Ken Jones latched onto the loose ball to score the winning try, converted by Gwyn Rowlands, to complete Wales's third victory in four meetings with New Zealand. Cardiff wing Gwyn Rowlands had made a major contribution with his kicking, as Wales triumphed 13-8. Ah, the good old days. We must again mention Dr. Gwyn Rowlands. He not only scored a try and conversion in Cardiff's 8-3 win over the New Zealanders, but on his 25th birthday a month later, he won his first Welsh cap, kicking a penalty and two conversions for Wales (a try was only 3 points, remember). Gwyn in the two games scored a try, a penalty and three conversions, 12 points of the Cardiff and Wales totals of 21. Cardiff and Wales were New Zealand's only two losses on a tour of 29 games in Britain and Ireland, although later France unexpectedly beat the exhausted tourists 3-0

My Proudest International
The Welsh team which I led to victory over the All Blacks at Cardiff in 1953

As an aside, Clem Thomas' cross-kick, like that of Gwyn Rowlands for Cardiff against the All Blacks, was a similar piece of quick thinking to that of Lloyd Williams of Cardiff, son of British Lion Brynmor of Cardiff, also a Wales scrumhalf. Lloyd was pressed into service on the wing in the 2015 World Cup pool game against England at Twickenham, as Wales were without 10 backs through injury – a perennial Welsh problem has been injuries to our best players. Whereas England had a choice of perhaps 50-60 players suitable for internationals, Wales never has more than perhaps 25, and long-term injuries affect Wales much more. George North had to move from wing to the centre, and Lloyd was the third-choice scrumhalf. During the game, backs Scott Williams and Liam Williams left on stretchers and wing Hallam Amos went off with an arm injury after 67 minutes, being replaced by Lloyd Williams. Even before the tournament started Wales had world-class players Jonathan Davies, Leigh Halfpenny and Rhys Webb ruled out. The Welsh forwards struggled against a stronger pack, and Johnny May's try was converted by Farrell, who also dropped a goal and kicked 4 penalties.

Wales changed their approach at half-time to try to reduce the number of set pieces. Biggar's kicking kept England from walking away with the match. England led 25-18 with 7 minutes to go, seemingly in control. A Welsh move saw Lloyd Williams pinned on the left touchline, but he looked up and cross-kicked for Gareth Davies to score under the posts. Biggar converted, and kicked one more penalty, scoring with all 7 kicks. In this Rugby World Cup Pool A game, Australia, hosts England and Wales were placed in the same group, although being ranked second, third and fourth respectively in the World Rugby rankings as of 21 September 2015. The draw for teams in groups was held, moronically, three years earlier, with Fiji and Uruguay being in the same group. In the other groups, South Africa and Scotland faced Japan, Samoa and the USA. New Zealand and Argentina played Tonga, Georgia and Namibia. France and Ireland played Italy, Canada, Romania. An easy passage for the top two teams in each group. It does not matter what sport, the authorities in charge are either inept, corrupt or both. Australia and Wales went through from this so-called '*Group of Death*' with England being eliminated. In the 2022 World Cup, Wales are again in the same pool group as England, Australia and Fiji.

In *The Guardian*, Paul Rees reported an interview with Bleddyn, 55 years after the 1953 New Zealand game, on 20 November 2008*: '*When Wales last defeated New Zealand, their players arrived in Cardiff from various parts of the country on public transport less than three hours before kick-off. They had a quick lunch at a hotel near the Arms Park and then walked down Westgate Street, mingling with supporters, to get into the ground. The year was 1953 but post-war austerity did not explain why players who filled stadiums were treated little differently from those who played on deserted park pitches. The contrast to today could not be more marked: the current Wales squad, preparing to face New Zealand at the Millennium Stadium, have been housed all month at a five-star hotel in the Vale of Glamorgan and they will arrive for Saturday's match in a luxury coach with a police escort.*

Bleddyn Williams, now 85, captained Wales 55 years ago, having led Cardiff to victory over the All Blacks at the Arms Park the previous month. He is the Welsh Rugby Union's guest of honour on Saturday, fittingly so, not just because of his exploits all those years ago but because then, when amateurism was sacred and its principles rigorously enforced, players were treated as second-class citizens with their legitimate expense claims constantly challenged. Why take the train when the bus was cheaper? Not that Williams, who was regarded in his day as the prince of centres, able to sidestep off both feet and the master of the outside break, envies the professionals of today.

*"I was glad I played when I did, you relied on your wits when you went into a game, not hours of analysis on the opposition. You played the game as you saw it and, while international players today are paid handsomely, and why not given the money they generate, fulfilment in my era came in a different way. Coaches today complain if they do not have more than a week to prepare for a match, but before we faced New Zealand in 1953, **we just had a one-hour run-out** on the Friday afternoon at Glamorgan Wanderers (a club in a western suburb of Cardiff). Players arrived at the ground by bus or train and returned home immediately afterwards, gathering again in Cardiff at 12pm on the day of the match. There were no coaches then and I suppose I took charge of the session.*

We just talked about a few things. Some of us had had the advantage of playing against the All Blacks for Cardiff and I had watched their game at Llanelli. I knew a bit about them anyway, having toured New Zealand with the Lions in 1950, but in those days it was about what you wanted to do, not stopping the opposition. They were more innocent times: you could walk among supporters to the ground because few recognised you. They were good (times) *to play in and you made lasting friendships."* Speak to a player after an international today about a certain incident in a match, and the common reply is: "I will have to look at the video."

In the 1950s video was just a Latin verb to be conjugated in a classroom. *"I have to admit that rugby today does bore me at times,"* said Williams. *"I played for the love of the game, and I just worry that all the time put in on the training field and all the days and weeks spent in hotels is creating a boredom factor. I only ever spent one night in a hotel before a home match, when we played in Swansea."* Wales have not beaten New Zealand since that December afternoon in 1953, six days before Christmas. They were not expected to do so then, despite Cardiff's success and the fact that the All Blacks had never won a match at the Arms Park. New Zealand, as now, were the top-rated team in the world and they were particularly strong in the forwards. They had been matched up front by Cardiff, but **Wales chose none of the club's pack**, although the back-row Sid Judd did play after Glyn Davies suffered an injury. (The wonderful Sid Judd scored a try both for Cardiff and Wales against the All Blacks).

"Club teams generally did better against touring teams than Wales," said Williams. *"Players knew each other while international matches outside the Five Nations were few and far between. A touring side had a distinct advantage because of the time they had spent together, but we were playing in front of 50,000-strong Welsh crowd. I cannot say I was surprised that we won, just the way we did: we were trailing 8-5 in the last 15 minutes, when the superior fitness of the All Blacks should have told, and our wing Gareth Griffiths was playing with a dislocated shoulder while I had torn ligaments at the top of my thigh."* Williams was not to play

for another two months after the victory over New Zealand, but it was his injury that led to the winning score after Judd had levelled the scores with a try. Clem Thomas, a back-row forward, had the ball on the wing and confounded the defence by kicking diagonally into the New Zealand 25. "I was standing next to Clem and, if he had passed to me, I could have done nothing," said Williams. "It was the cleverest and quickest bit of thinking I had ever seen from a forward. The ball bounced in space and Ken Jones (the wing) nipped in to score. I never thought then that 55 years on we would be waiting for our next victory over the All Blacks. I live in hope and, perhaps, the ball will bounce our way again on Saturday."' Bleddyn wrote *'I played the last 20 minutes in extreme pain, having torn ligaments at the top of my thigh. Indeed, that is why I had to cry off after being selected for the Twickenham match against England, and I did not play for nearly two months.'*

On Boxing Day 1953, the Neath-Aberavon derby had to be cancelled, and the Maesteg-Bridgend derby was abandoned in the second half. Those in 'rather late middle age' among us, who remember the state of pitches in those days, can easily understand what inspired Llanwrtyd Wells to hold its annual world championship bog snorkelling event. Of that afternoon, we read of Jack Matthews (*'a Wasp for the day'*) playing well <u>against</u> his beloved Cardiff: *'Skated to Victory – Boxing Day sees the commencement of the pantomime season at Cardiff Arms Park, and we had a spectacle that provided the thrills of a Christmas extravaganza. On a surface as slippery as the ice at the Wembley Pool, Cardiff skated to victory against a plucky Wasps side to win by 12 points to three, and the Principal Boy in this engaging frolic was none other than that bright-as-Buttons genius little Cliff Morgan. Handling the slippery ball with commendable certainty, he waltzed this way and that to completely mesmerise the opposition... he had a hand in three of the Cardiff scores.'* There were tries by Alan Barter, Gordon Wells and a drop goal by Alun Thomas, with Sid Judd touching down yet again, after a lengthy period off the pitch being treated for an injury. *'It was surprisingly good football in the quagmire conditions and the handling of the greasy ball by the Cardiff backs was exemplary.'*

From 1928 to 1973, Cardiff won 33 games against Watsonians, drew one in 1949, and lost only one, on 28 December 1953. Dave Phillips' headline reads *'Cardiff "14" Fail to Hold Watsonians. Cardiff, without six of their regular backs and further handicapped by the loss of Nicholls (injured) in the first half, suffered defeat by 13 points to 5 at the hands of the Watsonians, at Arms Park today.'* Centre Nicholls was taken off on a stretcher and taken to hospital after a crash-tackle, with Nelson coming out of the pack to go on the wing, and Alun Priday missed several kicks. Lloyd Williams made a try for C.D. Williams, but without internationals Bleddyn Williams, Gwyn Rowlands, Alun Thomas et al, *'a shadow Cardiff side lost suffered their fifth defeat of the season.'*

Cardiff were still the team to beat, and Bath reported for their home game (nearly always when Wales were playing England on the day) of 16 January, losing 20-9: '*Despite contributing four players to the Wales v England international, Cardiff comfortably amassed 4 goals and 3 tries without reply from Bath. The homesters were without Kendall-Carpenter and the injured Mike Terry. The pitch was in perfect condition for open Rugby, and the visiting backs had a field day. The Bath pack put in a fine performance, but were not able to provide Royston Collins with the necessary quick ball. In consequence, good attacking opportunities were lost. Individual efforts by Addenbrooke and Lewis towards the finish, did not bring the rewards they deserved. Cardiff remained well and truly on top. THUMBS DOWN v CARDIFF There was a flood of 'Letters to the Editor' following this encounter and we have included a few 'cuttings.' "It was indeed disappointing to see such a puerile display by our Bath side." "Having seen the game between Cardiff II and Bath, it was a treat to see rugby football as it should be played - but by the Welshmen. I only wish Bath could play more like it. Do the Bath players practise in the week, for practice makes perfect?" "This disastrous defeat may stand Bath in good stead if they can learn from it the necessity of quick heeling, the art of always being in position, both to check an opposition attack and to initiate their own." "I wonder how well advised the Club is in giving regular games to the young R.A.F. players who are in the neighbourhood for a very limited period." Several letters were in this vein, calling for the fostering of local talent.*'

On 23 January 1954, the fourth year in a row that Sale were given fixtures, they were beaten 31-3, '*with Beckingham outplaying Eric Evans, the English hooker, Cardiff's three-quarters took advantage of all the chances given to them.*' Both sides had a dropped goal, and John Llewellyn converted tries by J.D. Nelson (2), Alun Thomas (2), Cliff Morgan, Rex Willis, Derek Murphy and Sid Judd. Having scored 20 tries to one in four years, fixtures were discontinued against this excellent Lancashire side. Sid Judd, Gareth Griffiths, Rex Willis and Cliff Morgan each played three times against New Zealand, for Cardiff, Wales and the Barbarians. For the Baa-Baas loss against Cardiff, 16-0, Gwilym Evans' headline was '*Beckingham out-hooks Evans of England.*' **In the UK the All Blacks suffered only two defeats, to Wales 13-8 and Cardiff 8-3.**

Swansea held them to a draw 6-6, and Ulster also at 5-5. In a 36-match tour, the only other losses were 11-8 to South-West France and 3-0 to France. They beat Ireland 14-3, England 5-0 and Scotland 3-0. In their other 3 Scottish games, against strong representative teams, they scored 83-6. We must realise that Cardiff players turned out in a few charity games each season, fund-raising for good causes and other rugby clubs, where the 'Firsts' were expected to play, and of course there were pre-season trial matches for Cardiff, plus three Welsh trials to endure. There were also regular county fixtures, and in this season the Glamorganshire team included Cardiff's Cliff Morgan, Rex Willis, Bleddyn Williams, Gwyn Rowlands, Alun Thomas, Derek Murphy, Geoff Beckingham and Sid Judd. They beat Monmouthshire and drew with London Counties. Schoolteacher and backrow forward Judd scored 43 tries in 184 games, along with 30 conversions and 4 penalties, winning 10 caps. A Barbarian, he played three seasons of internationals and was Cardiff captain before he was 26. Judd was certain to go on the 1955 Lions Tour to South Africa but his health was failing. He was a wonderful number 8 or flanker, but becoming ill, Sid had to stop playing aged just 27 and died three years later from leukaemia.

Bleddyn, in many club match reports, is described as *'brilliant'* in this season. With 17 touchdowns he scored most tries, and wing Dr. Gwyn Rowlands scored 16 tries and kicked 33 goals to amass a total of 127 points. In just 30 games, back-row Sid Judd got 10 tries, Cliff Morgan 9, and 7 each came from Colin Bosley and Derek Murphy. The 'veteran' prop Stan Bowes was elected Athletic captain but was selected for the First XV no fewer than 36 times. Peter Goodfellow deputised, and the 'Rags' record was P35, W26, L6, D3, points 531 to 161. They had to use 68 players, and those who scored most tries were Derek Murphy 10, Colin Hewett and Bryn Mapstone with 9 each, and J. M. Griffiths (Gareth's brother), and Howard Nicholls 7 each. Bryn Mapstone of Taff's Well also played 7 times for the Firsts. Alun Priday was the leading kicker with 38 goals, and Bryn Mapstone was also successful with 22. Athletic XV caps were awarded to Bleddyn's brother Lloyd Williams, the remarkable prop Colin Howe and to Colin Bosley, John Dodd, J. M. Fitzgerald and E. Forster. Lloyd had played for the Firsts in 1952-53 and also this season, deputising for Rex Willis, and on Willis's retirement was soon to be a first-choice scrum half for Cardiff and Wales.

To celebrate a remarkable year, *'The Cardiff Rugby Supporters Club (President Percy F. Bush and G. B. Jones, hon. secretary) held an annual dinner in the Royal Hotel. The players who had triumphed over the All Blacks, club officials and the press were invited to a happy function. Amongst those who spoke at the gathering were Rhys Gabe of 1905 fame and Billy Cleaver. On the menu card was printed Cardiff's victory over the All Blacks, which was and will ever remain one of the finest games of all time.'* There was an annual dinner for decades after this, for the players who took part. A *Football Echo* headline indicates <u>the impossibility of Cardiff achieving an unbeaten season</u>: *'Cardiff's Mid-Week Fixtures.* **Wholesale Reshuffling Tarnishes that Record** *– Cardiff R.F.C. can be forgiven if they look with a certain amount of distaste at mid-week fixtures for, of their five defeats in 23 games this season, only one has been sustained on a Saturday, and that was a narrow reverse against Swansea at St Helens on October 17. Llanelly (8-3), Northampton (22-9), Combined*

*Services (18-9) and Watsonians (13-5) were all mid-week upsets in which "shadow" sides (often Cardiff in name and little else) were involved. The latest in the series was staged at the Arms Park on Monday when a side labelled "Cardiff" (but without seven of their recognised stars)' were beaten by Watsonians. 'To add to the tale of woe, Howard Nicholls was carried off the field suffering with concussion, and a 14-man team just could not manage to stave off the defeat. Without wishing to put forward any alibis – the "Team That Beat The All Blacks" shouldn't need any! – it does look as if wholesale reshuffles such as we saw on Monday are tarnishing the record of a side who have already **proved this season their claim to be considered the "Best Club in the World."**'* In the Swansea away defeat 11-9, both sides scored a try and two penalties, but Swansea converted their try. Cardiff had won the previous 6 games, scoring 15 tries to 3, and were to win the next 3, scoring 8 tries to nil. Thus in the 10-game sequence from October 1950 to December 1954, Cardiff only lost one match by a conversion, scoring 24 tries to 4. With a full team, the club would have been unbeatable).

* Bleddyn was reminiscing just before the 22 November 2008 game when Wales were soundly beaten 29-9, before 74,000 people in the Millennium Stadium, tiring badly in the second half. New Zealand performed the *haka*, and the Welsh team lined up facing them on the halfway line. The *haka* ended, and Wales were expected to turn away, so the match could start. Being informed that this was an act of submission, Wales stayed stock-still. Eventually New Zealand moved after the referee had implored both teams and threatened Wales with a penalty. Wales had the better of the game for about 20 minutes but lost 22-9. Sean Edwards then relentlessly forced Welsh players into becoming among the world's best-conditioned teams. Wales only lost 19-12 to NZ in the following year, and their fitness helped the Welsh towards Grand Slams in 2008, 2012 and 2019. Indeed, just a month after that first New Zealand humiliation, in the **2008** Six Nations, England were outscored 2:1 on tries as Wales won 26-19 at Twickenham. Then in Cardiff Wales scored 3 tries to nil, defeating Scotland 30-15, then outscored Italy 5-1 on tries, winning 47-8 in Cardiff. Ireland were beaten a try to nil in Dublin 16-12. The Grand Slam climax was in Cardiff, two tries to nil, 29-12 against France. That made 13 tries to 2 in total, 148 points against 66 – a well-deserved Grand Slam by the side that played all the rugby. Wales has won 12 Grand Slams to England's 13, France's 9 and Ireland's 3. When one considers that England has 17 times as many registered players, a far higher income and can call on the products of its former Empire – and often does – it is a fabulous record. There are around 2 million Welsh people living in Wales at present in a population of 3 million – a third say they are not Welsh. There are 56 million people living in England, the most overcrowded country in Europe after Malta, and 67

297

million in France. There are 5 million people in Eire and almost 2 million in Northern Ireland – both the nation and the region represent Ireland. Thus Wales, with c.2 million people, plays Scotland – 5.5m; Ireland – 7m; England - 56m and France - 67m. And rugby has always been a minority sport compared to soccer in Wales, with player numbers dropping annually.

Wales had not won the Grand Slam since 1978, when they achieved it in 2005, then 2008, 2012 and 2019. The **2005** season was marvellous, a thrill for the nation, scoring 17 tries, 151 points to 77. First England fell in Cardiff 11-8, Shane Williams scoring the only try. Next, in Italy 6 Welsh players scored a try apiece to a single try, 38-8. In France, Wales were under the cosh for the first half, with France scoring two tries in the first 14 minutes, and then Wales were constantly defending. Stephen Jones scored his second penalty in the 6th minute of injury time for France to lead 15-6 at halftime. I was down Trecco Bay for a Celtic Festival in a crowded, despondent room and then announced to everyone that *'We've got this!"* The Welsh defence had been tremendous to contain the French. Once Wales had settled, France were not going to score another try. Cardiff wing-forward Martyn Williams scored in the second and fifth minutes of the second half and France were facing a different team, Wales winning 24-18, restricting France to a dropped goal. The Grand Slam was in sight. Scotland were smashed away 46-22, six tries to 3, with Scotland scoring the last two tries. Wales were 38-3 up at halftime and eased off, not wishing to get injured for the final match, Scotland winning the second half 19-8. It was a breath-taking display of attacking, running, passing, skilful rugby. In Cardiff, Ireland were beaten 33-20, and there was some beer drunk in Cardiff that evening.

In the first game away in Ireland in **2012**, Wales scraped home 23-21, 3 tries to 2; in Cardiff Scotland were beaten 27-13, 3:1 on tries; England away were beaten 19-12, a try to nil; in Cardiff Italy lost 24-3, 2-0 on tries; and to finish the season, Wales scored the only try of the game, beating France 16-9. Points 109-58, 10-3 on tries. **2019** was the 4th Grand Slam since 2005, beating France away 24-19; Italy away 26-15; England at home 21-13; Scotland away 18-11; and Ireland home 25-7. One apologises for deviation, but Grand Slams are something else in rugby history.

After World War Two, the **Five Nations Championship** restarted in 1948 and was played up to 1998, Italy joining the following year. Wales won 5 **Grand Slams (1950, 1952, 1971, 1976, 1978)** – there would have been a sixth in 1972 but the Irish match was cancelled because of death threats. England also won 5, 3 coming in the 1990s thanks to a superb pack. France won 6, Scotland 2 and Ireland 1. 21 Grand Slams in 50 years. However, counting shared championships, Wales won 20, France 16, England 13, Ireland 8 and Scotland 6. In the **Six Nations**, from 1999 to 2020, Wales won **4 Grand Slams - 2005, 2008, 2012 and 2019.** France won 3 in 2002, 2004 and 2010; England won 2 in 2003 and 2016; and Ireland also won 2, in 2009 and 2018. This is a marvellous statistic from a poorly funded country. Wales, England and Ireland each won 5 Triple Crowns. Of the 22 Six Nations International Championships, England won 7; Wales 6 (2002, 2008, 2012, 2013, 2019 and 2021); France 5 and Ireland 4. (Championships are no longer shared). Wales pulls far above its weight in international rugby, at a time when regional rugby and poor funding has harmed the club game.

DR. JACK MATTHEWS OBE 21 June 1920 – 18 July 2012
1936-7 to 1938-39 - Welsh Secondary Schools rugby centre
1937 Welsh AAA junior 220 yds champion
1938-39 Senior Welsh Rugby Trial (aged 18)
1939 second in the Senior Men's AAA 100 yards; third in the 220 yards
1939-40 - 1944-45 Cardiff University Medical School, Royal Army Medical Corps doctor
1944-45 – Five Victory Internationals for Wales, captaining vs. France
1945-46 – 1953-54 Cardiff RFC, 180 games, 54 tries
Cardiff Captain 3 seasons: 1945-46, 1946-47, 1951-52
Cardiff Athletic 1952-53-1954-55, five games for First XV
Wales – 17 caps
Wales Captain vs France 1951
1950 Lions Tour of Australia and New Zealand – played **all six Tests** alongside Bleddyn in 5 tests.
1980 British Lions doctor
Cardiff RFC Chairman 1954-55
1981 OBE
1999 Cardiff Rugby Hall of Fame
2013 **World Rugby Hall of Fame**, alongside Bleddyn

'A cross between a bulldozer and a brick wall'; *'Man of Iron'* comments from 1950 Lions Tour

Jack played alongside Bleddyn Williams in 1938, and intermittently throughout the war years, before being capped for Cardiff in the first post-war season of 1945-46. Only 5 feet 8 inches, but 15 stone, he was 25 when he started playing for Cardiff, as captain, alongside his best friend Bleddyn Williams. In 1943, Jack was stationed as a RAMC doctor at RAF St Athan, just west of Cardiff, and fought future world champion 'Rocky' Marciano in an amateur boxing match. Marciano became a professional heavyweight after the war, winning 49 of his 49 fights, 43 by a knockout. He ended his heavyweight career having won all seven bouts as World Heavyweight Champion. Marciano's punch was tested and featured in *Boxing Illustrated* in December 1963: *'Marciano's knockout blow packs more explosive energy than an armour-piercing bullet and represents as much energy as would be required to spot lift 1,000 pounds one foot off the ground.'* Dr. Jack easily held him to a draw in a three-round bout.

On 20 July 2012, the *Western Mail* reported: *'Matthews recalled: "We had a great post-war side with Cardiff. Our home gate was 35,000, that was the average. Cardiff soccer were in the First Division then and we were getting more than them. Bleddyn and I had been playing together since 1938 and we've been friends ever since." Until just four years ago, the pair spoke every day and would continue to meet once a week for lunch to discuss rugby. "Everybody knows how tough he* (Jack) *was, but I played countless games with him and he was a beautiful passer, bloody quick, and a magnificent captain. He made Cardiff the side they were," said Bleddyn Williams in an interview shortly before his death in 2009. They had continued their devastating club partnership on the Lions tour to New Zealand and Australia in 1950. Matthews played all six Tests against the All Blacks and Wallabies, and it was the New Zealand public who christened him the "Iron Man", for his whole-hearted tackling against the home side. His association with the Lions did not end with his retirement as a player, and in 1980 he was named the Lions' first official doctor for the tour to South Africa. "There were a tremendous amount of injuries and there weren't many games where we had 15 men on the field. It was hard work," said Matthews years later.'*

David 'Dai' Richards, the excellent Swansea, Wales and Lions centre was Swansea's regular fly-half, but had been switched to centre by Wales because of the brilliant Cardiff partnership of Gareth Davies and Terry Holmes. Richards was 5 foot 9 inches and weighed 12st 10lbs. He pointed out to Simon Thomas in *walesonline* (*'The Tales of Dai Richards – The Rugby Star who's Glad He Played When He Did'* 28 April 2021) that during the late 1970's and early 80's, he *'spent 15 years trying to avoid people, whereas the modern game is about physical contact in midfield. It's a different game to the one we played, there is no doubt about that. It is so physical. "In my day, you didn't want contact. You would try and beat somebody or go to a weak shoulder and offload. <u>You wouldn't go to ground if you could help it, you would try to keep the ball in play and keep it alive</u>.* (The author's underlining – a bit different to today's ugly game.) *I don't think I would have been able to cope physically in the centre today, I would have had to go to play No 10.'* Chosen for the controversial 1980 Lions Tour to South Africa, Dai reminisced *'Gareth Davies and Ollie Campbell were the two outside-halves and they both got injured early on. So, I then played something like five games on the trot at fly-half, which I really enjoyed. What's remarkable about that trip was the back-room staff. It comprised precisely three people - team manager Syd Millar, coach Noel Murphy and doctor Jack Matthews. We didn't have a backs coach. The most senior guys took the session, whereas now it's almost one for one* back-up. And whoever was the physio at the particular ground we played, we would borrow him'.

Richards fondly recalled Dr Jack Matthews, who had been dubbed the 'Man of Iron' on the Lions' 1950 tour of New Zealand and Australia. 'It was about my third game, and I was playing against Natal in Durban and I had a twinge in my leg. I was thinking I was hoping this is not a hamstring. After the game I went back to the hotel and thought I had better go up and see Jack, before I went out to dinner. So, I knocked on his door and he came to answer it in a long silk dressing gown, cravat, cigar in one hand and a huge glass of brandy in the other. I said, "Sorry to bother you", but before I could finish my sentence he held his hand up and said: "Piss off, I'm having my break, see you in the morning." It's a Lions tour, I was the only fit fly-half and it was "don't bother me now, this is my down time, I'll see you in the morning". But that's the way things were in amateur rugby. I remember that incident so well. He was a picture when he came to the door, I can assure you. He was a hell of a boy, Jack, a top, top character. He was a great centre in his day, as tough as teak. He boxed against Rocky Marciano when he was in the services and drew with him. That tells you a little bit about the man, how tough he was. I loved Jack, he was a great guy. I had the greatest admiration for him'.

In the first Test in Cape Town, Richards was back in the centre, as Ireland's Tony Ward had been called up as a replacement No.10. The game ended in a 26-22 defeat, despite Ward slotting six kicks to add to a Graham Price try. Dai recalled, 'The forwards played very well. We probably didn't play as well as we should have done behind. We definitely could have won it. It was a real shame.' Only a week later, Richards' tour came to an early end when he dislocated his shoulder against Transvaal in Johannesburg. 'That was the end of me, I just remember being tackled and somebody fell smack on top of me and pressed my shoulder to the ground. There was nowhere for it to go. It just popped out. It wasn't a particularly nice experience. It was pretty painful. The muscles around the joint tend to contract when you have a dislocation. The physio - I don't know where we got this guy from - had his foot under my armpit trying to push it back in. Well, I was nearly passing out. It wasn't pleasant. Thankfully, Dr Jack told him to stop. He said medically that's not the soundest way to put a shoulder back in! I went off to hospital and they gave me something to knock me out. The muscles relaxed around the joint and it popped back in. I did ask whether I could stay on and try and play some part in the tour later on, but with the dislocation it would take too long.'

During an interview in 2008 'Dr. Jack' said he had delivered, "at least 7,500 babies, many during home visits in the middle of the night before a game", during his 50 years as a GP in Cardiff. He was always seen in company with Bleddyn Williams in his leisure time, watching Cardiff home and away or sitting in the clubhouse, chatting to all and sundry.

Martyn Sloman reminisced: '*As I was born in 1946, I must have seen Bleddyn Williams play; to my great regret, I cannot remember it. My father took me as a very small boy to the occasional Cardiff game but by the time I was able to follow the game, the greats of 1953 had retired. All I could do was ask for their autographs. Some 50 years later I was taking one of my sons to a Cardiff game. There walking along Westgate Street were Bleddyn Williams and Jack Matthews – on their way to take their seats. What was lovely is that there was not the distance of a pop-pass between them. I remember thinking that this was to way to grow old. Bleddyn was, needless to say, gracious in signing yet another autograph.*'

GARETH MEREDITH GRIFFITHS 27 November 1931 – 8 December 2016

1950, 3 caps for Welsh Secondary Schools
Won the Welsh Schools Senior boys 100 yards title in 10.8 sec; silver in the 220 yards.
Won the Welsh AAA Junior Men's 100 yards crown in 10.4 sec.
London Welsh RFC
Barbarians – **13** appearances*
National Service RAF 1949-51, played wing for RAF four times
Cardiff 1949-50 – 1959-60, 140 games, 74 tries
1953-54 St Luke's College, Exeter
Wales 1953-57, 12 games 5 tries
British Lions 1955, 3 tests against South Africa
1955-56 Loughborough University
*Apart from Tony O'Reilly of England in first place with 30 appearances, the next 9 appearances are English club players. 20 of the top 30 are English players (4 uncapped); Ireland have 3; Wales 3 (Rhys Williams, Phil Bennett and Tommy David); Scotland 3 and South Africa 1.

WRU OBITUARY: All Blacks slayer Gareth Griffiths dies:
He famously returned to the fray against the New Zealanders despite dislocating his shoulder in the second half. The doctor replaced the dislocation and Griffiths, then a 22-year-old student at St Luke's College, Exeter, demanded to go back on the field. Wales were losing when he left the field and Wales were reduced to 14 men against the tourists for 10 minutes. Gwyn Rowlands moved off the wing to cover Griffiths' centre position and Swansea flanker Clem Thomas switched to the wing while he was getting treatment.

In the book by Huw Richards, "Dragons and the All Blacks", which tells the story of the 1953 game, Griffiths explained how the injury happened and what the doctors did for him on the touchline before his brave return to the field. "I had the two centres coming at me with the ball. I don't know where Cliff (Morgan) *was, but Bleddyn* (Williams) *had to take the outside half," explained Griffiths. "I had to use what I used to call the 'basketball defence' where you pawed one of them to make him pass, but hoped to God you'd still be fast enough to get the other one. The problem was that when that happened you didn't hit him, he hit you – on this occasion it was (John) Tanner.*

I couldn't move my right shoulder or pick up the ball. When I told Bleddyn I couldn't move my shoulder, he said 'let's have a look' and then, 'you'd better go off.' "Nathan Rocyn-Jones, the WRU surgeon, told me to go and lie on the blanket on the touchline. I did as I was told and in a few seconds he put it back in. It was aching, but it certainly wasn't excruciating. You have to remember that all the muscles and the bits around them were warm. At 22, I still had a young body and Rocyn-Jones was an expert orthopaedic surgeon, so it was simple for him to put it right back. I never had any trouble with it after."

Wales just managed to hold out, as the All Blacks pushed for more scores, and the return of Griffiths lifted the Welsh team and the 56,000 crowd at Cardiff Arms Park. As Dr Gwyn Rowlands, his Cardiff clubmate, admitted, "what he did was exceptionally brave". The 13-8 win completed a dream double for Griffiths, who had been part of the Cardiff team that had beaten the tourists 8-3 at the same venue a month earlier. Even though he was a student in Exeter, Cardiff skipper Bleddyn Williams had asked him to come home to play with the Blue & Blacks in the build-up to the game. Griffiths had hoped to make a possible four appearances against the All Blacks, but in the end had to settle for three. The South-West Counties selectors decided against picking St Luke's students for their game, but he did play for Cardiff, Wales and then the Barbarians.

"Bleddyn asked me to come up for four or five weekends before the game. It was a long way, and I had to get special permission from the principal to be away, but it was worth all the effort," explained Griffiths. Born in Penygraig on 27 November 1931, Griffiths had none other than the former Wales and British & Irish Lions wing Willie Llewellyn as his next-door neighbour, when he arrived in the world. He learned his rugby at Porth County Secondary School and won a Wales Under-15 cap against England in 1946 at the age of 14. In 1950, he made three appearances for the Wales Secondary Schools, winning against Yorkshire Schools (14-3) and England (37-3), but losing to France (9-6). In the same side were future Welsh scrum-half Onllwyn Brace and one of Griffiths' future Lions teammates, Russell Robins.

As well as being a talented rugby player, Griffiths also excelled on the track. He won the Welsh Schools Senior boys 100 yards title in 10.8 sec, scooped silver in the 220 yards and won the Welsh AAA Junior Men's 100 yards crown in 10.4 sec... After leaving school he went into the RAF to complete his National Service and twice played for them at Twickenham in the Inter-Services Championships against the Army and the Royal Navy...

He also ran for the RAF and played rugby for them in France and Germany. After National Service he returned to Cardiff for a year before heading to St Luke's, where he was part of the famous side that became the first in British rugby to score 1,000 points in a season.... He made his Cardiff RFC debut at the tender age of 18 in an 8-3 win over Pontypool and went on to make 140 appearances for the club, between 1949-1960, scoring 74 tries. He was the eldest of four brothers who all played for Cardiff. J.M. Griffiths was a wing who played for the Rags and one game for the Firsts in 1953-54. Ritchie, a centre who won six Welsh Secondary Schools caps over three seasons, played 11 times for the senior side and David, a full back, played 5 times for the Rags and 6 times for the 1st XV before switching to Bridgend. David played at full back for the East Wales side that drew 3-3 with the 1967 All Blacks.

Vice-captain to Peter Goodfellow at Cardiff in the 1956/57 season, he also played for Llanelli in the 1960/61 season and made **13 appearances for the Barbarians**, including six on the 1957 tour to Canada and against the 1953 All Blacks. His Wales debut came in an 8-3 defeat against England in Cardiff in 1953 when he was one of six newcomers to the side. He went on to score three tries in the next three games in the Five Nations Championship as Wales finished second to England, the season after winning the Grand Slam. Five of his first six caps for Wales were on the wing, with the rest coming at centre. His three Test caps for the Lions in South Africa all came on the wing. Although not an original selection for the 1955 tour, he was called out to take over for the injured Scotland wing Arthur Smith and the sick Alun Thomas. He arrived on 18 July and made the most of his time on tour.

He scored in his first two games, against Transvaal and Rhodesia, and ended up with three tries in 12 games. He missed the victory in the first Test, but was picked to partner Ireland's Tony O'Reilly on the wing for the next three internationals. The Lions won the third Test, but lost the second and fourth games to leave the series tied at 2-2. Those were the only defeats Griffiths tasted in his 12 games in a Lions jersey...' A Welsh-speaker, he was selected for the Wales Athletics team on his return from South Africa. There followed a remarkably successful career in business management, living in Penarth with a holiday home in Newport, Pembrokeshire. His wonderful Art Deco home on the clifftop at Penarth has recently been completely renovated. He played in the winning team against the All-Blacks in 1953, and was the last survivor of the Cardiff winning team in that year. On his passing, Cardiff said in a statement on their website: 'He was a true great of the game and brought great credit on himself and Cardiff Rugby Club. Griffiths was born in Penygraig in the Rhondda, and went to Loughborough College where he excelled at rugby and athletics. His sprinting speed made him a dangerous and versatile attacking player, able to cover the wing, centre and full-back positions. He *joined Cardiff RFC in 1949 as a wing alongside the legendary centre partnership of Bleddyn Williams and Dr Jack Matthews.'*

CHAPTER 25 - '*THE WILLIAMS FAMILY (MORE THAN A RUGBY DYNASTY)*', *The Garth Domain* No.26 December 2004 - Don Llewellyn and Gerald Edwards.

In Bleddyn's greatest year, it is time to talk about the Williams brothers – their family background before, during and after the war, mainly in the words of brothers Brinley 'Bryn' and Vaughan. I was so pleased to meet author Don Llewellyn, film producer, rugby aficionado, historian, great patriot and promoter of the local Welsh dialect, and this book would have been impossible without the efforts of him and Gerald Edwards, to whom I am incredibly indebted. Gerald, a Taff's Well man and former rugby player, carried out the interviews and wrote them up. Let us start with the eight brothers and four sisters growing up in Taff's Well. In '*The Williams Family*' there is a long conversation between Bryn (Brinley) and Vaughan Williams, prefixed by an introduction by Don Llewellyn, that gives more family details: '*We learn from Bryn and Vaughan that their father was born in King's Road, Canton, Cardiff. Arthur Williams had been in the Glamorgan Yeomanry during the First World War, when he met their mother Nellie, who had been living in Gwaelod-y-Garth since she was five years of age. She had moved with her parents, from Ochrwyth in the Risca area, around 1903. Her father, Ted Roberts, who was a woodcutter, had come to settle at Bristol Terrace near the Gwaelod-y-Garth Inn. To get to the Gwaelod in those days, they would walk over Machen Mountain and drop down into the valley to catch the train, which ran on the Pontypridd, Cardiff and Newport line, (the old 'P.C. and N.' that ran through Machen). After coming through Caerphilly, they would alight at the halt near Glan-y-Llyn, and then cross the Taff by ferry.*' There was a ferry across the River Taff at this time, which enabled Arthur Williams from Taff's Well to court Nell Roberts across the river in Gwaelod-y-Garth, and after marriage they also initially lived at Bristol Terrace in Gwaelod (with her parents), where their daughter Dilys was born.

Later, Pont Sion Philip bridged the River Taff and the small boat service from the Ferry Inn ended. The next Williams children, three daughters and eight boys, were all born in a rented terraced house at Moy Road, Taff's Well. The four Williams daughters became Dilys Jones, Joan Roberts, Enid Pritchard and Mair Philips. Apart from his time in WW1, their father Arthur was usually a coal tipper in Cardiff Docks. Because of a feeder canal, ships could use Cardiff Docks at any time, despite the enormous tidal range, and there were permanent queues of railway wagons waiting to be unloaded and ships requiring the coal for export. Gangs of shunters ensured the constant flow of wagons for one 'tipper' to weigh it on the weighbridge, another would note the weight, a third man would move the wagon onto a cradle, and the fourth tipper would cant it through a chute to pour it into the ship's hold.

The wagon then ran back under gravity to the weighbridge for another weighing, so the exact amount of coal could be recorded. Dock charges and the wages of tippers and trimmers were based upon tonnage. Great care had to be taken not to break the large, friable coal, as customers would not pay for 'small coal' unless ordered. Thus, an anti-breaking (not braking) device, like a long box, was introduced into the chute and gently lowered into the hold. A cone of coal gradually built up, checking the impact of incoming coal. In this dark and dusty hold, the coal trimmers shovelled the coal sideways until the load was balanced, when another cone could be built up and balanced. It was back-breaking work, with the trimmers being paid by the colliery companies, and the shunters and tippers by the railway company. There were probably cold-water showers for the trimmers. It was a filthy, back-breaking job, with Arthur being described as a trimmer in several sources, rather than a tipper, and one imagines that Arthur Williams worked all the hours available to support his large family. Because of their continued exposure to coal dust, coal trimmers were far more likely to suffer from emphysema, lung and throat cancers and COPD than coal miners, severely shortening their life spans. Indeed, if Arthur Williams had been a coal trimmer, we may never have seen any of the Williams brothers. Arthur was a colliery clerk, and then a weigher and then a tipper in Cardiff Docks.

'Bryn also tells us that that his mother's father (Ted Roberts) had worked the lumber wagons up on the Brynau and later at Rockwood. He says that his grandfather must have been tough, for when he developed cancer of the tongue, he walked to Cardiff Royal Infirmary to have a part of it cut out. Returning home that same night he had gone to work "amidst the coal dust and all" unable to eat anything but a banana.' Edward 'Ted' George Roberts had been a collier when living in Gwaelod-y-Garth, so one supposes that his tongue cancer may have been caused by working conditions, and he then worked on lumber wagons. He would have walked there and back about 18 miles to Cardiff's Royal Infirmary. Ted Roberts was an imposing figure in a photo of the 1910 Taff's Well rugby team. He later joined the committee, and his son Tom Roberts was also a fine rugby player for the club. Another son, Roy Roberts, was to play for Cardiff, alongside the oldest of the Williams boys, his nephews Gwyn, Bryn and Bleddyn. There is a quote, 'It is clear that the natural aptitude for rugby possessed by the Williams brothers came from their mother's line.' However, their father's older brother by 18 years, Phillip, also played for

Taff's Well and Cardiff Athletic, and definitely had some influence. Of Arthur's daughter Nell Williams, née Roberts *She was a first cousin* of Ewart (Bill) Tamplin, another name from Welsh rugby's Hall of Fame and her own brothers also made a mark, with Roy distinguishing himself for Cardiff. The way in which this innate talent expressed itself is covered in the family's reminiscences, but here, in a conversation between brothers Bryn aged 84 and Vaughan, 73, we have a colourful evocation of other aspects of life in the remarkable village of Taff's Well during their younger days.* *However, Nell Williams (nee Roberts) was the cousin of Ewart 'Bill' Tamplin's father, with the same name, so the famous Bill Tamplin was a second cousin to the Williams brothers.

I repeat relevant parts of the dialogue between Bryn and Vaughan Williams, as it shows the sort of village life in which the boys and girls grew up – a forgotten, gentler and more innocent world. From the 1920s to the 1950s children had no toys except hand-me-downs, and there was little in the way of entertainment – this author had no TV or radio, not even electric light in the house in the 1950s. On Sundays a tin bath was unhooked from the backyard gate, and filled with hot water from pots boiling on the gas stove. Dad had the first bath, in front of the coal fire in the living room, followed by mum, me and then my younger brother. There was one toilet, outside in the tiny backyard. There was only gas lighting in the house, and even on the road, and televisions, phones, fridges, double-glazing, central heating and supermarkets were unknown. Most Welsh parents before the war lived hand to mouth, and a main ambition in the South Wales valleys was for sons not to go down the pits, but to become teachers. There was a massive exodus of qualified boys to become teachers in England. In the case of Barry, boys would want to work down the docks or join the Merchant Navy. Women's jobs, except in shops, were scarce. It is important to remember that our eight brothers and four sisters came from what today would be called poverty, but that was just natural for all of their generation. Children rarely stayed in the house unless the weather was really foul, as there was literally 'nothing to do' except read a library book. We had no radio or record player. However, everyone you knew was 'in the same boat', with little money. Only upon going to grammar school, did I and my friends from Cadoxton, meet boys who owned bikes and wore new clothes and whose fathers were 'professional' men. Very few married women worked – their role was the daily grind of shopping, washing clothes, feeding the family and so forth, with no vacuum cleaners, refrigerators, central heating, double glazing and so on. Working class kids – i.e. the massive bulk of British children - spent every available minute 'out', finding things to do, as explained by Bryn and Vaughan.

'**Bryn** – *When I was about eight years old, I remember I used to go with Ivor Williams' son Ken, who was the same age as me, down there* (to the River Taff) *by the baths.'* (Taff's Well had a swimming pool next to the thermal spring.) *That's where we used to throw stones at the Gwaelod kids and of course they would retaliate. Well Felix, Ken's brother, went down there one day on his own and he fell in, and you wouldn't know there is a cavern – and of course when he fell in, he went under it and they couldn't find him. They used grappling hooks and everything and even went down to Bale's farm, because on the bend in the river there was a spot, where if anyone drowned, they would be drawn into the side by the current. Oh yes, when those things happened, they would contact Ray Bale* or his brother George to take a look. I remember once going to Gwaelod when I was about three, according to my mother, and seeing a 'Penny Farthing' bicycle leaning against that little wall up the Zig Zag, and I wondered what the Hell it was! Somebody had come from somewhere with it. Fancy pedalling that up the Gwaelod Road!* *Ray Bale played for Cardiff, 176 times from 1934-35 (the first year that Gwyn Williams was a First regular) until 1948/49, playing alongside Bleddyn and Roy Roberts).

Vaughan – *I remember those four or five taps on the side of the road, where the Gwaelod people got their water.*

Bryn – *Yes, they were a feature of Gwaelod, weren't they. What about our side though – there's so many interesting things over here. That old Glyn-y-Llyn Station was a place of interest to us boys; it was one of the widest in the area, you know. The line was single-track with points (ground-frame) to send a passenger train down the line the same time as another train was coming up. It had a middle section and the one train would be shunted into this, to allow the other to pull alongside the platform.*

Vaughan – *Yes, and our old canal again. The canal bank used to be a thoroughfare. People would walk all the way to Melingriffith Works – do their shift, then walk all the way back.'* (Forges produced tinplate and iron at Whitchurch, Cardiff, between the River Taff and the Glamorgan Canal, and the factory was founded before 1750. Melingriffith became the **largest tin-plate works in the world** until 1806 and closed in 1957.) *'That canal was interesting no matter what season it was. The winters used to be so cold when I was young. Believe it or not, we used to go skating on the canal and play ice-hockey on it! Then there were those summers! I know they say we only remember the good things, but they were so HOT! And blackberries, well we used to go into the water – because the biggest blackberries were the ones that used to overhang the canal wall – not on the towpath mind – on the other side, we used to wade in to get them. And remember the moorhens there?*

Bryn – *And the dragonflies. We used to catch them and put them on our lapels! ... You know, a lot of good things have gone out of this valley. Today they'll do anything for so-called progress. That canal, for instance – just think what a wonderful amenity it would have been today. The original plan was for the new A470 to go up the valley on the other side of the river. Look at all the houses that would have been saved in Taff's Well and*

308

Nantgarw as well as that wonderful canal.

Vaughan – *I remember Mostyn Thomas of the farm up there on the Graig. He bought a house down by the Treble Locks, on the understanding that the road would go on the other side of the river. In the event, when he had to sell the place, he had less for the house, through compulsory purchase, than he had paid for it.*

Bryn – *"Spoil the Countryside" is their motto today. Anything for money. Money rules everything.*

Vaughan – *There's an awful lot gone. I remember from the 1930s, 40s and 50s. I've got some photographs of the carnivals galore in Taff's Well. Well, everyone used to dress up. You'd have all the excursions going to Barry Island – and to me Barry Island was the other end of the Earth, really. But there was something going on in Taff's Well all the time.'*

If I may interpolate, my favourite Welsh poet (along with David Jones) was the truly great Idris Davies, (1905-1953) who is, along with Jones in my book *100 Greatest Welshmen*. His *Gwalia Deserta* (*Wasteland of Wales*, 1938) was recommended as follows by T. S. Eliot... '*They are the best poetic document I know about a particular epoch in a particular place, and I think that they really have a claim to permanence.*' The long dramatic poem described the desert that industrial South Wales had become in the 1920s and 1930s. *Gwalia Deserta* shows a socially and politically committed poet, full of the imagery of mining-valley life in the terrible days of the 1930's. *The Bells of Rhymney* verses are his most widely known work – he was born in Rhymney, went down the pit at 14, and became a schoolmaster. Davies' *The Angry Summer* is a long book-poem about the summer of strikes in 1926 – a fabulous piece of work, leavened by a few verses of when the miners used to come down by train in their thousands to Barry on the weekends. As children in Cadoxton, Barry, at those times we used to avoid the crowded 'Island' like the plague, instead walking across the Docks heading to the adjoining (sewage-ridden) Jackson's Bay instead for a swim. (It was popular for cash-strapped parents because there was no shop selling ice-cream or sweets). In Davies' poem the light interlude on Barry Island was a popular poster with Welsh families having to leave Wales for work in England, and it begins thus:

Let's go to Barry Island, Maggie fach . . .
We'll have tea on the sands, and rides on the donkeys,
And sit in the evening with the folk of Cwm Rhondda,
Singing the sweet old hymns of Pantycelyn . . .'

Bryn – *I was thinking too of the Horseshoe Level – you know, on the side of the mountain just before you get to Mostyn Thomas's house you see it. It's a brick-faced curved ridge, horseshoe-shaped.*

Vaughan – *Yes, where that bit of handrail is on the right-hand side. If you look up to your right, you'll see an archway that is half-buried, that's what it is. The horseshoe ridge has recently been demolished. Another loss. Then* *there was the 'Big Pond' as we used to call it. It was a reservoir for the canal. Surplus water was released back into the canal when there was a water shortage during the summer months.*

Bryn – *Do you know that pond was about three-quarters of a mile around, and there used to be ducks there? Only once can I remember it being drained. At the top end, we used to go in there, no shoes on, nothing, only rolled-up shorts, and you could see all the eels going around.*

Vaughan – *Those eels used to come to the surface, and you could bash them on the head with a stick. There was someone down here in Moy Road, I can't remember his name, but his daughter's name was Heulwen and he had a sailing boat, which they used to tow up to the pond. But the most significant thing about that pond is this. Because it was a lovely spot, it was there that my oldest brother Gwyn, mind you I don't remember it myself, was training for the Taff Swim – and he trained for it up in the big pond.*

Bryn – *I'll tell you one thing. When Gwyn was training for the Taff Swim, he used to swim with me on his back! Of course, he was much bigger than me – well, he was like a man when he was playing schoolboy rugby.*

Vaughan – *I was thinking, Bryn, where I live now at Tyrhiw – I can recall a schoolboy international trial match being played there, and Bleddyn played fullback in that trial. Although he was an outside-half at school, that's where he was picked to play against England.*

Bryn – *Yes, was it 1937? The game against England was also played at Gloucester – and that's when the stand collapsed. Bleddyn was born in 1923, so it must have been 1937, actually. He started about 1941-42 for Cardiff. Of course, I played up in Cilfynydd – they were a great side to play for, too. I remember having Bleddyn with me one day up there, and the secretary thought he looked quite small in his striped Rydal School blazer. My answer was "Just put him on the field." I was playing outside-half for them – because Cardiff Rags had finished then, see, because of the war, and they couldn't get players. All the first team were in the Territorials – civilians, really, although they went to Singapore, mind.*

Vaughan – *One of the reasons Cilfynydd had such a good side in those days was the fact that a lot of them worked underground, and had not gone into the army, and of course they had guest players too, and that's how you went from Cilfynydd to Cardiff, isn't it?'* (Miners were a reserved occupation, too valuable to go to war, a complicated scheme which covered five million men in a wide range of jobs, needed to stay in Britain in the war. These 'scheduled' jobs also included railway and dockworkers, farmers, agricultural workers, doctors and schoolteachers. Bryn had the opportunity of working down the mine, but instead chose to join the Army, spending six years away).

Cilfynydd is just a few miles north of Taff's Well, sited on the ancient drovers' road, alongside the remnants of the Glamorgan Canal. The village

310

had been hit by tragedy. On 23 June 1894, its Albion Colliery was the scene of what was then the worst disaster in the South Wales Coalfield. The ignition of coal dust, following a detonation of firedamp, triggered a massive explosion, killing 290 men and boys. Of the 125 horses, only 2 survived. Many of the bodies were so badly mutilated that identification was virtually impossible, and there were instances of bodies being carried to the wrong houses. Almost everyone in the community lost someone in the disaster, with one family on Howell Street losing 11 members: the father, four sons, and six lodgers. The population was only around 3,500 people. In the Aber Valley, over the hill from the Taff Valley, at the Universal Colliery at Senghenydd in 1913, 440 miners died, including eight 14-year-olds – the rugby team changed its strip to black for decades. Glyn Davies played for Cilfynydd, then Cardiff after the war, but moved clubs as he was not guaranteed first team games. He then gained 11 Welsh caps from 1947-1951, while playing for Cambridge University, Pontypridd and Newport, before being replaced by Cliff Morgan in the Welsh team. Tiny Cilfynydd also generates international singing stars. Sir Geraint Llewellyn Evans, 1922-1992, was an internationally renowned bass-baritone. 1,700 people attended his funeral service at Westminster Abbey, with hymns sung in Welsh. Stuart Burrows, born in 1933, is a famous tenor from the village, again hailed across the world, and known as '*The King of Mozart.*'

Bryn – '*I'll tell you this, not many sides would beat Cilfynydd in those days. We beat Gloucester and oh! – we beat Pontypridd handsomely – what a local derby that was! Then I joined the Army, but I didn't let them know I was going. The last game we played was up on the Rec, as we called it, in Abertridwr. A charity game it as. Charity be buggered, they did everything but cut your head off with a scythe. But you know, as we said before, there's a lot of good things gone out of this valley. Just think of the characters that used to be around here: Mabon – Len Francis, and his brother too.*

Vaughan – *Oh, I remember the time of that heavy snow, '47 was it? Yes, '47. Do you remember, Bryn, when Lloyd went missing? Anyway our sister was living, squatting actually, in the 'Camp' at Rhydlafar. We looked everywhere for Lloyd, didn't we? Then we thought, as he was friendly with our sister's husband Dilwyn, Dilwyn Pritchard, that he might have gone over there to them, so we went up, didn't we Bryn, and it took us about four hours to get there. And when we got there, he was fast asleep in bed.*' Don Llewellyn recalls Rhydlafar in *Garth Domain 19*: '*Squatters moved into the vacated US Army Hospital and then the site was taken over for the Prince of Wales hospital, which, in due course, would lead the world in orthopaedic surgery...The local story begins with the departure of the Americans and the take-over by squatting families. Mrs Norma O'Brien tells of how she with her husband Doug (just home from the war), and* *without a home, were glad of the chance to put a roof over their heads. By the time the hospital was built, the O'Briens and the other squatting families had been accommodated elsewhere.'*

Bryn – *'Yes, he was asleep in bloody bed*!

Vaughan – *Mind you, Enid had managed to phone somebody in Taff's Well, to ask for a message to be taken down to my mother to say that Lloyd was all right, but the message had not been passed on. Anyway, Len and Jim – you know Len always had a red nose even when it wasn't cold, and as you know both brothers always had Wellingtons on. We walked across the footbridge – over where the rugby field was later. There was deep snow everywhere and we saw this pair of Wellingtons sticking up out of the snow, and somebody thought it was a pair of discarded boots. When they pulled on them, they discovered Jim fast asleep. There must have been some air-holes in there somewhere, but he was fast asleep!*

Bryn – *One time, I was driving along the road at night near Taff's Well Station, and there was Jim Francis right in the middle of the road, and I saw him just in time in my lights. Another time I saw him in the porch of the Park Hotel in Cardiff, dead drunk and sleeping on the steps. And there he was with the tools of his trade, which he always carried with him, his pick and his shovel! He also used to pretend to blow a bugle, and do you know, he always called me the 'Major'! When I would ask him how long he had been in the army, he would say, "Oh, for years, sir, for years!" But I'll tell you what, after Jim went to a home in Cardiff, he was altogether different. I saw him in the Taff's Well Inn one day, and he was all dolled up – he was like the Prince of Wales. I asked him, "Is that you, Jim?" and he said "Yes, Major, it's me." Len, though, was in a home up in the Hawthorn, wasn't he? I remember when I was at the 5th Welsh Club on Broadway in Pontypridd, who should tap me on the shoulder but Len. Well, he was the same, very smartly dressed. I have never seen such a transformation in all my life.*

Another thing from those years ago, Len and Jim used to work on the building sites, you know, and they had one of those builders' hand carts, the kind that had shafts in the front for the puller, and a bar at the back for somebody to push. Well one day we were up in Heol Berry, Gwaelod-y-Garth, and Len and Jim had their cart with them. Jim was pushing and Len was pulling, and of course it was bumping along, as the road was rough. Then they stopped and someone brought out an urn of tea. Well, they drank for a while, and do you know what Len did? Well, it didn't matter who was about. He took out his personal equipment, and standing there with his other hand holding the shaft of the cart, answered the call of nature there and then, in the middle of the road. "Len, for God's sake" I said, "what on Earth do you think you're doing?" He turned round and said, "Well, if you have to work like a horse, you might as well act like one."

Vaughan – *Yes, the characters have all gone. Take Jack Buttle.*

312

Marvellous man. There were those dances at Glan-y-Llyn Hall, and then there was the Georgian Club that Jesse Slee ran. We used to go there on Saturday mornings, and Jesse used to run film shows – like a matinee. Evan Williams did it after him.

Bryn – *Oh yes, Evan Williams, a kindly man who did so many good things for the village – along with Mrs Williams. They were both well thought of in the area.*

Vaughan – *Taff's Well, when you come to think of it, was self-contained, wasn't it, in those days – we had an undertaker, we had a tailor, we had four butchers, there was Thomas and Evans Universal Stores, three or four barbers, Paul Tripp the blacksmith, everything – you didn't have to go out of the village. Very few people went into town* (Pontypridd or Cardiff) *in those days.* (Remember that the Taff's Well population, having more building and incomers over the post-war years, is still under 4,000 people!)

Bryn – *The point has been made, that whereas the older residents are willing to talk, the newcomers are not so willing. Do you know the first thing they do, when they move into their new homes here? They build either an eight-foot fence or a six-foot eight wall – you know, so that they can't see over their neighbours. Years ago, washing day was a Monday, and people outside would shout up the lane to each other or wave – you don't see that today, do you?*

Vaughan – *Well, most of the homes in Taff's Well were terraced houses, you know, and people did talk. They sat out in the summer – they'd put the old chairs out and would be chatting with their next-door neighbours. And as I recall it, during those hot summers when we would go to the seaside, we would even leave the back and front doors open to allow a draught to go right through the house.'*

Bryn – *'And nobody ever lost any money either, although they would leave it for the milkman if they weren't there. And everybody was 'aunty' or 'gran' or whatever, even if you weren't related. It was a matter of politeness.*

Vaughan – *Yes, well if some mother was going shopping, her child would be looked after by a neighbour, hence 'aunty'. But you know when we consider what is happening in the world today, we know how lucky we were. Just imagine how we used to go camping up by the Brynau Brook. The point I'm making is that we'd be up there for a week, and our mothers wouldn't need to worry about us.*

Bryn – *Then there was Tom Morley, of course Roger Williams was his grandfather too. With Peter and Tom Morley, I used to go up to the barn you know, and the chickens were laying eggs there too, in amongst the hay. I had a dozen and a half eggs more than once, and they'd let me take them home to my mother.*

Vaughan – *There was another barn, just here opposite the house where Rhys Davies lived, you know, which had been Bryncoch Farm. Well, when*

313

they used to cut the grass where the Co-op Bakery is now, that is where Taff's Well used to play for a while. They would stack it here. Also, any excess from the meadow where Hillside Park is now. You know, from the orchard all the way to the top of Hillside Park.

Bryn – Yes it was a wonderful time for children up there near the little wood, especially during haymaking time with the men, on that meadow of Rhiw'r Ddar Farm. I recall taking Roger Williams's grandson Tom Morley, with the milk float drawn by Joey the pony, down to the Taff's Well Inn, to pick up a firkin of cider (a wooden barrel holding 86 pints), which had been delivered from Hereford. George Lovell, a Somerset man in charge of our haymaking, would tell us boys you could drop a coin in that cider and it would float!

Vaughan – I remember Roger Williams's horse. When we were kids, we'd run home from school in the summer because of the haymaking, and I used to lead the horse. He stepped on my foot once, and oh, he was a big Shire horse was Sam. Anyway, he had a growth in his side, and Roger wouldn't pay out for any vet – ever – you know. He went over to the farm and came back with a knife, and without hesitation stuck it into the horse's side. Oh, the pus and God knows what came out of it. The horse lashed out, but he was alright.

Then there was the matter of the evacuees (in the war). Well, we had some down here too and the name of one of them was John Wakin. Here was billeted just here near Bryncoch, with Mrs Morris. He was a tall, lanky kid, very quiet but he was animal mad. He always had something in his pocket, like a blindworm or something. During the war, the old Glan-y-Llyn Station was a warehouse for Bulmer's Cider, and we used to watch John Wakin – 'Wakey' – coming down the road, and he would be swaying about, and we used to wonder how he got like that. Then we found he had knocked a hole in the wall and tapped into one of the barrels. He would get a stem of that hollow grass that used to grow along the old railway line, and cut the ends off. He then stuck it through the wall to suck out the cider!

Bryn – Do you remember Jakey Davies's little cousin? He used to come down to stay and he always had creatures in his pockets as well – snakes, mostly. He was always coming down Moy Road, with a pocket full of them and you could see his pocket moving. He'd say "Put one in your hand, then, they're only grass snakes."

Vaughan – Then there was Angus Yates, 'Gus' we called him. He was a hell of a boy, and in school, come the end of the war and they were going back to their parents or whatever, we played a trick on him. We told him that as he was leaving, he had to go and see Mr Trigg the headmaster, and ask him for his 'cards'. That's exactly what he did. Then what about Bobby Jones, another character. He was a Communist, but he didn't care a damn who knew that. He was one of the kindest people I ever met, especially with the old folk. All in all, we had a good time, well we had a childhood

314

anyway didn't we, it's as simple as that. Mind you they were hard times. I remember my mother making trousers for us out of old blankets. We never had long trousers until we left school. I can recall the biting wind during those bitterly cold winters, when our legs used to chap on the inside.

Bryn – *The air-raid shelters were built in Taff's Well after I went to the army, I'm sure.*

Vaughan – *Yes, and there was one near here in Sycamore Street, and another on the corner by Llewellyn's. Do you know they stood on a bed of ash? They were built of brick, but they first laid a thick layer of rough ash, and the concrete base went on top of that. The reason for this was that in any blast, rather than the shell of the shelter disintegrating, the whole structure would be allowed to move on the ash base.*

Bryn – *Yes, those shelters must have been built after I went away. But I remember one of those raids when I was home on leave. I was hiding by the gate – you know, there was a door for the orchard which was never opened. I was coming down that way with Elizabeth (we were courting then) and she lived at the Legion Club then, and we were going down to see my mother – and the guns opened up over Cardiff! I pulled her under that gate, and it was pouring like rain – the shrapnel. You could hear it falling on the roof there.*

Vaughan – *Thinking about that bombing, I remember Dr Williams's house getting it, of course. Then there was one in Mrs Ford's just at the bottom of Moy Road and she took to her bed, and never got up, do you know that? There was another bomb in the canal and there were two where the soccer team play now. I remember Bleddyn coming home during a raid. Bleddyn was making his way home across the patch of waste land between the bridge and Moy Road, and he dived for cover right into the thick bed of nettles at the side of the path! He came home stinging – but safe.*

Bryn – *Bleddyn used to play for the schoolboys of course and I remember when we were in Cardiff, we always had fish and chips in Temperance Town. This was about 1932, and there were spotlessly clean little cafes there. We used to have what we called 'whale' and chips, the fish was so big. But the other thing I remember was those pitches at Sophia Gardens. No facilities, so you changed your kit under the trees on the side of the fields. Once I remember it was so cold that Del Harris had to rub Bleddyn's hands to get the circulation going again. There was great difficulty in removing his boots, because the laces were frozen solid. Oh yes, Taff's Well has changed. Do you know that in 1939 you could have bought two houses in Moy Road for a couple of hundred pounds?'*

('*Whale*' was cod, which could grow to six feet and live for 20 years. Overfishing in the Atlantic and North Sea, along with idiotic EU fishing policies, have meant that this once plentiful food is now expensive, with much smaller fish being taken, and far, far smaller portions in chip shops. Temperance Town was the unofficial name for a working-class inner-city

Cardiff area dating from the 1850s, and demolished between 1937 and 1954 to make way for Cardiff Bus Station. It was built on reclaimed land next to the Taff, on land owned by the teetotaller Colonel Edward Wood, who imposed a condition of sale that the selling of alcohol would not be allowed, thus the name.)

Vaughan – *'And it was the same in the forties and fifties – you could have bought them for a song. Now they are selling for nearly a hundred and thirty thousand pounds each!* (The 12 Williams siblings and their parents did not live in a large house. Their home in Moy Road, described as a 3-bed terraced house, sold for £114,000 in 2014. Cenydd Williams and his sister Mair assure me that the third bedroom was basically a *'small box room'*. In 2018 and 2019, eight similar 3-bed houses in Moy Road sold between £192,00, and £210,000.)

Bryn – *And a lot of these houses around here were originally allocated to people who worked on the railway. They've got them down in Radyr – they're the same as these, by Radyr Yard there.*

Vaughan – *Well, in Moy Road, up as far as next-door-but-one to us, they were all railway people. And you always knew them even without their uniforms, because of the waistcoat and the watch on a chain.*

Bryn – *Yes, they took everything to bed, including bloody whistles, I think.*

Vaughan – *Of course it was a job for life, on the GWR* (Great Western Railway).

Bryn – *Well, I worked myself for about four years on the railway before I went on the road* (i.e. working as a salesman) *– there wasn't much about in those days* (i.e. there were few jobs available). *They were a great crowd.*

Vaughan – *Have you seen all these books which have been printed, particularly the ones showing the old 'Puffing Billy' on the other side there. It would come over the crossing by Bale's and then to Tom Edwards's quarry, just before you got to the Tynant, for loading stone. But they had a trolley on that line, and we used to push it from where E.C. Cases used to be, down there by Laurence's under the viaduct, all the way up past the weir near the footbridge. It would take about a dozen of us to get it that far, and then we would jump on it and let it go. It would speed down past those houses below Gwaelod School and then we'd jump off by the bottom road. Pushing it up was hard work, but the ride was great – especially coming round the bend!*

Bryn – *Aye, that would have been a good name for that, 'Thomas the Tank Engine', it was very much like it, wasn't it?*

Vaughan – *And then the drams coming down full of coal from Rockwood, the same thing.* (Drams were iron wagons filled with coal or stone, originally taken to the canal on tram-roads for off-loading into canal boats or barges. Later they were coupled to trains. There is a 1991 photo of the last dram of coal being taken out of Maerdy Colliery). *When I think about it, we used to do some stupid things. On the Barry Line, too – the one that* used to go over the viaduct. It came around by Moss's and just above there, we used to jump onto a track and down by the gulley, and just before it went over the bridge, we'd jump off. When I think about it – if somebody slipped, they'd have had their leg off.

Bryn – And of course they'd have their brakes on and there'd be a lot of sparks.

Vaughan – That reminds me of something I saw in South Africa on our recent visit there. Marj and I went on what they call the Outeniqua Choo Tjoe steam train, along the coast from Knysna to George – about a two-hour trip. But they've kept the old trains there, you see, and they use them for carrying passengers and goods. This one goes twice a day, and it's packed.

Bryn – You saw no sign of the Shapiros, did you?

Vaughan – No, although I made lots of enquiries.

Bryn – I remember when we tied up in Cape Town, as we were going along down the gangplank, we could see a long line of cars. We thought they were taxis, but in fact they were locals anxious to take us around, and show us all the sights. It was my luck to be taken by this gentleman named Shapiro, a local businessman. Oh, we went all around – over Table Mountain and so on. We stopped with them a week – we didn't bother to go back on deck. I had a wonderful time there. Mind you, Apartheid was on then and you couldn't talk to the blacks and the women with the black children who were begging.

Vaughan – Yes, I know that Mrs Shapiro wrote to our father to tell him about you, and after he died, his daughter used to write, because you were away almost six years because of the war, weren't you? I have tried to trace that family, and although there were a lot of Shapiros there, I haven't as yet come across this particular one.'

The wonderful dialogue ends here, with a note from Don Llewellyn: 'Limitations of space force us to leave the chat between Bryn and Vaughan at this stage – but there is no doubt that they will carry on, for there is so much more to be said about life in the wonderful community of Taff's Well and other villages in the Garth Domain'.

Enid Pritchard was the sister who never missed a game at Cardiff. In *The Williams Family* she spoke of growing up in this very special family, being interviewed in hospital by Gerald Edwards after she suffered an unfortunate accident. She spoke of her mother's father: '*My grandfather Ted Roberts together with Dai Millward **initiated rugby in Taff's Well**. They used to play in the field next to where the soccer is now. My grandfather used to get Loma, my cousin, and I to go over there to chase the cows out of the field before they could play, and we'd get threepence for our trouble.*

My grandfather was a character. He would come out of the house and go up to the farm road – because he lived in Bryncoch, and he'd walk

317

diagonally across to get onto the road. It didn't matter who was coming, they had to wait for him to cross, pipe in his mouth, stick in his hand, he'd just go across in one direction like that – as if to say: "You can wait for me, I've lived here longer than you, before there were cars, so you can wait for me!" He was a case. He used to make alcoholic drinks from just about anything. We used to go and get nettles for him, and he'd make wine and say to us, "You can have a little sip, you're not twenty-one but you can have a sip." I remember he gave Bleddyn some when he was about eighteen, just to try it – but it flattened him! Oh yes, I miss 'Dad' – we always used to call him 'Dad-up-the-road', as against my father. He'd say, "Go on home now, Johnny the Bull is in that barn, and he'll get you if you don't go home before dark." Well, I used to run like blazes down the road, just in case that bull came out and chased me.

We didn't have much money, but we had a lot of fun. If we were indoors, my sister Joan and I would go upstairs, to sit and read or cut out things. If the weather was fine, we'd go trekking up into the woods, all of us, as kids. Bleddyn and Bryn used to help the farmer up the top there, you know, near the Black Cock. They'd have my cousin Loma and myself as handmaids, to go down to get potatoes for them to cook. It was very hot one summer, and we'd taken these up for them, because although the farmer used to give them a lot of stuff, there were some things they had to take themselves. The boys were more or less working for nothing, but were being fed. Some things they didn't always give them, so we had to take potatoes and things up there. We staggered up there one day and they gave us a drink of something, and we had no idea what it was. It was stone-cold cider! We glugged it all back and we didn't know whether we were coming or going. We walked back through a drunken haze! It tasted lovely, mind, because it was so hot that day, and it had come from the cellar up at the farm, so it was lovely and cold you know.

It has been fantastic, really, growing up in a rugby family. It was wonderful. You'd come home on a Saturday night after seeing the games, and the boys had been playing and there'd be an inquest around the table in the kitchen. Nobody would criticise anyone – there was just discussion about aspects of the game and whatever. Rugby brought you into a special group of people. Rugby people are nice anyway – you can travel with them, and you don't get the same problems you have with soccer. They visited home, and of course my mother's place was HQ you know – 'Open House.' Whoever it was, they'd go in and have a chat.

It was awful to see my mother Nell afterwards with Alzheimer's; and she didn't know you. It's heart-breaking, isn't it. But she lived until she was ninety-three, having raised twelve children in those days, without benefits or rent allowances or whatever they have today. The had too much pride in those days – in any case they wouldn't want it.' (Nell and her sisters and daughters used to watch all the games they could, but her husband was working all hours and overtime to support the family. Cenydd tells me that his father Arthur used to watch games when he could, but always standing on the terraces behind the posts, whereas his wife, daughters and various aunties were in the stand. Over the years it must have been a terrible strain for Arthur Williams to feed and clothe twelve children. Roy Roberts' son Mike tells me that Arthur Williams always wore a suit, a hat and carried a walking stick when not working. My own father also used to 'dress up' when not in work.)

'Yes, we had a lovely childhood. Nobody had much money, but nobody worried about it, for everyone was in the same boat anyway. It was wonderful going up the forest and playing around Castell Coch and in the fields round Tyrhiw Farm and whatever, but the thing was that no-one worried about you in those days, because they were safer times. Bryn and Bleddyn were much younger that Gwyn, but they didn't bother with the girls of the family so much. They were never unkind, of course, but somehow I had a special relationship with Gwyn. I was bridesmaid at Gwyn's wedding. Regarding the younger ones of course, I used to wash them and put them to bed, when my mother was out. Only the other day Elwyn was here, and he asked me if I remembered washing him and putting him to bed. Well, I couldn't lift him now, and that's for certain! When my grandmother, who was originally from the Chepstow area, was coming to Gwaelod-y-Garth to live, she was asked by a neighbour what was the name of the place to which they were moving. "Well, I don't know", she said, "but it sounds like GLORY BE TO GOD!"'

(Gilbert de Clare, the Norman Earl of Gloucester, built castles at Llantrisant and Caerphilly. Known as 'Red Gilbert', it is alleged that Castell Coch, Red Castle, was named for him. It was subsequently destroyed in a series of Welsh attacks. 500 years later the ruins were acquired by John Stuart, Earl of Bute as part of a marriage settlement. The Earls of Bute owed their status as the richest men in Britain, owing to vast area of Glamorgan and Monmouth, rich in coal and iron, being given to them by marriage to a Welsh heiress. Thomas Windsor, 1st Viscount Windsor had married Lady Charlotte Herbert, daughter of Philip Herbert, 7th Earl of Pembroke, the original heiress. Their grand-daughter, the Honourable Charlotte Jane Windsor (1746–1800), succeeded to the enormous Welsh family estates, and married John Stuart, 4th Earl of Bute. The Bute family restored Castell Coch and Cardiff Castle, and built Cardiff docks to export the mineral riches of the interior. In 1800, Cardiff had barely 1,000 people, but was to become one of the busiest ports in the world.

Similarly, in 1634 Richard Grosvenor had acquired valuable mineral and mining holdings in North Wales via marriage. In 1677, the marriage of the Welsh heiress Mary Davies to his son Sir Thomas Grosvenor, gave the Grosvenor family, now the Dukes of Westminster, the manor of Ebury,

500 acres of land north of the Thames, west of the City of London. We are talking about Mayfair, around Grosvenor Square, Belgravia, and the richest part of London. 300 acres of the original land which Miss Davies inherited, before she met her husband, remain with the family today, forming the Grosvenor's London estate which contributed to Gerald Grosvenor, the sixth Duke of Westminster's £9 billion fortune before his 2016 death. Today the Grosvenor Group runs £13.1bn of assets, with a £6.7bn property portfolio. Not only minerals but wealth has always left Wales.)

I was honoured to meet **Mair Philips** in Taff's Well, the youngest and only surviving daughter, and in *The Williams Family*, she recalled *'I remember when we lived at Moy Road. Every Saturday the youngest boys would be out there, polishing their boots and my mother would be cooking them bacon and eggs, so that they had a light meal before they were playing rugby in the afternoon. They were good times.'* Mair remembered that the four oldest boys, Gwyn, Bryn, Bleddyn and Vaughan (born 1918, 1920, 1923, 1931) were older than her (born 1936), and away so much, that she really only knew the four youngest brothers, Lloyd, Elwyn, Cenydd and Tony (born 1933, 1938, 1939 and 1941) really well. She remembers Gwyn coming home injured during the war, and him watching the village team, and the fact that Bryn, a salesman post-war, always brought back presents for the family in a suitcase, when home from his travels. They never really noticed that their home was crowded, with a tin bath brought in from outside for 'bath-night' once a week – virtually all families were the same.

Upon the Francis Frith website we read *'Taff's Well School - a Memory of Taff's Well: A memory shared by Mary Jones on Dec 19th, 2012:* 'My memory of Taff's Well School was that I lived in fear of most of the teachers except our headmaster Mr. D Harris and Miss Hall, they were the only two that stood out with having any real love of teaching children. If some of the others were around today, they would have been locked up for cruelty. Fortunately, I left that school when I was thirteen and went to College in Cardiff. I had many happy memories of living in Taff's Well and remember Ty Rhiw houses being erected, and as kids we use to call it "Tin Town" because of the construction, and we did not like the fact that they put houses on the fields that we used to sledge down in the snow. People from the valleys moved down to "Tin Town" and we did not know them, and they seemed a little strange to us.*

I loved going carol singing in Canal Row and the people were on the whole very generous with their pennies, sometimes some would give three pence, one house we use to go to where a lady lived on her own, we would just about start to sing when the window upstairs was raised and if we didn`t hurry, we would get water thrown on us, all good fun. My parents lived in Taff's Well for the rest of their lives, but I left when I went away to further my career. I still call back occasionally, just to see the old place, it has not changed for the better, as I used to love the old canal and the whitewashed lock cottages, with the lovely roses and sweet peas growing in profusion.'

On the same site, under the heading '*Swiss Cottage*', Roger Smith writes: '*I was born on my grandfather's smallholding alongside the River Taff; he had run it as a small pig farm/market garden. I can remember looking up at the viaduct and watching the trains running across it. The whole vale had such a magical quality about it. The castle upon the hill* (Castell Coch) *was such a special place to me in my childhood.'*

Carey Collings handed me a faded obituary from a Welsh newspaper, titled '***Nellie Williams – A Rugby Legend – Grand Old Lady Dies at age of 93'***, which reads, '*A South Wales woman whose eight sons became great names in Welsh rugby has died aged 93. Risca-born Mrs Nellie Williams, formerly of Moy Road, Taff's Well, died in a Llantwit Fardre old people's home where she had lived for the last two years. Part of a rugby-playing family herself, she played a key role in encouraging her sons to take up the game, and then to stick with it. **Her sons were Gwyn, who played for Cardiff against the All Blacks in 1953 and later went north to play for Wigan; Bryn, who played for Cardiff and Cross Keys; Bleddyn, who played for Cardiff, Wales and the British Lions; Vaughan, Cardiff Athletic and Neath; Lloyd, Cardiff, Wales and the Barbarians; Cenydd, Cardiff and the Barbarians; Tony, Cardiff and the Barbarians and Elwyn, who gained an Under-23 cap for Wales, was captain of the Welsh Schoolboys and who made a record number of appearances for the Cardiff side.***

Mrs Williams also had daughters Dilys, Enid, Joan and Mair. Mr Lloyd Williams of Pentyrch said that two of his mother's brothers, Mr Tom Roberts and Mr Roy Roberts, also played for Cardiff, and the latter was in the Pontypridd team too. Her father had played for Risca. "So, she was brought up in the realm of rugby and was instrumental in encouraging us all to take the game up," said Mr Williams. "She constantly kept us at it, though not in a heavy-handed way. She keenly followed our progress, and I remember that in 1963 when Elwyn and I played against the All Blacks she had broken her leg in a road accident but yet insisted on being carried by firemen's lift into the stand, with her leg encased in plaster. She was really amazing.'

Bleddyn's daughter Lynne reminded me that her grandparents were Welsh speaking, which accounts for the Welsh Christian names given to most of the Williams children, at a time when Welsh names were not at all in vogue in Glamorgan. There were 18 Welsh names and 7 English – Dilys Myfanwy, Gwyn Glyndwr, Bryn (Edward) Lougher, Bleddyn Llewellyn, (Enid Mary), (Joan Beryl), Vaughan (Ronald), Lloyd Huw, Mair Olwen, Cenydd Owen, Elwyn Rhys and (Anthony) David. Lynne also recalls Bleddyn telling her that his grandfather Ted Roberts was always bringing vegetables and eggs from his garden to the house in Moy Road, to help feed the family.

The diaspora of farmworkers and others from my 'bro', the Vale of Glamorgan, to seek work in the Industrial Revolution, is shown by the paternal grandparents of Arthur Williams. On his father's side, John Williams of St. Andrews (outside Dinas Powys) married Elizabeth Jones of Laleston and all their children and grand-children were born in Cardiff. On Arthur's mother's side, his grandparents were Richard Griffiths of Pendoylan and Margaret Lougher of Bonvilston, whose children were all born in Bonvilston.

CHAPTER 26 - CARDIFF SEASON 1954 – 1955

A GREAT SEASON - CLIFF MORGAN STARS FOR LIONS – CARDIFF TOP THE MERIT TABLE – BLEDDYN, *'THE PRINCE OF CENTRES'*, RETIRES – BLEDDYN REMINISCES

Bleddyn Williams P32 T14 = 42pts; **Lloyd Williams** P11; John Llewellyn P27 C10 P13 – 59pts (Taff's Well); Alun Priday P20 T1 C11 P6 = 43pts (Tongwynlais); Derek Murphy P3 T3 = 9pts (Pentyrch)

P48, W38, L5, D5. Points 676-243. Tries 148-41, Pens 31-28

From Danny Davies' magnificent history, the season review begins with sad news: *'This was quite a remarkable season, marred only by the untimely illness of our captain Sid Judd which restricted his appearances to 24 matches. Later the illness was to prove fatal, causing his death by leukaemia in the full flower of his manhood. Before his breakdown he was a most experienced forward already holding ten Welsh caps, and a candidate for the forthcoming Lions tour to South Africa in 1955'.* (In fact, Sid was a very strong candidate for the Lions captaincy). *'He was strong, aggressive, a good reader of the game and a most useful goal kicker. In fact, he was the type who asserted his qualities by his energetic example. Sid nominated Rex Willis to be his vice-captain.*

Alun Thomas left Llanelli and Cliff Morgan took up work in Dublin and joined Bective Rangers, which quickly became known as 'Morgan's Rangers'. Cliff was pleased to captain an International XV, more than half of them British Lions, to play Bective on its 75th anniversary in 1956. Colin Bosley left us and so did John R. Phillips our popular forward, who I seem to remember became a Benedick and joined Newport. But there was much good talent to contend for first team places, particularly amongst the

322

backs. At half back there was Rex Willis; Lloyd Williams and Colin Hewett both of whom could play in either half back position, there was Brian Mark and the versatile and devastating side-stepper Ken Richards. At three-quarter we were also strong, being able to choose from Gareth Griffiths, Haydn Morris, Bleddyn Williams, Gordon Wells, Howard Nicholls, Derek Murphy, Dr. Gwyn Rowlands and the Old Illtydian Peter Nyhan.' I should note there that Gordon Wells often played on the opposite wing to Ray Glastonbury, Cardiff being the only team in history to simultaneously have two *'cathedrals'* on its wings.

On 25 September 1954 Cardiff scored 3 tries against Aberavon, winning 15-9. (The team was to score 8 tries in the return fixture, winning 32-11, Aberavon scoring a try in each game). Two days later, on 27 September, a Jack Matthews XV, stuffed with Cardiff players and captained by him, played Penarth. Penarth had just beaten Bridgend and 5,000 spectators watched a thrilling 8-8 draw. Wilfred Wooller wrote: *'There was a galaxy of international talent, past and present, in Matthews' side for this fine open game, to celebrate the 75th anniversary of the Penarth club. The experience of old favourites Cliff Davies, Des O'Brien, Jack Matthews and Ewart Tamplin... and the brilliance of current stars Cliff Morgan, Clem Thomas and Rex Willis came to the team's aid. Penarth entered into the spirit of the game and a continuous stream of movements, some orthodox, some utterly fantastic, enlivened play for the spectators. Between spurts of unstoppable energy by Cliff Morgan came lovely runs by the Penarth right-wing Barry Griffiths. Veteran Frank Trott comfortably held his own against an excellent display by Kevin Bush... Skipper Bush, if anything, was as outstanding for his side as Cliff Morgan for the guests. Brian Joseph, a 19-year-old RAF man stationed at St Athan, shook Jack Matthews and his team of internationals at Penarth last night with his power play. Once Jack Matthews, the "iron man" of Welsh rugby fell to a crash-tackle by Joseph, a centre, playing his second game for Penarth. Although England hooker Nick Labuschagne won almost every set scrum and the Wales half-back pair of Rex Willis and Cliff Morgan made many openings, Penarth showed determination in defence...'* Brian Joseph played only one game for Cardiff, in 1955-56, and Penarth's fly-half Graham Jones had a Welsh Trial, but then immediately signed for Salford rugby league, where he played 200 matches. Penarth had a superb season, with a 55.5% winning rate of 17 wins and 8 draws, and drawing 3-3 with the Barbarians, the first time they had not lost to them for over 30 years.

Another charity match was played on the following day, 28 September, 3 days after playing Aberavon. (There were 3 games in 4 days for some Cardiff players). For this John Maunder Benefit Match, Cardiff played a Mr. Bleddyn Williams XV. Cardiff played a full team, less the players loaned to Bleddyn - C.D. Williams, Des O'Brien (the Irish captain who played for Cardiff), Frank Trott, Cliff Davies, Malcolm Thomas and Ken

Jones. Then on 2 October, with most players having been involved in 4 games in 8 days, Cardiff drew away at Newport, a try apiece. Cardiff won the next two but lost the last fixture at home, 11-6, 2 tries apiece. It was an excellent Newport side, the Cardiff victories being 6-3 and 6-0. The point is, that these two charity games, sandwiched between two official games, are unrecorded in Danny Davies' excellent history of the club. Players simply enjoyed playing, as there were few of the massive concussive hits we see today in 'clear-outs' and the like. Jack Matthews wrote about Bleddyn always being available for charity matches, often gathering players, e.g. to play at Llanelli in aid of the fund for the famous Albert Jenkins. For the young Cardiff forward John Maunder, seriously injured in a steelwork's accident, *'Bleddyn's only regret was that, as a contributor to a national newspaper on rugby football, he was barred from playing in the game by the laws of amateur football.'*

Lloyd Williams, in first-team absences, was either called up as outside half or scrumhalf, depending upon where he was needed. On 11 December 1954, *'Reshuffled Cardiff Romp Home'* was a headline for the 9-3 win over Quins: *'The phenomenal reserve strength of Cardiff was never more obvious than at Twickenham yesterday when, with six deputies, the unbeaten visitors handed out a good hiding to Harlequins, who fielded six internationals... Lloyd Williams and Colin Hewett struck up a happy partnership at once. Neither put a foot wrong, but I would prefer to see young Williams keep his feet when distributing.'* This writer well remembers that Lloyd often dive-passed, as did Gareth Edwards in his younger days, before the latter learned in New Zealand to deliver spin passes for better length and speed.

Cardiff topped the unofficial Welsh Merit table with 84.7%, winning 38 of its 48 games. The club was unbeaten for the first 22 matches, but on 13 December lost its ground record 11-3 to Cambridge University. The pitch was its usual lagoon-like state on the day, and Cardiff had wished to cancel the game. However, *'The official viewpoint is that if the game had been against anyone else it would have been definitely postponed, but the fact that the Light Blues were already in Cardiff forced the local officials to allow the game to be played.'* When the Final trial was being played, Moseley beat a depleted Cardiff team, 9-8. On 19 February 1955, after a period of frozen rugby pitches and postponements, Cardiff took Newport's ground record 6-0 by two dropped goals. All the 'Big Five' were in attendance. Newport then beat Cardiff at Rodney Parade in March 11-6 (2 tries apiece), and on tour at Birkenhead Park Cardiff lost 9-8 (a try each). Also in March, Cardiff completed the double over Leicester, winning 32-9, 7 tries to 2, with Gwyn Rowlands scoring 14 points. Bristol were soundly beaten 8 tries to 1, 38-3, and the same 8-1 try score was achieved against Aberavon, 32-11. At Easter, the Barbarians included seven selected 1955 British Lions and won 6-3. In April 1955, Gwyn Rowlands kicked 4 goals and scored 2 tries, 16 points out of Cardiff's 22-13 win over Coventry.

1954-55 Bleddyn's last game, Alun Priday following

May 1955 saw Bleddyn play his last game, made captain for the final match of the season at home to Llanelli. He was only 32 but had been carrying injuries for some time. Cardiff won 9-0, and the crowd ran onto the pitch and carried him off at the end. The St. Albans Brass Band played '*The End of a Perfect Day.*' Bleddyn was to enter a career in sports journalism and was President of Cardiff Athletic Club, being made an MBE in 2005. Cardiff also lost Jack Matthews to retirement and to the chairmanship of Cardiff, Sid Judd to illness, and Cliff Morgan was to play for Bective Rangers, '*Morgan's Rangers*', for some time. (Because his job moved him to Wicklow, Morgan joined Bective Rangers for the 1954/55 season and helped the club to win the Leinster Senior Cup in April 1955, its first victory in that competition for 20 years. In the cup final Morgan scored an early try to lay the foundations for an 8-0 win over an Old Belvedere team that included a young Tony O'Reilly in the centre. A few weeks later they were teammates on the Lions team that drew the series against South Africa 2-2. One South African journalists described Morgan as "*the best out-half ever to play in the country.*"

The game between Bath and Cardiff was cancelled owing to snow on the date of the England game, and 8 Cardiff men played for Wales, Bleddyn Williams (captain), Gordon Wells (first cap), Cliff Morgan (four times while with Bective Rangers), Sid Judd, Gareth Griffiths, C. D. Williams (first cap) and Haydn Morris. Wales beat England 3-0 at Cardiff; lost at Murrayfield 14-8, despite scoring 2 tries, like Scotland; beat Ireland 21-3 with 4 tries in Cardiff and beat France away 16-11. Wales shared the Championship with France, but had beaten them in Paris. Cardiff's Haydn Morris and Alun Thomas scored the only tries of the game. Bleddyn only played in the first international, succumbing to injuries, so maintaining his record of captaining Wales 5 times and winning 5 times. The Neath home programme for the Cardiff game on 19 March 1955 notes that Bleddyn had captained Wales against England that season, Rex Willis led against Ireland and Neath's great Rees Stephens was to lead the team in France.

Leading try scorers were Pentyrch's Derek Murphy 26, Gordon Wells 17, Haydn Morris 15, Bleddyn Williams 14, Gareth Griffiths 10, Howard Nicholls, Dr. Gwyn Rowlands and Ken Richards 8 each, and the captain Sid Judd scored 7 tries and kicked 23 goals (- this was in the first half of the season, as he was succumbing to illness). John Llewellyn kicked 24 goals, Ken Richards 17 and Gwyn Rowlands (after his return from Australia as a ship's Medical Officer) also kicked 17. Colin Howe, Alun Priday, Ken Richards, J. H. Thomas and Gordon Wells were awarded Cardiff caps. Malcolm Collins played in 44 of the 48 First XV fixtures, Geoff Beckingham in 42, J. D. Evans 42 and Eddie Thomas 41. These were hard men – and as they all had full-time jobs, and were not involved in full contact training in the 'big hit' type of rugby played today. Less full contact training = fewer injuries, it is not rocket science.

Peter Goodfellow, a great club servant, captained the Rags, with their best results since the war. P33, W28, L4, D1, **points 521-118**. Like the Firsts, they started really well. Up to the end of November 339 points were scored, but later in the season 6 matches were cancelled, with an effect on the final number of points. They were unbeaten until 11 December, losing 8-3 to Pencoed. Six Rags players were playing that day for the Firsts, as the first Welsh trial was being played. Peter Goodfellow moved up from the Athletic to captain Cardiff away at Harlequins, as 6 of the First's best players were absent in the trial. Cardiff still scored 2 tries to one, winning 9-3. 1954 saw the start of the annual floodlit exhibition matches against the Harlequins at the White City Stadium, which continued until 1959, but are not counted in the official games. Back to the 'Rags', Resolven were beaten by 12 tries, 8 converted by Alun Priday, to nil. Priday also scored one try. Priday kicked 58 goals scoring in all 137 points. Top Rags try scorers were C. L. Davies 18, R. T. Parsons 15, international Gareth Griffiths and Peter Nyhan with 8 each. John Dodd. Derek Murphy and J. H. Thomas scored 7 each, Ken Richards 6, Alun Priday and Bleddyn's brother Lloyd Williams 5 each. Lloyd was still unsure whether his position should be centre, fly-half or scrumhalf. He was to become a solid six-footer scrumhalf, and a great help to his back row.

Alan Jones was the captain of the Cardiff Juniors, in effect the Youth XV which achieved an outstanding P27, W23, L2, D2, points **442-52**. The Juniors/Youth were to feed youngsters via the Rags into the Firsts, and all four youngest Williams brothers – Lloyd, Cenydd, Elwyn and Tony, came into the premier team via that route. Newport organised the Welsh Sevens (Snelling) tournament in April 1955, and Cardiff entered a young team, of which only Gareth Griffiths and Gordon Wells had any experience of Sevens (at St. Luke's College). Gordon Wells was to play 7 times for Wales, and scored 119 tries in 254 games on the wing for Cardiff. The young Lloyd Williams was scrumhalf, Gareth Griffiths captained and Gordon Wells scored six tries as surprisingly Cardiff won, beating Pontypridd, Aberavon, Newbridge and in the final, Newport 8-3. The rest of the team were J.C. Crothers, J.H. Thomas, Ken Richards and Terry Donovan.

In a recent Ebbw Vale against Cardiff (not Cardiff Blues) programme, dated 25 November 2017, we can read: '*In the 50s tees were only used by golfers, rugby goal-kickers had to dig a heel in the pitch to place the ball. Our goal-kicker at the time was also our biggest player, not the most mobile of second rowers but a formidable presence. He was Ben Edwards, so reliably big and imposing they named a clock after him in Westminster. Speaking of whom, today's High Noon crunch match being played before lunch instead of before tea is most unusual. Perhaps we should call it a brunch match. Ben was a genial giant, and like another goal-kicking forward of the time, Cardiff's Bill Tamplin, he quickly placed the ball and invariably bisected the posts. Our clubhouse was not built in Ben's time and the space at the southern end of the ground was used for parking, an often dangerous place to be. In a game against Cardiff a long-range kick at goal by Big Ben flew like a missile, found its target, hit the visitors' bus, smashed a window and as there was no glazier on duty, the Cardiff team had a draughty journey home. Big Ben captained us on our first official visit to the Arms Park on September 29th, 1954 and Eric Finney, the great uncapped forward, packed down alongside him. Our pack was described in the Cardiff programme as "one of the heaviest in Wales and not lacking in speed". The attendance broke records for a mid-week game and with the kick-off at 5.15, a lot of workplaces in Ebbw Vale emptied early. The*

Cardiff skipper was backrow forward Sid Judd who kicked one of his side's two penalty goals and he was one of six Welsh caps in the home team, among them Bleddyn Williams who I never fail to mention in the programme when Cardiff are here.'

For the British Lions tour to South Africa, Rex Willis was invited to tour, but for domestic reasons was unable to accept. Rex had been the favourite to become the Lions captain. Bleddyn had announced his decision to retire, and would have gone on tour, but players aged over 30 were not wanted. (Where do they get selectors? From a primordial swamp?) Bleddyn had felt that the dry pitches would suit his game far better than the usual morass at Cardiff. Therefore, instead of 6, only 4 four Cardiff players were chosen: Cliff Morgan, Haydn Morris, Alun Thomas (who had just joined Llanelli) and Gareth Griffiths, who only flew out as a replacement, and was chosen for all the Tests, but only played in 3 of the 4 because of injury. There were 11 Welshmen in the squad of 31. Danny Davies was appointed honorary secretary of the Lions, and says he saw Cliff Morgan produce his best rugby of his career. Cliff Morgan did not play well in the Cardiff 1951 narrow loss to South Africa (over-kicking, as he freely admitted), and he had been very much under pressure from the balding flank forward C. J. van Wyk. However, for the British Lions against South Africa at Johannesburg in 1955, *'Cliff Morgan was in superb form and van Wyk never saw his backside for Johannesburg dust. He darted under van Wyk's clutches to score brilliantly and set the Lions on to a sensational win by 23 points to 22'.* There was a world record crowd of 100,000, and the Lions won despite an injury to Reg Higgins reducing the Lions to 14 men.

'After the South Africans squared the series in the second Test, Morgan was made captain for the third Test and inspired the team with a combination a stirring team talk and a great kicking game to a 9–6 victory, ensuring the series could not be lost, after which he was dubbed "Morgan the Magnificent" by the South African press. After his Lions heroics Morgan was made captain of Wales, and helped them win the title (although not the Grand Slam) in 1956.' The series was drawn 2-2. During the writing of this book, Haydn Morris, one of the oldest surviving Cardiff players, passed away at the aged 92. He scored 101 tries in just 129 games for Cardiff, gained 3 Wales caps, and on the 1955 Lions Tour scored 9 tries in 8 appearances, including a hat trick against Griqualand West, before injury halted his rugby and prevented him appearing in the Tests. In Nairobi in September, for the last match of the Lions tour, against an East African XV, Danny Davies, Cliff Morgan and Haydn Morris met Captain Howell Loveluck, who had played for Cardiff between 1939-40 and 1949-50. He was now a chaplain to H.M. Forces in Kenya, at the time of the *Mau Mau* Uprising. The gruelling 25-match tour had begun on 22 June and ended on 27 September.

Huw Richards posted on website *espn*, 3 September 2008 '*1955 Welsh Lions take a trip down memory lane.*' '*The tour took us back to a time when a Lions party took a day and a half to get to South Africa by air - and thought it rapid because previous teams had gone by boat, even if Russell Robins (Pontypridd) still has vivid memories of delays before take-off: "We got on the plane, got off again, got on again, got off again. I'd never been on a plane before in my life and was beginning to feel a bit nervous about it." Employers had to be asked to fund, or at least tolerate, several months off work and there were few perks for the touring player ... Players received an allowance of 5s (25p) per day spending money. Robins said, "The big thing we had in common was that we were all skint", while cheerfully admitting that a useful additional source of income was the sale of match tickets ... Tour Manager Jack Siggins decided that he needed a young and lively side to take to South Africa and initially wanted his fellow selectors to disregard and players over the age of 27. In the end, only one player over the age of 30 - Maesteg scrum half Trevor Lloyd - was included in the tour party ... This, we were reminded, was the tour that gave rise to Lloyd's Law, a fixed item of Lions custom and practice ever since, when Maesteg scrumhalf Trevor Lloyd, aware of the formidable competition for female company likely to come from the likes of teenage heartthrob Tony O'Reilly, sought and received assurances that no Lion should move in on a girl being chatted up by a team-mate.*

It was, recalled Gareth Griffiths: "Like being in a film, with myself as one of the actors. It was the holiday of a lifetime, lasting for four months" ... It was also an age when a player might have to play on in a Test after splitting his tongue - as Courtenay Meredith did: "I was throwing blood up, but you couldn't leave the field as there were no replacements and you'd be leaving your team with 14 men." ... There was, though, no sense of pressure from the Lions' previous history of failures - Robins said, "all we were concerned about was playing a decent game of rugby and enjoying ourselves" - perhaps because there were only three journalists accompanying the party. It was, all were agreed, the zenith of their careers to be British Lions - members of the party that broke a losing run extending back to the beginning of the twentieth century by drawing the Test series 2-2 and playing rugby whose brilliance is remembered to this day.

Had there been a toast to conclude the proceedings there can be little doubt it would have been to 'absent friends' - and to one in particular, Cliff Morgan. Not well enough to travel from his home on the Isle of Wight, he was nevertheless present, both through a letter of apology that showed that a mind with a poet's eye for the right word and the perfect phrase is still in excellent shape, and in the appreciation of his erstwhile team-mates who recalled his teaching them Afrikaans song Sarie Marais, so they could sing it while descending the stairs of the aircraft on landing at Johannesburg

Airport and, in Russell Robins words "was our real leader, on and off the field"... Their final tour record was: P25 W19 D1 L5. Points For 457 Points Agst 283. Tries For 103 Tries Agst 34. 750,000 fans paid more than half-a-million pounds to watch the 25 games in South Africa. They arrived at Jan Smuts Airport on 11 July and didn't leave Nairobi until 29 September, arriving home on 30 September. They travelled 25,000 miles from start to finish on their tour. Among the many tributes, Dannie Craven, who was chairman of selectors for the 1955 Springboks, stated: "They are the strongest touring side I have ever seen in South Africa. Their back play is a treat to watch." In the four Tests in 1955 there were 6 Welshmen in the 1st, 7 in the 2nd, 8 in the 3rd and 8 in the 4th.'

Russell John Robins (21 February 1932 – 27 September 2019) had captained Welsh Secondary Schools while at Pontypridd Grammar School, then attended Cardiff University. After he completed his National Service, Wales picked him at number 8, replacing their captain John Gwilliam. He played for his hometown Pontypridd 183 times, captaining them from 1953-56, and played in all four Lions Tests in South Africa, making the most appearances on that tour, 17 out of 24 games. Robins also played for the Barbarians 4 times. He could equally play second row, and in this writer's eyes, he was a superb player. He would have gained more recognition in travelling a few miles down the valley to play for Cardiff, but stayed true to his roots. On the WRU website we read: *'In February 1959, he switched codes and joined Leeds RLFC in a move that netted him a £2,000 transfer fee. At the time the then 27-year-old said: "I'm out of a job and must think about my future. It is this more than anything else that has influenced my decision." He had previously worked for the NCB and a firm of brewers. The Pontypridd secretary, Des Jones, was fulsome in his praise of Robins after learning the news of his departure. "We are very sorry to lose such a great player. We will hold nothing against him for he has been a great club man and a most loyal player. By refusing to leave Pontypridd before, he has brought great honour to the club by playing for Wales and the Lions," said Jones. He scored a try on his debut in rugby league and was at Leeds when they won their first Championship title in the 1960-61 season, coached by Welshman Roy Francis and playing alongside the great Lewis Jones.'*

BLEDDYN LLEWELLYN WILLIAMS MBE - 'THE PRINCE OF CENTRES' 22 February 1923 – 6 July 2009

Taff's Well

Rydal School 1937-1941 outside half

Cardiff Schools 1935-36, and 1936-37 captain aged 14 (no Youth teams then) - Dewar Shield winners

Wales Schools under-14s fullback 1937 (missed next year through injury)

Cardiff Athletic centre vs Ebbw Vale, aged 16, 1939 while at Rydal

Taff's Well First XV aged 16, 1939, fly-half against Chepstow, while at Rydal

Cilfynydd (with brother Brinley) 1941

Rosslyn Park 1941-42

RAF volunteered 1942 - November 1946

Welsh Services, Combined Services

Great Britain wartime XV

3 Wales Service Internationals vs England – 3 tries in the 34-7 win at Gloucester 1943; 3 tries in the 21-11 win at Swansea 1944; win 24-9 at Gloucester 1945

7 Victory Internationals Wales Dec 1945-April 1946 vs N.Z. Army (captain), England (2), France (2), Scotland (2)

Cardiff 1945-46 to 1954-55, 283 games, 185 tries

Club record 41 tries in 30 games in 1947-48

Wales captain, chosen for all 1950 season, but unavailable through injury

Cardiff captain 1949-50 and 1953-54

Cardiff, and Wales, captain in 1953 wins over All Blacks

Wales January 1947- January 1955 - 22caps, 7 tries - fly-half first game, then centre

Wales captain in five matches, four times in 1953 and once in 1955, in his final international. He led the side to victory in all five games

Barbarians 11 times (vs Thorneloe XV 1944, East Midlands 1946, Penarth 1947, Newport 1947, East Midlands 1947, **Captain vs Australia** 1948 (with cousin, Bill Tamplin), Newport 1948, East Midlands 1949, **Captain vs South Africa XV** 1952, East Midlands 1953, Penarth 1954, **Captain vs East Midlands** 1954. (Bleddyn was also chosen aged 19 in early 1943, but was ill).

British Lions vice-captain in Australasia 1949-50, playing in 20 of 29 games as centre and outside-half and scoring 8 tries. He played in 3 of the 4 Tests against New Zealand (missing the first through injury) and both Tests against Australia (Jack Matthews played in all 6 Tests). **Captain** in the **third and fourth Tests** against **New Zealand. Captain 1st Test vs Australia**

President of both Cardiff RFC and Cardiff Athletic Club

'He taught us the old-fashioned principles of courtesy and courage. His love of the open, running game set him apart: his glorious sidestep, his perfectly timed pass, his speed and strength, made him a very special world-class centre.' Cliff Morgan

*'... **the greatest of the post-war backs in the British Isles**.'* Clem Thomas, *The Sunday Observer*

'...the dominating figure of post-war rugby' – E.R.K. Glover

*'From the 1945-46 season until he retired at the end of the 1954-55 season, Bleddyn scored 185 tries for the Cardiff club, a truly great performance by one who was so keenly marked by the opposition, who recognised in him the principal danger-man and a potential scorer or maker of scores for other players. It is often said that the hallmark of a good centre-threequarter is based on the number of tries his wing scores. All I say about this is – ask any wing who has played outside Bleddyn, and the reply is always the same: "It has been a pleasure to play with such a centre. I have never had so much of the ball, and at the right time at that! And what streamlined passes!" ... Never let it be said that Bleddyn was an individualist; he was **the finest team player I ever knew**... He was considered one of the finest, if not the finest, three-quarters ever to visit New Zealand... It has been a great pleasure to contribute the Foreword to this entertaining book, written by one who will be regarded as a modern Prince of Threequarters, a grand sportsman and a true gentleman.'* – Dr. Jack Matthews, *'Rugger, My Life'*, Bleddyn Williams, 1956

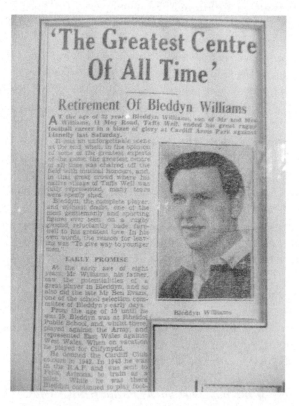

A newspaper cutting celebrating Bleddyn's career reads: *'THE GREATEST CENTRE OF ALL TIME – RETIREMENT OF BLEDDYN WILLIAMS - Retirement of Bleddyn Williams. At the age of 32 years, Bleddyn Williams,*

the son of Mr. and Mrs. Williams, 11 Moy Road, Taff's Well, ended his great rugby career in a blaze of glory at Cardiff Arms Park against Llanelly last Saturday. It was an unforgettable scene at the end, when, in the opinion of some of the greatest experts of the game, the greatest centre of all time was chaired of the field with musical honours, and, in that great crowd where his native village of Taff's Well was fully represented, many tears were openly shed. Bleddyn, the complete player, and without doubt, one of the most gentlemanly and sporting ever seen on a rugby ground, reluctantly bade farewell to his greatest love. In his own words, the reason for leaving was "to give way to younger men".

EARLY PROMISE. At the early age of eight years, Mr. Williams, his father, saw the potentialities of a great player in Bleddyn, and so also did the late Mr. Ben Evans, one of the school's selection committee of Bleddyn's early days. From the age of 15 until he was 19, Bleddyn was at Rheidol (Rydal) Public School, and whilst there played against the Army, and represented East Wales against West Wales. When on vacation, he played for Cilfynydd. He donned the Cardiff Club colours in 1942. In 1943 he was in the RAF and was sent to Felix, Arizona, to train as a pilot...'

There is a tribute to Bleddyn in a display cabinet at Taff's Well Rugby Club: 'One of the legends of Welsh rugby, Bleddyn played only once for Taff's Well in a "serious" game although he has appeared in many fun games such as the "Married vs Singles". His illustrious career with Cardiff has been succinctly described in Mr. Danny Davies's book upon Cardiff R.F.C. Bleddyn made his debut in 1938-39 against Ebbw Vale* in a match in which brother Bryn also played, and continued to season 1954-55, playing 283 First Team games. Captain of his Club 1953-54, he led the team to victory over the touring All Blacks. A Barbarian, Captain of Wales with 21 Caps, and member of the British Isles Touring Team to New Zealand and Australia 1950. Holder of Cardiff's highest scoring record of 41 tries in the season of 1947-48. One of the greatest centre three-quarters of all time.' *(Cardiff Firsts had no recorded fixtures with Ebbw Vale between 1931 and 1954, this game was a Cardiff Athletic fixture.)

The Cardiff RFC Hall of Fame website records: 'Bleddyn Llewellyn Williams knew from his days as a schoolboy rugby player in Taff's Well that Cardiff was the only club for him. His elder brothers Gwyn and Brinley had preceded him in Blue & Black colours before the war and, as the whole world of rugby now knows, five more of the remarkable Williams fraternity – Lloyd, Vaughan, Cenydd, Elwyn and Tony – would one day follow in his footsteps. But in the ten years from 1945 it was Bleddyn who achieved his life-long ambition of playing for the club and then became the unchallenged Prince of Centres. "As things turned out it was a natural progression for me" remembered Bleddyn. "I played for Cardiff in the Dewar Shield and then for Wales Schools at full back, which was a bit of a shock to the system to say the least, then went off to Rydal School and

333

captained the Anglo-Welsh Public Schools against the Welsh Secondary Schools at the Arms Park. I'd also had a game for the Rags at Ebbw Vale and a Cardiff XV at Chepstow, with Lyn Williams at fly-half and Wilf Wooller at centre, so I kept in touch with the Club during the war".

In fact, by 1945 Bleddyn Williams had already experienced a wide range of rugby for Wales in the Service Internationals and for the Barbarians, the RAF and even the Great Britain team that took on the impressively titled 'Dominions XV' at Leicester in the closing months of the war. So, it was no surprise when he saw out his service days at St. Athan that he found himself at the Arms Park and part of the Jack Matthews' Cardiff team of 1945-46. "Yes, Jack and I soon hit it off and, yes, we enjoyed playing together. We had done so before, for an East Wales team that played the British Army in 1943, but now we were playing week in, week out, and were just two parts of what was to become a complete club team.""

In an interview for the Cardiff Rugby Museum, Bleddyn remembered losing to the New Zealand Army, the 'Kiwis' 6-3 on Boxing Day, 1945, because the Cardiff hooker missed a penalty in front of the posts. However, he said the Cardiff team learned a lot from the game – *'they set a precedent, really, about what rugby should become, they were very fit, threw the ball about, they were all Army boys... From then on our average crowd was about 30,000, we played such attractive rugby that everywhere we went, we drew record crowds, and ever since then Cardiff have been well-known for their open play of rugby... we transferred our quality of rugby from this club, or whatever it was, to the Lions, and we still are considered the most popular travelling team, including the '71 Lions, because of the number of people we affected and how well we played... we didn't have any coaches and we drew the First Test, I couldn't play, I pulled a hamstring, and the Second Test was lost eight nil, we lost our wing forward after 10 minutes with a broken nose, no replacements, you see. The Third Test was 6-3, and the last was 11-8. We could well have won the last Test. Ken Jones scored a try in that Test, which is still considered one of the best...* (next speaking of his captaincy of Cardiff and Wales in 1953) *Bear in mind that in 1953 we didn't have any coach, it was many years later that coaches arrived. So we got together, we had experience of them in New Zealand... and we planned it, we thought that if we could tie up their wing forwards, man for man in the backs we had a better back division, so I thought we had better do this from the line-out, and if we could contain their back-row forwards in the back of the line-out, then on our throw, we threw to the back, tied up their wing-forwards, then we got it back and we scored two tries in the first twenty minutes, with open play, and all from inside our own half.*

And we believed that the best place to attack from was from our own quarter of the field. The defence is not so alert. Two great tries, and we beat them 8-3...There's a story at the end of it. John Llewellyn was our full-back, and he's from the same village as me, and he called a mark on our own goal line, so I said to him, and I asked the referee how long to go, and he said, "It's only a few minutes to go". So I said to John, "Make absolutely sure that, even if you gain a yard, put it into touch". And what happened? He sliced the ball into touch in goal. And of course, you had to restart the game, and it was a scrum on our goal line. (Note, not on the 5-yard line). *And their put-in. Anyway, the ball was put in twice, and we had to re-assemble again and Beckingham said to me, our hooker, he said "Skip, we'll get a heel against the head". And he did, and the ball went to Willis, to Morgan who put it to touch, and the game was over. But if they had put the ball in and heeled the ball there was a good chance that they would score a try and convert it, but they didn't, and we won the game. We had a great social life, that's why I can't get on at all with this modern game, the professionals, we never see the Cardiff players in here* (the clubhouse). *Well, what we did, we always stayed here after the game. We'd always stay for the first hour then go to the little pub right opposite here, the City Arms, and we used to have a bit of a drink there, as we knew the landlord very well, then we'd come straight back here, and we'd stay here until it closed. And all the supporters used to come here, and we'd have a great singsong, and this is what we did whether we played at home or away. The social life was very good.'*

The *Cardiff Hall of Fame* website continues: 'The 1947-48 season was a celebrated one for the club and its players. Under Haydn Tanner's inspirational leadership only two games were lost – at Pontypool in September and Penarth in March. Not that Bleddyn was one to worry too much about unbeaten records. Years later he was to write: "*Invincible records are generally a bad thing, for in pursuing a policy of maintaining an unbeaten record a team is inclined to pursue negative tactics.*" No one accused Bleddyn Williams or any of the teams under his influence of being negative. At 5 foot 10 inches and 13 stone, he seemed bigger on the field, and was a devastating tackler and runner. Throughout the season of 39 wins and 182 tries, we saw a free spirit and a range of ball-handling and running skills rarely seen over such a prolonged period. The culmination was in the final home game against Gloucester on 28 April 1948, with the team running in nine tries including 4 to Bleddyn, giving a record total for the season of 41. It was an individual achievement that was to remain unsurpassed for nearly 50 years.

The highlight of Bleddyn Williams' two periods of captaincy, and arguably the Club's greatest day, was the defeat of the All Blacks in 1953. Considering the dearth of newsreel film, the opening 20 minutes of the game on 21 November 1953 continues to be a remarkable place in the memories of those who were there, and in the imaginations of those who were not. It is now folklore that Bleddyn instructed his team to run at every opportunity, even from the deepest defence. Thus, after six minutes Cliff

Morgan broke from the scrum in his own 25 with the captain's words still ringing in his head: "*We have got to try things... if we fail, we fail, but we have got to be different*". And different it was, as Gwyn Rowlands cross-kicked and Sid Judd gathered to score at the Westgate St. posts. Different, again, when within minutes Bleddyn carried on another audacious Morgan break-out from defence and this time Rowlands keeps the ball and touches down himself in the right corner. 8-3 was the score-line and the historic final score, and the messages of congratulations poured in from all over the world. Four weeks later and Bleddyn did it again as he led Wales to a 13-8 victory over New Zealand at the Arms Park, No one has repeated the feat in the long years since.

For Bleddyn Williams, though, Cardiff Rugby Club was not just about the glory. "*It is a special club because it sets standards, particularly personal ones. I was so lucky in my playing days because everywhere I turned, I had role models. Off the field there were Hubert Johnson and Brice Jenkins, Les Spence and SC Cravos, Gwyn Porter and Arthur Cornish. On it, just think of the forwards we had from Les Manfield, Maldwyn James and Gwyn Evans in the early days, to John Nelson and CD Williams. And then there was Bowes! Stan could play tight and loose head and because of that, was a reserve on stand-by 19 times in one season. That was the sort of loyalty that was evident throughout the Club.*" The greatest role model and setter of standards, of course, was Bleddyn Williams himself. By the time of his retirement in the spring of 1955 he had long since been established as one of the legends of Cardiff Rugby. His final match was against Llanelli and at the end, another Cardiff victory secured, his teammates hoisted him on their shoulders, and the band played and the crowd sang, "*For he's a jolly good fellow.*"

In a brief summary, Bleddyn was educated at Rydal School, and while there captained the Anglo-Welsh Public Schools against Welsh Secondary Schools at Cardiff Arms Park. This author only recently discovered that his eldest brother Gwyn selflessly 'went North' to help pay for Bleddyn's public school fees. Known as the '*Prince of Centres*', Bleddyn scored 185 tries in 283 matches for Cardiff in 10 seasons, and 'gave' perhaps over 250 tries to his wing. '*He was club captain in 1949-50 and 1953-54, the latter gaining him legendary status with Cardiff's victory over New Zealand and, five weeks later, as captain again when Wales beat the All Blacks again at the Arms Park*'. Bleddyn played for Wales in the WWII Services Internationals, and the immediate post-war Victory internationals. When the Five Nations Championship recommenced in January 1947, he won the first of 22 caps in Wales' first game against England. He captained Wales five times and with five wins. In 1950 he was vice-captain of the British Isles in New Zealand, Australia and Ceylon, playing in 21 games, seven of them as captain, and scoring 13 tries. A popular Barbarian, he captained the club in two of his eleven appearances, which were the two main fixtures against Australia in 1948 and South Africa in 1952. He was on the Barbarian committee 1949-1951. Without the Second World War, his continuous generosity in passing to his wings to score tries when he was in a position to do so, and injuries, Bleddyn would have set many records playing rugby. Three of his brothers – Tony, Cenydd and Lloyd - were also Barbarians. No other family, save the Biggs of Cardiff, gave the Baa-Baas four brothers, and no other family gave *'the greatest rugby club in the world'* eight playing brothers.

In *The Williams Family* (1984), Don Llewellyn writes: 'If Bleddyn Williams had been playing in the present era, he would have been a megastar, although that is a term that the modest man would be disinclined to use, for he played in an age when there were different values in sport and, indeed, in life generally. That is not to say that there was no hero-worship in his time, for most small boys in South Wales, during the 1940s and early 50s, wanted to emulate the *"Prince of Centres"* and crowds of them swarmed onto the Arms Park pitch at the final whistle of matches, to jostle for his autograph. Bleddyn Williams was acclaimed as the best centre of his time and although his all-round game was universally admired, it was his magical side-step that captured the imagination of everyone. Such was his pre-eminence in the post-war game, that rugby scribes in their reports of matches introduced a degree of familiarity which had been unknown up to then, and not been seen since, for example, *"Cardiff were on the back foot at this stage and were staring defeat in the face, when BLEDDYN went off on one of his inimitable runs, leaving in his wake a posse of would-be tacklers before scoring under the posts."* In his Cardiff career Bleddyn scored 185 tries in 283 appearances. It is a matter of conjecture how many more he would have scored had he not chosen, time and time again, to give a scoring pass when it was clear that he could have crossed the line himself.'

This writer has the remains of a cutting titled *'Greatest Centre of All Time'* written shortly after Bleddyn's final game, against Llanelli – *'His total number of caps for Wales is 22. This number would have been far exceeded had there been no war. Injuries also prevented him on many occasions from representing his country, During the tour of Australia and New Zealand in 1950, Bleddyn was recognised as the greatest centre-threequarter ever to visit the Antipodes, and there was much regret among his numerous friends abroad that he was not included in this year's touring team.* (June to September 1955 – Bleddyn would have gone if chosen, but retired instead. The series was drawn, two Tests each). ***Presented with the Llanelly Tie.*** *Bleddyn leaves the game in perfectly fit condition. His club colleagues and officials parted with him with much regret, and, after the game against Llanelly on Saturday, he was presented with a Llanelly club tie by Ray Williams, the Welsh international, on behalf of the committee. On Saturday Bleddyn received letters, telegrams and cablegrams from all* over the world on the occasion of his retirement from the rugby game. This great and heroic personality who has played our national game so well and so brilliantly for his beloved country, quits the scene of his great triumphs still unspoiled, modest and unassuming. He is regarded in Taff's Well with affection and high esteem. That the Williams family will carry on this great tradition is certain, even to Bleddyn's younger brother, Tony, who to all appearances in the exact replica of Bleddyn.'

Gerald Edwards interviewed Bleddyn in 1984, for *The Williams Family*, titled '**Bleddyn looks back at a life of seemingly infinite variety, and it all began with Taff's Well**': '*Well, first of all it began with Taff's Well Infants and then I progressed through the other school, where the headmaster was Captain Walter Trigg. I have many fond memories of that time, including of course that of starting my rugby career. That was when I was eight years of age, and it all came as a result of Gwyn my elder brother playing for Taff's Well First XV, when he was just fourteen. Mr Trigg thought it quite silly that he should be playing senior rugby, when there should be an opportunity for him to get a schoolboy cap. As a result of that, a schoolboys' side was started in Taff's Well, for Gwyn's sake in fact – and I made up the numbers as an eight-year-old scrumhalf. I was very small, a little dwt* (Welsh for 'tot'), *really. Well, they thought I was too small, and dropped me from the line-up for the first game. Somewhere along the line I played Hell, I understand, so they put me back in, and I graduated from there.'*

In his biography, Bleddyn mentions his father's brother Phillip, who had played wing for Cardiff reserves around the turn of the century, and wrote '*My grandfather, Ted Roberts, the Risca and Taff's Well forward, also took pride in the family's sporting descent, and it was he who influenced me more than any other member of my family. His inbred passion for, and unsurpassed knowledge of, the game inspired me. I hung on every word of his colourful tales of the Monmouthshire and Glamorgan League games, and their very ruggedness of description fired me with a desire to play the game... Rugby for me really started with an old shoe wrapped in paper. It served bearably for a ball, but unless caught deftly our young "players" were liable to suffer a painful crack on the knuckles.'*

'I had a thoroughly enjoyable childhood in the village of Taff's Well. I was a bit of a 'loner' in some respects, because I used to do a hell of a lot of walking – over the Graig Mountain and so on. I was involved with Roger and Polly Williams, who owned Rhiw'r Ddar Farm, spending many an hour haymaking and helping to churn the milk and the cheese, which they made there. In the summertime, with other friends of mine we used to make 'tents', by bending trees over and intertwining the branches with ferns, and we'd sleep out in those. Then the family, well my father, bought me a tent and we pitched up at the Rhymney Woods, where we left it for a time. After a week or so, it disappeared. Then, on one of my sojourns to the

338

farm with Polly Williams, I went into the barn and there was my tent – so I nicked it back. They'd had no idea whose it was, and hadn't mentioned it, so I just took it back. I also remember taking the carthorses, Dolly and Sam, to Paul Tripp the blacksmith down near Canal Row.

Another thing I did in summertime was to go on the barges, that were taking flour to Hopkin Morgan's in Pontypridd. On arrival there, they always used to give me huge slabs of cake, because if they had anything left over from the day before, they used to give it to us. I fed myself quite often on cakes! Then the barges would be filled with chains, and we would take them down to the Docks in Cardiff. There was the Blayden family from Llandaff North, who had some of the boats and also the Frasers from the Treble Locks. Often, I would sleep overnight in the cabin, when they anchored up by the Cow and Snuffers (pub) in Llandaff North. This was right opposite the Tivoli Cinema, and as a kid I would go to the cinema and come back and sleep in the boat. We also learned to swim in that canal, and the big pond below Roger Williams's farm.'

Bleddyn credits his elder brothers Gwyn ('a veritable hero') and Bryn with training him and 'infusing confidence' in his abilities with a rugby ball. Only aged 15, Gwyn was playing regularly for Cardiff Athletic before joining the Firsts aged just 16. For two years, Bleddyn played scrumhalf before a growth spurt, and as outside half captained Cardiff Boys in 1936-37 to their first Dewar Shield victory in 12 years. Bleddyn played centre for the Rest of Wales against Wales in a Welsh Schools Trial at Aberavon, and his headmaster Captain R Trigg, summoned him to be told he was to play for Wales at full-back. Bleddyn was 'flabbergasted', never having played the position, and played against England at Gloucester. Del Harris, his Taff's Well schoolmaster, played for the village club and was also instrumental in helping Bleddyn learn the game, but Bleddyn's moment of real enlightenment came in seeing Cardiff fullback Tommy Stone. With brother Bryn, he had watched Cardiff in a charity game at Taff's Well on 2 October 1935, only winning 6-5. 'I saw Tommy field the ball direct from kick-off and side-step through the fast-following Taff's Well forwards. My eyes opened wide. *"I'm jolly well going to try that", I told Brinley excitedly. And I did. It came off and I had learned to side-step. I say learned, because although it came naturally, it had not been until I saw it being employed by someone else that I realised there was such a thing as a jink. At the height of my career, "Wizard of the Jink" was a frequent newspaper headline. All thanks to Tommy Stone.*'

'I used to enjoy the walk over the top to near the Black Cock Inn from Price's farm, and up into the forest near the Castle (this could be Caerphilly, but more likely Castell Coch, which makes for a circular route), where we used to pick wild strawberries. Those fields surrounding the forest used to have a mass of flowers in summer. It was a wonderful childhood. As a result of me being in that school side, and then getting into the 'Cardiff Town' team, as they called it in those days, I must have impressed someone – and later I was to find out his name – that I had something going for me as a rugby player. For, on the strength of that, one day, the Bursar from Rydal School, a public school in Colwyn Bay, arrived on our doorstep and expressed a wish to see my father and mother. It turned out that they wanted to offer me a scholarship at Rydal. My father worked down the docks and we were a large family, which would get even larger later, and it was clearly going to be difficult. However, they agreed at last, and off I went as a fourteen-year-old, travelling on the train, going first up to Shrewsbury and then, changing trains at Chester, I went on to Colwyn Bay, where I was met and taken to the school.

That started such a different form of life for me, for which I was terribly indebted, really. I loved every minute of the four years I spent there. It was a period of two years in Colwyn Bay, incidentally, because the war broke out and the school was taken over by the Ministry of Food. We moved to a hotel which was on the back road from Conway, or Conwy as it's called now, and Penmaenmawr. It's near the Sychnant Pass, a big building known as the Oakwood Park Hotel. There were over two hundred there – all under one roof. It was a fine place and another reason for enjoying our stay was that there was a nine-hole golf course nearby, so we were able to play golf as well! They were happy days, but I shall never forget my introduction to Rydal. I was put into a room with three other boys, at a private house next to the school called 'Ingleside.' I got into a bed which had been 'apple-pied' (made up in apple-pie order), and then found that a pound of tripe had been placed in it. So: *"Welcome to Rydal!"* I was fortunate because one of the boys was a fellow named David Owen, D.A.G. Owen, who became 'Dago' to us. His parents were Ladies and Gents Outfitters in Penmaenmawr, and those people were extremely kind to me. When we were able to go out on Sunday, they used to come and pick us up and take us home for Sunday lunch – they were wonderful people. I haven't seen Dago since we left school, but he lives in London, and we always exchange Christmas cards.

I was very saddened by one event which happened soon after my arrival at Rydal. I knew my mother's brother Teddy Roberts, who lived opposite us in Moy Road in Taff's Well, had not been well for some time. He had been a wonderful rugby player – he had played for Taff's Well – but although I didn't know it, he had TB. This is why, by then, he had not been able to work and so on, and I spent a lot of time with him. In letters from home, my mother, not wishing to spoil my first term at my new school, said simply that my uncle was 'not very well.' When I came home at Christmas time, I discovered that he had died three weeks after I left. I broke my heart, I must say, he was the youngest of the Roberts family, you see.' (Edward 'Teddie' Roberts was Bleddyn's uncle, the brother of his mother. Roy Roberts, the Cardiff player, was another brother, as was Tom

Roberts, the Taff's Well stalwart. 'Ted' Roberts was Bleddyn's grandfather, the father of his mother).

Sister Enid, in her account, made the point that Ted Roberts and Dai Millward 'started rugby' in Taff's Well. In *A View from the Garth*, we read '*Two outstanding forwards of this period were Tommy Howells and Ted Roberts. The team photograph of 1910 shows Ted in all his glory looking for all the world like Taff's Well's answer to John L. Sullivan. Ted was one of those larger-than-life characters that Taff's Well seems to have been blessed with in abundance. He particularly enjoyed the local derby game against Tongwynlais. In those days, just prior to the Great War, the main local derby was against Tongwynlais, rather than Pentyrch... In 1910 Ted Roberts was not to know that he was to play a major part in creating one of the great sagas of Welsh rugby, for Ted's daughter married Mr. Arthur Williams, a union that produced eight sons. Those sons were to become a legend in Welsh rugby, and one, Bleddyn, is **regarded by many as the greatest player in the history of the game**... It was not until the 1923-24 season that the Club lost its ground record when Bryncethin lowered our colours by 11-0. Taff's Well played one man short through most of the game and in these pre-substitute days this was indeed a disadvantage. Ted Roberts was a frequent supporter and kept his fellow-supporters entertained with his comments... Ted, of course, was interested particularly in the play of his son Tom, who had performed with distinction as a fullback until Percy Field returned to play for the Club.... There could only be one fullback, so Tom being very solidly built agreed to play in the forwards and performed marvellously as a hooker and wing forward... Throughout our history men have emerged that have been larger than life characters – Fred Harris, Fred Porter, Ted Roberts, Tony Bonetto, Elwyn Williams* (one of the Williams brothers), *Iorrie Jones. The list is impressive. Yet it was this diminutive, dapper little man* (Dai Millward) *who bestrides the history of Taff's well R.F.C. like a giant.*'

Bleddyn continued, 'Roy, another brother of my mother, well of course he played with us at Cardiff. Bill Tamplin was our second cousin, so there were three of us in that famous 1947-48 Cardiff side. The three of us played against Australia for Cardiff. Roy, when he left Cardiff, went on to captain Pontypridd. Around Rydal the fields were somewhat undulating, so we played only House matches there, and used to travel back and fore to Colwyn Bay for the main school games. Schools' matches were mainly played against Liverpool and Birkenhead sides, because there was very little rugby played in North Wales. One feature of that, was that the school acquired a yellow bus, similar to the ones used in the United States today. This one, though, had a canvas roof – it was an old charabanc really – and that was our means of transport to games. There was quite a steep hill going down to Conway so that was alright, but on the way back we would have to all get out and help push it up the hill.

341

I obtained a schoolboy cap in 1937 against England at Gloucester, and was chosen to play at fullback, the only time I played fullback in my life – then and never again! This was as a result of the idiosyncrasies of the selectors – you know, an *"I'll pick your boy if you pick mine"* sort of situation. I did play for Taff's Well when I was sixteen, when I was home from school. It was against Chepstow. I had played in a Welsh trial as a fly half when North Wales played East Wales at Ruabon, but later I broke a bone in my leg, and consequently I didn't get a Welsh Secondary Schools cap. In any case, that was the year I left to join the RAF.' W.R.U. referee and editor of Welsh Rugby, Fred Croster, recalled that during the war, Hubert Johnson was stationed nearby and skippered wartime games when he was able. Fred was also stationed in the area with the Army P.T. Corps and was 'lucky to get the occasional game with the club'. Danny "Massa Dan" Davies was a sergeant in the Home Guard and did much to round up players to keep the Cardiff club alive, along with schoolmaster Arthur Cornish and Brice Jenkins, arranging charity games. Bleddyn was 18 on 22 February 1941, and Croster recalled, *'Several of the club's traditional fixtures continued and I can well remember one game against the "old enemy", Newport, when a youngster came bursting into the dressing-room just two minutes before kick-off, wild with excitement. It was the 18th birthday of Bleddyn Williams who had raced back to the ground after registering for service with the Royal Air Force!'*

Bleddyn continues, 'Well, I had volunteered for the RAF' (aged eighteen, upon leaving Rydal), 'but in the meantime I had been playing some rugby down here' (South Wales). 'I had played one game for the Rags up at Ebbw Vale, and then I joined Cardiff and was all set to play for the Firsts, when a bomb fell on the Arms Park, leaving a large crater at the city end of the ground' (- 2 January 1941.) At this time, though, my brother Brinley, who was in the Army and stationed nearby, was playing for Cilfynydd – so he invited me to play there.

I joined the RAF, but had to wait about nine months before I could get in. I volunteered to become a pilot, and I went first to a block of flats near Lords' Cricket Ground. Whilst up there I was invited to play for Rosslyn Park. At that time, my co-centre was Claude Davey, who had captained Wales in the victory over the All Blacks of 1935, and I was to be the captain of the last Wales side to beat the All Blacks in 1953. We had a good team, and from there I went to Cambridge University, the RAF side of it, of course.' Bleddyn had only been in the RAF for 3 weeks, when he played against a New Zealand Combined Forces XV at Bedford on 2 January 1943, the RAF winning 25-19. He was able to play regularly for the Service until October of that year, when he was sent to the USA to train as a fighter pilot in Arizona. Before leaving, he had played for various teams, RAF Heaton Park, where Richard Jenkins, later known as Burton, was a fine wing forward. Bleddyn mentions in his biography being taught

342

flying by a Californian of Welsh descent, and staying with him in Los Angeles. Touring film studios, he met 'a host of stars' including Gary Cooper, Merle Oberon and William Bendix. During wartime Bleddyn had joined Cardiff, switching his position to centre, but often played outside half. He was offered £6,000 to play rugby league for Leeds – about £500,000 today, but turned down the offer. His oldest brother Gwyn had gone North to the league's best club at the time, Wigan, and later his younger brother Cenydd was to go professional with the best team of his era, St Helens. Gwyn later recalled that he went North to help pay for Bleddyn's Rydal School fees - Bleddyn seemed unaware of this. Bleddyn was to stay amateur and forge an outstanding centre partnership for Cardiff and Wales with Dr Jack Matthews, along with fly-half Billy Cleaver making up one of the most formidable midfield trios any nation has ever produced.

'There I did what was called the ITW, the initial training course. I got through those examinations and stayed on at Cambridge, first at St John's College and afterwards at Magdalene College. I did my initial flying at a place called Caxton Gibbet, which was a field outside Cambridge, and was next door to a pub which was 'The Gibbet', where they used to hang people. I passed my training, and this of course was the stage that they know if you are *'washed out'* or not – whether you aren't capable of judging height and so on.

An interesting feature of this, also, was that there were just two of us stationed at Marshall's Airfield, which is now Cambridge Airport of course. We were stuck in a Nissen Hut and the other boy was Billy Liddell, the great Scottish soccer international, a lovely man, a non-drinker and non-smoker. Unfortunately, Billy ultimately *'washed out'* as a pilot, but he went to South Africa as an observer (navigator). Eventually we went up to Heaton Park in Manchester, which was a holding unit for the RAF. Then I went to New Brunswick in Canada, another holding unit, and then to Arizona to complete my flying training. It was near a small town, about 18 miles from Phoenix, that I finally qualified as a pilot. I came back and was going on to advanced flying school, but we lost so many glider pilots at Arnhem, that they couldn't afford the time to train any more. In fact, there seemed to be a surplus of our lot, so "*you, you and you*" became volunteers to become glider pilots. I received my initial instruction with gliders at Shobdon in Herefordshire. We later progressed to the much larger troop-carrying glider, the *Horsa*.

Midway through the advanced glider training, I returned to Cradenhill, Herefordshire, to undertake an army course as a platoon commander. This was because, on landing, the glider pilot would assume command of the thirty or so infantry troops we had transported. In the event however, having been subsequently attached to the Headquarter Group, by virtue of the fact that I was to convey the radio equipment for the Airborne Division,

I was relieved of this responsibility, for what became known as *Operation Varsity*, for the crossing of the Rhine into Germany. I had to land as near as possible to a farmhouse, which was designated as our headquarters. It was a pretty horrendous flight, as you can imagine. There were over a thousand glider combinations, some coming up from France, which were American, and all the rest from East Anglia. I was stationed in Essex myself. Well, I ended up with my nose in the orchard!

 ArmyFlyingMuseum @armyflying · 21m ···
On 24 March 1945, Glider Pilot & International Welsh #Rugby player Bleddyn L. Williams set off from RAF Rivenhall in a Horsa Glider during Op Varsity. He would be sent home a week later by his CO to play in the Great Britain v. the Dominions game at Welford Road.
Enjoy today's 🏉

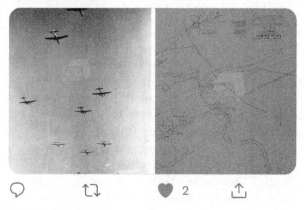

$\heartsuit$ 2

Tweet from '@ArmyFlyingMuseum'

Field Marshal Montgomery had put up a smokescreen, to safeguard the men coming across the Rhine by DUKW or whatever, and the RAF the night before had bombed Dusseldorf or some other city nearby, and that caused more smoke, so it was very difficult.' (DUKW was a manufacturer's code based on D the model year, 1942; U was the body style, utility [amphibious]; K was all-wheel drive; and W for dual rear axles. Called by everyone '*ducks*', the 6-wheeled vehicles were shaped like boats, and used to transport soldiers and equipment.) 'On top of that, the American parachutists who were supposed to come down at a different landing area, actually came down on ours, so we didn't only have Germans shooting at us, but we had to avoid the parachutists coming down. Anyway, somewhere along the line I must have received a bullet in the air-pipe system, so I had no brakes. When you land like that, you've got to go a bit, and I ended up in a reen, and my nosewheel snapped off. Fortunately, we were less than a hundred yards from the farmhouse which was our destination.' (A 'reen' is a running waterway, linking a ditch or stream to a river, used for drainage, and a common term on the Cardiff and Gwent Levels on the East Glamorgan and Monmouthshire coasts).

He reminisced later, again about the war, '*Although I trained as a pilot, I never got the chance to fly a Spitfire as I'd wanted to. Instead, I was retrained as a glider pilot. We were dropped over the Rhine in Operation Varsity and I was part of a 1,000-strong glider unit heading five miles inside German lines. There were a mass of 88mm guns firing at us and 98 pilots never made it home.*" In Bleddyn's biography, he wrote: '*There came the day, in that thick, swirling smoke, that was intended to cover the crossing of British and American troops as they swarmed across the Rhine, and I remembered the crashed glider in the long grass at Oxford. The smokescreen might have helped the Army; it was an additional hazard for the R.A.F. I cursed frenziedly as I nosed through the black curtain, my second pilot, Sergeant Graham Richmond, standing up in the cockpit without his safety belt and directing me in. He made a good job of it, for with German ack-ack bursts framing our progress, we lurched right through the wall of the farmhouse that was to be our H.Q. The "old firm" of Williams and Richmond had delivered the goods. Right to the doorstep! It was well for me that my particular foxhole was not investigated by any German counter-attackers. For my Sten-gun was distinctly bent, as well as being clogged with dirt. If Jerry had come along, I might never have seen the Arms Park again.*'

Having landed his glider, Flying Officer Williams spent the next 6 days living in a slit trench, wrapped in a parachute to keep himself warm. *Operation Varsity** on 24 March 1945 involved more than 16,000 paratroopers and several thousand aircraft, the largest airborne operation in history to be conducted on a single day and in one location. American pilot error caused their 513th Parachute Infantry Regiment to land on Bleddyn's drop zone, which he refers to above. The British 6th Airborne and American 17th Airborne Divisions then captured Rhine bridges, and secured towns that could have been used to delay the advance of the main British ground forces. The two divisions incurred more than 2,000 casualties but captured about 3,500 German soldiers. The operation was the last large-scale Allied airborne operation of World War II.

'I was there about a week, and it was my job to go around and find out names of those glider pilots who had not reported in – so that wasn't a very pleasant thing to do. There were lots of Germans who had been killed, still lying there – but more than that, it was a sad thing that a lot of our gliders had gone into the woods, largely because they had either been shot down, or had lost their way because of the smoke. In one or two cases we saw the pilots and troops all dead with broken necks. One of my mates, with whom I trained in Arizona, was originally in the Police Office in Bargoed. Well, we couldn't find him at all – that is, until I was walking through the barn, which was the casualty clearing station, and found my trousers being pulled. I looked down, and for a moment I didn't recognise him. Then it transpired it was Howard Curry, and what had happened to him was that he had landed in a wood, when carrying troops and a jeep and trailer. The jeep had gone through the bulkhead, killed his second pilot, and they found him (Howard Curry) wrapped around the axle. Howard was in a dreadful state. He ended up in the hospital here at Church Village' (a few miles west of Taff's Well), 'where he went through plastic surgery for two years, before going back into the Air Force! He stayed and made a life of it afterwards. He died just a few years ago.

As a matter of fact, something happened during our training for the Rhine action, which in a way prepared us for those visibility problems we were to face. We had a trial run, flying over the Cotswolds. My tug-pilot, via the communications along the towrope, said *"Bleddyn, we are in a bit of trouble – the fog has come down over our aerodrome and we are going to have a problem finding the place."* He decided we should fly to London, where it was a little clearer, to find Liverpool Street Station and fly down the railway line. Rivenhall aerodrome, our home base, was only about half a mile from Witham Station. He said, *"When we get to Witham Station, you pull off, turn left, go down the road and over the mess."'* (A mess is the designated eating place for the military.) 'Well, I was the only one who landed on that runway. That was a good experience for us and stood us in good stead, for what happened a fortnight later.

One extraordinary story is that before I had left the Rhine, I had been selected to play for Great Britain against The Dominions at Leicester, and this was to be on the Saturday following our arrival in Germany.' (One must remember that Bleddyn had not yet played in official games for Cardiff Firsts, and had played just a few games for Rosslyn Park. Bleddyn's selection would have been based on some spectacular performances for the RAF, Combined Services, Wales in the Service Internationals and for the Barbarians). 'So, on the Friday before the Saturday, I was walking around doing my job as usual, and Major Hugh Bartlett, who was our Commanding Officer, and who later captained Sussex at cricket, came along. He had been at Cambridge with Wilf Wooller and was a keen rugby man as well. He came up to me and said, *"Aren't you supposed to be playing at Leicester tomorrow?"* He followed that with: *"Pack your bags and get ready as quickly as you can."* They stuck me in a jeep and drove me to the Rhine, which was about five miles away, and crossing into Germany proper was the 53rd Welsh Division, and I went back in an empty DUKW the other way. A jeep met me there, and I was driven to Eindhoven in Holland, from where I flew on a transport plane to Brize Norton in Oxford – where, later on, strangely enough, I was stationed. Incidentally, I was stationed, as I said, in Rivenhall in Essex, and my RAF CO at that camp had flown his Oxford aircraft to Brize Norton, where he picked me up and flew me back to camp. By this time, my wife Violet, who was from Cardiff, was desperate – I had met her incidentally when I was working during the school holidays. She worked at Paton's just by the railway station in Taff's Well. Anyhow, my bat-woman had told her that only two had come back from the operation and she thought I was dead, so I arrived like an apparition at the door about midnight. There was joy all around, as you can imagine. Well, I travelled to Leicester the following day, accompanied by my wife and played. In fact, I scored a try and we won – but I was never sent back to Germany.' (He was exhausted with his travels, but Great Britain beat the Dominions 36-13 with Bleddyn scoring 1 of the side's 9 tries.)

I ultimately did a course of American gliders – they were much lighter than ours. They didn't carry as many troops, but we were due to go to Burma, where you would fly your gliders low into the jungle area, where a path would be cleared for you to land, and you would be snatched out. So, I did a course at Ramsbury in Wiltshire, where we were placed on the runway with a loop on a pole, and down would come a Dakota which would hook you up and snatch you off the ground. The rope would unwind, and you were away, but there was the danger of whiplash. Years later, when the eminent surgeon David Jenkins, who was later to die after crashing in a Tiger Moth (the kind on which I had originally trained), x-rayed me, and he was amazed to see the condition of my neck. He said, "*I can understand a prop forward having a neck like yours – but not a centre three-quarter!*"

Whilst I was on that course, my second pilot was a fellow named Graham Richmond. He was from up the Northwest, and I used to take him home with me at weekends when I was free. He'd stay at my wife's parents' house, and he used to play darts at one of the pubs, for pints, you see. Anyway, whilst we were on this course for going to Burma, we were walking through Bathampton one day, and suddenly he disappeared – and came back in a big Alvis car. I couldn't understand this at all, but I was soon to find out. He said, "*I'm getting married, Bleddyn, and would you be my Best Man?*" I agreed and come the day, I was picked up at Carlisle with a Rolls-Royce - the type that's hired for the day, you know – and I was taken to this huge mansion. It was then that I found out that he was a millionaire. His father had made his money in timber in Canada. Although I had lived with this chap for eighteen months, it was only then that I found out. Sadly, though, I learned from his sister who was living in Edinburgh – when I was up there playing for Wales against Scotland – that the marriage had only lasted about three weeks. Also, sadly, Graham died a young man.

Well, we were all ready to go to Burma, but first I was to play another game on the Saturday for the Welsh Services team, a mixture of professional and amateur players, a magnificent side. When I got back on the Monday morning, I found that the posting had been cancelled. Not long after that, of course, they dropped the Bomb and they obviously knew this was going to happen – so we didn't go. Well, I had finished flying so I got myself posted to St Athan' (- an RAF aerodrome 15 miles west, along the coast from Cardiff). 'I went there as the Assistant Physical Education Officer, and was there for over eighteen months, and was able to play for Cardiff.'

From 11 March 1939 until 18 January 1947, eight years, Wales did not play a full international match, but they did play games of international class that never brought full caps to those who took part in them. The Services Internationals saw the return of Rugby League players allowed, and were played for charitable causes. When Wales beat England 17-12 at Swansea in 1942, they were aided by the professionals Alan Edwards, the great Gus Risman, Syd Williams, Willie Davies, Trevor Foster and Gwyn Williams, the brother of Bleddyn, all superb players who had changed codes pre-war. (In April 1943, Gwyn was almost killed in North Africa). In 1943 Wales defeated England 34-7 and 11-9 with Air Craftsman, later Flying Officer Bleddyn Williams (RAF and Cardiff) making his debut. (Gwyn was supposed to be playing, but wished to head with his regiment to the Front in North Africa). Bleddyn's later partnership with Gus Risman in Services and other teams, he acknowledged, was a huge part of his rugby education. Post-war, Bleddyn scored an astounding 30 tries in 21 games in 1945-46, while still in the RAF. Bleddyn played in the last match to be organised by the war-time Inter-Services Rugby Committee, a British Empire XV v France at Richmond on 28 April 1945, before a capacity crowd. The French side contained 10 players who were later to be capped by their country, while their captain had been capped before the war. Almost all of the British Empire side were internationals and alongside Williams were four RAF colleagues. The Empire side won 27-6, and of particular interest is that the legendary Brigadier–General Jacques Chaban-Delmas, who had led the Resistance inside France during the war and played against the RAF in Paris, appeared on the wing. Bleddyn was also a member of the RAF team that played in the first Inter-Service fixture after the war, at Twickenham on 16 February 1946, when the RAF beat the Army 9-6.

'I came out of the RAF in November 1946. I was demobbed in Blackpool and so started to work in Cardiff. Firstly, I worked for G.V. Wynne-Jones, the commentator, who was in business. After playing several times for Wales, I was then selected for the British Lions – and that's another story. I had been injured in the final Welsh Trial in 1950 in Cardiff, when I tore all the external ligaments in my knee. Having been selected as captain, I missed all the Welsh games that season. Anyway, after being out of plaster for just a week, I returned to play for Cardiff at Bath, for a match in which I was expected to prove my fitness. It was Cliff Morgan's first senior appearance, and on the way there he had said, "*The best way you can prove your fitness is by scoring a try in the last minute.*" I didn't take much notice of that, but towards the end of the game I saw him speaking to the referee. He was actually asking how much time we had left and was told "*three minutes.*" Cliff turned to me and said, "*Are you ready to score your try?*". Anyhow, soon Cliff was beating his opposite number and one or two others. He went up to the fullback and I was outside him. He gave me the pass and I scored under the posts. The headline in the paper the next day was "*Williams is Fit!*" (Bath is, and was, one of the best English sides. In the 15 games from the 'miracle year' of 1947-48, when Cardiff scraped home by a try 3-0, to 1974-75, Cardiff won all 15, scoring 49 tries to 13, scoring 243 points to 69. Cardiff had a truly remarkable side.)

'Of course, when we went to New Zealand and Australia for the British Lions, we travelled by sea – five weeks aboard ship. I was able to use weights to strengthen my leg and everything was alright. We were away for six and a half months.' (Bleddyn made the trip although he was still struggling and needed to work on his fitness every day of the actual **six-week voyage** to New Zealand - the total length of the last Lions tour - plus a couple of weeks' rehabilitation on arrival to complete his recovery. Despite having missed the 1st Test because of the injury, he went on to play in 20 of the 29 matches on tour, scoring 12 tries, including one in the 1st Test against Australia. He captained the Lions in the 3rd and 4th Tests against the All Blacks as Karl Mullen, the tour captain, was injured.)

'Well, I worked for twenty years with GKN and was then head-hunted by Wimpey. I was approached by a man called Tony Prichard who was from Abertillery. He had obtained a civil engineering degree and was a keen rugby fan. It turned out that the Wimpey Group had an organization that involved rugby personalities, and this led to me being asked to speak at one of their dinners in London. The next thing was that Tony Prichard invited me to work for him in Birmingham. I pointed out that no-one knew me in Birmingham – whereas Cardiff would be a different matter. On being asked who I would recommend to go to Birmingham, I suggested David Duckham whom I knew quite well. David was offered the post and he accepted. Sometime later, I was taken on by Wimpey in Cardiff, and it was a wonderful company to work for. They allowed me to carry on as a freelance rugby journalist, and I was able to travel to South Africa, New Zealand and so on, for '*The People*' whilst working for them. I was there for fourteen years and finished as Marketing Manager for Wales. They were involved in housing, open-cast coal-mining and civil engineering. I retired in 1987, and as I wanted to cover the inaugural World Rugby Cup fully, I had requested to take my retirement a year early and this was granted, although they really wanted me to stay on.

When I came back from the World Cup' (in Australia and New Zealand), 'two partners in another civil engineering company, Brunswick Construction based at Mwyndy, Llantrisant, took me on. One of the partners was Paddy Gallagher, an Irishman who came over to fight during the war and never went back. Paddy said that they wanted to diversify, and they would like my knowledge of PR and Marketing work. I told him that I had retired, but he was very persuasive. What they wanted was for me to do selected jobs, so I joined them and stayed until I was 78. Now I am officially retired! I appreciate my good fortune in having been able to meet all sorts of thoroughly interesting people from all walks of life. Among my many good friends was Richard Burton, whom I first met when I was at Heaton Park, prior to going to America. He was in the RAF, fresh up from Oxford University and known then as Richie Jenkins. Later, whenever I was playing in London, Richard and Stanley Baker would come to our matches, and our friendship continued from there. I knew Richard's first wife Sybil, and also, later, Elizabeth Taylor who used to come to matches, where she and Richard would drink beer pint for pint with the others!

Stanley was a great friend too, and it was a huge sadness and traumatic experience when he died so tragically in San Pedro, Spain, in 1976.' (Ferndale's Stanley Baker was producer and lead actor in the 1964 film *Zulu*, and received a knighthood in 1976, but did not live to receive it. Baker's widow claimed that Baker was originally offered the role of James Bond, but turned it down, not wishing to commit to a long-term contract. She also revealed that he was going to star in *This Sporting Life*, but had to drop out when *Guns of Navarone* went over schedule. She says Baker never regretted losing the part of Bond to Sean Connery, but regretted not making *This Sporting Life*. A lifelong heavy cigar and cigarette smoker, he was diagnosed with lung cancer on 13 February 1976, and had surgery, but the cancer had spread to his bones and he died of pneumonia in Malaga on 28 June 1976. He told his wife shortly before his death, aged just 48: "*I have no regrets. I've had a fantastic life; no one has had a more fantastic life than I have. From the beginning I have been surrounded by love. I'm the son of a Welsh miner and I was born into love, married into love and spent my life in love.*" Ferndale RFC have a Stanley Baker Lounge in their clubhouse.)

'Anyway, back to my playing days. As a schoolboy I played for the Cardiff 'Town' team for two or three years, but as far as the Taff's Well team is concerned, we played mostly on the park, but occasionally on the other side of the river at Rhiw'r Ddar. In Cardiff we always played at Sophia Gardens, we'd go down by bus and strip under the trees, raining or not. Then after the game we'd wash our knees in the River Taff. Schoolboys were given free passes to watch Cardiff play, so it would be down to Wood Street for those wonderful chips, and then off to the Arms

Park to watch Gwyn playing. I saw him in the match against New Zealand in 1935, when he was seventeen. Then, having seen the game, we'd take a penny and get a seat in the "Gods'" (the highest, cheapest seats) 'at the Empire Cinema. We would sometimes watch the film twice and not get home until eleven o'clock that night. I was just eight when I started playing, and was a member of the Cardiff Town side that beat Aberavon in the Final of the Dewar Shield in 1937.' (The Dewar Shield is the oldest schools' rugby competition in the world, highly prestigious – Cardiff have won 22 of their 33 Final appearances.)

'I later played for Wales under-fourteens at Gloucester – but I was still small in 1937. Next thing, of course, was going to Rydal. We had a very good rugby side up there. I managed to get in the first fifteen when I was fourteen. I'd played for the Colts first of all and had clearly done well enough to be moved up to the seniors, where I was playing with 18-year-olds. In the first year I scored a try against Liverpool College, and I had beaten about four boys to get the try. My headmaster was the Rev. A.J. Costain, at the time. He used to parade up and down the touchline, shouting encouragement all the time. When I came off the field after scoring that try, he put his arm around me and said, "*Look here, Williams, that was a wonderful try you scored, beating four lads, but if you had given the ball to your wing, he wouldn't have had to beat anyone.*" That was a salutary lesson which I remembered for the rest of my life. The lesson was – if someone is in a better position than yourself, give him the ball – and that's the philosophy I followed. In the last but one season at Rydal we were unbeaten. I captained the side, the following year. I also played cricket for the school as a wicketkeeper, and I played with Billy Sutcliffe, who was the great Herbert Sutcliffe's son. He played fullback for us and captained the cricket side. In one of the games, I scored a century against one of the college teams. Herbert Sutcliffe had been watching, and afterwards he gave me a bat.

I played cricket for the RAF as well, and when I was at St. Athan we won the RAF Cup. We also won the Rugby Cup, but I didn't play regularly because I was playing for Cardiff. I felt I shouldn't be selected for the final, for it would be unfair to those who had played on Wednesdays and Saturdays. In the event, though, one of the backs cried off and I took his place, on the wing! And I actually scored a try. My main period at Cardiff started in 1945' (- then aged 22). 'I missed the first three weeks because of tonsillitis, and I had my tonsils removed in the RAF. I had suffered from tonsillitis for a long time. We had a marvellous Cardiff side. We played the New Zealand Kiwis on Boxing Day 1945 and made a lot of friends – and still have a lot of friends who played in that side' (- speaking 39 years later). 'This was the New Zealand Army team, which became the mainstay of their national side on returning home. We lost by a try to nil, but would have won if our hooker (Maldwyn James), who used to take the kicks in those days, hadn't missed one in front of the posts! Then we had a highly successful season with Dr Jack Matthews, my co-centre, who ultimately played with me for Wales and indeed the Lions. Jack was a great friend – still is a great friend. He was a wonderful rugby player.

One of the main highlights of my career was being selected' (as captain) 'to play for the Barbarians against Australia in 1947. It was the first match of what was to become a tradition. It came about because the Australians wanted to tour Canada on their way back home, and they didn't have enough money, and that match would raise the necessary funds. It was decided to hold the game in Cardiff, because a bigger crowd could be guaranteed there, than would be the case at Twickenham in those days. We beat them in a marvellous game.'

Actually, this was on 31 January 1948, the 34th and last game of a very successful Australia tour to Britain and France, before 5 games in Canada and America. Bleddyn's Baa Baas won 9-6 and included 5 Welshmen – all from Cardiff. They were Haydn Tanner, Bleddyn, Frank Trott, Bleddyn's cousin Bill Tamplin, and Billy Cleaver. Australia won their first 4 games before losing to Bleddyn's Cardiff, 11-3. They won the next 15 games including vs Scotland, losing by a point to a Lancashire and Cheshire XV, then winning 4 games, including against Ireland before losing to Wales 6-0. Australia beat England and won the rest of their 44 games except against France, London Counties, and Bleddyn's Barbarians, Wales and Cardiff. Bleddyn captained the Barbarians again in 1952 losing against South Africa, who had only lost one game, to London Counties 11-9, in a 31-match tour of Britain and France. They narrowly and very fortunately beat Cardiff 11-9, and were again lucky to beat Wales 6-3. Their strength was shown by wins against Scotland 44-0, Ireland 17-5, England 8-3 and France 25-3. South Africa scored 19 points or more 14 times, in days of lower scores.

'The second highlight was being selected to captain Wales in 1950 for the first time – although I had captained Wales in the 1945-46 season in an unofficial international against the Kiwis. Haydn Tanner should have been captain for that game, but he was in Italy at the time, and the Army wouldn't release him. So I stood in for him, I was just 22, but we lost that match to the Kiwis 11-3. Well, although I was chosen as captain for the 1950 internationals, I didn't play a single game because of injury. As a matter of fact, I captained Wales only five times – but I'm pleased to say we never lost any of those games. It was also a highlight that I was made captain of Cardiff in the 1949-50 season, and also again in 1953-54 when we beat the All Blacks. Three weeks later I captained Wales as well to victory over the All Backs, and that's the last time Wales defeated New Zealand.'

On 19 December 1953, Bleddyn was captain when Wales trailed the All Blacks 8-5 in the last 15 minutes, with Cardiff wing Gareth Griffiths playing on with a dislocated shoulder, and Bleddyn having torn thigh ligaments. Cardiff flanker Sid Judd crossed to level the scores 8-8 - tries were not awarded four points until 1971, and five in 1992. Then flanker Clem Thomas had the ball on the wing, and with no room for manoeuvre, he caught the All Blacks flat-footed, kicking crossfield into the New Zealand 25. Wing Ken Jones grabbed the loose ball to score the winning try to complete Wales' third victory, 13-8, in its four meetings with New Zealand. In 1953, Bleddyn played in the 5-3 loss to England in Cardiff, then John Gwilliam was dropped for missing relatively easy penalties to win the game. In his place, Bleddyn was selected captain for the Scottish game. He scored two tries, and Ken Jones one, in the 12-0 away win. Bleddyn was then captain in the 5-3 win against Ireland, Gareth Griffiths touching down, and again away in Paris 6-3, with Gareth Griffiths scoring two tries to a penalty. If Gwilliam had kicked just one of his penalties, it would have been a Grand Slam year. In 1955 Bleddyn captained Wales in the first international of the season, beating England 3-0, but it was his last game for Wales after 22 caps. Bleddyn later said of his Cardiff and Wales scrumhalf, Haydn Tanner, 'Among all the scum-halves I've seen or played with, he would reign supreme. He had a superb pass – the best I ever played with. His service was even better than Gareth Edwards'.

In 1955 Bleddyn wished to tour with the Lions again, this time in South Africa, when a decision was made not to select players over the age of 30. It cost the Lions the services of Bleddyn, their most experienced back. Bleddyn partnering England's centre Jeff Butterfield outside Cliff Morgan, at the height of his powers, and the superb Irish wing Tony O'Reilly outside him would have been terrific to see on good pitches. Having not been selected for the Lions, and having suffered from injury, Bleddyn then made the decision to retire for rugby at the relatively early age of 32. However, he regretted not playing just one extra year, as pitches improved. In Davies' history of Cardiff, Bleddyn leads the try scorers with 184, followed by Johnny Williams with 150. Of the family, fly-half/centre Tony scored 67, flanker Elwyn 46, scrumhalf/fly half Lloyd 21, fly half/centre Cenydd 20, flanker Gwyn 12 and Bryn 3.

Bleddyn returned to his early days in his 1984 account: 'I regularly went back to play for Rydal "Old Boys" as well. On one occasion, I took the whole of the Cardiff side and most of us were internationals. What's more, not one of the Cardiff group would take a penny in expenses. We went in cars, stayed the night in Llangollen and drove back the following day, and although the school provided food and beer after the game, not one of them would accept a penny in expenses. The next time I took a Cardiff side up there some years later, we picked them up from Pontypool where they had a match, and went from there by coach. That time they wanted money. The school provided fare for them, but all in all it cost me five-hundred quid! How attitudes have changed – and this was still in the amateur era, mind.

That was the difference between the people of our day – they were money-oriented even then.

I played only once for Taff's Well and that was when I was sixteen and home on holiday from Rydal. I heard later that there had been an interesting committee meeting at which Bob Lewis, the captain at that time, was told *"Bleddyn is home."* Bob's response was *"So what?"* It was then explained that they wanted to find a place for me. It turned out that I played at outside-half and Bob, the regular in that position, had to play in the centre! The match was up at Chepstow and we had to change for it at a pub, from which we walked down to the ground. All except the Chepstow scrumhalf, that is – having left his boots at the pub, he had to play in his shoes. They won the game by virtue of a drop-goal by the very same scrumhalf, whose shoe went over the bar before the ball! For the record, my first senior game for Cardiff was when I was eighteen. That was also at Chepstow and they took the full Cardiff side there. I played in the centre alongside Wilfred Wooller. Now I can reveal the identity of the man who recommended me for that scholarship to Rydal. Yes, it was Wilfred Wooller, a former pupil at Rydal himself, who had seen me play for Cardiff Schools, and decided to inform them about me. For years I did not know that it was he who had been responsible.' (No Chepstow game is recorded in Cardiff First-team records. Under records of charity/scratch matches however, there is an away game on 15 September 1937, Cardiff winning 21-6, scoring 5 tries to 2. It could not have been the first game, as Bleddyn was 14. In April 1970, again away in a charity match Cardiff won 44-18, scoring 10 tries. However, the Rags have played Chepstow many times in the past, including when Bleddyn's brother Tony was captain).

As an aside upon internationals in his playing days, Bleddyn wrote in his biography: *'For matches in Wales, the home team gather on the morning of the match, and this I feel is a mistake. In Britain, International teams are allowed to meet only once for a practice before each match, and this again I think is wrong. It is one of the prime reasons that we seldom see spectacular International Rugby, and the International tournament rarely provides football of the quality displayed by the leading club sides. This certainly could be remedied by allowing frequent practices and tactical discussions. When the British team went to New Zealand in 1950, we found our opponents had been preparing for us well in advance, playing together and planning together. This should be adopted by all the Home Unions, and would give national teams more opportunity of meeting touring Dominion teams on an equal footing. Under the present system, tourists always have the advantage.'* Bleddyn also remembers hard matches, such as against the Barbarians, taking place on the Saturday before internationals, and he and his fellows lacking their spark with so little recovery time.

E.R.K. Glover wrote on Bleddyn's retirement, *'When I left Cardiff Arms*

Park on Saturday, someone said to me, "I really feel at last that the War is over, now that Bleddyn has retired." And that, perhaps, sums up his place in the long saga of rugby football. He has, indeed, been the dominating figure of post-war rugby, although his fame, or rather promise, had been trickling through to us in the Services before the finish. Who will forget his play in those early years of peace? That wonderful side-step that every rugby player in the world knew about, but was powerless to stop - that toss of the head as he cleaved a hole in the opposing defence – the sure and fierce tackle just when it was needed. At his peak, Bleddyn was **unquestionably the best centre in the world**, and even when he was slowing up a little, the South Africans still rated him top in that position. Such an occasion as his retirement naturally calls for assessment of his qualities, and reminiscences of his achievements. Followers of rugby I met were full of both after last Saturday's game. But the predominating feeling was one of admiration for the standard of his conduct on the field.

Highest Tribute. One admirer, who saw the never-to-be-forgotten game between Wales and New Zealand in 1905, matched him with Gwyn Nicholls for gentlemanly conduct – a tribute which, to my mind, means more than all other honours in the game. It is, I hope, the thing that young players will remember about Bleddyn. Not many will be able to emulate his skill, but all players of the game can copy his behaviour on the field. With the modern tendency to rate results above all, it is appropriate that in his last game, he should have "made" a try for Rowlands with his break-through, and one for Thomas with his great tackle of Phillips. Bleddyn Williams will, I'm sure, rest content that his rugby epitaph should be "He played the game".'

SEASON	P	W	D	L	TRY	CON	PEN	DG	PTS
1945-1946	21	17	0	4	30	0	0	0	90
1946-1947	27	22	2	3	12	0	0	0	36
1947-1948	30	29	0	1	41	0	0	0	123
1948-1949	32	26	3	3	25	0	0	0	75
1949-1950	24	17	3	4	23	0	0	0	69
1950-1951	22	15	4	3	5	0	0	0	15
1951-1952	22	18	0	4	11	0	0	0	33
1952-1953	26	18	1	7	6	0	0	0	18
1953-1954	39	30	2	7	17	0	0	0	51
1954-1955	38	32	4	2	14	0	0	0	42
TOTAL	**281**	**224**	**19**	**38**	**184**	**0**	**0**	**0**	**552**

Post war, Williams had married Violet, and they had a son Bleddyn Ashley Williams and daughters Lynne and Leslie. After retiring in 1955, Bleddyn became a respected rugby journalist, writing for the *Sunday People* for 30 years, and being honoured with an MBE in 2005. He accepted the award with typical modesty, saying he owed it to his Cardiff team mates. In 1979, Violet had given him the 'kiss of life', after he collapsed with an embolism. Violet later died of cancer. A former President of his beloved Cardiff RFC, in later life he was President of the Cardiff Athletic Club, the owners of Cardiff Arms Park and Sophia Gardens. On 6 July 2009, aged 86, Bleddyn passed away at Holme Tower in Penarth, after suffering ill health for some time. In the many obituaries he was referred to as *'The Prince of Centres'*.

In response to a letter sent to the press, asking for information upon the Williams brothers, I received a lovely letter from Mrs. Margaret Darling, now living in Llandudno. Parts of it read: *'In August 1962 I met my husband at the Welsh Amateur Golf Championship in the Royal St. David's Golf Club, Harlech, where I lived. He was Captain of Whitchurch Golf Club, Cardiff, where he lived. We were married in November 1962 and Bleddyn was my husband's best man. He was married to Violet, who became my best friend, and they had a son Ashley and daughters Lynne and Lesley. We spent a great deal of time together, although they were all 20 years older than me. Bleddyn and Vi had a caravan in Mwnt, near Cardigan, and eventually bought a cottage in Gwbert-on-Sea, where we spent many summer holidays together.*

Bleddyn and Violet also accompanied us on our honeymoon to Paris! – where Bleddyn was reporting on the Wales v. France international. We spent every Saturday evening after the game at Cardiff Arms Park, in the company of Cliff Morgan, Rex Willis, Malcolm Collins, Jack Matthews and many others. My husband in his youth played for James Heriot rugby team in Edinburgh, where he was born' (Heriots Former Pupils RFC), *'but when war broke out in 1939 he joined the 8th Army under Montgomery and became Captain, and was mentioned in Despatches but war ended his rugby career.*

I have fond memories of visiting Bleddyn's mother in Taff's Well and often wonder how she brought up a family in such a small house, but in those days, they had no choice. She was a lovely lady, and I did get to know some of Bleddyn's brothers. Cenydd, I believe, became professional. Lloyd was married to Ann who I was very friendly with, they had two daughters but later divorced. Tony was the youngest, and I remember him getting married. Bleddyn was very friendly with the Welsh Stars at that time. I remember he and Violet picking me up on a Saturday night as Archie, my husband, was not very well, and when I got into the back seat, Stanley Baker was sitting there! They were also friendly with Richard Burton and Liz Taylor. I am now 81 years old and back living in North Wales. I believe most of these names have passed away. They were happy times, never to return, but leave me with such wonderful memories...'

Former Cardiff fullback Alun Priday reminisced recently about Bleddyn, *'Yes, we were fortunate to play the game at a time that it was a game and not a business, I find the game today is a bit boring as it is bash, bash,*

bash, how often does one see a centre make a break with a sidestep as Bleddyn did? I went on one occasion with Bleddyn, Stan Bowes and Geoff Beckingham to play up at Bleddyn's old school, Rydal and had the "pleasure" of playing centre marking Bleddyn. I knew when he had the ball, that a sidestep was coming, but could do nothing to stop him. His sidestep was so wide and his thighs so strong – it was an impossible job. Happy days.' And former Cardiff player John Harding emailed me of Bleddyn's later days: *'Bleddyn was Legendary. The Finest of Rugby Players, Sportsman and Gentleman. As President of Cardiff RFC and Cardiff Athletic Club, Bleddyn would continue to support and nurture the world standing of the famous CRFC and Cardiff Athletic Club. I was on the CRFC Committee in early 2000. As President, Bleddyn would attend Committee meetings. Bleddyn brought clarity and stability in decision making at every opportunity. A great pleasure to be in his company.'*

Finally, let me repeat J.B.G. Thomas's comment upon Bleddyn captaining Cardiff to beat the All Blacks in 1953: *'What a game it was. How magnificently the players performed. The voice was raised to cheer as Bleddyn Williams and his fellows split open New Zealand's defence like a destroyer's bow ripping through the flimsy hull of a crippled submarine. The rugby triumph which had eluded Cardiff since 1905 was achieved in a match full of excitement and glory accompanying a great sporting occasion.'* 'JBG' was a very fine reporter of the game.

*Operation Varsity

In Operation Varsity, Bleddyn flew a Horsa glider from RAF Rivenhall on 24 March 1945. The Airspeed AS.51 Horsa was a British glider used for transporting troops. Its fuselage was plywood, and fabric covered. Towed transport gliders were built in large numbers to air-land troops with their heavier weapons behind enemy lines, without using parachutes, and with far less scattering of the troops. Its honeycombed plywood floor was easily shredded by flak. These gliders were built quickly to be cheap and disposable. There were two models of the Horsa glider Model I (Mk.I) was the troop version, 67 feet long. It carried two pilots and 20 to 25 fully equipped troops with varying amounts of equipment. The Mk.2, the AS52 Horsa, had the flexibility to carry a Jeep or an Ordnance QF 6-pounder anti-tank gun. The Horsa was normally towed at about 100 miles (160 km) per hour by a C-47 Dakota transport or a Halifax bomber. Its American equivalent, the Waco CG-4A gliders were known as *'flying coffins'* and could only carry 13 soldiers. The role of gliders in Operation Market Garden was praised, although overshadowed by the failure to take the key bridge at Arnhem. Gliders were central to Allied invasions of Sicily, Burma, Southern France, Bastogne, and 'Operation Varsity', the crossing of the Rhine into Germany in March 1945. *'They were the only aviators during World War II who had no motors, no parachutes, and no second chances.'* - General William C. Westmoreland, U.S. Army.

It was a 'nasty' operation, and losses of airborne troops were high, because the landings took place in full daylight, rather than a 'normal' night-assault. Planners believed that a daytime operation had a better chance of success than at night, the troops being less scattered. However, landing paratroopers, and especially gliders, without the cover of darkness left them exceedingly vulnerable to anti-aircraft fire. The official history of the British Airborne Divisions highlights the cost, recording that of the 416 British gliders that landed, only 88 remained undamaged by enemy fire, and that 20-30% of British glider pilots were casualties. The American 194th Glider Infantry Regiment had two-thirds of its gliders hit by ground fire and suffering heavy casualties as they landed. The casualty rates were worsened by the slow rates of release and descent of the gliders themselves, and the fact that each aircraft towed two gliders, slowing them even further. As the time to release a glider unit was 3–4 times longer than a parachute unit, the gliders were vulnerable to flak, and many of the slow-moving planes towing them were destroyed. Both airborne divisions captured Rhine bridges and secured towns that could have been used by Germany to delay the advance of British ground forces. The two divisions incurred over 2,000 casualties, but captured around 3,500 German soldiers. The operation was the last large-scale Allied airborne operation of World War II.

'Rugby World says Farewell to "Jinking Prince" Bleddyn Williams
(*walesonline* 18 July 2009)
"*ADMIRATION for Bleddyn's consummate skills as a rugby player spanned generations.*" That was Welsh Rugby Union president Dennis Gethin yesterday as the sport's legends yesterday paid their respects to the "jinking prince" – the last captain to lead Wales to victory over New Zealand. Gerald Davies, Barry John, JPR Williams and Bob Norster were among those mourning Bleddyn Williams at Llandaff Cathedral in Cardiff. A simple floral arrangement of lilies and carnations sat on top of the ex-Cardiff, Wales and British Lions captain's coffin as four pallbearers carried the former centre into the cathedral to Edward Elgar's *Nimrod*, from the *Enigma Variations*.

The 86-year-old from Taff's Well, near Cardiff, died earlier this month at Holme Tower in Penarth. Leading yesterday's tributes was surgeon and former Wales hooker Dr Brian Rees, who said: "*It's been 200 years since the birth of Charles Darwin. His book Origin of the Species describes the process of evolution. Even the great Darwin couldn't have defined a better example of the human species than Bleddyn Llewellyn Williams.*" Dr Rees said it was "*ironic*" Williams died at the end of Lions' tour to South Africa, adding: "*I'm sure he would have been thrilled by their performances, their guts and determination.*"
Addressing the coffin, Rees added: "*On behalf of your many, many friends*

358

throughout the world, I thank you for your wonderful life and your sportsmanship and, most of all, for your Corinthian spirit."

Williams, a former pupil of Rydal School in Colwyn Bay was made an MBE in 2005 and was best known for his partnership with Dr Jack Matthews. He played 22 times for Wales and was undefeated in his five matches as captain. Four-hundred mourners, including Cardiff Blues chairman Peter Thomas and former Wales flyhalf Phil Bennett, listened to *Psalm 23* and sang *Cwm Rhondda* and *Calon Lan* in an hour-long service led by Cathedral Dean John Lewis. Paying tribute to *"caring, compassionate"* Williams' powers of observation and recall, WRU boss Gethin said he *"faced his final illness with the courage of a Lion".*

Gethin said: *"He was up-to-date, informed and great company. Sitting next to him in the stand for a Cardiff game was an education. He still read the game well and, while not completely in approval of the modern game, would applaud and recognise the skills of the modern player. One of my last memories of Bleddyn was at the new Stradey Park ground at Llanelli. Jack and Bleddyn marvelled at the new look and approved. What a shame they will not be able to do the same for the new Blues ground opening this season. Bleddyn was an encourager, not a criticiser."* Gethin added: *"As long as rugby football is played, his name will be remembered and revered. It seems from the time of his birth he was destined to become a prince."* The WRU chief said one of Graham Henry's first moves, when he was appointed Wales coach in 1998, was to visit Williams and Matthews. *"Henry was told on many occasions by his father who had seen them play in 1950 that they were without doubt the greatest centre pairing he had ever witnessed,"* said Gethin.

"We are all aware of Bleddyn's amazing rugby record for Cardiff, Wales and the British Lions. But his unique feat which will never be surpassed was of being captain of both Cardiff and Wales when both those teams defeated the 1953 All Blacks. Throughout his rugby life his mission was to do everything possible to enhance the name and reputation of Welsh rugby. He was as selfless off the field as he was on it." Williams will be best remembered for his jinking runs which flummoxed defenders. *"It was the jink that immortalised him. It seems the jink must have been devised with Bleddyn specifically in mind,"* said Gethin. *"His opponents knew the jink was coming but when it did come they were helpless to do anything about it. Knowing fathers winked at their sons, 'Watch Bleddyn'. And incredibly Bleddyn justified their expectations, tore the defence wide open and enhanced the legend."* Gethin said Williams was *"quick to exploit a try-scoring opportunity, but slow to take the credit. That was Bleddyn's style."* He added: *"A man without conceit, a firm believer in fair play and sportsmanship, his values were timeless. That underlying philosophy of his must endure and flourish for the benefit of all."*

In 2013 Bleddyn and his life-long friend and co-centre Jack Matthews were jointly inducted into the **World Rugby Hall of Fame**. The citation reads: *'The two Welsh centres formed a uniquely complementary and successful partnership at club, national team and Lions levels after the Second World War. They played together for Cardiff and Wales and they both captained their club and the country. They also played for the 1950 Lions in both New Zealand and Australia. Bleddyn Williams, the third of eight rugby-playing brothers, made his international debut against England in 1947 at fly half, the first of his 22 Welsh caps – the other 21 were at centre. He captained Wales in five Tests, winning all five, and remains to this date the only Welsh captain to boast a 100 per cent success record. He was vice-captain of the 1950 Lions and played in five of the six Tests, injury having prevented him from playing in the first Test. With Karl Mullen injured, he captained the Lions in three of the six Tests – two in New Zealand and one in Australia. He became a very successful rugby commentator and was awarded an MBE for services to rugby. Dr. Jack Matthews made his international debut in a non-cap Victory International against France, one of the five War Internationals he played in. Described as one of the fiercest tacklers in the game, he won 17 caps for Wales and six for the 1950 Lions, four in New Zealand and two in Australia. He captained both Cardiff and Wales and became the first Lions team doctor with the 1980 tourists to South Africa.'*

The Times Saturday July 11, 2009, Bleddyn's Obituary

LLOYD WILLIAMS BECOMES A REGULAR - VAUGHAN RETURNS FOR CARDIFF ATHLETIC

Lloyd Williams P15 T1 = 3pts; **Vaughan Williams** (Cardiff Athletic); John Llewellyn P3 C3 = 15pts (Taff's Well); Alun Priday P42 T2 C3 P2 = 18pts (Tongwynlais) – Gwyn Rowlands was the place-kicker and Alun was not the regular kicker until the following season; Derek Murphy P24 T16 = 48pts (Pentyrch)

P52, W35, L16, Dl. Points 612-360. Tries 130-61, Pens 27-34

52 fixtures! Can one imagine that in modern rugby? And even that amazing number does not reflect upon the number of games played by amateur players. Alun Edward Islwyn Pask (1937-1995) was an Abertillery flanker and number 8 capped 26 times by Wales, captaining the side 6 times. He also played in 8 British Lions Tests. Alun once played 65 times in a season. The Welsh first-class club season is now staccato, with far, far fewer games, international breaks, and for the regions the absurdity of incredibly costly away games for the squad, along with its legions of analysts, coaches, physios etc., travelling to South Africa, Italy, Ireland and Scotland. South African fixtures help promote rugby in South Africa but drain Welsh financial resources. The same can be said of other away games. The Irish game has been based upon four provinces, Ulster, Leinster, Munster and Connacht, and is financially healthy. The two Scottish regions are in centres of high population, Glasgow and Edinburgh. The two Italian teams, Benetton and Treviso generally struggle, like the Welsh teams. In the new United Rugby Championship, the four South African teams are the Stormers, Bulls, Sharks and Lions, who play at Cape Town, Pretoria, Durban and Johannesburg. This involves a great deal of travelling within the country, to virtually empty stadia with capacities of 55,000; 51,762; 52,000 and 62,567. This cannot help Welsh rugby, in any way, shape or form. Welsh home attendances for the URC are atrocious, not helped by intermittent fixtures, being shown at strange times, while also often being televised. Up until an away game at Ulster on 4 March, 2022, Cardiff had not played a game for 5 weeks. Then, missing an international weekend, they play twice in South Africa, returning for a home fixture on 26 March. The distance between Pretoria and Cape Town for the away fixtures is 1,500 km. In their first 5 Guinness Pro12 home fixtures of the 2021-22 season, the average gate at Cardiff was 7,244. Their game at Edinburgh had an attendance of just 500. There were 5 home games from 24 September 2021 to 26 March 2022 – FIVE home games in SIX months. No wonder attendances are poor, and the joy of travelling away to watch your team is dead. Apart from internationals, rugby as a spectator sport is dying in Wales.

In the 2022-2023 URC fixture list, Cardiff play Munster Sept 16-18 H; Glasgow Sept 23-25 A; Lions Sept 30-Oct 2 H; Scarlets Oct 7-9 A; Dragons Oct 14-16 H; Stormers Oct 21-23 H; Edinburgh Oct 28-30 A; Sharks Nov 25-27 A; Bulls Dec 2-4 A; Dragons Dec 23-26 A; Ospreys Dec 31-Jan 2 H; Scarlets Jan 6-8 H; Leinster Jan 27-29 A; Benetton Feb 17-19 H; Ulster Mar 3-5 H; Zebre Mar 24-26 A; Connacht Apr 14-16 A; Ospreys Apr 21-23 A. There will be cup games, but there are just 9 home games, spread between September 16-18 and March 3-5. The last three games are away. There is a 6-week period from the Dragons home game on October 14-16, of four away games, with the next home game on December 31-January 2 with the Ospreys. Of the away games, die-hard supporters might attend the three Welsh games, but you can forget Glasgow, Edinburgh, Sharks (Durban), Bulls (Pretoria), Leinster, Zebre and Connacht. It is a pointless experiment, not even replicated in any other team sport.

Back to normality. Cardiff again scored twice as many tries as the opposition but 'lost' on penalties, still preferring to run the ball and score tries. Malcolm Collins was captain, nominating Dr. Gwyn Rowlands as vice-captain. Collins had joined from Newport in 1949-50 and gained his First Team cap in that season. He was 6 ft. 2 ins, more than 16 stone, had a Final Welsh trial and was a reserve for Wales. Davies believed that he should have played for the full Welsh team, but he fell to the 'curse' of Cardiff forwards, also suffered by Geoff Beckingham, Elwyn Williams, Roy Roberts and many others. Cardiff captain Collins was the middle lineout jumper and played in 50 of 52 matches. He only missed Watsonians at Christmas, when there were 5 matches in 8 days, and St. Ives on the annual Cornish tour, where the team had 8 games in two weeks.

Bleddyn had finished playing, Cliff Morgan could only play in 8 matches, and Welsh triallist Arthur David Stanley 'Stan' Bowes had eventually retired to the Athletic (but was still often called upon). From the Cardiff Rugby Museum website we read: '*Stan Bowes, a legendary figure, played 184 games for Cardiff over twelve seasons 1938/39 -1955/56 scoring seven tries. A tough prop forward and character of the club he once reportedly almost pulled out of a game at Llandovery because the team he had been selected to play for were wearing Black and Amber. He refused to have Newport colours next to his skin and would not put the shirt on until somebody found him a Cardiff shirt to wear underneath the "Black and Amber rag."*' Born in 1917, he played for the Rags in 1937-38, and for the Firsts from 1938-39 to 1955-56, in his later years captaining the Rags, for whom is last appearance was aged 54 on 9 December 1961, home to Glynneath. Tony O'Reilly scored from 50 yards out for the Barbarians, with Stan soon giving up the chase. On O'Reilly's walk back before the conversion, he passed Stan, who told him '*I'd have caught you if your laces had snapped.*' I well remember the time when touch judges were one from the opposing club and one from the home club, and on retirement from the game, Stan was usually running the line, laughing at times. For the visit of Watsonians, he donned a kilt. A great man. Dai Hayward always referred to him as '*Unsinkable Bowes*', and on Stan becoming club chairman, he had the following business cards printed:

STAN BOWES – A Legend in his own time
World Traveller Bon Vivant Soldier of Fortune Oppressor of Champions International Lover Casual Hero All Round Good Guy Philosopher Wars Fought Revolutions Started Alligators Castrated Governments Run Uprisings Quelled Tigers Tamed Bars Empties Virgins Converted Computers Verified Orgies Organised

The Cardiff Rugby Club Former Players Association was formed in the early 1970's with Colin Howe, Stan Bowes and John Nelson the founder members. Stan was 'Cardiff' through and through. Rex Willis only played 23 times, with Bleddyn's brother Lloyd now playing in many First Team games. His older brother Vaughan, the fourth oldest brother after Gwyn, Bryn and Bleddyn, played regularly for the Athletic, but had his career affected National Service, and his rugby recollections are given at the end of the 1962-63 season. Vaughan played a few games of first-class rugby for Neath and returned to play for Taff's Well. Cardiff won its first 5 games, including beating a strong Romanian team 6-3, which was unbeaten on tour. Based almost entirely upon the excellent Bucharest team, it had just defeated Swansea 19-3 and drawn with Harlequins. One seems to remember that they were all Romanian Army men, in effect well-trained professionals. Cardiff's training usually amounted to an hour or two a week, led by the senior forward and senior back. And many players could not afford the time off work, if they lived a distance from Cardiff. Hardly any player had a car, unless it was a company one.

Then followed one of the club's worst periods in its history, losing 9 of the next 11 games. Newport won three times, and Cardiff had to put in an '*almost superhuman effort*' to halt a Newport 'grand slam', just winning the fourth game 10-9 at Newport (- two goals to a try, penalty and drop goal). However, in the first game, Cardiff had been 6-3 up at home, then lost both Rex Willis and Gwyn Rowlands and the 13 men lost 16-6. That hard-fought final win against Newport on 6 November sparked a revival, and the club only lost another 7 games. There was a 6-6 draw against the Barbarians. After six successive away games, there was a home game against Bath, Cardiff winning 11-0, and Bath Rugby Heritage reports for 21 January 1956: '*Cardiff were able to field an exceptionally strong side, as only Cliff Morgan and C L Davies were on duty with the national side. It was the first occasion that there was no Cardiff man in the Welsh pack. Cardiff Team:- A Priday, G Rowlands, G John, H Nicholls, D C Murphy, K*

Richards, B Mark, J D Evans, G Beckingham, C Howe, E Thomas, M Collins, J Crothers, P Goodfellow and E Lewis. Bath's hopes of recording their first win at Arms Park, against Cardiff, were rudely shattered this afternoon by two early Cardiff scores. The visitors played by no means badly but on a rain-affected pitch the Welshmen seemed quicker at taking their opportunities and handled the ball better. Bath stuck manfully to their defensive tasks, with Kendall-Carpenter saving a certain try. There was a fine all-round performance from Sullivan. Bath had the misfortune of losing Drewett near the end of the first half and Peasley had to deputise. Bath's plight worsened mid-way through the half when, in stopping an attack, Rees was injured and was escorted limping, from the field. Smith (M) had to come out to fill the second vacancy and it meant that Bath had only six forwards... The plucky 13 defended stubbornly... Cardiff threatened to score, but still, Bath kept them out: and Bath came out of the game with credit considering all things'.

Cardiff's season ended with five fairly easy wins over Gloucester 11-3, Leicester 20-5, Pontypool 16-8, Bridgend 13-0 and Aberavon 13-3. For the Leicester game, Cardiff were missing Cliff Morgan and several other First XV choices. Tries were scored by wing Howard Nicholls (2), outside half Colin Hewett (2), centre Gordon Wells and prop Colin Howe, with Malcolm Collins kicking just one conversion. Cardiff had lost away 6-3, again missing players.

Top try scorers were Gwyn Rowlands with 24 (and 28 goals, making 136 points), Gordon Wells 20, Howard Nicholls 18 and Derek Murphy 16. Ken Richards scored 9 tries and 34 goals, 117 points. **Malcolm Collins, the captain played in an amazing 50 of 52 fixtures, and 5 players played in 40 or more** - J. D. Evans 46, Colin Howe 45, Eddie Lewis 43, Alun Priday 42 and Geoff Beckingham 40. Collins may have played another 10 or so games, with Cardiff and Welsh Trials, and Representative and Charity matches. That level of playing is impossible in the far more violent modern game, with an emphasis upon brute force rather than flowing rugby. Cliff Morgan captained Wales in its four matches to win the Five Nations Championship, C. Lynn 'Cowboy' Davies won 3 Welsh caps on the wing, and Gwyn Rowlands played against France. Wales started well, beating England by 2 tries to nil, 8-3 away, with one try a 45-yard run by 'Cowboy' Davies. For the Wales - Scotland match on 4 February 1956, the South Upper Stand was opened, increasing the seating capacity to 12,800 and overall capacity to 60,000. Scotland were defeated by 3-0 on tries, 9-3 on points. Cowboy Davies and Cliff Morgan both scored tries. Then in Dublin, a defeat in front of a record 50,573 crowd, 11-3, with Ireland scoring the only try. Apart from Cliff Morgan and Lynn 'Cowboy' Davies on the wing, the other five backs were all from Newport, and there were four Neath forwards with Newport's Bryn Meredith hooking. However, somehow England smashed Ireland at 'Twickers' 20-0. The International

Championship is never, ever straightforward. France were beaten in Cardiff 5-3, a try apiece, with Cardiff's CD Williams touching down and Wales won the Five Nations outright.

Perhaps the strangest, among multifarious odd selections, by the 'Big Five' selectors over the years, was that of Rex Clive Richards (1934-1989) of Cross Keys, picked out of position as prop for the 5-3 win against France in 1956. He also played for the representative Crawshays XV. Despite not having played a full season of first-class rugby, Richards was chosen ahead of 'Stoker' Williams, who had just played all four Lions Tests in their all-Welsh front-row alongside Courtenay Meredith and hooker Bryn Meredith, that had out-scrummaged the Springboks. Williams had played too early against Ireland, after appendicitis, and was unthinkingly dropped for the French game. After his sole international, aged just 21, Rex Richards left Cross Keys and headed to America, hoping to make it big on the strength of his 'Tarzan' nickname, and had several film roles, including that of *King of Wongo* in 1958. His brother Bill Richards said although 'Tarzan's film *The Wild Women of Wongo* is generally considered a turkey, his brother narrowly missed out on at least one role that would have made him internationally famous: "*Just before he came home, he auditioned to play Tarzan and out of 1,000 people he got down to the final two, just missing out to Gordon Scott. He was nicknamed Tarzan when he played rugby at home, but when he got back he received a letter from America which said the name Tarzan was copyrighted and he should stop using it.*" It seems unfair to dismiss 'Tarzan' in a few words, so may I direct readers to the *walesonline* article 9 August 2009, '*The Incredible Story of Wales Tarzan... At an art workshop Viv Huskings had arranged with sculptor Michael Johnson, he had the chance to meet with a lot of the older generation from Cross Keys. It was here he discovered Rex had been given the nickname Tarzan long before his audition for the film. He revealed: "All of them had fond memories and admiration for the way he played rugby, carried himself in society and also his physical stature. One lady told me she was absolutely besotted by Rex and used to melt when he came into her father's café every Tuesday night after training. She said she had never set eyes on anyone since who could come close to Rex in looks and body. Women used to flock to Pandy Park on a Saturday, not to watch the rugby, but just to gaze in lustful adoration towards Rex." I was also told Rex used to high dive in aqua shows during the summer months and a few of the locals had paid for a trip to see him in Bournemouth. When I asked the group about his nickname, Tarzan, many said it came from a combination of his diving background, rugged looks and muscular physique.*' His is an amazing story, well worth reading.

'The Big Five' was the group of selectors, notoriously difficult to unseat, who seemed to have an agreement to pick their personal regional favourites to play for Wales as a 'quid pro quo', so that all parts of Wales were satisfied with the team selection. It quite often meant that the best team was not chosen. Somehow, I have in my possession a *South Wales Argus* of 12 June 1953, with the headline '*Welsh Union "Big Five" Unchanged*'. Well, what a surprise – there was more chance of the Pope turning Methodist. The article part-reads, '*The Welsh Rugby Union "Big Five" selection committee received a vote of confidence at the first meeting of the new general committee of the union.* (All the different committee members were on the same gravy train, turkeys not voting for Christmas.) *Last season's members – Messrs. Vincent Griffiths, David Jones, Ivor Jones, Hopkin Thomas and D.G. Williams – were the only five candidates - and were all re-elected. The match and referees' committees will also be unchanged.*' Communist Russia seemed to have appropriated the 'Big Five' selection procedures. D. Hopkin Thomas of Llanelli was also elected to the International Board. A small legion of functionaries and their wives accompanied the fifteen players, a physio and team manager – there were no coaches. Tactics were decided by the captain and senior team members, usually on the morning of the game. For interest – well it interests me – there was a small ad in that 1953 paper reading '*Monmouth (on the outskirts of town). For Sale, Attractive Cottage Property, with 2 living rooms, kitchen, 2 bedrooms, W.C. All mains services. Freeehold. Vacant Possession. Price £650 (no offers). Mortgage obtainable, or alternatively with Adjoining Property (let at 12/9 per week), price £700 (the two).*' For post-decimalised readers, 12 shillings and 9 pence is around 64 pence today.

My deceased father-in-law used to regale me with tales of these selectors and assorted committee men, when working for Cory Travel in Cardiff, and making arrangements for Welsh teams to travel. A small army of selectors, administrators and wives stayed in first-class hotels, and took precedence in booking flights. Sometimes in a case of over-booking, players had to take a later flight, never the 'anointed ones.' Players always shared a room, often in worse accommodation, and were watched like hawks. There was one reserve for a game, in these days, and he would only play if someone pulled out on medical advice on the morning of the game – he could be a back or a forward, and had to make his own way to away games. I remember on the 'killer', the overnight train to the Scottish match, that Glyn Davidge (- it may have been David Nash, one's memory is fuddled by both age and alcohol) was sitting, sprawled on the floor, with his back against a door of the buffet car, surrounded by bottles of beer. There were no cans in those days, and wine and spirits were expensive – he knew he would not be playing so had decided to enjoy the ambience.

The Rags, under Peter Goodfellow, had a better season than the Firsts: P39, W29, L4, D6 Points 571-184. However, Goodfellow was needed by the senior side 33 times in their 52 games, and Stan Bowes took over the captaincy. The only defeats were to Ogmore Vale 14-3, Newport United 9-

8, Bristol United 5-3 and Barry 20-16. The former international John Llewellyn kicked 27 goals. He played 7 seasons for Cardiff, 152 games, from 1950-51 to 1956-57. A Taff's Well schoolboy, he played for his home village, then Penarth and Cardiff and had a final Welsh trial. T. J. 'Tommy' McCarthy played 29 games, on his way to becoming the first choice outside half for the seniors, J. Crothers 27, Stan Bowes 27, F. C. Ferguson and R. Parsons 25 each, Brian Joseph 23, J. M. Fitzgerald 21, B. Sadler and the 'fifth brother' Lloyd Williams 20. Cardiff Junior XV played 28, won 24, drew 3 and lost 1, points 473-78. They were undefeated in Wales, a great omen for the club's future. In June 1956 Cardiff's new club house was opened.

One should also mention local club Penarth, on the coast, separated by the River Ely from the capital, which has supplied Cardiff with many players, and also has welcomed many Cardiff players into its team. In 1955-56, only 29 of its 332 points were scored by forwards, with the legendary scrumhalf Bernard 'Slogger' Templeman joining, taking most kicks and being an inspirational player over the following years. With 'the miniature tank' Templeman pulling the strings, Penarth beat Maesteg and Mountain Ash twice, and defeated Pontypridd, Newbridge, Neath, Abertillery, Bedford with their best win being beating Bridgend 22-0. It took the Barbarians over an hour to score a try, and Penarth were regarded as the best team in the Snelling Sevens at Swansea, beating Glamorgan Wanderers, Llanelli and Abertillery to reach the final in front of 10,000 spectators roaring them on. Sevens 'kings' Newport scraped home by a conversion 5-3.

CHAPTER 28 - CARDIFF SEASON 1956 – 1957

CARDIFF BEAT GERMANY AND ITALY AND TOUR ROMANIA - LLOYD WILLIAMS PLAYS OUTSIDE-HALF FOR CARDIFF AND SCRUMHALF FOR WALES – LLOYD HAS THREE WELSH CAPS - CENYDD WILLIAMS, THE SIXTH BROTHER, PLAYS FOR CARDIFF – '*CARDIFF'S HARDEST SEASON ON RECORD*'

Lloyd Williams P37 T6 = 18pts; **Cenydd Williams** P5 T2 = 6pts; John Llewellyn P7 T1 C15 P7 = 54pts (Taff's Well); Alun Priday P36 T3 C40 P20 = 143pts (Tongwynlais); Derek Murphy P36 T12 = 36pts (Pentyrch); Glyn Williams P15 T7 = 21pts (Pentyrch)

P50, W36, L12, D2. Points 627-346. Tries 134-66, Pens 31-21

Former Ghurkha captain and backrow forward Peter Goodfellow could also play in the second row, and played 240 times for the Firsts from 1948-49 to 1958-59. In 1953-54, Stan Bowes, in his fourth successive year of captaincy, had nominated Goodfellow as his vice-captain in the Rags. Goodfellow was then captain of the Rags in 1954-55 and 1955-56, but during his second year of captaincy he was called upon 33 times by the Firsts, with Stan Bowes captaining the Athletic in his absence. Goodfellow's performances saw him elected Cardiff captain in this season, and he was also to be the Rags captain in 1959-60. A remarkable and affable man, Goodfellow spoke fluent Urdu. He nominated Gareth Griffiths as his deputy. Lloyd Williams had a fine season, proving his versatility by playing in both half-back positions, and partnering Cliff Morgan for most of the season after Rex Willis was hurt against Swansea on 10 October. Rex could only play in 9 club matches, so Lloyd made 37 appearances. In November the Cambridge Blue forward William Roderick Evans, a formidable presence at 6 ft. 4 ins and over 16 stones, joined. He was known as 'Roddy', after his nickname at University, 'Roddy the Body'. Roddy gained 13 Welsh caps, touring with the Barbarians in 1958 and with the Lions in 1959. Glyn Williams joined from Pentyrch, a winger the same age as his friend Derek Murphy, and played 117 games for the Firsts between 1956-57 and 1964-65, scoring 43 tries.

Cardiff's first game was against Germany on 1 September, who were beaten 25-0, and in October Italy was defeated 8-3. It is strange that just over a decade previously these countries were fighting and killing Britons. (And, in the interests of parity, Britons were killing them.) In the Tuesday Cardiff Trial match before the Germany game, it was reported that *'another prospect is the sixth of the famous Williams clan of Taff's Well, Cenydd, brother of Lloyd and Bleddyn, who showed several of the family's traits in Tuesday's trial.'* The traditional Cardiff and District season opening game on 5 September was cancelled because of heavy rain, as it was in 1958 and 1963. Welsh weather... say no more. We don't have a weather forecast, it's a density of rain forecast. On 17 September, Cardiff played Leicester away, scoring 3 tries to 2 to win 18-9. Dave Phillips reported that Cardiff's *'rags and tatters'... 'triumphed with many stars missing from their line-up. Lloyd Williams played outside-half partnering a debutant scrumhalf 'little Leo Karseras'.* Karseras made only 13 appearances in 8 seasons, between this season and 1962-63. The 'strange-looking team', as usual, pulled away in the second half. From 1946-47 to 1972-73, in 20 games against Leicester, one of England's finest teams, Cardiff won 18, drew 1 and lost 1 (away 6-3). In 1947 they won 50-5, with 11 tries to 1; in 1949 22-6 with 6 tries to 0; in 1955 32-9 with 7 tries to 2 and in April 1956 20-5, scoring 6 tries to 1. Over the period Cardiff scored 64 tries to 18. Cardiff filled rugby grounds wherever they played.

Lloyd Williams had only made 43 appearances over the previous four seasons, biding his time in 'The Rags' but from this season he was a regular first-teamer, playing both scrumhalf and outside-half. At the start of the season, Dave Phillips reported that Lloyd again played outside-half, with Rex Willis scrumhalf in a *'magnificent encounter, with the Wizards' "Terrible Eight" and Cardiff's magic backs supplying thrills galore'.* Cardiff were losing to a penalty, when *'from a scrum Lloyd Williams got possession and kicked to the left wing, where Howard Nicholls took the ball and crashed over on the left wing.'* However, with scores 3-3, Aberavon were to *'experience the famous Cardiff second-half revival'* when *'after only two minutes play Cardiff set their supporters alight with a really superb try... Lloyd Williams made a straight break'* and *'passed to Gordon Wells, who used his prodigious speed to tear a gaping hole in the Aberavon defence and streak through. When challenged he handed to Eddie Lewis, who crossed for a try near the posts, which Priday had no difficulty converting... Beckingham's hooking experience enabled Cardiff to make full use of their more powerful backs,'* and Cardiff largely controlled the second half to win 8-3, 2 tries to a penalty.

The opposing fly-half was the Welsh international Cliff Ashton, and the game was on 22 September 1956, with both teams unbeaten, having each scored 111 points. The Aberavon forwards were intent upon *'subjugating'* Willis, and Cardiff tactics were to allow their opponents' 'tearaway' pack to tire itself out in the first twenty minutes. Indeed, Garry Owen wrote that *'in the early stages Rex Willis seemed in for a repetition of the Aberavon-Bleddyn Williams game, when he took a hammering that would have made Joe Erskine groggy.'* (Joe played for Cardiff Youth before turning to professional boxing, beating Henry Cooper twice on the way to becoming British Heavyweight Champion). Lloyd Williams, playing outside Rex, was built like a big wing-forward, unlikely to be put off his game by hard tackling. Aberavon, in their unbeaten run had beaten Llanelli, Abertillery, and *'a Cardiff-accented Bleddyn Williams XV.'* J.B.G. Thomas wrote, *'If I could watch every week Rugby football of the quality that Cardiff and Aberavon played at the Arms Park it would be my pleasure. It was a really hard match between two unbeaten sides, played in a magnificent spirit. Each side had everything to lose, and while the players fought to the end, they performed like true sportsmen, which was an object lesson for all, and particularly our New Zealand friends, struggling in the quagmire of victory at all costs.'*

A week later, under the headline '**Sparkling Cardiff Maintain Unbeaten Record'**, Malcolm Lewis reported that Cardiff scored 5 tries to Llanelli's 2 to win 21-13 on 29 September. *'Cardiff pursued their experiment of playing Lloyd Williams at outside-half... in the tenth minute the Cardiff backs clicked to take the lead. Receiving just inside his own half, Lloyd Williams cleverly made half an opening before transferring to Wells. The centre took it at top speed to complete the opening and the ball went via*

Griffiths to Howard Nicholls who, handing off Howells, burst away for a lovely try... The Scarlets "tearaway eight" kept on harassing Cardiff but the Williams-Wells combination was working very smoothly... Lloyd Williams tried a long kick out to his left. With Peter Davies out of position, Gareth Griffiths tore up at terrific pace and out-running Howells, he got the touch down as the ball rolled over the line... Llanelly's fate was sealed two minutes from the end when LLOYD WILLIAMS, eluding the covering back row, slipped over for a try under the posts which Llewellyn converted... Lloyd Williams fitted in very well at outside-half, acting as a perfect link and occasionally making the odd break.' On 3 October, Lloyd again *'teamed up well'* at fly-half to Willis against an *'immense'* Italian pack, Cardiff winning 8-3, two tries to one. Dave Phillips thought that *'Italy must shortly enter the international championship.'* The wheels started grinding, and only 44 years later Italy joined the Five Nations Championship, to make it Six Nations, in 2000.

Halifax visited the Arms Park on 13 October, and Cardiff scored 7 tries in a 36-14 victory. Dave Phillips reported that Cliff Morgan was now available to play, so Lloyd Williams moved to scrumhalf, owing to a long-term injury to Rex Willis. *'John Llewellyn had a terrific game and his try crowned a superb display, and I thought Lloyd Williams, back again at scrumhalf, was the best of the Cardiff backs.* Just two days, later, on 15 October, Cardiff beat Bective Rangers narrowly 8-6, Bective just having overcome Neath 25-3. Lloyd Williams made a try for Cliff Morgan to *'burrow'* over, but the Irish tactics of a rampant pack targeting the Cardiff backs almost took Cardiff's record. Dave Phillips wrote that *'Lloyd Williams was a sound scrumhalf, but the same could not be said for the rest of the Cardiff defence.' 'Lloyd Williams Shows the Way'* was John Billott's headline for the 19-9 win against Cambridge on 20 October. *'Scrumhalf Lloyd Williams tired of his backs wasting chances against Cambridge University. He "had a go" himself – and 10 points can be traced to his two open-side breaks from the scrum. Otherwise, Cardiff would have drawn 9-9... Lloyd Williams broke to send Wells in by the posts... Finally, Lloyd Williams flitted through for a try which Llewellyn goaled and Cardiff kept their unbeaten record – the only leading invincible club in Wales.'*

With Cliff Morgan returning to the team against Cambridge, Lloyd now settled at scrumhalf for the rest of the season. 27 October 1956 saw the headline *'Brave Neath Go Down To Brilliant Trio'*, with J.B.G. Thomas reporting an attendance of 25,000. *'One day Cardiff will lose their proud, unbeaten record. Such an event is inevitable with the club playing attractive, open Rugby but it will take a good side or extremely bad conditions to bring about their downfall. In defeating Neath by a goal, a penalty and three tries to two tries they showed they are on top again in British Rugby as they were in 1947-48, with the promise of a tremendous*

duel against Newport on November 10... with L. Williams and Cliff
Morgan combining like a great pair, the three-quarter line, now the best in
Wales, pulled out all the stops and produced a copybook display of attack
at speed. This Cardiff midfield trio of Morgan, Griffiths and Wells, so
smoothly served by the steadily improving Lloyd Williams, is a remarkable
one. It makes mistakes as must all attacking groups, yet such is its speed,
power and elusiveness, that such mistakes are cancelled out by brilliance.'
Another report describes *'one of the most amazing tries we have seen at the*
Arms Park this season. Cardiff attacked strongly and the ball was juggled
from wing to wing and back again, almost every man in the Cardiff side
handling before Wells put Cliff Morgan away. The little outside half raced
through to put Glyn John over in the corner for a try which was cheered to
the echo... Lloyd Williams gave Cliff Morgan an immaculate service...'

Cardiff maintained their 16-run unbeaten sequence in a floodlit match at
Harlequins, which is not recorded in their official games. They lost
Malcolm Collins with torn ligaments midway through the first half, and he
returned as a passenger, but the 14 men scraped home 8-6. Collins was out
for only six weeks with his injury – they made them hard in those days.
Away at Oxford on 3 November, Cardiff were without Cliff Morgan,
Gordon Wells and Gareth Griffiths because of a Welsh Trial, and missing
Collins, Nicholls and others through injury. Lloyd Williams, Roddy Evans
and the superb front row of Colin Howe, Beckingham and J.D. Evans were
somehow not selected for that trial, and Cardiff scored the only try in a 6-3
win. On 10 November came the much-awaited Newport game, following a
6-6 draw in October. There was a gusting wind, and the game left Dave
Phillips unhappy memories: *'This Series Has Become a Guerrilla War...*
Saturday's rough, tough battle was no exception to the general rule...
Gone was the brilliant attacking rugby that has lured newcomers to the
Arms Park in recent weeks. Instead of the champagne sparkle, we had the
dregs of "scrumpo." It may have had 30,000 partisan fans shouting their
heads off, but it was not rugby football. Heavy rain reduced the Arms Park
pitch to a slithery skating rink and few of the international backs on view
could master the circumstances to enhance their "cap" chances this
season. The game quickly deteriorated into a forward battle, intense and
unremitting...' Cardiff won 6-5, a try and a penalty to a goal. Arthur
Trembath reported *'Lloyd Williams grows in stature with every game.'*

On 24 November, near the start of the game against Blackheath, Gordon
Wells was injured, so the centre was shifted to the wing. After a few
minutes it became obvious to Cardiff's captain Peter Goodfellow that
Wells had concussion, so he led him off the field. Eddie Thomas left the
pack to go on the left wing and it was 3-3 at half-time, a Cardiff try to a
penalty. With 14 men, *'Williams and Morgan were successful at half-back'*
and there was the familiar second-half Cardiff revival. Blackheath scored a
try and the depleted Cardiff team added two goals and a penalty to win 16-

6. It was an excellent first half of the season, beating Bridgend 28-5, Swansea 24-6, Halifax 36-14, plus Oxford and Cambridge universities. (Cardiff scored 7 tries in the Halifax game, the only other three games against Halifax being all won, 16-7 in 1888, 27-9 in 1955 and 28-3 in 1958, a total of 23 tries to 4.) Against Halifax, *'Lloyd Williams, back again at scrumhalf, was the best of the Cardiff backs.'* On 15 December a headline was *'They Adopt "Soccer" To Beat Mud'* as under *'monsoon conditions'* Cardiff scored 4 tries and a dropped goal to beat Rosslyn Park in Cardiff. For this game, Lloyd again had Cliff Morgan outside him, and *'handling excellently in the conditions, tore away from a scrummage, drew the Rosslyn Park defence before passing inside to Cliff Morgan, which Priday converted to give Cardiff an unassailable lead.'* In the final minutes a white ball was introduced to try and differentiate it from the mud-covered players. *'Conditions were so deplorable that one would not have been surprised had the authorities called the match off.'*

The Arms Park was its usual bog-like state on 20 December, when a 0-0 draw was scrapped out with Ebbw Vale, and Dave Phillips wrote that *'conditions made handling out of the question.'* Older readers only will remember the horrendous conditions of the pitch in a wet winter. *'The battle-scarred Arms Park pitch was churning up badly and with rain pouring steadily, the game developed into an exciting mudlark with players slithering this way and that on the treacherous surface.'* Players were indistinguishable. *'At the interval Lloyd Williams added to the general bafflement by changing to a No. 6 jersey, the same as his half-back partner Hewett... Nine minutes from the end the players called for new jerseys.'* Colin Hewett was Lloyd's fly-half, wearing 6 instead of 10 in those days Lloyd often played fly-half so there was a large size number 6 shirt available somewhere for him. Hewett played 100 times for the Firsts between 1952-53 and 1959-60, scoring 22 tries.

On Boxing Day 1956, Cardiff scored 5 tries in beating Wasps 19-0, with a headline reading *'Cardiff The Top Team – And This Is Why! Until the snow-covered ground became a morass, Cardiff, inspired by the scintillating runs of Cliff Morgan, played the type of Rugby that has made them the **club team of the year**, and delighted the 6,000 crowd. Helped by the solid scrummaging of Geoff Beckingham and the accurate service of Lloyd Williams, Morgan was always on the move... Inside 25 minutes Cardiff had piled up their 19 points, with two tries each by Gareth Griffiths and one each from Lynn Davies, Gordon Wells and Lloyd Williams... Wasps could not handle the greasy ball and the Cardiff line was never really endangered.'* Cardiff were unbeaten until the 19th game of the season, losing away at Swansea 6-3 on 1 December. Cardiff had won the home game in November 24-6, 4 tries to 1. South African Universities (the Sables) beat Newport, and then Cardiff beat the students 18-8 on 9 January 1957.

Rex Willis was still injured. In the Second Welsh Trial, on 8 December, the 32-year-old former Ghurkha Peter Goodfellow captained the Possibles, the Whites, but was never capped, the eternal curse for Cardiff forwards. On his team were two members of the best front row in Wales, Geoff Beckingham and Colin Howe, along with Alun Priday and Gordon Wells. Beckingham yet again out-hooked the incumbent Bryn Meredith. (Geoff and Colin were joined by J.D. (John) Evans for the 3rd Welsh Trial on 5 January, again in the Whites). Three Cardiff players were in the Reds, Cliff Morgan, C.L. 'Cowboy' Davies and Gareth Griffiths. There were 8 Cardiff players, and on the same day the club played Harlequins at The White City Stadium. Rex Willis had damaged his wrist in a charity match, but Lloyd Williams still missed out on the Trial. On 8 December, missing these 8 players, plus those injured, a mainly Rags First XV lost away at Quins 17-11, in a two tries apiece game.

A long article in *The Football Echo* is headlined '**What About The Cardiff Pack?** – *The delight felt by Cardiff club selectors at having eight of their shining stars selected for the final Welsh trial at the Arms Park on January 5 is not unmixed with embarrassment! The "Big Five" have nominated an entire Cardiff back division… yet that particular line-up has never represented Cardiff this season. It is: Alun Priday (Possibles), C. Lynn Davies (Possibles), Alan Barter (Possibles), Gordon Wells (Probables), Gareth Griffiths (Probables), Cliff Morgan (Probables) and Lloyd Williams (Probables). It is a great tribute to the club that such a clean sweep of talent should have been made… but club enthusiasts are anything but happy. "What about the pack?" they ask, and point out that only Geoff Beckingham has made the final grade, despite some grand play by his pack colleagues this season. The greatest satisfaction is at the honour given to young Lloyd. Lloyd has played some grand stuff this season and thoroughly earns the distinction of being nominated Onllwyn Brace's No. 1 rival. **Out He Goes**. Powerfully built, the possessor of safe hands and capable of throwing a long and accurate service to the irrepressible Morgan, he might well succeed Rex Willis as Morgan's international and club partner. His display in the mud and the slush against the Wasps must have been the deciding factor in his favour and there is jubilation in Taff's Well that yet another of the famous "Williams clan" is on the fringe of international honours'.* However, 'the poor old forwards have reason to grumble' in their non-selection for the Final Trial.

Another '*Football Echo*' article ended with '*The best front row in British rugby is generally considered to be the Howe–Beckingham–Evans trio of Cardiff, although this does not seem to agree with the "Big Five's" own assessments!*' For this Final Welsh Trial on 5 January, again a mainly reserve team played Moseley away, each side scoring 3 tries but Cardiff losing by a conversion, 13-11. However, over Easter, the Barbarians humiliated Cardiff, its heaviest ever defeat, 40-0. Cardiff were missing

Cliff Morgan, Gareth Griffiths and Gordon Wells, due to tour to Canada with the Barbarians, but it was a dismal performance, easily the worst result in the team's history.

On the day of the England game, 19 January 1957, Cliff Morgan and Gareth Griffiths were playing for Wales, a day when Cardiff Firsts seemingly always played Bath away. We read from *Bath Rugby Heritage*: '*Bath last defeated Cardiff ten years previously – January 18th 1947 at the Rec. Cardiff included three Welsh internationals and several Trialists, and Bath did very well to lead by two goals to a goal and a penalty at half-time. As has so often been the case, the talented visitors turned in a superb second half performance, finally running off winners by 3 goals, a try and a penalty, to Bath's 2 goals, a try and a penalty. Cardiff's comparatively slow start, may be explained by their late arrival, after missing their train connection at Bristol. Cardiff's goal was quickly countered by a brilliant try from Bath's right-winger, Harrison. Curtis started the move, which was carried on by Silk, Ian Smart gathered the loose ball and produced a perfect cross-kick, which enabled Harrison to take at top speed. He kicked past two defenders and raced on to touch down between the posts. Curtis added the extras. Priday was having a good day with 'the boot,' and added a penalty to his earlier conversion. Bath's second try came from an overhead pass to Dolman, and the hefty winger was able to outstrip a confused Cardiff defensive line, for Curtis to again major. (Half-time 10-8) Cardiff came back in the second spell, crossing the Bath line three more times, converting twice. Curtis reduced the mounting arrears with a 45-yard penalty, and right on time Dennis Silk scored an unconverted try to narrow the gap to just 5 points. In the final minutes, Bath had the misfortune to lose Gordon Drewett with a serious leg injury.*' Cardiff won 21-16, 4 tries to 3.

On 23 April 1957, Cardiff lost to a penalty 3-0 away at Northampton, having scored 4 tries to 2 at home to beat them 14-11. However, Cardiff were missing ALL their internationals. There were two floodlit matches, the first on Bristol City's ground, where Bristol Rugby Club were beaten 20-13. J.B.G. Thomas wrote that it was '*A brilliant display of exhilarating open Rugby football in the highest traditions of the two clubs and crowned the Bristol Rugby venture into the floodlit world.*' The other floodlit game was at White City, where the Harlequins were defeated 8-6. Both games were 'exhibitions', not included in the official records, just like many of the charity games Cardiff played. Cardiff toured Romania in May and June 1957, guests of the Romanian Rugby Federation. 80,000 spectators saw Cardiff lose to Bucharest 'A', effectively the full Romania team, 3-6 and then beat Bucharest 'B' 9-6. It was a truly international year, with Cardiff playing Germany, Italy, South African Universities, penetrating the 'Iron Curtain' into Communist Romania, and some players touring Canada. The huge crowd in Romania on 1 June 1957, to see a club side, was a world record for a rugby match. (However, the game was a 'warm-up' before a soccer game between Romania and USSR at 'B' level). Cardiff's team ended what Dave Phillips called '*their hardest season on record*' against a New Zealand Navy XV, winning 40-10, when C. Lynn 'Cowboy' Davies scored 3 tries in 20 minutes, and Gordon Wells and Colin Hewett also scored hat-tricks. There were 50 official games and many unofficial ones.

Top try scorers were Gareth Griffiths and Glyn John with 18, Howard Nicholls 14 and Gordon Wells 11. Alun Priday kicked 64 goals, scoring 3 tries for 158 points. **Six players made 40 or more appearances**: Peter Goodfellow 48 of 50 official matches, J. D. Evans 46, Colin Howe 45, G. Beckingham and Eddie Thomas 43 and M. Gough 40. Lloyd Williams and Roddy Evans were given their First Team caps. The Athletic played 32, won 21, lost 8 and drew 3, points 465-183. Their captain F.C. Ferguson made most appearances, 29 matches, followed by Brian Sadler 24, the prop Stan Bowes 22 and the future Welsh international prop Kingsley Jones 21. Top try scorers were Derek Murphy and R. J. Parsons with 16 each, and of particular interest to us is that Cenydd Williams both played for the Firsts and was awarded his Athletic Cap, along with Glyn Williams of Pentyrch. The Youth/Junior team played 27, won 24, drew 2 and only lost to Aberavon, scoring a huge 475-68 points.

Cliff Morgan, Gareth Griffiths, Gordon Wells and Lloyd Williams played for Wales. Wales lost the first game, at home to England, the eventual Grand Slammers, by a penalty 0-3. Cliff Morgan was partnered with Onllwyn Brace, and the only other Cardiff player was Gareth Griffiths in the centre. Then Wales lost in Scotland 9-6, a try apiece, with Lloyd Williams replacing Onllwyn Brace to get his first cap, partnering Cliff Morgan. Then Wales's season turned around, narrowly beating Ireland in Cardiff 6-5, with the same Cardiff halfbacks and Gordon Wells on the wing. This was a rarity, as Wales were outscored on tries 1-0. France were beaten away 19-13, when Wales scored 4 tries to 3, with Lloyd again partnering an excellent performance from Cliff Morgan, for Lloyd's third international cap in his first full year for Cardiff First Team. From 1952-53 to 1963-64 he would play 310 games for the club. Wales finished equal second with Ireland and Scotland on 4 points, but second on points difference.

CHAPTER 29 - CARDIFF SEASON 1957 – 1958

'WE FELL TO THE WORLD'S BEST R.U. CLUB' (- PHIL
TRESIDDER AUSTRALIA'S REPRESENTATIVE) – LLOYD
WILLIAMS, THE FIFTH BROTHER, PLAYS FOUR TIMES FOR
WALES - CENYDD, THE SIXTH BROTHER, HAS HIS CARDIFF
FIRSTS CAP - ELWYN WILLIAMS, THE SEVENTH BROTHER,
PLAYS FOR CARDIFF YOUTH AND WALES YOUTH -
CARDIFF'S RUGBY BROTHERS – LES MANFIELD

Lloyd Williams P33 T1 = 3pts; **Cenydd Williams** P21 T3 = 9pts; Alun
Priday P36 T2 C25 P23 D1 = 128pts (Tongwynlais); Derek Murphy P33
T9 = 27pts (Pentyrch); Glyn Williams P3 T2 = 6pts (Pentyrch)

P47, W32, L7, D8. Points 483-214. Tries 110-35, Pens 29-22

1957-58 Lloyd is standing, first left. Cenydd standing opposite end of row

In his final season, the back-row forward Eddie Thomas was chosen
captain. He had given sterling service since joining from Neath in 1952,
and he nominated Cliff Morgan as vice-captain. A modest man, Cliff
always refused the Cardiff captaincy, possibly thinking that it might affect
his play. Eddie Thomas had played for Neath and Aberavon against the
Springboks in 1951, and for Cardiff in the victory over New Zealand in
1953, and was now to captain the team to beat the Third Wallabies. At the
season's end he retired after 217 appearances, and Cardiff's *Annual Report*

reflects that *'he worked as efficiently for the good of the club off the field as on it.'*

Upon 14 September 1957 Cardiff welcomed Bective Rangers, a team to which they only lost once, and drew with 4 times, in 21 home and away fixtures between 1889 and 1975. Dave Phillips reported that *'Cardiff emerged battered but unbeaten from their Arms Park battle with a lively Bective Rangers side, saved by fine tries from Cenydd Williams and Cliff Morgan... Cardiff made one sensational change, Cenydd Williams replacing Gareth Griffiths at left centre... then came a magnificent Cardiff attack. Cenydd Williams got possession, found the half opening and was through. He passed to Gordon Wells who tried to outstrip the Irish defence but was collared... After 14 minutes play Cardiff took the lead with a remarkable try. Once again Morgan tore away and made ground before passing to Gordon Wells, who lobbed a pass out to Ken Thomas on the left wing. The wing immediately passed inside to CENYDD WILLIAMS, who was over for an opportunistic try, which Priday was unable to convert.'* (Capitals in quotations are always as in the original text). Lloyd and brother Cenydd combined to save a try, and Cliff Morgan went over for the game to be won 6-3. *'Cenydd Williams, in his baptism of major football came through with credit.'* Eddie Thomas and Roddy Evans were hit by a flu epidemic before the home game against Aberavon on 28 September 1957, but Aberavon had to make eleven changes owing to flu, bringing in players from Taibach. Aberavon Harlequins and Glamorgan Police to scrape a side together. Lloyd Williams and Cliff Morgan played well, but the scratch Aberavon side were magnificent, scoring a try against Cardiff's 3, and only going down 17-3.

On 19 October, *'there was a tense, sometimes exciting and always relentlessly keen struggle'* in the home draw 3-3 with Newport. The two Welsh selectors should have been impressed *'by the manner in which Geoff Beckingham out-hooked Bryn Meredith in the second half'*, and Rex Willis had returned to play. *'Willis, already capped 21 times by Wales, has ousted the current Welsh inside-half, Lloyd Williams, from the Cardiff team.'* Upon 23 October, unbeaten Neath were outscored by 4 tries, with one converted, to a penalty, 14-3: *'Ken Richards, until he injured a leg just after the interval and transferred to the wing, combined effectively with Lloyd Williams at scrumhalf and centres Cenydd Williams and Gordon Wells.'* On 2 November, there was a hard-fought win against Oxford University, with Cenydd Williams taking over at right centre from Gordon Wells and Lloyd and Cliff again at half-back. Pentyrch's Derek Murphy scored a *'splendid try'* after inter-passing between the backs, in a narrow 11-8 win. 18 November saw Cenydd Williams in the centre away to Bective Rangers, with Brian Mark, not Lloyd Williams, partnering Cliff Morgan. In a fast, open game, Cardiff scored 3 tries to 2 and a penalty, for a 9-9 draw. The Irish Press reported *'the sparkling three-quarter line of*

Nicholls, Williams, Griffiths and Ken Thomas being of the highest calibre.'

Only 2 games were lost up to New Year, and there was a high number of 8 draws, including two against Newport, home and away, both 3-3. All the other draws were away: Ebbw Vale 3-3, Bective Rangers 9-9, Rosslyn Park 8-8, Coventry 3-3, Neath 3-3 and Bridgend 5-5. Davies believes there could have been *'room for conjecture here!'* In the New Year, Cardiff lost at home to Newport 14-6, with 6 players in the Welsh team in Dublin - Alun Priday, J.D. Evans and Howard Nicholls had their first caps, and the others were Cliff Morgan, W.R. 'Roddy' Evans and Lloyd Williams. Other losses were away at London Welsh 8-6, Llanelli 8-3, St. Ives 6-3 on the Cornish tour and Gloucester 3-0. Pontypool surprised Cardiff at the Arms Park 14-8, however. At Easter the previous year, there had been 3 *'disastrous'* defeats to the following teams, but this year the Barbarians were beaten 14-6 (tries 3-1), Harlequins 3-0 and Northampton 13-3 (tries 3-0).

At last, after 6 away fixtures, Cardiff resumed home-away alternate years games with Bath, so moved the date from the day of the England-Wales game. Since 1938 there had been 12 away and 3 home games, all won by Cardiff, 11 of which on the date of the England game. The Bath report for 19 April 1958 is as follows: *'Lost 0-17. Bath did their best to contain a powerful Cardiff side in front of a large and appreciative Arms Park crowd. However, the Welshmen were able to cross the Bath line 3 times, converting once and adding 2 penalty goals for good measure. Against the normal practice, Bath, the visiting side, changed to white jerseys to avoid a colour clash... The visiting forwards stood up to their mammoth task well, and although they could not do much about Cardiff's supremacy in the tight, John Robert's eight kept up the pace in the loose... Drewett had a fine game at the base of the scrum and had one fine diagonal run, before slipping the ball to Lavery. Unfortunately, the Bath winger was stopped by the brawny Cardiff cover.'*

The season's highlight was the 14-11 win over Australia on 14 December 1957, with Gordon Wells scoring two brilliant tries on the wing. Dave Phillips wrote in the *Football Echo*: *'This was the classic game we had all hoped. Cardiff's superior strategy once again confounded the enthusiasm and virility of this young Australian XV.'* The official press correspondent with the Australian team, Phil Tresidder of the *Sydney Daily Telegraph*, reported *'We fell to the world's best R.U. club... It would be churlish indeed, for any Australian supporter to suggest that Cardiff did not thoroughly deserve victory in this splendid match'*. Cardiff scored a goal, two tries and a penalty to a goal, a try and a penalty. At the time of the game, after 22 matches, Cardiff had won 19, drawn 2 and lost 1, to lead the unofficial championship with 90.9%. Llanelli were second with played 22, won 16, lost 6, for 72.7%, followed by Aberavon and Penarth. Newport were 9th. Cardiff went on to finish the season with another unofficial championship title, but only second row Bill 'Roddy' Evans was selected for the Lions in 1959, although out there he started four of the six Tests.

Captain Eddie Thomas led a 'Rags and Tatters' team against Rosslyn Park, defending an unbeaten ground record at Roehampton. *'Only Eddie Thomas survived of the Cardiff pack that shook the Wallabies – Geoff Beckingham, John Evans were in the Welsh Final Trial, and the other four were trial reserves in the grandstand!'* Often, when reporting Cardiff missing players for trials, there is no record of their players in attendance and thereby they were unable to play for Cardiff. Sometimes they might have up to 13 'Rags' players in the side, and for this game most of the backs were missing **as well as 7 forwards**. Rex Willis was injured in the second half, and Cardiff were down to 14 men. Rosslyn Park scored a pushover try against Cardiff's weakened pack, pushing them back 6 or 7 yards, and converted, to make the score 5-0 at half-time. Peter Thomas, later Cardiff's President and benefactor, had little chance to make an impression as hooker, with the shove against his pack throughout the game. Ken Thomas scored a converted try for Cardiff, then Rosslyn Park had a penalty for 8-5. Hewett scored after a thrilling run five minutes from the end of the game for the 14 men to draw 8-8. Remember, **this was missing around 13 first choice players, down to 14 men, away against an unbeaten top class English team**.

Upon 4 January 1958, Wales beat Australia 9-3. Ireland then beat them 9-6, England 9-6, Scotland 12-8 and France 19-0, in the tourists' 32nd match in 15 weeks. Against Wales, Australia scored a try in the first half, but Wales in the second half had a try by Aberavon wing John Collins, a penalty and a drop goal. The great Carwyn James played outside half for Wales as Cliff was injured, partnered by Wynne Evans, also of Llanelli. On 30 November 1957, Cardiff at Bristol scored 5 unconverted tries and a penalty to a goal and a penalty to win 18-6. The double was completed on 11 January 1958 to win 19-9, Cardiff scoring 4 tries to 2. Rex Willis was dropped, and Cenydd Williams was in the centre again. Glyn John touched down in the corner and *'... it was a mere formality for Cenydd Williams to send over Howard Nicholls for another corner try... Lloyd Williams started the move, the ball going through the hands of Eddie Thomas, Gordon Wells and Cenydd Williams before Nicholls crossed for his second try... With only a few minutes to go Cenydd Williams slipped an inside pass to Howard Nicholls which Priday converted.'* Like his brother Bleddyn, Cenydd knew that his job was to put his wing over. If Cardiff had a reasonable kicker and with today's points scoring, there would have been some amazing score lines. Cardiff's 9 tries in total against Bristol, if converted, would be worth 63 points. In the match, Cliff Morgan and Lloyd Williams were able to rehearse playing against England on the following Saturday - a 3-3 draw for unfancied Wales who were not given *'a snowball's chance'* for the game.

379

It was Aberavon away on 8 February, having beaten them 17-8 in September. Aberavon were defending their ground record. However, Cardiff won 12-9 in a thrilling battle, scoring 4 tries to a try and two penalties. Lloyd was scrumhalf to Hewett and Cenydd was in the centre inside wing Nicholls. On 15 February 1958, Cardiff scored 8 tries in a 30-0 demolition of Cheltenham at the Arms Park. (After 9 successive wins, the fixture was ended in 1960.) **Cenydd was playing outside-half** to his brother Lloyd, as Cliff Morgan had cried off, and Cenydd's left centre position was taken by Gareth Griffiths. The brothers combined well throughout the game... '*After 12 minutes Cardiff took the lead with a really smart try. Lloyd Williams, scrum half, cut inside the wide breaking Cheltenham wing forwards to race down the middle before handing on the brother CENYDD, who dived for a sparkling try... Cenydd Williams raced into the Cheltenham half and passed to Glyn John who made considerable ground. Before being tackled he managed to get his pass to Dai Hayward, who raced in unopposed between the posts ... Just before half-time Cenydd Williams sprinted through spectacularly before passing to Gordon Wells ... to Gareth Griffiths... C.D. Williams raced up to dribble over for a fine try... Half-time was 11-0. Wells scored two tries after sprinting to the line, and Cardiff were now going great guns, and an incisive break through by Cenydd Williams saw the ball pass from hand to hand until Howard Nicholls dived over. There was more 'blue and black magic' with a try from Roddy Evans, then another brilliant piece of concerted work by Cenydd Williams and Gordon Wells saw Glyn John dive over.*' Cenydd was usually playing fly-half for the RAF (with the legendary league player Alex Murphy his scrumhalf) and Combined Services, so was comfortable in the position. His preferred position, however, was left centre, the same as brother Bleddyn, with the opportunity of feeding his wing with tries. Combined Services would not choose rugby league players, so Cenydd had a variety of scrum-halves during his National Service.

Baldwin writes of Mountain Ash players who went to Cardiff, including the great Les Manfield and Haydn Morris: '*To pick one player as the most outstanding might seem fatuous, but I will risk that. John D. Evans, **described by the All-Blacks and the Wallabies as the finest prop in these islands** and supported in this contention by countless other people, must rank as that player.*' 'JD' Evans won his first cap in the 1957-58 season, which coincided with a 14-8 loss to Newport. Six Cardiff players went with JD to Dublin - Alun Priday and Howard Nicholls were also getting their first caps – plus Cliff Morgan, Lloyd Williams and British Lion W. R. (Roddy) Evans, who claimed he learned everything about propping from 'JD'. John D. Evans was then playing for what the Australians called '*the greatest club in the world.*' It seems that he was surely victim to the club apportionment system of the 'Big 5' of the time, for he surely should have had more Welsh caps. JD played an incredible 338 games for Cardiff from

380

1951-52 to 1960-61. Fellow Cardiff prop Colin Howe even now (2020) rated him as '*the best*', and with Cardiff often providing a good few half-backs, three-quarters and fullbacks, its forwards often, like John Evans, Elwyn Williams and John Hickey, lost out in international selection.

The 16 March 1958 Cardiff-Newport programme reads: '*It is unfortunate that today's final clash of the season, with our close rivals and near neighbours, should take place on the day when Wales play Ireland. Both sides have representatives in Ireland, but Cardiff suffer most with six of their players appearing in the red jersey and one of their number standing by as reserve. Normally, the fixtures between the two clubs are so arranged that the dates do not clash with Inter-national Fixtures, but on this occasion the Wales v. Ireland Match was fixed for a week earlier than usual. However, both sides have strong reserve strength, and we feel certain that the standard of rugger on view today will not suffer. It gives the Cardiff Club the greatest possible pleasure to congratulate the three new "caps" from Cardiff Club who are playing for Wales this afternoon. There can be no finer clubmen in Wales than Alun Priday, John Evans and Howard Nicholls who represent all that is good in Welsh Rugger, and they have fully earned the great honour of playing for their country. We wish them and their colleagues a happy and successful game today. Cardiff have not been defeated by a Welsh side this season and Newport will no doubt hope to end this record. Of the three matches played between the two clubs the Blue and Blacks have won one, with two drawn. It is significant that in all three matches the highest score by either side has been three points. If the weather is kind today it is quite likely that the points scored will exceed the total scored in the previous three matches.*' And yes, Cardiff lost 14-6. The previous scores were 3-0 (A), 3-3 (H), 3-3 (A). Cardiff were missing seven players against Newport in this loss - Lloyd Williams, Alun Priday (his debut), Malcolm Thomas, John Evans, Cliff Morgan, Howard Nicholls and Roddy Evans. Wales beat Ireland in Dublin 9-6. 3 tries to 1. The club losing only losing 7 games, five away, and drawing 8, <u>all away</u>, was a successful season, when three Trials and five Internationals (including Australia) were taken into effect.

'Roddy' Evans a real handful in the lines-out – there was no lifting allowed, so his height was a major advantage. A solicitor from Porthcawl, Cambridge Blue 'Roddy' Evans was educated at Cowbridge Grammar, won 13 caps for Wales and played 18 times for the Lions, on the 1959 tour to Australia and New Zealand, playing in four of the six Tests. Throughout the International season, Cardiff had to call on the Rags to fill the gaps during trials and internationals. Wales drew 3-3 away to England, with the half-back pairing of Lloyd and Cliff being a success, but England took the Championship with a point more than Wales. England fielded their strongest post-war team. Wales then beat Scotland in Cardiff 8-3, with tries by Gordon Wells and Aberavon wing John Collins, and Ireland in Dublin

9-6 with tries by Bryn Meredith, Neath centre Cyril Roberts and Abertillery's flanker Haydn Morgan. A win against France in Cardiff would have taken the Championship but Wales lost 16-6 in front of the 60,000-capacity crowd. It was France's first win at the Arms Park in 50 years of trying. Lloyd and Cliff were the half-backs in all matches, and Geoff Beckingham played in the French match in place of the injured Newport Lion, Bryn Meredith. It was Cliff Morgan's 29th and final game for Wales.

'Is this the Hurried End for Cliff the Great?' is a press headline after game away at Llanelli on 31 March 1958. *'Cliff Morgan's wonderful rugby career may have ended in sad anti-climax five minutes after the start of last night's match. Cliff limped off the field in obvious pain... he damaged his ribs against France on Saturday. Nobody could have blamed Cliff for standing down last night, but he did not want to disappoint his favourite Stradey Park crowd... it was rugged and exciting... Cardiff's 14 men conceded eight points against the wind... Cenydd Williams, Cardiff's deputy stand-in outside-half, started several good moves, but Cardiff's best chance was thrown away by wing Glyn Williams. An even-time sprinter, Williams intercepted near half-way. He had a clear run-in, but stopped at the crowd's shout of "Knock-on". If it was a knock-on, the referee had not seen it; but Williams realised that too late.'* **'Cardiff's best backs were Lloyd Williams, Cenydd Williams and Gareth Griffiths'** in the 8-3 loss.

A strong Barbarians side, with 14 internationals, faced Cardiff on 5 April 1958, in *'a rain-swept gala match'*. Cardiff were in their wonderful **change strip of red shirts**, surely after 60 years it is time for them to return? With a blue and black chevron and a black collar? Cardiff supporters could wear them for Wales matches. The pink Cardiff Blues away strip of recent times has not been overly popular in terms of sales and seemed to have coincided with defeats. Psychological studies have shown that red shirts give a male team an advantage. Cenydd and Lloyd were the half-backs. Dai Hayward may have been wrongly judged for a tackle on England scrumhalf Dickie Jeeps, for the Baa-Baas to score with a penalty in front of the posts, but Dai made up for it with an opportunistic try soon afterwards. The Baa-Baas scored a try for a half-time score of 6-3. Cenydd and Gareth Griffiths were combining well, and Priday put over a penalty to equalise. *'Cardiff would not be denied and when Cenydd Williams feinted to run one way, Gareth Griffiths caught the Barbarians on the wrong foot and was over for a fine try... Cenydd Williams gained more ground to take Cardiff well inside the Barbarians' 25... Gareth Griffiths kicked high towards the Baa-Baas' posts, and from the ensuing scrummage CENYDD WILLIAMS dodged and weaved his way through some feckless tackling, to dive over for a grand try which Alun Priday converted with a magnificent wide-angled kick, to give Cardiff an eight points lead'* and win 14-6. (I have always said that Cenydd was my favourite Welsh centre, as he eased through defences like Barry

John – helped by his experience as a fly-half. My other favourites were Gerald Davies and Maurice Richards, before they moved to the wing – and as wings they never 'died' with the ball, coming inside and linking up. Then in more recent years, Jonathan 'Foxy' Davies of Llanelli – like the others a world-class player who at their peak would be a first choice for any international team of their era.

Cliff Morgan and Geoff Beckingham announced their retirements, along with Rex Willis and Eddie Thomas. Cliff said he would tour South Africa with the Barbarians, to end his career. Try scorers were Howard Nicholls 20, Gordon Wells 14, Glyn John 13 and Ken Thomas 9 each. Alun Priday, with 49 goals, a dropped goal and 2 tries gained 128 points. That marvellous prop Colin Howe played in 41 of 47 games. Club caps were awarded to centre Cenydd Williams, wing forward D. J. 'Dai' Hayward, prop Kingsley Jones (to play 14 times for Wales) and Ken Thomas. David John 'Dai' Hayward was to play 325 times for Cardiff, play for Wales and serve Cardiff RFC for 40 years. Some of my greatest memories are of Hayward operating in tandem with Elwyn Williams harrying opposing fly halves. They were like big sheepdogs, herding the poor player into the other's grasp. Dai Watkins, the Newport outside half, could make fabulous breaks, but Newport often lacked a centre or wing forward to support him. He was only 5 ft. 6 ins, and I remember him having a nightmare on a sticky pitch at Rodney Parade – he would find one of the Cardiff pair in his way, hesitate, and get tackled by the other. Facing these two, four times a season, and with Barry John now being picked for Wales, he went North in 1967, for a truly glittering career.

Peter Nyhan captained the Athletic XV to another terrific season – Pl. 33, W.27, L.3, D3. Pts 548-147. Newport United won twice, and Bristol United once, three were drawn and the rest won. Derek Murphy touched down 13 times and Ray Glastonbury 11. New caps were awarded to V. Davies, G. T. Ellis, Ray Glastonbury, Cliff Howe, George Spear and Peter Thomas (R.A.F.). Ray Glastonbury played 25 times, Cliff Howe 22, Peter Thomas and G. T. Ellis 21, George Spear 21 (and 10 games with the 1st XV), Derek Murphy 15 (and 10 with the 1st XV). **Elwyn Williams was the Cardiff Youth captain**. All four youngest Williams brothers played for Cardiff's Youth/Juniors team. Three Cardiff boys represented Wales Youth, Elwyn Williams, J. Regan and Tommy McCarthy.

CARDIFF RUGBY BROTHERS

With the appearance in Cardiff Youth of Tommy McCarthy and the seventh Williams brother, Elwyn, one of Wales' greatest uncapped players, it is time to mention other notable brothers who played together for the team. I noted earlier the unique record of 6 (perhaps 7) Turnbulls and 4 Griffiths brothers. We may as well trundle along this unknown pathway as, believe me, it is interesting. Please note again that there were never more than 15 players in a team, with no substitutes allowed until 1969 – it was far, far more difficult to get into the team, let alone make the required number of appearances for a first-team Cardiff cap:

BIGGS – 7 – Three Cardiff Captains in the first 'Golden Era' - Brothers in Cardiff's First XV for 22 consecutive seasons – Youngest Player Capped by Wales for over a Century – The Incredible Maori Tourists - 4 Brothers play for Barbarians, Cecil, Norman, Elwyn and Selwyn (a record only equalled by the Williams brothers)

We potter back through the decades to, and it again seems impossible, seven brothers who played for Cardiff, in their great decade of 1886-87 to 1906-07. The Biggs were a rich family who lived in the very up-market Park Place, Cardiff. E.P. (Elwyn) Biggs was a Barbarian and played in 57 games for the Firsts, scoring 10 tries from 1886-87 to 1893-94. J.J.E. Biggs played 18 times, scoring 4 tries from 1886-87 to 1892-93, and in 1922 was Lord Mayor of Cardiff. The wing Norman, outside-half Selwyn and centre Cecil were **all Cardiff captains**, **all Barbarians**, and Norman and Selwyn were capped for Wales 6 times and 9 times respectively. **Elwyn was the fourth Baa-Baa**.

Norman Witchell Biggs (1870-1908) went to private schools and Cambridge, where he beat the world sprint champion Charlton James Blackwell Monypenny over 100 yards. (The latter was the 27th Laird of Pitmilly, to the uninitiated, a title dating back to Ricardus de Moniepennie in 1211. (At least you will have learned something from this book.) Biggs played in 166 games for Cardiff, scoring 107 tries, from 1886-87 to 1898-99. Norman Biggs was at the time the youngest player capped by Wales, aged 18 years and 49 days when he played against 'New Zealand Natives' – the Maoris - in 1888. (It was not until 2010, 112 years later, when in 2010 Tom Prydie, aged 18 years and 25 days beat the record, after only two first-class appearances for the Ospreys. It was a very strange decision, not replicated in any other country in over a century of international rugby). The Welsh backs were tremendously heckled by spectators at Swansea, particularly the Cardiff youngster Biggs, as they faced the much bigger Māori team. Swansea had lost 9 of the 10 previous games to Cardiff but had beaten them easily, three weeks before the international. Their supporters were thus not too happy with the strong Cardiff presence in the Welsh team. However, on 22 December, Wales won 8-0 with 3 tries worth 2 points each and a conversion. In a punishing schedule in a bitterly cold month, the Maoris then beat Swansea and Newport on 24 and 26 December, but on 29 December Cardiff won 8-3. To be fair, the Māoris must have been utterly exhausted. Four games in 8 days against strong opposition in freezing conditions were unfair. Let us further develop the concept of 'unfair' in rugby, after the Biggs brothers entry.

384

Norman Biggs played for Cardiff from 1886–87 to 1898–99, but also captained Bath in 1899-1900 and played in the early 1890s for London Welsh. In 166 matches for Cardiff, he was one of their highest scoring players. In his captaincy season of 1893–94, he kicked 58 conversions, scored 25 tries and two dropped goals for 199 points. This was a club record for eight decades, until 1972–73 season when it was beaten by John Davies. He scored 107 tries in 166 games. Norman played in all 3 games in the 1893 Triple Crown team. In the first international of 1894, against England, Wales were beaten badly, losing 24–3. Interviewed after, Biggs was asked why he had failed to tackle Harry Bradshaw, who scored the first try. His answer was, *'Tackle him? It was as much as I could do to get out of his way!'*. In his final Welsh game in 1894, Cardiff supplied all four three-quarters against Ireland in the 3-0 loss – Biggs, Dai Fitzgerald, Jack Elliot and Tom Pearson. The next international saw brother Selwyn play for the first time. Norman also played cricket for Glamorgan, like his brother Selwyn.

Norman was a police officer in the Glamorgan Constabulary, and after the outbreak of the Second Boer War, Biggs volunteered and was posted as a private to the Glamorgan Yeomanry, for service in South Africa. Biggs engaged in 57 skirmishes with his unit coming under daily sniper fire, and was shot through the thigh, on patrol, on 11 October 1900. From 26 November to 18 December, he was on the hospital ship *Simla*, returning to England for treatment. Norman was commissioned as a second lieutenant, then promoted lieutenant in 1801 and attached to 4th Battalion Imperial Yeomanry in South Africa. He was then either wounded again or fell ill, as *The Times* reported on 26 September, that he had been discharged from hospital and returned to duty in the week ending 8 September. He sailed for home on the steamship *Goorkha*, leaving Cape Town on 19 July 1902. Biggs was then commissioned as a lieutenant in the 3rd Battalion Welsh Regiment on 13 June 1903, and seconded to the Colonial Office and posted to Northern Nigeria as a superintendent of police in a military area on 10 February 1906. Now promoted to Captain, in 1908, 20 years after his first cap, he was killed by a poisoned arrow during *'a native ambush in Sakaba'*, north-western Nigeria - surely the most unusual death for any Cardiff and Wales player. No, we will rephrase that – for any rugby player.

Fly-half Selwyn Hanam Biggs (1872-1943) scored 46 tries for Cardiff in 176 appearances in 12 seasons, from 1889-90 to 1900-01. He played 9 times for Wales, including in the 1900 Triple Crown year, and played cricket for Glamorgan. In 1894, 1896 and 1898 he appeared for the Baa-Baas. Cecil Fleming Biggs (1881-1944) played mainly as centre 173 times, for Cardiff, scoring an amazing 111 tries from 1898-99 to 1906-07. He was captain in 1904-05, and Davies calls him *'one of the great uncapped Welsh players.'* After a season and a half playing for the Athletic, Biggs was the second highest try scorer in his first full season in 1900-1901 with 16 tries.

A Barbarian, he was top scorer for the next three seasons with 16, 16 and 24 tries. Despite playing for Cardiff in the 1905-06 season, Biggs missed the Cardiff win against the All Blacks. Next season saw Cecil facing South Africa. All the Cardiff team were internationals – it was one of the 'Golden Eras' – and only Biggs and Dicky David were uncapped. Biggs was injured in the first few minutes, so Cardiff won with, realistically, 14 men. Lieutenant Geoffrey N. Biggs was much younger and away with the Army, but played one game for Cardiff, alongside his brother Cecil, against the Barbarians on Boxing Day 1906. Elwyn Biggs made 57 appearances from 1886-87 to 1893-94. His brother J.J. E. Biggs played 18 games for the Firsts from 1886-87 to 1893-94. I am adding a seventh brother to the six noted by Davies, W.H. Biggs, who played twice in 1878-79. Indeed, the **Biggs had players in Cardiff's Firsts for 22 consecutive seasons**, 1886-87 to 1907-08, often providing 3 brothers in the same team. Three played together against the Baa-Baas on Boxing Day 1892.

The MOST UNFAIR RUGBY TOUR of ALL TIME

Before travelling to Britain, the Māoris played 9 top New Zealand clubs, then played Melbourne twice, only losing to Auckland and Otago and drawing with Melbourne once, between 23 June and 15 August 1888, then embarking for Britain. After a gruelling two-month voyage by sea, their 26 players had 74 games in 6 months in Britain, 3 a week, against all the top clubs and England, Wales and Ireland – without the use of substitutes – it seems inhuman. These were the same players who began playing in New Zealand on 23 June 1888. Their fixtures in Europe were October 10 games; November 13; December 13; January 13; February 11; March 14. They won 49, lost 20 and drew 5. And remember, there were no buses/coaches – all travel was by steam locomotive. On 17 December they beat Wigan and on 19 December lost to Llanelli. That train journey alone would have taken many hours, with several changes on very slow trains. When they were not playing, they were travelling on trains. There were very few steam buses, as internal combustion engine buses did not appear until 1895. Then, after 11 games in New Zealand and Australia, travelling to Europe for 74 games without a break, they sailed off to Australia where their first game was on 24 May 1989, and they won all 14 matches, ending that part of the tour on 24 July before sailing home to New Zealand.

Here they cruelly had 8 games in 17 days from 7 to 24 August 1889, only losing the very last, to Auckland. One game every two days – no wonder they lost. They could not be allowed to go unbeaten in their own land... Just 26 players, no substitutes, **107 games away from home from 23 June 1988 to 24 August 1989, with around 4 months at sea**. The tour organisers would be prosecuted today. The only gaps in their schedules were sailing ships to and from New Zealand to Australia twice and to and from Australia to Britain. (They may just have been on the first steamship to sail the route, the *Australasian*, which began operating in 1888 and took 50 days for the crossing. The first passenger liner was the *Osterley*, running from 1909, which took 45 days passage.) The voyages from and to Australia took at least 4 months of this schedule. Their effective on-land playing time, ignoring travel was around 9 months – for 107 games – 3 games a week wherever the 26 went. One has to admire them. What great men! Please see, for details of this terrifying schedule: https://en.wikipedia.org/wiki/List_of_1888%E2%80%9389_New_Zealand _Native_football_team_matches – this team needs to be remembered.

McCARTHY – 5

T.J. 'Tommy' McCarthy was an admirable fly-half, always looking to release his backs, capped by Wales Boys and Wales Youth, and was a Welsh triallist. Tommy played 150 times for Cardiff from 1958-59 to 1966-67. In his first season he scored 4 tries in one game for the Athletic against Hampshire Police and was quickly drafted into the Firsts, going on to score 37 tries in his career. Tommy had to leave the field in the first half of the infamous 1960 Springboks game, being swung around in a tackle and breaking his collar bone. He emigrated to South Africa, joining Johannesburg's famous Wanderers club. All the brothers were backs, and John F. McCarthy played from 1954-55 to 1956-7, winning his 'Rags' cap with over 60 matches and playing twice for the Firsts. Denis played from 1961-62 to 1965-65, for both the Extras, and the Athletic, playing 50 times for the Rags. The greatest loss was Gerard, an outside half from 1952-53. He was killed in an accident while on National Service at Brecon. Gerard had captained Cardiff Schoolboys in three seasons, no less, and played 11 times for the Athletic. All four brothers played for Wales Youth. The final boy, Michael, had just one game for the Athletic in 1968-69 alongside Tommy.

CORNISH – 5

Fred Cornish of Grangetown, Cardiff, played 98 times from 1895-96 to 1898-99 and earned four Welsh caps. His son Don also played for Cardiff. They were related to four brothers who all played for Cardiff. The most famous was Robert A. (Arthur) Cornish, a Cardiff University student, who captained Wales twice in his 10 games. Arthur was 21 when WW1 ended and played 267 times for Cardiff Firsts, from 1919-20 to 1932-33. He was honoured with being one of the eight Welsh players asked to play for an England/Wales XV against Scotland/Ireland in the 1923 Centenary Match at Rugby School. Arthur became Chairman of the Welsh Selectors. Scrumhalf Robin Cornish was an Athletic player, but turned out 6 times for the Firsts in 1924-25, and his brother George, a forward, played 3 times for the Firsts in 1923-24. W.W. 'Willie' Cornish, a forward, captained the Athletic in 1923-24, and jointly in 1924-25, and received his First XV cap, playing 157 games from 1919-20 to 1924-25. Don Cornish played 6 times for the Firsts from 1920-21 to 1923-24, and many times for the Reserves. He mainly played for Grange Baptists, preferring to remain loyal to the Baptists. Cornish Close, in Grangetown, Cardiff, their family home, was named for Arthur and his four brothers, who were known locally for their contribution to rugby, baseball and cricket within the city.

GRIFFITHS – 4

There is a profile of Gareth Griffiths in this book, the Penygraig centre or wing who played alongside Bleddyn, playing 140 times for Cardiff from 1948-49 to 1959-60, scoring 73 tries and winning 12 Welsh caps. A Barbarian, he was a Lion in 1955. His brother Richard 'Ritchie' was a schoolboy international centre who gained his Athletic cap in 1958-59 and played 35 times for the Firsts. J.M Griffiths was a wing, who played 17 times for the Athletic from 1953-54 to 1956-57, while a student at Aberystwyth University. David Griffiths, a fullback, joined in 1965-66, playing 11games, mainly for the Athletic, before joining Bridgend which he served 'with distinction'.

HARDING – 4

Six brothers played for Canton and Canton Wanderers in Cardiff, of whom four played in Cardiff's pack. Charles only played for the Firsts once, in 1897-98, but Ernie played 87 times from 1902-1909, earning a First Team cap. Hubert only played twice, against Bristol and Moseley in 1902-03, and Joe played mainly for Cardiff Reserves from 1901-1905, but also appeared 26 times for the Firsts.

CRAVOS – 4

The moustachioed Stephen 'Steve' Cravos, a forward, played 120 games from 1886-87 to 1895-96, and his four sons played for Cardiff. Lawrie only played a few games for the Athletic, but Frank Cravos, in his only appearance for the Firsts, as a wing scored the winning try in a 6-5 win against the Barbarians, on 27 December 1920. (That must be a great 'pub' boast – "I played once for Cardiff and my try beat the Baa-Baas".) Victor 'Vic' Cravos was a utility back, and like many utility backs over the years, such as the under-appreciated James Hook, seems to have suffered for his versatility, playing for the Extras and Reserves as well as 7 appearances for the senior team from 1921-22 to 1928-29. However, the forward Sydney C. 'Syd' Cravos played from 1924-5 to 1931-32, captaining the Reserves in 1925-26 and the Firsts in 1929-30. A Barbarian, he played 112 times for Cardiff and later was the club chairman. The Cravos and Cornish families knew each other and often would play in the same team. More information on this family is given towards the end of Chapter 43, in the article: *The*

HANCOCK – 3 – *'one of Cardiff's Three Greatest Seasons'*
This was a famous family in Cardiff, for many reasons. Frank E. Hancock played 50 times from 1884-86. Cardiff were short of a back, and asked him to play in 1884 – and he scored the only two tries. For the next game away to Gloucester, the club did not want to lose him, so played Frank in the centre of their back line, **giving the world the 'four three-quarter' system** in 1884. *'The Cardiff System* used 7 backs instead of 6, brought in passing instead of dribbling as the dominant characteristic of the game, and led to Cardiff and Wales domination over the next two decades. Cardiff drew the Gloucester match, but for the six remaining games played with four across the threequarters, two centres and two wings. The selectors were impressed, and 8 Cardiff players, including Hancock and 3 Cardiff backs, were then chosen for Wales. Previously, rugby had been a forward-dominated affair, but speedy, passing backs now made a difference. In 1884-85, Cardiff was proclaimed *'the best team in South Wales, West of England and Midland Counties'*. Frank was captain in 1885-86, and with the new system the club won 26 games, drew none and only lost the last match of the season.

He was 'idolised' by his team, and advanced *'the passing game'* to the distress of opponents. *'**Not one Welsh club scored a try against the Blue and Blacks,** Cardiff's line was crossed only four times in all, thrice by Moseley in two matches and once by Gloucester. Swansea were beaten four times with a total of 4 goals, 8 tries, Newport by 10 goals, 3 tries in two matches, Llanelli 6 goals, 4 tries in one of two matches. Gloucester 4 goals, 6 tries to one try in two matches, Neath beaten 7 goals and a try to nil, and Cheltenham College destroyed by 7 goals, 5 tries to nil. Strong clubs from the North of England, who were later to secede to the Northern Union professional code, Runcorn, Dewsbury, and Castleford were among the victims.'* It was *'one of Cardiff's Three Greatest Seasons'*. Cardiff's Seconds had their second successive unbeaten season. Frank captained Wales, playing four times, but retired aged only 26 at the end of the season.

The first international where the four three-quarter system was tried by Wales, was against Scotland, in 1886 with six Cardiff players in the side. However, the experiment was not successful. It was brought back against the New Zealand Natives team in December 1888, when Wales won by a goal and two tries to nil. Wales fully adopted the formation in 1888-89, but the other home nations not until 1893-94. Gwyn Prescott writes: *'An English rugby columnist of the 1890s wrote, after one particularly heavy defeat: "Our* (English) *methods, like our 'rulers', are antiquated ... After Saturday's lesson the contagion will spread, and in a few years' time we will doubtless see the 'Welsh game' played throughout England.'''* We can see the attraction of *'the Cardiff System'* with more entertaining matches, and people of all sizes now being able to play instead of predominantly big men. In 1875 there had been only a few football or rugby teams in Wales, both comprised mainly of young former public-school boys. However, by 1892 there were 70 rugby clubs in South Wales, and by 1905 Cardiff alone was home to an amazing 200 teams. Coal and iron exports had seen the port's population rise from less than 1,900 in 1901, to over18,000 in 1851. (It was almost 60,000 in 1971 and over 160,000 by 1900. Edward VII gave city status to Cardiff on 28 October 1905, in recognition of the fact that it was one of the great economic and industrial successes of the age. By 1915 it was the biggest coal-exporting port in the world.)

Frank Hancock's contribution to the game saw him inducted in 2011 to the IRB (International Rugby Board) Hall of Fame. Frank's brother Froude played for just 9 times for Cardiff, mainly playing for Blackheath and Richmond, and was capped by England and was a British Lions. Froude Hancock was a founder member of the Barbarians in 1890. His brother E.L Hancock just had 2 appearances for the Cardiff. The family was connected with Cardiff's Hancock's brewery, makers of HB beer, sold in its 505 pubs. (The Cardiff brewery was taken over by Bass Charrington in 1968, and most production moved to Burton-on-Trent, with HB worsening in quality. Brains of Cardiff bought the brewery site in 1999, after selling its 1882 brewery in central Cardiff to become 'the Brewery Quarter' site of restaurants and apartments. After then brewing Brains at the old Hancock site, that site is being redeveloped into another mixed retail and housing site. Brains opened its new brewery in Tremorfa, Cardiff in 2019, but hit financial trouble. There must have been multi-million pound deals from the sales of their two prime Cardiff sites, but in December 2020, Brains sadly put 99 pubs up for sale, and another 156 were handed over to Marston's Brewery on a 25-year lease-back deal. I mention this because pubs are dying – youngsters do not go to pubs as in the old days. Supermarket alcohol is taxed lower and is very cheap; and business rates are exorbitant on pubs.

When in university, I and three other Cadoxton boys palled up with four Geordies. They came down for an England game and before the match we were in the Half-Way in Cathedral Road. I had the 'kitty' and looked after the beer buying. I went up to buy 4 pints of Brains SA on a tray, locally known as 'skull attack', and gave them to the Geordies. I also bought us four pints of normal Brains Bitter, or 'Light' as it was called. The beers looked the same in the crowded pub. This went on for several rounds, before we left the pub to walk to the Arms Park. They were 'all over the place', and they knew that we Welsh could 'take our drink' far better than them. We never told them that I had supplied them with the stronger SA. And they call the Welsh 'devious'. I prefer the adjective 'cunning' in the medieval sense of 'knowledgeable'. Another fairly irrelevant memory, but relating to the death of old-established breweries, is the 'Summer of 76'.

Lord, it was hot, and everyone over 60 remembers it. Brains had very few pubs outside Cardiff. The other Cardiff breweries, Hancocks and Rhymney, ran dry of beer, as did Whitbread and other big breweries. I was brought up on keg – yugghhh in these days – so I had to drink Brains Dark, Light and SA – all real ales and all gorgeous. Brains had their own well in their brewery at St Mary Street, Cardiff, so had a continuous water supply, and their sales exploded. They seemed to keep most of their new custom. Incidentally, around 1973 Brains was the only brewer in Britain that sold more Dark than Light (mild than bitter), and their strengths were equivalent. The Crown pub in Skewen, near Neath sold a brewery-barrelled mixture of half and half Dark and SA – MA? it was a superb pint. I could ramble on forever, but that's the end of this little diversion. (And Theakstons, before takeover, in one pub in Hutton Rudby sold a mixture of Old Peculier and Bitter – again superb but gone. It may have been called Standard).

MORGAN – 2 + 3

W.L. Morgan played 75 times from 1905-06 to 1911-12, often as scrumhalf to the great Percy Bush, gaining one Welsh cap. His brother Teddy only played once for Cardiff, living in London and playing for London Welsh. The Wales selectors wanted to see Teddy, and also Willie Llewellyn of Penygraig play with the Cardiff backs, to see if they could 'fit' to play for Wales, in the threequarters alongside Cardiff's Rhys Gabe and Gwyn Nicholls – heroes of the past. The experiment worked, and a fortnight later, wing Teddy Morgan scored the winning try for Wales, 3-0 against New Zealand in 1905, their only loss on tour. (Cardiff was easily their closest game, NZ luckily winning 10-8). Their three nephews all played for Cardiff. A Cambridge Blue, Guy Morgan played 8 times for Cardiff in 1931-32 and 1932-33 and gained 8 Welsh caps. Noel Morgan played for the Athletic, as did Rex Morgan.

POWELL – 3

J.W. (Wick) Powell was a wing who played 26 times for the club in 1919-20, and gained 4 Welsh caps in 1920, but went North. He returned to become licensee of the Cardiff Arms Hotel, which was in Quay Street, near the ground. His brother Jack was also a wing and played 97 games between 1921-22 and 1925-26, gaining one Welsh cap. A third brother, Willie, played a few games for the Reserves in 1919-1920.

SWEET-ESCOTT – 3

The brothers were the sons of the Rector of Penarth. R.B. (Ralph) Sweet-Escott played from 1889-90 to 1895-96 as a centre or half-back. He played 148 games for Cardiff, 3 games for Wales and was club captain in 1895-96. Cecil was also a half-back, between 1898-99 and 1899-1900, playing

50 games for the Firsts. Selwyn played 29 games in the three-quarters between 1890-91 and 1893-94. All the brothers also played many times for the Reserves. A Cambridge Blue, Ralph was a founder-member of the Barbarians in 1890

BOWCOTT - 3
A Cambridge Blue, Harry Bowcott was an outside half who played 113 times from 1926-27 to 1935-36, gaining 8 Welsh caps and touring New Zealand with the Lions in 1930. His scrumhalf was often brother Jackie, also a Cardiff High School product, who partnered Cliff Jones at Cambridge and played 45 times for Cardiff from 1929-30 to 1936-37. A third brother, Bill, only played once in 1926-27 but is not in Davies' list of Cardiff First XV players.

There are not only fathers and sons who played for the club, but also many pairs of brothers. (I shall only record up to where the Williams brothers stopped playing). **In just one season, 1926-27, 7 pairs of brothers played for the Firsts**: H.M and W.H. Bowcott; Jim and Tom Burns; Syd and Vic Cravos; from Taff's Well, Fred and Trevor Lee; E. 'Ted' and Jim Spillane; B.R. and Kevin Turnbull; and D.M. 'Dai' and Llew Williams.
   From 1881-82 to 1886-87, Charlie **Arthur** played 163 times, captained the club and played for Wales twice. Fred Arthur in the same period only played 10 games, and Charles' son Willie captained the Extras in 1922-23. Arthur **Bassett** played 101 times from 1935-36 to 1938-39, gaining 6 Welsh caps, playing with Gwyn Williams and Wilfred Wooller. Jack Bassett joined the club from 1935-36, playing 5 times and gaining an Athletic cap. He was winding down his career, alongside his brother, after playing for Wales 15 times and being a British Lion in 1930. Jim **Burns** gained two Welsh caps in 1927 and played 108 club games from 1924-25 to 1929-30. Another forward from Newtown, Cardiff, his brother Tom played 42 games from 1925-26 to 1931-32. (The great boxer, '*Gentleman Jim*', '*The Peerless*' Jim Driscoll was their cousin.) Jim Burns' son Tom (Jr.) was also a forward, captaining the Welsh Secondary Schools and playing 8 times for Cardiff.
   Percy **Bush** is one of the club's legends. He and his brother Fred gained Reserves caps together in 1899-1900 and sometimes played together in the threequarters, but Percy moved to half-back and began a stellar career from 1898-99 to 1909-10. Percy played 171 times for Cardiff, but Fred only 8. Percy was club captain 3 times, played for Wales 8 times, and toured New Zealand and Australia in 1904. Jim and Walter **Casey** of Newport both achieved Cardiff caps, Jim playing 166 times from 1906-07 to 1912-13, and Walter just 18 times from 1907-08 to 1909-10. Charles and Cyril **Cross** were the sons of Cross Brothers Ironmongers in Cardiff's St Mary Street, with Charles playing 14 times from 1934-35 to 1935-36, and Cyril
392

36 times from 1931-32 to 1932-33. They played more for Glamorgan Wanderers, in northwest Cardiff.

Willie **Davies** of Kenfig Hill was Cardiff's fly half in 1938-39, and played 31 matches, but turned professional, and then war came. His brother Cliff was a great prop from 1945-46 to 1951-52, gaining 16 Welsh caps and touring NZ and Australia with the 1950 Lions. He played 190 Cardiff games, and for the Barbarians and was known everywhere as '*The Bard of Kenfig*' for his singing on (and off) tour. Born in December 1919, he was 20 when war started, and lost six years of his rugby career. Cardiff High School's C.R. **Davies** played for Wales as a prop in 1934, but played for Cardiff only 6 times from 1929-30 to 1934-35, also playing for London Welsh and Bedford. Another product of Cardiff High, his brother back-row forward Selby Davies played 105 games, in a career affected by war, from 1935-36 to 1945-46. Whitchurch's **Randall Davies** was a scrumhalf who played 37 times from 1905-06 to 1908-09, and partnered with fly-half Percy Bush, but turned professional with Wigan. Brother Alfie Davies was another scrumhalf who partnered Danny Davies 8 times, but played mainly for the reserves.

A typical Gareth Edwards try for Wales at Cardiff Arms Park. He scored 20 for his country in the course of winning 53 caps.

Gareth Edwards against Scotland

From Gwaun-Cae-Gurwen, scrumhalf Sir Gareth **Edwards** MBE achieved every honour in the game, and is one of the greatest players of all time. He played 195 times for Cardiff, from 1966-67 to 1977-78, scoring 426 points. Gareth played 53 times for Wales and 10 times for the British Lions. During his career the Welsh side dominated the Five Nations Championship, winning the title 7 times, including 3 Grand Slams. Edwards' try for the Barbarians against the All Blacks in 1973 at Cardiff Arms Park, is regarded as the greatest try ever. His partnership with Barry

John for Cardiff and Wales was consistently the best half-back pairing this writer has seen. When Barry retired aged 27 (far too early), there was a seamless transition with Phil Bennett of Llanelli.

In 2003, in a poll of international rugby players conducted by *Rugby World* magazine, Edwards was declared the greatest player of all time. In 2007, former England captain Will Carling published his list of the *'50 Greatest Rugby players'* in *The Daily Telegraph*, and ranked Edwards the greatest player ever: *'He was a supreme athlete with supreme skills, the complete package. He played in the 1970s, but, if he played now, he would still be the best. He was outstanding at running, passing, kicking and reading the game. He sits astride the whole of rugby as the ultimate athlete on the pitch'*. Edwards was prominent in the Welsh team that virtually dominated European rugby in the 60s and 70s. He is one of a small group of Welsh players to have won three Grand Slams including Cardiff's Gerald Davies and Gethin Jenkins, JPR Williams, Ryan Jones, Adam Jones and Alun Wyn Jones. I have a 'Grog' statue entitled *'The Quadtriple Crown'*, from when Wales won the Triple Crown in 1976, 1977, 1978 and 1979. In 1975, Wales beat France away 25-10 (5-1 on tries; England at home 20-4 (3-1 on tries); Ireland at home 32-4 (5-1 on tries) but narrowly lost in Scotland, 12-10, scoring the only try of the match in front of a world record crowd of 104,000. They won the Championship with England having the Wooden Spoon. They scored 87 points against 30, 14-3 on tries, so almost had a fifth consecutive Triple Crown. Gareth's brother, outside-half Gethin Edwards, scored a try and drop goal on his debut for the Rags in 1971, and had a First Team cap, playing outside Gareth, and toured with him to Rhodesia, but after 17 games joined Neath.

Both **Fletcher** brothers usually played for Glamorgan Wanderers, but from 1930-31 to 1934-35 forward P.J. 'Phil' Fletcher made 15 appearances for the Firsts and gained an Athletic cap. R.J. 'Bob' Fletcher played half-back or centre 28 times from 1903-04 to 1904-05, and also had his Athletic cap. Edwin and Thomas **Franks** played for Dinas Powys before making just 10 senior appearances between them from 1902-03 to 1934-35, and played for Cardiff Reserves before both headed to Pontypridd for more first-team games.

The speedy wing Ray **Glastonbury**, from Bedwellty, played 51 games from 1957-58 to 1961-62 for Cardiff, before turning professional with Workington. He was Workington's top scorer in 1962-63 with 41 tries, and played rugby league for Wales. His elder brother Blandford also played on Cardiff's wing, just 9 (or 11) games in 1958-59, then played for Glamorgan Wanderers and Pontypridd. Ray **Glover** played 52 times from 1946-47 to 1949-50, and also gained an Athletic cap. Also a forward, Fred Glover gained an Athletic cap, playing 60 games for them, but could not break into a very good First team pack. Dennis **Hickey** (1959-60 to 1962-63) was an excellent forward, playing for the Seniors 44 times until ill health caused his retirement. John Hickey first played for the Athletic in 1961-62 and has both Athletic and First caps. He was a superb blind-side wing-forward who 'took no prisoners', playing 214 games for the Firsts from 1963-64 to 1974-75. He was their vice-captain in 1969-70 and captain in 1970-71, and Rags captain in 1974-75. He played for the East Wales team that drew with the All Blacks – the All Blacks were incredibly lucky, as they admitted. I knew the man when he finished playing, and he died in 2015 after a long illness. Their father Jim had played club rugby for St Peter's in Cardiff, but appeared for Cardiff Firsts, aged 19, in only one game, against the Barbarians in 1921.

Tom **Holley**, a back-row forward, played 10 times for the Firsts, and 76 times for the Athletic between 1938-39 and 1946-47, his service in the War affecting his career. His brother Arthur played in the Athletic in 1938-39. Tom was a devoted club servant, acting as masseur, also for the WRU, and used to give myself and friends left-over quarter oranges at half-time. D.E.J 'Jack' **Hughes** played 43 times for the Firsts in 1932-33 and 1933-34, gaining First and Athletic caps. Brother Arthur won his Athletic cap in 1932-33, but they both had joined from Newport and it seems they returned to play there.

C.M. **Ingledew** only played two games for the senior side in 1898-1899. Hugh Ingledew was a half-back from 1897-1898 until 1891-92, playing 69 times and winning 3 Welsh caps. Like Ralph Sweet-Escott, he was a **founder member of the Barbarians** in 1890, serving Cardiff for many years after his rugby career ended. The Barbarians were conceived in 1890 at an Oyster bar in Bradford, and they decided upon a motto for the club: *'Rugby football is a game for gentlemen in all classes, but never for a bad sportsman in any class'*, ensuring that the Barbarians did not discriminate upon class, race, creed or colour and the only qualification to be a member was that you were a good rugby player and a good sportsman. The ethos was that rugby should be an attacking game and that the Barbarians must always exhibit a style which demonstrated a commitment to hard, clean, attacking Rugby.

The Barbarians, much later, came later to play touring nations, and their annual Easter tour began at their 'spiritual home' of Penarth on Good Friday, followed by Cardiff RFC on Saturday, Swansea on Easter Monday and Newport on the Tuesday. There was a beautiful grey-stone Edwardian Esplanade Hotel, opposite the Pier on Penarth Promenade, disgracefully demolished for an ugly red-brick block of flats in 1970. All I can remark is that I have never met a poor town planner. 'The Esp' had been the spiritual home and headquarters of the Baa-Baas for over 75 years. On one night, the team had encouraged a cow to take up residence on the top floor. Before breakfast next morning, the tour manager asked the forwards to carry it down and release it where they found it. Cows cannot go downstairs, only up. Their two greatest games, that some readers will remember well, were the 1961 defeat of the unbeaten Springboks by 6-0, the only side to defeat them, with Haydn Mainwaring's magnificent try-saving tackle; and the 1973 match versus New Zealand, won 23-11, the greatest performance ever by a Barbarian team. Cliff **Jones** played for Cambridge, Cardiff and Wales as a splendid fly-half, but a series of injuries affected his career, and he only played 22 times for Cardiff between 1932 and 1939. He became a WRU selector. Brother Glan only played one senior game in 1936, but his son Kingsley played prop for Cardiff 190 times, for Wales 10 times, was a Barbarian and a 1957 British Lion.

Tredegar's Roger **Lane** was a number 8 or wing-forward playing 299 games from 1970-71 to 1980-81, a Welsh triallist, and set a record of 16 tries in a season for a forward (along with Mervyn John), beating Les Spence's 12. He scored 86 tries for the club. On the 1876*cardiffrugby* website, a discussion of Cardiff's best uncapped players features Elwyn Williams, his brother Tony, John Hickey and Roger Lane. Stuart had played for the Athletic in 1971-72, and re-joined Cardiff's Firsts in 1973-4. A strong open-side wing-forward at 6 foot and 14 st. 7 lbs, he could also play on the wing, and played 5 times for Wales 1978-80, being chosen for the 1980 Lions tour. He was expected to play in the Tests, but broke his leg in the first minute of the opening game in South Africa. Thus, the unfortunate record of the shortest career of any Lions tourist. He was an excellent Sevens player. Stuart Lane played 158 times from 1973-74 to 1981-81, like his brother a prolific backrow try scorer with 44. Stuart was playing No. 8 in a match report on the WRU website entitled '*The Greatest Cardiff Win Ever?*' (16 April 2003): '*January 8, 1977: Cardiff 25 Llanelli 15 - Llanelli arrived at the Arms Park that day with the unbelievable record of only one defeat in 32 cup-ties and tournament winners four years in a row from 1973. Led by Phil Bennett they had star names like J J Williams, Ray Gravelle, Roy Bergiers and Derek Quinnell in their ranks. But Cardiff had great players of their own such as Gareth Edwards and Gareth Davies at half-back, Barry Nelmes, Alan Phillips and Gerry Wallace in the front row and a captain par excellence in Gerald Davies. A capacity crowd of 15,000 saw the Scarlets race into 12 points lead by half-time and their cup invincibility looked secure. Everything changed in a remarkable third quarter when the Blue and Blacks scored 19 points in 18 minutes. A text-book tackle by Alex Finlayson on Gravelle led to a try by Chris Camilleri. Gerald Davies had taken over the kicking duties and converted the try and added a penalty goal. Then the skipper returned to his more usual role, side-stepping past several opponents to give Nelmes a scoring pass. Cardiff were suddenly 13-12 ahead but there was more to come with a second try from Camilleri and another by Gareth Davies.*

In The Observer next day, Clem Thomas wrote, "It proved not only a fabulous and passionate game but a remarkable rugby experience, for it must rate as perhaps the best club match I have ever seen"'.

Fred **Lee**, the Taff's Well village policeman, like the village's Tom Lewis, captain of Wales, was chosen for the final Welsh trial in 1926. Fred was reported as being *'like a tank'* and was reported as *'the best forward on the field'* in Cardiff's game against the Maoris in 1927. He played 68 First team games from 1924-28. He was known by Danny Davies for his conviviality, especially on tour, *'with a penchant for ample sauce'* – i.e. he 'liked his pop' – i.e. he enjoyed a pint... or two ... or eight. A full-back, Trevor Lee played 12 times from 1925-26 to 1929-30, but many more games for the Athletic. On one occasion for the Firsts, against Cardiff and District, he kicked 12 conversions and a penalty, and saw his fourteenth kick bounce back off the crossbar. It is still the club record. Cardiff scraped home in that match 66-10, scoring 12 converted tries, 1 try and a penalty – today's score would be 90-10. Trevor moved on to Penarth.

Porthcawl's J.C.M. 'Clem' **Lewis** played for Cambridge University, Cardiff and Wales. From 1909-10 to 1923-24 the outside-half played 229 times for Cardiff, and 11 times for Wales. A double Cambridge Blue, he joined from Bridgend, and was also a Barbarian. Without the Great War, his statistics would have been stellar. He was born in June 1890, so he lost the years when he was 24 to 28. He was capped before and after his war service, captaining Wales twice in 1923. In his First Team debut in 1921, brother Ivor Lewis scored 4 tries against Pontypridd, but only played 7 times for the senior side. Dr. Jack **Matthews** OBE was Bleddyn Williams' best, and inseparable friend, for most of his life, playing together at centre in a world-famous playing partnership for Cardiff, Wales and the British Lions. He played 180 times for Cardiff between 1945-46 and 1953-54, captaining the club 3 times, and playing for Wales 17 times. Bleddyn and Jack were inducted together into the World Rugby Hall of Fame in 2013, being called by World Rugby *'a uniquely complementary and successful partnership at club, national team and Lions levels after the Second World War'* Both captained Cardiff and Wales, made their international debuts in 1947, and were first choice for the Tests in the Lions squad that toured Australia and New Zealand in 1950. Jack's brother Mansel Matthews was a centre for Bridgend but had a game for Cardiff Athletic in 1946-47.

The forwards Billy and Jack **McIntyre** played for Cardiff from 1897-98 to 1903-04, Billy playing 81 times for the First XV and Jack 18, with both receiving First Team caps. The twins Alun and Elfed **Morgan** were props from Nelson, both gaining Rags caps in 1963-64, and both playing for four years, playing 3 and 6 games for the Firsts respectively. D.C. (Derek) **Murphy** from Pentyrch was a fine wing, playing 162 games from 1950-51 to 57-58, and had a Welsh Trial. Dennis, a centre, won an Athletic cap in 1951-52, playing two seasons, but a work change took him to Swansea. Known as the *'Prince of Threequarters'*, Gwyn E. **Nicholls** played 24 Tests for Wales at centre between 1896 and 1906, 10 times as captain.

Between 1892-93 and 1909-10 he played 242 times for Cardiff, captaining the team in 4 seasons. A Barbarian, he was the only Welsh player in the 1899 British Isles team (not known as the Lions until decades later), and was the star for Wales during their first '*golden era*'. (A professional man, like most of the international players from the other three Home Nations, Gwyn could afford to leave home for six months. Most Welsh players could not take time off work). Gwyn captained Wales to three Triple Crowns, and to the famous victory over the All Blacks in 1905. On 26 December 1949, gates bearing his name at Cardiff Arms Park were officially opened. Danny Davies remembers him as '*the greatest gentleman and Rugby sportsman I had ever met.*' S.H (Sid) Nicholls won his First Team cap, playing 108 games as a forward from 1886-87 to 1891-92. He played for Wales 3 times, once against the Maoris in 1888. Gwyn's son Geoff played for the senior side 7 times in 1934-35, also winning an Athletic cap.

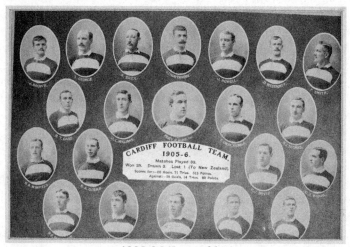

1905-06 'Invincibles'

Howard **Poole** was scrumhalf between 1925-26 and 1931-32, making 154 appearances. Along with Maurice Bowcott, he toured with the 1930 British Isles team to NZ and Australia, although never winning a Welsh cap. His brother Jack, a fullback, played for Glamorgan Wanderers, but played some games for the Athletic between 1929 and 1931. The second row Percy **Rayer** played against the All Blacks and won his Cardiff cap in 1924-25, and played 42 games for the Firsts between 1922 and 1926. The prop Willie played twice for the Firsts in 1923-24. From Cardiff High School, John and Willie 'Bill' **Roberts** gained Blues for Oxford and Cambridge respectively, outside-half Willie captaining the latter against his brother in the 1928-29 Varsity Match. Bill Roberts played 31 times for Cardiff Firsts from 1926-27 to 1936-37. John played for Cardiff 101 times from 1924-25 to 1931-32. A Barbarian, he played 13 times for Wales. Both brothers played against England in 1929, John on the wing. John Roberts went to China as a missionary in 1931.

Ted **Spillane** was a forward and his brother Jim a halfback or centre. Ted played 84 times for the Firsts from 1923-1929, and was nicknamed 'Sherbet'. Jim Spillane only had 9 first team games from 1926-28 but more than 50 Rags appearances. Ralph C. **Thomas** played centre 45 times for Cardiff, earning his cap in 1905-06, playing for Percy Bush's 'Invincibles' who only lost to New Zealand 10-8. A forward, Leonard Thomas was loaned from Penarth to play just one game for Cardiff in March 1906. Gwyn Nicholls, Dai Westacott, Cecil Biggs and R.A. Gibbs were being rested for the Irish international the following Saturday. Cardiff were losing at Leicester 3-0 when Leonard Thomas, described as 'a furious gladiator' beat five or six Leicester defenders to touch down. The 3-3 draw preserved the unbeaten season. Hywel **Williams** of Cardigan was a Welsh triallist who played 26 games for the Firsts and Athletic between 1960 and 1963, then transferred to play for Neath. Nick Williams scored 6 tries for the Athletic against Llanelli Wanderers in 1970-71, and played 9 times for the Firsts and many times for the Athletic between 1968 and 1972 before joining Glamorgan Wanderers.

LESLIE 'LES' MANFIELD DFC 1915-2006

A war hero, Les Manfield played for Cardiff and Wales in 1939-40 to 1948-49, and his brother and son also played for Cardiff. Like Haydn Morris from Mountain Ash, 'Les' Manfield joined Cardiff aged 23 in 1939-40. The son of a railway worker, he played for Wales Under-15s in 1930. He was such a good player that he had made a senior appearance for Mountain Ash against Aberavon at the age of 15, yet four years earlier he had just recovered from scarlet fever, which had left him with a weak heart. From *walesonline* we read '*He went to University College, Cardiff, graduating in Chemistry and taking a MSc course, skippering the rugby side and guesting for Neath, Bridgend and Penarth. Les moved to Carnegie College, Leeds, for a PE course, and as a boxer he reached the UAU semi-finals and won the light-heavyweight Welsh Universities College title in 1937. His weight rose from 12 to 14 stones, and former Mountain Ash player Haydn Coopey, secretary of Otley RFC, asked him to play. After just one second-team appearance, he played first-team rugby at Otley and also appeared for the UAU and Yorkshire County. England invited him to a trial and in 1939 he was at Twickenham to see Wales lose 3-0, but he chose Wales instead. Les said, at that time: "My sympathies lie with Wales, where I learned my football. I had cheered every Wales match for some years." On February 4, 1939, he gained a Wales senior cap in the middle of the back row in a 11-3 win over Scotland on Cardiff Arms Park. The*

Ireland game - a 7-0 win in Belfast - was to be the last full international for eight years.' Against Scotland and Ireland, Les was representing Otley and Mountain Ash.

By 1942 he was a 27-year-old Flying Officer and played in Services internationals against England at Swansea and Gloucester, also appearing in a British Red Cross game at Swansea for the Wales Services. In 1942, Manfield was posted to Cairo and spent three years in the Middle East, flying Wellington bombers with 104 Squadron, rising to the rank of squadron leader. Les was hit by flak twice whilst flying over Tobruk. While navigating an SOE operation to Crete, his plane crash-landed in the sea after its engines failed. He went back into the plane, attempting to bring the rear-gunner out. Manfield and three other crewmen survived at sea for two days before being picked up by a motor torpedo boat. On 4 April 1943, Manfield was awarded the Distinguished Flying Cross for his work in a Special Operations Unit. He left 282 Wing Cairo in 1945 and returned to Britain, as a course commander at the Empire Air Navigation.

Just before Christmas 1945 he played for Wales against France in a Victory International at Swansea and two weeks later played against the 2nd NZEF 'Kiwis', the famous New Zealand Army side in Cardiff. In further Victory internationals he played against England at Cardiff, Scotland at Swansea, England at Twickenham, Ireland at Cardiff, Scotland at Murrayfield and France in Paris during 1946. He broke ribs in the final trial of the 1946 season, but played in Cardiff and Wales victories over the touring Australians in late 1947. Les was one of only four men to play for Wales before and after the war (- the others being 'Bunner' Travers, Haydn Tanner and Howard Davies). In 1948 he played in all the Five Nations games, at 34 years old becoming the second oldest man to have played for Wales. Les played in the forwards 71 times for Cardiff, a great friend of Bleddyn Williams, retiring in the 1948-49 season. A hero, he must have been some player.

Rob Cole's obituary in *The Independent* reads: *'The Welsh rugby international Les Manfield was one of the few players to represent his country on either side of the Second World War. He won the first of his seven caps in a victory against Scotland at the Arms Park, Cardiff, in February 1939, before heading out to Egypt to serve as a navigator in fighter planes. He had the First World War fighter pilot Ira "Taffy" Jones to thank for getting him into the air. In 1939 Manfield volunteered for war and became a PT instructor at RAF St Athan, after giving up his job as a schoolteacher at Cowbridge Grammar School, but wanted to get into the thick of the action. Invited to play for an Ira Jones XV in a special rugby game at Richmond, Manfield greatly impressed his fellow countryman. "Is there anything I can do for you?" asked Jones after the game. "Get me into a bloody plane," said Manfield. His 6ft 3in frame was more suited to playing at No 8 for Cardiff and Wales, than to fitting into the cockpit of a fighter plane. So large was the man mountain from Mountain Ash, that in training he had to put his parachute on his knees. His first assignment as a navigator was in Egypt with 104 Squadron. The crews stopped on the way at Malta, and he got his briefing under the wing of the plane on the landing strip. "When you get to Cairo, turn right at the Pyramids and the base is just in front of you." That base was the airstrip being built for the El Alamein push.*

Manfield's time in Egypt was a mixture of bombing raids and special operations, flying secret agents behind enemy lines. There was also a bit of time for rugby. Just to prove the war had not blunted his playing skills, Manfield captained Cairo Welsh to a 22-3 St David's Day win over England in 1945 and a month later a 6-3 triumph over a Rest of the Empire XV at Alexandria. Manfield hated the heat and the flies in Egypt and regularly resorted to reading from the Bible his mother had given him'.

His son John, another Cardiff player, remembered that his father was: *'once saved from a nasty injury by the buckle on his parachute, as he lay prostrate on the floor of his Wellington bomber. As the navigator, he was also the bomber. He was lying flat, looking through the bomb sights, when a piece of flak came through the bottom of the plane. It hit Dad and took off a piece of the rear-gunner's boot.' 'On a raid over Tobruk on 5 October 1942, Manfield's plane had to turn back because the flak was so heavy. They weren't hit, but their second engine failed and they had to ditch into the Mediterranean. "It was like hitting a brick wall," recalled Manfield. All bar the rear-gunner emerged safely from the crash landing.'* Les swam back into the flooding fuselage to try and rescue the rear gunner – *"I found him in the aft part, but couldn't get to him. We had to get out",* he recalled with sadness. *The four survivors found themselves in a dinghy in pouring rain and 15ft seas. To make matters worse, the fumes from the fuel made them violently sick and they found that the rations in the life-raft had been stolen. They were adrift for two days before being found by a Motor Torpedo Boat (MTB). About 30 minutes after they were picked up, a message came over the radio telling the skipper to abandon the search. Manfield was flying again within a couple of days. In a six-week period, 104 Squadron lost 126 men killed in action or missing.*

His work with the Special Operations Unit earned Manfield the DFC in 1943, for his pinpoint accuracy in leading his pilots to the exact marks for the drops. Less than a year after he had led Cairo Welsh to their victory over the Rest of the Empire, Manfield was facing the New Zealand Army side - for Wales at the Arms Park - although the 6-3 margin was reversed on this occasion. He also figured in five uncapped wartime internationals between 1940 and 1942 and seven "Victory Internationals" in 1946. A schoolboy international from Mountain Ash Grammar School, Manfield had declined a trial for England to play for Wales. A hugely powerful player, he figured in the last two games Wales played before war was declared and then in the wins over the touring Australians, alongside Bleddyn Williams for both club and country in the 1947-48 season. He played throughout Wales's 1948 championship campaign. Manfield returned to teaching after the war, first at Cowbridge Grammar School, then at Mountain Ash Grammar School, where he ended as deputy headmaster.' Brother Ron was a fullback who only played once for Cardiff Firsts in 1946-47 and joined Pontypridd, finding opportunities limited at Cardiff. John, the son of Les, was a backrower with Secondary School caps, who played for Cardiff Athletic and 22 times for the Firsts from 1971-72 to 1973-74, and moving on, gained a Wales 'B' cap in 1977.

CHAPTER 30 - CARDIFF SEASON 1958 – 1959

LLOYD WILLIAMS IS VICE CAPTAIN AND PLAYS FOR WALES - THE SEVENTH BROTHER, ELWYN, HAS HIS ATHLETIC CAP - THE EIGHTH BROTHER, TONY, HAS A WALES YOUTH CAP – CLIFF MORGAN IS *'THE GREATEST WELSH PLAYER OF THE 1950s'*

Lloyd Williams P36 T1 Pts3; **Cenydd Williams** P24 T2 Pts6; **Elwyn Williams** P14 T1 Pts3; Alun Priday P40 T4 C37 P16 Pts134 (Tongwynlais); Glyn Williams P2 (Pentyrch)

P44, W22, L15, D7. Points 382-319. Tries 76-54, Pens 22-26

Elwyn Williams began playing for the Firsts, becoming a regular choice in the following season. A natural wing forward, he sometimes played number 8 when Howard Norris or Eddie Thomas were not available. This disappointing season saw Cardiff's closest try differential in its history, and they also lost the penalty count. C. Derek Williams was from Canton Grammar School, its fourth old boy to be captain, after R. A. Cornish, L. M. Spence and Peter Goodfellow. Nicknamed *'Seedy'* by the irrepressible Stan Bowes, Williams was a double Oxford Blue in rugby and cricket. Playing rugby for Berkshire in 1948 he was the county's half-mile champion, and the torch bearer from Berkshire to the White City, London, for the Olympic Games. Because of business commitments, Derek Williams was sometimes away from Cardiff, playing for London Welsh and Neath, but still played 248 games for Cardiff from the 1945-46 season onwards, and won two Welsh caps. 'Seedy' played for Cardiff against the Springboks and All Blacks, and then came out of retirement in 1957 to help Cardiff beat Australia. He stayed on for one more season, being elected as Firsts Captain. Open side wing forward is a good position for a captain, involved with both forwards and backs, but Williams had lost four superb players through retirement. The halfbacks Cliff Morgan and Rex Willis, the seasoned hooker Geoff Beckingham, and last season's captain Eddie Thomas had all ended their Cardiff Firsts careers. The greatest son of the small Rhondda village of Trebanog, Cliff Morgan, was later named the greatest Welsh player of the 1950s by the WRU. However, in the previous season Lloyd Williams had comfortably succeeded the great Rex Willis as scrumhalf. A senior cap was to be awarded to hooker Terry Donovan, a great club servant with 90 Firsts appearances between 1952-53 and 1961-62, previously unable to oust Geoff Beckingham.

1958-59 Elwyn, third player from left, middle row.
Cenydd and Lloyd 2nd and 3rd players from left, front row

'CD' chose Lloyd Williams as vice-captain, and Lloyd was the only Cardiff player to be capped by Wales in this year. It was the worst post-war season for Cardiff, with a remarkably low number of points scored and a high number of points by the opposition. Meirion Roberts in the centre and Howard Norris at prop/No.8 were awarded Cardiff caps, and were later to play for Wales, to make 225 and 413 Cardiff appearances respectively – great players this writer enjoyed watching. Meirion Roberts, in tandem with the 'sixth brother' Cenydd Williams, made a great centre pairing. On

28 November 1958, Elwyn Williams was number 8, flanked by captain C.D. Williams and Dai Hayward against Bristol, in a 6-6 draw. Cardiff scored the tries, Bristol the penalties. A couple of seasons after Lloyd had played several games at outside half, this was Cenydd's turn, with Lloyd supplying him. Cardiff later won the Bristol home fixture in April 6-3, scoring the only try. In later seasons, the back row settled down for some years as Dai Hayward open side, Howard Norris number 8 and Elwyn blind side wing forward. Norris often switched to prop, number 8 and second row, depending upon circumstances, and was to hold the record number of Cardiff appearances.

This is no longer seen. Players have become 'specialised' as the game has become regimented and boring. Welsh people are becoming disenchanted with the game. You now find a great atmosphere and constant singing at Cardiff City and Wales football home games. Fabulous. You may as well be at a funeral at some of the Welsh region and Wales rugby games, however. Props could then play on either side of the front row with few worries; centres could play left and right or inside and outside; outside half, scrum half, centre and wing positions could be inter-changeable. Of the Williams brothers, Elwyn Williams could play in three positions across the back row, and moved when needs must to centre or wing. Tony Williams played outside half, centre and wing. Lloyd Williams played scrum half and outside half, and Cenydd and Bleddyn outside half and centre. The eldest, Gwyn, played wing forward for Cardiff, and loose forward and wing for Wigan.

In this poor season, with again many draws, Coventry were beaten away 28-9, with 5 tries and 2 drop goals, but the Baa-Baas scored four tries in their 21-0 win. Newport beat Cardiff 11-0, 9-8 and 19-5 before trying at the Arms Park for their first ever 'quadruple.' Cardiff had lost their 3 previous matches to Aberavon, Newport and Llanelli, but on a poor pitch, then just about avoided the 'disgrace' of being the only Cardiff side to lose four times in the season to their nearest rivals, with a 0-0 draw. The fixtures had begun in 1876-77, went to 2 fixtures a year in 1880-81, and such was the game's drawing power, to four games a season in 1887-88. Newport came close several times to winning all four, and Cardiff had achieved it in 1887-88, 1905-06, 1947-48 and 1951-52. I was in attendance the last time at the Arms Park when Newport had their last chance to win all four games in a season, and they hammered Cardiff relentlessly, with the home side scraping a lucky draw, knowing how much it meant to the huge crowd.

Top try scorer was Glyn John with only 12 tries, 4 coming at Christmas in the Watsonians game, with 6 from Ken Thomas and Gordon Wells, and 5 each from Meirion Roberts, Colin Hewett and Ken Richards. Alun Priday kicked 134 points from 53 goals (over a third of the team's points) and scored 4 tries. It is worthwhile to note that not many fullbacks in this era were scoring tries, staying around their 25-yard line, until J.P.R. Williams changed the role into a more aggressive, attacking one. Alun Priday also played in 40 of the 44 matches, followed by C.D. Williams and Dai Hayward with 39, Lloyd Williams with 36, despite international appearances, and prop Kingsley Jones with 35. The miserable try-scoring record should be put in some perspective. The previous season, with just 3 more games, the score was 106-35. From 1945-46 to 1973-74, games varied in number from 40 to 53, but the tries for: tries against numbers were: 149-44; 122-32; **182-22!** (1947-48); 146-33; 121-38; 97-32; 106-41; 141-45; 138-44; 148-41; 130-61; 134-66; 106-35; **76-54** (1958-59); 91-40; 114-43; 81-29; 100-39; 119-40; 144-53; 128-32; 158-62; 137-45; 120-54; 120-62; 133-72; **175**-66; **158**-67; **190**-61 (1973-74). Cardiff has always scored far more tries in a season than the opposition, but this was a bad year indeed.

Wales 5, England 0, 17 January 1959 – on what might have been 'the nastiest, foulest day of them all'. A picture epitomising the quagmire conditions in which midwinter rugby often took place at Cardiff before the 1970s.

The Rags were again captained by centre Peter Nyhan and it was a much better record. Peter Nyhan was a great friend of Colin Howe and Lloyd Williams, and Lloyd's widow Lynne tells me that they were so inseparable that they were known as *'the Three Musketeers'*. The Athletic record was P36, W31, L3, D2, points 614-154. To lose only 6 matches in two seasons was a great achievement, and wing Ray Glastonbury scored 22 tries, Peter Nyhan 16, Gareth Griffiths' brother Ritchie Griffiths had 10 and G. T. Ellis 9. Fullback George Spear kicked 39 goals and scored seven tries for 104 points. Athletic caps were awarded to Graham Buck, Graham Davies, Ritchie Griffiths, Steve Hughes, R. Parkhouse, Jim Sweeny, the hooker W. J. 'Billy' Thomas, the very useful fly-half Thomas 'Tommy' McCarthy, and back-row forward Elwyn Williams. The eighth brother, A. D. 'Tony' Williams was playing stand-off and centre for Cardiff Juniors/Youth, following three of his brothers, and was capped by Wales Youth.

The 1958-59 season was an excellent one for nearby Penarth, beating Northampton away, Bridgend, Newbridge, Bridgwater and Albion, Abertillery and Swansea. 'Slugger' Templeman was 'the catalyst' in a team that in Easter 1958 lost to the Baa-Baas by a single point, and in Easter 1959 drew 3-3 with the Baa-Baas, the team that on that 1959 Easter Tour defeated Cardiff 21-0, Swansea 18-11 and Newport 15-5. Loose-head prop Henry Jacobs was Penarth captain, having played 16 times for Cardiff and many times for the 'Rags.' In the Five Nations, France had 5 points, Wales, Ireland and England 4 points each, and Scotland 3 points. Wales started well, overcoming England 5-0 in January (Dewi Bebb try, converted), but in front of over 70,000 people lost 6-5 in Scotland. Wales then beat Ireland 8-6, but were beaten 11-3 in Paris. Lloyd played in the first three games, and his size and strength served as a virtual third wing forward in defence. For the fourth match, the bad defeat in France, he was replaced by Newbridge's Billy Watkins, who just gained the one cap. '*The Big Five*', as the Welsh selectors were known, were often people with little experience of picking the right rugby team, as pointed out several times by 'J.B.G.' in his columns and books.

Aged only 30, the great back row forward Sid Judd died of leukaemia on 24 February 1959, three years after his illness forced his retirement from the game. He had joined Cardiff in 1946, playing 184 times in 10 seasons, and scoring 45 tries until illness forced his retirement. Capped 10 times by Wales, he scored tries in both wins by Cardiff and Wales over the All Blacks in 1953. Many fund-raising events were held by the club for the teacher's family, culminating in a Past v. Present match at Cardiff Arms Park on 30 April 1959. The Past XV included Billy Cleaver, Jack Matthews, Les Manfield, Cliff Davies and Stan Bowes, and the problem was choosing who to play, out of the many players, such as Wilf Wooller, who volunteered to come out of retirement for the game. J.B.G. (Bryn) Thomas wrote at the end of a fulsome obituary: '*He was a great footballer and a brave man.*' There was also a match played on 20 April 1959, for the Sid Judd Memorial Fund, between a Welsh Schools XV and a Cardiff & District Boys XV. On the front page of the programme is a eulogy from Ieuan C. Price: '*I first had the pleasure of meeting Sid Judd when he presented himself at Splotlands School as a keen student-teacher from Carmarthen Training College; one of the most likeable and sincere teachers I have had the pleasure to meet and work with. Sid will always be remembered as an outstanding International and Cardiff Club player, but we must not lose sight of the fact that he was also a first-class teacher. A product of Cardiff High School, where he captained the First XV, Sid gained Secondary School caps in '45 and '46. After military and college service, Sid became an esteemed member of Windsor Clive Schools, where he devoted his skill and many of his "out of school" hours to coaching and helping his boys in the game he loved. He was an extremely popular and valued member of the Cardiff Schools' Rugby Committee, and this match has been arranged as a tribute to his services... My Committee and I hope that the game will be as Sid knew rugby – open, hard, clean.'*

CLIFFFORD ISAAC 'CLIFF' MORGAN OBE CVO 7 April 1930 – 29 August 2013
Cardiff (on leaving Tonyrefail Grammar School) 1949-58, 202 appearances, 39 tries, 1 penalty = 120pts
Bective Rangers 1955-56
Barbarians 1950-58 – 17 games
Wales 1951-58 - 29 games 3 tries
British Lions in South Africa 1955 all 4 Tests – *'player of the series.'* The South African newspapers dubbed him *'Morgan the Magnificent'*

John O'Sullivan's obituary in the *Irish Times* 30 August 2013 reads:
*'**Cliff Morgan: One of sport's great entertainers** - The former Cardiff, Wales and Lions outhalf brought such pleasure to people with his talent on the pitch and later his work as a broadcaster.'* There is a picture titled: *'10th August 1955: Welsh rugby union outhalf Cliff Morgan is tackled by Koch whilst playing for the British Lions against South Africa at Johannesburg. He was voted player of the series after the tour, retiring three years later when he went on to a career as a radio broadcaster with the BBC.'*
"*This is Gareth Edwards, a dramatic start. What a score! Oh, that fella Edwards. If the greatest writer of the written word could've written that story, no one would have believed it."* It is rare that the soundtrack to an iconic sporting moment is as evocatively memorable as the television footage. Cliff Morgan's lilting voice that betrayed a rising sense of excitement was perfect accompaniment to Gareth Edwards' try in the Barbarians famous victory over New Zealand in 1973. Morgan (83) died yesterday. The Welshman's defining moment as a commentator had occurred in slightly fortuitous circumstances. Bill McLaren had been scheduled to call the game but had fallen ill. Morgan blazed a trail from a brilliant player to a superb commentator, one of the first to do so.
The only son of Clifford and Edna May Morgan, he was born in Trebanog in the Rhondda Valley. He began playing rugby at Tonyrefail School and ascribed his development to rugby master Ned Gribble, whom he describes as the man "who did more than anyone to shape my future in rugby". A wonderful talent, he was one of the greatest outhalves to play the game and in the eyes of Ireland's Jackie Kyle, **the greatest**. The two men opposed one another on Morgan's debut for Wales at Cardiff Arms Park on March 10th, 1951. They shared a lovely vignette which Morgan told repeatedly through the years. He recalled: "*I felt a hand gently touch my shoulder. It was the man I was having to mark, the maestro Jackie*

Kyle. He put an arm around me and whispered as fondly and genuinely as an uncle would: "I hope you have a wonderful, wonderful first cap today, Cliffie."

He went on to win 29 caps for Wales and also toured with the 1955 British & Irish Lions playing 15 matches, all four Tests - the series ended 2-2, the first time that century that the Springboks hadn't won it – and scored a brilliant try in a 23-22 victory in the first Test before a world record crowd of 96,000 in Ellis Park, Johannesburg. His fellow Lions tourist, Tony O'Reilly, would later say of Morgan: "He is a man apart because of his gaiety, his grandeur, eloquence, because of his skills as a football player, and his generosity to other players, which was enormous. He is not a selfish man in life or on the field. To me he is **simply the greatest of them all.**_"_ *The Welshman made 202 appearances for Cardiff between 1949 and 1958 with a brief one-year hiatus when he played for Bective Rangers. He won the Leinster Senior Cup and the heart of an Irish air hostess Nuala Martin, to whom he was married – they had two children Catherine and Nicholas – for 44 years until her death in 1999. He is survived by his second wife Patricia Ewing.'*

'Maurice Mortell Snr, a wing who won nine caps for Ireland, scoring five tries (1953-54) played alongside Morgan at Bective Rangers. He recalled: "Cliff was an engineer and was transferred from Cardiff to a company called Wire Ropes in Wicklow Town. Ireland's Grand Slam (1948) and Triple Crown winning number eight Des O'Brien was captain of Cardiff at the time but having been educated at Belvedere College recommended Old Belvedere to Cliff. However Belvo only took in former pupils of the school and those of Clongowes if I recall correctly. It was a closed club in that respect. I knew Cliff from playing for Ireland against Wales and had struck up a friendship. He came to Bective and Cliff provided that missing piece of the jigsaw that allowed us to win the Leinster Senior Cup. Hughie Church, a great scrumhalf joined us from Terenure, a junior club at the time. Cliff raved about him, 'Hughie bach,' little Hughie. Huge crowds came to Donnybrook to watch the Welsh wizard. He was a wonderful player whose first and last instinct was to run the ball. I remember in a first round cup match against Monkstown he fielded a kick at goal behind our posts. Instead of just touching down, he opened up, weaving past several tacklers before giving me the ball on our 25 yard line. I had to run the other 75 yards. As I made my way back slightly winded I can still see Cliff smiling and hear him saying: 'I'll teach you how to play.' I have very fond memories." Ironically the team that Bective beat in the 1955 Leinster Senior Cup Final was Old Belvedere, the team to which he might have gone instead. Morgan scored a try to boot.

Mortell explained: "Jim Murphy O'Connor won a lineout ball, Hughie fired out a great pass and Cliff touched down under the posts, swerving between the opposing outhalf and centre. He met Nuala (Martin) at a dance while he was here and she stole his heart. Within a couple of days of arriving he'd organised a choir in Bective. He was a wonderful raconteur who could captivate a room."

Morgan said of his time at Bective Rangers. *"No question at all the most enjoyable rugby of my life was at Bective Rangers. In the early fifties there was little coaching and few training sessions. People played because they loved the game. To win a cup final and to learn how to deal with disappointment as did Joe Molly when he missed the final in 1955; these are the things that make rugby a game apart."* Morgan suffered a stroke at 42, which temporarily left him speechless and paralysed down one side, but it did not stop him from going on to have a 30-year career in broadcasting, 11 of which were as the popular host of Sport on BBC Radio 4. He was also one of the captains, alongside Henry Cooper, on television quiz show, A Question of Sport. In one of life's crueller moments for a man who'd entertained so many with his voice he contracted throat cancer in 2005 and had his larynx removed, which limited his speech. It's better though to celebrate his life. Cliff Morgan was a wonderful entertainer on and off the pitch'.

CHAPTER 31 - CARDIFF SEASON 1959 – 1960

ELWYN WILLIAMS GAINS HIS FIRST XV CAP - CENYDD WILLIAMS OUT FOR MUCH OF SEASON – 'RAGS' AND YOUTH FIFTEENS STEAL THE HONOURS – FOUR WILLIAMS BROTHERS APPEAR FOR CARDIFF – THE START OF THE HIGH TRY 60s

Lloyd Williams P17 T1 Pts3; **Cenydd Williams** P8 T2 Pts6; **Elwyn Williams** P31 T7 Pts21; **Tony Williams** P1; Alun Priday P39, T1, C31, P17 Pts116 (Tongwynlais); Glyn Williams P24 T8 Pts24 (Pentyrch)

P44, W26, L10. D8. Points 428 - 285. Tries 91-40, Pens 22-36

Tony Williams made his first appearance for the Senior team, learning his 'apprenticeship' in the Athletic team. The Empire & Commonwealth Games were held in 1958 in Cardiff, with the Empire Pool (now sadly demolished) being built for swimming, and the Arms Park used for athletics. The rugby pitch had to be re-laid with fresh turf, unfortunately in soaking conditions, and the South Stand side of the pitch was badly affected. Water could not drain near the touchline, where the running track had been, so there was a muddy slick from end to end of the field. The adjoining Sophia Gardens, Glamorgan cricket's home, had to be used for some games. Rain from the west has always been a curse for Welsh rugby pitches, and also for Glamorgan Cricket Club, losing more days of play than other county. Thankfully, much of the precipitation is dumped over the 'Emerald Isle' before it passes over Cymru.

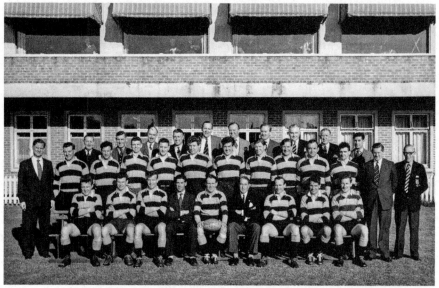

1959-60 Elwyn third from left middle row. Cenydd and Lloyd
second and third from left front row

This season was a real improvement, as demonstrated by the 36 successful penalties kicked by the opposition to try and win games. Many sporting Welsh boys attended the rugby-oriented teacher-training St. Luke's College, Exeter, so many that it was sometimes called St. Leek's, and one such was Rhondda's Gordon Wells, a fast wing with a sidestep that allowed him to come inside and keep the ball in play, *'the Cardiff way'*. He had joined in 1952-53, was a Baa-Baa and had 7 Welsh caps, touring South Africa and Rhodesia in 1958. Wells was elected captain, and was to play 254 games before finishing with the Firsts in 1961-62. Danny Davies used to wittily address Wells as *'my artesian friend'* – rugby players seem to have been more articulate in the past. Gordon nominated a great prop from Mountain Ash, John Davies Evans as vice-captain. He was always referred to as 'J.D'. and between 1951-52 and 1960-61 played in 338 First Team games, very often in tandem with Geoff Beckingham and Colin Howe. 'JD' played for the Barbarians in 1957 but only had 2 Welsh caps, both in 1958, and was in the 1953 Cardiff team that beat the All Blacks. His value to the team was shown by the number of appearances over 10 seasons – 21 (of 46), 40 (of 48), 36 (of 49), 42 (of 48), 46 (of 52),

410

46 (of 50), 36 (of 47), 23 (of 44), 42 (of 44), 4 (of 43). In his last but one season, he only missed 2 of 44 games. A wonderfully fit player, indeed.

It was a better season, but finding an outside half to match Lloyd Williams at scrumhalf was a problem, with no fewer than five being tried. However, local boy Tommy McCarthy played 28 times and thankfully became established as a first choice. A truly great asset was the second-row D. E. J. 'Danny' Harris, another St. Luke's product, joining from Pontypridd. A hard man, in two seasons he played 52 times, scoring 6 tries before being attracted North, a great loss. He gained 6 of his 8 Welsh caps with Cardiff before joining Leigh RLFC. Gareth Griffiths played only 7 times before winding down, to play for the Athletic with his brother Ritchie. Ken Richards left, and owing to National Service, Cenydd Williams took part in only 8 games. Brother Elwyn was now a regular First XV player.

There was a bad loss at home to Oxford University 22-0, and Cardiff lost 9-3 away to Neath. An excellent Newport team beat Cardiff 12-3 and 12-8, and the third match was luckily drawn 6-6 before a 3-0 away defeat. The previous year Cardiff had lost the first 3 games and drawn the last, but better was to come. In the following four seasons after this one, they only lost one of 16 games. The results were 60-61 WDWW; 61-62 WDWD; 62-63; WWLD; 63-64 WWWD. Incidentally, on Easter Monday morning, wing Ray Glastonbury played for the Rags against Cardiff H.S.O.B., and in the afternoon for the First XV against the Harlequins. However, there were doubles over Harlequins, Pontypool, Llanelli and London Welsh, and a 10-10 draw with the Barbarians. Apart from Newport's great season, it was an average year for Welsh rugby, with the Five Nations results being a loss to England away 14-6, a win at home to Scotland 8-0, a win in Dublin 10-9 and a home defeat to France 11-3. France and England shared the title, with Wales third and Ireland did not win a game. No fewer than 29 Cardiff players scored tries, led by Gordon Wells with 16 and centre Meirion Roberts with 11. Alun Priday kicked 48 goals and scored a try for 116 points. First Team caps were awarded to Elwyn Williams (who also played many games for the Athletic), Tommy McCarthy, Graham Davies, Ray Glastonbury, Danny Harris, hooker W. J. 'Billy' Thomas and wing Glyn Williams. Dai Hayward played in 43 of the 44 fixtures, with Gordon Wells and J.D. Evans 44 each.

Although an average season by Cardiff standards, there was now great expectation, from the performances of the Athletic and Youth teams. The Youth Fifteen, formerly known as Cardiff Juniors, had its best season since its foundation in 1949-50: Pl 26, W23, L1, D2. At Sevens, they won both the Llandaff and Bridgend Tournaments. During the season no fewer than 11 former youth players assisted the two senior sides. Peter Goodfellow captained the Firsts in 1956-57, and became 'Rags' captain in this season, having been captain before in 1953-54 with Stan Bowes, captain in 1954-

411

55, and again sharing with Stan in 1956-57. Both often appeared for the Firsts in these seasons, Goodfellow playing 240 senior games between 1948-49 and this season. Danny Davies makes the point that Goodfellow's Athletic team surpassed Haydn Tanner's 1st XV record of 1947-48, scoring 210 tries (via 40 scorers) to 182. Tanner's team record was Pl 41, W 39, L 2, Points 803-161. Goodfellow's team Pl 41, W 39, L 2, **Points 853-175**. *'Had the new four points value of a try from 1971-72 applied to 1959-60 the Athletic XV points would have been 1,063 in 41 matches.'* Davies points out that *'Even on this assumption this splendid achievement was to be surpassed in seasons 1972-73 and 1973-74'*. And who was to be captain in those two brilliant seasons? The eighth Williams boy, A.D. 'Tony' Williams.

On 3 March 1960, Bernard 'Slogger' Templeman became the seventh Penarth player to be selected for the Barbarians, having dropped three goals at Rodney Parade against Newport, and Penarth Chairman John Heslop drove him up for the game. According to Chris Thau, Heslop did not wish Templeman to be overawed, being surrounded by so many famous faces in the changing room. *'John made a point of obtaining the ear of the Barbarians captain David Marques, the England line-out expert. "I'd like you to make young Slogger feel at home" explained John. "When you give your team talk, could you…" he hesitated. "Would you mind", he continued, lowering his voice, "using some of the words that 'Slogger' will identify with; just a bit of effing and blinding here and there. It may not be the way you have it in the Baa-Baas, but it's the way we have it in Wales…"* East Midlands were beaten 25-17.

Then at Easter 1960, came the climax of Templeman's leadership of Penarth. It was the first game, as usual, of the Baa-Baas' annual four-match tour of Wales. Former RAF fly-half Tony Wilding played on the Penarth wing in this game and recalls the crowded Penarth dressing-room – *'There was no team talk, and anyway Slogger was not the type of guy to give speeches. "Let's get on with it, guys", was all he said. He was a brilliant player yet a law unto himself. If he could not do anything with the ball, then he will give it to you. I have been a few times on the end of his suicide passes* (when playing fly half). *I remember once against Neath when I had my ribs broken following one of his passes. But on the day Slogger could do nothing wrong, and this is how we won a great match.'* J.B.G. Thomas covered the game, held in mud and rain, where Penarth *'inspired by Templeman'* adapted better to the conditions. Before half-time each side scored a converted try 5-5, and each side touched down in the second half, but Slogger Templeman converted again to make the score 10-8 - Penarth's first win in 40 years over the Barbarians. Penarth's long-standing and perhaps parsimonious secretary, Lot Thorn, was asked for a photo to be taken before the game, and refused, saying *'A photo? You must be joking! You are not worth a photograph'*. Thus, there is no photograph of the winning team.

A day later the Baa-Baas drew 10-10 with Cardiff, then lost to Swansea 16-0 and beat Newport 11-9. (I will just mention Tony Wilding, a fly-half at Cowbridge Grammar School, as he was set to join Cardiff, but was concussed in his first trial match, and after hearing nothing for a month, joined Penarth. He should have played for Welsh Schools, but the *'usual political machinations'* i.e. horse-trading between selectors obstructed the *'most talented outside-half in contention'*. He enjoyed a fruitful Penarth partnership with 'Slogger' Templeman.)

Yet again Penarth performed well in the Welsh Sevens and the Arms Park, beating Pontypridd, Cardiff, and the favourites Newport by 20-5! They then lost to the winners Llanelli, stuffed with internationals, 20-14. Penarth scored more tries in the tournament, 49, to Llanelli's 44. The team remembered that after beating Cardiff, the wonderful ex-POW Les Spence, a great Cardiff player and sometime President, went into the Penarth dressing room and showered them with strong language. The team sat back, both exhausted and bemused, at this legend in the game berating them. Eddie Donovan recalled that his team was 'shell-shocked'. Then Les grinned all over his face, congratulated them and producing a bottle of champagne from behind his back for the team. And after Penarth beat Newport, he again invaded the Penarth dressing room, to much laughter. Penarth, almost adjoining Cardiff along the coast, guessed what was coming after they had just thrashed Cardiff's 'old enemy' – but this time **two** bottles of champagne were produced. These were happier days for most rugby teams – playing for enjoyment.

CHAPTER 32 - POST-WAR TAFF'S WELL RFC

PENTYRCH WIN THE MALLETT CUP THREE YEARS IN A ROW – BRYN AND VAUGHAN WILLIAMS ARE REGULAR PLAYERS – STEVE FENWICK PLAYS FOR TAFF'S WELL – THE 'INVINCIBLE' SEASON OF 1960-61 - THE NEW CLUBHOUSE – LLOYD, ELWYN AND TONY WILLIAMS PLAY AGAINST TAFF'S WELL – ELWYN COACHES 'IKE' STEPHENS TO PLAY PROP - TRAGIC FIRE OF CLUBHOUSE

We left Taff's Well RFC just before war, noting their Cardiff player and Welsh international Tom Lewis, along with Cardiff player Gwyn, the oldest Williams boy, and his uncle Roy Roberts MM, who played for Cardiff before and after the War. Their captain Fred Porter was asked to play many times for Cardiff, and gained a Cardiff Athletic cap, but had

413

concentrated on his local club. In 1947, there is a photo of the Taff's Well School team, with Lloyd Williams wearing his Cardiff Schools cap, and his brothers Elwyn and Cenydd are also in the team.

PC Douglas H. 'Doug' Jones joined Taff's Well rugby club in 1946, and soon headed south to play on the wing for Cardiff. He played mainly for the Athletic but made 30 appearances for Cardiff Firsts between 1947-48 and 1949-50. He left to get more games of first-class rugby. There was a dreadfully cold winter in 1947, restricting everyone's appearances at all levels. According to '*A View from the Garth'*, regarding Doug Jones: *'His play earned him recognition by the Welsh selectors, and he was picked as reserve for the National Team. When one of the wingers cried off, the scene was set, for another Taff's Well 'old boy' to achieve the ultimate aim of all Welsh players and gain a cap. The selectors, however, however, decided otherwise and brought the redoubtable Jack Matthews home from holidays and played him on the wing, although he was, or course, a centre. Thus was Doug Jones 'robbed' of glory.'* In 1947-48 he had scored 22 tries for Cardiff in 29 appearances, including one against Australia, but because of incredibly strong competition for the wing positions, vanished into the Athletic, only playing once more for the Firsts, in 1949-50. He moved on to play for Aberavon, Swansea and Maesteg.

From 1947 to 1951 local boy Tony Bonetto played rugby for Taff's Well, then at age 18 along came National Service, which saw him playing for the R.E.M.E., Western Command and once guesting for the RAF against Cambridge University. Moving to his wife's hometown, he captained Treharris in 1953, as a rather large scrum half, then in 1954 played wing forward and prop for Pontypridd. Their top points scorer, renowned as a 'kicking machine' he was known as '*Boot Bonetto.*' Injuring his knee in the Snelling Sevens, playing for 'Ponty' against Bridgend, Bonetto thought his career was ended, aged just 24. Now on the Taff's Well RFC committee, he went to watch them play at Caerphilly, and the team was a man short. He offered to play, but had no boots, and was loaned a pair of brand-new white plimsolls, now known as trainers but in South Wales always referred to as 'daps'. Wary about testing his knee, he played No. 8, then moved to second row and ended up as hooker. '*The resurrection was made complete in the final moments when "The Boot" slid over for the winning try. He should have been renamed "The Dap" there and then!*' He then resumed his playing career with the club.

The club celebrated Bleddyn's first Welsh cap on 18 January 1947, '*delayed by World War II and that has to go down as another of Hitler's war crimes!*' Bleddyn's life was celebrated in a nine-cell graphic in the *Sunday Pictorial* on 19 January 1947. The text describes Taff's Well as '*The centre of good rugby'*. Iorwerth 'Iorrie' Jones, who had played with Gwyn Williams and Roy Roberts before the war, was an 'iron man' character, and a useful boxer, captaining Taff's Well for three successive

414

seasons after the war. Another gem was unearthed in J.E.G. (John) Llewellyn, born in Glan-y-Llyn, Taff's Well, who played for the school, then the club and then Penarth before joining his friend Bleddyn at Cardiff. He played 152 times for Cardiff, including the 1953 defeat of the All Blacks, from 1950-51 to 1956-57, having a Final Welsh Trial at full back, and returned to play for the village. Many players across the nation served two years of National Service in the late 1940's, 1950s and up to its end in 1963, and tried to get back to their club to play when possible.

SUNDAY PICTORIAL
JANUARY 19, 1947

Bleddyn Williams' First Welsh Cap

It would be remiss here not to mention the achievement of Taff's Well's great rivals, Pentyrch, on the other side of the Garth Mountain. In 1952 at the Arms Park, they won the Mallett Cup for the third successive time. There would have been four brothers playing in this Welsh-speaking team, but the eldest brother Maelgwyn Williams had gone to play for Pontypridd, alongside Tony Bonetto. His brothers, all from Craig Gwilym Farm - Glyndwr, Illtyd and Glanffrwd Williams - all played in the pack. The Mallett Cup, for Cardiff and District clubs, has been played for since 1894, excepting war years, the oldest rugby cup in Wales. Of the 15 clubs in the 1894 competition, only Cardiff, Barry, Canton, Whitchurch, Llandaff and Pentyrch survive. In the first final against Canton, the 19-year-old Gwyn Nicholls played in the Cardiff win. Cardiff's great clubman Tom Holley MBE won two finals, playing for Spillers in 1937 and the Dockers in 1948. Over 50 teams now take part.

Vaughan Williams missed over two years playing, because of National Service, but he and brother Bryn were regulars throughout the 1950s for Taff's Well. In 1950 *'Local stars were brought together in a special match to celebrate Bleddyn's return from the British Lions tour of New Zealand.'* Bleddyn is pictured wearing his Lions jersey, sitting between his brother Bryn and Dai Porter, in the middle row of a photo of the team he raised, to face Taff's Well. Many players are mentioned in Peter Thomas' book on the club, and one story is well worth recounting, a team talk reported in the press: *'An overweight and unfit 17 stone veteran No. 8 forward of Taff's Well RFC was selected to play for the 2nd XV and in view of his 1st team experience he was elected acting captain for the day. Aware of his limitations in company with the much younger and fitter 2nd team players, and knowing full well it would take every effort on his part, to even keep up with the referee, he decided to give the team a pre-match tactical talk in the dressing room. "I think it'll be a fast game today, boys, so we'll 'ave to slow 'em down a bit in the scrums. There's only one way we'll beat 'em in the loose, so don't forget – you tackle 'em and I'll fall on 'em."'*

Gerald Edwards recalls (in *The Garth Domain* No24, June 2004), that the Castle Inn/Hotel *'was one of the major social centres of Taff's Well. Many a four (or more) pint starter was supped here **before** a Taff's Well rugby match. The Castle was not a particularly big building but at the rear were stables, and I believe a coach house. I do know for certain that it was a very friendly changing room, where only two or three could move to pull a shirt on etc. at the same time. The shower wasn't built to dispense a lot of water, and showers had to be taken in pecking order – I knew my place! Camaraderie gone mad, but it was "Great!" A vivid memory as a youngster was standing at the side of the Castle Inn and hearing Iorrie Jones and his brother "Rugger" Jones singing Cyfri'r Geifr! (- 'Counting the Goats'). Edwards then mentions the Anchor – 'A guess on my part is that the Anchor name is derived from one of the many metal industries, that abounded in the lower part of Gwaelod. It is a comfortable club with a skittle alley. The landlord at the time, Mr. Williams, allowed the rugby* *team (having been moved out of the Castle Inn) to change for matches. It was light, but still cramped and we didn't have to duck flying skittles. After a number of changes, the Anchor opened with the sale of hot meals and no skittle alley. The eyebrows were more than raised when the Anchor started selling Mongolian cuisine.'*

In 1959-60 John Llewellyn, the superb Cardiff fullback, was instrumental in acquiring a piece of land, next to the Taff, which became Cae'r Afon, the new pitch. In January 1961, the unofficial clubhouse, the Castle Hotel, closed, so a new clubhouse was built, its cost and that of the adjoining ground being around £11,000. Built of cedar wood rather than brick on cost grounds, and completed by Christmas 1962, it was initially heated by oil stoves, and known as 'The Paraffin Club'. It took an immense amount of hard work to make the pitch fit for purpose, and it was in an attractive position. Bryn Williams helped form a Youth Team in 1960, and one of its early players was Steve Fenwick, who captained Wales, was a British Lion, and whose brother Chris was an excellent centre for Taff's Well Firsts for many years. On leaving Caerphilly Grammar Schoolboy, Steve played for Taff's Well in the 1968-69 and 1970-71 seasons, before achieving greatness in one of the great Welsh teams.

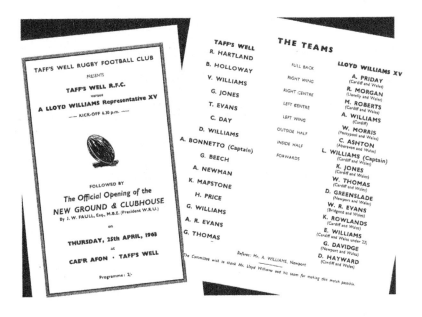

Steven Paul Fenwick (born 23 July 1951) joined Taff's Well RFC, where he thoroughly enjoyed his two years. Steve never lost links with the club, where his two brothers also played, and left all his playing memorabilia for a trophy cabinet. It was destroyed in the tragic 1999 fire, along with all Bleddyn Williams' treasured items. In 1971 Steve switched to nearby

Beddau where he played 51 games. (Playing for Barry Youth, a Beddau player and this writer were singled out and being spoken to by the referee in the first half. I was looking innocently at the ref, when the Beddau bloke stepped back, and swung a haymaker to knock me unconscious. When I came to, the game had been abandoned before half-time as 29 players were brawling. In the clubhouse after, some old blokes said it was the best game they'd seen for ages. Beddau means graves. I wonder how many visiting rugby players never left there?) Steve moved from Beddau to Bridgend instead of the expected route to Cardiff, and won 30 international caps in the centre, a record at the time. He scored a try against France after 5 minutes on his debut, scoring 9 points. He played in all four Tests in the 1977 British Lions tour to New Zealand, and captained Wales in the Centenary game against the All Blacks in 1980. A Barbarian, his only flaw was that he should have joined Cardiff... His regular co-centre, Ray Gravell of Llanelli, was a bundle of nerves before a game, but Steve was placidity itself. One could even say that he had an air of insouciance about him, if one wanted to impress the gullible. Steve had all the gifts of a modern centre, being able to kick, break and tackle, a great player.

P. L. MYNETT,   B. L. WILLIAMS,   B. W. C. LEWIS,   J. I. EDWARDS,   A. Z. JONES

BLEDDYN PRESENTS THE AUTOGRAPHED BALL HE USED WHEN CAPTAIN OF CARDIFF THEY DEFEATED THE 1953 ALL BLACKS

Bleddyn presenting match ball from
1953 New Zealand game to Taff's Well RFC

'Goggo' Beech's Taff's Well team had an unbeaten season in 1960-61. These *'Invincibles'* had Tony Bonetto now playing hooker, 6 inches taller than his props 'Goggo' Beech and Alan 'Oofer' Newman. The second row was Keith 'Twit' Mapstone and Graham 'Fledge' Field, small for the position but mobile. The back row was No. 8 Brian Thomas, who had played hooker for London Welsh, and flankers were chosen from Gordon Bunn, Garth Williams or Gordon Thomas, the latter having played for Glamorgan Wanderers. Backs included Vaughan Williams, one of the Williams brothers, back from playing for Pontypridd, Gwyn 'Id' Davies, 'Tessey' Evans, Trevor Toghill and Graham 'Jite' White. During the 1960-61 season the ground records of Machen and Pontypool United were taken. Twenty-five years later there was a reunion of the players, committee members and supporters associated with that season, including Tony, Bryn, Cenydd and Vaughan Williams.

A long article, in the pink sports edition of the *South Wales Echo*, known as *'the Football Echo'*, Saturday 20 April 1963, was headlined: *'Now Taff's Well have a home of their own.'* Brian Wall reported: *'Taff's Well take on the stars of the Welsh rugby world next Thursday in a match which marks the biggest day in the club's history. Robert Morgan, Meirion Roberts, Keith Rowlands and Glyn Davidge will be there – so will Dai Millward. The last name may not mean much to the majority of Welsh rugby fans. But it means a lot in Taff's Well where, for 40 years, Dai Millward was "Mr. Rugby." And next Thursday night, when WRU president Wilfred Faull officially opens Taff's Well's new ground and clubhouse at Cae'r Afon, Dai's mind will doubtless roam back over the years to 1921 – and a meeting in Harry Field's shop. For that was the time and place that the present Taff's Well Rugby Football Club came into being. Dai Millward was appointed secretary, an office he was to hold until 1960. Getting started was no problem to the rugby men of Taff's Well. It was keeping going without a regular ground that gave them their biggest headache.*

Only Assets - *For in those early days of struggle and strife Taff's Well had as much chance of owning their own ground and clubhouse as they had of beating the Springboks. Their only assets were the skill of the players and the enthusiasm of their officials. And you had to be enthusiastic to serve a club, whose home games often depended on the frame of mind of a local farmer. If the farmer was co-operative, then Taff's Well had a field to play on. If not – well, the club just had to cancel the match.* (Older club members remember clearing pitches of cowpats on the morning before a game. Some gave their children pocket money for the task). *Dai Millward was the man who had the tricky task of negotiating with the farmers, and he remembers ruefully that every year, Taff's Well had to call off several home games. This insecurity of tenure cost the club some attractive fixtures, but it did not sap the spirit of the players or officials. Indeed, Taff's Well is one of those clubs which have always been fortunate in having able administrators. Mr. Millward, who now serves Welsh rugby as a clerk at WRU headquarters in Cardiff, was the doyen of them all, of course, but the names of George Wibley, Harry Field, George Handley, Bill Liddington, Ted Roberts* (the grandfather of the Williams brothers), *Ted Knight and Arthur Pearce will also be remembered...*

WRU Members *-... a photograph of the 1892 side still survives, and it is a fact that Taff's Well were members of the Welsh Rugby Union in 1900. Dai Millward can go back as far as 1900 when he helped form – and played for – Glanyllyn Juniors. This team started their activities with a Christmas Day match against Garth Seconds. Glanyllyn eventually developed into Taff's Well Juniors, playing on Rhiwddar Field and holding their meetings in Jack Powell's café. For a few years after World War I, there was no senior rugby side in Taff's Well. Then a few members of the pre-war junior team approached Dai, and in 1921 Taff's Well RFC was born. They competed in the Cardiff and District Rugby Union and although forced to "gipsy" from the Rhiwddar Field to Tyrhiw, to Caeglas and then back to Rhiwddar, it was not long before WRU status was regained. And, although the grounds varied, the club found regular changing quarters in the Castle Hotel* (now redeveloped). *This had the disadvantage of being a long walk from the nearest pitch – but at least it was permanent.*

Star Players *- Another problem was that the club's collection of tin baths had to be filled with water, and then carried upstairs to the changing rooms. But spartan conditions often produce star performers and among Taff's Well's outstanding players of this period were Bleddyn Thomas, Fred Porter, Trevor Phillips and Phil Rowlands.* (Fred Porter played 22 games for Cardiff, 1925-26 to 1927-28; and Phil Rowlands played 44 times 1920-21 to 1923-24). *To reach one of the pitches, on which the club played for a time, the team and officials had to cut steps into the side of a steep bank. They cut 'em – and started climbing. In those between-the-war-years Taff's Well built up a reputation for good football and good fellowship. They had an invincible season and turned out players of the calibre of Reg Field, Percy Rudge, Tommy Gist, Jack Culliford and R.W.C. "Bob" Lewis, now president of the club. A lot of their products graduated to Cardiff and two of them, forwards Harry Rees and Tommy Lewis, won their Welsh caps from the famous Arms Park club.* (Rees had 169 games for Cardiff from 1933-34 to 1938-39; Tom Lewis played 206 times from 1923-24 to 1932-33).

The Williamses *- But Taff's Well's strongest link with Cardiff is the Williams clan –* **the finest footballing family in the land***. Gwyn, Bryn, Bleddyn, Vaughan, Lloyd, Cenydd, Elwyn and Tony – all have turned out for the club at some time or other. It is Lloyd Williams, who is taking a star-studded team to Taff's Well next Thursday, a team which includes his brothers Tony and Elwyn. But to own a ground and a clubhouse seemed a remote possibility, even after the Second World War, when the indefatigable Dai Millward quickly started the ball rolling again. Prominent players in those early post-war winters were Glyn Russell* (rated the best uncapped hooker in Wales), *John Llewellyn* (later to play full-back for Cardiff) *and Bryn Williams* (now vice-chairman of the club).

(Bryn is the second oldest of the Williams boys, and John Llewellyn played 116 games for Cardiff from 1950-51 to 1956-57, including the win against the All Blacks in 1953). *Iorrie Jones (now club chairman) was an outstanding player, who just wouldn't stop playing. He carried on for so long that he even played in a few matches with son George, a member of the current first team!*

Bad Patch – *Around 1950 Taff's Well suffered the sort of bad patch which strikes every club, but in the years that followed playing standards steadily improved, and in 1960-61 Taff's Well RFC went through the season undefeated. Taking in part of the previous season, the club actually went some 60 matches without defeat. The skipper of the invincible team was Gordon Beech, who received strong support from Graham White, Graham Field (now assistant secretary) and Trevor Toghill. Invincibility was fine for the team's prestige, but the big target was still a home ground of their own, particularly as there was talk of Rhiwddar Field being taken over as a building site. In 1959 a committee had been formed to examine the possibility of purchasing a piece of land which could provide a permanent home for the club. Various sites were inspected before the search ended at Cae'r Afon. John Llewellyn played a vital part in securing the freehold of the 4½ acre site, which, when bought, was a jungle of bushes, small trees and scrub.*

Site Cleared – *Some do-it-yourself hard labour saw the site cleared and then the experts moved in, levelling and seeding to produce a first-class playing pitch.'* (However, players remember the first few years when pieces of brick and rock regularly resurfaced on the new pitch). *'During this time negotiations were going on for the erection of a clubhouse, and in September 1962 building work started. All Taff's Well's ambitions were turning into achievements. Another of this season's achievements (the importance of which should not be under-estimated), is the formation of a youth team under Reg Feld and Fred Porter. Already there is a familiar name in the youth line-up – Ashley Williams, the son of Bleddyn. Tony (The Boot) Bonetto, who re-joined the team from Pontypridd, has the honour of leading the first team in this, the most memorable season in Taff's Well's history. Supporting him are such forward stalwarts as Keith (Twit) Mapstone, Alun Newman, Gordon Thomas and Garth Williams, while behind the scrum Clive Day, Vaughan Williams* (Bleddyn's brother) *and Terry Evans are still going strong.* (Bryn Mapstone, a cousin, played for Cardiff).

Committee Men – *The administration of the club's three teams is in the hands of a capable committee headed by Iorrie Jones, Bryn Williams* (Bleddyn's brother), *Alan Jones, Arthur Millward (son of Dai) and Graham Field. All are looking forward to next Thursday, when WRU President Faull sets the seal on Taff's Well's success story by opening their ground and clubhouse. Taff's Well would naturally like to celebrate* the occasion, with a win against Lloyd Williams' All Stars – but the result really doesn't matter. As Dai Millward stresses "The things that matter most to Taff's Well are the spirit in the club, and the way they play the game".'

In the same paper the main report was upon Cardiff City hammering Sunderland 5-2, with Mel Charles, the brother of John, having a superb match. And in a tournament in Brussels, Tylorstown Rugby Club played Belgian, Italian and German teams, before defeating Stade Français in the final. That's right, Stade Français. So tiny Tylorstown (Pendyrus) in the Rhondda Valley has an unbeaten record against the cream of French rugby, and later produced John Bevan, the wonderful Cardiff, Wales and Lions wing. And one of my childhood favourites, Del Shannon was appearing at Sophia Gardens, supported by Johnny Tillotson (*'Poetry in Motion'*) and the Springfields (before Dusty went solo). All for tickets ranging from 6/6 to 11/6 (– shillings and pence in proper coinage). I also feel I must mention another article, headlined *'Young Yorath Turns on a Star Display – Thirteen-year-old Terry Yorath came unexpectedly into the Cardiff Boys Senior XI, when they met Rhondda Boys in the return leg of the Welsh Shield, this week. With normal winger Curtain calling off through injury, Terry, a pupil at Cathays High School, filled the breach and his footwork and intelligent thinking were a feature of the game. Having won the first leg 4-0 away the Cardiff side made certain of a semi-final place with a 5-0 win...'* A Grangetown, Cardiff, boy, Terence Charles Yorath (born 27 March 1950) played for Leeds United, Coventry City, Tottenham Hotspur, Vancouver Whitecaps, Bradford City, Swansea City, and Wales. He later became a football manager for Bradford City, Swansea City, Cardiff City, and Sheffield Wednesday, and managed Wales and Lebanon. Yorath was awarded 59 Welsh caps from 1970 and captained Wales 42 times. Yorath was popular amongst the Wales players and fans, and guided them to wins over Brazil in 1990 and World Cup holders Germany in a European Championship Qualifier in 1991. Under Yorath, Wales attained what was then their highest ever FIFA ranking of 27th in August 1993. In 2011 Wales football fell to its lowest ever ranking of 117th, but had a spectacular and unparalleled rise to a remarkable 8th in the world in 2015 and is 19th in June 2022.

On 25 April, 1963, Lloyd Williams arranged a XV to play Taff's Well, to celebrate the official clubhouse opening. Welsh international Lloyd captained, playing alongside Cardiff players - his brothers Elwyn (who had captained the Wales under-23 team) and Tony. It was an international team including Cardiff and Wales players Alun Priday, Meirion Roberts, Ken Jones, Dai Hayward, Howard Norris and Keith Rowlands. Other players were Robert Morgan (Llanelli and Wales), Bryn Meredith (Newport and Wales), W. Morris (Pontypool and Wales), Cliff Ashton (Aberavon and Wales – in the programme, but replaced by Lloyd Williams), D.

422

Greenslade (Newport and Wales), W.R. Evans (Bridgend and Wales) and Glyn Davidge (Newport and Wales). The only non-internationals were Tony and Elwyn Williams. In 1951 'the Boot' Bonetto had played his first game for Taff's Well, and was still playing, captain for this game. Under the headline '*Taff's Well Celebrate New Club*', J.B.G. Thomas reported: *'Despite a wet evening and extremely greasy conditions, there was an excellent open and attractive match at Taff's Well last night. It was a special match to celebrate the opening of the new and attractive Taff's Well clubhouse, watched by a large crowd of enthusiastic spectators. Lloyd William's XV, including ten internationals and three British Lions, provided the greater part of the open play and won comfortably by six goals and four tries to two goals, a penalty and a try.*

However, Taff's Well showed excellent spirit and deserved their three scores late in the match, as a result of their tenacity. For the International XV the three Williams brothers Lloyd, Elwyn and Anthony, each scored two tries against their village team, and one of them, Anthony, was marked by brother Vaughan, playing for Taff's Well, while another brother, Brinley, acted as touch judge. Another player to enjoy himself was British Lion and former Wales captain B.V. Meredith who emerged from his retirement at short notice, to hook for the International XV and join D. Greenslade and H. Norris in the front row. Lloyd Williams, who led the side, played at outside half with T.B. Williams (a Cardiff player) at scrumhalf.

At half time the score was 26-5, but by collecting 11 points in the closing stages, Taff's Well managed a respectable score of 42-16 in favour of the internationals. Before the match the spacious clubhouse was opened at the Cae'r Afon ground by Mr. J.W. Faull, for the Welsh Rugby Union. And the occasion was a great one for the former referee, David Millward, who has been connected with the club for many years.' The brothers Elwyn, Lloyd and Tony scored two tries each – 18 points - against their village club, with Dai Hayward and Robert Morgan scoring one each. There were two other try scorers for the 'Internationals', but were not recorded by 'JGB'. Alun Priday kicked 3 conversions, with Dai Hayward, Robert Morgan and Elwyn each converting one. Taff's Well tries were scored by T. Evans, G. Thomas and G. Williams, with Tony Bonetto kicking a penalty and two conversions.

In 1965, 14 years after his debut, Bonetto converted 3 of 5 tries when the team defeated Stade Français, the first continental rugby team to visit the club, 21-0. The former Cardiff international centre and current selector Alun Thomas played for the visitors, the *Western Mail* suggesting he had *'picked the wrong side'*. Tries came from Brian Nash (2), with George Jones, Colin Riley and Hugh Christopher also touching down. A return was arranged for 1966, the first time Taff's Well had travelled overseas, but the score is missing from Peter Thomas' account. *'After the game we were royally entertained at Harry's Bar at a dinner that was endless'*. The veteran Bonetto was so overwhelmed by French hospitality that he gave away his watch, suitcase, clothes, and returned to Britain in his underpants. Ah – the spirit of 'coarse rugby' will always survive as long as there are rugby tours.

In 1969, the 17-year-old Ian 'Ike' Stephens came from neighbouring Tongwynlais to play at No. 8. Elwyn Williams, the current No.8, convinced Ike to move to the second row and then to prop, and as the youngster gained muscle, his ambition to play for Wales grew. First class clubs, especially Cardiff, came to ask Ike to play, but he joined Bridgend at the end of the 1974-75 season. Playing for Taff's Well, '*On a trip to Staines in 1975 he amazed and delighted the English by making a masterful speech in Welsh. Little did they know it was complete gibberish, made up on the spur of the moment. It did not include a single Welsh word! The rest of our team were completely doubled up with laughter. When 'Ike' left the club for Bridgend he was greatly missed on and off the pitch. He was, however, always there for our annual club dinner, until in 1983 he was unable to attend, as he was with the Lions in New Zealand. The dinner would not have been the same without him, so Carey Collings designed a completely life-like and life-sized cardboard cut-out of 'Ike', dressed in a club blazer. He made a moveable mouthpiece, so that we could practise our ventriloquism. It was a great success, and the cut-out bought more beer than 'Ike' usually did.'*

'Ike' Stephens always remained close to the club, and he played for Wales B, then 13 times for Wales, and for the Barbarians and the British Lions in South Africa in 1980 and in New Zealand in 1983. He was 28 years old on his debut for Wales in the 1981 game against England, after touring with the Lions. Ike had served Taff's Well for six years before joining Bridgend. If this unbiased author has one criticism of his career, it is that I wish he had joined Cardiff. Ditto Steve Fenwick. I asked JPR Williams once, over a pint or two in the Vale of Glamorgan pub in Cowbridge, why he never joined Cardiff after leaving London Welsh, to work as a surgeon and play for Bridgend. He replied, '*Because my father would have killed me.*' JPR's dad was a doctor who had played for Bridgend. Local allegiances are wonderful. This author can never understand why people who have never been to Manchester support Manchester United. My allegiances have always been to Cardiff Rugby Club, Cardiff City Football Club, and Wales in anything. All else is unimportant. But all people should be like that – your allegiance, your love, must be for your '*bro*', your neighbourhood, the surrounding places that shape you. I understand why Monmouthshire people support Pontypool or Newport or Ebbw Vale, even if they are playing poorly and lack resources. Your '*bro*' comes first. On 4 March 2022, Cardiff Blues were smashed in Ulster 48-12, and the following day the Dragons

(Newport) were hammered by Munster 64-3. But we still support our clubs - '*things can only get better*' – now where have I heard that before? Oh, that's right, it was Sir Anthony Charles Lynton Blair's 1997 election campaign song. One is unsure that the blatant lies underpinning the 2003 Iraq Invasion made anything better. Right, back to rugby, and a terrible incident.

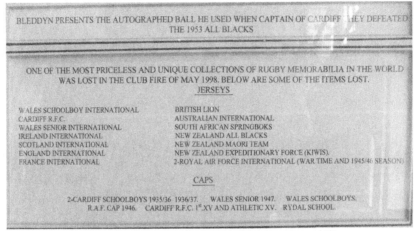

Board in clubhouse listing Bleddyn's memorabilia

In May 1968, Taff's Well clubhouse was accidentally burnt to the ground. The fire was started at night, by a faulty socket in the floodlighting system, where the switch was on the outside wall of the timber-framed clubhouse. The prized trophy cabinets of the British Lions 'Ike' Stephens, Steve Fenwick and Bleddyn Williams were destroyed. Carey Collings recalls that it is the only time he saw the perpetually smiling Tony Williams angry. In Bleddyn's cabinet were international shirts and the match ball from when he captained Cardiff to beat the All Blacks in 1953. A new board in the club now lists what else was lost. It reads: '*One of the Most Priceless and Unique Collections of Rugby Memorabilia in the World was Lost in the Club Fire of May 1998. Below are some of the Items Lost*' – the following were all Bleddyn's. '*JERSEYS Wales Schoolboy International; Cardiff R.F.C.; Wales Senior International; Ireland International; Scotland International; England International; France International; British Lion; Australian International; South African Springboks; New Zealand All Blacks, New Zealand Maori Team; New Zealand Expeditionary Forces (Kiwis); 2 – Royal Air Force International (War Time and 1945/46 Season) CAPS 2 – Cardiff Schoolboys 1935/36 1936/37; Wales Senior 1947; Wales Schoolboys; R.A.F. Cap 1946; Cardiff R.F.C. 1st XV and Athletic XV; Rydal School.*'

Thankfully, former player Gwyn Davies stepped in and secured funds to build a new clubhouse, with houses being built upon Cae'r Afon. The club owed £25,000, and luckily club treasurer Laurence Bonetto had the electricity supply inspected and insured a few weeks before the fire. The new ground, with floodlighting, was named Cae Gwyn, Gwyn's Field, in gratitude. There were major problems with the ground being full of metal, concrete slabs etc., and excavation, resurfacing and drainage were required. Gwyn set a club record of 6 tries in a game and is the club president. A very fast and strong wing, he was offered trials with Llanelli after that game, but preferred to stay with his club, and team-mates he had known since school.

CHAPTER 33 - CARDIFF SEASON 1960-61

LLOYD WILLIAMS CAPTAINS AGAINST THE SPRINGBOKS - THE DARKEST GAME IN CARDIFF'S HISTORY - LLOYD, CENYDD, ELWYN AND TONY PLAY FOR THE FIRSTS - TONY WILLIAMS HAS HIS ATHLETIC CAP - LLOYD WILLIAMS CAPTAINS WALES AGAINST FRANCE - CARDIFF ARMS PARK FLOODED

Lloyd Williams P32 T1 Pts3; **Cenydd Williams** P14 T1 Pts3 (National Service); **Elwyn Williams** P35 T5 Pts15; **Tony Williams** P8 T4 Pts12; Alun Priday P39 T5 C31 P25 Pts152 (Tongwynlais); Glyn Williams P12 T3 Pts9 (Pentyrch)

P43, W30, L8, D5. Points 498-240. Tries 114-43, Pens 25-23

Although Cenydd was finishing National Service, and Tony still playing most of his rugby for the Rags, the four Williams brothers played 92 games between them in this season, with Lloyd and Elwyn playing over 30 games each, and both were to face the Springboks. Lloyd Williams had been vice-captain in 1958-59, and was captain in 1960-61 and 1962-63, nominating the prop Kingsley Jones as his vice-captain in both seasons. Kingsley Jones and Meirion Roberts gained their first Welsh caps against South Africa in December. The centre C. H. A. (Cyril) Davies joined from Llanelli, but had a bad knee injury playing against England on 21 January and was out for weeks. The season started with a 13-match unbeaten run. Before Christmas Cardiff won 3-0 and drew 3-3 with Newport, and then defeated them 17-3 away and 16-9 at home, scoring 7 tries in the last two matches. Until February 1961, pitches were almost unplayable with one of the wettest winters on record. With the WRU using the Arms Park 6 times a season, at least 22 Firsts home games plus Rags and other fixtures, Cardiff's pitch had little chance to be match playable, but fixtures went ahead. There were doubles over Llanelli, Gloucester, Harlequins and London Welsh, and three wins on the Cornish tour.

Sunday 4 December 1960. On the previous afternoon South Africa beat Wales 3-0. During the night the Taff burst its banks and Cardiff Arms Park lay knee-deep in water

Cardiff were unbeaten when they faced South Africa upon 29 October, and I can honestly recount that the Fifth Springboks was the most unsporting team I have witnessed, in around 65 years of watching rugby and playing from the age of 13 to 40. Colin Howe recalls being swapped in his prop position, to prevent the young Kingsley Jones facing the giant and aggressive Piet du Toit in the scrums. J.B.G. Thomas reported, '*Few who watched could have foreseen the manner in which the game was to be played, the Springboks forwards played fiercely and relentlessly to maintain possession, but not long after the start, D. J. Hayward was crocked.*' Fullback Alun Priday recalled: '*What a game that was. We went into it unbeaten in 13 matches and there was a crowd of 50,000 packed into the Arms Park. After about 10 minutes I caught a highball under the old North Stand and send it back into touch, but as I turned to walk back to my position I was hit by an almighty tackle and laid out... the rest I can't remember.*' He was very badly late-tackled by left-wing Francois du Toit 'Mannetjies' Roux, and speaking to Alun recently, he has very little memory of the game, being concussed and playing from memory. I and

427

friends from Barry were about 20 yards away from that premeditated attack by 'the human torpedo' Roux – we could see it coming – there was no intention to play the ball. The tackle was shoulder-height and Priday had turned away. The referee, Gwynne Walters, ignored any sanction, as Priday lay prostrate – it was simply 'not done' to send off a tourist. The match was 12 minutes old. It is the only time I heard a Cardiff crowd booing. At the end Alun Priday told the press *'Every tooth in my head is loose and I don't know which leg to walk on.'*

With Hayward a passenger and Priday concussed, Tommy McCarthy at stand-off was illegally swung off his feet as he almost made a break. He damaged his collar bone (and dislocated his elbow) and was off the field after 35 minutes. *'After that, the game deteriorated into a brawl and Cardiff, reduced to 14 men when fly-half Tommy McCarthy went off, held on bravely for a 13-nil defeat.'* Wing forward Dai Hayward was a *one-armed passenger* after just 5 minutes, and the versatile wing-forward Elwyn Williams moved into the centre when Tommy McCarthy was helped off in the 35th minute, as Gordon Wells moved from wing into the centre, and centre Cyril Davies took over at fly-half. *'Cardiff faced a very grim task in the second half but played most gallantly and continued to attack by running with the ball when possession could be gained. Conversely, the Springboks were prone to kick and even earned slow handclaps from the crowd. But our handicap was too much for a gallant thirteen* (counting the concussed and limping Priday as an active participant) *and South Africa ran out winners by two goals - one from a penalty try awarded by Gwynne Walters the referee, and one penalty goal to nil. It was not a popular victory. The South Africans were accused of rough play, but they complained bitterly to me* (Danny Davies) *about unfair press reports which had gone to South Africa.'*

Complained bitterly? If the game had been televised, it would have put youngsters off playing rugby for life. It was utterly appalling. Cardiff is proud of never in its history being considered a dirty team. Its ethos is passing, running rugby, even at the cost of losing some games. Cenydd Williams was lucky, with National Service, to miss the game – it is memorable for being horrible. I have been lucky to meet Alun Priday, and told him I remember the foul tackle upon him just like it happened yesterday – such was the shock at the time. As mentioned, Alun cannot remember a thing about the game after being smashed in the first few minutes, not even limping.

5 minutes – future international wing forward Dai Hayward 'trampled' on and injured, a 'one-armed passenger'; **12** minutes - international fullback Alun Priday knocked into 'Kingdom Come', by a shocking late tackle, limping and concussed; **15** minutes - *'Colin Howe, the short Cardiff prop, was soon punch-drunk and a passenger'... 'injured and often standing up in the set scrums in a dazed condition'* – J.B.G. Thomas; **35**

428

minutes - Tommy McCarthy illegally swung around and carried off the pitch with badly torn muscles in his left arm, a black eye, cut nose and a damaged collarbone.

The small hooker Billy Thomas, despite a **gouged eye**, amazingly took an equal share of the ball from set scrums, and until McCarthy was 'scragged', making a break before passing to his centres, the South Africans never looked like scoring. While he was on the ground, prior to leaving the game, South Africa picked the ball up and the flanker Hopwood touched down, in their only move of the match. The Cardiff backs were caught out of position, expecting to attack, and the injured open-side wing forward Dai Hayward was missing, so the backs had no cover. Conversion, 5-0. In the second half, only Cardiff, as in the first half, tried to play the ball, with breaks by centre Cyril Davies, and co-centre Meirion Roberts being caught inches from the line after good work by wing Ray Glastonbury. With just 14 men, of whom only 11 were still capable of playing, captain Lloyd Williams was 'harshly penalised' by the inept referee at a scrum (see J.B.G. Thomas's oddly titled, '*Springbok Glory*') for a penalty in front of the posts. 8-0. The pitch was in good condition, and J.B.G. Thomas wrote: '*This should have been the turning point and the opening of floodgates for continuous Springbok attacks. Unfortunately, their rigid approach remained unchanged, and they merely banged the ball into touch ahead of their forwards or allowed them to continue rushing and charging through like a herd of mad buffaloes.*'

Cyril Davies, now playing outside half, and wing Gordon Wells made some breaks but lack of supporting players meant that moves fizzled out. It seems that the Springbok forwards were on a mission to destroy the Cardiff pack, with hardly any of their backs contributing to the game. Indeed, their manager said that they did not 'open up' the game, defending his team's tactics to the South African press, '*because the Cardiff defence was so good.*' What? A make-shift fly-half in Cyril Davies; Elwyn - a wing forward in the centre; fullback Priday limping lame and concussed; the other wing forward Dai Hayward not being able to tackle or support his backs; a hooker with a gouged eye; the prop Colin Howe described as 'punch-drunk' and missing their out-half Tommy McCarthy with a serious elbow injury, cracked collar-bone, black eye and cut nose? Surely some mistake... Toward the end of the game, little Roux, who should not have been on the pitch, punted the ball over the Cardiff line, and he and Gordon Wells dived for it. Little Roux was bumped by the more solid Wells as they both dived. The pusillanimous referee gave a penalty try, and then there was a penalty to make the score 13-0.

Dai Hayward recalls in *Taff's Acre*, '*I will never forget the shock and feeling of sheer helplessness at being rolled back yards in the first few scrums. To this day, Cardiff prop of that vintage Colin Howe tells me that he still wakes up screaming in the middle of the night at the spectre of S.P.*

Kuhn and P.S. Du Toit bearing down on him in the set scrums. On that day, the Springboks took no prisoners...' Lloyd Williams recounts that he thought Cardiff could beat them, but *'What I didn't bargain for was the absolute hammering we were about to receive from their pack of forwards. It was an incredibly physical match and I was flattened time after time. But others fared even worse.'* The life and soul of the party after matches, Colin Howe vanished that day after getting changed. There was none of the usual socialising in the Cardiff clubhouse after the game, with what was South Africa's First XV. The teams were:-

CARDIFF-Alun Priday. Gordon Wells, H. M. Roberts, Cyril Davies, Ray Glastonbury, Lloyd Williams (capt.) and T. J. McCarthy. Kingsley Jones, W. J. Thomas, C.T. Howe, D. E. J. Harris, W. G. Davies, D. J. Hayward, Howard Norris and E. Williams.

SOUTH AFRICA-L. G. Wilson. M. J. G. Antelme, J. L. Gainsford, A. I. Kirkpatrick and F. Roux; C. Nimb and R. J. Lockyear, S. P. Kuhn, G. F. Malan, P. S. du Toit, J. T. Claassen, A. S. Malan (Capt.), H. J. Pelser, G. H. Von Zyl and D. J. Hopwood.

Reg Pelling reported in the *News Chronicle*: *'**Brutal, unsporting, stampeding elephants**. All-in wrestlers. Anything but good rugby types. Those are some of the more printable terms being used in Wales to describe the Fifth Springboks. The complaint is not that they beat Cardiff, but they should use such borderline, strong-arm and ruthlessly negative means to accomplish it... This match was nothing more than a slogging brawl punctuated by late tackles, obstructions, line-out barging and heedless, needless trampling upon men.'* Wilf Wooller wrote in the *Daily Mail*, *'the Cardiff dressing room after the match looked like a battle clearance station. A continuation of the present tactics and style of play by Avril Malan's men must lead to trouble on and of the pitch, and possibly serious injury'*. Pelling commented *'I saw the **red-rimmed gouges made by football studs** when Dai Hayward was helped out of his jersey afterwards... and Alun Priday came out of the bath to tell me that every tooth in his head was loose and he didn't know which leg to stand on.'* And J.B.G. Thomas wrote that the game was *'To the Springboks the victory – **to Cardiff the glory**... a tragedy for South African rugby... Cardiff were battered into submission by the most vigorous South African pack in my memory.'* (For younger readers, 'vigorous' was always the polite adjective used in this time to mean 'dirty'.) In the *Sunday Times*, Vivian Jenkins commented, *'The H-bomb holds no terrors after this. The South Africans beat Cardiff all right, by two goals and a penalty goal to nil, and indeed more than beat them. **They mangled them, reduced them to pulp, heroically though the Welsh side resisted**; but as for pleasing the Welsh spectators, the tourists took off on as many wrong feet as the proverbial centipede.'* The tourists' manager, Ferdie Bergh, said *'I saw very few incidents in the game which justified the adverse publicity.'* The South

African press blamed Cardiff, and their captain, Avril Malan told the *Johannesburg Star*, '*The All-Blacks played cleaner football in the last Test series than this Cardiff pack.*' This quotation comes from the Stalinist brand of truth.

Cardiff always prided themselves on being a clean team, their forwards were always there to get the ball into the three-quarters. I saw the game, and 62 years later well remember the events. It was horrible to watch. The Cardiff forwards were kicked and beaten, with a 7-man pack and a passenger in the first quarter, then the vital positions of fullback and outside half were 'taken out'. And the Springbok forwards were having too much 'fun' to think about playing rugby. The 13-0 score was a miracle, a moral victory against a team that has over the decades favoured brutality to rugby – ask any Lions tourist.

Away at Oxford, on 5 November the Dark Blues were beaten 16-14 (4 tries and 2 conversions to a try and 3 penalties), when 8 Cardiff players were playing in the first Welsh trial at Swansea. On Saturday 3 December, the Springboks returned to Cardiff Arms Park to play Wales. The Cardiff pack, effectively down to 6½ men with Elwyn Williams removed to play centre and wing, and Dai Hayward one-armed, had been valiant against South Africa five weeks previously, but only Danny Harris and Kingsley Jones were chosen for Wales – a stunningly ridiculous selection by 'The Big Five'. The Cardiff centres Meirion Roberts and Cyril Davies were selected, but Lloyd Williams, who in effect played like another wing forward for Cardiff against the Springboks, was stupidly omitted. I repeat, 'stupidly'. Playing like, and built like, a wing-forward, Lloyd had played superbly, but selectors can be incredibly, let's say it again with an adjective, 'stupid'. This is not an over-exaggeration. Tony O'Connor of Aberavon was instead chosen scrumhalf, 5 foot 7 inches (1.71m) and 11 stone 9 pounds (74kg) – Lloyd could look after himself at 6 foot (1.83m), tall for those days, and 13 stone 3 pounds (84kg). In the Wales game, '*This was a really rainy season but on this particular day, there was a howling gale of wind and rain relentless in its fury which turned the ground into a veritable quagmire, making it completely impossible to play normal Rugby. But the match was played in the morass and South Africa won by a penalty goal to nil scored in the first half with a gale behind them.*' Danny Harris, Cardiff second row, was adamant that he had scored a try, but nothing was given. It seems that referees always used to bend over backwards to please touring teams. But just ask any British Lions tourists if that in the case when they toured. Ken Richards, the Bridgend fly-half just missed with a drop goal. Fifteen minutes from the end of the game, the referee asked both captains if they wished to abandon the match. Terry Davies of Llanelli wished to play on, as Wales had a gale behind them. '*The next day, Sunday 4th December the River Taff burst its banks. It overflowed the bank near the club's bowling green and in a few hours the whole area of Cardiff*

431

Arms Park was under three to four feet of water'. On the Sunday morning the pitch was under four feet of water, with damage being done to the Athletic club and many club records destroyed.

Lloyd Williams was hurt in the match with London Welsh on 17 December and was absent until the Aberavon away match. Both sides scored 2 tries, but Cardiff lost 12-6. After the South Africa loss, the battered Cardiff team lost away to Wasps, Ebbw Vale and Bristol, and at home to Swansea, the Barbarians and Bridgend. After playing Bristol in exhibition games at Bristol City's Ashton Gate under lights in 1956 and 1957, there were two attempts to play Bristol at Cardiff City's Ninian Park in 1960, both postponed because of 'atrocious weather', and then Lloyd and Elwyn Williams played in the unofficial 19-14 loss in March 1961. South Africa were unbeaten until their last match of the tour, when they lost 6-0 to the Barbarians at Cardiff, to tries by H. J. Morgan and W. G. D. Morgan. It is remembered for the heavy shoulder-on tackle (legal then) by Swansea's full-back, Haydn Mainwaring, stopping a try by captain Avril Malan. '*Malan was shouldered off the field by Brian Jones, Mainwaring and Ronnie Dawson the captain, and in the evening was made an honorary Barbarian.*' All I can say is that none of those concerned saw the Cardiff game. The 'Springbok head', awarded by the South Africans to teams who beat them, was given to Penarth Rugby Club and Penarth Golf Club, the annual Barbarians' hosts in Penarth. In season it can be seen in the rugby clubhouse and in the summer leaves for the golf club. Penarth upped their game against Cardiff in this year, with Alun Priday's penalty 5 minutes from time giving Cardiff a narrow 6-3 win. In Easter 1961, Penarth almost beat the Baa-Baas again, with Templeman having a superb game after a short interlude with Pontypool, losing 26-22. It was 18-8 to the Baa-Baas at half-time, then 26-17, but to be fair, Penarth won the second half 14-8. As with Cardiff, families play for Penarth, including five Chandlers up to 2011.

Mention was made of playing conditions in this season. On 14 March 1961, Cardiff had to play Bristol at the Cardiff City football ground, Ninian Park. Lloyd Williams captained, Cenydd partnered Meirion Roberts in the centre and Elwyn was blind-side wing forward, alongside No.8 Norris and open-side Hayward. Underneath the teams, the programme reads: '*This match was originally scheduled for November 3rd 1960, but the atrocious weather at the time caused postponement to the next date, November 22nd. On this latter date the weather was again most unkind, and a further postponement was necessary. It is hoped that tonight's match will be played under ideal conditions of weather and lighting and that our supporters will be well compensated for their previous disappointments.*' Cardiff lost 6-5 by a converted try to a try and a penalty, an extremely rare loss against Bristol. Bristol never won more than two games on the trot, and most of those very close games. Cardiff had winning sequences of 18,

14, 7, 8, 9, 16 and 4 games, with four 3-win sequences, from 1888-89 onwards, scoring 419 to 148 tries, and only losing 27 out of 142 matches. A quick diversion - regarding 1888-89, it was the only season when Cardiff played Gloucester 4 times. The scores were 0-0 (A); 3-3, a try apiece (H); 0-0 (A) and Gloucester won the final game, in Cardiff, 13-11, converting 2 of their 3 tries, while Cardiff only converted 1 of their 3. It was so, so close to an impossible 4 draws in a season. Not a lot of people know that...

Leading Cardiff try scorers were Gordon Wells 21, his 'fellow-Cathedral' Ray Glastonbury 11, Cyril Davies and Tommy McCarthy 8 each. Alun Priday totalled 152 points with 56 goals and 5 tries. Priday was one of the rare fullbacks who scored tries at this time – until JPR Williams broke the mould, many were content to patrol their own 25-yard line for most of the game. Two years later, Alun bagged 9 tries, possibly a record in top-class rugby at that time for a full back. Cyril Davies and Brian Davies earned 1st XV caps, Cyril being helped by Cenydd Williams' absence on National Service. D. J. 'Dai' Hayward played in 40 out of 43 games, followed by Alun Priday 39 and prop Colin Howe 38. Lloyd Williams captained Wales against France, and other Cardiff players featuring for Wales were Cyril Davies, Danny Harris, Kingsley Jones, Meirion Roberts, Alun Priday and the small but dynamic hooker W. J. 'Billy' Thomas. Meirion Roberts also played for the Baa-Baas against the Springboks. The Athletic XV, under Harry Morgan also had a good season: P32, W24, L6, D2, Points 395-139. Athletic XV caps were gained by George Davey, Alan Drew, the excellent flanker John Hickey, Leo Karseras, number 8 John Selway and A. D. 'Tony' Williams. Tony played 8 times for the Firsts, and three of his brothers were also playing for Cardiff this season, Elwyn, Lloyd and Cenydd. Les Hewer captained the Juniors XV, who only lost one game – Pl 23, W 20, L 1, D 2, Points 507-51. Four played for the Welsh Youth, Les Hewer, Ian Jewell, Colin Prescott and B. Harris, and again the youth team won the Cardiff & District Youth Sevens. There was still great promise coming through the ranks.

Wales came second to France, level with Scotland but with a superior points difference. Wales beat England at home, 6-3, with 2 tries by North Walian, Swansea's Dewi Bebb. Cardiff players were centres Cyril Davies and Meirion Roberts, and forwards Kingsley Jones and Danny Harris. Away to Scotland, Wales lost 3-0, with Cyril Davies dropping out. Alun Priday, Meirion Roberts and Kingsley Jones played when Ireland was beaten in Cardiff 9-0, with 2 tries from outside half Ken Richards. Belatedly, Lloyd Williams was awarded his first cap, away against France, with Meirion Roberts again keeping his place, and Billy Thomas also winning a first cap. Dewi Bebb and Alun Pask scored two tries. The game could have been won but for missed kicks. The 8-6 loss, by a conversion to France, meant that the Championship was very narrowly lost.

I spoke to Colin Howe, and he affirmed that he, Peter Nyhan and Lloyd

Williams were known as 'the Three Musketeers', and that they did everything together, something substantiated by Lloyd's widow Lynne. Colin passed away during the writing of his book, but was really enthused about being remembered. He told me, '*I played 263 1st team games over 10 seasons - 333 games total - The South Africa game was the 1960-61 season. I played most games at tight head with Geoff Beckingham and 'J D' Evans. I'm always proud to say, I had my 1st Team cap in Bleddyn's last season 1954 -55. Great player! Lloyd was captain when we played S. Africa in 61 - dirty game! My nicest memory was beating Australia in 1957-8. If you are in touch with Cenydd please give my best! Fine player! Regarding South Africa, no subs then, Elwyn moved to centre so 7 men in the pack! I am 90 in Feb but memory not too bad! It was the same front row for 6-7 seasons with JD Evans and Geoff Beckingham. I had trials for the Probables and Possibles, and have photos of Richard Burton and Sid Judd after the OZ game. I'm on the CRFC Heritage Committee. I was an apprentice at the Royal Ordnance in Llanishen when aged 17 to 18, and was Llandaff Youth hooker. I met Meirion Roberts at Mountain Ash, when J.D. Evans was 2nd row there. I was at Pontypool for 3 seasons, it was too difficult to get into Cardiff, I played 5 times against Cardiff, then joined. I hurt my shoulder the 3rd season at Ponty, but my name was getting known. The big aim was to play for Cardiff, and I was walking down St Mary Street, and met Colin Hewett, the Welsh Secondary Schools scrumhalf, substitute to Rex Willis, when I was aged 20. I asked if I could have a go and he said write in, so I wrote to the Secretary, Brice Jenkins, and got a postcard to report for Cardiff Trials.*

I was playing for the Rags by the season end, 1953 when we beat All Blacks and I played in a few 1st team games, Bleddyn's last season, lovely footballer. Bleddyn's brother Gwyn Williams was in the Somerset Police, lived in Taunton, the youngest player to play a touring team. The Williams' mother came to every match. I knew Bleddyn quite well, and played with Tamplin. My 1st tour of Cornwall was Tamplin's last tour. Post-war we fought like dogs to get on tour and play 3 games in 4 days, St. Ives, Penzance and Camborne, and the pub crawl was led by Tamplin. Great bloke to play with. "Leave it to me", to sort out any nonsense from opposing players. I wanted to go into the Royal Navy for National Service, as I had been in the Sea Cadets, and was tested A1 but downgraded because of a perforated eardrum, caused by childhood measles. I was sent to see a specialist who tested eyes instead of ears, and somehow avoided National Service. After the Oz game in 57, I was offered £2,500 to go to Wakefield rugby league. I was 25-26, and if not married I would have gone. After the Oz match the players walked arm in arm to the Royal Hotel for dinner. What a difference to the South Africa game. I had to switch to loosehead vs Du Toit, to accommodate Kingsley Jones on the tight head. Hard. Boots flying. Kuhn was dirty, stamped on my chest. Billy Thomas

434

said "we'll have the bastard", but his punch missed Hopwood and hit Pelser. Danny Harris was a hard man. I had pint though with Du Toit and saw him do his party piece. He picked up a 17 stone prop from floor and sat him on the bar of the Angel there. Jim Mills went up from the Youth to the Rags when I was captain, then went North in his second year in the Firsts' (1964-65).

Prop Pieter Stephanus du Toit, like hooker Gabriel Frederick Malan, was noted for 'vigorous play'. The latter 'figured in many small "incidents" during the tour and he received several warnings from referees.' Du Toit was 'perhaps the most controversial' Springbok. 'Du Toit played in all four Tests against the All-Blacks in 1960.amd there was a tremendous to-do in the Second Test when he a Whineray were engaged in a considerable amount of "nonsense" as opposing prop forwards. Referee Mike Slabber reported duToit's play as being unfair and outside the law, and for a South African referee to do this to the South African Board caused world-wide interest and word of du Toit's activities came to Britain ahead of him. Whether or not we prejudged him does not matter, but his scrummaging was one of the reasons for setting the Cardiff match alight.' (- from Springbok Glory). Regarding the England game, Louis Duffus of The Star, Johannesburg, reported: 'I was disillusioned. As a virtual non-partial observer I saw the only excessive roughness perpetrated by the South Africans – with three individual reprehensible tactics employed by Abe Malan, Johan Classen and Frik du Preez... I was not prepared for the grim over-robust almost vicious tackling of the Springboks,' they 'made line-outs a farce, handling redundant, and which obliterated the joy of passing and running with the ball.' Malan was 'sternly reprimanded by the referee, and South Africa won by a goal. Their fly-half, Dave Stewart, passed the ball to his 'centre Kirkpatrick perhaps three times and to his other centre, Gainsford, once'.

A Note on Roux – lest he be forgotten

A Guardian article, 'Sharp reminder of O'Driscoll inaction' by Jon Henderson was posted on 6 Nov 2005. 'History tells us that, like everything else under the sun, rugby players doing unspeakable things to each other is nothing new. Which is not to excuse the actions of Tana Umaga and Keven Mealamu, whose presence in the All Blacks party now in Britain has reignited the controversy of the spear-tackle on Lions captain Brian O'Driscoll, but to wonder why more robust efforts have not been made to eliminate them. Lions backs in particular have been targeted over the years, including Phil Bennett of Wales, captain and fly-half of the 1977 British Isles team to tour New Zealand. Clem Thomas, for years the distinguished rugby correspondent of this newspaper, wrote of the second Test on that tour: "It was evident that the All Blacks were giving Bennett

435

special attention and he was put down fiercely, with one late tackle by Eveleigh producing a huge dust-up." An even stronger echo of the O'Driscoll incident comes from the tour of South Africa in 1962 when the England fly-half Richard Sharp, a tall, elegant runner who had been capped by his country while still at Oxford University, had a cheekbone smashed in the game before the first Test. Sharp's purring runs, his effortless acceleration enabling him to exploit the smallest gaps, were central to the Lions' plans to win a series in South Africa for the first time since 1896. As it turned out, his injury ruled him out of the first two Tests and although he returned for the third and fourth Tests, he lacked the incisive edge that made him a special player.

*If Sharp's problem was a recurring image of the Springbok centre Francois 'Mannetjies' **Roux** bearing down on him, he could have been excused. Roux's **brutal, head-high tackle** on Sharp was what broke his cheekbone in the match against Northern Transvaal. Even without photographic or TV evidence to fuel the subsequent debate, it raged every bit as fiercely as the one over O'Driscoll's manhandling by Umaga and Mealamu. One English newspaper ran a cartoon with a South African tackling a Lions player in the dressing-room after the game, with a second Lion exclaiming: "I wish you'd cut out these late tackles." The tenor of most of the other comment was less droll with the small but feisty Roux, a fighter pilot with a reputation as a reckless tackler - he had executed a **dangerous tackle on Alun Priday** in Cardiff the year before - accused of deliberately putting Sharp out of action'. (For 'reckless' substitute filthy). 'Even some South Africans were said to be upset by the decision to pick Roux for the first Test.'... 'Francois Roux du Toit attained a certain grisly fame in rugby when he made a tackle or the English flyhalf, Richard Sharp, or such severity that the latter's jaw was broken... An even stronger echo of the O'Driscoll incident comes from the tour of South Africa in 1962 when the England fly-half Richard Sharp, a tall, elegant runner who had been capped by his country while still at Oxford University, had a cheekbone smashed in the game before the first Test... Brian Vaughn the manager of that 1962 British Lions team was so appalled by the viciousness of the tackle, that his first reaction was to bring his team off the field in protest. Happily, this calamitous idea was not proceeded with.'* His very late tackle upon Alun Priday, after the fullback had cleared to touch, was described as being like *'a guided missile'* and it is still vivid in my memory. However, *'Roux is regarded as a 'true legend' in South Africa, and is featured in a book as one of the twenty greatest Springboks.'* The *espn* website today states that the diminutive centre/wing was *'renowned for being a reckless tackler'*. To be honest, he made up for his lack of height by being overly and illegally aggressive.

Of the 1974 Lions Tour to South Africa, we read in Wikipedia: *'The test series was beset by violence. The management of the Lions unilaterally declared that in their opinion the Springboks dominated their opponents with physical aggression because of their famous size advantage, 'off the ball' and 'blind side' play. In the build-up games, and in McBride's previous tours of South Africa, provincial sides had tended to use their physical size, late tackling and dirty play to deliberately intimidate and* **injure Lions players prior to Test matches.** *McBride again saw this tactic of targeting certain players being used by the provinces in 1974, and decided that the '99 call' (originally the '999 call' but it was too slow to shout out) was meant to show that the Lions were a team and would not take any more of the violence being meted out to them. It was intended to show that the Lions would act as one and fight unsporting behaviour with more of the same. The idea was that the referee would be unlikely to send off all of the Lions if they all attacked. At the 'Battle of Boet Erasmus Stadium', in Port Elizabeth, one of the most violent matches in rugby history, there is famous video footage of JPR Williams running over half the length of the pitch to launch himself at Moaner van Heerden after such a call. According to McBride, the 99 call was only used once, as it sent out the message that the Lions were willing and more than able to respond in kind and protect themselves.'* Lorenzo Bruno Nero Dallaglio OBE, known as Lawrence, has often remarked upon the professional South Africa players being brutal and dirty against the 1997 touring Lions. Doddie Weir's tour was ended by *'an act of thuggery, when Marius Bosman deliberately stamped on his knee.'* *'The stamp on Doddie was a cold-blooded act totally out of context with the game,'* said a furious Ian McGeechan at the time, the Lions coach. In the first few minutes of the Second Test in 2009, known as the *'Battle of Pretoria'*, Schalk Burger put his fingers into the eyes of British Lion Luke Fitzgerald. It was one of many acts of foul play that were ignored. And there's more… and more. Indeed, *'plus ça change, plus c'est la même chose'* (- the more things change, the more they stay the same - an epigram by Jean-Baptiste Alphonse Karr in the January 1849 issue of his journal *Les Guêpes* (*The Wasps*).

CHAPTER 34 - CARDIFF SEASON 1961 – 1962

LLOYD CAPTAINS CARDIFF, AND WALES TWICE – TONY WILLIAMS HAS HIS FIRST XV CAP - FOUR WILLIAMS BROTHERS PLAY TOGETHER FOUR TIMES FOR CARDIFF'S FIRST XV

P42, W27, L10, D5. Points 390 - 197. Tries 81-29, Pens 21-23

Lloyd Williams P34 T3 Pts9; **Cenydd Williams** P20 T4 Pts12; **Elwyn Williams** P28 T5 Pts15; **Tony Williams** P30 T1 Pts3; Alun Priday P38, T2, C38, P18 Pts136 (Tongwynlais); Glyn Williams P33 T10 Pts30 (Pentyrch)

Lloyd Williams and Kingsley Jones were captain and vice-captain for a second successive season. Two splendid international forwards left with J. D. (John) Evans retiring and Danny Harris turning professional. The international wing Gordon Wells also retired after 17 games, and the team lacked a cutting edge. All four youngest Williams brothers; Tony, Cenydd, Elwyn and Lloyd played together four times in Cardiff First XV matches. Three of the brothers played together, probably over twenty times. On the *rugby relics* website I discovered a Neath-Cardiff programme from the Rhys Stephens collection, which gave the Cardiff team in the away loss 6-0, to 2 penalties by Grahame Hodgson. At Cardiff, the home team had won 14-0 on 9 September, scoring 3 tries. In the loss on 23 December 1961, the Cardiff team was fullback Alun Priday; Tony Williams at right centre had Gwyn Williams on his wing; Cenydd Williams was inside left wing Gordon Wells; half-backs were Geoff Davies outside Lloyd Williams; the front row was altered in the programme, as Kingsley Jones was not available, to Howard Norris, Billy Thomas and Colin Howe; second row Keith Rowlands and Malcolm Gough; back row Elwyn Williams, John Selway and Dai Hayward. Missing were, apart from Kingsley Jones: international backs Meirion Roberts and Ray Glastonbury; fly-half Tommy McCarthy and Number 8 Cliff Howe. Neath were always hard opponents, especially at the Gnoll. In the years from 1878-79 to 1974-75, in 156 fixtures, Cardiff won 92, lost 47 and drew 17. Cardiff scored 331 tries to 171, with 46 penalties apiece.

A. D. 'Tony' Williams gained his First Team cap, along with second row Keith Rowlands from Llanelli, who soon was to play for Wales, and was chosen for the Lions tour to South Africa with Kingsley Jones. Because of the state of the pitch, and three Christmas matches cancelled owing to frost, it was a low scoring season. Davies points out that '*the W.R.U.'s joint usage of the Cardiff Arms Park, mainly in the second half of seasons, made it impossible for the Cardiff club to arrange a regular home and away fixture list like that of other Rugby clubs; the playing condition of the ground was far from perfect.*' This was a horrible year for weather, with nearby Penarth missing out two months of fixtures and playing their first match of 1962 on 2 March.

In January, fixtures were resumed with Bath, again on the date of the Wales-England game, and Cardiff won away 8-0. Lloyd Williams captained Wales, and his team-mates Malcolm Collins and Kingsley Jones also played. Bath reported: '*Bath were soon 5 points in arrears, when a long touch throw found Davies at outside half, who had the pace to cut*

438

through Bath's midfield defence, exchange passes with Morgan and touch down under the posts. Priday converted. Cardiff scrum half Lloyd Williams was prominent, when initiating slick Cardiff attacks, which Bath were hard pressed to repel. Several Cardiff players combined in a forward rush, and Bath offended when halting the incursion. Priday put the visitors further ahead with a penalty. In direct contrast to Cardiff's innovative, high-speed play, Bath were utterly orthodox in their build up. Nevertheless, it was greatly to their credit, that they continued to hold such a talented side. Davies continued to be the main "thorn in Bath's side" wriggling through at will. In every aspect of back play, Cardiff were yards faster and much cleverer than the home side, and it seemed only a matter of time before further tries came... Cardiff's close marking knocked Bath completely out of their stride. However, the Bath pack refused to yield, and battled it out and kept the score within bounds to the final relieving whistle.'

This was a mixed season, but there were two wins and two draws against Newport, all close games 9-3, 3-3, 5-0 and 6-6. Brilliant rugby was displayed in the Easter matches with Cardiff beating the Barbarians (10-0) and Harlequins (13-3). The double over Llanelli featured a 5-try, 19-0 away win, but a hard-fought 8-5 home win.

John Huw Williams, Cardiff wing 73 times from 1964-65 to 1968-69, loaned me his programme of the Swansea-Cardiff game of 17 March 1962. The programme reads '*Our old friends and rivals from Cardiff are slowly but surely recapturing some of their past glory and they come to St. Helen's this afternoon with a very impressive playing record.*' As a student, John was allowed to appear for other clubs, and in this instance, he kept the programme because Swansea won at home 9-0, John Huw Williams scoring the only try of the game against his own club, after Swansea drew 0-0 at Cardiff. In the programme John has crossed out Dewi Bebb's name, and written in his own on the left wing as Swansea's number 5. For Cardiff, captain Lloyd Williams was 7 at scrumhalf and Elwyn Williams numbered 15, blind-side wing forward. Alun Priday, fullback was number 1, as numbering was the reverse of today. A former international, Harry Morgan, captain of the 'Rags' partnered Lloyd. There is an ad in the programme for Glamtax, a '*uniformed chaffeurs*' service, not quite the equivalent of today's stretch limo's. We may see Cardiff's record against Swansea for the period of this book, during which Swansea never achieved a 'double'. In 1936-37 there were 4 games, all won by Cardiff, who went on to do the double in 1945-46, 1947-48, 1950-51, 1951-52, 1954-55, 1957-58, 1962-63, 1963-63, 1969-70, 1973-74 (a treble) and 1974-75. 10 doubles, a treble and a quadruple to none. And this against one of the best four clubs in Wales. Swansea have always been stern opposition, as evidenced by the playing record from 1876-77 to 1974-75. In 227 games, Cardiff won 115, lost 85 and drew 27, points for 1,649 and against 1,442. Swansea scored more penalties, 74-66, more dropped goals

39-31 and more goals from a mark 5-1. However, the try count was Cardiff 342 – 275, a total in Cardiff's favour, as with all other teams they played throughout their history.

Away at Gloucester, the home team scored two penalties to win 6-0. On April 12 there was an away thumping at Pontypool 16-3, although Cardiff were only outscored 2-1 on tries. A third successive away game was lost at Ebbw Vale, although a try apiece, 6-3. In T.S. Eliot's words, April was '*the cruellest month*', with a fixture pile-up because of the bad winter. Top try scorers were Pentyrch's Glyn Williams and Gordon Wells with 10 each, Meirion Roberts and Dai Hayward 6 each, and Ray Glastonbury and Les Hewer with 5 apiece. Alun Priday again scored more than a third of Cardiff's points with 56 goals and 2 tries. In 42 matches, Malcolm Gough and Alun Priday played 41 and 39 times respectively.

Harry Perrott Morgan, a Cambridge Blue, had joined aged 28 from Newport, and had won 3 Welsh caps, but only played 53 times in 5 seasons for Cardiff from 1958-59 to 1962-63. He captained the Rags in 1960-61 and 1961-62, and in the latter season the record was Pl. 41 W. 27 L.6 D.8 Pts. 511-241. Two 'Rags' matches that had to be postponed were both played away on 30 April, Maesteg Celtic being beaten 22-3 in the morning and Cilfynydd 24-11 in the afternoon. The team must have been exhausted. The former Cardiff High School Old Boys full back Alan Drew top scored with 137 points from 49 goals and 4 tries. Leading try scorers were Steve Hughes 19 and Les Hewer 10. Harry Morgan played 10 games for the Firsts, and 30 times for the Rags, and Alan Drew played 4 times for the Firsts and 26 for the Rags.

Colin Prescott captained the Youth XV – Pl.22, W.15, L.4, D.6. Pts. 307-60. In this impressive season the captain Gareth Jones, Islwyn Matthews and Jim Mills gained Welsh Youth international caps. 'Big Jim' Mills gained a certain notoriety in his Rugby League career when he left Cardiff Firsts in 1965, going on to play 17 times for Wales and 6 times for Great Britain. He played for 15 years, and in 367 appearances the prop scored 61 tries. Amazingly, in his last 3 years, returning to Widnes, he touched down 21 times in 93 games, retiring aged 36. Big Jim was 6ft 4in and 18 stone in his playing days, known as an 'enforcer' and was sent off around 20 times. Ben James, in *walesonline*, 11 January 2021 interviewed Jim: '*He initially started out as a football goalkeeper in school, before a teacher with some solid rugby union stock spotted some untapped potential in the young Mills. Sid Judd, the former Wales flanker, was the first of many who'd change the course of Mills' journey with his intervention. Mills recalled "Sid scored a try for Cardiff against the All Blacks in midweek, before scoring against them for Wales on the weekend. He played the All Blacks twice in a week, scored both times and won both matches.* One day he said 'Come here, Millsy. You come and play rugby. You're too big for soccer!'" From there, Mills was set for a life in rugby. Judd promised the* *young Mills a trial for Cardiff schoolboys, if he'd pop to the fish and chip shop to get him such lunch. "Well, I believed him and from then on, I was asking him every week where my trial was! Eventually he got me one and from there, I was in the Cardiff schoolboys."* *Actually, Cardiff beat NZ 8-3 on 21 November 1953, and Wales won 13-8 on 19 December.

Mills went on to play for the Cardiff first-team nineteen times, with a future in union looking on the cards, until a chance meeting on Westgate Street set him on the path north. "There was a fella stood across the road on Westgate Street," recalls Mills. "I found out later it was Eddie Davies, a scout at Halifax. Colin Dixon had recommended me as he'd played in the youth with me, before going to Halifax. This Eddie Davies came across to me and asked if I would be interested in playing rugby league. I said I might do, and he said that's all he wanted to know. Then he just walked away. So I carried on as usual and went down through the gates to the Arms Park as I would normally do, thinking nothing of it. I think we were playing Coventry that day. The next thing I know, there's all these directors down from Halifax offering me £4,000."

Mills admits he wishes he'd stayed in union a little longer, to push for a Wales cap and see how far he could have gone in the sport. However, the money was too good to turn down for a 19-year-old working on a farm and so north he went. The new code took some getting used to. Not yet 20, Mills started out a little homesick before eventually getting to grips with his new sport. But eventually, he made his mark - with spells at Halifax, Salford and Bradford seeing him picked for the famous Ashes-winning Great Britain side of 1970...' Mills played in Australia for two years, but returned home, *'to the most successful part of his career at Widnes. There, he won virtually every honour going as Widnes found cup success throughout the decade. The pinnacle was the Challenge Cup victory in 1975 - a 14-7 win over "red-hot favourites" Warrington. The two try-scorers that day - Mills and John Bevan - were two men who'd been on the same side years ago for Cardiff youth. It's a good indication of the talent Welsh rugby league boasted at the time - as was their performance in the 1975 World Cup. They defeated England in a match later dubbed the 'Battle of Brisbane' - a loss that would ultimately cost England the title. "They thought they were going to hammer us," he recalls. "Their coach, Alex Murphy, came on the TV the night before and said there wasn't a Welsh player who would get in the England side. Well, that was the end of them!"*

In the Five Nations Lloyd Williams captained Wales in the away 0-0 draw with England, and Kingsley Jones also played. However, Wales lost 8-3 at home to Scotland with Lloyd again captaining and Meirion Roberts returning to the team. Lloyd was dropped, and it was his thirteenth and last game for Wales (1957-1962), and his third as captain, all in this 1961-62 season. Wales then beat the Championship winners France 3-0 in Cardiff

441

with Meirion Roberts and Kingsley Jones playing and Keith Rowlands gaining his first cap. Wales drew 3-3 in Ireland, with Keith Rowlands the only Cardiff player. With just one loss, Wales finished equal 3rd.

FOUR WILLIAMS BROTHERS PLAY FOR CARDIFF FIRST XV

In this season, Neath were beaten with 3 tries, 14-0 at home, but Cardiff lost to 2 penalties from international fullback Graham Hodgson, 6-0 away on a frozen pitch on 23 December 1962. Cenydd was to leave next season, but he played with his three brothers in the away defeat. Wearing 1, Alun Priday was fullback, with Gwyn Williams and Gordon Wells on the left and right wings; Cenydd and Tony Williams were left and right centres; outside half was Geoff Davies and scrumhalf Lloyd Williams; there was a great front row of Howard Norris, Billy Thomas and Colin Howe; the second row was Keith Rowlands and Malcolm Gough; and the back row Dai Hayward, John Selway and Elwyn Williams. It was not a full-strength Cardiff side. Cenydd still remembers the loss, as an injured player meant that Cardiff were down to 14 men for most of the game. This caused the versatile Elwyn to move from wing forward to play in the backs, which would have been a nightmare for any commentator. Indeed, if Lloyd had passed to Gwyn Williams, and it was transferred along the re-adjusted threequarters of Elwyn, Tony and Cenydd, there would have been a sequence of play between five Williams.

Clem Thomas was a Swansea flanker, who played 26 times for Wales from 1946 to 1959, and was a British Lion in 1955 in South Africa. As the tour started, he was taken ill and had an emergency appendectomy, but recovered in time to play the last two Tests. Tony O'Reilly, writing after Thomas's death, felt that if Thomas had been available for all four games the Lions might have won the series rather than drawing it 2–2. He was some player, and became an eminent rugby writer upon retirement. In a *Sunday Observer* (now *The Observer*) article, Clem Thomas wrote a long article, probably late January 1962, just before the Scotland game, under the headline: '*Triumph of Mr. Trigg* – *Welsh rugby folklore is immensely richer for the Williams family of Taff's Well. It has contributed to the Cardiff Rugby Club eight brothers, seven of whom have played for the Cardiff first XV, and one for the second XV, affectionately called "The Rags". Their representation in this famous club reached its climax a week ago when no fewer than four brothers played together against Newport: Cenydd and Tony in the centre, Lloyd at scrumhalf and Elwyn at wing-forward.*

Their connection with the club was first established by their father's brother, Philip Williams. Then, in turn, followed Gwyn, the eldest brother, who, as wing forward and centre, played for Cardiff when only 16 and played against New Zealand in 1935 at the age of 17. At 19 he turned *professional for Wigan and became a Rugby League international. Brinley was next to play for Cardiff – at centre and wing. His was a short-lived first-class career because of the war. Brinley, at the age of 40, still plays for Taff's Well where he is a member of the committee. After Brinley came the most famous of all the brothers – Bleddyn. He is one of the all-time greats of Welsh Rugby. Twenty-two Welsh caps, with countless others missed through injury and the war, vice-captain of the British Lions in Australasia in 1950, and, to my mind, **the greatest of the post-war backs in the British Isles**.*

*A brilliant individualist with the famous side-step, his greatness, nevertheless, lay in his vast knowledge of the game and his ability to see all games in perspective. Not only was he the best three-quarter I ever played with or against, but he was also the **best captain** I played under.* (Bleddyn won all five games as captain of Wales – I blame 'the Big Five' as usual, for his not being captain in his other seventeen internationals. He missed another 15 internationals because of injury, otherwise his appearance record would be 37). *It was Bleddyn's captaincy which led Cardiff to the famous win over the All-Blacks in 1953 and, later in the same season, led Wales to victory against the same side. The turning point of the latter game came 15 minutes from time when Wales were losing by eight points to five, and for 20 minutes the All-Blacks had laid siege to the Welsh line. The Welsh forwards and half-backs were not able to get the ball away.*

During a stoppage in play Bleddyn walked up to us forwards, begged for one quick heel, and instructed Willis to leave out the heavily marked Cliff Morgan, and push the ball straight out to himself in the centre. At the next scrum the ball was won and pushed out to Bleddyn, a side-step beat the close-marking All-Blacks and a long, left-foot kick found touch near the half-way. At last, the siege was raised. In the next six minutes a penalty goal by Rowlands and Ken Jones's try gave us a narrow, and somewhat fortunate, win by 11 points to 8. (Clem Thomas graciously omits the fact that it was his cross-field kick that gave Jones the winning try).

The remaining five brothers are still contributing to the family's rugby history. Lloyd, the present Cardiff captain, with 12 Welsh caps, is one of the most powerful scrum-halves in the game and regarded as the best captain in Wales at present. Cenydd, Elwyn and Tony, 23, 21 and 20 respectively, have yet to play their best rugby. (The four brothers often played in the same team). *Vaughan is the only one of the brothers not to have played for the first team. He is centre for the second.* (The Cardiff Athletic brother, Vaughan, had played usually as centre from the age of 15 for Taff's Well, then during two years National Service, played outside-half for the British Army of the Rhine and the Guards Brigade, but centre for London Welsh firsts and Pontypridd, both first-class clubs. He gained his cap for the 'Rags', but competition to pay for the firsts was so intense that he preferred getting regular games outside the club).

Bleddyn, with his customary modesty, maintains that the best footballer in the family was Gwyn, the eldest. Bleddyn says that it was Gwyn who pushed the rest of them into rugby history. When Gwyn first went to Taff's Well school – to be followed by the rest of the family – the school had no Rugby team, but the headmaster Walter Trigg, recognising that in Gwyn he had an outstanding athlete and footballer, started a Rugby team in order to realise the potential of this remarkable boy. Little could Mr. Trigg have imagined what he was starting.'

As mentioned, in some passages of play, a commentator would have had to say '*and it's Williams to Williams, back to Williams, now Williams and out to Williams'* etc. when the four boys played together. In the 98 years that the book covers, Cardiff's First XV has featured the following surnames: 82 Jones; 75 Davies; 64 Williams; 62 Thomas; 48 Evans; 38 Morgan; 24 Lewis; 18 Rees; 17 James, Jenkins; 12 Roberts; 10 Morris, Phillips; 9 Hughes, Griffiths, Smith; 8 Hill; 7 Biggs, Edwards, Harding, Llewellyn, Turnbull; 6 Bowen, Cornish, Hopkins, Nicholls, Owen, Richards.

CHAPTER 35 - CARDIFF SEASON 1962 – 1963

SOME NARROW DEFEATS MAKE FOR AN AVERAGE YEAR – ELWYN PLAYS 39 TIMES – THE LAST SEASON THE FOUR BROTHERS APPEAR - CENYDD WILLIAMS GOES NORTH, A RECORD FEE FOR A NON-INTERNATIONAL – HIS CAREER PROFILE

P43, W26, L12, D5. Points 467-227 Tries 100-39 Pens 23-17

Lloyd Williams P34 T4 Pts12; **Elwyn** Williams P20 T5 Pts5; **Tony** Williams P20, T5 Pts15; **Alun** Priday P41 T9 Con 43 P21 Pts176; Glyn Williams P22 T11 Pts33 (Pentyrch); **Cenydd** Williams – his last season P38 T3 Pts9 - Total P115, W71, D17, L27, T19 = 59 points

A downturn in Welsh and Cardiff fortunes occurred around this time, although a year later Cardiff managed to come within a point of beating the All Blacks again in 1963, scoring the **only try** of the game. However, the slump began to end in 1964, when Wales shared the Five Nations title with Scotland, after which Wales won the Triple Crown and the title in 1965, followed by another championship in 1966, although the Grand Slam still eluded them. These successes helped Cardiff centre Ken Jones and prop Howard Norris win places on the Lions tour to New Zealand. Later that year (1966) Cardiff beat Australia 14–8 with a 'full house' of a goal, try, drop goal and penalty to a try and penalty, although Wales were not able to repeat the feat a month later, losing 14–11, 2 tries apiece).

1962-63 Tony is on left of middle row, Elwyn and Lloyd on far right

10 Welsh players were in the Lions party of 33, touring South Africa, in May-August 1962. Of the 7 Welsh forwards, only Keith Rowlands and Kingsley Jones were from Cardiff. The Welsh backs were Dewi Bebb of Swansea, Ken Jones of Llanelli (later Cardiff) and Aberavon scrumhalf Tony O'Connor. The 5ft 7inch O'Connor was wrongly picked instead of Lloyd Williams for Wales against South Africa in December 1960. He was chosen in the next 2 games, against England and Scotland, then dropped for captain Onllwyn Brace, Lloyd Williams, Lloyd Williams, Lloyd Williams, before O'Connor played against France in March 1962. Six days later he was chosen for the Lions, although only playing in one of Wales last five games. Tony O'Connor played his last international in Wales's next game against Ireland, making just 5 appearances for Wales, and did not play in the Lions Tests. He was succeeded by Pontypool's Clive 'Top Cat' Rowlands, who played 10 games in succession as captain of Wales. Allan Lewis of Abertillery than had a game before another 4 by Rowlands, then 5 by Allan Lewis, followed by Cardiff's Billy Hullin wining a cap. After another game by Allan Lewis, a certain young gentleman named Gareth Edwards, the Cardiff scrumhalf, went on to create all kinds of records. It was a gruelling Lions schedule, with the first game against

Rhodesia at Salisbury (now Harare) on 26 March, then a game in South Africa on 31 May. There were 8 games across South Africa in June, including a 3-3 Test. July saw another 8 games with a 3-0 Test loss. There were 7 games in August with 2 tests, losing 8-3 and 34-14. The tour ended against East Africa at Nairobi on 28 August – 25 games in 105 days, at different altitudes and in sweltering temperatures. Because of the tour, forwards Keith Rowlands and Kingsley Jones played in only 17 and 10 matches respectively for Cardiff. More details on this tour are given in the section on Cenydd Williams later in this chapter.

Former Newbridge Grammar schoolboy David John Hayward (1934-2003) was captain, and the prop (Charles) Howard Norris his vice-captain, both forwards. It was a just reward for the excellent, hard-working Hayward, who had played for Wales under-15s, Wales Secondary Schools, Newbridge and Loughborough College. 'Dai' Hayward had joined Cardiff in 1957-58, and usually was pack leader in his 325 games for the Firsts. Dai represented Wales 6 times, and toured South Africa with Wales. He first represented Wales in 1949, in a 41-8 win over England under-15s at Bristol, followed by a 41-0 win over South of Scotland at Cardiff. One has no idea why 'Dai' is not in Cardiff RFC's 'Hall of Fame' – I watched him play in tandem with Elwyn Williams many times, forming to my mind the best back row in Welsh rugby at the time with Number 8 Cliff Howe.

His obituary in *The Independent* reads in part: '*Dai Hayward was one of the most combative flank forwards in rugby of his era. The former Cardiff and Wales back-row man was renowned as a destroyer of opposing back divisions in the late Fifties and Sixties.*' It neglects his creativity in a running, passing back row, scoring 50 tries. Dai spent almost 40 years with Cardiff as a player, committeeman, and club chairman in 1985-86. His obituary tells us: '*despite his great reputation as a destroyer, there had been no senior cap; he may have suffered from his reputation and partly through his game against the 1960 Springboks, recognised as one of the dirtiest matches of all time. Cardiff lost 13-0 and Hayward reputedly threw the opening punch, although the "Boks" threw a good deal more. Hayward was trampled on and had one arm hanging loosely and totally unusable from the first quarter.*' To be fair, that '*first punch*' was **only reported in the South African press** and totally missed by all the Cardiff players and 40,000 spectators. 'Fake news' is not a new occurrence. South African newspaper reports, written by men who had never attended the game, stated that '*Cardiff started it*'. It is simply untrue – Cardiff's forwards are there to feed their backs. Hayward was never a dirty player, and who in their right mind would start a fight with a monstrous set of forwards? The reputation of South African packs – and backs – is lamentable. A highly intelligent man, Dai suffered dementia in his 60s, Lloyd and Tony Williams died early from the same horrible disease, and Elwyn later suffered from it.

446

The centre and wing Cyril Evans joined from Llanelli, but as in the previous season, it was a low-scoring team. On 12 September 1962, Cenydd played outside half against Penarth, with Lloyd scrum half, in an 8-3 win, Cardiff scoring a try. On 6 October 1962, at home Cardiff scored two tries, one converted, to beat Newport 8-0. Cenydd was left centre, Lloyd scrum half and Elwyn open side wing forward, swapping with captain Dai Hayward. This may well have been a ploy to contain Newport fly-half, the brilliant David Watkins. The same formation was used in a narrow win against Bective Rangers that month, in a run of 13 unbeaten games against the Irish side, and again against Ebbw Vale on 15 December in horrible conditions at home, in a win by two penalties, 6-0. On 26 December, Cenydd, Lloyd and Elwyn were yet again in action together against Wasps, scoring 5 tries to 1 in a 17-5 victory. In a long run of all three of these Williams brothers playing for the Firsts, in February 1963 there was a home draw with Aberavon, 6-6, with Cardiff only scoring penalties to Aberavon's tries. On 16 March at home against Swansea, Hayward and Elwyn again swapped positions, and Tony Williams came in for Cenydd, in a 17-9 home win, Cardiff scoring 4 tries to 1. Cardiff had won away in December 9-8, 2-1 on tries.

There were many cancellations owing to frost and snow in an 'Arctic winter'. Cardiff Athletic had 10 successive cancellations from 26 December to 2 March, and the Firsts XV did not play a match in January. Straw protected the pitch and I seem to remember to be one of the boys helping to clear the pitch for the England international – it was certainly a game around this time, when we had really bad winters. Despite scoring twice as many points as opponents, with 100 tries being scored, Cardiff had a middling season for results, losing 12 games of 43, albeit some narrowly. (3-0 to a penalty at Bridgend; scoring 4 tries to 3 at Bristol but only converting one, losing15-14; 6-3 at Gloucester, 1 try to 2; at Neath 6-5; and home to Newport 6-5, a try apiece). Easter was poor, with defeats by the Barbarians, Harlequins and Bridgend. However, Bristol were beaten at home by 5 converted tries to a try 25-3, with the away match cancelled because of frost; London Welsh were beaten at home by 6 tries, 29-0 and away by 4-1 on tries, 14-8; 6 tries to 2 were scored in the Swansea games 9-8 (A) and 17-9 (H); and 7 tries to 1 against Wasps 8-0 (A) and 17-5 (H). (That last score-line may seem strange, but 8-0 was a goal and a try, and 17-5 was a goal and 4 tries against a goal. In modern scoring, instead of a total points score of 25-5, we would have 39-7).

Top try scorers were centre Meirion Roberts with 12, Pentyrch's wing Glyn Williams 11; Alun Priday, Dai Hayward and Steve Hughes 9, and Cyril Evans 8. Penryn were beaten on tour 39-0, with 8 tries, Dai Hayward scoring 3. In that game on 23 April 1963, full back Alun Priday beat Wilfred Wooller's record of 163 points set in 1938-39. Priday ended the season with 176points made up of 9 tries, 43 of which were converted, and

21 penalty goals. 9 tries in a season was a splendid return in these days of defensive full backs. In all, Alun scored 33 tries. His value to the club is shown in the 7 times Alun scored more than a hundred points in a season, compared to the team's total – 1962-63 176:467 (38%); 1956-57 158:627 (25%); 1960-61 152:498 (30%); 1961-62 136:390 (35%); 1958-59 134:382 (35%); 1963-64 134:568 (24%); and 1957-58 128:483 (27%). In 1954-55 playing for the Rags, he again scored more than 100 points, including 5 tries, 137:521 (26%). Strangely, in 5 seasons of these seasons he scored 136, 134, 134, 128 and 126 points, the last for the Athletic. That is some 'grouping'. Alun played for the RAF in National Service, Wales twice, and the Barbarians. His value to Cardiff Firsts between 1952-53 and 1965-66 is shown by his number of appearances in these years: 2, 12 (his National Service years), 20, 42, 36, 36, 40, 36, 36, 39, 39, 38, 41, 34, 22, 7. His was an immaculate presence at fullback, and 9 tries in a season from a fullback was a real rarity at top level.

First team caps were awarded to centre Cyril Evans, No.8 Cliff Howe, wing Steve Hughes and prop John Price, previously captain of Penarth. All were brilliant additions to the club. Alun Priday played in 41 of 43 matches, followed by the indefatigable Elwyn Williams and prop Howard Norris with 39, and centre Meirion Roberts 37. Dai Hayward and Howard Norris* won their first Welsh caps, playing alongside the irreplaceable pair of Kingsley Jones and Keith Rowlands. The Cardiff chairman's report for the season reads: '*So ended a strange season - a season badly affected by Arctic conditions for nearly three months, a season when Cardiff, inspired by precept and example by the skipper Dai Hayward, played open attacking football, trying always to make the games attractive for the spectators and enjoyable for the players. It is difficult to explain the falling off in form at certain periods.*'

The Athletic XV were captained by the prop Colin Howe, dropping down to help the team, and he played the most games, 29 of 32, plus 5 for the Firsts when called upon. Their season was worse affected than the Firsts by the weather, playing 11 games fewer. Pl 32, W 19 L10 D 3. Pts 342-193. Top scorer was full-back Alan Drew with 78 points from 4 tries and 29 goals. Cardiff Youth could only play 16 games, winning 12 with 4 drawn, in an unbeaten season scoring a very, **very impressive points total of 303-36**. Captain Islwyn Matthews, David Ivens, Geoff Jones and Jim Mills received Welsh Youth international caps, and Jim Mills began playing for the Athletic XV. Danny Davies records a bombshell statement, with the W.R.U. flexing its muscles - '*In May 1963 the W.R.U. informed the club that the limitation of the number of matches on the Cardiff Arms Park was not satisfactory, and that eighty acres of land near Bridgend were available for a national ground. A contract had been signed with the Dunraven Estate. The subject became one of national interest, and particularly to the city of Cardiff, where international matches had been* *played since 1884. The management committee and all relevant bodies including our city council made it clear that every endeavour would be made to retain the Welsh international matches in Cardiff.'*

*A Note on Howard Norris

On the Cardiff Rugby Hall of Fame website, we read: '*Charles Howard Norris was prepared to make any sacrifice to play for Cardiff. He would even risk his job in the days when the top players worked by night or day Monday to Friday, fitted in a couple of training sessions and then played twice a week on Wednesday and Saturday afternoons. "When I left St Luke's College, Exeter I started teaching in Cadoxton and was quite happy there until one fateful day I asked if I could leave at three o'clock to join up with the Cardiff team going to London by train for a floodlit match with the Harlequins. I didn't think there would be a problem because I wasn't teaching a class for the last lesson that day – so I went. Imagine my surprise when I got back to find I had been suspended for four weeks and the full weight of the redoubtable Alderman Llewellyn Heycock, Chairman of the Glamorgan Education Committee, was on my case!" To cut a long story short, Cadoxton's loss was Llanharan and then Llanharri's gain. For Howard Norris was a gifted teacher, admired by pupils and colleagues, and a long and professional career blossomed. As did his career and reputation with Cardiff Rugby Club as he achieved his life's ambition.*

"*Let's make no bones about it*" said Howard, "*Cardiff was the only club for me. I was brought up in the Rhondda and Wells and Kingsley Jones were near neighbours. Gordon was a star in the Porth County School rugby team when I was still in my first year there, but these fellows were my heroes as well as my friends and gave me a goal to aim for.*" And nothing would deter the young Howard Norris. After winning Welsh Secondary Schools caps in the second row alongside Roddy Evans, and with the future Cardiff club-mates Meirion Roberts and Cyril Davies in the centre, Howard went to St Luke's and, true to form, turned down a lucrative job offer in Exeter before returning to South Wales. "*I had played in the Club trials in August 1953, again with Roddy Evans, and got a game with the rags at Usk before going to college, and then I went into the RAF, but I always knew that one day I would try again to get into the team on a regular basis,*" admitted Howard. That day finally came in September 1958 and Howard recalled how he heard of his first selection. "*The Club captain that year was CD Williams, and he went out of his way to see me and tell me personally that I was picked for Cardiff – what a wonderful thing to do.*"

The first game was against Penarth and Howard remembered the pack that played that day: "*J D Evans, Billy Thomas and Colin Howe in the front row, Roddy (almost inevitably!) and Peter Goodfellow in the second*

*row, and me packing down with John Nelson and CD in the back row –
what a start for me – I was so proud!" Howard Norris clearly made a big
impression because he then played 34 of the remaining 37 games that
season, an exceptional record for a Club debutant. It was a case of
beginning as he meant to continue, as for the next 12 years he rarely
played less the 30 Club games a season; indeed, he thought nothing of
playing in 44 of the 49 official games in 1964-65, an incredible
achievement for someone who was by then a prop forward. "Yes," he said,
"it was a long career, but a happy one. I actually played in all three rows
of the scrum before gaining my caps and a Lions tour as a prop and I also
had, I think, the unique distinction of playing for Cardiff against all four
major touring teams, including the Springboks twice." Such was Howard's
commitment to the Club, that he said his Welsh and Lions caps pale into
insignificance, alongside the honour of captaining Cardiff and breaking
the career appearance record at the time.*

*"Of course, it was wonderful to play for Wales, and of course it was a
great experience to tour with the Lions in 1966 and be good enough to play
three Tests against the All Blacks. I was also tremendously proud to lead
the Barbarians pack against the unbeaten All Blacks at Twickenham in
1967 and we only lost in injury time. There were five Cardiff players –
Gareth Edwards, Gerald Davies, Keri Jones, Barry John and myself – in
the Baa Baa's team that day and we all wore our Club socks. And yet to be
part of the Cardiff set-up for so long, with successive committees made up
of ex-players for whom maintaining the Club's reputation and standards
was paramount and the most important thing to me." Howard Norris was a
caring and generous man, one who would break off from talking about his
own career to extol the virtues of opponents as much as team-mates.
Mention Newport and a broad smile would come over his face. "I have a
tremendous affinity with the Black and Ambers. Like us they were inspired
by individuals as much as their history. Dai Watkins – a great and lovely
man when he was tormenting us, especially Dai Hayward, on the field of
play; Des Greenslade was the best tight-head I ever propped against; and
Bryn Meredith, what can you say about him – what a hooker! But they
almost ruined my life in 1969 when they won the first three games and I
was captain. I pleaded with the boys before the fourth match, 'Please don't
let me down... not me... Not the first Cardiff captain to lose to those Black
& Ambers b—s four times", and they didn't let me down – a glorious 9 all
draw." For his part, Howard Norris never let anyone down as he carried
the Cardiff flag to the four corners of club rugby in these islands. It was no
surprise when he devoted countless hours to committee work after his
retirement. And it was absolutely no surprise to anyone when he was a
hugely popular choice for the first Hall of Fame.'* Howard Norris played
413 games in 14 seasons for Cardiff and was captain in 1967-68 and 1968-
69. He has the record number of appearances for Cardiff, followed by Alun

Priday and Elwyn Williams. Howard had 3 Lions Test caps on the Australasia Tour 0f 1966, but only 2 Wales caps, in 1963 and 1966. Surely some mistake…

CENYDD OWEN WILLIAMS b. 20 July 1938
Cardiff Juniors (now Youth)
Taff's Well
Cardiff Athletic cap 1956-57, played for First XV in that year
Cardiff First XV Centre, Outside Half 1956-57 to 1962-63
First XV cap 1957-58, 115 appearances, 20 tries
National Service 1959-1962
RAF XV, **Combined Services XV**, tour of Rhodesia and Kenya 1962
Barbarians Centre vs Cardiff and Leicester
St. Helens Rugby League 1963-69 Centre, Full Back, Wing 108 Appearances plus 4 as sub, 34 tries, 102 points (joined aged 24)

Cenydd spells his name Cennydd, but all reports and programmes name him as Cenydd, so I have kept that spelling to avoid confusion. He is named after the sixth century saint Cennydd/Cenydd, who is remembered at Senghennydd, over the hills north-east of Treforest and also at Llangennith/Llangennydd in the Gower, where his feast day was celebrated on 5 July, with the effigy of a bird on a pole. Wales has around 950 saints dating from the fifth to seventh centuries, while Anglo-Saxon England was

still pagan. Cardiff RFC's website records: '*Cenydd Williams was one of eight brothers from Taff's Well to play for Cardiff. He was equally at home at centre or outside half. After starting with Cardiff Juniors, he progressed through the ranks and gained his first team and Athletic Caps. Like brothers Bleddyn, Lloyd and Tony, he played for the Barbarians making his debut in 1961 against Leicester. In all he played 115 games for Cardiff, scoring 20 tries, before turning going to play rugby league with St Helens.*'
In the 1984 history of Taff's Well R.F.C. we read: '*Cenydd gave excellent service to Cardiff R.F.C. from 1956-62 and was equally at home at centre or outside-half. A neat, almost classical player. He graduated via Cardiff Juniors and gained 1st XV and Athletic caps. He represented the Barbarians and made 112 professional appearances with the St. Helens Club. During his time with Cardiff, Cenydd turned out for Taff's Well on many occasions, in one memorable match he scored five tries, all under the posts, Mappy kicking the conversions. He still follows the fortunes of the club from his home in the North of England.*'

I often watched Cenydd play outside-half, but more often partnering Welsh international Meirion Roberts in the centre for Cardiff, and I believed he was the better player, never seeming to die with the ball, a graceful runner with a marvellous swerve, handing tries on plates to his wing. He started playing for Cardiff aged 17, then lost two years through National Service, and left for St. Helens aged just 24. It is typical of the Williams brothers that I told him he should have played for Wales, and his immediate response was, '*No, that should have been Elwyn. Elwyn should have played for Wales*'. (Incidentally, in the rugby league press he was usually reported as 'Ken' Williams. Similarly, in the Cardiff programmes and match reports, Alun Priday was usually anglicised to Alan). Cenydd was approached to go North when on his National Service, but an overseas tour was coming up with Combined Services, so he refused. To go overseas to Africa must have been a dream – very, very few people travelled overseas – package tours did not really exist until the early 1960s. Cenydd was in the last ever National Service intake and played in 4 Inter-Service games; in 1961 he played centre with the great Alex Murphy at fly half, and Booth at scrumhalf - the RAF lost to the Royal Navy 9-3, but beat the Army 19-11. In 1962 Cenydd moved to fly half, as Murphy had left the Service, but Gloucester's Micky Booth was still at scrum half and this was a Championship winning year, after a win against the Royal Navy 16-6 and victory versus the Army 19-14. Alex Murphy – one of rugby league's 'legends', wanted Cenydd to join the great St Helens team, which Cenydd eventually did in 1963.

11 Moy Road, where Cenydd and his 11 brothers and sisters grew up, had a small bathroom, two double bedrooms, a box-room and an outside toilet. Arthur and Nell had a bedroom and the youngest daughter Mair the box-room. Squeezed into one bedroom were Cenydd, Lloyd and Vaughan

in one bed, and the youngest brothers Elwyn and Tony in a smaller bed. He recalls the immense strength of Gwyn being able to lift a brother on each arm into the air, and recalls that Bleddyn always said that Gwyn was the finest footballer of all the brothers (-football used to refer to rugby football). Cen remembered his first game for Taff's Well, on the wing when he was 15 years old. He also recalls driving with Bleddyn to play at Leicester for the Barbarians, but the match being snowed off. While in the RAF there were regular telegrams asking him to play for Cardiff, and the RAF were happy the let him go, as his was the last National Service intake.

He is extremely proud of his two years playing for the RAF, when they beat the Army and Navy in 1961-62 to win the Services Cup. Asked to recall his favourite games, they were against Bective Rangers 17-0 in 1958 when Cardiff scored three tries, and the away win in 1962, 8-0. Arthur Williams never took advantage of free Stand tickets to watch his sons play rugby at the Arms Park, preferring to stand behind the posts if he had time off work. He probably wanted to attend with his mates, who could only afford the cheaper tickets behind the posts. There have been comments that Arthur, whose older brother Philip had played for Cardiff Athletic and Taff's Well, was not overly interested in rugby. But in a tribute to Bleddyn we read: '*At the early age of eight years, Mr. Williams, his father, saw the potentialities of a great player in Bleddyn, and so also did the late Mr. Ben Evans, one of the school's selection committee of Bleddyn's early days.*'

And everyone noticed that Arthur's wife Nell, and their daughters Enid, Joan and Dilys, and some of Nell's sisters were always in the stand sitting together. They sued to take Roy Roberts' young son Mike with them.Nell used to make tea with cheese sandwiches for everyone after matches. She also invited all the boys and their wives for Sunday teas, which had to take place in separate sittings at Moy Road. Cenydd's memory of Gwyn is that, like Tony, he was always smiling, even after he came home from 6 months in hospital. Gwyn married one of his nurses, and eventually retired in Swanage, Dorset. Bryn was away with the war for years, but became a salesman and always arrived at Moy Road with a rucksack of liquor and fruit. Jean recalls Bleddyn as '*a lovely, lovely man*', who went to St Helens to see Cenydd play. Vaughan was a very good centre, and Elwyn, '*on his day, was unbeatable*'. Elwyn worked at Forgemasters in Taff's Well, and Cen believes that his not being picked for Wales was because of the selection biases of 'the Big Five' the selectors. It was a case of trying to please supporters from different areas of Wales, that each selector represented, that often led to the wrong team being chosen. Cenydd was closest to his other youngest brothers, Elwyn, Tony and Lloyd, who possessed '*a very good dive pass*' – this was in the days before spin passes. Jean Williams loaned me a scrapbook she used to keep, with photos of Cenydd in various teams including the Combined Services, the RAF, the Barbarians, Cardiff and St Helens. One newspaper cutting celebrates Tony joining Cardiff, with a picture of the eight brothers, headlined '**1-2-3-4-5-6-7-8- The Fantastic Rugby Family Williams**: *What a line-up! Here is rugby's most famous family, the eight Williams brothers, sons of Mr. and Mrs. Arthur Williams, of Taff's Well, Glamorgan. They have all played Rugby for Cardiff at some time or other – and most of them represented Wales, at least in Schoolboy or Youth fifteens. From left to right they are: Tony, just 20, and the latest to play for Cardiff; Bleddyn, the best-known of all, who was capped 22 times; Cenydd; Elwyn; Lloyd, Welsh international scrumhalf who captains Cardiff; Vaughan; Brynley; and Gwyn, whose career as a Rugby League player was ended by a war wound.*' There is also a photo of Cenydd, in '*The Football Pink*', captioned '*Cenydd Williams, Cardiff's outside-half, gets in a kick to touch during today's game with Rosslyn Park at Cardiff Arms Park.*' This was taken probably in December 1958, with Cardiff scoring three tries and winning 9-3. Cenydd was aged 18 years and 1 month, playing fly-half for the greatest club in Europe. He played for the Athletic aged 16 and won his first team cap aged 17.

There is another newspaper cutting, alongside which Jean Williams has written, '*1961-62. Best year so far, has played for Cardiff, RAF (champions first time in 30 years), Barbarians and Combined Services*'. The article reads '*Jenkins puzzles his old pals – Newport 9 RAF 6 – Former Newport skipper Leighton Jenkins, now a flying officer in the Royal Air Force, took his Services team to Rodney Parade last night, to help toughen them for their Twickenham games against the Royal Navy and the Army. Under his leadership the Air Force showed that they were making it tough for any kind of opposition. They gave Newport one of the hardest games of their season and it was as much as Newport could do to keep the R.A.F. off in the second half. Newport had a 9-0 lead, but the airmen successfully fought back so successfully that they were able to collect two tries –*

*Cenydd's Try – First came from Cenydd Williams, younger brother of Lloyd Williams, Wales captain. Jenkins got the second. Norman Morgan first put Newport ahead with a penalty goal which brought his points total to 18 in three matches, clear evidence that he has made a complete recovery. Then came tries by Brian Jones and Peter Rees. For the last 15 minutes of the first half the R.A.F. were without full-back Glyn Hopkins, of Leicester, who got a cut on the back of the neck which needed a couple of stitches. Alex Murphy, the St. Helens outside half, who will play for Great Britain against France in the Rugby League International at Wigan, a week on Saturday, had a great match. But the **star of the R.A.F. back division was Cenydd Williams**, who kicked skilfully to touch and defended resolutely.*' Cardiff's Ray Glastonbury played alongside Cen, and with Leighton Jenkins, the three also played for the RAF Sevens team.

'**Cenydd Bids to Save a Family Record**' is the headline of a newspaper article subtitled '*Jim Hill Spotlights Club Rugby*' – '*Wales Rugby selectors today travel to Twickenham to watch R.A.F. three-quarter Cenydd Williams begin a cap bid – in defence of his family's footballing honour! Crop-haired (owing to National Service, of course) Cardiff centre Cenydd, who switches to fly-half against the Navy, is the "mystery" player, selectors have earmarked to fill the left centre vacancy against Ireland. Though the Dublin game is postponed by the smallpox scare* (in the Rhondda), *23-year-old Williams still goes under the Big Five microscope with an **odds-on chance of clinching a delayed first cap** against France in Cardiff on March 24.* (Cenydd was actually 22 and 3 months old). *It adds up to a golden opportunity to restore the Rugby reputation of the legendary Taff's Well Williamses.*

All eight brothers have played for crack club Cardiff – four are in the present Cardiff first team and two, brilliant centre Bleddyn and skilful scrumhalf Lloyd, have captained Wales. But the family pride was jolted this week when selectors left out 27-year-old Lloyd and named Aberavon's Tony O'Connor against the Irish. A cap for Cenydd will avenge this "slight" from the Big Five. In the meantime, big brother Lloyd will be preparing a more personal answer to the men who dropped him. With three weeks to go before Wales meet France, Cardiff's tough scrum worker has plenty of time to thrust himself back into the cap reckoning. The Big Five have virtually written off the team they picked to play Ireland – as if it had never been chosen. They will meet to pick a new team to play the all-conquering French maestros strictly on current form and the needs of the moment. Today, as well as the inter-services game at Twickenham, selectors will be talent spotting at Wales' top derby games – Newport v. Cardiff and Ebbw Vale v. Abertillery. Closest watch will be kept on these cap challengers to Cenydd Williams – Meirion Roberts (Cardiff), Brian Jones (Newport), Roy Howell (Abertillery) and Ebbw Vale centre pair Dennis Evans and Ray Knott. Newport meet Cardiff for the fourth time this season, and, still waiting for a win, were forced into a late team change yesterday.'

Jean notes in her scrapbook under the cutting '*Much to our disappointment, neither Cen nor any of his brothers made the Welsh team. Wales however did very well, they beat France three nil, who until this were unbeaten.*' The French away game was in 1962, Wales winning by a penalty goal from Kel Coslett. France won the Championship. Alan Rees of Maesteg was chosen as outside-half, with Llanelli's Ken Jones and Cardiff's Meirion Roberts playing in the centre. In 1962, the RAF beat both the Navy and Army teams, much to Cenydd's delight, but in 2019 the RAF lost to the Army 59-0, which demonstrates the power of the RAF in Cenydd's time. In 1961-62 Cardiff beat Newport twice at home, 9-3 and 5-0, and drew twice away 3-3 and 6-6, scoring 4 tries to 2. These were always hard games.

Upon the same day as the France-Wales draw, 24 March 1962, Cenydd played as the RAF outside-half in the 19-14 win against the Army. Stand tickets were 7 shillings and 6 pence, and Twickenham was a sell-out. The RAF had beaten the Navy 12-6 there upon 3 March, and thus won the Inter-Services Championship. The winning team stayed at the Waldorf Hotel and dined at the Café Royal on 3 March. The menu was *Filet de Sole Belle Meuniere*, followed *by Selle d'Agneau Rotié, Panachee Bergere* and Pommes *Rissolées*, finished off with *Ananas au Kirsch, Bombe au Grand Marnier, Friandises* and *Café*. A far cry indeed from Fish and Chips in Taff's Well.

In the Coventry-Cardiff programme for 16 September 1961, backs are numbered from 1 Alun Priday at full-back, via Cenydd at Left Centre, 4, to the scrumhalf Leo Karseras at 7, and the forwards numbered from the prop and captain Kingsley Jones at 8 to the number 8 at 15. (Karseras only played 3 times for the Firsts). On 1 April 1961, the 22-year-old Cenydd had been chosen to play for the Barbarians, having played around 50 games for Cardiff, and they won at Cardiff 19-11, scoring 5 tries to 3. (His appearance is not noted on the official Barbarians website). However, in the following year, Cenydd was in the Cardiff team and they won 10-0 with two converted tries. Jean Williams writes *'Cardiff had a victorious Easter, after suffering a few bad games. However, with the return of RAF players Cenydd Williams and Ray Glastonbury, to help them out, they played a magnificent game to beat the Barbarians 10-0 (Easter Saturday). Cen was thrilled to beat them. When he played for the Baa-Baas they won, so it was nice to think you can beat them when you play against them. There was a terrific write-up about the game, alas I lost it, that is why I am writing about it. Easter Monday Cardiff beat the Harlequins 13-3. I have a write-up about this which you will find on the next page.'*

Upon 17 March 1962, LAC (Leading Aircraftsman) C. Williams played at outside half, number 6, for the RAF at Leicester. Upon the same day Cenydd is mistakenly in the Swansea-Cardiff programme playing left centre alongside his usual partner, Meirion Roberts, with Elwyn and Lloyd in the team. The Cardiff outside-half was Harry Morgan, who made only 52 appearances from 1958-59 to 1962-63. There is a rugby headline, *'CENYDD WILLIAMS A BARBARIAN – Cardiff centre Cenydd Williams has been invited by the Barbarians to play for them against Leicester on December 27 in the annual Mobbs Memorial match, writes John Billot. This is the first time Cenydd has played for the world-famous Barbarians, but he has impressed with his consistency this season, particularly while playing for the RAF in Scotland where the Barbarians selectors saw him in action. On Saturday, during the Cardiff-Ebbw Vale game, we saw the entire midfield formation composed of brothers. When fly half Geoff Davies was injured, Cenydd Williams moved from the centre to deputise and blind-side wing forward Elwyn Williams replaced him in*

456

the centre. So the Cardiff line-up was: Scrumhalf, Lloyd Williams; outside-half, Cenydd Williams; and centres Elwyn Williams and Tony Williams. This must be another record for the Cardiff club.' Geoff Davies had been kicked behind the ear, but *'shook off his concussion and returned to play on the wing.'* Stationed at RAF Abingdon, the 23-year-old Cenydd still had six months National Service to complete. Cen is down on the Barbarian website as having played Leicester Tigers in March 1962. His appearance for them against Cardiff, in a winning team is not mentioned. His wife Jean said that he was pleased to play in a winning Barbarian team against Cardiff and also be in the Cardiff team that beat them 10-0 on Easter Saturday, 21 April 1962. Two days later saw the Easter Monday Harlequins game.

Cen's play at fly-half for the Combined Services prompted Cardiff to play him at outside-half instead of his preferred position of centre. This Easter Monday (23 April 1962) report is by the late John Billott, one of the greatest rugby scribes, headlined: *'Cardiff and Quins Play It Tight – Cardiff 3-0-13 (one penalty) Harlequins 1-0-3 (one penalty). Cardiff, after their forward domination to beat the Barbarians, applied similar measures. The Harlequins, after their 22-0 win at Swansea, were out to prove that Cardiff's iron pack could at least be bent. This forward struggle was always absorbing, though we have seen so many such encounters that we can be excused our intolerance of the lack of back play. Venturesome bid True, the second half supplied more running behind the scrum, and Harlequins full-back Wilcox regularly strode into the three-quarter line as an extra attacker, in a venturesome bid to inspire a try. Perhaps if Hayward had been taken off the field, Quins would have achieved their aim. Hayward did more running about that anyone else; in fact, probably more running than any other two men. His wing-forward play continues to be devastating. Alas, it also devours our hopes of attacking back play. Cardiff were similarly subjected to hostile infiltration by Harlequins' spoilers. Scrumhalf Lloyd Williams could not provide a service for McCarthy to run onto and this slowed Cardiff's backs. McCarthy and the resourceful Cenydd Williams were the best home attackers and Gibbs was a penetrative Quins' centre.*

Militant forward Tight-head prop Wrench was a militant Quins' forward, who found time to express personal differences of opinion with two of Cardiff's hardest workers, Norris and Gough. Again, Elwyn Williams impressed. I have never seen this Cardiff blind-side breakaway play other than with outstanding efficiency. He had a hand in both Cardiff tries and made the second for number eight Cliff Howe. The first he owed most to Cenydd Williams' ripping burst and an in-pass put McCarthy diving in, to be carried over by his momentum. Priday, who was every bit as sound as British Lion Wilcox, converted both tries and kicked an excellent wide-angled penalty goal. Wilcox supplied the Quins' points with a penalty kick. It was a hard contest, as the players will testify. But a crowd in holiday mood prefer something to talk about, other than tight rugby. Still, we shall see Statham (- the great fast-bowler, Brian Statham) on the Arms Park next week – and cricket cannot come quickly enough after this kind of Easter rugby fare.'

Five days later, on 28 April 1962, 23-year-old Cenydd was playing outside-half for the Royal Air Force against a Hartlepool Rovers XV containing three British Lions in the R.F. Oakes memorial match, with the RAF winning 24-6. Cenydd then went on his 3-week tour of Africa with the Combined Services as their outside-half, and then returned to 'Civvy Street.' Cenydd kept his programmes, and after winning the first four games, is still disappointed at losing the final game to Rhodesia 24-16. Like Cenydd, the centre HJC (John) Brown, was also a Barbarian. Upon HJC Brown's website (www.hjcbrown.com/combined-services.htm), written by Alan Hughes, we read of Cenydd's tour: *'The Combined Services team flew in an RAF Hastings aircraft staying at El Adem in Libya before arriving in Nairobi. The Hastings was an uncomfortable noisy aircraft, and the journey was hard. As daylight broke, we found that we were over Lake Victoria – a magnificent and welcome sight! Playing in Salisbury, Rhodesia* (now Harare, Zimbabwe) *Bulawayo and Kitwe, they stayed on military bases or in private homes, and were well entertained. HJC recalls that he was one of six players who sat up all night playing cards, to be picked up by minibus at 6.00am, then taken to a Safari Park. Not surprisingly the party fell asleep and saw no wild animals! The matches generally were easy for the team, which had many top-class players in it. The team visited Victoria Falls and had a picnic on an island with crocodiles swimming around! ...*

On the Combined Services Tour of Rhodesia and Kenya, the final match in Salisbury was watched by the British Lions Touring party, en route to South Africa. Little did he (H.J.C. John Brown) *know that he had already been carded as first reserve for the Lions, which he discovered on returning home... About 2 weeks later he was called upon to fly out to replace Richard Sharp who had been badly injured in an illegal tackle. To join the Lions, HJC flew on a South African Airways Boeing 707 overnight, stopping in Rome and Brazzaville. On arrival in Johannesburg, he was taken to meet Richard Sharp in hospital. He said "Richard's face was an absolute mess due to the tackle from M. Roux. He looked as if he had been in a car crash. It was the **worst rugby injury** I had ever seen". Richard returned home soon afterwards ending his tour.'*

This is the very same wing, Francois du Toit *'Mannetjies'* Roux, born 1939, whom I saw late tackle Alun Priday in 1960 – a little coward of a man, indeed. Mannetjie means 'little man' in Afrikaans, and he made up for his lack of size by other methods. Wikipedia notes: *'He possessed a great deal of pace and was a ferocious defender, despite his lack of size.*

He was perhaps best known for his tackle on England and British Lions flyhalf Richard Sharp, while playing for Northern Transvaal (the Blue Bulls) in 1962, which broke Sharp's jaw or cheekbone. Controversy seemed to follow him almost throughout his career, with Roux achieving notoriety on the demo-ridden 1969-70 Springbok tour of the United Kingdom for kicking one protester in the backside and hurling the ball at another.' Nothing about the Priday tackle by Roux, the dirtiest I have witnessed in over six decades of playing and watching the game.

I shall quote a little more, to show the character of the amateur Lions tours of those days: *'Moving on to join the* (Lions) *team at their hotel, HJC soon realised that, as rugby is a religion out there, they were being treated like royalty. Best hotels were booked, with full choice of a la carte menus (no healthy food rules in those days!), invitations to private parties at incredible homes, yachts, race meetings – the full works. HJC recalls that the out-of-pocket expenses permitted to be paid to the players was 50p a day (£3.50 a week) but in truth they did not need more, with everything laid on. As players we did not need to touch our kit, which was all done by the Baggage Man. HJC records his full admiration for the travelling UK rugby writers, who also stayed at their hotels. They observed matters without them ever 'going to press', which today would make front page news. They were definitely 'One of the boys.' Willie John McBride, or Bill as he is known to his friends, had his 21st birthday on tour, and usually played in the Wednesday team as did HJC. They became good friends on tour and HJC was not surprised when he went on to become the legend he is now.'*

'HJC' Brown's particular memories are *'1. Riding an ostrich and standing on its egg. 2. Swimming in the sea in Durban, surrounded by shark nets. 3. Shooting antelope and game birds which were cooked by the hotel and served up for dinner. 4. Attending the many braiivleis (barbecues) to eat his favourite food – grilled meat. 5. Being driven in large American cars at 100mph on the open road only to drop to 20mph to crawl through small villages. 6. The effect of altitude on breathing which made the lungs feel as if they were going to burst. Craftily the SA authorities planned the tour so that we played at sea level, then up to 6000ft ASL* (above sea level) *for the next match and then back to sea level and so on.* (- author's underlining) *7. The additional distance one could kick the ball at altitude. 8. The grass burns on the knees and legs received when playing on dry turf. The next day, they stiffened up and had a very significant effect on free movement.'*

And Bleddyn Williams came to the rescue: *'Playing in Rhodesia, HJC had received a tackle which left him with a very sore toe! On returning home, he saw four doctors, in four different hospitals, had countless x rays only to be told that it was bruised. HJC knew that something else was wrong, so whilst on a course at RAF St. Athan near Cardiff, he went to the*

Cardiff RFC clubhouse one evening, and met Bleddyn Williams. When told of the toe problem, Bleddyn referred him to the Cardiff and Wales renowned physiotherapist Ray Lewis. Within 5 minutes, Ray discovered that he had dislocated the end digit of the toe, pulled it back, put some zinc oxide plaster on it and sent on HJC his way. HJC says "without his help I may not have been able to join the Lions."' The above is a small portion of a wonderful tribute to HJC, as he was known, including the fact that he had bobsleigh medals and incurred 32 stitches after an IRA attack on his mess at Aldershot. One wishes there were websites like this for most of Wales's former players.

Fortunately, I managed to discover on the web a programme for the first game in Cenydd's RAF-Combined Services tour, against East Africa. There is a picture of the 23-year-old SAC (Senior Aircraftsman) Cenydd O. Williams down to play fly half. He was 5 ft 11 ins and 178 lbs, having played for Cardiff, the RAF and already for the Barbarians. There is no photograph of his Cardiff team-mate LAC Ray Glastonbury, down to play on the left wing. Like Cenydd, he was 20, Ray played for the RAF, and was 5 ft. 10½ ins, and 172 lbs. There were three England triallists, but only two internationals, N.S. Bruce, the Scotland hooker; and F/O (Flying Officer) Leighton H. Jenkins, the Welsh lock forward. Jenkins had been Newport captain when they beat Australia in 1957, scoring a try in the 11-0 victory, faced the All Blacks twice, played 5 times for Wales and was in Cliff Morgan's side which won the Five Nations in 1956. Jenkins captained Cenydd in Cenydd's two years playing for the RAF, and had stayed in the RAF after National Service. He rose to become Squadron Leader and then Wing Commander in 1979. Another Cardiff and RAF player on tour was LAC Peter Thomas, again aged 20, 5 ft 7 ins and 161 lbs, who played 45 times for Cardiff between 1957-58 and 1969-70. The 1962 games were all in May, so the Combined Services squad of just 24 players, missing HJC Brown, had 5 games on rock-hard surfaces in 15 days, following a gruelling journey and involving miles of travel on poor roads:

5 May - East Africa (team from Kenya, Tanganyika and Uganda) at Nairobi, the capital of Kenya - W 36-17

9 May - Northern Rhodesia (now mainly Zambia), at Kitwe, Zambia - W 19-15

12 May - Federal Combined Services at Bulawayo, now Matabeleland, Zimbabwe - W 17-10

16 May - Southern Rhodesia (now part of Zimbabwe) at Gwelo, now Gweru, Zimbabwe - W 22-14

19 May - Rhodesia at Salisbury, now Harare, Zimbabwe - L 16 – 28

Indeed, the present distances involved were Nairobi to Kitwe 1,350 miles by road through Tanzania; Kitwe to Bulawayo 709 miles by minibus; Bulawayo to Gweru just 104 miles by car; Gweru to Harare 173 miles by minibus.

On 26 December 1962, Cardiff defeated Wasps at home 17-5, 5-1 on tries. The following day was their traditional 27 December game against Watsonians. Cardiff often played in red shirts against Watsonians, and it seems strange that red has not been kept as their usual change strip, as the capital of Wales. Red with a blue and black V of the front of the shirt would be fitting, rather than the walking multiple advertisements carried by their successor, the Cardiff Blues. The Blues often played in pink in away games – not really a rugby colour, but their Welsh Championship ground sharers, Cardiff, thankfully still kept to blue and black. (As of 2021, the 'Blues' appellation has been thankfully scrapped, and the Blues are now Cardiff Rugby/Rygbi Caerdydd, and Cardiff are once more Cardiff RFC.) Lloyd Williams was rested, Elwyn switched to number 8 to give Cliff Howe a breather and Cenydd played outside half. Jean Williams only has a cutting of the game's first half, with Cardiff only leading 6-0 at half-time. Malcolm Lewis reported that Cardiff had to make eight changes, two positional, as in the space of 4 days they had 3 games. And modern players speak of playing too much... Watsonians had defeated Newport on the previous day. Meirion Roberts made a break and passed to Cyril Evans for a try in the first minute. Lewis writes: '*Scrum half Brian Williams, making only his second appearance of the season, was providing partner Cenydd Williams with a beautiful long, accurate pass. From one of his passes Cenydd cut away in great style, stumbled but immediately recovered to continue on a defence-splitting run. He was only halted at the last moment by a timely tackle from McNish...*'

Inspired by Cenydd's distribution, Cardiff ramped it up in the second half and won 35-3, 8-1 on tries. Two days later, upon 29 December 1962, Cardiff beat Gloucester 11-0 at home, with Cen still playing outside-half, alongside his brothers Lloyd and Elwyn. The Gloucester match programme notes that Cenydd against Watsonians, was '*adroit at Stand-off. This win of 35 points to three was indicative not only of first-class attacking team movements, but of notably apparent leadership by the captain, Dai Hayward.*' One report on the Gloucester game was headlined '***Williams Boys are the Stars at the Arms Park***, and another report by W.E.N. Davies reads in part: '*Brothers Excel for Cardiff – I doubt whether the pitch was really fit for play for the players had great difficulty keeping their feet, and any sudden movement was apt to result in a "base over apex" performance, with not an opponent within yards! Full marks, therefore, to the teams for giving us quite an entertaining game. Cardiff deserved to win, for in the first half their backs overcame numbed fingers, to produce several excellent rounds of passing. In addition to the tries scored, there were several near misses that could be readily excused on such a day. Gloucester were rarely in the hunt in this period and one expected further Cardiff scores in the second half.*

Gloucester changed their tactics at the interval, however, and from then on had as much of the game as Cardiff. Indeed they came near to scoring on a couple of occasions. One – by Meadows – was only foiled at the corner flag, and another field length movement deserved a score. In the second half, Gloucester tightened up the forward battle to prevent the Cardiff backs being put in possession. They also made use of the long kick up field – a useful weapon on a surface that made the bounce quite unpredictable. When the Cardiff backs did attempt to handle, the cold had done its work and many passes were understandably dropped. In the first half the whole Cardiff back division was superb. **L. Williams** *was a tower of strength and scrumhalf while his brother,* **C. Williams**, *gave a great display of straight running at outside half. Roberts and Evans were probing runners in the centre, and the wings had a go at every possible chance. Priday was safe as ever at full-back and controlled matters in the opening period. Hayward and* **E. Williams** *were always on the ball. Gloucester's main strength lay in the forwards who fully held their own after the interval. Long, Hudson and Ford were great workers. Behind the scrum Booth was outstanding, and besides kicking intelligently in attack, was always popping back to save his defence... Priday kicked a 40-yard penalty after 15 minutes, and then* **C. Williams** *made a perfect break to split the Gloucester defence and send Roberts in for a simple try. Just before half-time* **L. Williams** *made a similar effort to present* **C. Williams** *with another easy try which Priday converted. The second half was scoreless, but full of interest with Gloucester right back in the game.'*

Tudor Jones wrote under the headline *'Talent Show by Cardiff - Cardiff 11pts Gloucester 0:* **Talented Cardiff brothers Lloyd and Cenydd Williams could be the Welsh half-back pair before the season ends**. *And Wales needs the culture and experience of Meirion Roberts to help their teenage speed men against England. These were the big lessons hammered home in this top-class match played in Arctic conditions. What a tragedy that 22-year-old* **Cenydd Williams**, *brother of the immortal Bleddyn, had not been switched to fly half by Cardiff earlier in the season. Another Cardiff hero was Captain Courageous Dai Hayward. Once again, the ability of Cardiff full-back Alun Priday gleamed as the bull-dozing Gloucester forwards drove through. Cardiff have also an all-star back division, the only flaw being the ability of centre Cyril Evans to take the ball at vital moments. Crafty, clever Cardiff used the bone-hard ground to gain length with long raking kicks... Welsh selectors must have wondered about their decision in dropping* **Lloyd Williams** *for the final Welsh trial next Saturday.*

Three times he burst through to rip big holes in the Gloucester defence, so well marshalled at full-back by Alan Holder... Gloucester centres Ron Pitt and John Bayliss danced through like ballerinas, and only the great covering defence of Cardiff forwards Hayward and **Elwyn Williams** *saved*

462

the line. *Cardiff's first try, scored by Meirion Roberts, helped fans forget the cold.* **Lloyd Williams** *fed his brother* **Cenydd**, *who raced 40 yards, before sending Roberts over for the try of the match. Later* **Cenydd Williams** *put in a thrilling twenty-yard sprint to race for Cardiff's second try. Priday converted one and kicked a penalty goal. It was a fairy-tale comeback for Cardiff prop forward Kingsley Jones. After delaying his return to top rugby, when he returned with the British Lions from South Africa, he chose this game to prove he is back in form. Cardiff centre Cyril Evans was just robbed of his moment of glory. In a thrilling sprint against Gloucester full-back Holder, he dived head-first into a pile of straw but was too camouflaged for a try to be awarded.'* There you are, games on 26, 27 and 29 December, on a frozen pitch, against Wasps, Watsonians and Gloucester, and Cardiff scored 15 tries to 2.

On 8 January 1963, J.B.G. Thomas chose his Welsh XV for the final trial, in a long article, and under the headline: '***Cenydd Williams would be the right man at fly-half*** *– It is the ambition of every Welsh rugby follower to see England beaten at rugby football, and the real reason for this is that England are hard to overcome... The England match is important because virtually it decides the fate of the next season for Wales... It is the Triple Crown that appeals most to Welshmen...* (Thomas goes on to heartily recommend Meirion Roberts in the centre as an automatic choice) … *the outside-half position is also one that will give the Welsh selectors considerable difficulty because they appreciate, as do all Welshmen, that young David Watkins, of Newport, has considerable potential, but can he and the two "runner-in" centres work smoothly against the anticipated spoiling defence of England? There was a complete lack of cohesion, when these three played together against Canada, and naturally the final trial provides them with a further opportunity of cohesion and accuracy in running and passing, the value of which was so rightly emphasised by R.T. Gabe, one of the game's greatest handlers. -* **Has judgment and skill** *– I feel now that had Cenydd Williams, of Cardiff, played at outside-half this season he would be almost* **an automatic choice**. *He revealed during the holiday matches strength, judgment and skill, while playing in the position, and Cardiff's power behind the scrum was largely due to his smooth working with Meirion Roberts in the centre*

These points cannot be ignored, and if the trial match does not produce an international outside-half then surely **the selectors must resort to Williams**. *He was, incidentally, an outstanding success for the Combined Services in the position during the May tour of East Africa. Another problem exists around the scrum half position. And here I would adopt the unusual policy of nominating two players – one for dry conditions and one for heavy weather. This could be applied to both halfback positions, and on a dry day Watkins could be paired with either O'Connor or Rowlands. I would nominate the Williams brothers for heavy going. The Indian Summer*

463

being enjoyed at the moment by Lloyd Williams, suggests that on a heavy Arms Park, he and his brother would be the most suitable candidates...'

Thomas goes on to recommend Dai Hayward as open side wing forward – *'Even so it is particularly hard luck on a player of Hayward's ability, for he would be snapped up readily by the other countries, and be an automatic choice for Wales, but for the remarkable ability of Haydn Morgan... I would nominate Alun Pask as the Welsh captain. He is technically equipped for the job.'* Ex-paratrooper Haydn Morgan, nick-named 'The Red Devil' because of his hair, played open-side to Pask's number 8 for Abertillery, played 4 times for the British Lions (with 2 Tests each in New Zealand and South Africa) and 27 times for Wales. A Barbarian, he was a difficult man for Hayward to replace. Alun Edward Islwyn Pask played 23 times as blind-side flanker for Wales and 3 times as number 8. A Wales captain, he played in 3 of the 4 Tests in South Africa in 1962, and in 1966 both Tests against Australia and 3 of the 4 New Zealand Tests. This was the man Elwyn Williams was up against for a Welsh cap until around 1967. JBG Thomas picked his team for the game against England to include Cenydd Williams, as outside-half to Tony O'Connor.

In 1991, England won in Cardiff for the first time in 28 years, the previous time being 1963. Richard Seekts reported in 1963 – *'Britain was in the grip of its coldest winter since 1740, and outdoor sport had more or less been wiped out by the weather for five weeks, but the Cardiff authorities were determined to put on a show for both spectators in the ground and for millions of television viewers who, with little else to do in such conditions, watched the match. 30 tons of straw were removed from the pitch on the morning of the match, the dead ball areas were shortened to six yards due to frozen patches and the white paint for marking the lines froze during pitch preparations. At kick-off the temperature was minus six degrees. Both teams remained indoors to keep warm while the National Anthems were played; the match started immediately they took the field. In addition to the long lay-off, neither side had managed any meaningful practice, and 13 players were making international debuts. Four of Wales' forwards and both half-backs, captain Clive Rowlands and David Watkins were getting their first game at this level.*

Wales made a frantic start and had scoring chances aplenty in the first 10 minutes, but it was a chaotic scene of handling errors and players skidding around on the icy turf, and none of their chances were converted to points. Just getting the match underway was, said The Times, "a wonderful triumph of mind over matter and its justification was a highly entertaining game witnessed, because of lack of competition, by more millions on far-flung screens than would ordinarily have been the case."... As the second half wore on, it became apparent that several Welsh players didn't care for the arctic conditions. Conversely, England were galvanised by their lead, their defence becoming more ferocious, with Rogers and his

464

back row colleagues in devastating form. England's second try had an element of farce as Rogers hoofed the ball up field where Phillips and Hodgson, competing for it, both skidded straight past, so enabling the following John Owen to collect and score near the posts. Hodgson got Wales on the scoreboard with a penalty, Sharp responded with a drop goal from a scrum on the 25-yard line. Finally, Wales scored a try when flanker David Hayward found a way over from a line-out, a couple of yards from England's line. It had been rich entertainment, albeit in extraordinary circumstances. Remarkably, there were no serious injuries, though several players finished with cuts and friction burns from the ice. England went on to win the Five Nations Championship in 1963, only a 0-0 draw with Ireland denying them a Grand Slam. For Wales, it was the wooden spoon, despite a win over Scotland.' Dai Hayward had his long-awaited cap, but alas for Cen, it was not to be.

In 7 seasons interrupted by injury and National Service, Cen scored a try every 6 matches for Cardiff. He preferred playing left centre, but was also a brilliant outside-half. In either position, he made tries rather than scored them.

	P	W	D	L	T	Pts
1956-1957	5	3	0	2	2	6
1957-1958	21	15	3	3	3	9
1958-1959	24	13	4	7	2	6
1959-1960	8	2	2	4	2	6
1960-1961	14	10	2	2	1	5 (inc 1 con)
1961-1962	20	12	3	5	4	12
1962-1963	23	16	3	4	5	15
Total	115	71	17	27	19	59 (inc 1 con

Cenydd did not even have a trial for Wales in any of the 4 centre or 2 fly-half berths going in the Reds and Whites. Speaking subjectively, he was a fabulous player, better for Cardiff than his international co-centre Meirion Roberts. Alex Murphy, one of the greatest rugby league players of all time, played scrumhalf to Cenydd's fly-half in the RAF, and was instructive in getting St Helens to chase for his signature at any cost. It was a decision, easier than one would think, to sign professional forms and head North for Rugby League, foregoing the 'glamour' of Welsh caps. 'Cen' was only a bad leg break away from never playing Union again, or being out for well over a year, like Elwyn, with little money coming in. He had recently married Jean and was living with her parents in their house in Rhydfelen (-as Cen calls it – Rhydyfelin is a made-up name for the village just north of Pontypridd). There were poor unemployment or sickness benefits in those days, and absence from Cen's work as a fitter and turner at Forgemasters in

Taff's Well, could easily have led to his being sacked. Reporters and politicians these days seem to think that it was much simpler and affordable to buy a home in the 1950s, 60s and 70s – it definitely was not. Wages were low, interest rates were far higher than today, and youngsters had to save and save (and save) for their first house. No-one went on foreign holidays or bought designer clothes. If young people were lucky to have a car, it was an 'old banger', carefully nurtured to keep it on the road for years.

Nobody except the upper classes bought 'brands, and at least into the early 60s, holey socks would be darned. Men and women had few pairs of shoes and changes of clothes – austerity was bred into children born in and after the war, with a built-in anxiety never to go into any debt, except an affordable mortgage on a house. Children were an incredible expense. Eating out was a real rarity, as was shopping for anything but basic necessities. Televisions were programmed in black and white and expensive. There were no supermarkets, washing machines, freezers, fridges, packaged meals, fast food outlets (except for Wimpey) and foreign takeaways. No-one stored meals, but food items were bought on a daily basis from a local grocery store. The only 'takeaway' was the chip shop, and even that was a rarity for many people. This writer's generation has kept out of the debt trap all their lives, tried desperately never to be reliant upon any state aid, and been rewarded with the lowest State Pensions in Europe, *'the lowest in the developed world'* - £8,000p.a. In the OECD, the Netherlands pays a pension worth 100% of average earnings; Portugal, Italy and Austria all over 90%; Spain 82%, and the UK is in 24th place with 29%. The OECD average is 62%, which means that the British pension should rise to £15,000 to reach than figure. Young Cenydd and Jean made a decision, that today's generation, like their teachers with little knowledge of post-war history, will find difficult to understand. One needs sometimes to add perspective, for younger generations to understand the past.

It was reported on 31 January 1963, *'**Gone – Cenydd Williams turns pro.** – Welsh rugby's best-kept secret was out in the open last night when Cardiff centre Cenydd Williams signed professional forms for St. Helens Rugby League Club. The fee? That's still a secret, but Cenydd, a 24-year-old fitter and turner, is reported to have received between £3,000 and £4,000. He is the second member of the famous Taff's Well family to turn professional, after brother Gwyn, who joined Wigan in 1938. Bleddyn Williams, former Cardiff and Wales skipper and most brilliant of all the brothers, said today: "I'm sorry to see Cenydd go of course, but he must look after himself. It was up to him and entirely his own business." Cardiff R.F.C. Secretary Frank Trott was astonished when I broke the news to him this morning. "It's come as a great shock" he said, "We valued his services highly and thought he would go places." Cenydd was certainly on the fringe of Welsh international honours and St. Helens can congratulate* *themselves on a real capture. At 5ft. 10½in. and 13 stone, Williams is ideally built for the hurly burly of the 13-a-side game, and St. Helens expect him to solve a centre problem which has existed since the break-up of the Doug Greenall – Ray Gullick partnership. Cenydd has an old friend up north in the person of the brilliant scrum half Alex Murphy. These two played together with great success in their RAF days.'*

Bleddyn wrote in his column for *The People*: **'***Reluctant Welsh fly-half joins old chum*** *– The race by the Rugby League to sign Union players, before the Cup deadline expires is reaching its climax. St. Helens stole a march on their rivals in mid-week, when they signed Cenydd Williams, the Cardiff, Barbarians and former Combined Services centre or fly-half. And, incidentally, a young brother of mine.* **The fee of £6,000 is probably the highest ever paid to a non-international.** *Cenydd has a five-year contract, and joins Kelvin Coslett, the former Welsh international full-back, Tom Van Vollenhoven, the ex-Springbok wing three-quarter, and British Rugby League Test players Mike Sullivan and Alex Murphy. Young Cenydd will be no stranger to Murphy, who is considered to be one of the greatest of all League scrum-halves, for they regularly teamed up for the Royal Air Force during their National Service days. Cenydd, who is known as the reluctant fly-half because of his dislike for the position, has been tipped for the Welsh cap this season and is the second of us eight brothers to turn professional. The other, and by far the best player in this family, is Gwyn, who played senior rugby for Cardiff when he was 16, and joined Wigan at 20 in 1938. Gwyn's career was tragically cut short. He was severely wounded in the North Africa campaign serving with the Welsh Guards.'*

Back playing for Cardiff after his tour of Africa and the end of his National Service, Cenydd had talked the offer over at length with his wife Jean, and they decided that a professional career was the best option. I was lucky to meet Cenydd and Jean on 29 August 2020, when we took refreshments in the Griffin Inn, Eccleston, St Helens. I phoned to book the meal and a room for the night, and told the person who answered the phone that I wanted to book a table for a former St Helens player, Cenydd Williams and his wife. He answered, *'he's a legend'*, and gave me a double room for the price of a single. To be honest, I have had so much joy writing this book, talking to former players, and have made some lifelong friends. I loved watching Cenydd play – and to meet him was fabulous for me. I have met, over the last decades, well over 100 former rugby internationals, of whom only two were less than enjoyable company – and that opinion was shared widely. All the others were marvellous, humble men.

On National Service with the RAF at Abingdon, Cenydd had played outside-half to the legendary St Helens scrumhalf Alex Murphy, and inside the camp had been approached by a St Helens scout, who had somehow got through security checks. Cenydd was offered £4,000 to head North, by club director and secretary Basil Lowe, who with his wife, took Cenydd for a drink and made the offer. Cenydd refused, as he wished to go with Combined Services on tour in Africa. Professionals like his friend Alex Murphy, although they could play for the RAF, Navy or Army, could not play for any Combined Services team. A year or so later another scout came along to Cenydd's home, with the 22-year-old Cenydd now back at Cardiff RFC, and asked Cenydd to telephone the St Helens chairman. Cenydd replied he had no telephone, and walked with the scout who made a reversed charges call, from a nearby telephone box. The chairman offered Cenydd £5,000, and Cen thought for a few moments and asked for £6,000, thinking it would be refused. However, the chairman offered the amount. Cenydd talked it over with Jean for two days and they made the enormous decision to leave friends and family. Kel Coslett, the Wales full-back went to St Helens at the same time, aged just 21. Cliff Morgan was offered £5,000 several times in his career to turn to rugby league.

Cenydd Williams playing for St Helens, first left, kneeling

It was a move Cenydd and Jean never regretted – it was a five-year contract, and they thought they would return home, but liked the area and the people so much, that they stayed in Lancashire. To place a modern-day perspective upon £4,000, Cen and Jean bought a new £4,000 house on a new small estate in a village near St Helens. They could have bought a semi-detached on the same estate for £2,000. The equivalent today would be perhaps £600,000 for two such houses. For young Cenydd and Jean to move from living with her parents, to a brand new four-bedroom house and garden in a nice village, must have been bliss. I always thought that league players were then professional, but Cenydd said they were semi-professional, and they still all had day jobs, for instance Kel Coslett was a truck driver for St Helens Corporation. When Kel broke his leg, he worked as a packer, standing up all day, which helped strengthen his leg. Cenydd said that training was '*a bit of a joke*', just two hours a week, with one set of weights that no-one used. There was '*no coaching*' – it was up to the players to sort themselves out, just as in Union. There were great Welsh players in the team including Bobby Wanbon, John Mantell and Bob Prosser, but Cenydd laughed when he saw their primitive training regime.

Dave Dooley, of Saints Heritage Society wrote this pen picture of Cenydd: '*One of Alex Murphy's team-mates in the RAF XV, Cen Williams was a classy Welsh centre who played rugby union for Cardiff and toured with the Barbarians. He turned professional with St. Helens and scored two tries on his debut against Bramley on 23rd March 1963. He played centre to the great Tom Van Vollenhoven on a number of occasions, but was forced to retire after a cartilage operation in 1969. Cen is the brother of the famous Welsh rugby union centre Bleddyn Williams. Following his brace of tries on debut he bagged another pair in the same season in the away fixture at Halifax. His smart play produced a regular place in the team during the next season, 1963/4. That campaign produced a brace of tries against Hull KR and a starting place in the Western Divisional Championship Final victory over Swinton. Moreover, both Vollenhoven and Killeen benefited from his silky skills. Nine tries from 26 matches continued his run in the first team in the 1964/5 season but the next three seasons saw only sporadic outings in the first team as competition for the centre berths reached red-hot proportions. Cen's next major Final was the 1968 Lancashire Cup Final when the Saints ran riot in the second half to crush Oldham by 30 points to 2. On that day he played on the left wing, aged 27, and scored a try. In all this fine centre's play led to 34 tries in a career of 108 matches at the Saints - an impressive strike record!*'

In his first match vs. Bramley, aged 22, Cenydd played with the Welsh former union international, Kel Coslett, and the game's stars Tom van Vollenhoven, Alex Murphy and Ray French. In his first season, Cenydd played 8 matches, scoring 7 tries. In 1963-64, he scored 8 tries in 35 games, and the following season 9 tries in 34 matches. Dennis Whittle wrote in the St. Helens newspaper '*The Star*' of '***A Hot Welcome for Tourists*** *… I did manage to chance upon the accompanying pictorial pearl of the Saints' team which faced Australia on September 28, 1963, and battled magnificently before losing 8-2, with home points coming via a penalty goal from Kel Coslett. Obviously fully psyched up for their showdown with the Kangaroos, the Saints' squad reads: Coslett, Keith Northey, Ken (Cenydd) Williams, Mick Mooney, Geoff Heaton, Tom Van Vollenhoven, Peter Harvey, Cliff Watson, John Tembey, Bob Dagnall, Dick Huddart, Ray French, Keith Ashcroft... Pride of place must go to Welshman Coslett who took the professional ticket as a full-back from*

Aberavon in 1962, and went on to make 530 appearances for the club, in which he kicked 1,639 points, including 214 for a total of 452 points in a season 1971-72, all of which are records. In addition, goal king Kel skippered Saints to Wembley success from the loose forward position against Leeds in 1972 – when he won the Lance Todd Trophy – and again against Widnes in the "Dad's Army" clash of 1976 when he demonstrated his versatility by wearing the number 10 shirt. Coslett's fellow "Taff" Williams (Cenydd) *had many rousing games in the centre after coming to Knowsley Road from Cardiff, where he was a member of the famous rugby-playing family which included his Welsh international three-quarter brother Bleddyn.'*

The Star, on 26 December 1996, carried a long article by Dennis Whittle commemorating the 30th anniversary of Cenydd's first two full seasons with the club: **'Saints' Twin Triumph'** - *... it was inevitable the pages of the club yearbook for 1965-66 found me knee-deep in nostalgia while reliving a golden age when a first ever Cup and League double loomed large on the horizon. Supporters' attitude for such soaring success had been whetted by a previous season when Saints won the League Leader's Trophy with 56 points from 34 games; Lancashire Cup and League; plus Woodbine Sevens Trophy, along with runners-up spot in the Top 16 competition. So it could be safely said that Saints were well and truly set to take off in the chase for the game's major honours, and a glance at the stars who earned them and the officials who lent a guiding hand makes compelling reading.'* 'Ken' (Cenydd) Williams is included in the 'stars' who played that season, and *'Van Vollenhoven could manage only 11 tries from 22 outings in a campaign dogged by injury.'* Cenydd, following the example of brothers Bleddyn and Tony, always thought it was his job to put the wing over, rather than score himself. Van Vollenhoven was a winger, like his fellow South African Len Killeen, who scored 140 goals and 26 tries in 43 appearances. In 1965-66, *'notable games in the club's calendar included September 15 when New Zealand were defeated 28-7, with the results against the old enemy Wigan being lost 17-8 at Central Park, and won 17-10* (at home.) *...There was a Wembley victory for Saints, and they duly obliged and added the Championship, League Leaders, and Lancashire League crowns for good measure. Stirring times indeed!'*

In 1965-66, a season affected by injuries, Cenydd only played 10 games, scoring 3 tries, but in 1966-67 touched down 24 times. Another season with injuries followed, restricting appearances to 11 games and two touch downs, and in his last, 1968-69 year, 'Cen' scored 3 tries in 23 games. In October 1968, in front of 17,000 fans at Wigan's Central Park, St Helens won the Lancashire Cup 30-2 against Oldham, with Cen coming on as substitute. 'Ken' (sic) Williams was full-back against Wigan, because Kel Coslett had switched to playing loose forward in the Floodlit Trophy Final in December 1968, played at Wigan. Coslett kicked two penalties to

470

Wigan's two pens, but Cliff Hill scored the winning try for Wigan to win 7-4. On the wing for St Helens was the former Cardiff Rugby player Frank Wilson, and Welsh internationals John Mantle and John Warlow were in the pack. Wilson could play wing, centre or fly-half, and scored 310 tries in 528 games for St Helens. Cenydd's last game was against Doncaster in 1969. 34 tries, 102 points in 112 matches is an excellent return for a centre in those days of muddy pitches. Cen retired at Rainford, a village near St Helens. His record at St Helens is as follows:

Season (Official Matches)	Tries	Matches
1962~63	7	8
1963~64	8	35
1964~65	9	34
1965~66	3	10
1966~67	2	24
1967~68	2	11
1968~69	3	23
TOTALS:	34	145

Season (Other Matches)	Tries	Matches
1964~65	0	1
1965~66	0	1
1967~68	0	1
1968~69	1	1
TOTALS:	1	4

To demonstrate how St. Helens was the top club in rugby league, we read: *'The 1968–69 Rugby League Lancashire Cup competition was the fifty-sixth occasion, on which the Lancashire Cup completion had been held. St. Helens won the trophy by beating Oldham by the score of 30-2. The match was played at Central Park, Wigan, (historically in the county of Lancashire). The attendance was 17,008 and receipts were £4,644. This was the second of two consecutive Lancashire Cup final wins for St. Helens, and what is more,* **the seventh of the seven occasions on which the club will win the trophy in nine successive seasons.** *Cen scored a try and Kel Coslett kicked six goals.'*

Cenydd played fullback rather than centre in the 1968 BBC2 Floodlit Trophy which they lost 7-4 to Wigan, and St Helens' record reads:
*   Championship Winners: 1931-32, 1952-53, 1958-59, 1965-66, 1969-70, 1970-71, 1974-75
*   Challenge Cup Winners: 1955-56, 1960-61, 1965-66, 1971-72, 1975-76
*   League Leaders' Shield Winners: 1964-65, 1965-66
*   Regal Trophy Winners: 1987-88
*   Premiership Winners: 1975-76, 1976-77, 1984-85, 1992-93
*   Lancashire Cup Winners: 1926-27, 1953-54, 1960-61, 1961-62, 1962-63, 1963-64, 1964-65, 1967-68, 1968-69, 1984-85, 1991-92
*   Lancashire League Winners: 1929-30, 1931-32, 1952-53, 1959-60, 1963-64, 1964-65, 1965-66, 1966-67, 1968-69
*   Charity Shield Winners: 1992-93
*   BBC2 Floodlit Trophy Winners: 1971-72, 1975-76

When Cenydd, known as Ken by everyone, played for St Helens in the 1960s, it was the club's Golden Era: '*With a galaxy of stars including Tom van Vollenhoven, Alex Murphy, Dick Huddart and Vince Karalius, the 1960s was a decade of great success for the Saints. In Prescott's first season as coach, he lifted the Lancashire League in the 1959-60 season. During this decade, the recognisable 'red vee' strip first appeared in 1961 for the final against Wigan. St Helens won this epic 12-6, and the kit has since become synonymous with the club. They won the Lancashire Cup in the 1961-62 season, with a 25-9 success over Swinton seeing yet more silverware come St Helens' way under the management of Prescott. After his departure in 1962, Stan McCormick led the club to retaining the Lancashire Cup in his first year, again beating Swinton; and St Helens made it a quadruplet of Lancashire Cup successes with wins against Leigh in 1964, and once more Swinton in 1965, this time under coach Joe Coan. The 1965 New Zealand tourists appeared at Knowsley Road on Wednesday 15 September.*

Saints inflicted a 28-7 defeat on their visitors, their biggest loss of the tour. A League and Cup double was achieved under Coan in the 1965-66 season, whilst they lost the Floodlit Trophy final against Castleford. St Helens were beaten by Wakefield Trinity in the 1967 Rugby Football League Championship Final at Station Road, Swinton on 10 May 1967 by 20 points to 9 in a replay, after a 7-7 draw, 4 days earlier. This would be Coan's last year in charge at St Helens after a highly successful period as boss. He was replaced by Cliff Evans. Evans' first full season in charge at the club saw him win the club's eighth Lancashire Cup in 1968; winning 13–10 against Warrington after a replay. St Helens retained the Lancashire Cup the year later, whilst also winning the Lancashire League for being the highest placed Lancashire side in the National standings, and they also reached the final of the Floodlit Trophy that season, where they

472

were beaten 7-4 by Wigan. The 1969-70 season would be the year that Evans would leave his post, but not without winning a National Championship, beating Leeds in the final after finishing third overall.' (- from Wikipedia and St Helens RFC). The eldest Williams brother Gwyn joined arguably the <u>best</u> Rugby League team of the time, Wigan, in 1938, and the only other Williams brother to head North, Cenydd, joined arguably the <u>best</u> Rugby League team of the 60s, St Helens.

CHAPTER 36 - CARDIFF SEASON 1963-64

CARDIFF UNLUCKY AGAINST ALL BLACKS - ELWYN SCORES 10 TRIES - LLOYD PLAYS 38 GAMES AND RETIRES – LLOYD'S PLAYER PROFILE AND REMINISCENCES

P45, W33, L9, 03. Tries 63-27. Points 508-254. Tries <u>119-40</u>, Pens 26-24

Elwyn Williams P35 T10 Pts30 (Davies states 9 tries once and 10 tries twice); **Tony Williams** P13 T1 Pts3; **Alun** Priday P34 T1 C34 P20 D1 Pts134 (Tongwynlais); Glyn Williams P2 T2 Pts6 (Pentyrch); **Lloyd Williams** his last season P38 T3 Pts9 - Total P308, W199, D39, L70, Tries 22 Points 66

Dai Hayward and Howard Norris were captain and vice-captain for a successive season, but somehow in September, 4 of the first 5 games were narrowly lost: Ebbw Vale 6-3 (H); Bridgend 8-6 (A); London Welsh 14-11 (H), with Cardiff scoring 3 tries to 2; and Coventry 6-5, a try apiece. In the return fixtures, Ebbw Vale were beaten 3 tries to a penalty, 9:3 (A); Bridgend won again, with a penalty 3-0 (H); London Welsh were defeated 13-3 (A), 3 tries to 1; and Coventry were hammered 4 tries to 1, 22:6 (H). There were some really superb newcomers to bed into the team, and results improved greatly, with Cardiff scoring twice as many points as the opposition. The Welsh international outside half Cliff Ashton came from Aberavon; the hooker Garry Davies from Treherbert; the brilliant wing Maurice Richards joined as a centre, much like Gerald Davies; another centre Mike Horgan joined from Pontypridd; a wing Ritchie Wills left Newport for Cardiff; and a wing and Welsh triallist Byron Thomas came from Tredegar. The remarkable prop John O'Shea joined from Newbridge, an Under-23 Welsh international. Billy Hullin, a nuggety scrum half, left Aberavon and earned his Athletic XV cap, soon to be the regular Firsts player. All the new men except Garry Davies and Billy Hullin gained First XV caps in this year.

There were doubles over Aberavon, Pontypool, Llanelli, Swansea, Gloucester and the Harlequins. Newport, the only conquerors of the New Zealand tourists, were narrowly beaten three times (14-6 A, 3-0 H, 8-5 H) and the postponed fourth game was played upon 29 April, an 11-11 draw. It was a fair result, as they suffered from 'Cardiff disease', with 4 of their greatest players, David Watkins, Brian Price, Stuart Watkins and Peter Rees going on the Welsh tour to South Africa in May 1964. Dai Hayward was omitted for the same reason. Thankfully all 3 Easter games were won including the Barbarians 21-3, scoring 4-0 tries. After losing 6 of their first 19 games, Cardiff played Wilson Whineray's Fifth All Blacks on 23 November, in front of 50,000 people. The visitors' pack had another world class forward, Colin 'Pine Tree' Meads and unfortunately at full-back one of the greatest goal kickers, the great Don Clarke.

Captain Dai Hayward trained the team, until they were confident that they could match Bleddyn Williams' Cardiff that beat the All Blacks in 1953. The 10th anniversary of the match was celebrated with the annual dinner in Cardiff's clubhouse, the night before the game. However, shortly before the dinner the news of John F. Kennedy's assassination came through. It was a sombre evening, and next day Cardiff could field 9 Welsh internationals: full back Alun Priday, centre Meirion Roberts, prop Kingsley Jones, hooker Billy Thomas, prop Howard Norris, second row Keith Rowlands, wing forward Dai Hayward, and half backs Lloyd Williams and Cliff Ashton. As usual against Cardiff, the 'Fifth International' in the British Isles, New Zealand played their Test team. Hayward led the Cardiff pack superbly, and the team were on top for the first half. However, Don Clarke kicked a penalty from 50 yards. Cardiff kept pressing, with the superb back row of Hayward, Cliff Howe and Elwyn Williams constantly pressurising scrum half Chris Laidlaw and the Maori outside half Herewini. On his own line, Herewini mishandled a pass and Cliff Howe touched down, with Priday converting. In the course of the game, **Priday missed no fewer than four kickable penalties**. Cardiff led 5-3 at half time, but Herewini dropped a goal from 35 yards, so Cardiff won on tries but lost the game 6-5. Lloyd and Elwyn Williams had fine games, and the best team lost. (Modern scoring 7-6 to Cardiff!)

The great reporter John Billot, in his 'All Blacks in Wales' recorded, 'A goal kicker would have beaten the All Blacks. But Alun Priday missed four first half penalty shots, three of them from quite reasonable range. Ironically Priday had broken the club's scoring record the previous season with 176 points.' The wing Maurice Richards, just over 18 years old, had first played for the Rags in May 1963, and just five days later had become an automatic choice for the Firsts, usually in the centre, where he played against New Zealand. He switched to the wing permanently, when internationals Gerald Davies and D. Ken Jones were the Cardiff centres, with Keri Jones on the other wing, probably giving Cardiff the best threequarters line in the world. Maurice Charles Rees Richards toured with the British Lions in South Africa, and gained 9 Welsh caps in 1968 and 1969, having scored 4 tries in a game against Gloucester in 1967. In 1966-67 he scored 33 tries in 38 games. He then scored a sensational **4 tries in one game against England** in 1969. After scoring 97 tries in 171 games for Cardiff, Maurice Richards turned to rugby league in 1969, playing for Great Britain and Wales and scoring 302 tries in 511 matches.

Maurice told Paul Rees: '*My sixth game for Cardiff was against the All Blacks. I remember fielding a kick and getting a knee in the back from Waka Nathan as I fell to the ground. I was raked so hard the marks took seven weeks to disappear. **Short-arm tackles were part of the game and players used any means they could to win.** It is much better now and refereed well... Running out on to the Arms Park was special. When I was a kid it seemed the only place where rugby existed.*' How on Earth he was ignored by the Welsh selectors for 5 years after his All-Blacks game, when he was playing the finest rugby of his life, is beyond every Cardiff supporter. The All Blacks lost only one match on tour, to a very fine Newport team on 30 October, by a dropped goal from Welsh international John Uzzell, who later joined Cardiff. The All-Blacks' manager said '*It was Newport all the way. They were the better side and we did not look like scoring*'. The 1963 All Blacks were undefeated in 36 of their 37 tour games, and the crowd of 25,000 at Newport's Rodney Parade had witnessed that one defeat on a rain-soaked pitch. This was one of the finest touring sides to visit Britain, and Cardiff should have beaten them. On 21 December, Wales lost by a penalty and a drop goal, 6-0, with only Dai Hayward and Kingsley Jones representing Cardiff. One can call the selectors lots of names about their choices for this game, all of them correct if accusatory. In their last match in the UK, the All Blacks cut loose at the Arms Park, beating the Barbarians 36-3.

The Welsh team drew at Twickenham 6-6, 2 tries each, with centre Ken Jones the only Cardiff player. They then beat Scotland in Cardiff 11-3, 2 tries to 1, with Dai Hayward back in, along with Ken Jones. There was then a splendid win in Dublin 15-6, 3 tries to 0, Dai Hayward keeping his place but Ken Jones being replaced by a young John Dawes. In the final game at Cardiff, Dai Hayward again played, with Ken Jones switched to wing, and Wales were 11-3 down to France at half time but drew 11-11, a try apiece. Unbeaten Wales shared the Championship with Scotland, who had lost against Wales, but Wales scored more points and had a greater points difference. Lloyd and Elwyn Williams were involved in almost every game, but Cenydd had gone North, and Tony filled in at centre, fly half and sometimes wing, while mainly playing for the Athletic and scoring 8 tries. He was to play centre against Harlequins but was shifted to the wing just before kick-off in 2-try, 8-0 home win in March.

Cardiff's leading try scorers were wing Steve Hughes 16, No. 8 Cliff

Howe 12, and flanker Elwyn Williams and wing Ritchie Wills with 10. Cliff Howe equalled Les Spence's record for a forward set in 1936-37, but Les Spence had also converted a try. Cliff Howe played most, in 40 out of 45 games, then prop Howard Norris 39, Lloyd Williams 38, prop John O'Shea 37, Graham Davies 35 and Dai Hayward 33. Alun Priday and Howard Norris became Barbarians. Veteran prop Colin Howe was Athletic captain again, with another good record: P35 W24 L5 D6 Pts 443-172. Taff's Well, home of the Williams boys, was defeated 30-3 and 33-9. In the season, Tony Williams (also playing games for the Firsts) scored 8 tries, along with Ritchie Wills and Glyn Ellis. Scrum half Billy Hullin and Chris Jones each touched down 7 times. Athletic caps were awarded to Ron Hill, Billy Hullin, Chris Jones, Gareth Jones and Jim Mills, all former youth players, and to prop forward twins from Nelson, Alun and Elfed Morgan, and H. D. Powell. Junior (Youth) XV results were: P26 W16 L7 D3 Points 258-101, with two members capped by Wales.

I saw Colin Howe propping many times – he joined Cardiff from Pontypool in 1952, then played 273 games, plus 70 for the Rags, before retiring in 1964. He captained the Rags for his last two seasons, and played in that disgraceful Springboks loss in 1960 and the Australia win in 1957. His long-time partners in the front row were hooker Geoff Beckingham and prop John Evans, known as JD. Beckingham played 331 times for Cardiff, beating the All Blacks in 1953 and the Wallabies in 1957, but winning only 2 Welsh caps because of the presence of Lion Bryn Meredith. 'JD' played 338 times for Cardiff over 10 seasons, also winning 2 Welsh caps. We should also mention a stalwart of this pack, the second row Malcolm Collins, who first played in 1949-50, winning his club cap, and regularly played 40 or over games a season, retiring after 306 games in 1958. A Barbarian, he played against the Springboks and All Blacks, and in five Welsh trials but never won a cap. **In the season of his Cardiff captaincy, he played 50 of the 52 games on the official list**. The front row members mentioned above also all played more than 40 games a season for the Firsts quite often, plus many unofficial charity games. Among dozens of such fixtures, a Cardiff Invitation XV was taken by Bleddyn Williams to play Bridgwater, captained by Dr. Jack Matthews and featuring the inimitable Stan Bowes.

In this year, St. Helen's staged its last international until a Test match between Wales and Tonga in 1997. The decision to abandon Swansea for Welsh rugby internationals in the 1950s was caused by capacity problems, only holding 50,000 spectators; long delays for players and spectators travelling west along the A48, especially at Port Talbot (the M4 was not operational in Wales until the 1980s, and the Briton Ferry dual carriageway was not replaced by the final stretch of motorway until 1993); and higher revenues from games at Cardiff Arms Park. Swansea Corporation, which owned the ground, were willing to raise the capacity to 70,000 or even

82,000, but wartime bomb damage forced a revision of building priorities. Even now Swansea has more difficult access than Cardiff for large-scale events.

LLOYD HUW (Christened HUGH) WILLIAMS 19 October 1933 - 25 February 2017
Taff's Well School - outside half
Caerphilly Secondary School
Cardiff Schoolboys 1946-49 – three Dewar Shields
Cardiff Youth 1949-52 scrumhalf
Wales Youth vs France 1952
1952 (23 January) - 1954 National Service,
1952-54 RAF XV, Combined Services XV
1952-1956 Cardiff Athletic 64 appearances (1952 alongside brother Vaughan vs Gloucester)
1952 Cardiff First XV aged 18, outside half, then scrumhalf
Cardiff First XV 1952-53 to 1963-64, 12 seasons, 22 tries, 308 games
Cardiff Captain 1960-61, 1961-62
Barbarians vs Newport 1956-57
Welsh captain 3 times, **13 Welsh caps** 1957-1962
1999 inducted into Cardiff Rugby Hall of Fame
Height 6 feet (183cm) Weight 13st 3lbs (84kg)

Lloyd Williams has his Wales Youth cap against France, 1952

At Taff's Well, an entry in a Display Cabinet records: '*Lloyd Williams is a staunch member of Taff's Well R.F.C. He has represented Taff's Well in the past, when on occasions he was not playing for Cardiff. Indeed, Lloyd played one game for Taff's Well Second XV at a time when he was the Welsh International scrumhalf. His career with Cardiff began in 1952 and continued to 1964, during which time he twice captained Cardiff, and gained 13 International Caps, three of those games as Captain. Strong, perceptive and inherently combative, this was the man to have in your side when the going got tough. Just before retirement, in 1963 Lloyd brought an International XV to Taff's Well to Cae'r Afon to commemorate the official opening of the clubhouse and ground.*'

From the Cardiff RFC website: '*One of eight brothers from Taff's Well who all played for Cardiff, Lloyd served a long apprenticeship at the Arms Park playing for Cardiff Schools, then the Youth team, the Athletic in 1951 - 52 before making his first team debut at the age of 18 in September 1952. Over the next four years he was limited to 43 appearances, but had many fine seasons ahead of him, playing 310 first team games before retiring. In 1960 and 1962 he was first team captain and later served as a member of the rugby committee.*
Lloyd gained 13 Welsh caps, making his debut against Scotland at Murrayfield in 1957, his last international was also against Scotland in 1962 at Cardiff. He captained the Welsh team on three occasions. In 1956-57 he represented the Barbarians against Newport.

There is no substitute for good timing, and Lloyd Hugh Williams' entry into the Hall of Fame coincided with his fiftieth year of service to Cardiff RFC. "I played for the Rags for one season in 1951-52, then 12 years with the first team, then 26 years on the committee, and now I've had the great honour of being a vice-president for eleven years", said a very proud man at the time of his induction. He first came to fame as a fifth of the eight brothers to play in the Blue & Black and went on to be a quality player and captain of Wales in his own right. Mention Lloyd Williams to anyone who saw him play, and they will immediately recall his lovely dive pass from the base of a scrum or lineout, his remarkable strength around the fringes of the pack that earned him the title of 'ninth forward', and, more than anything his courage in every game he played. Breaking into the Cardiff team at scrumhalf in the early 1950s was no easy thing, even for Lloyd Williams, who won the Dewar Shield with Cardiff Schools and played for Wales Youth against France, and was good enough to represent Combined Services.

"At that time the first choice was of course Rex Willis and his very capable deputy was Brian Mark, so I knew I would have to wait for my chance", remembered Lloyd. The first team debut eventually came in September 1952 against Nantes and Cognac and then the first of many memorable games against Newport. In the following seasons he made

seven, ten, eleven and fifteen appearances, enough to gain valuable experience and build a steady reputation for himself, but never quite enough to win the first team cap awarded for 20 games a season.' Lloyd only ever wanted to play for Cardiff, and was patient while regular international Rex Willis played from 1947-48 to 1957-58, and the reliable club servant Brian Mark made 95 appearances from 1949-50 to 1957-58. Lloyd was happy with his previous experience of playing outside half, which added to his knowledge of half-back play, and regularly played for the Rags in his first four seasons from 1952-53, although making 43 appearances for the Firsts. However, in 1956-57 he took over as the team's regular scrum half, and in the following 8 seasons, from 1956-57 to 1963-64, his First XV appearances were 37, 21, 36, 33, 32, 34, 34 and 38, making 308 games in all, with 22 tries.

'But even in those formative years there were days to remember, include the near-miss to end all near-misses. A letter arrived in the post one day in November 1953, from the Club secretary Brice Jenkins. It contained a card that said. "You have been selected to play for Cardiff against New Zealand..." But before I could give a cheer, I suddenly spotted a handwritten addition in the bottom corner saying "Reserve"! Rex Willis was, of course, the scrumhalf in that famous win, but Lloyd would one day play his own part in the history of the Club's games against touring sides. Meanwhile, another significant match, that he was certainly very much part of, occurred in March 1956. Newport were chasing their first-ever fourth win in a season against their arch-rival and at the last minute Willis withdrew with an injured shoulder. Into the Rodney Parade cauldron stepped Lloyd Williams. "It's a match and a day I will never forget," said Lloyd. "I thought I'd be playing for the Rags against Senghenydd that day, but found myself in a situation where Newport had a dozen bottles of champagne lined up, and I had the responsibility of supplying our key man Cliff Morgan with the ball." It was a challenge that Lloyd proved equal to. Though six points down early in the match, and the Newport back row hounding Cliff at every turn, Cardiff recovered firstly through Lloyd's break that gave Eddie Thomas a try, and then another swift pass from him, that allowed Cliff to put Gordon Wells over for a second score. With both tries converted Cardiff held on for an unlikely win – and Newport had no use for the champers. Instead reports at the time suggested that "Cardiff should have collared that bubbly and toasted their young scrumhalf." Cliff Morgan certainly did, for as he left the field he put his arm around Lloyd's shoulders and said, "Thank you – you helped make this victory possible."

The Hall of Fame entry continues: 'Less than a year later, Cliff Morgan and Lloyd Williams were running out together at Murrayfield as Wales's half-backs against Scotland. To complete the happiest of stories it was his big brother Bleddyn who gave Lloyd news of that first cap. "I had just returned from playing for Cardiff in Aberavon, and was in the foyer of the

Athletic Club when Bleddyn phoned JBG Thomas at the Western Mail, then came over to me and said, 'You're playing for Wales next week'. It was a very emotional moment." Lloyd was to partner Cliff in his final seven games for Wales, but shortly after Cliff retired Lloyd found himself in the international wilderness. *"I didn't play for Wales for two years then one day there was a knock on the door and there again was Bleddyn – always a bringer of good news. "You're back in the Wales team in Paris on Saturday", he said, "and you're captain!" This time I really did have to sit down.* It was hardly surprising that Wales turned to Lloyd Williams for leadership because for two seasons from September 1960 he was an outstanding club captain. He took his team into the ill-fated struggle against the Springboks that year unbeaten after 13 matches, and in eight matches against Newport under his leadership, the Club won five a drew three. The great landmark though, was against the Barbarians in 1964, when he reached his 300th First Team appearance and the Club celebrated in style with a magnificent 21 points to three victory. Six weeks later he took his bow for the final time, with 310 games and another 64 for the Athletic XV to his name. *"In fact"*, said Lloyd, *"I once worked out that between the **eight Williams brothers played 1480 games for the Club.**"* Some record.'

SEASON	P	W	D	L	TRY	CON	PEN	DG	PTS
1952-1953	7	6	1	0	1	0	0	0	3
1953-1954	10	6	1	3	0	0	0	0	0
1954-1955	11	8	1	2	0	0	0	0	0
1955-1956	15	10	0	5	1	0	0	0	3
1956-1957	37	28	2	7	6	0	0	0	18
1957-1958	21	15	2	4	1	0	0	0	3
1958-1959	36	17	6	13	1	0	0	0	3
1959-1960	33	17	8	8	1	0	0	0	3
1960-1961	32	23	5	4	1	0	0	0	3
1961-1962	34	22	5	7	3	0	0	0	9
1962-1963	34	20	5	9	4	0	0	0	12
1963-1964	38	27	3	8	3	0	0	0	9
TOTAL	**308**	**199**	**39**	**70**	**22**	**0**	**0**	**0**	**66**

John S. Williams reminisced in *The Garth Domain* June 2008 that he was born in Morganstown, next door to the rugby-playing brothers Roy and Emlyn Cook, the latter who played for Cardiff a few times in 1950-51 and 1951-52. He then moved as a child to live next to the Williams' family, before returning to Morganstown and playing for Penarth. John then went to play on the left wing for Taff's Well. *'At that time Vaughan Williams was left-centre and Lloyd Williams was scrumhalf. 'It was strange how things worked out. Lloyd and I went into the RAF on the same day, 23rd*

January 1952. Both of us went to Hednesford in Staffordshire...' **Bleddyn, Bryn, Vaughan, Cenydd and Tony all preferred the left-centre position, although, like Lloyd, all were excellent outside-halves**. Elwyn could easily have been a back, also, and Gwyn played wing when he went to rugby league. The brothers were not only superb players, but versatile.

LLOYD'S STORY (from *THE GARTH DOMAIN - THE WILLIAMS FAMILY*, 1984) by Gerald Edwards and Don Llewelyn

'The decline of rugby over the last few decades has been due to several factors, including the disappearance of Grammar Schools and the growth of interest in indoor sports. The conversion to Comprehensives brought about a totally different situation, as fewer and fewer teachers were willing to turn out, unpaid, on Saturday mornings to teach the game. From then on, the players just weren't coming along. Then what really hit it on the head was the arrival of the professional game, which changed rugby almost overnight. Suddenly small clubs were paying players the equivalent of, if not more than, they would get from a top-class side, and this helped to stop the natural flow as well. At the top level, crippling amounts of money were paid out to bring over New Zealanders, South Africans and Australians. Although this happened in England too, here it cut the legs right off our home-grown players, so to speak.

Regarding the Regional or Provincial system, which is presently in place, there's plenty wrong with it. Pumping money into it appears not to be the answer. People like Leighton Samuel, who have put up a lot of cash, without getting a penny out of it, can only pay so much. The situation as far as Cardiff is concerned is complicated, by the fact that so many people wanted to drop the name, and for them to be known just as 'The Blues', to satisfy people who didn't want to be associated with Cardiff. Well, I think the capital city should be proudly represented by its own name, after all the Cardiff Club has been around for 128 years. I actually think the names of the other Welsh clubs should have been retained too. And I think eventually we will have those names again: Newport, Swansea, Llanelli and Cardiff.' (The new names for the regions were the Newport-Gwent Dragons, Neath-Swansea Ospreys, Llanelli Scarlets and Cardiff Blues. After 20 years, by 2020, they generally went by the names of Dragons, Ospreys, Scarlets and Blues, although all older supporters still called them Cardiff, the same as Cardiff RFC, their feeder team at the same ground. As of 2021, the Blues reverted to Cardiff Rugby/Rygbi Caerdydd, and brought back black into their playing strip. However, a quick perusal of strips for sale seems to indicate navy being used instead of the traditional black.)

'And I really don't believe that all this runs the risk of the teams in the other towns falling into the arms of Rugby League, as has been suggested by somebody.' (Rugby League had the same problem of falling

481

attendances as Welsh Rugby Union clubs, but a switch to a summer season has reinvigorated the game). 'If you think about our allegiances for a moment, you have to remember that in the twelve years or so I played with Cardiff, many of our players came from Pontypridd... and the Bridgend area too. There were lots from the Rhondda as well who bypassed Pontypridd to come down to us, not to mention those from the Llanelli area! As far as our fortunes on the international stage are concerned, we have to face up to the fact that since our successes of the 1970s, other nations have caught up with us, and in fact gone past us. From that time, they started to take up training and coaching much more seriously than they used to. Also, as a nation, we don't have many big men. Just think of those huge English forwards for a start, Johnson, Grewcock and so on, men who are not only six feet seven inches tall, but also very athletic. When we produce the odd giant, he is usually lacking coordination. He might be a good line-out jumper, but is slow around the field.

There are lots of inexplicable things going on today, as well. Why, for instance, are players put on the field with two or three minutes to go? I just don't see the purpose of that – unless someone is hurt, of course. It seems that it might be done just to be able to award a cap. Well, I think that devalues the honour. Mind you, I think the team selectors in my day used to make some strange decisions – probably for the same reason. I remember that after we lost to Scotland in Edinburgh in 1957, by a freak dropped goal by Arthur Dorwood, several changes were made, unnecessarily in my view. We had been twice in the lead in that match, but we lost 9-6. Low scores were a feature of rugby in those days. Take the match Cardiff lost to the All Blacks in 1963, also by a dropped goal. New Zealand had a penalty after I was given offside. It's also history that Don Clarke kicked the resultant penalty from the halfway line.' (Long-range penalties were very rare at this time.) 'I remember standing under the posts and willing it not to go over – but it did. It crept over the bar. Then we scored a try which was converted, but Mac Herewini dropped a goal to win the game 6-5 for the All Blacks. You know, we more than held our own in that match, and came so close to repeating what had happened ten years earlier in 1953, when Bleddyn's Cardiff side beat the tourists. The '63 All Blacks were themselves to fall victim to a dropped goal by 'Dick' (John) Uzzell, giving Newport a victory in terrible conditions.

Anyway, back to that Scotland game in 1957. That was the match in which I gained the first of my 13 Welsh caps. I had taken over the scrumhalf berth from Onllwyn Brace, to partner Cliff Morgan. It was the game in which the great Ken Jones gained his 44th cap, a record at the time. That was on February 2nd. Then it was the Ireland match at Cardiff the next month, which we won 6-5. Later the same month we beat France in Paris, in a comparatively high-scoring game – 19-13!' (England won the Grand Slam and Wales were second. Wales had earlier been beaten 3-0, with

482

England scoring a penalty at Cardiff. In Paris, winning 19-13, Wales scored 4 tries to 3, with the rare occurrence of three Welsh forwards touching down – John Faull, Bryn Meredith and Ray Prosser.)

'In the following January, Australia played Wales in Cardiff, and unfortunately for me Cliff Morgan withdrew through injury. The selectors decided to give first caps to Carwyn James and Wynne Evans, the Llanelli half-back partnership. Wales beat the tourists 9-3, but two weeks later Cliff and I were back to face England at Twickenham. The game was a 3-3 draw, despite England fielding what apparently was their strongest side since the war. Cliff was brilliant that day with his tactical kicking. In fact, everyone played well. There are a couple of interesting and amusing memories of that game. Firstly, we had to play in trial match jerseys, without the three feathers, because someone had packed the wrong kit! Then in the evening a squad of souvenir hunters entered Twickenham and sawed down the crossbar, over which Terry Davies had kicked a 45-yard penalty and took it away. Then I played for the rest of 1958 and in the England and Scotland matches of 1959.' (In 1958 England won the Five Nations on 6 points, with Wales again second, on 5 points. Scotland were beaten at home 8-3 (2-0 on tries) and then Ireland away 9-6 (3-1 on tries), but France won in Cardiff after a 3-3 halftime score, 16-3, scoring 2 tries to 1).

'Cliff Ashton of Aberavon, getting his first cap, was my partner for the England game on January 17th, 1959, which we won 5-0 by virtue of Dewi Bebb's marvellous try, in what was his first international appearance also. That was the game when the crowd really started to sing *during* a game. We lost to Scotland 6-5 at Murrayfield, a try apiece. We could have won that game if things had gone according to plan. We were attacking, and Cliff Ashton had indicated that he was going to go for a dropped goal. I put the ball in the scrum and Bryn Meredith swiftly hooked it. I managed to get the ball away with difficulty, but Cliff had to readjust and made a 'snap' drop of it. We thought it had gone over but it dipped just beneath the bar. We then beat Ireland 8-6 in Cardiff. We had to tackle for our lives in that game, and our defence came in for a lot of praise. I seemed to spend sixty of the eighty minutes just stopping the Irish forwards on the rampage. Wilf Wooller was kind enough to say that if it hadn't been for my tackling and that of Terry Davies, Wales would have been swamped. Guess what happened for the next match which was against France in Paris. They dropped me!

They moved Malcolm Thomas to outside half and brought in Billy Watkins of Newport at inside half. **For the first time in the post-war years, there wasn't a single Cardiff player in the Welsh side. To me it was unbelievable, it made you wonder what the Hell you had to do.'** (Wales lost 11-3 in France, who won the Five Nations with 5 points - Wales were joint second with 4.) 'I was then out of the Welsh team for two years. I thought, well that's the end of it now, you know. Billy Watkins was followed by Colin Evans of Pontypool. I was captain of Cardiff during that time: 60-61 and 61-62. I played one game against the Springboks'. (Captaining Cardiff in the 1960 'bloodbath'.) 'Onllwyn Brace had been back for a couple of games, and then I was reserve at the game against South Africa in which Tony O'Connor played. Unfortunately for Tony, he was penalised for putting the ball in the scrum 'wonky', and the resultant kick gave the tourists a 3-0 victory. After that game the great flood at the Arms Park took place, after torrential rain hit Cardiff. I was asked to play for the Barbarians against the Springboks, but by that time I was injured and had to decline. O'Connor kept his place in the Welsh side for a couple of games, but then Onllwyn Brace was back for the Ireland game which Wales won 9-0. I remember that evening well, for Bleddyn and I went to see Cardiff City playing Spurs in a very important game...'

(I must digress here, because I was at this game, and for Cardiff City fans, it was the strangest season on record. In the First Division (– now the Premiership) Cardiff had just been promoted from the old Second Division (- now the Championship) and had only lost 3-2 away to Tottenham Hotspur, who this season were to achieve the first 'Double' of the modern era, winning the League and FA Cup in the same season. But in front of 45,463 fans, Cardiff beat Spurs at Ninian Park 3-2, in a great game, with Barry's Derek Tapscott scoring, along with Hogg and Walsh, against Allen and Dyson. Spurs only lost 7 of 42 fixtures. Cardiff were now sitting comfortably in the First Division table, but the sequence from that great performance up to the end of season was a miserable L, L, L, L, D, L, L, D, D, finishing 15th of 22 teams with 37 points. That run of games after playing Spurs was to be ominous. The next season Cardiff City were relegated by a point, just above Chelsea, in 21st place with 32 points. Again, there had been a dreadful end to the season, and no fewer than 14 of 42 games were drawn.)

'... On the following Monday evening I heard a knock on the door, and I could see it was Bleddyn, so I assume he'd come to pay for some tickets I had got him for the match on Saturday. I opened the door and was taken aback when he said, *"Congratulations, you've been picked for France."* My response was simply *"Oh."* *"Indeed"* he said, *"And captain!"* My brother knew this because he was writing for *The People* and had just come from the meeting. However, I didn't hear from the WRU until the Thursday – and even then, there was no mention at all of the captaincy. Therefore, my return occurred on March 25th 1961 against France at Stade Colombes, partnering outside half Ken Richards. That was Terry Davies's last game for Wales and Alun Pask's first. Both sides scored two tries, but we lost the match 8-6.

I was captain again and partnered Allan Rees for the England game in January 1962 at Twickenham, a 0-0 draw. In the dinner that evening I was sitting next to the Leader of the House of Commons and 'Sir' somebody or other, 'President of the RFU.' (This was C.H. Gadney, who had refereed the Welsh win over the All Blacks in 1935.) 'I thought *"Oh blimey"* – but it didn't go down too badly – for a feller from Taff's Well! For the Scottish match I was captain once more. We were preparing for that on the St Peter's ground down Newport Road when one of the 'Big Five' walked by. I simply said to him *"Alright"* – and his response was *"It had better be alright tomorrow."* I knew what he meant. We lost the game 8-3, but I think minds had been made up in any case. This man was a Lions selector, and there was a tour coming up. The Ireland game was postponed because of the Smallpox scare, but I was dropped anyway and Tony O'Connor was back for the home match against France. I was not to play for Wales again, but continued to play for Cardiff for another couple of seasons. I finished in 1964 when I was thirty. I thought that I was playing now more with the head, than with the will. I'd had a good run over twelve years, appearing for Cardiff 310 times. They allowed me to stay as a registered player for a year, they do that in case you change your mind. And then I packed it in and joined the club committee, on which I served for twenty-two years, and for part of that time as Cardiff's representative on the East District Committee.

I started playing rugby, of course, with Taff's Well schoolboys. They had restarted the side in September 1945 when I was nearly twelve, and also played for Cardiff Boys. We played for the latter on a sportsground of one of the factories down at Penarth Road. I remember playing there against Caerphilly, and playing for them was John Llewellyn's brother-in-law, Dai Edwards from Tongwynlais, who had a schoolboys' cap that year. It was 1946 before everything settled down, and by then I was playing with a chap in the Cardiff Boys' side called Gerry McCarthy. Anyway, Del Harris came up to me and said, *"Would you like to play scrumhalf?"* I was then selected to play against Pontypridd at Taff Vale Park. I remember little about the game, except that at the first scrum I put the ball in and when it came out, I passed it and that was that. I suppose I was hooked, no pun intended. I played altogether for three years in the Cardiff Schoolboys side. We won the Dewar Shield in three successive years. In 1949 the Cardiff Youth started up and I became part of that. This means that by the time I finished in 1988, I had been attached to the Cardiff club in one way or another for 39 years.

However, in 1952 I went into the RAF, and first went up to Padgate to kit out and then to Hednesford, a training camp in Staffordshire, not far from Stoke. I was told to go down to the Flight Office and I began to wonder why. I was told they'd had a request from Cardiff, asking for me to play for them on Saturday. Well, I'd been playing for Cardiff Youth up until then, and explained that I knew they wanted me to play in the Final of the Youth Cup against Aberavon at Maindy Stadium. I was permitted to come home, and found instead that I was playing for Cardiff Athletic. Vaughan played that day as a matter of fact – it was against Gloucester. I went back to camp, then a week or so after I was sent for again.

All this was unheard of, because I was there really for square-bashing. Anyway, I had a weekend off because of the jabs that I'd had, but soon I was told that I'd been selected to play for the Welsh Youth against France. I was told that if I went, I'd have to be 're-flighted' to make up for lost time. After being away almost a week, I returned to the camp. I walked in and they said, *"Where have you been?"* *"Playing rugby in France"* I answered. *"Oh, alright then"*, they said, and I passed out the following Tuesday – I hadn't even fired a rifle! In fact, I didn't do a lot of things the others did. I left there towards the end of March, quite near the end of the season really, and I was posted to RAF Pershore in Staffordshire. I thought the Group Captain, the head of the Flying Training School was selector of the RAF side, but I only found out recently, when a book came out, that he was Secretary of the RFU and had been for some time. So I stepped right into it, didn't I!

I became the 'blue-eyed boy' there, so I played for the Station, and the Command. He said to me just before Christmas *"I think you had better take your uniform with you, because I have a feeling you are going to be picked to play for the Combined Services in the South of France."* It turned out then that I played for the Combined Services before I played for the RAF. I was then picked to play for the RAF against Swansea, which became a regular fixture. After that I played in the inter-service game and we beat the Army and the Navy. I came out in 1954. I think I played for Command until Christmas, but I didn't play any more RAF matches.' (Lloyd also played scrum half in both Inter-Service games in 1953, a draw 3-3 against the Royal Navy and a 11-3 defeat to the Army.) 'When you look back over a career in rugby, you can feel amazed at just how many matches you will have played. In those days, of course, you had to be quite seriously hurt before you came off the field, because there were no substitutions in those days. I fractured my cheekbone three times, but I don't remember being taken off the field.

I didn't go straight into the Cardiff side, although I did play my first game when I was 18. There were one or two times when I was called up at the beginning of the season. Cliff Morgan was playing in a charity game for Jeff Butterfield in Bristol, and Glyn John hadn't turned up, and minutes later I was running onto the pitch to play for Cardiff against Bridgend, at outside half. Rex Willis was playing scrumhalf, of course. We hammered Bridgend (28-5), and then the following Saturday I played for the "Rags" – the Firsts were at Coventry and were to play Leicester on the Monday. I went up and played against Leicester, and the other games I played were against Aberavon, Newport, Swansea and Llanelli – I played seven games altogether in that 1956-57 season. Rex then became injured, I went back to scrumhalf and then found myself playing for Wales in that position.

The hardest men I ever played against were the South Africans. Eighteen months ago, I went to South Africa and we spent Christmas and New Year there. We were with a chap I'd met when I was over there with Cardiff, as a committeeman in 1979. Well, he had a barbecue, and he invited Lionel Wilson, who was full back for the Springboks in 1960. He was recalling with pride their win over Cardiff, who had been unbeaten up to that match. That had been over forty years earlier – so you can see how important it was to them. **Mind you,** *they had to clog to beat us. No doubt about it.* **And they had help from Gwynne Walters the referee.** I mean there were several incidents where he should have stepped in. Their right-wing Roux hit Alun Priday virtually when the ball was crossing the touchline, and Walters didn't do a bloody thing about it. We were playing attacking rugby, and they were tightening everything up. It was a bruising game and we were battle-worn.' (The author's opinions on this game are shared with everyone in his experience who saw it. It was a total disgrace that must never be swept under the carpet. Later Springbok teams may have tried, but none came close to that level of thuggery.)

'I've been proud to be part of this unusual family of so many rugby players, and people have often said that the story should be told. I've been thinking about my mother's influence on us. Just imagine all that washing – and Taff's Well played in white shirts! My father, well, he hardly went to a game, but my mother went regularly. When we played New Zealand in 1963, she'd had an accident. I think it was the one when she was talking to her brother Roy Roberts, on Glan-y-Llyn Square, and a motorbike came over the hill, went around Roy, and hit her. She broke her leg, but anyway she went to the match – they gave her a fireman's lift up to the stand. She used to go down on the bus, and she didn't miss many games, you know. All eight boys played for Cardiff – between us all we had 1,480 first team appearances. I don't suppose that record will ever be broken. Bleddyn and Elwyn were Schoolboy Internationals. Elwyn, Tony and myself had Youth caps. Three of us played for the RAF and Combined Services. Myself, Bleddyn, Cenydd and Tony played for the Barbarians. Bleddyn and I had senior caps, and both of us enjoyed the captaincy of our country. We are proud also to be part of the Cardiff Hall of Fame.'

Welsh Rugby **May 1968**: Sports Profile of **LLOYD WILLIAMS - CARDIFF, WALES and the BAA-BAAS - OF THE GREAT WILLIAMS FAMILY** by Fred Croster

'For those who may not know, there is, to the north of Cardiff, indeed, where the River Taff flows through the gorge which made Cardiff possible, a small village with the picturesque name of Taff's Well. That is the geographical name, so called because of the healing waters at the well for

487

which it was quite famous. In the lifetime of most of us, however, that self-same village has become even more famous as the birthplace of the Williams family, who have, and still are carving out a page in the story of Welsh rugby which is completely unparalleled. In chronological order, number five in the family was born in 1933 and christened Lloyd Hugh; a name destined to add even more lustre to the family story. As did all the others, Lloyd went first of all to the small local village school, Ffynnon Taf, so called after the River Taff which flowed alongside. In this picturesque and important artery of the Welsh coaling valleys there is only just room for the river, the canal which once carried the coal barges down to Cardiff from Merthyr, the railway line which followed and the road. Fortunately, behind the school there is just enough room for a playing pitch, and it was here, still in use and conspicuous to all passers-by, that Lloyd and all the Williams's received their initial baptism into the world of Rugby Football.

Here, the so-important fundamentals were correctly laid down and this might be a particularly apt comment at this time when the Welsh Rugby Union's coaching schemes are so much in the news. Lloyd Williams, as the others, was guided on the right lines during the very earliest, formative years, to such effect that these things become almost second nature and I am in sympathy with those who say that it is in these early days that the fundamentals have to be laid down.

The Headmaster then was Major Walter Trigg, now passed on, and an ardent rugby man. He was, in his time, chairman of the Cardiff Schools' Rugby Union and a W.R.U. referee. The man who had most to do, however, with the early coaching of these lads was Del Harries - one of the quiet, sincere men of rugby who usually make the greatest contributions. This was certainly so in Del's case. He had the gift of bringing out the very best in boys and men, and in addition to all that he did for Taff's Well and Cardiff Schools, he became a well-known W.R.U. referee, a Cardiff Schools Selector, then Chairman and later followed Viv Phelps as secretary, when Viv moved on to become the Welsh Schools secretary. Del, one of the finest men I have known, was singularly unfortunate in other ways. He lost his wife, and then he himself died suddenly and sadly at quite an early age. He had been appointed to succeed Walter Trigg as Headmaster and just lived for his school and schoolboy football.

It was when he returned from war service with the R.A.F. that the local schools rugby restarted and Lloyd Williams immediately came under his wing. Not big then, but quite fast and elusive, Lloyd played at outside half and then to bring exceptional honour to this small school, as the tender age of 12 he was selected for the representative Cardiff Boys' XV. He was actually picked in the centre, with John McCarthy of another great Cardiff Rugby family as outside half. Cardiff Schools at this time were going through a truly wonderful era. They won the Welsh Schools' Premier

Trophy, the 'Dewar Shield' in seven successive years and Lloyd Williams played for them for three. This was made possible, firstly because of his so early and young start, and because of the advancing of school leaving age. The outstanding team, from full back was: (the legendary) Billy Boston, W. Carter, Tony Free, (Taff Well's) Bryn Mapstone (played 7 times for Cardiff), Derek Grindle, Gerrard McCarthy, Lloyd Williams, T. Nicholson, Terry Donovan (played 90 times for Cardiff), Joe Erskine (yes, the future British and Empire Heavyweight Champion who also gained a Welsh Boys Club Cap later on), W. Cornish (Arthur Cornish's nephew), W. Clayton (gained his cap), Bernard Walsh and Ralph Jones (an Ely boy who became a Welsh Schools Boxing Champion). Lloyd Williams went from school straight into the brand-new Cardiff Junior Section... This enterprise was to lead the way in Welsh Youth Rugby... Bryn Mapstone, Derek Grindle, Joe Erskine, Ralph Jones and Terry Donovan, went with Lloyd from the School XV into the Cardiff Youth XV.

At the age of 16, Lloyd was selected to represent Wales in their first Youth International; this was at scrumhalf, against the Welsh Secondary Schools and then against Munster. In the following season - 1952, the Welsh Youth played the French Youth for the first time... It was Lloyd's turn to be called up and he also went into the R.A.F. like Bleddyn. He was posted to Persham, near Worcester, not too far away, and at the age of 18, in September 1952, he played his first game for the Cardiff 1st XV. His second game was against great rivals Newport and he managed to put in three appearances for the Blue and Blacks that year. Although we always think of Lloyd as being a very big man, it is interesting to note that at this time, at the age of 18, at the beginning of his Service life, although a shade under 6ft. tall, he only weighed 12 and a 1/2 stone. It must have been the "Good Life" in the R.A.F. which caused him to develop. It really was a good life then, as rugby football, in very good company, played such an important part. He played regularly for his station, the R.A.F. Representative side and the Combined Services, and particularly remembers the match against the French "B" side in France, in season 1952-53. With him were Vic Tindle, Mel Channer, Bob Stirling, Peter Yarrington, Bob Weighill - all English internationals; Rhys Williams of Llanelli, Wales and the British Lions, Jimmy Greenwood of Scotland and the Lions, plus Cardiff Colleagues, Alun Priday and Dr. Gwyn Rowlands, who were of course Welsh internationals, later.

These two years in the R.A.F. were not only enjoyable, but provided the opportunity to gain invaluable experience of top-level rugby. He was still, during this time, playing the odd game for the Cardiff club when Service duties permitted, but his first full season at the Arms Park, excepting his Youth Days, was in 1953-54 when he came out of the R.A.F. Established in the Cardiff side at that time was Rex Willis; that very good scrumhalf Brian Mark was also playing well, but Lloyd still managed to almost gain his "Rags" Cap. Season 1953-54 will always be remembered at the Arms Park, for the wonderful win against the All Blacks. Brother Bleddyn was, of course, the successful Cardiff skipper. What a unique honour it would have been if Lloyd had played. Both he and Brian Mark were standing by. Lloyd did gain his full "Rags" Cap, the following season 1954-55.

These were great days in Cardiff's proud history, with names that have become part of our rugby heritage. Rex and Cliff Morgan were the half backs, and in season 1956-57, Lloyd well remembers one particular Saturday, early in the season, when he had been picked to play for the "Rags". Jeff Butterfield had arranged a special game at Bristol, Cliff Morgan was invited to play, and at the last minute Lloyd found himself on the field, to play for the 1sts, at outside half, at Bridgend. That season he played 6 or 7 games as partner to Rex Willis and he must have made quite an impression. In fact one National paper carried the headline "Lloyd sets a pivot poser for Cardiff". It went on to state that Cardiff had a problem which many clubs would like to face. It was the choice between brilliant Welsh international Cliff Morgan, and their sturdily built and quickly developing Lloyd Williams. As we all know, Lloyd obtained all his honours as a scrumhalf, but his versatility stemming from his previous excellent schools grounding, was to stand him and Cardiff in good stead on a number of occasions.

In October 56-57, Rex was injured against Swansea, Cliff was back in the side and Lloyd Williams took rapid advantage to secure the key scrumhalf position. He was selected for the Final Welsh Trial that year, but after 20 minutes, had to go off with a badly cut eye. He was selected as reserve against England in January 1957 and then proudly gained his first Cap against Scotland the following month. At this time, many readers will remember, there was considerable rivalry between him and Onllwyn Brace, "Onkers", as he is fondly called by many. This rivalry was not in any way personal, they were and still are very good friends, but you know how the popular Press love to build up these things. The controversy was based on their respective and distinctive qualities and I, personally, well remember being in the Cardiff Clubhouse on the occasion when Lloyd was selected to play for Wales in preference to Onllwyn. Lloyd was thrilled beyond measure, naturally, at having been chosen and deeply touched when a telegram was handed to him. It was from Onllwyn, who had been dropped and contained a simple, sincere message of congratulations and good will. The hallmark, surely, of a great sportsman. Wales lost 9-6, to Scotland in that game, despite the galaxy of Welsh stars on display. These included: Cliff; Malcolm Thomas: Ken Jones, playing in his last international at the end of his illustrious career; Rhys Williams; Bryn Meredith; Ray Prosser and so on. In that same season, Lloyd was selected to become a member of the Barbarians and played for them against Swansea on Easter Monday and against Newport on Easter Tuesday. On that Easter Saturday he had played for Cardiff against them, in the 'black weekend' as the Baa-Baas won by 40 points. Who on the Arms Park will ever forget it? He also played for the Baa-Baas later that year in Ulster.

Lloyd about to stop a 'forward rush' against England in the Arms Park mud of 1959

'The pitch resembled a lake' according to John Billot. Wales won 5-0, Dewi Bebb touching down after only 5 first-class matches in south Wales.

A good season then, and our profile subject gained the unusual distinction of gaining his Welsh Cap before he had gained his own, Cardiff Club, Cap. It may not be widely known that to gain a Cardiff Cap, it is a requirement that no fewer than 20 games have to be played for the team in one season. An honour, purposely not lightly won. The following season, 57-58 saw Lloyd firmly established in the Cardiff and Welsh sides. That was the season of great disappointment, many will remember. With Clem Thomas as skipper, Ireland and Scotland were beaten, but before them, in the first international, against England at Twickenham, the result was a 3-3 draw. This was a game that I, myself, will never forget, as I was the Welsh Touch Judge - the first time that the present system of having a referee to run the line in an international was adopted - and it was the game when Terry Davies hit the upright when by all that was holy and unholy it should have gone over. I can see that damned ball in my sleep even now. Sailing beautifully, to go between the posts, my flag was already being raised, when a freak gust of wind, right across the way it had been blowing, caused it to turn and cost Wales the Triple Crown. "Heart-breaking" is the biggest understatement I can think of at the moment. Tenby R.F.C. supporters were so incensed at this, that on the following Sunday morning, they cut down the crossbar and carted it back to Wales. It was later replaced by Terry Davies himself, from his timber yard.

The game will be remembered for Cliff Morgan's line kicking. As can happen so often at "Twickers", the wind was blowing down one side of the pitch and up the other. Cliff summed this up from the start and used it to tremendous effect. For some reason England never tumbled to it. Nim Hall was their outside half if I recollect. Cliff was in great form and was never once caught in possession - the point of this little anecdote is - for Cliff to have such a good game - who provided him with so much "Good Ball?" Lloyd Williams, and I think he was never really given enough credit for the part he played. December brought the Australians to Cardiff and for this attractive game the Cardiff selectors saw fit to recall Rex Willis in preference to Lloyd Williams - a selectorial quirk which was to be repeated nearly 10 years later as on the recent Australian Tour, younger brother Tony was similarly not selected - Phil Morgan being chosen instead. These things can happen; I know, I was one of the Cardiff selectors then.' (Tony was recovering from a bad injury, but was 'devastated').

Lloyd Williams, big and strong, could play the ninth forward game fearlessly. A scrum half with a longer than usual pass, he was a member of the famous Taffs Well family who provided eight brothers, all top notch players for Cardiff, including, of course, Bleddyn. Lloyd in action against France in 1958.

Lloyd Williams against France, 1958

'Lloyd was, however, back in the Welsh team which met France at Stade Colombes... This year was that of the British Lions Tour of New Zealand and Australia and all Wales felt that one of the scrum halves had to be Lloyd Williams. He had had quite an outstanding season; big and strong, with a wonderful service, he seemed ideally suited to stand up to the hurly burly of this, quite arduous tour. The All Blacks were expecting him, but the selectors thought otherwise, and this must rank as probably the greatest disappointment of his playing career, The scrum halves who were selected were Dickie Jeeps of England - no one grumbled at this - and Stan Coughtry of Scotland.' (Coughtry was injured early on, and Andy Mulligan of Ireland replaced him, with Croster believing that Lloyd was incredibly unfortunate not to go on tour). 'There was some consolation as, for the following season, that unforgettable character, double and nearly triple Oxford Blue, C.D. Williams was the Cardiff captain and he chose as his vice-captain Lloyd. One momentous game in that season was that between Cardiff Present and Cardiff Past for the Sid Judd Memorial Fund.

Season 60-61 saw the fulfilment of many ambitions, to make up for some of the previous disappointments. Lloyd was elected Cardiff captain, and will never forget, as indeed will many of us, the Cardiff game, or shall I say "Battle" against Avril Malan's Springboks? South Africa won decisively by 13-0, but what an epic struggle it was. Gwyn Walters was the referee and my friend Gwyn has often said since, to me, that in some ways it was a nightmare and taught him lessons which he never forgot.' (In this writer's perception at the time, the referee was too cowardly to send off at least two or three South Africans, but it was simply 'not done' to offend touring nations.) 'From the first whistle the "Boks" went in with everything they had, determined to win and this they did; with Dai Hayward a passenger with a shoulder injury from almost the first line-out; Tommy McCarthy as outside half, another passenger, forced to go off in the first half' (with what Croster euphemistically calls a 'shoulder bump'); full back Alun Priday laid low with one of the latest, late tackles ever, and that was how it went.' (These three – the vital positions of outside half, an international fullback, and an international open-side wing forward, were all deliberately? incapacitated.) ''That was the game when that so likeable, well-nigh indestructible, prop, and good friend, Colin Howe, spent the whole game in "Close Combat" with one "Du Toit". As I have mentioned somewhere before, Colin vanished completely after the game - those of you that may know him, will know what an amazing event that it; some of us swore that he just crawled into a corner to die playfully. Lloyd himself performed wonders that day at the base of the scrum, displaying qualities even in excess of those we knew he already possessed. They were all needed, of that there is certainly no doubt, but, sadly, the ultimate result was never really in doubt, with only 12 fairly fit men left in the Cardiff side.

Lloyd was reinstated into the Welsh team and was awarded the supreme honour of captaining his country. The last home international was against Scotland and to me, personally, it was quite something, to see this personality, whom I had watched develop all the way up from his very early school days, lead the Welsh team out on to the Arms Park turf. He gained 13 international caps in all, and this was during the period when the "Big Five" varied between Lloyd, "Onkers", Tony O'Connor and Wynne Evans; not an easy task to "Get in". Again, the following season, he was elected as skipper of the Cardiff side. This was something quite exceptional. If my memory serves me right, only brother Bleddyn and Dr. Jack Matthews had previously been so honoured.' (Croster 'misremembers' in modern parlance, as Bleddyn was captain in 1949-50 having been being vice-captain in 1947-48 and 1948-49. In 1953-54, Bleddyn was again captain, having been vice-captain in 1950-51. Jack Matthews captained in 1945-46 and 1946-47. Previous captains in successive years were H.J. Simpson 1883-85; Gwyn Nicholls, a 'treble' 1898-1901; H.B. Winfield

493

1901-1903; Percy Bush 1905-1907; and Wilf Wooller 1938-40, although the 1939-40 season had only two games. Club 'greats' Dai Hayward and Howard Norris later 'did the double' in 1962-63/1963-64 and 1967-68/1968-69 respectively).

'The team settled down really well this year, and they responded well to the calls made on them. Dai Hayward succeeded Lloyd as skipper the following year - the year of Wilson Whineray's All Blacks and their closest shave of the tour (- old rivals Newport were the only team to beat them, with Jack Uzzell's drop goal). They scraped home against the "Blue and Blacks", by 6-5. A drop goal and a penalty, to a Cliff Howe try, converted by Alun Priday. What a game that was, and what a fright that great New Zealand team had. Is it, I wonder, only coincidence that the East Wales team, coached by Dai Hayward, gave the last All Blacks such a close shave? The following season, Lloyd Williams decided to retire, decided to go out at the top, and call it a day... His playing career thus spread over twenty years; in the last seven of them he had always played for the Cardiff first team, and in all played in the region of 300 games for the senior side. Although officially retired, during the following season he was invited to play for the Co-optimists, and then, in a very special match, arranged to raise funds for the 1958 Empire and Commonwealth Games, held in Cardiff. A Welsh XV met The Rest of Great Britain and Lloyd was invited to play. This will go down as one of the outstanding memories of his long career; another is the great Welsh victory over France, in France, when he was the skipper, in 1957, when in a cracker of a game, Wales won 13-11. Graham Powell of Ebbw Vale scored one of the best tries, under the posts to clinch the victory.

When asked for particular comments, the reply was, that it was part of **the Williams way, to always minimise the making of mistakes and to ensure that good results will always come from good play**. How true this is. One of the biggest of modern scrum halves, Lloyd Williams will always go down in Welsh Rugby history as one of the longest passers of the ball ever. This did not come by accident, but by the correct use of the techniques of passing - feet position, body alignment, holding of the ball, follow through, etc., in combination with his strength, surprising mobility and speed, ability to kick well with both feet, tackle and defend, a break which almost always led to a score, and tactical reading of a game, has earned him a very special niche. "Kicking into the Box" brought many a good try. After the game against Ireland in terrible conditions in 1959, he was dubbed the 9th forward, so well did he save and save and save. This title, though well meant, did tend to make the uninitiated assume that his attributes were only under these circumstances. Not true at all; Lloyd was every bit as good when conditions and the going was good. Now a member of the Cardiff Committee, Lloyd is intent upon "Putting back into the game". He was on selection for a couple of years, is not now, but of late, has devoted considerable time into helping Gareth Edwards to "Get that service right". Observers will have doubtless noticed that there has been a considerable improvement therein... Having, as do we all, to work for a living, Lloyd is now a rep. with the Lancashire Tar Distillers - a job that enables him to get abroad, meet all his old friends and good for business too.'

CHAPTER 37 - CARDIFF SEASON 1964 – 1965

ELWYN PLAYS IN 45 OF 48 OFFICIAL GAMES - FLOODLIGHTING ESTABLISHED – VAUGHAN WILLIAMS PLAYER PROFILE

Elwyn Williams P45 T8 Pts24; **Tony Williams** P25 T5 Pts15; Alun Priday P22 T2 C25 P7 Pts77 (Tongwynlais); Glyn Williams P2 (Pentyrch)

P48, W30, L12, D6. Points 644-329. Tries 144-53, Pens 21-30

In May 1964, Wales undertook – for unknown reasons except a holiday for the committee and their wives - a tour of South Africa. On 12 May they beat East Africa 26-8 in Nairobi. They were not impressive against Boland in South Africa, winning 17-6, then were hammered by South Africa 24-3 in Durban after drawing 3-3 at half-time. Wales then lost to Northern Transvaal in Pretoria 22-9, before winning at Bloemfontein, 14-6 against Orange Free State. Thankfully, the only Cardiff player involved in the 23-man squad was Dai Hayward. Wales won the Five Nations Championship. They defeated England 14-3, 3 tries to 0 (H), beat Scotland 14-12, 2 tries to 0 (A), beat Ireland 14-8, 2 tries to 1 (H) and lost to France 22-13, 3 tries to 4 (A). Keith Rowlands was the only Cardiff representative, in the final two games against Ireland and France, probably a season record for the lowest appearances by Cardiff players in a Welsh team. However, Fiji toured Wales and on 26 September played a Welsh XV, which included Maurice Richards and Dai Hayward, in a 13-try thriller, Wales winning 28-22.

For Cardiff's 1964-65 season, centre Meirion Roberts was captain, and prop Howard Norris was vice-captain for a third time. A Cardiff High School product, Meirion played for Wales 8 times, was a Barbarian and made 225 First XV appearances. Another Cardiff High School boy, Cambridge Blue A. R. 'Tony' Pender joined to play in the back row, playing 151 times for Cardiff. Fly Half/Centre W. H. 'Billy' Raybould and second row Lyn Baxter (290 appearances), also began played for the Firsts. Penarth Captain John Price, Glamorgan No. 8 in three successive winning finals, joined Cardiff, where he played for the Firsts 76 times from 1964 to 1968. All eight September matches were won including Pontypool (A)16-3, Bristol 23-3, London Welsh 48-6 (12 tries), Penarth 35-3, Coventry 19-9, and Gloucester 16-9. Cardiff took an excellent team to Pontypool Park, 5 September 1964, and John Huw Williams' match programme gives the team, numbered from Alun Priday, fullback at 1, to David Hayward, open-side wing forward at 15. One wing was the man who was to go on and break Bleddyn's record of tries, Steve Hughes, and John Huw Williams was on the other. Centres were Meirion Roberts and the great Maurice Richards, before he swapped to the wing, as later did Gerald Davies. Fly-half Tommy McCarthy partnered scrumhalf Billy Hullin. The front row was Howard Norris, Billy Thomas and Tony Pender – out of position, he was a back-rower. Second rows were John Price and Graham Davies; and the back row comprised Elwyn Williams, Cliff Howe and Dai Hayward.

The programme notes read: '*Games between Cardiff and Pontypool have always been productive of thrilling and brilliant rugby, and we feel that today's match will be no different.*' Cardiff scored 4 tries to 1 penalty, winning 16-3, and in the return at the Arms Park won 11-9 to take the double. Intriguingly Cardiff were outscored 3-1 on tries in this second fixture, and would have lost 15-13 with today's scoring. However, Cardiff's record against one of the nation's premier clubs is outstanding, in 121 games winning 83, losing 25 and drawing 13, scoring 1,346 points to 681 between 1907-08 and 1974-75. Pontypool won 60-58 on penalties, but Cardiff scored 281 tries to 115. Pontypool achieved a double over Cardiff 3 times, all before WW2, while Cardiff achieved 28 doubles, one being a treble, 18 since the War. The Koh-I-Noor Restaurant in Pontypool was in the programme offering '*Indian, English & Chinese Dishes*', surely years before its time. Against Coventry on 19 September, Tony Williams partnered the great Maurice Richards in the centre, winning 19-9 at home, 5-0 on tries. Against Gloucester on 23 September, Tony was again centre in a 16-9 home win, 3-0 on tries. Elwyn was playing in nearly every game. Full back Alan Drew scored 71 points in the month.

However, on 3 November, Newport inflicted the first loss, 10-5 in Cardiff. Cardiff then lost away 15-13, but won at home 11-0, with the fourth match on 6 March 1965 being cancelled, owing to frost and snow. Neath did the double over Cardiff, their sixth and seventh wins in succession. The two games versus the Baa Baas were lost 12-8 and 14-11. Davies does make the excuse for some defeats, that Cardiff was not able to turn out its best teams, but Cardiff had the best points scored, 644, for a decade. On 7 November, Tony and Elwyn were in the team that scored 4 tries in a 19-0 home win against Oxford University. On 28 November 1964, Tony and Elwyn played in the 16-3 defeat of Llanelli, 4-0 on tries. There were then a 6-0 away defeat to a penalty and a drop goal, and an away draw 5-5, each side converting a try. In the fourth game, Cardiff at home won 14-8, 4-1 on tries. The four games against Llanelli ended with Cardiff winning 9-2 on tries, when tries were still only worth 3 points. Tony was coming into the side as a regular now, playing with Elwyn in a Floodlight Alliance 9-3 win over Bridgend on 2 December 1964. They played in the 15-6 victory over Ebbw Vale on 19 December, and against Liverpool on Boxing Day, winning 11-9, 3-1 on tries. At this time, Meirion Roberts and Maurice Richards were the first-choice centres, but Tony still managed 25 appearances. The next 7 seasons he made 34, 31, 36, 40, 25, 36 and 16 appearances for the Firsts before winding down his career.

Maurice Richards with 18 was the top try scorer, Steve Hughes 17, scrum half Billy Hullin 12, Meirion Roberts 11 and Tony Pender 10. Alan Drew scored 45 goals and 3 tries for 111 points, but also scored 115 for the Athletic. Elwyn Williams played in 45 of 48 matches, Howard Norris 44, Meirion Roberts 41, Maurice Richards 35, Dai Hayward 33, Steve Hughes and Billy Hullin both 33, and John O'Shea 32. Keith Rowlands played for Wales against Ireland and France. Club caps were awarded to Garry Davies, Alan Drew, Billy Hullin and Tony Pender.

As well as playing regularly for the Firsts, Alan Drew was Athletic captain with a record of; P38 W32 L5 D1 Points 725-194, the highest number of points since 1959-60. All losses were close: Bristol Utd. 8-6, Newport Utd. 9-6, Pontypool Utd. 10-5, Gloucester Utd. 6-3, and an unexpected loss in the Silver Ball semi-final 5-3 to Llantwit Major. Top try scorers were Billy Raybould 11, Frank Wilson 10, and G. Mainwaring and Tony Williams with 8 each. Most appearances were Ian Robinson 27, John Hickey 22, Elfed Morgan and Harry Ridgewell 21 each. Athletic XV caps were awarded to Lyn Baxter, John Davies, Roy Duggan, W. H. Raybould, Harry Ridgewell, John Huw Williams and Frank H. Wilson. Glyn Williams of Pentyrch played his last game for the Firsts in this, his 9th season, scoring 43 tries in 115 games on the wing. 55 of his games came in the seasons 1961-62 and 1962-63, when he scored 21 tries. During this time, he was a regular for the Athletic. The Youth XV under David Evans had the following record: P26 W20 L5 D1 Points 466-154. They won the Welsh Youth Open Tournament at Bridgend, only conceding 3 points. Wing P. Lyn Jones scored 27 tries in 21 matches, and Terry Stephenson 26 in 23 games, and Stephenson played three times for the Welsh Youth.

Floodlighting was established at the Arms Park on 7 October 1964, with a second game against the Barbarians celebrating the occasion. Baa-Baas fixtures began in 1891, and from 1901 to 1921 there were two fixtures a year, then returning to annual games played at Easter, on the visitors' Easter Tour of South Wales. Up to 1975, Cardiff had won 58, lost 29 and drawn 4 of the 91 fixtures scoring 269 tries to 162, and 1,208 points against 708. The floodlit game had been a necessity, because of the effect of television and its effect on fixtures, with decreasing receipts for all major clubs. Cardiff won the Floodlight Alliance Tournament of the senior

Welsh clubs having floodlighting, beating Ebbw Vale, Bridgend, Cross Keys, and in the final Llanelli by 14-8. Danny Davies records: *'Our St. Albans Military Band was playing as brightly as ever; Sousa's marches were never entirely forgotten. It is a great joy to have this band still with us, continuing to improve with sound, and dress to please us all.'* I, for one, miss the communal singing, led by the silver band, at all internationals and for Cardiff games. Supporters used to arrive early at the Arms Park just to sing along and stamp their cold feet, especially at Christmas. To younger readers, believe me, winters used to be freezing.

As the *'crachach'* (posh people) had their seats in the South Stand, near where the teams came out to play, the silver-haired conductor John Williams used to lead the singing on that side of the ground. When the singing was not fervent enough, I remember him marching the band over to the North Terrace, to great cheers from that 'cheaper' side of the ground, and howls from the South. A few hymns later, he brought them back, smiling. At every game, we used to have verses of *'Rachie'*, with at least two-part harmony – choirs sing it in four parts – and we always used to sing it on the coach when playing rugby:

I bob un sydd ffyddlon
  Dan Ei faner Ef
Mae gan Iesu goron
  Fry yn nheyrnas nef
Lluoedd Duw a Satan
  Sydd yn cwrdd yn awr:
Mae gan blant eu cyfran
  Yn y rhyfel mawr.
(chorus)
I bob un sydd ffyddlon,
  Dan Ei faner Ef
  Mae gan Iesu goron
  Fry yn nheyrnas nef.

It is one of the most stirring pieces of music ever written. (Check it out on YouTube.) However, it has been replaced by the chorus of *'Hymns and Arias'* and some bored oaf shouting *'Oggy, Oggy, Oggy.'* Equally mindless spectators respond *'Oy, Oy, Oy'*. *'I bob un sydd ffyddlon'*, it isn't. Max Boyce references the stadium singing his song – *'And we were singing Hymns and Arias, Land of My Fathers, Ar Hyd y Nos.'* *'Land of My Fathers'* is the stirring National Anthem, *Mae Hen Wlad fy Nhadau*, and *Ar Hyd y Nos* is a lovely hymn, first published in 1784, translated as *All Through the Night*. Apart from our 1856 *National Anthem*, and perhaps *Sosban Fach* and *Calon Lan*, the singing has died at the Millennium Stadium. I seem to remember years ago, *The March of the Men of Harlech* (*Rhyfelgyrch Gwŷr Harlech* in Welsh), being sung. First written down in the 18th century, the first lines are: *'Wele goelcerth wen yn fflamio, A thafodau tân yn bloeddio, Ar i'r dewrion ddod i daro, Unwaith eto'n un.'* Like *Rachie*, it is a stirring song. Cardiff City and Wales football supporters have taken *Men of Harlech* and *Yma o Hyd,* the Dafydd Iwan song, to their hearts. There are some spirited renderings on YouTube, with a great performance at the 2022 National Eisteddfod.

Thankfully, while Welsh singing at rugby games has atrophied to virtual non-existence apart from the Anthem, English supporters can only resort to a black spiritual lament, *'Swing Low Sweet Chariot'*. All rugby players over the age of fifty will remember it was sung on rugby coaches, accompanied by rather outré impressions of what was going on in the song. Now, of course, possibly a majority of spectators have never played the game – in the 50s, 60s and 70s, tickets were freely available to schools whose players at all levels could buy one, and to rugby clubs, again where players could buy tickets. Nowadays possibly half the people watching do not know what is happening, it has become such a complex game. The rule book used to be 12 pages – now it is 160. But I digress. Q. Who never lost while playing on the Arms Park? A. The St Alban's Military Band.

Cardiff's St Albans Band began in 1895, when blast furnace men from the East Moors Steelworks formed a drum and fife band. The following year, second-hand instruments were bought by parishioners' subscriptions and a brass band was formed by St. Peter's Church. In 1913, woodwind players were added to form a military band. In 1919 the band began playing at soccer matches in Ninian Park, but being rugby enthusiasts, were soon playing at matches at Cardiff Arms Park. Despite military calls on bandsmen, the silver band kept going throughout both wars. In 1919-20 they began playing before Cardiff games. In the Second World War the band became known as Band of the 22nd. Battalion Home Guard Unit of Guest Keen Iron Works. They performed before the Kiwis in 1945, and in 1948 they played *'Now is the Hour'* to the Wallabies and Barbarian sides. From 1958 until 1987 they played at all Cardiff and Wales matches. Even at Cardiff matches, the spectators sang along. The concert band now regards itself as a community band – its absence is a loss of yet another tradition. Max Boyce refers to them in *'The Incredible Plan'* about the funeral of William McGonagall Morgan, the relevant verses being:

'Then he had this idea... he'd go in disguise
He had it all drawn up and planned
And he went to the game, to his family's shame
As one of the St. Alban's Band...

The refs came in four double deckers
It was going exactly to plan
And the St. Albans Band came in lorries
And the police in a Griff Fender van!

I'll never forget the day of the match
The likes of I'll ne'er see again
When Queen Street was full of Alsatians
And the pubs full of ambulance men...

The funeral was held on a Monday
The biggest I'd ever seen
The wreaths came in four double deckers
There was one from Prince Charles and The Queen.
(Sorry!... 'The Prince of Wales' and 'The Queens')
There were sprays there from three thousand policemen
And one from the St. Albans Band
And the bearers were refs with Alsatians
Dark glasses, white sticks and tin cans.'

VAUGHAN RONALD WILLIAMS 3 August 1931 - 2005

Taff's Well reserves 1947, aged 16, then First XV centre
National Service – 2 years, not 18 months - 1950-52
British Army of the Rhine (BAOR) XV vs British Army 1951
Welsh Guards, and Guards Brigade XV outside half 1950-52
London Welsh Firsts* 1950-52 (during National Service)
Cardiff Athletic 1952 (playing alongside Lloyd)
Taff's Well 1952-56 centre
Cardiff Athletic 1955-56 centre
Neath Firsts 1955*
Llantwit Fardre 1956-57 Captain
Pontypridd First XV* 1958 centre
Taff's Well 1958-63 (64 games unbeaten), then committee member

*Neath were on Cardiff's fixture list from 1878-79, with two fixtures a year. Mike Price, secretary and historian of Neath R.F.C. informs me that Vaughan made his debut in the early 1955-56 season, but returned to Cardiff after a few games. London Welsh games with Cardiff began in 1885, with just one annual game. Although the first game with Pontypridd was in 1878, games were sporadic in the time of this book, with only 33 games. Mike also tells me that *'Bleddyn played one game for Neath - at outside-half against an RAF XV at The Gnoll on Boxing Day, 1940 scoring two tries in a 28-8 victory. Incidentally, Jack Matthews played two games for Neath too - the first when at Bridgend County School, a nil-nil draw with, strangely, Cardiff in May 1939 - his tackling must have been good then as he kept Wilf Wooller out; then on Easter Monday, 1942 in a 16-nil win over the RAF. So the famous pairing actually played for Neath - a good quiz question methinks! Lloyd told me that Bleddyn was convinced that Gwyn would have played for Wales but he was wounded (head) in the* *war when serving with the Welsh Guards.'*

Vaughan was the only brother to be denied playing schoolboy rugby, because of the war. Alongside a picture of Vaughan at Taff's Well R.F.C., we read: '*Of all the "clan", Vaughan is the Williams who has been most associated with Taff's Well as a player. Although playing the occasional game for Cardiff and Neath, Vaughan was primarily a Taff's Well player, being an important member of the "Invincibles". A strong running centre, he was capable of a devastating break. When his playing days were over, Vaughan contributed to committee work. He is well-known as a fervent supporter, whose comments from the touchline are both varied and colourful. Vaughan desperately wants our teams to do well, and woe betide any opposing player or referee that gets in the way of our success.*'

The first memory of Vaughan's early rugby career is recorded by the greatly missed Don Llewellyn of Pentyrch (*The Garth Domain* March 2006): '*Everything west of the river was in our parish, but when we crossed that footbridge, we were in Taff's Well – our neighbouring village with which there was friendly rivalry but also a great amount of mutual respect. We learned from an early age, about the remarkable prowess of young rugby players in Taff's Well and envied them for having such a rugby-oriented school. My memory of Pentyrch School was that all sport was frowned upon, let alone rugby. Nevertheless, we did play the game in the village as kids and two memorable matches took place against Taff's Well, one in the Autumn of 1945 and the other in the spring of 1946. The teams were meant to be restricted to players under fourteen years of age but in the event, both sides included some over-age lads. The first match took place at Pentyrch, and I played at scrumhalf for the home team. Opposing me was Ivor Rowlands who was older and cleverer than me. It might have helped though if someone had told me that my function was to pass the ball to our outside half Denis Murphy.*' (- a brother of the great Cardiff wing Derek Murphy, who himself had played for Wales Youth). '*However, I'm pleased to say my uselessness didn't prevent Dennis scoring two tries, that helped us gain an unexpected victory. My one nightmarish memory of that game is of Vaughan Williams tearing down the wing with only myself to beat. It was a case of "serve me right" for having kept myself away from the play! I can still hear the roar of expectation from the crowd on the touchline, as I moved in for the tackle. I blinked and the great Vaughan was scoring under the posts!... In later years playing as hooker for Pentyrch, I was to experience the full might of the Taff's Well rugby machine at senior level – also to admire it.*'

The CRFC website tells us that Vaughan '*was not as successful as his older brothers and only played three times for the Blue and Blacks but he remained loyal to his village club, Taff's Well.*' Like his younger brother Cenydd, Vaughan first played rugby for Taff's Well aged just fifteen. Tony tells us Vaughan was an Athletic player, and to get into the Firsts he would have had to replace Bleddyn or the great Jack Matthews, and that National Service affected his club career. Despite this Vaughan had a full season with Cardiff Athletic, and also played first-class rugby for London Welsh, Neath and Pontypridd. In February 1952, he may have faced his brother Bleddyn, but the Cardiff-London Welsh fixture was called off owing to the death of King George VI.

In 'The Williams Family', 1984, Vaughan entertainingly recounts his career, under the heading 'A Long Time Ago'. 'Perhaps my first clear memory of rugby was when my elder brother Bleddyn was home on holiday from Rydal School in 1939. I was eight and not yet old enough to play in the school team, although I played touch rugby with all the other kids in our street, Moy Road. Those of my age had never played in an actual team, so when Bleddyn was home, I asked him to write down the team positions on a piece of paper. We did have an old rugby ball, which was more like an out-of-shape soccer ball, but it served our purpose. Then it was over to Roger Williams's field where we slapped up sides. Nobody wanted to play in the forwards; each saw himself as a fly-half, or centre, or even flying wing! There were too few of us to form two full sides, but we made the most of it. There was one hazard though: Roger Williams's wife Polly. We thought she was a bit of a demon, for whilst we were playing happily, a shout would go up: *"Look out, Polly's coming!"* and we would scatter and make a bolt over the old railway bridge, to the safety of Moy Road. Often, Polly would confiscate our one and only ball, but we found where she used to put it, and that was the water gutter, just above the pigsty at the farm. Needless to say, we used to nick it back! I am sure she used to put it where we could see it, so maybe she wasn't such a demon after all.

Then war broke out in the September, and that was the end of *my* dreams of playing for the school team. I saw my three elder brothers, at different times, go off to war: Gwyn into the Welsh Guards, Bryn (after training as an infantryman) to the Army Service Corps and Bleddyn to the RAF. When Bryn left, no-one in the family imagined that we wouldn't see him again for almost six years. He served in North Africa, and the Middle East, helping to fight Rommel, and then on to Iraq, Lebanon, and the rest. Gwyn also saw action in North Africa, and was badly wounded by a sniper's bullet. Who knows what Gwyn would have achieved, if this tragic thing had not happened. He had begun his first-class rugby career when he was seventeen, the youngest man ever to play for Cardiff. He was also the youngest ever to play against a touring team, for he was still just seventeen years of age when he appeared for Cardiff against the All Blacks of 1935. There were good and bad times during the war years. Rugby was very much curtailed, but there were a few memorable internationals in which amateur and professional players were allowed to play in the same team. I remember being taken to Gloucester to see an England v Wales match in which Bleddyn, Haydn Tanner, Gus Risman, Alan Edwards, Jim Sullivan and other household names turned out. Wales trounced England that day. I was also privileged to see the Army v South Wales at the Arms Park. Gwyn was in the Army team and Bleddyn played for South Wales. It was said that the captain of the Army side told Gwyn: "*brother or not, you must nail him*", and Gwyn's reply was: "*I have to catch the little B****r first!*"

The news of Gwyn's injuries devastated us as a family. I can remember when the telegram came, and my mother (bless her) was overcome with grief. It was a long time before we knew the extent of his wounds, and that it would change his life for ever, but we are grateful that in spite of all that, Gwyn was to survive and live until he was 79 years of age. The same cannot be said for other boys in the village who, tragically, were never to return home. There were hardships at home, of course. Everybody was affected by the rationing of food and clothing. The winters as I remember them were bitterly cold – we had icicles on the inside of the house as well as the outside! Mam could make a meal from practically nothing; some little meat and bones from Dougan the butcher, and other things like blackberries in the Autumn. She made trousers from old blankets for us to go to school, and we wore DAPS even in winter, to save what decent boots we had for the severest weather.' ('*Daps*' is a South Wales term for what posh people called plimsolls, always thin-soled, white canvas, cheap footwear used in gym at school – today's multicoloured, multi-material, multi-technology, multi-expensive 'trainers' did not exist for decades.) 'Then there were bombs – I can remember when and where each one fell.

Among my good memories of the war years are those long warm summers when, as kids, we would spend many happy days camping up alongside the Brynau Brook. My mother saw very little of us during school holidays, and only once would we go to the seaside, on the annual outing to Barry. As soon as school was over in July, out came the tent, a few tins to cook in, a loaf of bread, some spuds, and a box of matches, then up to a lovely green patch beyond the Brynau to pitch our tent. We had everything: a wood fire, the brook, the woods and the weather. We tickled trout in the Brynau, wrapped them in clay from the bank, and cooked them in the oven we made out of a Jacob's biscuit tin, that we had from Mrs Arnold's shop, next door to us in Moy Road. Then with free-range eggs from Roger Williams's farm, Rhiw'r Ddar (we knew where the hens laid them!), trout, spuds, plus the loaf from mam – what more could you want? The water in the Brynau in those days was beautiful to drink, clear as crystal. We swam in the culverts and, altogether, despite the hard times, we had a wonderful childhood.

To make up for the lack of rugby, the youngsters of Taff's Well, Nantgarw, Tongwynlais and Pentyrch used to slap up sides to play each other. The rivalry was intense. I can well remember playing on the old ground at Pentyrch, just off Mountain Road, with the Murphy boys in their team. It wasn't too bad playing with the slope, but what bothered me was the bog with all the bulrushes etc., down at the far end, an area where a wing could disappear from sight! We would walk up to Pentyrch, before playing, and back to Taff's Well after the game, but it was great. I left school in July 1945 and that meant working to help towards the family, so a week later I started in a smelly and dirty job at a factory on the Treforest Estate and stuck it out for a while.' (Vaughan, like most working-class boys, left school at 14. My father left school at 14 to join a Merchant Navy ship, the *English Trader*. A couple of days out, she grounded on some rocks, and he became the youngest seaman to be rescued by a Breeches Buoy. All six ships, all from South Wales ports, that he served on in the 6 years before the war, were lost to enemy action. He managed to get back to Wales via the Panama Canal, with no convoy escort, to try and join his brother in the Royal Navy. However, the recruiting office discovered that he had learned to spot-weld at sea, and immediately sent him to weld planes and tanks in England.)

'After the war I remained with Taff's Well 1sts and 2nds, until I was called up to do my National Service in 1950. I had put down to join the Navy, but I found myself reporting for duty at Caterham Barracks for the Welsh Guards (my brother Gwyn's regiment). Then it was "*short, back and sides*", getting kitted out and the JABS, oh boy those jabs! Our feet never touched the ground for the next two months and boy, oh boy, we were fit. Being a Welshman in the Guards I was expected to play rugby. It all went well but one thing did upset me. A month before I was called up, my mother had bought me a new suit from McQuistins in Park Place in Cardiff. It had cost her £5, a lot of money in those days. Anyway, after we were kitted out, we were given a SANDBAG with a label on it to send our civvy clothes back home. I sent mam a note saying how sorry I was, to have to send it that way. The Brigade rugby team recruited players from the Guards Depot, through which all sections, the Coldstream, Grenadiers, Welsh, Scots and Irish Guards passed. Our team played sides from the local area, plus teams from other Army units, also some RAF sides. The fact that matches were played on Wednesday afternoons suited me, as I had been invited to play with London Welsh, whose home ground that time was at Herne Hill, and I managed to turn out for their Firsts a few times. Then followed my transfer to Pirbright, where in the summer months there were plenty of forced marches, assault courses etc., which made me very fit indeed. I then joined my battalion and headed for West Germany where we would be based at Wuppertal. Before we boarded the train at Waterloo Station, our company commander had us marching up and down the platform. With nothing said by the CO except to bring us to attention at the start, we marched and counter-marched with precision, leaving the crowd which had gathered, spellbound. That made us all feel ten feet tall.

It is inevitable that in a Welsh regiment there will be more than one Williams, so we went by our numbers. In my case it was 02. One day I had

504

intended going to a carnival in Wuppertal, but was intercepted by our sergeant-major Rees (or 'Piggy' Rees as he was known – but not to his face). He called my name "*02 Williams*" and I turned on my heels and slammed my feet down. "*Sir*", I said, thinking to myself "*what the Hell have I done now?*" Sgt. Major said "*I understand you have applied for driving lessons – get back to your room and change into your work clothes and report to the MT yard at the double.*" "*Yes sir*" I answered and off I went. After three weeks of driving lessons, I could turn my beloved nippy Jeep on a sixpence. Then I progressed to a Bedford 15-cwt truck, then the TCVs' (Troop-Carrying Vehicles) 'and finally the Bren-gun carriers, tracks and all. I was transferred to HQ Co. and being a driver, for one thing, I was excused guard duty. I had truck-duties though, and one night I had to pick up a cinema manager (who was a British civvy) from his home in Solingen, about 15 to 20 miles away. Returning home with him I was asked in for a cup of tea and began my return journey to the barracks. I had gone only three or four miles when, on changing down, the gear stick came away in my hand completely. Unable to re-insert it, I had to drive the next 15 miles or so in bottom gear. I was shattered on arrival at base, but everyone else was tickled pink and had a good laugh.

By the time the rugby season started over there in October I was very fit, as a result of training for athletics during the summer months. I was entered (ordered, actually) to compete in the 100 metres and the 200 metres. Our rugby side was a mixture of regulars and conscripts (officers, NCOs and other ranks), and did very well as a team. We were much fitter than our opposition and ran them off their feet. On one occasion when I was playing stand-off, the scrumhalf was CSM' (Company Sergeant Major) 'Dando, who had played with my brother Gwyn in the Training Battalion earlier in the war. Our giant RSM' (Regimental Sergeant Major) 'Piggy Rees was in our second row. We won the 2nd division championship and later met the Yorks and Lancs Regiment in the BAOR' (British Army of the Rhine) 'Final in Hanover. That 2nd division was not second rate as understood from league football – this was simply the name of the Army Division. I am pleased to say that we won handsomely and that I scored a couple of tries. A few weeks later I had a letter from my mother, to say that she had seen the highlights of the game in the Capitol Cinema in Cardiff, on a Pathé Newsreel!

I came home on leave in March 1951 for 14 days, and on the day I was due back, Wales were playing Ireland at the Arms Park, 2 o'clock KO.' (Bleddyn was playing, alongside Cardiff's Jack Matthews, Cliff Morgan and Rex Willis. Wales drew 3-3, having previously hammered England by 5 tries to 1, 23-5, and then lost surprisingly to Scotland 18-0. Bleddyn had returned for the Ireland game, after missing the first two through injury, so Vaughan took the chance of seeing his brother play. Bleddyn then missed the 8-3 loss to France, but was back for the very unlucky defeat to South

505

Africa, where he scored a try in the 6-3 game). 'Just when my train was about to leave the station, I sent a telegram requesting a two-day extension to my leave. My request was refused, and I thought *"to Hell with it – they can only shoot me once!"* I watched the game and was back on the train on the Monday, and arrived at Wupperal on the Tuesday. After a night in the guardhouse cell, I was up before the CO in the morning and found myself confined to Barracks for a week. I did two days only, for on the Friday, I was on my way to play in the BAOR Sevens Finals. Not a bad three weeks!

We were paid in BAFS money, which we could only spend in the NAAFI or the Church Army.' (British Armed Forces Special Vouchers - BAFSVs – were a military currency issued to prevent British pounds being used in black markets overseas.) 'Everyone in the company had a weekly ration of cigarettes, so I bought all the packets I could from the non-smokers in our company, and sold them on the corner of two streets in Wuppertal for a healthy profit. After that I was never short of a few bob.' (A bob was a shilling coin, equal to 12 pennies, worth a twentieth of a pound, in real money. A pound then would be worth £35 today, so 10 'bob' would be worth £17.50). 'There was a shortage of all things in Germany, as there was back home. One thing the locals did have was nylon stockings' (from the American GIs), 'so it only meant exchanging some cigs for them, and I was able to send nylons home to my youngest sister Mair. With money in my pocket, I was able to travel around to see other cities and towns – what was left of them, for this was 1951 and they were still in ruins. After Dusseldorf, Dortmund, Duisburg and Essen, I went with a friend Peter Collins from North Wales, on a visit to Cologne. I remember crossing the Rhine by Bailey Bridge – the original bridge was still in the river. I enjoyed our visit to the cathedral in Cologne, although we had to apologise for not removing our caps on arrival there. In the summer the Battalion was down in Sennelager, an area very similar to Salisbury Plain, for very real manoeuvres, which allowed me to experience a little of what war was all about. I had seen much of the devastation over there, but still held the view that the Germans got what they asked for.' (Sennelager still has a large British Army barracks. It was briefly occupied by the Americans after the War, which explains the availability of nylons, a very rare and black-market commodity in post-war Britain.)

'I was then assigned to the Company Commander as his driver and remained at his beck and call. On one occasion, I had to collect him (in my best bib and tucker) at the station in Paderborn, and bring him back to Sennelager, where I was told to get some food. I knew the Quartermaster Sergeant (- 84 Williams had been my Battalion's loose-head prop). He told me to call him when I had eaten the main meal, for he was making some plum duff with strawberry jam. I duly went to see him and was greeted by a blast – he had put the tins of jam into the container, an open oven, without first piercing them. The explosions caused my best uniform and my person to be covered with strawberry preserve. The suit was ruined, and I still have marks on my hands and arms as souvenirs of the incident. I reminded 84 Williams of this, years later when he got on the same bus as me in Whitchurch – he lived just behind the Common.

In October 1951, the Battalion was visited by Edward, Prince of Wales, who was Colonel-in-Chief of the Welsh Guards. At the match the next day between the Battalion and the RAF, the players of both teams were lined up to be introduced to the Prince. He shook hands with each of us. I dislocated my finger in that game, making a tackle – and it remains disfigured to this day. I was to play one more game, in Hanover. I was called to the CO's office, to be told of my selection at centre for the whole BAOR, against the British Army based in the UK. I was the only player from the Battalion to be picked for that game. The arrangements were as follows: Call 04-30 hrs; B/fast 05-00 hrs; T/port 05-30 hrs; Train No. D123; Depart Dusseldorf 06-55 hrs; Arrive Hanover 12-44 hrs; Arrange to have two haversack rations for journey. A six-hour train journey, picked up at the station, kick-off 14-00 hrs, December and no lights! My opposite number was St John Rees who had played for Cardiff.' (Full-back D. St John Rees made 76 appearances from 1945-46 to 1949-50, gaining his first team cap in that first season alongside such luminaries as Bleddyn, Bleddyn's cousin Bill Tamplin, Dr Jack Matthews, Billy Cleaver, Les Manfield, Billy Darch, Dr Glyn Jones, Maldwyn James, George Tomkins, Hubert Jones, W.G. Jones and Cliff Davies.) 'Vaughan adds: "I was the only 'other rank' in our team, the others were either officers or NCOs. It was a low-scoring game and we won by a few points."

I was not given any instructions about my return journey, so right after the match I made my way to the station, and arrived back at Dusseldorf after midnight, where I had to ring the Barracks for them to come and pick me up. During that long journey back, I had time to think about other things and one of these worried me. My mind wandered, and noting the big black steam engines which pulled the coaches, I wondered if they were the same locomotives used to transport the unfortunate Jewish people to their fate at the Death Camps. I will never find out, but it did worry me. We were encouraged to mix with the local people, and make friends, but I found that very difficult to do. How could I make friends with the people who had shot my brother Gwyn? I know war is war, and it's "kill or be killed", but I still found it hard. Some 40 million died in the Second World War, all because of some brainless idiot who wanted to rule the world.

National Service was supposed to be 18 months, but the Government decided to add a further six months, so during this period I was doing my extra time. I didn't mind too much. I left for home in the middle of December for some leave that was due to me, and reported back to Caterham on 2nd January 1952, ready for my demob on the 4th. I can honestly say, that despite some of the difficult times, I did enjoy the Army, and I wish that National Service had been continued, because it wouldn't have done any harm to the youngsters of today to have some discipline restored. Maybe then it would be a better place to live in.' (In 1952, brother Lloyd was called back from National Service for a game and played alongside Vaughan for Cardiff Athletic vs. Gloucester). 'After I was demobbed, it was time to start working for a living again, and to play rugby of course. After a while, I got myself a place in the Taff's Well team and stayed until the 1955-56 season, when I moved to live in Llantrisant. Then I made friends with John Watkins, the Pontypridd hooker, who persuaded me to join Llantwit Fardre, his old club. I did so eventually and would be joined by two other Taff's Well lads, Ivor and David Rowlands and also Reg Francis from Nantgarw. Before joining Llantwit, I had a season with Cardiff, playing for the Rags, mainly. I was a permanent centre by this time, but **there was no way I was going to break into the Cardiff side**, not with Bleddyn and Jack being there!

Anyway, I enjoyed my spell with Llantwit, but I did have a trial with Neath. I played four or five times for them, and then when I wasn't sent a card, which was the usual way to inform players that they were picked or not, I rang the secretary of Neath, and his reply was "*I think you should return to Llantwit Fardre.*" I still don't know what was behind it, but it seems that someone had 'put the boot in'. In those days, the so-called first-class clubs were accused of poaching players, but that was not the case with me, as I had applied to Neath for a trial. Anyway that was the end of that. I played in a mid-week match for Llantwit against Pontypridd. It was a tight game and I scored what I considered to be a perfectly good try, which would have won it for us, if only the referee (from Pontyclun) had allowed it. I was the only one near the ball when I touched down, so how could a referee who was far away and unsighted, judge that I had not grounded it properly? Yes, there were bent refs in those days too! The players that I remember at Llantwit Fardre were great, like Sid Davies, Dennis Coakley, Billy Lougher, Peter Farr, Bill Tapp, John and Bill Williams, Dai Andrews, Norman Pulford, Gwyn Breeze etc. As you can see, I still remember them.

At this time, I was asked by Mr Rees, who lived at Weir House, on the corner of Cardiff Road and Sycamore Street in Taff's Well, if I would be interested in playing for Pontypridd. I said I would give it a go, and this led to me playing four or five games for Ponty. Graham White, the Taff's Well centre cum fullback, should have been playing for Pontypridd in one of those games, but just before the start, Bernard Hedges, the Glamorgan cricketer and Glamorgan Wanderers' fullback, walked in. Our captain said: "*Hello Bern, fancy a game?*" Bernard said he wouldn't mind, and Graham was told to change back into his clothes. I was gobsmacked by this and that was the last time I played for Pontypridd. So, it was back to my first love,

Taff's Well, and to spend the rest of my playing days there.

One could say the club should have changed its name to Taff's Well Wanderers. The present ground is their fifth to my knowledge. Ty Rhiw. The ground is where I live today, on the bungalow site at Brynau Road. It would be interesting to those who are not aware of it, as to how the players got to the pitch. The ground had been made available to the club by the Thomas family, who had Ty Rhiw Farm, just a short distance away. The two teams, after changing at the Castle Hotel in the village, had to walk into the lane at the back, turn right, then left, past what used to be called the Castle Field (the old fairground site), then through the gap between the houses in King Street, over the railway crossing, then down the long path between the allotments, and the field where the Co-op bakery used to be. When they reached the end, they had to climb over the stile and onto the canal bank, turn left, and follow the towpath to Woods' Lock, turn right over the stone bridge of the canal, through the three-cornered field, over the crossing of the old Cardiff railway, under the arch by the Rhymney Cottages, then climb the 60-odd steps that had been cut out of the bank, over another stile, and onto the field; all this before a ball had even been kicked!' (This writer is exhausted, just reading about that trek).

'The next ground was but a short distance away, just over the first railway crossing and into the field, where the Co-op bakery used to be. The point I would like to make is that this area was large enough to have three playing pitches, plus plenty of room for a clubhouse. I think there was a small payment due to Roger Williams (or Dai Parry) for the lease of the land. Now it came to pass, that all of this land was offered to Taff's Well RFC by the farmer, for the princely sum of £1,000, but it was turned down by the long-standing club secretary, because it was "*an awful lot of money*". A chance in a million was thus lost. What price would it be today? In those days there was always a game between the 'Married Men and Single Men' on Christmas morning. Many had a right old rollicking for turning up late for their Christmas dinner, but I remember one of these occasions for a different reason. In the pre-match 'pass-about' and 'kick-about', someone kicked the ball high into the air and down it came, hitting the unfortunate Lynn Cross on the head. He went out like a light and was carried off before the game even started.' (In those extremely cold winters, sometimes the ball was like a lump of concrete – honestly.) 'He soon recovered to enjoy a pint in the Castle and have the mickey taken out of him.

Ground 3 was near Rhiw'r Ddar Farm. No. 2 had been lost, because there was now a new railway to be built through the ground, linking up Taff's Well station with the old Cardiff railway, just before Moy Road. The Co-op bakery, and Moy Road Industrial Estate came later. We played on Rhiw'r Ddar until the early 1960s. Once again it was a marathon to get to it, but not so many obstacles. But what we *did* have was cowpats by the score. Many a time we had to go early and clear the pats before we could start the game. It was during this time that the club had its best record ever. In 1959-60 we were unbeaten until the second half of the season; in 1960-61 we went undefeated. It would be the middle of 1961-62 before we were to lose. In all, we had gone **64 games without defeat**.' (In *The Williams Family* booklet there is a photo of Vaughan in the Taff's Well '*Invincibles*' XV of 1960-61, and also one of him in his Welsh Guards uniform, holding his bearskin.) 'There were quite a number of different players used during this time, but the mainstays were: Graham White, Brian Holloway, Gwyn Davies, myself, Terry Evans, Trevor Coghill, Alan Jones, Gordon Beech (captain), Tony Bonetto, Alan Newman, Graham Field, Keith Mapstone, Ivor Dimond, Gordon Thomas, Brian Thomas, and last, but not least, the great man himself Iorrie Jones. That was the basis of the side, but there were many others who played their part when other players were either injured or unavailable, for whatever reason. There was also constant pressure from other players in the club; those who spring to mind include Garth Williams and Clive Day. I apologise to those players I have left out, and to those I have forgotten.

They were great times. In those days, if we played up in Pentyrch, we made a day of it, and stayed till late, but after home games, the last into the tin bath came out dirtier than when he went in! Then there was a quick dash home, and back to the Castle – in later times it would be the Anchor – for a sing-song. If you weren't there by six o'clock, you wouldn't get a seat. A new ground, our fourth, was purchased, across the river via the footbridge near the station. This had been an old Council tip, covered with weeds and you name it. It took a year for club members, including players, to clear it. Unfortunately, someone had a brainstorm and decided that what was needed was a dozen or so lorry-loads of 'black duff', waste from the Upper Boat Power Station, to spread over the top. This led to the ground becoming like concrete – and after rain, it was a lake. It was years, really, before the problems were solved. A clubhouse was built during this time, our first ever, so we became independent from the pubs in the village. I played in the first game on the new ground – but should never really have played, because it was full of small stones and very little grass. I split my knee open on one of those stones, causing me to be out for a month or so. I did, though, play in the OFFICIAL opening of the ground, when my younger brother Lloyd brought an international team to play us in the April of 1963. For many years afterwards, there were great times at the club, and great games. It was during the early 60s that I decided to hang up my boots. I had played for almost twenty years, and enjoyed every minute of it, but I wasn't to finish with the club. I took a seat on the committee and started to help in that direction.

Cae'r Afon' (River Field) 'was now going to be the home of Taff's Well RFC for the next 30 years. The glory days were to be those back in the late

60s and early 70s. First there were those Welsh Cup games against Llanelli and Swansea – both of which we lost by just a few points. Then our Silver Ball Final triumph against Pyle. My younger brothers Elwyn and Tony joined us from Cardiff, bringing with them the likes of Peter Flood and second row Stephenson. Also, there was Ike Stephens of course, who went on to be a British Lion. We had Sam Fear, Ken Blackman, Chris Fenwick (Steve's brother), Carey Collings, Peter Thomas, Gwyn Davies, Dai Owen, Jack Jones, Clive Day, Gwyn Bowden, Martin the outside-half (- I can't remember his surname – I must be getting old, Colin Riley and many more. That pitch was no. 4. What can I say about pitch no. 5? A magnificent new clubhouse and ground, a large carpark, plus a second pitch at Glan-y-Llyn. The playing fortunes of the team have gone back a little, but that may be due to some curse that Dai Millward has put on them for bringing rugby league to the club. (Only joking!) I have been to the club on a few special occasions, and have to say that I am both impressed and pleased with it. Once again, to all those people whose names I have left out or forgotten, I apologise, but for every one of you, may I say it was a pleasure and a privilege to have played with you all, but as I said at the beginning – it was a long time ago.' – Vaughan Williams 1984.

His sister Mair remembers Vaughan being really ill for months, with doctors taking no notice and eventually prescribing antibiotics. He was taken to East Glamorgan Hospital on a Friday, the day before Lloyd's daughter was married at Miskin, and on Monday Vaughan was told he had leukaemia, so was transferred to the University Hospital of Wales, the Heath, Cardiff. He died three days later on the Thursday, aged just 74, with Mair and his family around him. From diagnosis to an untimely death – three days.

CHAPTER 38 - CARDIFF SEASON 1965 – 1966

KEITH ROWLANDS CAPTAIN - GERALD DAVIES AND D. KEN JONES JOIN – ELWYN PLAYS 40 GAMES - ALUN PRIDAY'S CAREER ENDED AND PLAYER PROFILE

Elwyn Williams P40 T7 21pts; **Tony Williams** P34 T5 15pts; Alun Priday P7 T1 C3 P7 Pts 33 – retired after an illegal punch. Alun Priday career total P408, T33, C328, P184 plus 2 drop goals – points 1,316

Pl 47, W 35, L 9, D 3. Pts 583-198 <u>Tries 128-32</u>, Pens 24-23

Keith Rowlands, the red-haired 6ft 5ins second row, had joined from

Llanelli in 1961-62 and was a seasoned Welsh international, and in 1962 had played in 18 of 24 games in the Lions tour to South Africa. Rowlands was an excellent captain, with wing Steve Hughes, in his last season, rewarded with the vice-captaincy. The team had some excellent newcomers for this season. T. G. R. (Gerald) Davies played for Loughborough College, Cardiff and London Welsh, and was one of the greatest Welsh threequarters of all time. Originally a centre, his switch to the wing meant that he still possessed a swerve and sidestep to always keep the ball in play. He played 62 times for Cardiff, and in 1968, Gerald went to Cambridge University for three seasons, captaining the Dark Blues. He then joined London Welsh before moving back to Cardiff for work and re-joining Cardiff. Nine times capped wing Robert Morgan joined from Llanelli to attend Cardiff Teacher Training College, playing for Cardiff Firsts 19 times, before re-joining Llanelli the next season. Then there was the brilliant centre, D. Ken Jones, who had played for Llanelli for the previous five seasons, an Oxford Blue, Wales Schoolboy international, Barbarian and British Lion, who played for Cardiff 104 times from 1965-66 until 1970-71.

The Newport-Gwent Dragons website records: '*A master of attack who scored some outstanding tries for Wales and the Lions, his creative genius knew how to unlock even the tightest of defences. His daring approach thrilled crowds around the world. He scored two tries in 14 games at centre for Wales and three in six Tests for the Lions in South Africa, Australia and New Zealand.*' Another Cardiff Teacher Training College product, John Huw Williams, was called by Davies: '*a splendidly balanced running wing*' and had been mainly in the Rags until this season. 'John Huw' played 73 games from 1964-65 until 1968-69. W. Clive Evans, '*a brilliant but short flank forward from Bridgend Sports Club*' also joined, playing 94 times until 1972-73. All received First XV caps this season, along with Lyn Baxter. All the new boys started the new season with a run-out for the Rags against Bonymaen on 18 September, winning 57-3. Of the 13 tries, Ken Jones scored 3, Gerald Davies 2, John Huw Williams 2, Chris Jones 2, and John Price, Tommy McCarthy, Les Gauntlett and Tony Williams 1 each. Tony Williams kicked 8 conversions. With their glut of excellent backs, Cardiff scored four times as many tries as the opposition this season.

On 11 September 'Old Rugby Roma' of Italy, with players from France, Romania and Czechoslovakia visited, and were beaten 14-3 in a fairly grim match, a decade after Romania had been beaten 6-0. The South Wales Echo reporter Malcolm Lewis called the game '*like Spaghetti without the Bolognaise*'. On 29 September, Cardiff lost to a reviving Bridgend 3-0 (A), then lost 14-5 (A) and 9-3 (H), after winning 16, drawing 2 and losing 4 of their previous 22 fixtures. Alun Priday's jaw was broken in a disgraceful off-the-ball punch in the first Bridgend game, on 29 September, so from the season's start, his captaincy of the Athletic went to John Davies. Fullback Alun James Priday was a product of Whitchurch Grammar School, like Gareth Bale, Sam Warburton and Geraint Thomas. The foul punch, from behind, really ended a career where he would have otherwise made a record number of appearances for Cardiff. Alun could only return to play 7 more games towards the end of the season, then retired after 410 games in 14 seasons, scoring 1,799 points and gaining just 2 Welsh caps.

(Apart from a spell of 12 unbeaten games in the 1950s, the 93 games with Bridgend, dating from 1879 to1975, have been close, with Cardiff winning 49, losing 35 and drawing 11. Bridgend easily won the penalty count 54-38, but Cardiff scored 174 tries to 106, and 857 points to 643.) In the April 1966 loss to Bridgend 9-3, Elwyn played at 13 (then the number for blind-side wing-forward), but Tony Williams played left wing to Maurice Richards' centre, because players were missing. Right centre was Gerald Davies, and his wing was John Huw Williams. Both Richards and Davies are remembered as wonderful wings, but had spent some years as centres, while Tony is remembered as a centre and outside-half. Cardiff lost 17-11 to Cambridge University with Dennis Gethin kicking 11 points for the Light Blues, the year before he joined Cardiff to replace the sadly retired Priday, and he made 109 appearances until 1970-71. Cardiff also lost to Oxford (A) 9-0; Llanelli (A) by a dropped goal and a penalty 6-0, (but won 14-3 at home, 2 tries to 0); Swansea 3-0 (H), a penalty (but won 6-5 away, a try apiece); and Neath 6-5 (H) 1 try each, (but won 6-3 away, scoring the only try).

On 9 October, Tony played outside half to Billy Hullin in the 17-3 defeat of Northampton, 4-0 on tries. Ken Jones and Maurice Richards were centres, and Elwyn as usual partnering Dai Hayward. On 23 October, there was the same line-up at home to Cambridge University, but Cardiff lost 17-11, 2-2 on tries. From programmes *on rugbyrelics.com*, Tony played outside half, and Elwyn in the back row against Ebbw Vale, on 30 October 1965, in a 16-0 home win, Cardiff scoring 4 tries. The brothers were in the same positions in the 13 November 1965 win over Newport, 11-3, 2-1 on tries. Other games where Tony played fly half, from just a few programmes, were against Pontypool, 20 November, 36-8 home win, 8-1 tries; Swansea, 4 December, 3-0 home loss to a penalty; Liverpool 27 December 11-3 home win, tries 3-1; and at home to Coventry 8 January 1966, 6-5, tries 2-2. Tommy McCarthy only played 15 games at fly-half this season, and 10 the next, before retiring, which accounts for Tony's many outside half appearances.

Against Llanelli in the 14-3 home win on 26 February, Elwyn was playing as usual, and Tony was partnered by scrumhalf John Every, in the absence of Billy Hullin, who had just become the father of a second daughter. With a marked over-representation of girls being born to players, the programme noted '*a remarkable paucity of the male species*' among the Cardiff team, which one player attributed to *'the quality of the liniment the players rub on before the game!'* Playing for Llanelli, before he joined Cardiff, was *'an interesting player to watch ... B. John, who impressed critics and spectators alike with the quality of his play throughout this season.'* There was also a pen picture of the great Maurice Richards, an excellent cricketer who won the Welsh Under-19s long jump, and the hop, step and jump, and had been offered trials with Tottenham Hotspur, but was concentrating upon rugby and his accountancy studies.

Elwyn and Tony Williams were playing in the 6-5 Neath loss on 9 March, but the service from Every to outside-half Tony was erratic – Every only played 6 times for Cardiff. Then again, few scrum-halves performed well against a well-drilled Neath pack. However, the appearance of the great Gareth Edwards in the next season solved that particular problem. And in the season after that, the appearance of the superb Barry John was to limit Tony's games as the Firsts' outside-half. As regards 'the old enemy' Newport, Cardiff won 17-8 (A), won 11-3 (H), and lost 8-0 (A), scoring 6 tries to 2. In the 11-3 win, Brian Anthony played full back for Cardiff, and his brother John was full back for Newport, probably a unique occurrence in first-class rugby. Only three games were played against Newport this season, and the final game of the previous season as cancelled because of frost and snow. John Huw Williams' programme for the February home game against Bristol, Cardiff having won away 3-0, refers to the weather as *'February fill-dyke'*. With Maurice Richards playing centre and Elwyn at blindside, Cardiff ran in 6 tries to win 27-0 in the mud. Their record against Bristol from 1888 to 1975 reads Played 142, Won 108, Lost 27, Drawn 7, Points for 1,874, Against 791. Bristol scored 56 penalties, one more than Cardiff, but Cardiff won the try count 419-148. Elwyn played in the thrashing of Ebbw Vale away, 42-8, 8 tries to 2, on 6 April 1966, but the home game was only won 3-0. The Ebbw Vale programme explained – *'Unfortunately both sides will be somewhat weakened, because whilst Cardiff send some of their first team players to the Gala Sevens, we are sending a few of ours to the altar. We wish Arthur Lewis, Ritchie Wills, Gareth Howls and Len Dimmick very happy marriages and may all their troubles be little ones.'* Cardiff have been lucky to have strength in depth over the years, probably more than any other team in the period of this book. On 11 April, Harlequins put on a great display at Cardiff, both teams touching down twice, but Cardiff kicking a conversion to win 8-6.

In a season of 47 games, winning 35 and drawing 3 was a reasonable return. The backs sparkled, scoring 128 tries against 32, a 4:1 ratio. Indeed, Cardiff once again had a low penalty to try ratio, kicking 24 against 23. Cardiff played to entertain, helped by the magnificent Maurice Richards with 17 tries, followed by wing Steve Hughes 15, Billy Hullin 11 and Robert Morgan 10. Wales prop John O'Shea played 44 times in 47 matches, followed by Tony Pender, Billy Thomas and Elwyn Williams on 40. Captain Keith Rowland was capped for Wales. Howard Norris and D. Ken Jones were selected for the 1966 British Lions tour, to New Zealand and Australia. Specialists Newport were beaten in the exciting final of the Welsh Snelling Sevens at Cardiff by 23 points to 20, after extra time. This used to be a 'great day out', with big crowds, with no alcohol on sale.

Cowbridge Grammar School's John Davies, a Welsh Secondary School cap, had travelled with Wales to South Africa in 1956, had been a forward with Pontypridd and London Welsh, and took over as Rags captain from the injured Priday. Their playing record of: Pl 37 W 30 L 7, Points 476-176, like the Firsts, had an impressive try ratio of 98-24, c.4:1, and an almost identical penalty ratio of 25-24. Like Alun Priday, fullback Alan Drew suffered a broken jaw, but he scored 4 tries and kicked 17 goals in his restricted games. Leading 'Rags' try scorers were John Huw Williams 12, P. Lyn Jones 10 and Frank Wilson 7. New Athletic caps were Robert Furness, John Harding, P. Lyn Jones and Gwyn Thomas the prop from Swansea, who had played 17 1st XV games, as well as 13 for the Athletic. Peter 'Pies' Thomas played hooker in 9 Athletic games this season and in 11 for the 1st XV up to 1967-68, and is 'a huge figure in Cardiff rugby history'. He was nicknamed 'pies' after his family company firm 'Peter's Pies', to distinguish him from another early 1960's Cardiff hooker, who himself became known as Peter 'RAF' Thomas. John Harding reminisced in an interview for Cardiff Rugby Museum that he started playing for Cardiff's Third team, known as the 'Tatters', in the early 60s, as the Athletic were the 'Rags', so you had 'rags and tatters.'

Then, being selected for the Rags, John Harding said, 'was a big moment for me. The Rags were a well-respected top-class club side, British Lions and Welsh players consistently came through them. They could challenge first-class sides. Putting that jersey on, every game was the most important game of your opposition's life, every team you played, it was their match of the season, and it was the same playing for Cardiff Firsts, and so it was never an easy game. I was at a wedding on a Saturday morning, and the priest came out and asked, "Is there a John Harding here?" I said "Yes", and he said, "There's a telegram and it came through this morning, and it's an invitation to know you've been selected for Cardiff." Seems somebody dropped out, and it was my opportunity to get in. And it was amusing, you see, because suddenly all the wedding guests were waving me off. That was the thrill of my life, my sporting life. It was against Aberavon away, they were always tough, and so we get to Aberavon, I put the number 8 jersey on, it was a great thrill. And on the pitch, I was told about their full-back, "He's quite a new player, but he's good". We kicked off, and I ran down the pitch, the full-back caught it, he kicked the ball to touch, I tackled him, and the ref warned me. (laughs) And I tell you what, that did me the world of good. People thought, hey ho, he's got a bit of

515

good in him. But I was never a dirty player, that wasn't in my system... Fine club, right place, the club was in the right place. I didn't go to Cardiff as many players as many players have gone to Cardiff, looking for a Welsh cap. I went to Cardiff because it was my club, it was wonderful. It's my home.' The versatile Alun Priday was again captain of Cardiff Cricket Club and the former Japanese POW Les Spence captain of Cardiff Athletic Club Bowls. Steve Hughes and Meirion Roberts retired, along with Dai Hayward, but Dai later changed his decision and was elected captain of Cardiff Athletic XV in 1966-67.

PETER THOMAS

The club's major benefactor over the years, Peter played for the Public Schools Under-18s, then Cardiff Youth for two years, joining at the same time as the famous Ian 'Robbo' Robertson and Jim Mills, later to become a rugby league legend. He then played for Ebbw Vale for two years, before returning to Cardiff. Peter Thomas was Chairman of Cardiff Rugby from 1996 until the game went professional in 2000-2001, continuing in that role as Chairman of Cardiff Blues. In 2019 Peter stepped down as Chairman, but remained a major shareholder in the company, with the honorary position of Life President of Cardiff Rugby. There follows 22 August 2021 interview on the Cardiff rugby site:

'Peter Thomas' lifelong love for Cardiff and Blue and Black'
FIRST TEAM NEWS

'Peter Thomas is relishing an exciting new era at Cardiff Rugby as the Blue and Blacks fully embrace their rich history and heritage following the recent brand realignment - a move he describes as the club 'coming home'. The Cardiff Rugby Life President has dedicated more than 50 years to the capital city outfit. First, as a hooker playing 11 times for the first team and predominantly the Rags, then as a patron and the club's first chairman from the outset of professional rugby in 1996. He held that position until January 1, 2019, when he was succeeded by Alun Jones, and took the honorary role of Life President while remaining on the board. Cardiff Rugby remains one of Thomas' great passions and he is still actively involved in the club and life in general at the Arms Park. And to see the first team run out in the famous Blue and Black once more is something that fills Thomas with immense pride.

"It's like coming home, quite frankly," said the 78-year-old. "I played for the club in the 1960's with Gareth (Edwards), Barry (John) and Gerald (Davies) and it was a great period of my life. If you go anywhere in the world, New Zealand for example, and mention Cardiff Rugby, rugby people would know about Cardiff Arms Park. It's heritage. You go back to 1876 and all the great names that have played for Cardiff. I suppose going into the regional rugby era we embraced that and changed the name. But

I'm thrilled we are going back to Cardiff Rugby and I know our sponsors and suppliers are the same. Cardiff Rugby is known throughout the world and this is a great, new beginning for us. The name Cardiff Rugby speaks for itself. It has great presence, tradition and heritage. Cardiff Rugby has produced more British & Irish Lions than any other team. I think it's over 60 Lions and I think next to us is Leicester with something like 40. "Everywhere you go in the world, people mention Wales and they think of rugby and Cardiff and the Arms Park. You can't buy that brand. From a business point of view, it's absolutely everything. We want to add to that tradition. I played in the amateur era, but to go back to that tradition now is just wonderful."

It is that deep respect and love for Cardiff Rugby that keeps Thomas involved in the club and he is determined to taste success once more. Through his playing career he played with many of the greats of the second golden era of Welsh Rugby and the club were still frequently referred to as 'The Greatest', in the 1990s came multiple cup successes and touching distance of the first ever European crown, while during the regional era Cardiff have twice won the European Challenge Cup and the EDF Energy Cup once. Many of those successes have been largely thanks to the substantial investments Thomas has made and while the focus today is on being self-sustainable, he believes now is the start of an exciting journey. He continued: *"It's always been a great passion of mine. When I played for the club my mentors like Bleddyn Williams and Jack Matthews – all these sorts of wonderful guys – gave so much to us. When I was asked to come back in 1993 as a patron in the amateur game, it was for very much for me and my family a great love and passion. It's a great honour to be a part of this club. We talked a few weeks ago – Alun, myself, Nigel Walker, Richard and Dai – and I reminded them that it was back in 2006 that we started to develop a side which in 2010 won the Amlin Cup in Marseille. When I think back to the players we had in the team that day – and no disrespect at all to our current team – it was very good. We had a front row of Taufa'ao Filise, TR Thomas and Gethin Jenkins. We had Paul Tito, Maama Molitika, Xavier Rush and Martyn Williams. Sam Warburton was on the bench! "It took four or five years to get to that stage and in our conversation last week I said to Dai 'We need to start now.' We know the areas we need to strengthen. We haven't replaced Xavier Rush except temporarily with Nick Williams. We've got Navidi who can play No 8 and one or two other boys in the back-row, but Dai knows where he's short. But look at the exciting backs we've got; Mason Grady, Ben Thomas, Max Llewellyn, Jarrod Evans, Tomos Williams, Josh Adams. They're exciting players coming through but for us to get up there and compete in the play-offs and in Europe, it's going to take three seasons."*

Thomas is acutely aware that further investment is still required if Cardiff Rugby are to compete in the latter stages of Europe once more and

Welsh rugby is working collectively to increase incomes to the professional game. Chairman, Alun Jones, has also called on the club to find further revenue streams and exploit all opportunities to harness a greater self-reliance. But Thomas is confident that the foundation blocks are in place and he has been delighted with the impact and leadership shown by Dai Young following his return as director of rugby. He added: *"We are hopeful but also realistic. We are not ready this year. There will be changes and Dai will conduct those. He's already explained what we need to do so we are very hopeful and excited, but very realistic about where we'll be this season. There are two things in life which run a business and that's people and product. One of the best things which has happened in Welsh rugby recently is the nomination of Nigel Walker to the Welsh Rugby Union as rugby development director. He is a brilliant rugby brain. He's an Olympian and he will make great changes to the game and the national team. With Dai, he's gone away, learned the game, and come back. The coaching staff he has with him here is getting better and better every year under his guidance and tuition which I'm sure will show its rewards. Dai and I go back over 26 years since I brought him back from rugby league in 1996. He was with us for 14 years as a player, assistant coach, and coach. He went away to learn what it's like to work in a different environment, different and difficult circumstances and now he's back as a mature, No 1 director of rugby. We're very lucky to have him. He's a very different person to what he was nine years ago. He's calmer, far more mature and organised, and very realistic in his approach to the game. I'm delighted and very excited about the future."*

Without Peter Thomas' financial and other assistance over the decades, Cardiff may well have either folded or belong to the W.R.U. One can only hope and pray that his optimism is well-founded, against a current background of court cases for major illnesses being caused by the 30-year movement from a running game towards hard-contact rugby. And whenever Eddie Jones calls for his England XV to be 'brutal', I shudder. At time of writing, 7 August 2022, South Africa, with their 6-man forward 'Bomb Squad' among their 8 replacements, have beaten New Zealand soundly.

ALUN JAMES PRIDAY
Born 23 January 1933 Whitchurch, Cardiff
Tongwynlais RFC 1949-1951
410 games in 14 seasons for Cardiff 1951-1963
1799 points inc. 33 tries
RAF during National Service
Wales 1958 (won in Ireland 9-6), 1961 (won in Cardiff 9-0)
Barbarians 1963-64
Captain Cardiff Cricket Club 1964-65

Although born in Whitchurch, north Cardiff, fullback Alun Priday played his first senior game, aged 16, for Tongwynlais, just a couple of miles from Taff's Well. It was against Cardiff's Butetown team, the CIACS. He remembers, *'But when I was laid out, my mother ran on to the pitch waving her umbrella. I banned her from watching again and when I was capped, she went shopping!'* Alun was inducted into Cardiff RFC's Hall of Fame, from which we have the following information. 'Alun Priday had his eyes on Cardiff from an early age, *"My father brought me to the Arms Park in 1945 and I saw Dr Glyn Jones scoring a try in the corner, and from that moment I was hooked – it was always my ambition to play for the club and seeing the wonderful 1947-48 team in action made me even more determined."* The ambition and determination reached fruition by the time Alun was 22 years old as he won his first Athletic XV cap in 1951-52 and then his First XV cap for 20 games three seasons later. The real red-letter day though was Easter Monday 1953 in his first game to the senior side against the Harlequins.

"I remember every moment of it" he says proudly. *"We won 15-3 with Cliff Morgan, Haydn Morris, CD Williams and Lloyd Williams scoring tries – it was a great day in my rugby life."* Before the end of that season he got another game against Cheltenham, and then 12 more the following year before establishing himself as a regular in 1954-55. *"I wasn't at that stage doing much goal-kicking because Ken Richards, Gwyn Rowlands and Sid Judd shared the duty when John Llewellyn wasn't playing, but I was just happy to be in the team"*. One of Alun Priday's greatest moments of his entire playing career comes in fact from those early days, when, he insists, the team performed in a way that represented all that was best about team spirit. *"There was a Welsh trial match in Llanelli and eight of our first-team regulars including Cliff, Rex, Bleddyn, Gareth Griffiths and Gordon Wells, almost an entire back division, were involved in it. But that didn't stop us going to Twickenham and beating the mighty Quins. I soon realised that men like Peter Nyhan, Howard Nicholls, Malcolm Collins and Eddie Thomas were the backbone of the club."*

Alun was recognised as one the most reliable last lines of defence in Welsh rugby, ideally suited to the catching and kicking role that was typical of the 1950s. As a safe pair of the proverbial houses under the highball, his trademark low, spiralling kicks to touch always kept his team going forward. He was soon attracting attention of the national selectors in both England and Wales. *"I was invited to attend an English International trial in Bristol in December 1956 but opted instead for in Swansea the following week and then played in the Probables in the final trial of January 1957"* he remembers. He eventually won his first cap in Ireland the following year and then another in 1961. He was unfortunate in that his peak years coincided with the career of the brilliant Llanelli and Lions full-back Terry Davies, but no one doubted that Alun was himself a player of true class. "*To play week in, week out for Cardiff was the nearest thing you got to International rugby at that time and you could only have to think of the four games each year with Newport, or the annual glamour match with the Barbarians, and of course the big touring teams every three or four years to realise just how challenging it was*", he says. "*Have no doubt about it, my aim was to be in peak condition for the games in Newport, home or away. Sometimes we won, sometimes we lost, but we always knew we'd been in a game.*" Alun is unnecessarily modest about his own part in the three titanic struggles against the great touring teams in 1957, 1960 and 1963. First of all, he shared in a great win over the Wallabies, which was to set him on his way to his cap in Ireland three months later. And then he played, however unwittingly, a central role in the tough game against Avril Malan's Springboks in 1960.

"*What a game that was. We went into it unbeaten in 13 matches and there was a crowd of 50,000 packed into the Arms Park. After about 10 minutes I caught a highball under the old North Stand and send it back into touch, but as I turned to walk back to my position I was hit by an almighty tackle and laid out... the rest I can't remember*" he readily admits. In fact, he been late tackled by Springbok left-wing Mannetjies Roux, described by more than one watcher as a '*guided missile*', and has very little recognition of what happened to the rest of the first half.' (Dai Hayward was also a passenger from the tenth minute.) 'After that the game deteriorated into a brawl and Cardiff, reduced to 14 men when fly-half Tommy McCarthy went off with a dislocated elbow, held on bravely for a 13-nil defeat. At the end Alun Priday told the press "*Every tooth in my head is loose and I don't know which leg to walk on*".

Agony of another kind was to follow in his next game against a touring team in 1963. Another capacity crowd saw the All Blacks taken to the wire, thanks to mighty effort by Cardiff pack, who created the only try of the game for No.8 Cliff Howe, but were pipped by a penalty and a dropped goal. Alun Priday converted Howe's try, but is still hard on himself for missing two or three medium-range kicks that might have won the game. But no one else would agree with him, as his general play that day was again magnificent. Alun Priday played his final game, his 410th for Cardiff, on 29 September 1965 at Bridgend when his jaw was broken in a controversial incident. Appropriately his last touch was as he made the bravest catches, under pressure. '(With no substitute, Cardiff lost 3-0). 'He took his leave from the playing field but was soon back at the Club as a much-respected committeeman and then Secretary for 17 years, Chairman for two and is a Vice-President. No one has any doubts that he is worthy of his introduction into the club's Hall of Fame.'

Alun told me '*Cenydd and Elwyn and Tony are the last of the famous*

*Williams Brothers, who all played for the Blue and Blacks - what a rugby family, **I played with 6 of them** either for the Rags or the First XV'*. Alun scored 1,799 points for Cardiff Firsts, and would have surpassed that but '*it was a prop by the name of Brian Jones who punched me, and broke my jaw in that game at Bridgend. I had just kicked for touch when Gary Protheroe first came past me as I kicked, then Brian Jones following Gary, did the business. I must say Bridgend Committee came to my home after my week in hospital to apologise and they suspended Brian Jones. It is a long time ago but Diurbar Lawrie, the Bridgend Secretary was a real good friend and whenever we met, he again apologised.*' We must never forget foul play. Publicity is its worst enemy. Some teams in the past have revelled in their reputation for being 'hard' – far better to be remembered for playing rugby. To be honest, the Cardiff, Newport, Swansea and Llanelli teams - the traditional 'Big Four' of Welsh rugby, have a better reputation than many other teams.

CHAPTER 39 - CARDIFF SEASON 1966 – 1967

FOURTH AUSTRALIANS BEATEN - DEBUT OF GARETH EDWARDS, THE WORLD'S BEST PLAYER - TOUR OF SOUTH AFRICA - ELWYN MISSES WALES CAP WITH BROKEN LEG

Elwyn Williams P6 T4 Pts12 - having broken his leg in the sixth game, then recuperating; **Tony Williams** P31 T5 Pts15

Pl 47 W 35 L 9 D 3 Points 691-322 Tries 158-62 Pens 42-38
Pl. 5 W 2 L 2, D 2 Pts 84-71 (South Africa Tour)
Tot 52 W 37 L 11 D 4 Pts 775-393

Elwyn Williams badly broke a leg playing away in the 9-5 win at London Welsh on 10 September 1966. He could not play for 18 months until 18 March 1967, and it was an injury which his team-mates, many supporters and reporters, felt stopped his playing for Wales that season. It was a bad break, and play stopped immediately as players heard the sound of it. If we examine his Firsts appearances from his debut in 1958-59 to 1968-69, his last full season for the Firsts before stepping down to the Rags, we can see his importance: 14, 31, 35, 28, 39, 35, 45, 40, 6, 17, 37. Elwyn missed all but the first 6 games of this season, and also missed half of the following season recuperating.

The Lord smiled on Cardiff this season for backs, the world class Gerald Davies and Maurice Richards easily swapping between centre and wing;

521

and John Huw Williams was a wing much admired by Danny Davies, scoring 27 tries in his 73 games for the Firsts. The superb international centre Ken Jones, known as DK (David Kenneth) joined from Llanelli.

Keith Rowlands was captain again, but on 31 December Keith also broke his leg, again to London Welsh in the 6-0 (H) win. He spent New Year's Eve knowing that his season was over. Scrum half and vice-captain Billy Hullin took over the captaincy. The previous season, both full backs, Alun Priday and Alan Drew, had their jaws broken. Alun had finished with the Firsts after missing most of last season owing to his controversial injury against Bridgend, and Alan Drew also finished playing at the end of this season. Luckily, the full-back Dennis Gethin, who had kicked Cambridge to victory over Cardiff in the previous season, joined, and was to play 109 times for the Firsts. Phil Morgan joined and played 25 times, in just this season, temporarily solving an outside half problem. Ken Jones (DK) played 22 games for Cardiff this season, gained 13 Welsh caps, and for the British Lions played 3 Tests in South Africa, 2 in Australia and 1 in New Zealand. The speedy wing Keri Jones came from Cardiff Teacher Training College, playing 60 times until 1967-68. Keri Jones only played 2 games this season, then concentrating on athletics to run in the Commonwealth Games in Jamaica. Keri scored 30 tries in 58 games in the next 2 seasons, toured with the British Lions, played 5 times for Wales and was a Barbarian. He soon joined Wigan rugby league club, scoring 38 tries in 57 matches up to 1972. Keri also won caps for Great Britain (RL) in the 1970 Rugby League World Cup against France and New Zealand. Frank Wilson, a local boy and a superb Athletic wing, only played a few games for the Firsts before 1967-68, when he made 24 of his 37 Cardiff appearances, scoring 22 tries in total. He moved to St. Helens aged just 23, and touched down 176 times in 310 games. He was a massive loss to Cardiff and Welsh rugby union. However, there were still plenty of centre and fly half opportunities for Tony Williams, and even scrum half Gary Samuel had a few outings at centre because of representative calls on the threequarters.

The versatile Gary 'Sambo' Samuel had joined in 1965-66, playing 112 games until 1974-75. Gary would have played more, but at the start of the season, the *'greatest scrum half of all time'*, and frequently voted the *'world's best player of all time'*, had joined Cardiff. Studying at Cardiff Teacher Training College, on 10 September Gareth Edwards played his first game for the Rags, winning at Briton Ferry away 30-5, and scoring 3 tries. In his next game, a 6-6 away draw with Bristol United, he scored all 6 points with a try and a penalty. On 17 September, he played for the Firsts at home to Coventry, and sparkled in the 24-6 home win, Cardiff scoring 5 tries to nil. Danny Davies records: *'I well remember entering these personal feats in the club's official records, and thinking, "We've got something here!" Gareth made his first overseas tour with Cardiff, to South Africa in May 1967, and was to make another six: to South Africa,*

522

New Zealand, Canada and Rhodesia for the British Lions: for the Barbarians to Canada; and Rhodesia for Cardiff. Having played with, and watched some of the club's great scrum halves for more years than I care to remember - Tommy Dean, Bobby Delahay, Maurice Turnbull, Haydn Tanner, Rex Willis and Lloyd Williams, I now rate Gareth as the best of them all. Present day Rugby has been revolutionised - for the better -and accepted coaching methods and law changes have involved the scrum half more than any other player of the team, particularly around the base of the scrum, the line out, and at - and in - the rucks. Gareth is superior in all the essentials, well-built and strong, courageous and a most determined runner. He has the longest of passes, is a prodigious kicker of the ball and crafty touch finder.

Many thousands of Rugby men and countless millions of sportsmen have been fortunate to see him in the flesh and on television, scoring two of the most memorable tries in Rugby history. The first, his 80 yards solo run for a try for Wales against Scotland at Cardiff in 1972, and the culminating try after a 90 yards movement by the Barbarians in their greatest and most brilliant victory over New Zealand at Cardiff in 1973. At the time of writing, Gareth has already captained Wales eight times, holds 35 Welsh international caps, and is currently touring as vice-captain of the most successful Lions of all time in South Africa; playing at the peak of his career as did Cliff Morgan on the Lions Tour to South Africa of 1955. He is now rated as the **world's best scrum half**, and I heartily concur. I would indeed like to see him as captain of the Cardiff Rugby Club before retiring from the game he has so much adorned.'

Cliff Morgan said: 'Of all the players I've known during 50-odd years involvement with the game, Edwards stood head and shoulders above the rest.' Bill Samuel, his teacher at Pontardawe Grammar School, converted Gareth from a centre to scrum half, and helped him develop all the skills, and more, necessary to be the best in that position. Gareth became an accomplished gymnast, Welsh Schools Long Jump Champion, 220 yards Hurdles Champion, and won the Welsh Games 110 yards hurdles. Facilities were sparse, but experts said that with practice he could pole vault for Great Britain. The *Western Mail* voted him the most promising athlete in Wales. The Swansea football manager, Trevor Morris, went to Gareth's parents' home in Gwauncaegurwen to ask him to sign professional forms to play soccer. On a scholarship to Millfield, he broke the English Championship record for the Low Hurdles, beating Alan Pascoe, who won medals in the Olympic Games (silver), the European Championships (gold, gold, silver, bronze), the Commonwealth Games (gold, silver, bronze) and the European Indoor Games (gold). All in all, Gareth could compete in any sport. In rugby he realised that his pass could be quicker and longer, so practised and practised the spin pass to give his fly halves a quicker delivery and more space.

It would be remiss not to recount the well-known story of how Gareth, always a Cardiff player after Millfield and Cardiff Training College, met Barry John, then a Llanelli player vying with Newport's Dai Watkins to be Welsh fly-half. Ross Harries recounts the story:

'*Barry John: I was picked to play in the trial for the international against Scotland (on 4 February 1967) and the scrum half in the Probables was Gareth Edwards. I didn't know him personally, though I knew of his growing reputation. He phoned me and suggested that we get together for a practice session before the trial.*

Gareth Edwards: So down I went to the West, and after a bit of a search I found out where he was staying. I climbed the stairs, knocked on the door and went in to find him lying on his bed, looking rough. He'd been out at a party all night and had forgotten that I was coming. Worse than that, he couldn't remember where he'd put his boots. But he got up and we went out – me in my pristine Cardiff College tracksuit and polished boots, him in a skanky old T-shirt, gym shorts and trainers. The pitch was a soggy bog and I thought the whole thing was going to be a disaster, but I was determined that we'd get used to playing with each other. "I reckon I can get the ball out to you from pretty much any place" I remember saying to him (in Welsh). *"How do you want the ball?"*

Barry John: It was a bleak Sunday morning, with the rain pelting down. I could see that we would get on well and there seemed to be little point in hanging about in the rain, so I said (in Welsh), *"Look, Gareth, you throw 'em – I'll catch 'em. Let's leave it at that and go home.*

Gareth Edwards: That was the BJ plan. But you know what, it worked. He had this incredible easiness of the mind. He backed his own talent and he gave off a constant calm superiority. He was powerful and quick – much more powerful than he looked – and had the ability to accelerate from a standing start, which is so hard to defend against. His kicking was superb and he always had time on the ball. That's something I'll always remember. He always had time. To my shame I have to admit that I was quite a poor passer of the ball back then – but as he said that filthy day in Carmarthen, I just had to throw the ball in his direction and he would do the rest. He really was that good.' Barry hurt his knee in the trial and confessed to a bad game against Scotland, wishing he had dropped out. Cardiff's Billy Hullin was preferred to Gareth at scrum-half. In the next internationals the half-back pairing was Watkins-Allan Lewis (Abertillery); Watkins-Edwards; Watkins-Edwards (the 'Keith Jarrett game, won 34-21, where Newport's out-of-position fullback Jarrett caught a long lick and ran 50 yards for a magnificent try, converted all 5 Welsh tries, and kicked 2 penalties); and then John-Edwards against New Zealand began their remarkable pairing of 23 games for Wales, with just one match missing in 5 years. Dai Watkins had been named squad captain for a training session at Neath before the All Blacks game, but told the surprised players that he was off to Salford RL, leaving the fly half spot open to Barry.

On 3 September Cardiff beat a West German XV, 41-3, with wing John Huw Williams scoring 3 tries and Dennis Gethin kicking 8 goals. On 1 October, Newport were beaten by 3 goals (converted tries), 3 tries, and a penalty, 27-0 (H). Somehow, after that hammering, Cardiff lost to Newport 8-0 (A), and 17-0 (H) before salvaging a 3-3 draw (A). For an unbiased commentator like this author, Cardiff won the series on tries 6-4, which is one of the reasons I have used Danny Davies' seasonal try tallies of for and against. Running rugby and tries from open play has always been the 'Cardiff way', and indeed, the 'Big Four' of Cardiff, Newport, Swansea and Llanelli have always nurtured attacking back play. Cardiff Training College were defeated 21-6 on 22 October. The college team included Gareth Edwards, Gary Laycock, David Griffiths and Roger Beard, all of whom joined Cardiff.

Grogg of Gareth Edwards

Ray Cheney had joined Cardiff from Newport and kicked 3 conversions and 2 penalties against the training college. A Porth boy, Cheney had played centre forward at soccer for Ton Pentre and Wales Youth, attracting the attention of Tottenham Hotspur FC. National Service in the RAF intervened, for whom he played rugby, and returning to 'civvies' he set a club record of 169 points for Pontypool, also playing against the Springboks. He switched to Newport from March 1963, scoring 40 points in 11 games, and hitting the cross bar with a drop goal attempt in the superb 3-0 win over the All Blacks in 1963. In that 1963-64 season he again set a club record of 171 points, and the following season broke that record with 224 points. He was reserve Welsh full back 23 times. Ray then played for Cardiff 69 times, beating the Australians in 1966, and played for Crawshays RFC and cricket for Monmouthshire County Cricket Club. With the loss of Alun Priday and Alan Drew, the club really needed such a fine full back.

Cardiff beat Australia for the fourth (of four) games, 14-8 on 5 November. The team was well coached by Roy Bish, and Keith Rowlands and Lyn Baxter controlled the lines-out. Nuggety scrumhalf Billy Hullin '*was a match winner, outsmarting his opposite number Ken Catchpole, scoring a try and a drop goal. He also made the break for Ken Jones's try, which Ray Cheney converted and also kicked a penalty goal.*' For Tony Williams, the most bitter disappointment of his career was not playing, but he had only just returned after a bad injury. Australia beat Wales and England. I must mention the following awesome fact – Cardiff Rugby Club – forget the modern 'Blues', never lost to Australia winning 6 out of 6 games:

1908 W24-8 (Wales won 9-6)
[1945 W28-3 Australian Air Force]
1947 W11-3 (Wales won 6-0)
1957 W14-11(Wales won 9-3 1958)
1966 W14-8 (Wales **lost** 14-6)
1975 W14-9 (Wales won 28-3)
1984 W16-12 (Australia beat England, Wales, Scotland, Ireland)

For the match at home against Neath in December, the reputation of the Neath pack was such that **Cardiff asked for a non-Welsh referee**, and a neutral referee from Ireland, Paddy D'Arcy was appointed. Cardiff won 9-6. The game away was drawn 3-3, Unfortunately this fixture, especially at Neath, used to see what was euphemistically called 'over-vigorous' play, causing Cardiff to cancel fixtures for 3 seasons from 1968-69 to 1971-72. This writer saw many Cardiff games at this time – Neath had a team that was not overly liked by most of their opposing teams. Of course, all was not sweetness and light in some fixtures. Mutual respect meant that Cardiff-Newport matches rarely exploded into violence, and Cardiff, Llanelli and Swansea all had reputations as clean, running teams to uphold. However, the Neath game was 'something else', and a recent article places it in context.

Anthony Woolford's piece in *walesonline*, 10 April 2018, was headlined: '*The hardest and most feared rugby teams in the whole of Wales - Matches cancelled, fears "someone could get killed" and referees walking off during the middle of matches.'* Maesteg, Tredegar and Ebbw Vale were 8, 7 and 6 respectively in the 'table' of 'hard' teams, followed by Newport at 5: *'Never afraid to take a backward step in the fisticuffs stakes, Newport's most notorious match came at Bristol in 1985 when* **referee and police officer Supt George Crawford walked off in the first half complaining that it was like "street violence" on the field, and never came back.** *A replacement referee was found to complete the game. Weeks later a visit by Fiji to Rodney Parade was again marred with violence. Fijian second row Savai was sent off after a huge fight broke out among four different sets of players. Savai was seen butting Newport captain Watkins and was dismissed by referee Owen Jones. Shortly afterwards, Watkins was flattened by a kick to the stomach, which led to an exchange of words between the officials of both teams.'*

Fourth was Treorchy – *'You had the Treorchy back row of the early 1970s whose boast was that no half-backs had scored against them for three years and they put 11 outside-halves off the field during that time,'* said Chris Jones, *'the man whose disciplinary rap sheet had more weeks on it than the Julian calendar... So all you did was wait for the referee to turn his back and then boot, punch, stamp, gouge and whatever you wanted to. That was the way it was and every team had its hard men.'* Third was Pontypridd, whose Sardis Road ground was termed *'The House of Pain'*.

In the context of Cardiff cancelling fixtures, Neath were placed second: *'You could go back to the 1950s when brutal scrummager Courtenay Meredith strutted his stuff to the following decade when* **in 1967 fixtures with Cardiff were put on hold after one infamous match that left Welsh legend Gareth Edwards fearing someone could get killed.** *"I honestly thought someone was going to be killed," recalled the Lions great. "There was a great closeness among us as players but also a great rivalry between our clubs. It was hard to believe that you could batter yourselves to death one week and then be comrades in arms the next Saturday."'* The top place was occupied by Pontypool – *'Pooler were so notorious in the 1970s, 80s and early 90s under the reign of Ray Prosser and then Lions hooker Bobby Windsor, some chose to break off fixtures with them. London Welsh did so in 1973 after one infamous game at Old Deer Park when the Exiles ended the game with 12 men, and later on Bristol were said to be incensed by one match at the fortress named Pontypool Park when a young outside-half among their ranks by the name of Stuart Barnes was subjected to some rough stuff. They didn't even have a full fixture list among the top Welsh clubs back in the day. Former Wales and Bridgend centre Steve Fenwick recalled in the book "Nobody Beats Us": "In between internationals we played Pontypool away. It was a bastard of a fixture. They were ruthless and games against them were like the Alamo. They would pound us for 80 minutes and it was the one game I would tell my wife not to book anything* *for the Saturday night as I might be in hospital or limping back home.'"*

Cardiff's tour of South Africa was a real success, except for the refereeing in their loss, as a tired team, in the last game to Northern Transvaal. Against a strong Eastern Province team, Cardiff had scored 29 points in the first half alone, winning 34-9 (6 tries to 1). Maurice Richards on the left wing scored 3 tries and kicked 19 points. Cardiff were reported as being *'fantastic'* with tries *'the like of which I have never seen'*. Gareth Edwards was asked to play full back, and South African commentators admired *'the classical centre play of Gerald Davies and D. Ken Jones'*. Jones played on two Lions tours. On 6 May 1967 Cardiff drew 11-11 with South West Africa; in 10 May North West Cape Districts lost 23-12; on 13 May Eastern Province was thrashed 34-6 (6 tries to 1); Southern Universities beat a tired team 14-11 on 17 May; and on 20 May a very disgruntled team had **"no chance"** – according to those who took part - of beating Northern Transvaal, losing 25-5. It was one of those games where there was little point in playing.

Leading scorers were Ray Cheney with 151 points from 61 goals; the superlative wing Maurice Richards with 117 points from 33 tries and 8 goals; Ken Jones 23 tries and John Huw Williams with 9. Lyn Baxter made most appearances, 43 of 47 matches, and John Hickey, Tony Pender, Maurice Richards, Billy Hullin, Gerald Davies, John O'Shea, W. J. 'Billy' Thomas and W. Clive Evans all played 30 matches or more. Elwyn Williams could only play 6 games, recovering from his broken leg, and he gives an account of his disappointment in missing Welsh caps in his own words, later in this book. First XV caps were awarded to W. J. Carling, Ray Cheney, John Hickey, Ken Jones and Phil Morgan. Hooker Billy Thomas retired at the season end after 268 appearances. Graham Davies left for Bridgend, and Phil Morgan decided to turn professional. Gerald Davies, Billy Hullin, John O'Shea, Gareth Edwards and Billy Raybould, who was now with London Welsh, all gained their first Welsh caps.

Dai Hayward had put off retirement to captain the Athletic XV but was injured in the third match and did not play again until the sixteenth. They achieved the **best points record** of any reserve team in Cardiff's history: 977 points scored against 227, an average of 25 points a game, when tries were only 3 points. They scored **221 tries against 28!** Again, they refused penalties, scoring only 22 against 35. Rugby players will understand these statistics – they are amazing. At the modern game's 5 points for a try, they would have scored 1419 points, over 37 per game. The Rags played 38, won 34, lost 3 and drew 1. The Athletic also won the prestigious Glamorgan Silver Ball Competition, winning all 12 matches, and beating Aberavon Quins in the final 7-0. Their only other win came in the following season, and Taff's Well won it only once, in the 1975-76 season with Elwyn Williams back coaching and playing.

The famous Bassett brothers played for Cardiff before the war, and their nephew Robert Bassett this year set a scoring record of 101 goals and 4 tries for the Athletic - 228 points; 6 goals, 1 try for the Firsts -18 points; and 8 goals, 1 try -21 points, for the Extras XV; 267 points for the three Cardiff teams. Bassett kicked 10 goals and scored a try against Cardiff High School Old Boys. The Athletic obviously could not choose a single 'man of the year' and awarded it jointly to captain Dai Hayward, coming back after injury, and 'Bob' Bassett. P. Lyn Jones scored 28 tries (6 against Old Penarthians), Steve Hughes 24, Frank Wilson 15, John Uzzell 14, back row Roy Morgan 13 (plus 3 for the Firsts) and Brian and Bernard Evans 10 each. Bob Bassett made most appearances, 26 followed by Roy Duggan, Steve Hughes, Tommy McCarthy and Gwyn Thomas on 24, Dai Hayward 23, Ian Robinson 22, and P. L. Jones and Gary Samuel 21 each. Athletic XV caps were gained by Robert Bassett, Roy Morgan, Gary Samuel and Peter 'Pies' Thomas, whose 16 appearances with The Rags and 8 for the 1st XV qualified him.

For those who don't understand the 'Pies' nickname, Peter, his brother Stan and their father built a national savoury foods business, Peter's Savoury Products, and sold it in 1988 to Grand Metropolitan plc for over £95m. You can still see 'Peter's Pies' being sold. Peter then became heavily involved, like his brother, in property development. Peter and his wife, Babs, are major benefactors of the performing arts in Wales, and he was appointed CBE in 2012 for services to business, sport and charitable work in Wales. Peter put £14 million into Cardiff and the regional team Cardiff Blues over the years. In the enforced regional reorganisation Cardiff Blues became the first team, and Cardiff RFC a feeder team in the next level down, the Welsh Championship. It was a sad, useless, pointless affair, which has led to dwindling crowds at all levels of Welsh rugby. Peter spent 25 years as Chairman of Cardiff Rugby, from when the sport became professional in 1995, was President of Cardiff Blues and is now Life-President of Cardiff Rugby.

Another Peter Thomas, known as Peter 'R.A.F.' Thomas., captained the re-formed Extras XV (the 'Tatters') and the results were the best of their three seasons so far. Thomas held an Athletic XV cap for 1957-58 and had toured East Africa with the Combined Services, with Cenydd Williams and Ray Glastonbury. Danny Davies makes the comment with which many of the older generation agree, about 'Thomas RAF' *'having, like Lloyd and Cenydd Williams, Alun Priday and others, done National Service the withdrawal of which was not, nor has been, in the national interest of our country.'* Alun Priday was again captain of the Cardiff Cricket Club, and Davies quotes from its report: *'Cardiff Cricket Club, whose removal to Sophia Gardens in 1966 saddened the hearts of many cricket and Rugby sportsmen. With the erection of the new huge gaunt concrete stands for the club and the Welsh Rugby Union, the Cardiff Arms Park lost its original character of more than a century.'* The wonderful old Arms Park (some of us fondly remember the dog track and the adjoining county cricket ground, Sophia Gardens) was pulled down for a new National Stadium, to be itself later replaced by the Millennium, now Principality, Stadium.

CHAPTER 40 - CARDIFF SEASON 1967 – 1968

BARRY JOHN'S DEBUT – *'THE GREATEST FLY HALF'* - SIX CARDIFF PLAYERS CHOSEN FOR LIONS TOUR - CARDIFF NOT GIVEN CHANCE TO BEAT ALL BLACKS – LLOYD WILLIAMS AND STAN BOWES PLAY FOR THE EXTRAS

Elwyn Williams P17, missing the first half of the season with a broken leg. Having scored tries in every season, 39 tries - this was the only blank try season in his record; **Tony Williams** P36 T6 Pts18

Pl 46 W 32 L 12 D 2 Pts 703-314, Tries 137-45 Pens 36-41

C. Howard Norris had joined Cardiff in 1958, via Porth Grammar School, St. Luke's College Exeter and National Service, and gained the game's highest honours. He understood all aspects of forward play, beginning in the back row, then playing in the second row before becoming one of the world's outstanding props. In those days, 6 foot and over 16 stone made for a well-respected front row forward. He played only twice for Wales, but toured New Zealand with the Lions in 1966. Howard played in the first 3 Tests against the All Blacks, and it may be a **record that he played more times in Lions Test Matches than for his country**. One could yet again make a case for international bias against Cardiff forwards, when their backs nearly always featured strongly in Welsh teams. He made a club record First XV appearances of 413 (or 415, Davies gives both figures) up to November 1971. Norris was a popular choice as captain, and chose Gerald Davies as vice-captain. In December 1967 Howard Norris was the Barbarians pack leader, comfortably drawing with the unbeaten All Blacks 6-6 at Twickenham, until the fifth minute of injury time, when the Baabaas' full back S. J. Wilson missed an easy kick to touch. New Zealand scored a try direct from the miskick and fortunately won 11-6.

From Cardiff Youth and the Athletic, the wing Alec Finlayson became a regular first teamer, and Ian Lewis joined from Cardiff Training College, J. H. James joined from Cambridge, and second row Maurice Braithwaite from Pontypridd. The *'glittering prize'* to join the club was 22-year-old Barry John, a seasoned Llanelli player already capped 3 times by Wales.

Davies writes: *'Like Cliff Morgan on the Lions tour of 1955, and Gareth Edwards perhaps in 1974, Barry appears to have reached the peak of his Rugby brilliance in New Zealand in 1971 where he was crowned so to speak - "King John", thus becoming royally superior to our great "Prince of three-quarters" Gwyn Nicholls, 1891-1910. The best of Barry John's Cardiff predecessors, P. F. Bush, J. Clem Lewis, Cliff Jones, W. B. Cleaver and Cliff Morgan, each had their own characteristic style of play, and to assess the best of them all would need comparing like with like. None of them had the benefit of an inside half anywhere near as incomparable as Gareth Edwards. But what Barry possessed, and they did not, was an elusiveness and deception, born of apparently ample time in which to move, he was expert in the touch finding technique between the two 'twenty-fives', his goal kicking approach was simple, speedy and accurate; he was one of the club's best drop goal kickers and kicked four in one match against his old team Llanelli in November 1970. Undoubtedly, Barry John and Gareth Edwards were the greatest pair of half-backs in the club's history'.*

I believed it was impossible for Wales to replace Barry, who retired much too soon, but another gem, the late Phil Bennett of Llanelli succeeded him. They were very different – Barry glided, Phil scurried, but both seemed to have time on the ball, both were excellent tactical kickers and both were match winners. I just missed Cliff Morgan, but Barry and Phil are the greatest outside halves in my experience – a pleasure to watch. And both, like nearly all former Welsh internationals, converse with you as if you were a long-lost friend. (I was in the Llanelli Scarlets clubhouse a several times a few years ago, and Gareth Jenkins, Phil and his wife and Chico Hopkins, invited me to sit at their table after the games, not knowing me from Adam, and including me in their chatting.) Upon 3 October 1967 Cardiff played a British Isles team, for the benefit of the dependants of forward Cliff Davies, winning 13-8.

The first 8 games were won, and up to the end of December only four matches were lost, to Newport 11-6 (A), Ebbw Vale 3-0 (H), Llanelli 11-6 (A) and Neath 16-6 (A). I mentioned previously a problem with playing Neath. The first game, won by Cardiff at home on 6 September was, according to Davies, *'a travesty of good football. Neath started off with very much robust intent and some rough play, which, after some repetition, invoked many calls and boos from the crowd to "send him off". The game deteriorated and Randall Davies was ordered off the field and later sentenced to three months suspension by the W.R.U.'* Cardiff won 9-6, scoring the only try of the match. This second match, away, with Neath followed the example of the first, was lost 16-6, with Cardiff missing their best players. **Fixtures were cancelled, by Cardiff, for three seasons,** until 1971-72 in the interests of (Cardiff) player safety. In this second game, Tony Williams captained the team from centre, with Elwyn playing open side to John Hickey's blind side wing forward. John Huw Williams' Neath programme reads *'We extend a sincere welcome to Cardiff R.F.C., captained today by Tony Williams. Our visitors are enjoying a very successful season and at present head the Welsh unofficial table. Five Cardiff players appear for the Barbarians against New Zealand at Twickenham this afternoon, and we wish Keri Jones, Gerald Davies, Barry John, Gareth Edwards and Howard Norris a happy and successful match. Neath members will have an added interest in Keri Jones, as he commenced his first-class career with Neath some four seasons ago. Included in our visitors' side are three Internationals, John Uzzell, Billy Hullin and John O'Shea, former Cambridge Blue Dennis Gethin, who has played some grand games for Neath in the past, and wing Frank Wilson who scored the East Wales try in Wednesday's exciting game against the New Zealand Tourists at (the) Arms Park. We look forward to a good game of rugby, worthy of the tradition of both our clubs.'* Yeh, right. Other clubs (and their supporters) of that era that played Neath will remember an 'All Black' team that took no prisoners. The cancellation of fixtures, from the second 'unsavoury' match on 16 December 1967, lasted until 15 September 1971, almost 4 years.

Along with those five great players, Cardiff were also missing from the game Tony Pender, Dai Hayward and Maurice Richards, i.e. eight of their first team. Plus Elwyn Williams, their first-choice flanker, still recovering from his broken leg. **Only 6 of the Cardiff team were regular First XV players**. Previous games had been bad-tempered over the years, and as followers of Welsh rugby will know, no team enjoyed playing at The Gnoll. And non-Neath supporters generally stayed away. In 156 games against Neath, from 1879 to 1975, Cardiff won 92, lost 47 and drew 17, scoring 1,496 points to 839. Neath drew 46-46 on penalties but Cardiff won the try count 331-171. Cardiff lost to Llanelli 11-6 (A), and 6-3 (H), allowing Llanelli to become unofficial Welsh champions instead of Cardiff. Despite being top of the unofficial table for almost the whole season, the loss of six Cardiff players selected for the British Lions at the end of the season allowed Llanelli to overtake Cardiff. Cardiff again finished second behind Newport the following year, with Maurice Richards the only Lion to make more than 20 appearances for Cardiff. Many of Cardiff's 12 losses were affected by injuries, and the non-availability of their star players.

After losing 11-6 (A), a try apiece, and drawing 8-8 (H) with Newport, Cardiff came into some real form. They then won 18-3 (A), 4 tries to 0, and 26-3 (H), 6 tries to 1, a season total of 12 tries to 3 against their nearby rivals. These things matter to some of us. London Welsh were easily beaten, 5 tries to 2, 27-12 (H), but Cardiff had five players in the Welsh team, in the away game played on the morning of the England-Wales match, and London Welsh won 14-6. The game was so exceptionally full of flowing attacks that a London sportswriter called *'Rugby for the Gods'*, and another noted a spectator saying, *'After that there doesn't seem any point in going to the international, does there'*. The Barbarians were beaten 16-11, 4-2 on tries, by another weakened Cardiff team. Another reduced team was sent on a French tour, losing 11-8, 13-3 and winning 12-9. Davies relates: *'Such tours at the end of a strenuous season, against strong and augmented opposition should never be undertaken. The results, particularly when we cannot send our strongest players, are most damaging to the club's reputation... According to press reports, the accommodation provided for some of our players, officials and club supporters was of the very lowest category of quality, two in a bed and so on, and of "red lamp" standard. It should be - never again!'*

If the club had been given its regular game against leading touring teams, it could well have beaten the All-Blacks – instead they made up over half the East Wales team that was far superior on the day, when New Zealand escaped with a draw. If TV footage still exists, there is the proof. Mike Pearce at *sportsdragon.com* reports that it was a hastily assembled East Wales side and that the match had originally been scheduled for the Saturday, but heavy snow fell throughout Wales, *'and the icy snow-covered terraces would have been a danger to spectators, so the match was called off. 40,000 turned up on the following Wednesday afternoon, a week before Christmas, to watch a match which was expected to be an easy win for the unbeaten all-conquering All Blacks. It was an overcast day and the pitch was greasy, the more mobile East Wales pack made the New Zealand forwards look ponderous, and the All Blacks half backs were put under a great deal of pressure throughout the game. In the 22nd minute Lyn Baxter won a line-out and Barry John tried a dropkick, it swerved away to the left of the posts, but Frank Wilson followed up to beat Thorne to the touchdown. Shortly afterwards the home side could, and maybe should have, been awarded a penalty try when a diagonal kick intended for winger Keri Jones saw him race to the line with McCormack, only for the New Zealander to barge him out-of-the-way as they reached the ball.*

Later in the first half Wilson went over for a try for the Welsh, only to be called back for an infringement. A try was only worth three points in those days, so it was three nil to East Wales, the score remained the same at the end of the half. In the second-half East Wales launched attack after attack on the All-Blacks line. Several kickable penalties came their way which they missed, resulting in Captain Gareth Edwards taking over the kicking duties and missing two kickable penalties himself, from fairly easy positions. 10 minutes from time, and against the run of play, came the Steel try that saved the All-Blacks' blushes. Lochore raced away from the scrum on halfway with Davies in support, Davies passed it out to Steel, and with the cover defence coming across and 50 yards to go, a try did not look likely, but Steel beat off his tacklers to score probably the best, and definitely the most important try of the tour, to level the scores at 3-3.

East Wales continued their onslaught on the All-Blacks line, and there was almost a sensational finish, when Barry John's last second drop goal grazed the right upright. It was felt the home side should have won this game and deserved to do so but the All Blacks hung on in there and saved their unbeaten tour record.' Gareth Edwards missed two easy penalties, and reminisced: *'I was barely 20 years old, though it was only a few months later that I captained Wales for the first time. Dai Hayward, the former Cardiff and Wales wing forward, was asked to coach the East Wales side, though coaching was very much in its infancy then. He said we'd better meet up and have a chat about the game, so we met in what was then the Cockney Pride, a pub in Cardiff, where over a lunch of curry and chips, we discussed our tactical approach to this enormous event. I can still remember Dai's opening line: "Well boys, there's no point complicating anything. If we get hold of the ball, let's move it"'.* Upon a greasy pitch, the far more mobile East Wales pack outplayed the New Zealand forwards, putting the All-Blacks half backs under pressure throughout the game. *'Had we won it, against one of the greatest teams I ever played against, people would still be talking about it with great reverence. It was a wonderful performance by a side that had been put together literally in a week.'* (Source - Mike Pearce, https://thesportsdragon.com/2017/10/03/east-wales-the-team-that-tamed-the-mighty-1967-all-blacks/). One rests one's case – the full Cardiff team would have beaten them. The eight Cardiff players were Keri Jones, Gerald Davies, Frank Wilson, Barry John, Gareth Edwards, John O'Shea, Lyn Baxter and John Hickey. In fact, New Zealand played no club sides, just regions in this tour, and after 2 wins in Canada, they beat 9 British regional sides and Wales, England, Scotland and France, before drawing with East Wales and only just beating the Barbarians.

For the last few weeks of the season, Cardiff lost more games, as a record number of 6 players were selected for the Lions to tour South Africa with the British Lions: Gareth Edwards, Gerald Davies, Barry John, Keri Jones, Maurice Richards and John O'Shea. The tour party was ravaged by injury – as with ALL South African tours - and Edwards, John, Ireland's Mike Gibson and Gerald Davies never appeared in a Test team together. Indeed, *'Star back Barry John broke his collar bone in a **dangerous tackle** in the first Test'*. Targeting the best players has been an unfortunate theme is rugby up to the present day. Tourist John Taylor wrote in 2013: *'it was hard to believe this is the man* (Cardiff prop John O'Shea) *who still holds the unique distinction of being the only Lion ever to have been sent-off. I can say 'distinction' because it was truly farcical. We were playing Eastern Transvaal at Springs, in front of the most hostile small-town crowd you can imagine. A scuffle broke out amongst the forwards (handbags - no damage) and Tess* (O'Shea) *was isolated by half a dozen home forwards.*

When the dust settled the home referee singled him out (the only Lion involved) and dismissed him. Suddenly thousands of oranges - they cost nothing and every spectator seemed to have a bag of them - rained down on him as he made the long walk back to the dressing room. Willie John rushed down from the stand to offer protection, dealing peremptorily with one idiot as he tried to attack Tess, and this was the genesis of the infamous '99' call six years later in 1974. McBride was determined nobody would ever again be isolated, so when the call came everybody had to pile in, so that the referee could never single out one offender. It worked - there were some really ugly brawls in '74 but nobody received their marching orders.'

For this season, Wales at last appointed a coach for the team, David Nash, who only lasted a year as Wales won one, drew one and lost three of their games. He was succeeded by the former scrumhalf Clive Rowlands from 1968-74, who achieved in 29 games – W18 D4 L7. The British Lion John Dawes succeeded Rowlands from 1974-79 and went even better, admittedly with a team that had grown under Clive. In 24 games Dawes' record was W18 L6. From Cardiff, Keri Jones, Gerald Davies, Barry John, Gareth Edwards, John O'Shea and Maurice Richards all played every game for Wales in this season. Thus, because of internationals from 13 January to 23 March, their Cardiff appearances were limited. Wales drew 11-11 (A) with England, with captain Gareth Edwards and Bobby Wanbon scoring tries, then defeated Scotland 5-0 (H), with a try by Keri Jones. Wales then lost 9-6 (A) to Ireland. Keri Jones scored the only Welsh try in the 14-9 (H) loss to France, who won the Grand Slam. With a total points difference of only minus 3, Wales somehow came fourth, but they were on the verge of becoming a great team. Cardiff's leading try scorer was wing Frank Wilson with 17. He was a Llandaff North product who turned professional at the end of the season, after just 37 appearances for Cardiff. At St. Helens RL he scored 176 tries in 310 matches, and played 14 times for Wales RL. P. Lyn Jones scored 15 tries, Gerald Davies 10, Maurice Richards and Barry John 9 each (plus 9 dropped goals for Barry). Billy Hullin was also a Welsh international and scored 6 tries. Dennis Gethin scored 157 points, from 66 goals and a try. Barry John, Maurice Braithwaite, Dennis Gethin, Roy Morgan, Ian Robinson, John Uzzell and Frank Wilson gained First XV caps.

Second row John Price had joined from Penarth in 1962-63, and now captained the Athletic, to a brilliant record of **P33 W30 D2 L1: Pts 700 - 140**. The record was all the more impressive because of the number of times Rags players were called upon to play for the Firsts. The defeat was at home to Taibach, 6-3, after losing the excellent scrumhalf Gary Samuel early in the match and playing with 14 men. However, the Rags reached the Silver Ball Final, meeting Taibach at Bridgend, and revenged that unfortunate loss by 27-3. Price used 69 players, of whom 49 scored, leading try scorers being the sturdy wing P. Lyn Jones 16, Alec Finlayson 13, John Uzzell 13, Frank Wilson 12 and John Huw Williams and Roy Duggan each 8. Goal kicking was shared amongst Ray Cheney, Bob Bassett, Ian Lewis and Dennis Gethin. Meirion Davies, John Evans, Mike Knill and Gerald Morgan were awarded caps. The Cardiff Extras XV was often raided by the Athletic, as was the Athletic by the Firsts. In the process of rebuilding the national rugby ground, most of all the Cardiff sides' games were played on Glamorgan's County Cricket former ground Sophia Gardens. It was not a great season for the Extras, Cardiff's third team: P22 W12 L8 D2. When the Extras were short of players, Stan Bowes and Lloyd Williams played several times. Lloyd had last turned out for the Firsts four seasons previously, but the wonderful prop Stan Bowes, with 184 Firsts appearances, had made his last appearance in 1955-56. Petty Officer Stan Bowes first played in 1938-39, so lost most of his career through war service. Stan played in the 1944 Services International when Wales beat England 24-11, but never achieved a full cap, and is fondly remembered by a dwindling band of supporters running the line for Cardiff in the 1960s (and laughing as he tried to keep up with play).

CHAPTER 41 - CARDIFF SEASON 1968 – 1969

TONY WILLIAMS VICE-CAPTAIN - CARDIFF WIN THREE MAJOR SEVENS EVENTS - TONY WILLIAMS *'SEVENS PLAYER OF THE YEAR'* – ELWYN *'A COMPLETE FOOTBALLER'* PLAYS 300 GAMES – MAURICE RICHARDS

Pl 45 W33 L9 D3 Pts 648-317 Tries 120-38, Pens 49-37

Elwyn Williams P37 (of 45) T5 15pts; **Tony Williams** P40 (of 45) T9 27pts

This was the last season where the youngest brothers played in virtually every game, totalling 77 appearances and 14 tries between them. Tony had another two years playing regularly for the Firsts, then joining the Athletic and Taff's Well, but his brother Elwyn made only ten First appearances in the next three years, owing to a new coach wanting heavier forwards playing 'the New Zealand way'. There was, unlike in the present era, in this season a welcome change in the laws, then known as the 'Australian Dispensation' to encourage running with the ball rather than kicking. (One does not know why 'the Mark' still exists, by the way). When the ball was kicked directly into touch, without bouncing, from outside the 25-yard line (in European, 'the 22'), the line-out was now to be taken parallel to the point of kicking, rather than the point of crossing the touchline, favouring running clubs like Cardiff. In 2022, there was another change, called the 50:22 Rule: '*If a player kicks the ball from his own half and it bounces before going out of play in the opposition 22, his team is given the throw into the resulting line-out, in a prime attacking position.*' To be quite frank, the rules/laws have become an ever-growing sclerotic accretion, like the English judicial system, and need ripping up and starting again to make them comprehensible to anyone. There could also be an average weight limit per man of, say, 15 (89kg) or 16 stones (95kg) at club and international level respectively. There could still be the 20 stone, 6foot 7inch behemoths, but there would be compensating two 14 stone men in his team to keep to the limit. The game has developed in favour of massive men, taking it away from the capabilities of normal size people.

The old wooden North Stand, dating from 1934, was demolished in the course of rebuilding works in the summer of 1968. In the next season, 1969-1970 Cardiff began formally playing on the adjacent former Glamorgan Cricket Ground, now renamed the Arms Park, as the new National Stadium was completed, which was reserved for internationals and the like. Howard Norris was captain again, nominating the experienced Tony Williams as vice-captain. Tony, the youngest Williams brother, was comfortable playing anywhere in the backs, probably preferring outside half, but usually playing centre. Danny Davies reminds us that it was then 15-man rugby, sometimes 14 or 13, not, as now, any number between 15 and 23 players participating, with a forwards and backs swapping on the hour: '*September 1968 did not presage a very good season as we lost, rather unusually, four matches - to Bridgend (H), Coventry (H), Gloucester (A) and Aberavon (A), but we were beset by injuries, and in **three of those matches we were reduced to fourteen men before half-time**, which again prompted agitation for a bye-law to provide for replacements.*' Cardiff lost to Bridgend 11-6 (but won away 10-6); to Coventry 6-3 (and lost away 14-11, again missing players); to Gloucester 15-6 in a game of no tries (no second fixture); and to Aberavon 6-3, a try apiece (but won at home 13-6). Without injuries and representative appearances, a full Cardiff team could have possibly achieved an unbeaten season.

On 16 October 1968, Cardiff scored 8 tries to 2 at the Arms Park, defeating Pontypool 35-9, in modern scoring 51-13, winning the away game 11-5. The Cardiff home programme noted fixture congestion, and added: '*Cardiff make four changes from the team which drew 6-6 at Northampton last Saturday. Maurice Richards is not available for mid-week games and his place is taken by Alec Finlayson, whilst Tony Williams has a reoccurrence of an old neck injury and will be replaced by Roy Duggan. In the pack a rota system is being operated in the second row, which means that John Hickey replaces M. Gay. It is interesting to note*

537

*that **Elwyn Williams plays his 302nd game for the first team** this evening. We congratulate him on passing this milestone of 300 games, which is a wonderful achievement and underlines the consistency of his play over many seasons. **A complete footballer**, he has come back after breaking his leg two seasons ago and he has loyally served the Cardiff Rugby Club in a manner, which is in keeping with the remarkable record of the Williams family.'* In 121 fixtures between 1908 and 1975, Pontypool achieved the double over Cardiff 3 times, all before WW2. Cardiff achieved 7 doubles and 3 trebles before that war, and 18 doubles after. Cardiff won 83 games, lost 25 and drew 13, scoring 1,346 points to 681. Pontypool won on penalties 60-58, but lost the try count 281-115.

Regarding the Coventry 6-3 loss, John Huw Williams loaned me his programme. Among its notes we read, *'The Cardiff Team again has enforced changes, from the side which defeated Bristol 19-9 on Wednesday, although the Pack remains intact. The absence of Billy Hullin, who was married yesterday, and the injury to Gary Samuel is aggravated by the fact that Gareth Edwards is playing for Roger Young's XV in Ireland. However, he will be available next week, which will ease the Selectors' injury worries. They have had plenty of scope for experiments recently, but there has always been a good record in the Club of reserves rising to the occasion, so let us hope that this proves the case today. There is certainly plenty of competition for places, which is always a healthy sign.'* The fourth-choice scrumhalf, A. Canham, only played two games for the Firsts, both in this season, as Cardiff were juggling appearances of the internationals Edwards and Hullin and another great scrumhalf Gary Samuel, who would have walked into most other clubs as their first choice.

Replacement of injured players, up to two players per team, was added to the 1968-69 Laws, too late for these Cardiff losses. Mike Gibson was the first official replacement in a test match, replacing the injured Barry John in the opening minutes of the Lions' First Test against South Africa in 1968. (However, replacements had been used unofficially in New Zealand, South Africa and Australia before this time). Tactical substitutions of up to three replacements were then introduced in 1996, and now we have no fewer than 8 replacements sitting on the bench, most or all usually appearing at some stage in the game. When on the committee of Llanybydder Rugby Club, I was quoted in a two-page article in the Western Mail, on the problems of fielding full teams – *'We don't need a bench, we have a stool'*. The WRU seems out of touch with smaller clubs, who receive minimal support, unless they have a large enough catchment area for mini and female rugby teams. However, the massive drop-off of youngsters at age 12 has never been addressed – it is because the game is too 'brutal', something which the England coach Eddie Jones, encourages it to be. In New Zealand, young players are allocated teams by size, not age, allowing for confidence to build before any growth spurt.

Scrum-halves British Lion Gareth Edwards and Gary Samuel were injured, and Cardiff's other British Lions returned to play well after the season's start. Edwards only played 10 times, but the indomitable Billy Hullin filled the scrumhalf void in this, his last season, making a total of 154 appearances since 1963-64. Of the other Lions, Gerald Davies went to Cambridge after the tour, playing only twice for Cardiff; Barry John only had 14 games and John O'Shea 11. Maurice Richards managed 23 appearances, but the other Lion wing Keri Jones turned professional upon his Lions Tour return. Lyn Baxter's Welsh tour to Argentina, coupled with injury later, meant he only played 19 times. Apart from injuries to other players, Cardiff lost a great deal of playing time from 7 truly great players – the best half-backs in Europe, and probably the world, John and Edwards; two superb wings, Maurice Richards and Keri Jones; a world class centre/wing, Gerald Davies; and two of their best forwards, O'Shea and Baxter.

1968-69 Tony and Elwyn win Harlequins Sevens

Cardiff lost to Swansea 6-3 (A) in a try-less game in December. However, the replay in Cardiff in March, with a more complete team, was a massacre 27-5 (H), 6:1 in tries, in today's scoring system 39-7. Newport was yet again the problem. For the first Cardiff-Newport game of 5 October 1968, John Williams' scarlet-uniformed St. Albans Military Band celebrated 50 years of playing, and leading the singing at Cardiff Arms Park. Cardiff lost the first 3 games 11-6 (H), 9-6 (A), and after a frost cancellation 6-3 (A). For the fourth match, once more Newport came to the Arms Park determined, for the first time, to beat Cardiff four times in one season. These four games in a season had started in 1880-81, and Cardiff had achieved the feat four times. The largest crowd of the season saw Newport outplay Cardiff on 16 April 1969, scoring 2 tries to 1, and after a quarter of an hour of the second half, the score was 9-9. As Dannie Davies records: *'for practically the rest of the game they were camped almost permanently inside Cardiff's twenty-five and looked as if they must win. But it was not to be, and by desperate tackling and covering, Cardiff held out to the end, thus once again thwarting Newport's efforts, they were better on the day.'*

Cardiff were equally determined not to be the first side in history to lose all four games, with Newport players being held up on the line, and my mate muttered *'Bloody Hell, Barry John's tackling!'* In the words of Max Boyce *'I was there'*, and Newport were desperately unlucky, never achieving the quadruple. Eleven days before, the Barbarians had been defeated in a thriller, 20-16, 3 tries each.

Dennis Gethin beat Alun Priday's season record of 176 points for a full-back, with 199 points from 80 goals and one try. Wing-forward Mervyn John beat the try scoring record for a forward, with 13 against the 12 of Les Spence and Cliff Howe. Mervyn John also scored 9 tries for the Rags. Other top try scorers were Alec Finlayson 18, Maurice Richards 13 and Tony Williams 9. Tony Williams played in 40 out of 45 matches, Denis Gethin 39, John Hickey 38, Elwyn Williams 37, Ian Robinson and Howard Norris 34, Garry Davies and Maurice Braithwaite 33, Ken Jones 24 and Maurice Richards 23. New First XV caps were awarded to prop Roger Beard (33 games), wing/centre Alec Finlayson (29) and flanker Mervyn John (25). Cardiff won three major 'sevens' tournaments, Davies recording: *'**most of the credit was due to the astute and intelligent leadership of our captain, Tony Williams**.'* In the first Sevens, for the Lord Wakefield Trophy, in the Harlequins Invitation Sevens, Tony captained his versatile brother Elwyn, John Huw Williams, Nick Williams, Meirion Davies, Billy Hullin and John Hickey. The 'Quins' were defeated in the 4 September 1968 final, 21-13. In the Welsh (Snelling) Sevens on 26 April 1969, Barry John scored a record number of points to gain the Everson Award. Billy Hullin touched down in the final minutes in a great final against Llanelli to win 17-13. This was a great day out for rugby supporters, with everyone cheering 'minnows' against the better clubs. The following Saturday the Welsh National Sevens were staged on the Cardiff Arms Park for the first time, and Neath were beaten 11-3 in the Final. Tony Williams earned the accolade of *'Sevens Player of the Year'*.

Ex-Cowbridge Grammar School, Aberystwyth University College,

Pontypridd and London Welsh, the forward John Davies was captain and pack leader of the Athletic, leading it to yet another great season: Pl 30 W 27 L 2 D 1 Pts 677-184. The try count was 151:27, a ratio of almost 6:1, with Cardiff kicking 19 penalties against 22. Terry Stephenson touched down 7 times against Cilfynydd, equalling a 72-year-old record, and Chris Jones set a forward record of 14 tries. Many of the Athletic also appeared for the Firsts. This was the final season of the three-year Extras XV experiment (a 'third team), and 35-year-old Dai Hayward, who had joined from Newbridge in the Summer of 1957, had still not retired, dropping down from the Rags to the 'Tatters' and becoming captain.

On the international front, this was so nearly what would have been a well-deserved Grand Slam year – Wales was on the cusp of another Golden Era. Scotland were hammered 17-3 (A), with 3 tries by the Cardiff half-backs John and Edwards and the Cardiff wing Richards. Then Wales won 24-11 (H) against Ireland, with 4 tries from Morris, Taylor, Watkins and D. Williams to 1 by Gibson. Attendance was only 29,000, as the National Stadium was still incomplete. Then Edwards and Richards scored tries, to 1 by Campaes of France in an unlucky 11-11 draw (A). The great fly-half Phil Bennett became the first replacement used by Wales when he replaced Cardiff's Gerald Davies, then a centre, when Gerald dislocated his elbow with four minutes remaining. On 12 April, against England, Maurice Richards became the third player to score **four tries** in a match for Wales. John added another try against 3 penalties by Bob Hiller, as England were put to the sword 30-9 (H). The Championship saw **14 tries to 2 in 4 games**, with a points difference of 48. France had the Wooden Spoon, with just one draw against the outright champions, Wales.

This 1969 Triple Crown paved the way for the 1971 Grand Slam, which was won by a team widely regarded as the greatest side ever to wear the Welsh jersey. The 'Super Seventies' included Grand Slams in 1971, 1976 and 1978 and Triple Crowns in 1971, 1976, 1977, 1978 and 1979. Had the game in Ireland in 1972 not been cancelled, that otherwise undefeated campaign could have ended with another Grand Slam. Four Cardiff players were selected for the 1969 Welsh tour to New Zealand, Australia and Fiji: Gareth Edwards (vice-captain), Barry John, Gerald Davies and Maurice Richards. As regards Maurice Richard scoring 4 tries, on his international debut Willie Llewellyn of Llwynypia had achieved it in 1899, also against England, and went on to captain Wales, beat the All Blacks and play for the British Isles - the Lions precursors. R. A. 'Reggie' Gibbs of Cardiff repeated the feat in 1908 against France. Six other Welshmen have done the same since, in a multiplicity of international fixtures, but none against top class international opponents. Maurice Richards was truly something else. He also scored 4 tries against Gloucester in the 1966 home win 37-6, where Cardiff scored 10 tries to 1 (Only 2 were converted, and if all were converted modern scoring would be 73-5.) Cardiff won away 25-6, 5 tries to 0. Scoring **15 tries to 1**, against one of England's premier teams, shows what we have lost by trying to work out a successful formula for rugby. English and French teams are well-funded, but Welsh reorganisation started with the formation of the Welsh-Scottish League in 1999-2000; which begat the Celtic League to include Ireland 2001-02 to 2004-2006; which begat the Magners League 2006-07 to 2010-2011; which begat the Rabo Direct Pro 12 to include Italy 2011-12 to 2013-2014; which begat the Guinness Pro-12, 2014-2015 to 2016-2017; which begat the Guinness Pro-14 to include South Africa 2017-2018 to 2019-2020; which begat the Guinness Pro-12 when South Africa dropped out 2020-2021; which in 2021 welcomed back South Africa for the Guinness Pro-14 Rainbow Cup and the Rugby Championship. Absolute bloody nonsense. When the Welsh regions play in South Africa, you see huge stadia with a few thousand people watching. The logistics and costs involved are horrendous.

It was a tragedy that after 171 appearances and 97 tries since 1963-64, the 3-Test British Lion, and 9-Welsh caps wing Maurice Richards turned professional at the season's end. He then played for Great Britain at rugby league, and holds Salford's 'Most Career Appearances' record with 498 games (956 points) as well as being the club's record try scorer. He is one of fewer than twenty Welshmen to have scored more than 200 tries in their rugby league careers, and rates alongside Gerald Davies as the best wing this writer has seen. From the age of 24-30 he played for Salford with distinction – what records would he have managed in Rugby Union?

MAURICE RICHARDS 2 February 1945 –
Cardiff centre then wing - 1962-63 to 1968-69 – 171 games 97 tries
Wales 1968-69 – 9 games 7 tries (inc. 4 in 1 game vs England)
British Lions 1969 - 3 Tests inc. 1974 NZ and Australia tour
Salford RL – 1969-1983 – 498 games, 956 points (most career appearances and most tries for Salford)
Wales RL 1969-75 3 tests
Great Britain RL 1975

Paul Rees, in *The Observer* 17 February 2019 wrote: '*They used to say the wind blew hardest at Cardiff Arms Park when it was trying to catch Maurice Richards. It had no more success than the England team that arrived in the Welsh capital 50 years ago, chasing a share of the Five Nations title but left resembling the rubble where the North Stand had been. Richards ran in four tries in a thrilling 30-9 victory in 1969, equalling a Wales record that still stands. Wales scooped the Triple Crown and the Championship. That afternoon's demolition of England was the start of a golden era for the men in red, but before the end of the year the 24-year-old Cardiff wing, a 1968 Lion who had still to reach his peak, had left Wales and his job at Port Talbot steelworks for rugby league, where he would become Salford's record try scorer and appearance holder in a 14-year career. When the names of the players of that vintage are read out, Richards's is not prominent, yet he was one of the finest wings of any generation, a sinewy, deceptively strong runner with instant acceleration and a sidestep that left many a defender struggling to work out what had gone wrong; a player ahead of his time who, without question, would be as successful in the modern game, born to score tries.*

Mervyn Davies, who won his first cap in 1969, picked Richards in his dream Welsh XV. "*Maurice had everything,*" wrote the former Wales captain in his autobiography. "*Physique, determination, speed and a shattering side-step. I shall never forget the try he scored in the second Test against New Zealand in 1969 (a few days after a stunning hat-trick against Otago) having beaten Fergie McCormick with an inside feint and outside body swerve that left the full-back rolling on his back, he outpaced four covering defenders to reach the corner flag.*" Richards's club colleague, and another household name in Wales, Gerald Davies says: "*I know he left union early, but Maurice has not been given the acknowledgment that one of the greatest wings I have ever seen deserves.*"

Of his exploits that day in April 1969, Richards, who still lives in Manchester, wonders if anyone would be interested. "*I have always believed in looking forward because looking back is a waste of time,*" he says. "*The game is different, professional for a start. When I left, I never thought union would go that way, because loose rucking meant it was too dangerous a game to earn a living in.* "*My sixth game for Cardiff was against the All Blacks. I remember fielding a kick and getting a knee in the back from Waka Nathan as I fell to the ground. **I was raked so hard the marks took seven weeks to disappear. Short-arm tackles were part of the game** and players used any means they could to win. It is much better now and refereed well. I remember the game against England with huge pride. It still gives you a warm feeling. In those days, Cardiff played on the Arms Park. I lived in the Rhondda and the club was on a pedestal there. I never dared to think about playing for them and it was a difficult decision to leave in 1969. Who knows what I would have gone on to achieve had I stayed, but I count myself fortunate to have played six years for Cardiff and been capped by Wales and the Lions followed by 14 happy years at Salford. I have no regrets.*"

When Wales faced England in 1969, their coaching revolution had just started, but teams were not allowed to meet up more than 48 hours before a match, and in effect had one training session to prepare. Wales stayed in the Angel Hotel and names who were to become world-renowned – Barry John, Gareth Edwards, Mervyn Davies, JPR Williams, John Dawes and Dai Morris – made the short walk down Westgate Street to get to the ground that Saturday. "*I always slept well before a game,*" Richards recalls. "*Walking to the ground was part of the experience and running out on to the Arms Park was special. When I was a kid, it seemed the only place where rugby existed. When I was seven my grandfather [Edwin Rees, a professional footballer with Charlton Athletic and Bradford City in the 1920s] and my stepfather took me to see Cardiff play Newport. One of their forwards stooped to pick up the ball and Cliff Morgan darted between his legs to scoop it up. I was hooked. It was all coming together for Wales in 1969. Clive Rowlands was the coach, an inspirational figure who knew what it took to win, we had a terrific set of forwards, halfbacks of a kind you will never find again and flair behind. Added to that was footballing ability, players who knew how to use the ball strategically. Put it all together and things happen, as it did that day against England. I scored the tries, but it was the forwards who won the game. They destroyed England's pack."*

The sides went in 3-3 at half-time. Bob Hiller had given England the lead with a penalty, before Richards scored his first try after his opposite number, Ken Plummer, was caught in possession five metres from his line and Barry John forced a turnover. Wales had been playing into the wind, and with it breezed to victory. John scored their second try, helping himself to a Keith Jarrett pass intended for Richards, and weaving away from four tacklers, before Richards rounded Plummer to finish a passing move and then outmuscled him after JPR Williams was held on the line. Richards's fourth was his best, coming into midfield 35 metres out after a lineout, powering through a tackle and stepping away from another before outpacing two defenders. It was the hapless Plummer's first cap, a replacement for the injured Keith Fielding, who was to join Richards at Salford. Plummer had to wait seven years for his second, but gained 4 caps. *"Ken Plummer was not to blame for what happened,"* says Richards. *"I was introduced to him at a Varsity match some years later; I don't think he was pleased to see me. I am not sure I touched the ball more than four times: it is about being in the right place. Look at some of the tries Wales and England have scored this year from kicks. Some tries are down to flair, others to hard work, perseverance and reading the game."*

Such was Richards's try in the draw in France that had thwarted Wales's grand slam hopes, chasing Gareth Edwards's chip over a scrum into space after the right wing had rushed up. *"I suppose I could have had five (against England) had Barry not intervened,"* says Richards. *"He had a habit of ghosting through tacklers. He did not seem to do anything but the end product was tremendous; what a player."* He had to settle for four, equalling the record for a Wales player against England set in 1899 by another left-wing, Willie Llewellyn, who came from Tonypandy, where Richards went to school. *"I was not aware of the record,"* says Richards. *"It was low-key in those days. We had a dinner after the match and I drove home after it. The next day was a normal Sunday, apart from a photographer wanting to take a picture of me and my wife, Lesley, and the following day I was at work in the steelworks in Port Talbot. The game is at a different level now because people have to sell it.*" It was Richards's sixth cap and he was to win only three more, two against New Zealand and one against Australia, finishing his international career as he had started it in 1964, in an uncapped match against Fiji. "*I was very unhappy with the refereeing on that tour,*" he says. "*It so depressed me that I asked myself if I wanted to experience it again. The answer was no.*"

Richards left Cardiff after scoring 97 tries in 171 matches, garnished by 12 in 13 matches in a Wales jersey and five for the Lions. He played 498 times for Salford and scored 297 tries, was capped by Wales and Great Britain. He once scored four tries against Gloucester, but it is for his feats half a century ago that he will be remembered. (https://www.wru.wales/2020/04/on-this-day-maurice-richards-gives-england-the-run-around/) Maurice spent his Rugby League career with Salford with a record 498 appearances for the 'Red Devils', and holds the Club record for most tries with 297. "*Wales had bigger wings than centres then, with Stuart Watkins on the right,*" says John Spencer, one of England's centres in 1969. "*I remember Maurice running straight at me. I tackled him hard, but was nearly knocked out as he stepped at the last moment. I lay on the ground pretending I was not hurt. He was incredible with the ball in hand. Ken Plummer did not pretend to be the greatest defensive player, but no one would have stopped Maurice that day.*" Nor the wind.'

CHAPTER 42 - CARDIFF SEASON 1969-70

TONY WILLIAMS IS THE FOURTH WILLIAMS BROTHER TO BE A BARBARIAN, A RECORD - TONY WILLIAMS IS SEVENS '*PLAYER OF THE TOURNAMENT*' AGAIN

Elwyn Williams P2; **Tony Williams** P25 T10 Pts30

P43, W32, L8, D3. Points 672-379 Tries 120-45, Pens 55-41

Work was still ongoing on the new National Stadium (- Cardiff RFC retained the rights to 'The Arms Park' name -), which was not fully completed and well over budget, until 1984, an ugly concrete throwback of a design. However, by 1997 it was considered too small, and in 1999 had been demolished, causing further problems for Cardiff's rugby clubs, with the new Millennium Stadium opening, on a North-South alignment instead of the East-West of the grounds of the Arms Park and the National

Stadium. (Yet another strange decision by the W.R.U. – building an over-budget national stadium, considering it too small after 13 years, and demolishing it after 15). The new Millennium rugby ground was renamed in 2016 as the Principality Stadium, but is still referred to as 'The Arms Park' by older generations. It is splendid visually, on the banks of the Taff in central Cardiff, the only national stadium in the centre of a capital city. It has a sliding roof to protect the pitch, but very, very average food and drink facilities with long queues. (In Real Madrid's Bernabeu and Barcelona's Camp Nou, one has multiple choices of excellent refreshments, with multiple suppliers and few queues. It is also wrong that alcohol is served throughout games, spoiling the atmosphere for those who go to watch rugby. Also, visiting teams always seem to want the roof open, and there are freezing winds affecting spectators in some seats. Many former rugby players will not go to games any longer. One wonders if the WRU has ever conducted a market survey of rugby fans who understand the modern game – if they can find any.)

With 5 Welsh caps, the British Lion prop John O'Shea was captain, and he chose wing forward John Hickey, who had risen via the Youth and Athletic, as vice-captain. This author met John Hickey a few times over the years, and he said he never went back to watch a game, or enter the clubhouse when he stopped playing, after 218 First XV appearances between 1963-64 and 1973-74. Hickey, one of this author's favourite players, was to captain Cardiff in the following season, and the Athletic in 1974-75. He was the very definition of a 'hard' flanker, a man anyone would prefer to have in their team than to play against. The two-footed kicker Robin Williams joined from Cardiff Teacher Training College, as did the superb wing John Bevan who made up for the much-regretted leaving of Maurice Richards.

Ferndale's Bevan was fast, a solid 13 stone, who could score from anywhere. However, he was another massive loss to Welsh rugby, heading North in 1973 after just 35 games, and scoring 25 tries. Bevan joined Warrington aged just 23. He had won the Grand Slam with Wales in 1971, and toured Australia and New Zealand with the British Lions. He played in 14 matches including the First Test, scoring 18 tries. The 17 he scored in New Zealand equalled the record of Tony O'Reilly. Bevan is fondly remembered for his role in the Barbarians' victory over New Zealand in 1973, during which he scored a try. In September 1973, Bevan joined Warrington for the then massive signing on fee of £12,000 (around £400,000 today). He made 332 appearances for Warrington, scoring 201 tries playing centre or wing, and played for Wales and Great Britain. Known as 'The Ox', for being unstoppable, he retired after 13 seasons. Like Maurice Richards, he was a one-off. Newport's excellent Welsh international wing Stuart Watkins also joined Cardiff, and played 34 games in two years before retiring from first-class rugby. Despite these men

546

coming in, Gerald Davies had returned to Cambridge. Barry John and Gareth Edwards both suffered injuries and were unable to play as a pair until the win against Harlequins on 30 April 1970. **In the first 24 games, 4 scrum halves and 7 outside halves were tried in various permutations**. Thus the season had a problematic start. By 1 November 1969, Cardiff had lost 4 games, to Bridgend 6-0 (H), Coventry 13-5 (A), Northampton 9-0 (H) and Oxford University 13-9 (A, 2 tries each).

South Africa were touring, and more than 100 people had been hurt in '*the Battle of Swansea*' in November 1969, protesting about Apartheid, when Swansea lost 12-0. A month later, on 13 December in Cardiff, a strong police presence ensured that protests were fairly minimal. However, the Swansea incidents were reported across South Africa, and Nelson Mandela's guards became more brutal towards prisoners, as it dawned upon the South African public that the world at large hated Apartheid. The summer cricket tour by South Africa to the UK was cancelled as a result, and overseas tours by all its teams virtually curtailed. The greatest disappointment in years was Cardiff's 17-3 loss to the Springboks, probably the worst performance I have witnessed between Cardiff and a touring team (I do not include Cardiff Blues, the recent regional side, in this volume). Club chairman Brian Mark wrote in his 1969-70 Annual Report: '*On that day the Cardiff team fell well below expectations and was soundly defeated by a superior side. It was a pathetic performance against a touring team and it was not so much the defeat but rather the manner of it that made it difficult to bear.*' Danny Davies wrote that he heartily concurred – it was such an unusual occurrence, calling it a '*stigma*' on Cardiff's history. The game was played at the new National Stadium, with the new North Stand still incomplete, in front of a 28,000 capacity crowd.

The Barbarians beat Cardiff 30-28 in a terrific game on 28 March 1970, fielding 15 internationals, and England's Tony Jorden kicked 18 points. Penarth had lost 42-6, and after the narrow Cardiff defeat, two days later Swansea also lost 24-8 and then Newport lost 24-6. The Barbarians always played their first team against Cardiff, all internationals: 9 Englishmen, 4 Irishmen, a Scot and a truly outstanding Welsh player, including 8 British Lions: Anthony Mervyn Jorden E, full-back (educated at Monmouth): Keith Fielding E, John Spencer E and Lions, Chris Wardlow E, Mike Bulpitt E, Phil Bennett W and Lions, Roger Young I and Lions, Ian McClauchlan Sc and Lions, John Pullin E and Lions, Phil O'Callaghan I, Peter Larter E and Lions, Mick Molloy I, Fergus Slattery I and Lions, Tony Bucknall E, Peter Dixon E and Lions. It should be remembered that it was then more difficult to selected for the Barbarians, than to play for one's country. The Barbarians play in black and white hoops, but players wear their club socks. Membership is by invitation, and in Tony Williams' era, players were all from the British Isles, but as of 2011, players from 31 countries have played for the Baa-Baas. Traditionally, at least one uncapped player is selected for each match, who nearly always goes on to play for his country. The Baa-Baas began their annual fixtures in Wales in 1891 against Cardiff, and an Easter Tour soon developed of Penarth on Good Friday, Cardiff (Holy Saturday), Swansea (Easter Monday) and Newport (Tuesday). The Penarth fixture was discontinued in 1986, and unfortunately those with Swansea, Newport and Cardiff in 1996. In 1995 Cardiff had won 75-33, and in the final 1996 game 49-43. Professionalism has ruined such high-scoring, entertaining games, where both players and spectators are seen to enjoy themselves.

On 30 March, the Baa-Baas beat Swansea 24-8, and in that morning's *Western Mail* there was an article by J.B.G. Thomas, with pictures of Bleddyn, Lloyd, Cenydd and Tony, headlined:

Baa-Baa brothers – Williams family may hold record

'By inviting Tony Williams, youngest of the famous Williams brothers of Taff's Well, to play for them against Swansea today the Barbarians have honoured four of the family. Bleddyn, Lloyd and Cenydd were previously made Barbarians, and rugby statisticians "Jock" Wemyss and Danny Davies were checking records yesterday to see if any family had a larger representation in the Baa-Baas' history. Wemyss said "As far as we can ascertain there have been three lots of brothers, the Biggs, of Cardiff, the Gibsons. of Northern, and the McGregors, of Pontypridd. The four Williams brothers must be a record!"

Tony Williams has been a popular player and a loyal servant of the game, and the honour is a fitting reward. The Barbarians include 10 internationals against Swansea. Team: B.J. O'Driscoll: K.J. Fielding, A.D. Williams, C.S. Wardlow, M.P. Bulpitt; P. Bennett, R. Young (capt.); C.B. Stevens, R.F.S. Harris, P.J. O'Callaghan, M.G. Molloy, T.A. Moore, W. Lauder, P.J. Dixon, J.F. Slattery. The Barbarians are keen to win all four matches on this tour, a feat last achieved in 1949 when they won 14-11 (at Penarth), 6-5 (Cardiff), 10-3 (Swansea) and 6-5 (Newport). The previous occasion of four victories was 1935. This is a high-scoring tour, with the Barbarians having totalled 72 points in two matches. But Swansea have a habit of rising to the occasion as they did in 1957 after the 40-0 defeat of Cardiff!' (There were actually 4 Biggs brothers, Cardiff players, selected for the Barbarians).

Cardiff achieved doubles over Swansea, Pontypool, Bristol and London Welsh. There were also three wins and a draw with Newport: 8-0, 9-0, 14-3, but a home draw 3-3 prevented a whitewash. Resilient prop Howard Norris played his 400th game for Firsts. Gareth Edwards captained Wales against South Africa, and in the last minute of the game, scored a dramatic try to enable Wales to draw 6-6. Darren Devine, in *The Western Mail*, walesonline 17 October 2015 reported: *'A decade of dominance would follow when Wales would collect three Grand Slams and five Triple Crowns... in its own way, Wales' draw with South Africa at the start of the*

'70s golden age was just as significant as the European rugby accolades that would follow. It was Wales' seventh meeting with the Springboks and they had never managed anything better than restricting South Africa's margin of victory to three points. Sixty-four years later Gareth Edwards, Wales' youngest captain at just 22, led a depleted side out at the Arms Park in a match many critics had suggested should not be played, because of the country's brutal oppression of its black population through Apartheid. Among the Welsh ranks was fly-half Phil Bennett, who got his first full Welsh cap in the contest. He had made rugby history a year earlier when he became the first substitute to appear in a Welsh international.

Bennett, 26, from Felinfoel, in Carmarthenshire, played on the wing - a position he had not occupied since his early secondary school days and one he would never again find himself in for Wales. In those days, wingers threw the ball into the line-out and Bennett had scant preparation for the role he was unaccustomed to. He said: "After a few sessions of practice they [teammates] said ... 'Phil, throw it in on the day and let's hope for the best.' Wales started quickly, playing towards the West Stand in the first half, which remained scoreless. As had become the norm for Wales-South Africa fixtures at the Arms Park during the era, conditions were muddy and all but ended any hopes of witnessing an expansive, expressive game both sides were capable of.

In the build-up the then 21-year-old Bennett remembers the advice offered by a team-mate to cope with the prospect of facing the bruising Boks. "I can remember one of the Welsh forwards saying to me, 'Phil, don't worry - when they [Welsh fans] sing the anthem, think of your family, your wife, your children, your mother and believe it or not you'll open your eyes and look at the opposition and they won't look so big - they'll shrink a little bit'. "The anthem was magnificent, and I felt so proud. I opened my eyes and had a look at the South African lot and they weren't getting any smaller." The match came to life in the second half, with a score against the run of play in the far corner of the West Stand by South Africa's Syd Nomis. Conditions made a game of running rugby virtually impossible and H.O. De Villiers and Edwards traded penalties. Deep into injury time, with Wales trailing by three points to South Africa's unconverted try and an earlier penalty, Edwards splattered down in the far corner at the East Terrace levelling the match at 6-6. The match nearly became Wales' first victory over South Africa, when Edwards stepped up with confidence for the conversion after his try.

But the heavy leather ball, saturated from the dampness of the field of play, fell six feet short of the posts and slightly wide. For the young Bennett, there was no sense of apprehension before kick-off, in facing a formidable opponent Wales had never overcome. But at the end there was pride in achieving something that had proved beyond his Welsh rugby

549

forebears. He added: "At the end of the day if you come off the field against South Africa and you've drawn 6-6 we said, 'Well, we haven't done too badly'. "That was the kind of feeling I had. Honours even, shake hands and we've done Wales okay." Three years later, Bennett was part of a British Lions set-up that triumphed over the Springboks. But it would be almost another three decades before the first Wales victory came over South Africa in 1999 - in part because Apartheid meant the sides didn't meet for 24 years after the draw in 1970.'

Wings P. Lyn Jones and Alec Finlayson with 13 were top try scorers, followed by flanker Mervyn John 12, and Stuart Watkins and Tony Williams with 10. Vice-captain John Hickey played in 35 of 43 matches, P. Lyn Jones 33, Mervyn John and Alec Finlayson 32, Lyn Baxter 30, Ian Robinson 29, and John O'Shea, Howard Norris and Tony Williams each played 25 times. Billy Hullin and John O'Shea both captained a Barbarian XV. John Davies was reappointed captain of the Rags, having made 49 appearances for the Firsts from 1964-65 to 1968-69, and their record was P32 W26 L6 Points 656-243 Tries 132-37, while having to call upon no fewer than 73 players, often including Youth players. The leading try scorers were Gabe Servini with 13, Terry Stephenson 12 and Brian Coles eleven, fly-half Servini getting his cap along with Paul Barry, John H. James, Lindsay Lewis and Wyn Llewellyn. The Youth had its best season since 1963-64: P31 W21 L8 D2 Points 513-186. A squad system had been set up, and organised coaching was centred at Whitchurch Secondary School. This year, Danny Davies noted the link between Cardiff and Taff's Well: *'Obituary. John Llewellyn passed away. John Llewellyn, a most likeable young man served Cardiff in the period 1950-57. John (his full initials J. E. G.) will be remembered as Cardiff's gallant full-back in its glorious win over New Zealand in 1953-54. After his retirement John worked hard - and with success - to enable Taff's Well Rugby Club acquire its own ground and clubhouse and enhance its reputation.'*

In May Cardiff again won the Welsh National Sevens, *'Tony Williams once again earning the accolade of "Player of the Sevens Tournament", his display was an example of his Sevens craft and skill for the youngsters'.* In the Five Nations, Wales beat Scotland in Cardiff, after being 9-5 down half-time, scoring 4 tries to 1, 18-9. Tries were still worth 3 points, so the modern score would be 26-11. John and Edwards were playing superbly in this and following seasons for Wales. Wales were down 13-3 half-time at Twickenham, but destroyed England in the second half, winning 17-13, scoring 4 tries to 2. The Irish game in Dublin was cancelled because of IRA threats to the Welsh team, ruining Welsh chances of a probable Grand Slam, as France were then beaten 11-6 in Cardiff, with J.P.R. Williams the Welsh kicker, although Phil Bennett was fly half – Barry John was injured. Ireland were smashed 23-9 (4 tries to 0) the following year, as Wales easily took the Grand Slam (13 tries to 3).

WELSH NATIONAL STADIUM AND CARDIFF'S NEW ARMS PARK OPENED – WALES GRAND SLAM - THE OTHER CARDIFF RUGBY TEAM: THE STORY OF THE RAGS

Elwyn Williams P1; **Tony Williams** P36 T3 Pts9

P44, W29, 10. D5. Points 699-429. Tries 120-62, Pens 49-45

After a year as vice-captain, captain was John Hickey who had joined in 1963-64, after playing for Llandaff Youth and the Cardiff & District Union Club, Canton. About 6 ft. 2 ins, and over 14 stone, he led from wing forward by example, having already played 170 times for the Firsts, and fully deserving of a Welsh cap. He nominated Gareth Edwards as vice-captain. The season featured the official openings of the Welsh Rugby Union's National Stadium and Cardiff's new club ground alongside. On 10 September Cardiff Athletic played its first home match with Bristol United, the first time the new club ground was used. It was formerly the pitch of Glamorgan County Cricket, adjacent to the new National Stadium. However, the new Arms Park was not 'officially' opened until October 1970, when the First XV played the W.R.U. President's XV, including seven British Lions. Cardiff beat the W.R.U. President's XV 17-8. The President's XV had internationals Tom Kiernan of Ireland, W. Lauder of Scotland, and Ray 'Chico' Hopkins, Ian Hall and Billy Raybould of Wales. Soon to be capped were four outstanding Welsh players, J.J. Williams (then Bridgend), Alan Martin (Aberavon), Terry Cobner (Pontypool) and Tommy David (then Pontypridd).

Before the game, 18 former Cardiff captains paraded across the pitch. I have placed in bold type the players from Taff's Well and the Williams' cousin Tamplin. The great men were the fly-half and club statistician Danny Davies (1925-26); **Tom Lewis** (with Taff's Well connections 1932-33); Tommy Stone (1935-36); Les Spence (1936-37); Wilf Wooller (1938-39, 1939-40); Dr. Jack Matthews (1945-46, 1946-47, 1951-52); **Bill Tamplin** (the Williams' cousin 1950-51); Rex Willis (1952-53); **Bleddyn Williams** (1949-50, 1953-54); Malcom Collins (1955-56); Peter Goodfellow (1956-57); Eddie Thomas (1957-58); **Lloyd Williams** (1960-61, 1961-62); David Hayward (1962-63, 1964-65); Meirion Roberts (1964-65); Keith Rowlands (1965-66, 1966-67); Howard Norris (1967-68, 1968-69); and John O'Shea (1969-1970). Other captains featured in the 1930-1975 period of this book have been: Bernard Turnbull (1930-31); G. Jones / R. Gabe Jones (1933-34); Archie Skym (1934-35); A.H. Jones (1937-38); Haydn Tanner (1947-48, 1948-49); Sid Judd (1954-55); C.D. Williams (1958-59); Gordon Wells (1959-60); John Hickey (1970-71); J.H. Jones

(1971-72); Gerald Wallace (1972-73); Garry Davies (1973-74) and Mervyn John (1974-75).

A.D. 'Tony' Williams was captain of the Athletic in 1972 and 1973, and usually the Cardiff 'Sevens' captain. First team vice-captains relevant to this book were Taff's Well's **Harry Rees** (1937-38); **Ray Bale** (1945-46); **Bleddyn Williams** (1947-48, 1948-49, both times with Tanner as captain, and 1950-51 under his cousin Bill Tamplin); **Lloyd Williams** (1958-59) and **Tony Williams** (1968-69). Between 1949 and 1974, one of the Williams brothers or cousin **Bill Tamplin** was captain or vice-captain of the Firsts or captain of the Rags, in 11 successive seasons. All these players were Welsh, with a majority from Cardiff and surrounding areas – this always inspired a local crowd. In today's professional game, whether Rugby Union, Rugby League or Football (then known as 'Soccer' in Wales – 'football' meant rugby), a high proportion of players in a team comes from anywhere under the sun. Amateur rugby meant local players playing for love, with men they grew up with – and playing for nothing, especially in the case of Cardiff.

Cardiff lost 6 and drew 3 matches by the end of November, often fielding weakened teams, but also because of a disastrous tour to France, sending a half-strength team to represent Cardiff. Danny Davies writes: '*I am sure that, with the knowledge of our strong fixture lists in mind and calls on the players, our committee will in future investigate the strength of the opposition before sending teams to France to play representative, provincial and other very strong French combinations and so avoid damage to our reputation*'. For the 41-6 trouncing against Auvergne, the worst defeat in Cardiff's history, among the players missing were Barry John, Gary Samuel, Gareth Edwards, Alec Finlayson, Lyn Baxter and Gerald Wallace. After 1 December however, only 3 more matches were lost... '*One of the best performances was the win by 14 points to 12 at home against Coventry with a weakened team, our three-quarter line and about half the pack having been injured. Barry John's boot won Cardiff's home game with Llanelli, his 4 drop goals in the match (the club record) for 12 points stopping Llanelli's 9*'. Barry's brother Clive was Llanelli captain on the day.

After an 8-year break in games, Cardiff played Bath at home upon 28 December 1970, winning 26-11. The Bath report reads: '*John Bevan scored for Cardiff after three minutes, but Walkey levelled with a finely angle penalty. Bath rallied strongly after the disastrous 20 minutes that followed. In the opening stages, they seemed more preoccupied with coming to terms with the bone-hard conditions, and quality of the opposition. In consequence, Cardiff established a 17-3 lead, and in some respects – the game was up! But Bath rallied bravely, even after losing Phillips with concussion, just before half-time. Polledri also withdrew briefly after a succession of knocks. Phil Hall stood back deep, operating*

552

in a combination of a temporary fly-half – and extra full back. By now, skipper Heindorff was handicapped by a back injury. Remarkably, with Walkey, Hannell and Carter in the forwards and Lye at scrumhalf, Bath began to rally. Waterman and Beese tackled valiantly and for the first time Cardiff were in check.

There was one lovely break out when Polledri got away on the right: "He found a rather surprising partner in hooker Alan Parfitt, who took time off from his duties in the tight to handle and run like a threequarter and in the process, sell possibly the best dummy of the afternoon." This was Bath's first try and after a counter-try for Lane of Cardiff, Parfitt was again in the action: "Parfitt intercepting a pass on halfway again sent Polledri storming away on the right, and after Jenkins had handled, was up to score his second try, which Walkey converted." Cardiff had the last word, when Edwards dropped a remarkable goal, but at least Bath had salvaged something of their reputation.' (Cardiff had won the 12 previous games, and 5 of the 6 before those, only losing 8-5 away with a weakened team in January 1947, as Bleddyn Williams, Jack Matthews, Billy Cleaver, Les Williams, Haydn Tanner and Gwyn Evans were playing against England.)

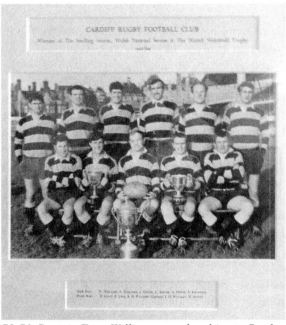

1970-71 Captain Tony Williams was the ultimate 7s player, Elwyn is second from left, standing

Against Cambridge University, former and future Cardiff player Gerald Davies scored 5 tries in their 22-6 win against a scratch Cardiff team.

However, against Newport in February Barry John and Edwards were at last back in tandem, scoring 14 points in Cardiff's 17-9 home win. Cardiff had drawn 6-6 (H) and lost 6-3 (A) but won the last game 13-8 (A) against a very good Newport side. Top try scorers were: P. Lyn Jones 15, Neil Williams and Roger Lane 13, and John Bevan 10, Bevan playing in just 11 matches. Back row Roger Lane equalled the record of Mervyn John's 13 tries for forwards. Barry John scored 114 points, including 9 dropped goals. New caps were awarded to Neil Collins, Meirion Davies, Gareth Edwards, Mike Knill, Roger Lane, Gary Samuel and Gerald Wallace. Ian Robinson made 43 appearances in 44 games, and captain John Hickey 36, despite missing the last 5 games through injury. The Athletic XV was captained for the third successive season by John Davies and their record was P31, W22, L6, D3, Points 541-254, Tries 118-33, Pens 23-36! Captain John Davies was hurt against Bridgend Sports on 6 February and out for the rest of the season, so announced his retirement and prop Howard Norris took over until the end of the season. Owing to injury in the First team's opening match with South Wales Police, Howard had to wait until 1971-72 to beat Alun Priday's match record, with 413 appearances to Alun's 410. Leading try scorers were Neil Collins 11, Nick Williams 10, Stuart Watkins 8, P. Lyn Jones 7 and J. H. James, D. Ken Jones, Ian Lewis and John Regan each 5.

Elwyn Williams, who had already played in more than 300 matches with the 1st XV, took part in 21 matches for the Athletic XV. His path to the Firsts was blocked by the excellent wing-forwards Mervyn John and Roger Lane, but Elwyn was a one-club man – plus Taff's Well of course. In the Rags' final match of the season with Barry, Robert Windsor played, plus another 4 matches for the Athletic and 4 for the Firsts. Unfortunately for Cardiff, hooker 'Bobby' Windsor, the 'Duke' left for Pontypool, Wales and British Lions honours. Six Youth players helped out the Rags, and Athletic XV caps were won by Peter Davies, David Hoyle, Ian Lewis, John Regan and Stuart Watkins. Cardiff Juniors (Youth) XV had another superb season: P26, W23, L3. Points 624-86. Four gained international caps - Steve McCann, Roger Harris, Martin Pengilley and David Morris.

Wales won the Triple Crown and **Grand Slam**, and three of Cardiff's players who participated were John Bevan, Barry John and Gareth Edwards. These, together with the justly renowned Gerald Davies* (now London Welsh) also toured with the British Lions to New Zealand and Australia. Wales defeated England in Cardiff 22-6, 3 tries to 1 (- try by John Bevan and 2 by Gerald Davies, 2 drop goals by Barry John, 2 conversions by John Taylor, penalty JPR Williams). Scotland were beaten away 19-18, 4 tries to 2 (- tries by Gareth Edwards, Barry John, Gerald Davies, John Taylor, 1 conversion each by John and Taylor, penalty John). Ireland were beaten at home 23-9, 4 tries to 0 (2 tries each by Gareth Edwards and Gerald Davies, conversion John, 2 penalties John). France

554

were beaten away 9-5, 2 tries to 1 (tries by Edwards and John, penalty John). All in all, 13 tries to 4 was indicative of Welsh rugby at this time, with Edwards and John playing superbly. Wales scored 73 points against 38, with tries still 3 points. If tries were 5 points as today, Wales would have scored 101 points, averaging 25 points a game. If we include Gerald Davies as a Cardiff player, Cardiff players scored 12 of the 13 tries. Barry John shared kicking with J.P.R Williams and John Taylor, and kicked 2 drop goals, 2 conversions and 3 penalties, so Cardiff players (including Gerald) scored 55 of Wales 73 points.

*I always regarded Gerald as a Cardiff player, as he played for Cardiff for five seasons; then London Welsh with the odd game for Cardiff, for four seasons; and ended his career with four seasons back at Cardiff. He played 167 times for Cardiff, scoring 73 tries, 12 conversions and 9 penalties for 322 points. A British Lion and Barbarian, he changed from centre to wing on a Lions tour, and I never saw him forced into touch. Thomas Gerald Reames Davies - ('Reames'? There's posh for you -) was Cardiff captain in his last three seasons, from 1975-76 to 1977-78, an achievement only equalled by the great Gwyn Nicholls from 1898-99 to 1900-01. An estimated 15,000 saw Cardiff at Pontypool on 14 January 1978. On a muddy pitch, Cardiff captain Gerald seemed to skate across the surface, on the few occasions when the ball reached him. Pontypool had the best pack in Wales, with four British Lions, and were 'all over' Cardiff, who were stuck in their own half for most of the game. Cardiff captain Gerald touched down in the first half, having only had two passes, and at halftime told his team to move the ball whenever possible, keeping the play away from Pooler's feared forwards. In atrocious conditions, he managed to touch the ball three times in the second half. Three tries. It was a totally unfair result for the home team, as Gerald was a genius on the day. Five touches, four tries. Pontypool scored 11 points to Gerald's 16. They don't make them like that anymore. Sorry, Pontypool, if Gerald had been on your side it would have been a massacre.

On the 1971 British Lions tour of New Zealand, Wales supplied 8 of 15 backs and 6 of 19 forwards. Coached by Carwyn James and captained by John Dawes, it was a gruelling schedule, with some very serious foul play by Canterbury a week before the First Test. 'The tour had started inauspiciously, with a loss to Queensland on 12 May and a tight win over New South Wales before the New Zealand tour began. There were then 10 games before '*The Battle of Canterbury*', intended to soften up the Lions. Wisely, Carwyn James, the outstanding Lions coach and former Llanelli and Wales outside-half, rested Barry John, with the First Test a week later. The Lions had swept all before them in New Zealand including demolishing Wellington 47-9, who were one of the great powerhouses in New Zealand rugby. Against Canterbury, the Lions soon lost their first-choice props. The Scot loose-head Sandy Carmichael was a devastating force in the Lions' front-row, so in an early scrum his opposing prop Alister Hopkinson landed uppercut after uppercut flush on the prop's face. Carmichael left the field with both his eyes closed and his face broken, his tour over. He said *"By the time I came off the pitch, both eyes were pretty well shut. Ian McLauchlan came towards me to see how I was, just as I went to blow my nose, but it was blocked and because the sinus was cracked the air blew into my eye socket which inflated like a balloon."* Irish tighthead and pack leader Ray McLoughlin took offence at the violence, but broke his thumb punching Canterbury hardman No.8 Alex Wyllie and was also out of the tour. Those two were soon joined on the Lions injury list by the great flanker Fergus Slattery, who was blindsided in a line-out by Hopkinson and had his front teeth cracked down to the root.

Slattery remembered, *"I didn't have a clue where I was. I went to Peter Dixon - the England back-row, at the next lineout and asked 'Where are we?' He looked at me all agitated and said, "We're in bloody Canterbury!" About ten minutes later I asked him again - but he'd just been smacked and had no idea. I only realised where I was in the final quarter of the game."* John Taylor watched the game, commenting *"Canterbury treated the game as a war, the invader to be repulsed at all costs. The game was a disgrace to rugby."* The violence carried on all through the game, and at one point the Lions even considered walking off the pitch. Willie John McBride, who captained the Lions in South Africa four years later, knew what was coming because he had been on the wrong end of a ferocious beating by Canterbury in the 1966 tour. *"I said to the guys, look, there are two ways this is going to go now. We either go back to the dressing room and forget about this or we stand and fight. And I'm going to stand here and fight."* Welsh lock Delme Thomas said *"That was, without doubt, the dirtiest game I ever played in."* Gareth Edwards was targeted and was punched in open play, recalling *"Before he tried to take my head off, Grizz* (Alex Wyllie) *warned me. I'd beaten him off the base of a scrum and he said, "Hey scrummy, you do that again and I'll break your neck. I've been quoted as saying I've only been scared twice playing rugby. Once was playing for Cardiff against Neath and the second was that Canterbury match."* And according to Scottish lock, the late Gordon Brown, *"The Canterbury forwards seemed prepared to stoop to the lowest level of gutter thuggery. With Hopkinson, Wyllie and Penrose in the driving seat, they kicked, punched and elbowed anyone in a red jersey who came near the ball. It was a wonder that nobody was killed."*

The Lions won 9-3 on 26 June with tries by Arthur Lewis and John Bevan. There followed another 3 wins before the fired-up All Blacks won easily on 10 July. Another 4 wins followed before New Zealand were beaten 13-3 on 31 July. After 3 more wins, on 14 August a 14-14 draw saw the Lions win the series 2-1. It is easily the most exciting Test series that this writer's generation recalls. The John O'Shea sending off on a previous tour, and the Canterbury game on this tour, inspired the next Lions team, to tour South Africa in 1974, to look out for each other instead of passivity in the face of illegal attacks. As *The Guardian* later reported: '*In the early matches, against provincial and select XVs, the Lions endured an intense examination of their physical and mental fortitude. For several decades, touring teams had suffered similarly. This time, the Lions would fight back, and the battle cry "99" would be written into rugby folklore. It was the simplest of strategies: "getting your retaliation in first", as the skipper put it. When a Lion was in trouble, his team-mates would hear the abbreviated call of "999", the phone number for emergency calls back home. The results were not pretty. And they worked.*'

The 1971 tour remains the only occasion where the Lions have returned victorious from New Zealand. All four Cardiff players started the first Test, and all except Bevan played in the other three Tests. Despite only playing in the first Test, John Bevan became the Lions' record try scorer (including matches against club teams) with 17. Barry John was given the title '*King Barry*' by the New Zealand press after scoring 30 of the Lions' 48 points, and in him and Edwards, Cardiff had the best two half-backs in the world.

THE OTHER CARDIFF RUGBY TEAM: THE STORY OF THE RAGS
Steve Coombs, 27th Apr 2021, CF10 Arms Park Rugby Trust website

This marvellous article begins with two quotes by Gareth Edwards, and contains photos from the Cardiff Rugby Museum website, which are not included here. Gareth tells us "*I started in the famous Rags, the second team, in a game at Briton Ferry. Next there was a visit to the Memorial Ground to play Bristol United and finally, I shall never forget the day I achieved my ambition, to wear the Cambridge blue and black of Cardiff's first team.*" The Cardiff international outside half and centre Mark Ring then commented, "*I used to love playing for the Rags because here was a mixture of youth players and experienced old heads... It meant that whenever we went up the valleys to play a club that wanted our blood just because we were Cardiff, we always had a few tough nuts on our side who we could rely on to look after us if things got nasty. That gave us the confidence to go out and play. The idea was to take that confidence with you into the first team...*"

Steve Coombs' article follows: 'Sometimes nicknames just stick. When on March 1st 2021, Cardiff Rugby Chief Executive Richard Holland referred to Cardiff's Welsh Premiership team as the Rags, he was invoking a name which has stuck to Cardiff Rugby's other team for 80 years. We have Syd Cravos to thank for this. Truly great clubs need their fair share of men like Syd. He was the son of Steve Cravos, who had played for Cardiff between 1886 and 1896 and shared the same style of fine moustache which makes his father stand out in team photos of the era. His brothers Frank and Victor also played for Cardiff. Originating in Trieste on the Adriatic, they were a family of characters. They were said to keep a liqueur from every nation in the world stored in the Butetown offices of their shipping firm, for the purposes of entertaining visiting ship's captains. It was a family of men who loved good company, a good joke and Cardiff Rugby. Like his father, Syd played for the club over a hundred times. Eventually he would become chairman. When he passed away, his family had been associated with Cardiff Rugby for nearly a century. But more than anything, he was a man who represented and captained The Rags. Fitting then, that it was Syd who was credited with coining their enduring nickname.

The name Rags comes from the battered, used jerseys they were given to play in. It is easy to imagine Syd, the clubhouse wit, holding court in the Pavilion that once stood at the river end, joking about the state of the kit he'd been given to play in. But of course, the story of the other Cardiff team (it seems disrespectful to call The Rags a "second" team...) begins much earlier than the 1930s. The first accounts we have of Cardiff's other team are from the second ever season of the club's existence. With Cardiff Rugby itself the product of a merger between two clubs (Glamorgan FC and Cardiff Wanderers, both of whom also ran Second XVs) it's little wonder that there were sufficient players for more than one XV. The other team was officially formed in 1879 as Cardiff Seconds. In his early history of the club, CS Arthur states that by the 1882/83 season the seconds had become thought of as a nursery for the first team. By 1884/85 the team had really started becoming a serious club side in its own right. Under the captaincy of a Mr Cholton James **they didn't lose a game all season and on 1st April 1885 – to their delight – they beat the Cardiff first team**.

This set the trend. Cardiff's other team wasn't simply a way for scratch teams of leftover players to get a game. It was a testing ground for promising players, an essential steppingstone before joining the Cardiff first team (what these days is called "development") and also a respected team in its own right. They were **unbeaten once again the following season**, under the captaincy of Dan Jones, who remained captain for six seasons. This was the era of Frank Hancock and the evolution of the Cardiff *"passing game"*. Just as the Cardiff first team reigned supreme, the other team's results were exceptional. Like the firsts they rarely lost and their points scoring records were consistently remarkable. In 1885/86 they swept all before them scoring 17 goals, 43 tries and only conceding 3 tries all season. It was said that Dan Jones could easily have become a prominent first team player, but he preferred to lead the other team which by 1898 had officially adopted the name Cardiff Reserves. Big names of this golden period like Gwyn Nichols and Percy Bush all made their debuts for the Reserves.

Players could become stars whilst playing for Cardiff Reserves. In 1911, the top try scorer was Charley Bryant, who became an Ireland international even whilst remaining a Cardiff Reserves mainstay. After World War 1 there was a period of rebuilding. Then as the 1920s began, cash was tight as plans to purchase Cardiff Arms Park from the Marquis of Bute were put in place. In 1922, the Easter tour which the Reserves had long enjoyed couldn't go ahead. In 1925, Cardiff adopted a controversial – and certainly very unusual - "two first XVs" policy. There would be no Reserve team. Instead, both Cardiff teams would be branded as a first team. Naturally the smaller clubs used to only being given fixtures against the reserves enjoyed the privilege of nominally having a Cardiff first team on their fixture list. It was argued that the volume of quality players available to Cardiff made such a strange undertaking practical. But the concept only lasted five seasons of inconsistent results which harmed the club's reputation.

It was in 1931/32 that the official name of Cardiff Athletic started to be used in place of Cardiff Reserves. But thanks to Syd Cravos's inspiration, to everyone they were the Rags. Soon after, fittingly, the great doyen of Cardiff Athletic Club Hubert Johnson took over as captain. By 1937/38 the Rags were once again invincible. The following season, Bleddyn Williams made his debut for them at the age of 16. After the Second World War, there was once again a period of rebuilding, but the importance of The Rags was quickly re-established. Also established was the tradition of older first team players stepping into The Rags to help along the younger, up and coming players. Stan Bowes captained The Rags for several seasons as he aged. His form was such that the old warhorse was eventually called up back to the first team. Dr Jack Matthews then came out of retirement to captain the Rags for several games.

By the time they celebrated their own centenary year in 1979/80, The Rags were not only treasured as a Cardiff institution, but well known by players from other areas as a valuable route into elite rugby. Gerald Davies cited the existence of the Rags as a major reason why he felt he was better off trying to advance his career at Cardiff than at any other club. "*With Cardiff, blessed as they are with a second string XV, the Rags, you could always be sure that if you did not get into the first XV a watchful eye could be kept on you and this would allow for continuity and progression.*" In Mark Ring's autobiography "*Ringmaster*" the value of the team in the 1980s is explained in detail: "*The Rags was the perfect place to start a rugby career.... You had older seasoned stalwarts on their way down from the top of the game mixed with youngsters trying to make their way up. Older heads like Ian Robinson... and captain Terry Charles were the kind of people who had a huge influence on me.*" By that time, selection for The Rags came via a series of intense trial matches at Sophia Gardens. Ring himself played his way into the Rags side in one of these games. Alongside him was an unknown dreadlocked winger from Butetown who notched up a hat-trick – Gerald Cordle. Cordle was an example of a player who had not been spotted at Youth team level, but could still find a way into elite rugby via The Rags.

Rugby of course changed quickly as the 1990s progressed. The 1995/96 Season Report noted, *"Early in the season a longstanding tradition came to an end with the abolition of the "Rags".* It had been decided that the club needed to focus its resources on a smaller, elite first team squad. But you can't keep a good team down. Six years later, in the early 2000s, it was realised that clubs needed a system for nurturing young talent (relearning a lesson first understood in the late 19th century...) and a Cardiff Under 21 team was formed. Naturally, this team became known unofficially as The Rags. When in 2003 the Cardiff first team was rebranded as Cardiff Blues, the Cardiff Under 21 team formed the basis of the team branded Cardiff RFC which was to play in the Welsh Premiership. Once again, the Cardiff club was running two teams both branded as a first team. And once again the situation never quite pleased anybody. Inevitably, even though it was never an "official" nickname, many always referred to the Premiership team as The Rags.

Fittingly, given the unique history of the Rags, the Cardiff Premiership team has been supported and managed by a group of committed Cardiff Rugby lovers, giving up their time on a volunteer basis. No one more than they deserved to enjoy the Welsh Premiership title in 2009 and the cup win in 2019. The Rags were on course for a potential league and cup double in the 2019/20 season. Then the pandemic happened. It isn't confirmed when rugby at Welsh Premiership level will begin again. But it is clear that a period of rebuilding, much like the periods after the two world wars, will be necessary. It is also clear that with the team becoming integrated with the professional arm of the Cardiff Rugby organisation, the Rags will yet again be reinventing themselves. Cardiff Rugby academy manager Gruff Rees, himself a former Rags player, has spoken about how much he is looking forward to these changes. It seems likely that we will again see a team of hugely promising young players taking the field supported by a few old heads. A nursery for the first team, but also a respected team in their own right. Same as it ever was. Syd Cravos would approve.'

The Start of the High Try 60s and 70s

Cardiff	Tries	Tot.Pts	vs	Tries	Tot.Pts
1959-60	91	428	vs	40	285
1960-61	114	498	vs	43	240
1961-62	81	390	vs	29	197
1962-63	100	467	vs	39	227
1963-64	119	568	vs	40	254
1964-65	144	644	vs	54	329

1965-66	128	583	vs	32	198
1966-67	158	775	vs	62	393
1967-68	137	703	vs	45	314
1968-69	120	648	vs	54	317
1969-70	120	672	vs	62	379
1970-71	133	699	vs	72	429
1971-72	175	1058	vs	66	516
1972-73	158	963	vs	67	499
1973-74	190	1086	vs	61	511
1974-75	134	870	vs	58	561
Total		2102			814

From 1971-72 the value of a try was raised from 3 to 4 points, and from the above, we can see that Cardiff were scoring far more tries in this period. However, we must mention the incredible strength of Cardiff Athletic, the 'Rags', at this time. In the same years, their try count was an amazing: 210-33; 91-19; 114-43; 77-32; 101-27; 155-28; 98-24; **221-28**; 173-23; 151-27; 132-37; 118-33; 157-45; 213-49; 209-34; **220-25**. **While the First XV scored 2.6 times as many tries as their opponents, the 'Rags' managed a multiple of 4.8** (- 2,440 tries to 507).

In four of these seasons, the Athletic only lost 8 games out of 137, with 4 draws in 1966-67, 1967-68, 1968-69, and 1974-75, soring 670 tries against 98, an incredible ratio of 6.8:1. There was one loss in 1967-68, 5-3 to Taibach, owing to Cardiff scrumhalf Gary Samuel being carried off early in the match. However, in the Silver Ball Final, Taibach were despatched 27-3. The Rags that season often included some marvellous former and future first-teamers, for example John Price, John Huw Williams, Mike Knill, Dennis Gethin, Ray Cheney, Frank Wilson, John Uzzell and Alex Finlayson. The Athletic only had two losing seasons between 1884-85 and 1974-75, in 1892-93 and 1929-30. The team was the bedrock of Cardiff success.

A Welsh Golden Era

19 years after the fifth Grand Slam in 1952, the sixth Grand Slam of 1971 heralded a new dawn for Welsh rugby. They had an unfair share of world-class players such as Gareth Edwards, Barry John, Mervyn Davies, John Taylor, JPR Williams, Gerald Davies, Graham Price, Bobby Windsor, Alan Martin, Steve Fenwick, Ray Gravell, J.J. Williams and John Dawes. Most had gone to training college to become teachers. There were 11 Welsh players in the victorious 1971 Lions Test side in New Zealand and 6 Welshmen in the successful 1974 Lions Test team in South Africa. In the 70's, 9 of the 10 matches against England were won; 8 of the 10 against Scotland; and 7 wins and 1 draw against Ireland in 9 games. France in

Paris were the greatest rivals, Wales winning 6, drawing 1 and losing 3 in 10 matches.

CHAPTER 44 - CARDIFF SEASON 1971 – 1972

BARRY JOHN RETIRES 'TOO SOON' – CARDIFF HAS THREE CAPTAINS – MANY INJURIES AND MISSING 'STARS' - BARBARIANS HAMMERED - THE RHODESIA TOUR – CARDIFF WIN THE SEVENS AGAIN

Elwyn Williams P6; **Tony Williams** P16 T4 Pts16

Pl 53 W 39 L 14 D 0 Pts 1058-516. Tries 175-66, Pens 58-59

A Welsh Merit Table was formed in this year, with Pontypool, Newport, Bridgend, Llanelli, Neath, Aberavon, Swansea, London Welsh and Ebbw Vale all agreeing to meet each other once in a season. Cardiff demurred, although they already played all these teams, and Newbridge replaced them to make a 10-club league. It may be that Cardiff wished to keep control of its fixture list, but this is speculation. In a fairly disappointing season, fullback John 'Army' Davies scored a club record of 209 points in his first year at the club. And at long last, the try value was increased from 3 to 4 points. The veterinary surgeon John H. James, a wing forward, had joined Cardiff in 1967-68, and gained an Athletic XV cap for 1969-70. He was chosen as Firsts captain for 1971-72, but before the season started, he injured his thumb and hand, vaccinating himself instead of a cow. James was unable to play until late in the season, taking part in only 2 games, and then all 5 matches of the Rhodesian tour.

Vice-captain Alec Finlayson took over until he was hurt against Newport in February, and prop Roger Beard then became captain until John James returned. Ian Robinson was injured in the first game and out of action for 11 matches. In the programme notes for the Northampton match on 9 October, Dai Hayward wrote: *'We have more walking wounded than Napoleon on his retreat from Moscow.'* In the final Welsh Trial of 1 January, Lyn Baxter dislocated his elbow touching down for a try. Davies records: *'He was going great guns at the time and lost an almost certain Welsh cap which all the experts predicted.'* Back row Roger Lane and wing Wayne Lewis, who was also hurt in the trial, along with Cardiff's three British Lions John Bevan, Barry John and Gareth Edwards made up Cardiff's five other players in the trial.

With a multiplicity of injuries, and the absence of John Bevan, Barry

John and Gareth Edwards until late in the season, Cardiff were defeated 4 times by 1 October, to Coventry 22-10 A (but winning the return 22-15, scoring 5-3 on tries); Pontypool 15-12 A (but scoring 3 tries to 1 in that game, and also winning 19-6 H and 10-3 A in the same season, scoring in those games 5 tries to nil); Abertillery 15-3 A (Abertillery scoring the only try) and Newport 7-4 A (a try each). Newport won the next game 6-0 at the Arms Park, with a converted try, the try now worth 4 points. However, a full Cardiff side then won 17-3 A, 3 tries to 1, and 25-6 H, 4 tries to none). Llanelli and London Welsh beat a depleted Cardiff on the mornings of international matches, and the day before Wales-Scotland, Heriots won 9-8, Cardiff scoring 2 tries to 1, owing to no available Cardiff player being able to kick simple penalties or conversions.

Cardiff lost in mid-October to Ebbw Vale 21-18, despite scoring 2 tries to 1, as Ebbw kicked 5 penalties. However, in the return fixture at the Arms Park in January, Cardiff fielded *'quite a weak team'* and scored 5 tries to nil, winning 26-6. Luckily, on 4 December the Lions Barry John and John Bevan at last returned to the team and played against Swansea – *'they provided the necessary attacking spark; the whole team raised its standard and the Cardiff crowd witnessed some sparkling Rugby'*. Cardiff won 38-6 at home, outscoring the All Whites 6 tries to 1. A week later, Gareth Edwards returned to play against Harlequins at Twickenham, where Cardiff won 19-12, 3 tries to 1. The home game was won 11-3, 2 tries to 0. John Bevan, Gareth Edwards and Barry John made an immense difference when playing for Cardiff, having in Davies' words: *'covered themselves with glory in New Zealand and Australia, and had played leading roles in the success of the Lions, in the Test series with the All Blacks. In New Zealand alone Barry John amassed a total of 180 points, and he, together with Gareth Edwards as scrum half were rated as the world's greatest pair of half-backs; Barry was acclaimed "King John". The powerful running of John Bevan produced 17 tries and made him top scorer. All three received the unanimous praise of the Rugby world, much so in Wales and through the television media. They were given a 'Welcome Home' night by the Rugby Club, with vocal support from the C.A.C. Male Voice Choir. Barry John "donated" his record breaking, kicking boots, to the club museum, and Gareth his British Lions jersey.'*

On 23 March, *Bath Rugby Heritage* reported their 15-6 loss at home to Cardiff: *'There was a very large crowd for this evening game, but expectations of top rate entertainment were never realised. Gate takings amounted to £150. Waterman's first penalty did put Bath in the lead after six minutes, but five other kicking chances were missed, including a long-range effort by Walkey. A penalty to Cardiff allowed the teams to cross over on level terms. Fourteen minutes into the second half, Waterman contributed a further penalty to complete Bath's scoring effort. Cardiff turned the tables very effectively in the last quarter.'* Cardiff scored 3 tries and a penalty to 2 penalties.

It is such a pity that nearly all club matches from this era were not televised, but a taste of watching the game is given in Paul Rees' account of the return match with Coventry. In *The Guardian* 28 March 2020, Rees wrote '*My Favourite Game: Cardiff v Coventry at Cardiff Arms Park, 1972. Barry John, a mixture of Machiavelli and Napoleon, bamboozled and outplayed one of the strongest clubs in Britain with his match-winning brilliance. The deft, tactical kicking of Cardiff's Barry John was one of his many skills that made him arguably the finest outside-half of all time. There are many images of Barry John, but a personal favourite is of the outside-half sitting on the ball where the touchline met the 22, on the side of the main stand, as Cardiff slid towards defeat against a club that was then one of the strongest in Britain. He wore the insouciance of someone watching his dog retrieve a stick, as he waited for a Coventry player to revive from the ministration of what passed then for a medic, someone armed with a bucket of water and a sponge. It took a while and, with Cardiff having been awarded a penalty, the opposition retreated behind their line in readiness for John's attempt at goal.*

There did not seem much to concern them, leading 15-3 against a side they had beaten 22-10 at Coundon Road the previous September. They fielded seven England internationals with two other players, Peter Preece and Geoff Evans, winning their first caps later in the year. Cardiff had two asterisks, but what a pair, John and his half-back partner Gareth Edwards.' (An asterisk against a name in a team in the programme denoted an international player). '*They had only recently returned to action after a long lay-off, following the successful Lions tour to New Zealand. It was not a vintage period for the Arms Park club, whose vet captain John James did not play all season after jabbing himself with cow vaccine. But they had John, in his prime at 27. He was to make his final break four months later – for freedom after feeling trapped by fame, having been hailed as the King after his return from New Zealand and treated with royal reverence. While Edwards was a player who tended to reserve his best for Wales and, protecting his hamstrings, ration his club appearances, John treated each match the same, there to be won, by whatever means it took.*

As he sat on the ball, he plotted. Part of the reason that made him stand out was that he thought a few moves ahead of everyone, a mixture of Machiavelli and Napoleon whose slight frame disguised his fierce competitiveness. As the sponge-man made his way off the field, John slowly rose to his feet and addressed the referee, who nodded in response. Casually, he bent down to address the ball before tapping it and running to the line as his opponents, who had not checked whether he had indicated he was going for goal, gawped incredulously. He showed his mortality by missing the conversion, but the crowd sensed the turning of the tide and became vocal. Cardiff's pack, full of gnarled forwards who either just failed to get a Wales cap or, in the case of the second row Ian Robinson, collected two in 1974, got on top. Four of the Coventry team had been part of the England side that had collapsed next door the year before, and they had a feeling of deja vu as John's boot put Cardiff in front, on a day when he went through the card.' (John scored every way possible, try, conversion, drop goal, penalty.)

'And then came the coup de grace. Few club matches were televised then, confining most of John's feats with Cardiff to memory, which can play tricks, but the sight of his making an arcing run to the spot where he traded a penalty for a try remains indelibly imprinted. It became clear, as three defenders converged on him, that he was not going to make it but still he went on. At the point just before the three pounced on him, he passed blindly out of the back of his right hand. Chugging up in support, the No 8 Carl Smith did not have to break his stride, only catch the ball with the defence occupied elsewhere. It was only a friendly, but the reaction to the 22-15 victory was as if a league had been won. A week later, John and Edwards were at Twickenham, helping Wales to victory over England, another day, another collar.' (Incidentally, this was not a friendly but an official match).

Danny Davies wrote of a justified grievance against a score-line in the Coventry away game that season: *'On 29th March under floodlights at home we lost to Bridgend by nine points to seven. The captain, unfortunately, gave away a penalty in the last minute, and Bridgend's Ian Lewis, the former Cardiff outside-half kicked the goal to win the match. This defeat definitely put paid to Cardiff's hopes of winning the Welsh Unofficial Championship. We were definitely robbed of victory at home to Coventry, early in the season. In the first half of that match, John Bevan our splendid international wing was definitely late tackled, and put out of the game. Yet with fourteen men we were leading until the very closing minutes, when David Duckham was given a run down the touchline and had reached our twenty-five, where he was obviously pushed into touch. Alas the Coventry touch judge, right on the spot, failed to put up his touch flag. Cardiff lost the match – a defeat hard to take.'* (In top-class games, there were very rarely neutral linesmen/touch judges. One was usually a former player of the home team, and the other his counterpart for the visitors).

Cardiff outscored a strong Barbarians team, stuffed with 14 internationals, on 1 April 1972, by 7 tries to 1, 43-10. John Regan made a brilliant break and scored a try but was injured, and left the field after 13 minutes. However, *'Cardiff played with sustained brilliance and achieved one of the greatest successes in its long history'*. Barry John's boot kicked seven goals. Penarth had beaten the Baa-Baas the day before, the second time in 51 years, with John Huw Williams, the former Cardiff wing, and Penarth captain in 1972-73, featuring strongly. Danny Davies succinctly wrote that the Baa-Baas were '*massacred*' by Cardiff's 14 men.

Gareth Edward's brother Gethin partnered Barry John at half-back several times, and both went on the 22-player Rhodesian tour in May, along with Tony Williams. All 5 matches were won, including a 24-6 win (4 tries) in the final game against Rhodesia at Salisbury on 27 May 1972. The enjoyable tour began against Mashonaland, won 14-13 (2 tries apiece) on 17 May; then a 44-13 win (13 tries) against Goshawks on the same day; then a 60-14 win (13 tries) against a Midlands Selection on 20 May, with the penultimate match vs. Matabeleland on 22 May, a win by 74 to 3 (14 tries). In the tour Cardiff played 5 games in 11 days scoring 42 ties against 4, but drawing on penalties, 4-4, scoring 236-44 points. As mentioned, it was an 'enjoyable' tour, with visits shoe-horned in, to the Kariba Dam, Victoria Falls and game reserves. The Welsh (Snelling) Tournament was won again, beating Pontypridd 22-0, Maesteg 16-0, Neath 10-6 and in the final Bridgend by 15-4, with John Bevan scoring 5 tries in the event. Cardiff scored 11 tries against 2. There were unofficial games against Pentyrch, originally away but played at the Arms Park at Pentyrch's request, won 29-7, 5-2 on tries; away at Tonyrefail, won 23-7, 3-1 on tries; away at Pontypool, won 10-7, 2-0 on tries; and home against Cardiff Training College, won 7-6, a try apiece.

Leading scorers were P. Lyn Jones 17, Wayne Lewis 16, Gareth Edwards 13, Neil Williams 11, Steve McCann 10, and Roger Lane and John Regan 9. Barry John scored 2 tries and kicked 43 goals giving him 122 points. 53 matches were played, with Mervyn John playing 51, Roger Beard 46, Carl Smith 43, Garry Davies 41, Ian Robinson 39, Roger Lane 35, John Regan 33, and Lyn Baxter and Wayne Lewis 31. First XV caps were awarded to John Davies, Wayne Lewis, Steve McCann, John Regan, Carl Smith, Gwilym Treharne and Neil Williams.

Centre John Uzzell had joined Cardiff from Newport in 1967-68, already with 5 Welsh caps. His dropped goal for Newport had defeated the 1963-64 All Blacks in the mud, their only defeat on tour. He captained the Athletic to: P37, W31, L6. Points 898-338. Before he retired in 1973-74 Uzzell had played 54 games for the 1st XV, gaining his cap, and 117 games for 'The Rags'. It was an excellent season. Former Newport and Wales wing Stuart Watkins scored 14 tries, Martin Pengilley 10 tries and 40 goals, P. Lyn Jones and Peter Flood 10 tries each, John Uzzell 7 tries and 2 dropped goals, and also Neil Collins and Elwyn Williams each scored 7 tries. From 1969-73 Elwyn played only 12 first team games, having played 37 in 1968-69, after his season and a half out with his broken leg. He could have played for any other club in Wales, but stayed with Cardiff, out of favour with the first-team coach Roy Bish. Cardiff Juniors had another superb season, scoring189 tries: Pl 30, W 25, L 4, D 1, Points 1,006-142.

Scotland and Wales did not travel to Dublin to play Ireland because of the escalating political situation. Some Welsh players received death threats from the IRA. Wales won 3 out of 3, finishing top of the table scoring 67 against 21 points. England played 4 games and had the Wooden Spoon, with no points and a deficit of -52. Wales easily won at Twickenham 12-3, 1 try by JPR, converted by Barry John and 2 pens by John, to a penalty. Wales scored 5 tries to 1, 35-12 beating Scotland at home, with tries from Gareth Edwards (2), Roy Bergiers, Gerald Davies and John Taylor, 3 conversions and 3 penalties from Barry John. France were then destroyed by 4 penalties from Barry John, and 2 tries from Gerald Davies and John Bevan to 2 penalties 20-6. It seems as if Wales would have cruised to another Triple Crown and Grand Slam in this year, without the Irish 'Troubles'. Hywel Francis wrote in '*London and the Miners' Strikes of the twentieth Century*': '*The Wales-England game at Twickenham in 1972 had a special quality. A striking miner, Dai Morris of Tower, was on the victorious Welsh side. My father was convinced that it was divine intervention on behalf of the Welsh miners. Many years later, just weeks before my father died in 1981, he had a lift into the Wales-England game at the National Stadium with the Mayor of Rhymney. As he got out of the mayoral car, who should be getting out of the nearby car of Alun Priday, secretary of Cardiff Rugby Club, but former prime minister, Edward Heath. My father introduced himself, explaining that they last met in Downing Street during the miners' strike of 1972. My father simply said, 'We beat you then in 1972, we beat you last week (Margaret Thatcher had done her now forgotten U-turn on pit closures), and we'll beat you again today!*' (Wales won 21-19 on 17 January 1981.)

The biggest blow to Welsh rugby was that in 1972 Barry John announced his decision to retire at the age of 27, unhappy with his celebrity status after his second Lions Tour. One relieved opponent noted that '*It was always reassuring to see Barry go through a door and not through the wall.*' Danny Davies reported: '*It was with much regret from his club point of view, and that of all his Rugby fans, that Barry John decided to retire after the end of the season to take up a commercial career with television and writing. He retired at the pinnacle of his Rugby fame, and with Bevan and Gareth Edwards had shared in a British Lions success, the Triple Crown and the Grand Slam for Wales within the space of his last twelve months of Rugby.*' Barry had taken a post as a rugby correspondent, so could never play or coach rugby union again, deemed to be a 'professional'. Rugby league players returning home, even when retired, were often turned away from their old clubhouses as they were 'tainted' by professionalism. Crackers.

There was something of a catastophe when Barry John retired prematurely, the greatest back that this writer has witnessed, but he had an incredibly talented successor for Wales, the Llanelli outside-half Phil Bennett. Having seen far more of Barry than Phil, I am prepared to admit that Phil – an absolutely lovely man - was Barry's equal, very different in style but equally effective – whereas Barry seemed to saunter through defences, Phil jinked and darted. I have met Barry on several occasions – when making a break he used to study the position of the defenders' feet to know which side to pass him – how many of us have the time to do that while playing in close quarters? The late Phil Bennett and his wife, Chico Hopkins and other great rugby players would chat to me as if I was their equal when I managed to go to Parc y Scarlets. Great rugby players are almost all great men, with no veneer of arrogance that one may find in other sports. I also met Carwyn James, the superb coach on the successful 1971 Lions tour of New Zealand, whom Barry had known from his Llanelli days. Everyone in Wales knows that Carwyn should have coached Wales. However, he wished to select the team, which was *verboten* to the Big Five. All I can say is that, being given a lift in a car by him as a rugby-mad youngster, aged about 12, Carwyn talked to me as if I was a grown-up – which was very unusual in those days. And impossible for grammar schoolteachers.

In 1972, aged only 27, Barry John retired, citing media attention and unfair expectations as reasons. With 25 Welsh caps, he scored 90 points from 5 tries, 9 conversions, 13 penalties and 8 dropped goals. His British Lions tour cemented his reputation, and that of Gareth Edwards, and the world's best half-backs, and he scored for the Lions a further 30 international points. Barry only played 5 seasons for Cardiff, in 93 matches, scoring 24 tries and 30 dropped goals. Unfortunately, after the superb Welsh team of the 1970s, there was to be a 27-year wait for more Grand Slams in 2005, 2008, 2012 and 2019. These later triumphs were in the Six Nations, and Wales is the only team to have won four such Slams. England has won 13 Grand Slams in the 4, 5 and 6 Nations; Wales 12; France 9; Ireland 3 and Scotland 3, an incredible achievement for a nation with a seventeenth of the players to choose from as England. Wales has currently (2020) has won the same number of Nations Championships as England (22), with Scotland 13, France 12 and Ireland 10.

In 1997, the first 13 inductees into the International Rugby Hall of Fame included Barry John, Gareth Edwards, Cliff Morgan and JPR Williams. Other Cardiff inductees have been Gerald Davies (1999) and Gwyn Nicholls (2005). The other Welsh inductees were Carwyn James (1999), Mervyn Davies (2001), Phil Bennett (2005) and Ieuan Evans (2007). New Zealand has the most honoured players with 18, followed by Wales with 10, of which 5 were Cardiff players – Barry, Gareth, Gerald, Cliff Morgan and Gwyn Nicholls.

Barry John Retires Too Soon

I must repeat that I have never seen such an unflustered player as Barry – he was always calm, always was in space or made space – he was the George Best of rugby, incredibly good, in my opinion the best back in my lifetime. It did not matter whether he played for Cardiff, the Barbarians, East Wales or Wales – he was the player that always caught the eye. Simon Thomas interviewed Barry and Gareth for the Western Mail and walesonline on 24 November 2017 - Gareth and Barry 50 years on: '**The greatest rugby duo ever tell the story of their immortal partnership.** *They even had their own catchphrase: "You throw it, I'll catch it!"*

As they look back half a century on their first game together for Wales, Gareth Edwards and Barry John find themselves asking the same question: "Where on earth has the time gone?" For it was indeed 50 years ago this month that a half-back partnership which was to take the international stage by storm was born. Appropriately enough, given the events of this weekend, it was New Zealand who provided the opposition as the two young men received an introduction to All Blacks rugby, as well as to each other. They were just 20 and 22 at the time, with only two caps apiece to their name, when they took the field at the old Arms Park on a wet and windy day in November 1967. It was to be the start of something very special. They were to play 23 games together for Wales - separated just once over the next five years - while there were five Test outings in tandem for the Lions, including all four matches on the triumphant 1971 tour of New Zealand. So, 50 years on, what are their recollections of how it all began? "Our paths really first crossed in Maesteg, of all places, when we went up against each other in a Probables v Possibles towards the end of 1966," recalls Edwards. "Then, lo and behold, they chose me and Barry to play together in the final trial before the Six Nations in Swansea."

That in turn led to a meeting which was to spawn one of the most memorable quotes in Welsh rugby history. "I was a bit concerned about my passing," explains Edwards. "People were saying it was a bit suspect and asking if I was ready. "So I rang Barry up to ask if there was any chance of having a run out before the trial and he said to come down to Carmarthen, where he was in college. "So I went down only to find he had forgotten all about it! He couldn't find his boots. He just had a pair of soggy track shoes and the pitch was soaking wet because it had rained for 48 hours." Barry takes up the story: "It was pouring with rain. We were absolutely drenched and I had daps on. "We were like two little seagulls out there. "I was slipping and sliding and, in the end, after about 10 mins I just said to him - "I was slipping and sliding and, in the end, after about 10 mins I just said to him in Welsh: 'Gareth, you throw it, I will catch it'. It was just a simple line I said at the time without realising how often it would be quoted in years to come. It's unbelievable" Simple or not, it worked. "I never looked back after that," said Edwards. "It was remarkable what was kindled from that moment onwards."

Their first outing, in that trial, was only to last 15 minutes as John took a stud to the inside of his knee and while both men were to feature during the Five Nations, it was with different partners. So it wasn't until fate took a

569

hand the following autumn that the partnership was born in the Test arena. "We met up as a squad down in Neath a couple of weeks before for the New Zealand game," said Edwards. "It was a dark and dreary Thursday night down at the Gnoll. "Then, all of a sudden, we were hit by the bombshell. "Dai Watkins had been named as squad captain, but then, as we were all getting changed before training, he said: 'Boys, I have got something I need to tell you, I am off to Salford. "He walked out and that was it. We were all stunned. "But it meant the path was clear for Barry and me." John quips: "I chipped in £50 to send him to Salford. He hasn't thanked me!" So come the game against the Kiwis, it was the young Cardiff half-backs who were handed the reins, while also being pitched together off the field. "I remember we shared a room together at the Angel, which was to become the norm over the years," said John. "For breakfast in the morning I was toast, marmalade and coffee and Gareth was toast, honey and tea. I would have to make all the arrangements. He would say 'you are the fly-half, get on with it'. So I was always the one who had to ring up for it. It was a big responsibility that!"

The game itself had a very different context to today, as Edwards explains. "Back then, we were the only side to have beaten New Zealand more times than they had beaten us. It was 3-2. So they came with a mission. 1905 still rankled with them. We were all so excited at the prospect of playing the All Blacks. We had grown up with the tales of yore and they came over so infrequently. It's not like today." Come the day of the game, the Welsh weather had taken its toll on the Arms Park pitch. "It had been raining like hell and the pitch was like a paddy field," said Edwards. It's hard for people to appreciate how conditions could be in those days." "It was terrible," confirmed John. "The old word was quagmire. People playing now wouldn't know what it was all about. You used to run on to the pitch and there would be puddles all over the place and there would be the colours of the rainbow because that's where the petrol had dropped from the tractors trying to flatten it out. If you had a mouthful of that, you were in trouble!" Playing into a strong wind in the first half, Wales restricted New Zealand to 8-0 at the break and when John slotted a smart drop goal to cut the deficit to five points, they looked in with a real shout. "We had the wind with us and we were putting a lot of pressure on them," said Edwards. "There was a feeling we were getting to grips with it and they were a bit shaky for a while."

It looked as though Stuart Watkins had scored a try for Wales, but referee Mike Titcomb ruled it out. (Watkins believed he had scored a perfectly good try.) But then a mix up under the posts off an attempted Fergie McCormick penalty gifted the All Blacks a try and there was no way back for Wales on a day when the Kiwi scrum proved its technical expertise in a 13-6 victory. "It was hard, tough rugby and it was going the full 15 rounds," said John. "They were a wonderful side." "We had our chances," said Edwards. "Paul Wheeler, of Aberavon, missed a couple of penalties, I missed a couple. And Barry John wasn't even taking kicks in those days! To rub salt in the wounds, our skipper and hooker Norman Gale kicked a penalty. He toed it through the posts. I think he was fed up with giving the penalties to us! I just remember the huge disappointment at not beating New Zealand. It still rankles with me as a missed opportunity."

It wasn't to be the last of those for the young half-backs during that winter, as they also found themselves paired together for East Wales and the Barbarians against the All Blacks. A late John drop goal attempt just shaved the posts at the Taff End during a 3-3 draw in the East Wales game, with Edwards' recollection being: "**We completely outplayed them**. We should have won. We were really sick." And the Baa-Baas led 6-3 in the dying minutes at Twickenham, only for the Kiwis to score two late tries to maintain their unbeaten record on tour. "How the hell we lost that one I will never know," says John. Edwards adds: "Those games were a hard lesson of playing New Zealand and how difficult they are to beat, but a great introduction to All Blacks rugby. "What was apparent was how slick and quick they were and how they took their chances very well. Much like today really."

From those beginnings, the half-back combination was to really blossom as the pair shared in glorious triumphs for Wales and the Lions. So to what do they put down their enduring success? "I suppose it's like any partnership that just clicks," said John. "You can go to Morecambe and Wise or to Ant and Dec in modern times. "The point is you see, our backgrounds were almost identical. His father was a miner, my father was a miner. When I walked into his house in Gwaun-Cae-Gurwen, it was like walking into a house I had seen a million times before. I would go in and there would be a nice little bit of cake and a cup of tea his mother would have there always ready. Our upbringing was the same and upbringing equals values, what's right, what's wrong. Our values were basically the same and responsibility goes with that. There was our upbringing, our outlook towards the game and also the fact we spoke Welsh. That played a good part. I would call 'i'm chwith, i'm chwith, i'm chwith', to my left, left, left, or 'tu ol, tu ol', behind, behind. It was like a shepherd with a sheepdog really. Beeb, beep, beep! I could cut off his pass wherever I wanted, it was so lovely coming to me. It's like a piece of string, I could cut it off there, there or there or let it glide."

Paying tribute to his former partner, he adds: "It's like having a saucepan with all the ingredients in. Gareth had so many ingredients in there and when they all combined to perfection the potency of that was like an explosion. He had so much awareness and skill. You could have played fly-half outside him, Simon." Perhaps not! As for Edwards' assessment of John, it's equally glowing. "We used to have a great laugh," said the man who turned 70 this year. "He was called the king and he just loved it and *fed off it. There were times when he became more and more outrageous in the way he played. Nothing was beyond him and it strengthened the team, his manner. It was brilliant to play with him. When he said he was going to retire, I was so disappointed. I did my utmost to try and get him to reconsider." But we are all still left with the memories of a pairing that was born that November day in 1967. "Can you believe it is 50 years? You can't," said Edwards. "Where has the time gone? When you are young, a week in school was a long time and summer holidays lasted for ever. When I look back, I don't need to close my eyes. I can visualise some of those moments as if it were yesterday. They are very vivid. It feels like just the other day. It was a wonderful time."*

CHAPTER 45 - CARDIFF SEASON 1972 – 1973

TONY WILLIAMS CAPTAINS THE ATHLETIC - ELWYN RETIRES TO PLAY FOR TAFF'S WELL – ELWYN WILLIAMS PLAYER PROFILE – ELWYN'S STORY

Tony Williams P8, 4T Pts16; **Elwyn Williams'** last season P3 – total games 339, tries 44 points 132

P49, W35, L12, D2. Points 963-499. Tries 158-67, Pens 46-55

Elwyn had been playing for the Athletic for the previous three seasons, and decided this would be his last, before going back to coach and play for Taff's Well. An extremely mobile player, as his 44 tries prove, he could have easily left for another first-class club when the coach Roy Bish, with his new insistence upon playing an All-Blacks style of aggressive contact rugby, did not pick him for the Firsts. Bish joined as Elwyn was recovering from his broken leg, playing 6 games until he broke it badly at the start of the 1966-67 season, and then 17 games at the end of the 1967-68 season. In 1968-69, Elwyn was back in the thick of things, playing 37 times. Aged just 29, at the start of the 1969-70 season, he was to play in only 12 more First XV games in his final 4 seasons with the club. However, Elwyn was Cardiff through and through, and stayed on as a regular Athletic player. And his performances at Taff's Well were to be astounding. Prop Gerald 'Gerry' Wallace had joined Cardiff in 1965-66, having been at Cardiff Teacher Training College with other Cardiff regulars Roger Beard, Ken Jones, Gareth Edwards and Gary Samuel. Gerry was elected captain and chose Mervyn John as his vice-captain. Already a Welsh trialist, Wallace was selected for Wales on its tour of Canada in May/June 1973. Cardiff won the W.R.U. National Sevens in September, beating Glamorgan Wanderers, Maesteg, Kenfig Hill and then Bridgend in the final 21-14. Tony Williams was not in the squad, but was to reappear the next year. Barry John had retired, but the brilliant young Keith James joined from Newport, making a splendid debut in the 32-12 win against Cardiff Teachers Training College. Keith was picked for Wales B against France B, and gained his 1st XV cap.

Cardiff's seventh heaven

TONY WILLIAMS, youngest of eight brothers who have all played for Cardiff—Bleddyn, No. 3 in the line and 18 years Tony's senior, is the most famous of them—delighted the Williams family on the opening Saturday of the season.

Then, at the Stoop Memorial Ground, Twickenham, he led Cardiff to victory in the first invitation Sevens tournament promoted by the Harlequins.

Lord Wakefield of Kendal ("Wakers" of old, who has won more England caps—31—than anyone else) presented a cup for the competition, and personally-handed it over to a delighted Tony *Continued on 21*

"Rugby World" photographer Peter Stuart took this cheerful picture of the victorious Cardiff seven—that's Tony Williams behind the Wavell Wakefield Trophy —and the photographs overleaf.

Winners of the Harlequins Wavell Wakefield Trophy. Elwyn is middle back row, captain Tony kneeling in front of the trophy

Danny Davies' chapter heading for this season was **'Cardiff's Rough Game with the Sixth All Blacks'** New Zealand had played extremely 'vigorously' trying to win against a wonderful Llanelli team on 31 October 1972 – I have talked with Gareth Jenkins, the late Phil Bennett, Ray 'Chico' Hopkins and others about the game – and Llanelli deservedly won 9-3. To be honest, some of the play was worse than nasty. That is being polite. It was a terrific Llanelli side, and their opponents were thuggish. Every Llanelli player suffered some sort of injury, with Gareth Jenkins in particular being subjected to some terrible kicking. A few days later, on 4 November, the All Blacks came to the National Stadium to play Cardiff, knowing that two successive defeats would make them pariahs on their return home. Captain and prop Gerry Wallace could not play, in a horrible game where Cardiff were battered, losing 20-4, 3 tries to 1. In his Annual Report, chairman and former player Danny Davies wrote: *'The game turned out to be a complete disaster. It was far below the standards and reputation of both sides as it could have been, and resulted in an unsatisfactory and unsavoury exhibition which did no credit to either side. It was a big disappointment to players, administration and members alike and we must look to our laurels the next occasion we receive a visit from a touring team.'*

Just four days later, on 8 November Newport were beaten in Cardiff 24-3, 4 tries to 0, and 3 days later was the date of the Final Welsh Trial. Only 5 regular 1st XV players were therefore available on 11 November, because of injuries or trial appearances, to play Auvergne in Provence. The team were smashed 36-0. Two years previously, missing nearly all the First XV, Cardiff had lost 41-6 and Danny Davies had inveighed against such games harming Cardiff's reputation, saying that such matches should not be played without a reasonable first team. It may well be that the committee wanted a free holiday with their wives, however. The return journey was in gale conditions in an old aircraft, causing it to land at Bournemouth *'after a severe and frightening buffeting. The committee decided to review this fixture.'*

Against Wales on 2 December 1972 All Blacks scrumhalf Sid Going chipped the ball forward close to the touchline, with his pack chasing *'like a great black blanket'* according to commentator Bill McLaren. The ball fell to the 17-stone prop Keith Murdoch who launched himself at the try line as three Wales players approached. The try was awarded, but the Wales players insisted the ball had not crossed the line. That put New Zealand 10-0 ahead, and 13-3 up at half-time. The match ended Wales 16, New Zealand 19, with all the Welsh players believing that they should have won the match. Wales played all the rugby. John Bevan scored a try to match Murdoch's and Phil Bennett kicked 4 penalties to Joe Karam's 5. It was Murdoch's last rugby game. At the Angel Hotel a few hours later, he punched a security guard at the hotel, in the face, before disappearing for several years. No great loss to rugby.

On 27 January 1973 in Cardiff, unbeaten New Zealand played the final game of their tour in Britain, against a Barbarian team including 5 Welsh threequarters and 2 forwards, coached by the great Carwyn James. It was a thrilling encounter of attacking rugby, considered to be the best rugby union match ever played, and featuring *'the greatest try ever'*. After two minutes, New Zealand winger Bryan Williams kicked the ball over Phil Bennett's head, who ran back to scoop it up. Everyone in the ground prayed that Bennett would just 'hoof it' as far as possible, into touch, as he was near his own goal line. Instead, Phil side-stepped four onrushing tacklers, heading upfield, before, with his way blocked, passing left to his ultra-safe attacking full back, 'JPR' Williams. Bryan Williams illegally tackled JPR around the neck, but JPR managed to offload the ball to English hooker John Pullin. Thankfully the referee played advantage, and Pullin passed to John Dawes, who made ground before passing to Tommy David and Derek Quinnell, all quickly moving upfield to around 20 yards from the All-Blacks' line. Quinnell passed the ball left, intended for John Bevan, but Gareth Edwards intercepted the pass, finishing with a diving try in the left-hand corner, 22 seconds after Bennett picked the ball up. Commentator Cliff Morgan was only asked to broadcast 2 hours before the game as Bill McLaren was ill, and Cliff's commentary is itself sometimes described as '*the greatest ever*':

'*Kirkpatrick to Williams. This is great stuff. Phil Bennett covering. Chased by Alistair Scown. Brilliant! Oh, that's brilliant! John Williams, Bryan Williams* (referring to the All-Black wing almost taking off JPR's head) *Pullin. John Dawes, great dummy. To David, Tom David, the half-way line! Brilliant by Quinnell! This is Gareth Edwards! A dramatic start! What a score! Oh, that fellow Edwards!*' Steaming up from well behind play, Gareth Edwards was just praying that his hamstrings would hold out as he took the ball, intercepting the pass meant for John Bevan. Immediately after, at the game's restart, Cliff Morgan said '*If the greatest writer of the written word would have written that story, no one would have believed it. That really was something.*' Often called '*that try*', it is often voted the best try in history.' Barbarians' coach Carwyn James is credited with stimulating Phil Bennett to make his trademark swerving and sidestepping runs, was a wonderful Llanelli coach, and was also the most successful British Lions coach, but never coached Wales, as he insisted upon having total control over the team selection.

In a feast of rugby, much better than any of today's games, David Duckham was excellent, and both John Bevan and John Dawes almost touched down. Fergus Slattery and John Bevan scored tries to make the halftime score an unbelievable 17-0. The pugnacious little wing Grant Batty scored two tries in reply, before Bevan scored his second try and then JPR Williams touched down. The Barbarians won 23–11, 4-2 on tries, with Phil Bennett kicking 2 conversions and a penalty. There were 7 Welshmen in the Barbarians, responsible for 19 points (tries were now worth 4 points). They were: London Welsh full back and British Lion John Williams, always known as JPR; Cardiff wing and Lion John Bevan; London Welsh centre and former Lions captain John Dawes; Llanelli's fly half and future Lion Phil Bennett; Cardiff scrumhalf and Lion Gareth Edwards; the future British Lion and as yet uncapped Llanelli and former Pontypridd wing forward Tommy David; and Number 8 Derek Quinnell, uncapped by Wales when becoming a British Lion in 1971. What a team. What players. What a game. Phil Bennett was an absolutely charming, humble man, a joy to talk with. And I once shared a changing room with Tommy David and Steve Fenwick, in their later rugby league days, when they were training for Cardiff Dragons – their banter had everyone in stitches.

A former player I know reasonably well, via the Vale of Glamorgan pub in Cowbridge when I lived there, was John Peter Rhys Williams MBE, FRCS. Let us quickly examine his career, because he, more than anyone, made the full back an attacking rather than defensive force. Always playing with his socks rolled down, with long hair and sideburns, he preferred playing flanker, with a 6-foot build to play in the forwards, but was always a full back for Wales. After Bridgend Grammar School and Millfield, he could have played professional tennis, but took up amateur rugby seriously to allow time to study to become an orthopaedic surgeon. Aged just 19, in 1969 he was capped in the 17-3 win against Scotland, and played 55 times for Wales until 1981, 5 as captain, and in 8 Tests for the British and Irish Lions, his last cap in 1981. Utterly fearless, he played in a 'Golden Era' for Welsh rugby, winning 6 Triple Crowns in 1969, 1971, 1976, 1977, 1978 and 1979; and 3 Grand Slams in 1971, 1976 and 1978. In 10 England-Wales matches, JPR never lost, scoring 5 tries.

For the 1971 Lions, he won the series against New Zealand with a (very, very rare) long-range drop-goal, and was prominent in the 1974 'invincible' series against South Africa. JPR did not go on the 1977 Lions tour to New Zealand, having been advised to concentrate upon his medical career, and was one of the inaugural inductees of the International Rugby Hall of Fame in 1997. In his fifties, JPR was playing for local team Tondu's 3rd XV, at last in his favourite position of flanker – he loved tackling. Only 7 recent era Welsh players have won 3 Grand Slams: London Welsh JPR Williams Cardiff's Gerald Davies and Gareth Edwards 1971, 1976, 1978; Cardiff's Gethin Jenkins, Ospreys' Ryan Jones and Adam Jones 2005, 2008, 2102; and Osprey Alun Wyn Jones 2008, 2012, 2019. In another 'Golden Age, 1908, 1909 and 1911, Johnnie Williams, Billy Trew, Dickie Owen, George Travers, Jim Webb and Tom Evans won the Slam. England have won 13 Grand Slams; Wales 12 - 1908, 1909, 1911, 1950, 1952, 1971, 1976, 1978, 2005, 2008, 2012, 2019; France 9; Ireland and Scotland 3 each. When one considers that England has 17 times as many players as Wales, plus can call on its former colonies and Empire to pack its team, Wales punches well above its weight, in a country where soccer is a far more popular sport. Indeed, beginning in 1950, Wales have won 9 Grand Slams to England's 7, and narrowly missed a tenth in 2020 when France scored in overtime.

Cardiff had beaten Newport 18-14 and 24-3, but the third game, won 19-10 (2 tries to 1) was again marred by violence. Then, Davies writes: '*The fourth and final match at Rodney Parade was quite remarkable, it was played in a drizzle which made conditions rather slippery towards the end, but never in my own experience have I seen the Cardiff Club gain so much possession of the ball against Newport, and they attacked time and again yet failed to cross the line against a very gallant Newport defence, yet, with about a minute from time near Cardiff's 25, a kick from Gareth Edwards was charged down, and a Newport player with a forlorn hope of saving the game (Cardiff led 6 points to 3 at this last minute) kicked high and towards the left hand corner with a following wind, and it bounced into the in-goal area where S. McCann had positioned himself. Steve seemed to have the ball safely covered to touch down for a minor, but it slipped past him somehow and a Newport player, following up out of the blue, dived on the ball about half a yard from the dead ball line and scored a try which at the very last fence and in the very last seconds, saved Newport from the stigma of four defeats.'* 7-6 to Newport.

On 29 March under floodlights at home, Cardiff scored the only try of the game, but Bridgend won 9-7. Cardiff captain Gerry Wallace gave away a penalty in the last minute, and Ian Lewis, Cardiff's former fly half, kicked the goal to win the match. A game that rankled with Davies is when Cardiff lost 19-18 and *'were definitely robbed of victory at home over Coventry early in the season. In the first half of that match. John Bevan our splendid international wing was definitely late tackled, and put out of the game. Yet with fourteen men we were leading until the very closing minutes, when David Duckham was given a run down the touchline and had reached our twenty-five where he was obviously pushed into touch. Alas the Coventry touch judge, right on the spot, failed to put up his touch flag. Cardiff lost the match - a defeat hard to take.'* Maesteg were defeated by the club's record score of 77 – 9, but it is not included in Cardiff's official games. Harlequins (A) were beaten 47-8, Cambridge University (A) 36-10 with a weak team, and Pontypool 37 - 10. John Davies set up a new points record of 209, from 4 tries and 81 goals, and Steve McCann scored 21 tries, with Alec Finlayson on 20 (4 against Harlequins). Mervyn John and Roger Lane each scored 16 tries, a record for forwards. Gareth Edwards touched down 13 times and kicked 3 goals in only 25 games. Keith James and Leighton Davies gained First XV caps. Four players were selected for Wales B against France B - Alec Finlayson, Roger Lane, Ian Robinson and Keith James, Wales winning 35-6.

Under Tony Williams, Cardiff Athletic's record was P38 W33 L5. Points 1,165-400, setting a record number of points in a season for Cardiff. Cardiff scored 210 tries against 49, over four tries per game and four times as many as the average of opposing teams, but their opponents scored twice as many penalties, 47-25. Top try scorers were P. Lyn Jones 22, Elwyn Williams in his final season 14*, the captain Tony Williams, John Uzzell and John H. James 11 each and Gareth Lewis 10. Leighton Davies scored 100 points and 86 with the 1st XV. P. Lyn Jones amassed 122 points and full-back Phil Jenkins scored 93. Four of Tony's team gained Athletic caps, Will Attwill, Jeff Jenkins, Don Llewellyn and the hooker John Thomas. Cardiff Juniors record was P22 W18 L4. Points 735-133, a match average of 33-6 points.

ELWYN RHYS WILLIAMS 6 November 1939 – 31 August 2022
Height 188cm – 6 ft 2 ins
Weight 81kg – 12 st 10lbs
Blind-side wing forward, no. 6 (plus 7, 8 and an ability to play in the backs, earlier in his career in the back row he was numbered 13, 15 and 14)
Wales Under-15s
Captain Cardiff Youth 1957-58
Wales Youth
Wales Under-23s 1962
Wales Final Trial 1962
Over 100 games for Cardiff Athletic
339 games Cardiff First XV 1958-59 to 1972-73, 44 First team tries (*Elwyn scored 14 tries in this, his final season with the Athletic, second only to wing P.L. Jones)
Taff's Well Player-Coach 1973-74 to 1977-78 'The Silver Years' with 3 District Cups and the Silver Ball Trophy, playing with brother Tony
Glamorgan Wanderers Coach 1978-1981
Cardiff Youth Coach 1981-1984
Cardiff First XV Coach - Offered position of twice, but had work commitments.
Taff's Well Coach 1985-88

'Elwyn and Dai Hayward were the best pairing of wing forwards in Britain' – John Huw Williams

In the clubhouse at Taff's Well there is a display cabinet which reads: *'ELWYN An excellent back-row forward who served Cardiff from 1958-1972, making 339 1st XV appearances, Elwyn was probably one of the most versatile forwards to play for the Cardiff club. He was selected for the Welsh Schools and Youth teams, and helped Wales Under-23 defeat Canada at the Arms Park in 1962. In 1973, he returned to Taff's Well as player/coach, and what an impact he made. He was, in great part, responsible for the marvellous period of success from 1973-76. It would be a great surprise if there is a more conscientious coach in the W.R.U. It is not in his make-up to let anyone down.'*

After playing for Cardiff Youth and captaining the side in 1957-58, Elwyn's debut for the first team was the following season. In 1962, he played for Wales Under-23s against Canada, and also had a Welsh Senior

Trial. He played from 1958/59 to 1972/73 for Cardiff, scoring 44 tries in 339 games for the Firsts, and more for the Athletic (Elwyn scored 21 in two seasons, but records are incomplete). Elwyn played with distinction in the terrible 1961 Springboks game, being forced to switch to the backs, and played against New Zealand in 1963. Aged 26, he broke his leg, when on the point of being picked for Wales, and missed almost two seasons from 1966-68, plus the Cardiff tour of Rhodesia. However, on his return, he played 37 games in his next complete season for the Firsts. Elwyn usually played blind-side wing-forward if the speedy Dai Hayward, Tony Pender or Mervyn John were playing, or open-side if playing with the no-nonsense John Hickey.

Elwyn Williams

In his 15 seasons, he also played over 100 games for the Athletic at the start and end of his Firsts career. He played for, and coached Taff's Well after leaving Cardiff, playing and winning trophies until he retired in his 40s.

John Harding tells me: '*Elwyn was a class player; fast, fit and strong. He was a well-balanced ball carrier with fine footwork that would outsmart defenders. A demon back row cover tackler. As a No.8, I would delight having Elwyn alongside me in the scrum and lineout, for defence strength and attack opportunities. In the blur of running through opposition, I would hear his word "switch'. Instinctively a pass could be released to Elwyn without even seeing him. He was right there. Elwyn was a supremely confident player and team player.'* Elwyn was the player, that all the younger brothers thought should have played for Wales – it was a pleasure to watch a constructive wing forward, a player before his time. Cardiff Rugby Club *History Players Archive* gives his statistics:

SEASON	P	W	D	L	TRY	CON	PEN	DG	PTS
1958-1959	14	10	1	3	1	0	0	0	3
1959-1960	31	17	7	7	1	0	0	0	3
1960-1961	35	23	5	7	5	0	0	0	15
1961-1962	28	17	3	8	1	0	0	0	3
1962-1963	39	23	5	11	3	0	0	0	9
1963-1964	35	27	2	6	9	0	0	0	27
1964-1965	45	30	4	11	8	0	0	0	24
1965-1966	40	29	2	9	7	0	0	0	21
1966-1967	6	6	0	0	4	0	0	0	12
1967-1968	17	11	0	6	0	0	0	0	0
1968-1969	37	26	3	8	5	0	0	0	15
1969-1970	2	1	0	1	0	0	0	0	0
1970-1971	1	0	0	1	0	0	0	0	0
1971-1972	6	5	0	1	0	0	0	0	0
1972-1973	3	1	0	2	0	0	0	0	0
TOTAL	**339**	**226**	**32**	**81**	**44**	**0**	**0**	**0**	**132**

ELWYN'S STORY (his account from *The Williams Family* - December 2004)

'At Taff's Well School, they put me on the wing to play in the Under-15s, when I was ten years old and I thought that was a bit much. Even so, I enjoyed it and the fact that my brothers had been playing for Cardiff drove me on. Mind you, they used to say, *"You're not as good as your brother"* and that gave me an incentive to do something about it. I was at the school in the days of headmaster Walter Trigg (only just, mind) and then Del Harris took over – he was the one who really sorted *me* out. It was both Del Harris and 'Mousey' Jones who took us. Well, I then continued my schooling at Treforest and at that time, along with Cenydd, played for Pontypridd Schoolboys. Cen was 13 and I was 12. Despite there being only a year between us, Mr Davies, the man in charge, had thought I looked a bit young, and he asked my brother how he thought I would fit in. *"No problem"* said Cen, *"he can play"*.

I played in the centre then with Cenydd, for about a year and a half. Then Mr Davies said that they didn't have any 'second rows' who were tall enough, and he asked me to help them out. So, I went from centre to the second row of the pack! At the time, actually, it didn't make much difference to me. In actual fact in later life, when I came into Cardiff, it turned out to be a big asset because I was in the back row, and they used me for jumping at the back of the line-out, so we had three jumpers in the side. When I was at Pontypridd, I had a cap for the Under-15s. Afterwards they wanted me to play for Pontypridd Youth, but my brothers were down in Cardiff. Cen was playing with Cardiff Youth and Lloyd had played just before that, so it was an incentive for me to go down there. I had a Youth cap then as well – just before my 18th birthday.

The senior side – well, the 'Rags', wanted me to play for them towards the end of the season, but I thought better and decided to wait another six months. The following year I started with the Athletic, and just before my 19th birthday I had progressed to the Firsts. I played against The Wasps in my first game. (Wasps were beaten 20-10, 6 tries to 2 at the Arms Park). I played No. 8, believe it or not. I had been a flanker for the 'Rags', but they put me at No. 8. I was light for that position, mind, but I was a jumper at the back of the line-out and they used to do a lot of 'peel-offs' in those days. I think I played fourteen times for the Firsts in my first season with them – it was the hardest season I ever had, well physically anyway. Players who had been around a long time didn't worry about the fact that you were only 18 or 19! In another season I had matured, but I suppose there must be some young players who begin asking themselves, "*why am I taking all these bumps?*" and then sort of faded away. I had a 'Rags' Cap for that first season. Then CD Williams retired, and I took over from him at blind-side in the Firsts. I was with Dai Hayward in the back row. Cliff Howe (No. 8) came up from Bridgend.

I was thinking about this recent talk, about players coming down from the Rhondda Valley to play for Cardiff. Well, in those days we had Keith Rowlands, Howard Norris, Kingsley Jones, who had all come down from the valleys. Then there was Maurice Richards a little bit later, Mal Gough in the second row – they were from the Rhondda Valley, not to mention players like Cliff Morgan, Gareth Griffiths, Gordon Wells, JD Evans. It was amazing for me to be in the same side as several who had played with Bleddyn. Those I had watched as a young boy – now I was playing with them! It could have been overpowering in a way. It was thoroughly enjoyable though.

As far as my play was concerned, I always believed in getting to the break-down as quickly as possible, trying to win the ball and putting pressure on the opposition. The game has changed slightly now, *they don't go running around the field as we did in those days.*' (author's italics) 'They say they are fitter, but I'm not so sure about back-row forwards. In my day, wherever the ball was, you had to be. If a centre had the ball, you had to make sure you were supporting him. So, you had to be fit and a good ball-handler. Those years we had, in Taff's Well School, brought out the best of us you know. They taught us the basics – and *the basics are the main thing in rugby.*' (Again, author's italics. Today we have giants with hands like dinner-plates, who cannot grasp a light, clean, dimpled ball, let alone pass it. Lord knows how they would have handled the heavy, sodden lumps of leather of the old days.) 'If everybody does the basics well, then you've got a good team. If you have an extra bit of speed and a bit of a sidestep, then you can do other things. That's what it's all about. When I eventually gave up the game and started to coach, this is what I concentrated on. If you have a man who can give perfect passes off his right hand but can't pass off his left, then you've got problems. You have to go back to basics in that situation.'

After first playing 14 games in his first season, 1958-59, over the next seven seasons (1959-60 to 1965-66) Elwyn averaged over 36 games a season for Cardiff. Then, in 1965-66 he played in the first six games, breaking his leg and not coming back until the last 17 games of 1966-67. After missing these one and a half seasons after his leg break, Elwyn played 37 times in 1967-68. However, Roy Bish, a former Aberavon player, had become Cardiff's first ever coach in 1965, and now favoured more bulky forwards to emulate the New Zealand style, with forward dominance taking over from more risky three-quarter attacking. The style was euphemistically called 'Fifteen-man Rugby', and was more formulaic, with free-passing back movements being replaced by structured plays. Elwyn remarked, later in this chapter, '*You were supposed to adopt the All-Blacks position of driving at the opposition and laying the ball on the ground.*' (This was anathema to a ballplayer like Elwyn, always looking around with ball-in-hand, of how to continue an attack. Copying New Zealand and South Africa, with big players intent upon contact, has made rugby into the sad, boring, complicated and brutal spectacle that fewer and fewer people are watching and playing today. From an early age, Elwyn could play in the backs or across the back row, and his skill set today would be highly regarded. Elwyn moved uncomplainingly into the Athletic team of his beloved Cardiff from 1968-69 to 1972-73, only playing 11 times for the Firsts in those years. At least in the 'Rags', away from Bish's eye, he could play rugby as it should be played, scoring 14 tries in his last season. What a bloody waste – he was only 28 when he lost his regular first-class career – and could have walked into any other top-class team. Using his average 36 games a season, Elwyn missed 55 games with his broken leg, and possibly another 144 when playing in the Rags for 4 seasons. Without the broken leg and the arrival of Bish, he could have played over 500 games for Cardiff. Elwyn continues his story):

'Well, I went back to Taff's Well, and was a player-coach for five years.

It happened because 'Rugger' Jones and Brian Lancaster came to see me. This was around 1972 and I was living up in Abbey Close at that time. They came to see me and asked if I would like to come down and play. Well, I thought I'd come to the end of my playing days with Cardiff; I was getting picked then just about two out of every three games for the Athletic with one or two for the firsts as well. I was 33 by then so I considered it was an ideal situation for me to come and help Taff's Well. I wasn't meant to be a coach at Taff's Well, mind. The idea was for me to play, but when I got there, I could see the need to do something like coaching – so that's how it happened. I got them all together and started giving them training sessions, and from there they appointed me coach and that was it.' (Former players remember Elwyn making them run up nearby hills, but it paid off, with the club being possibly the fittest at their level). 'Mind you, it was a learning curve as far as I was concerned to start off with. I had intended doing it for just one year, mind, but we were doing well, and the following year Tony came. Of course, we played Swansea here the first year in the Cup and that was a good game, you know. Everybody enjoyed that. Then the next year Tony was with us, and we played Llanelli. I had a cut in that game and had to go off.' (An account of these games is given in the chapter upon Taff's Well and its 'Invincibles'.)

'We had some good years in that period, winning the District three times and we also won the Silver Ball, of course, with Ian Stephens as a youngster. Ian was playing in the second row early on and then he wanted to play Number 8. I said "you're not going to play number 8. I'm number 8 because I'm there – and I'm the coach so you've had it!" In actual fact, we needed a loose-head prop. We had a tight-head prop but needed a loose-head and he was the ideal type of player. He was a totally dedicated youngster. Do you know that at the end of training sessions he would have somebody on his shoulders, a lot longer than anyone else? Jack Jones, our tight-head prop, took Ian under his wing and showed him all the different things he needed to know. As a tight-head who used to come up against loose-heads, Jack knew what was wanted and could tell Ian the ins and outs of it. Ian, as you know, became a British Lion.

Well, from that start we had three really good years. The next two were mediocre really. They were alright but not too special. At the end of the fifth year, I had an offer from Tommy Coombes, who'd been the Wanderers scrumhalf. He said "we would like you to come down there" – so I thought that the five years was long enough for a coach to be with any side. So, I was down there with Glamorgan Wanderers on a three-year contract but it went into a fourth year.' (Glamorgan Wanderers, based in western Cardiff, was then considered a first-class club, with 5 fixtures with Cardiff in the 60s and a few in the 70s). 'I like to think that they improved a little bit. I was supposed to be coaching the firsts and second strings only, but the thirds used to turn up as well. They had numerous reserve sides at the Wanderers and the promotion system from the thirds to the seconds, and from the seconds to the firsts, worked very well there. They were very good at the Wanderers. I mean I didn't get paid or anything, apart from expenses – but they were very appreciative, and I enjoyed it. It was the first senior side I had coached. Well, they had been part of what was called the 'first class' system but they weren't at the forefront by any means – although they did beat Cardiff at the beginning of the season I left. It was the side that I had coached, so I was pleased about that.

At this time (brother) Lloyd told me they wanted a coach for Cardiff Youth. I thought about it then decided OK, that's what I'll do. It was nice to go back, you know, to coach a team that I had actually played for, so that's what I did. And of course with a team like Cardiff, you have a big turnover of boys – but the Wanderers weren't very happy with my leaving them. They saw it as someone going down, from what they considered a first-class side, to coach a youth set-up. I must say they were very kind to me during my time at the Wanderers, Sir Tasker Watkins the president and others.'

(The Right Honourable Sir Tasker Watkins, VC, Knight Grand Cross of the Order of the British Empire, DL, 1918-2007, was 20 years old when war broke out, and had played for **Cardiff Athletic** and Glamorgan Wanderers before the Army as an outside half. After serving as a private, he was commissioned as a lieutenant in the Welch Regiment in 1941. He was in action at the Battle of the Falaise Pocket, where he won the Victoria Cross. His active service ended a few weeks later in October 1944 when he was badly wounded in the battle to liberate the Dutch city of 's-Hertogenbosch. When he was the Welsh rugby coach, Graham Henry always pinned Watkins' citation on the wall of the Welsh changing room before Six Nations games. The son of an engine-fitter from Nelson, a few miles north of Caerphilly, Watkins had qualified as a teacher just before war broke out and enlisted as a private. Leaving the army with the rank of major, with a VC, he read for the bar when demobbed in 1946. He was called by Middle Temple in 1948 and started practising in common law on the Wales and Chester Circuit. After taking Silk in 1965 he moved to chambers at No. 1 Crown Office Row in the Temple. He was knighted in 1971 and was sworn of the Privy Council on his appointment to the Court of Appeal in 1980. Deputy Chief Justice for some years, he was appointed GBE – Knight, Grand Cross of the British Empire in 1990. He was President of the Welsh Rugby Union from 1993 to 2004, overseeing the switch from the amateur era to professionalism and the move from club to regional rugby in Wales. Like nearly all who participated in that war, Tasker Watkins preferred not to speak about it, but aged over eighty, he gave an interview to *The Daily Telegraph*: '*You must believe me when I say it was just another day in the life of a soldier. I did what needed doing* *to help colleagues and friends, just as others looked out for me during the fighting that summer... I didn't wake up the next day a better or braver person, just different. I'd seen more killing and death in 24 hours - indeed been part of that terrible process - than is right for anybody. From that point onwards I have tried to take a more caring view of my fellow human beings, and that, of course, always includes your opponent, whether it be in war, sport, or just life generally.'* One 2007 obituary said that Sir Tasker Watkins had been *'The Greatest Living Welshman'.*) This quote is a deliberate repetition of one earlier in the book. What a life.

Elwyn continued, 'Whilst I was back with the Youth, I was approached on two occasions with a view to coaching Cardiff Firsts. I would have liked to do that of course, but my problem was my job, so I had to decline. At that time, I wasn't working nights, but I was working afternoons and one weekend in three, so that made it a bit difficult. I had time off for the games on a Saturday, only by each time taking two hours of my annual leave, so that I could get down there. Training sessions were the main problem, having to miss one in every three weekends. This had been my problem with Cardiff Youth as well. I managed to coach the Youth for three years somehow, and we got into the Esso Welsh Cup on three occasions when I coached them. We didn't win the first year, but we pushed Llanelli out. The following two years we firstly beat Llanelli in the semi-final and the following year we beat them in the final. We didn't have outstanding players, but they played as a team.' (Elwyn's record with Taff's Well for five years and later three years, Glamorgan Wanderers for three seasons and Cardiff Youth for three, all in his spare unpaid time, shows how good a coach Elwyn would have been in the professional era.)

'It's frustrating to watch players today, who have obviously been coached to drive forward to draw in defences, but too often they don't seem to have the vision to see that something might be *"on"* – such as a four or five man overlap outside them. They could draw the immediate defence and pass to take advantage of an overlap. They don't appear to look to see what's on. Look at the advantages they have today with video recordings and so on, to enable them to go over moves, and to show those wasted opportunities. And then there's the other advantages they have today. For instance, I never saw any weights at Cardiff – we made up our own weights from the Forgemasters for training in Taff's Well. Today of course players start weight-training young, and they become bigger built. Highlights of my rugby career obviously include playing against South Africa in 1960 and New Zealand in 1963. There were just a few low points: I broke my leg when I was twenty-six and lost the chance to play against Australia in that year. I also missed a trip away to Rhodesia because of that broken leg. It was a particular set-back at that time, because I think I'd scored about four tries in three games at the beginning of that season, and then I broke my leg when we went up to play London Welsh at

Crystal Palace. Then of course I had to play myself back into the side. I came back from the break, starting with the Thirds, then the Seconds and then I was selected for the Firsts, but this coincided with a different style of forward play.

You were expected to adopt the All-Blacks method of driving at the opposition and laying the ball on the ground,' (This 'innovation" was the start of the decline of running, open rugby, needing big attackers to 'clear out', pick up the ball, and begin the process again, retaining and battering until a defensive gap showed. Equally big defenders were needed to try, with big 'hits', to dislodge the ball and gain possession. Theoretically, a team in possession can keep the ball forever.) 'Roy Bish, for whom I had a lot of respect, mind, had come back from New Zealand with this new method, and I'm afraid it didn't suit me. I wasn't big enough to start with, and in any case **my style was trying to beat players – not driving into them**. On my return, I was playing well, sticking to my own style, but gradually it all petered out, when I was told they didn't want to risk me on hard grounds, and so on.' (Interestingly, the All Blacks, the best team in world rugby, and all the clubs in New Zealand, have reverted to shifting the ball as soon as possible, having moved to a more entertaining non-contact ball, where forwards and backs are equally comfortable with the ball, and supremely fit. Comparing the *Aotearoa* to the Celtic-Italian-South African Pro-14 is like watching breath-taking high-speed cavalry manoeuvres rather than trundling predictable tanks. The New Zealand Super Rugby Aotearoa features the top five teams (Blues, Crusaders, Hurricanes, Chiefs and Highlanders) competing in 10 rounds of two games per round, leading to a championship final. There was a wonderful result when the Hurricanes beat the Highlanders on 26 March 2021, 30-14. New Zealand full-back Jordi Barrett scored all the Highlanders' points, with 3 tries, 3 conversions and 3 penalties – wow! Just a pity he could not also put over 3 drop-goals…)

'Well, the truth is that when I was operated on by Harold Richards, an eminent surgeon, who was a member of the club, actually, he transferred a piece from my ankle to my tibia, saying that if it should break again, it wouldn't be in the same place! All I can say is that I was still playing rugby at forty years of age. Having started in the 1958-59 season, by the time I parted company from Cardiff I had made 339 appearances for the Firsts and over a hundred for the Rags, so I felt I had served the club as best as I could. Although I would have liked to coach Cardiff, and as I have explained, it was just not possible – were I to have my time all over again – I would willingly have it all over again for I thoroughly enjoyed it all.' Elwyn was a terrific player, and a wonderful man.

In the Chairman's Report for 1984-85, Stan Bowes wrote: '*the Youth XV succeeded where the First XV failed… we must thank … coaches Elwyn and Tony Williams…who have brought so much credit to the Club with their victory…* Elwyn's Cardiff Youth team scored 8 tries against Bath Youth at the Arms Park, winning 42-3. Cardiff Youth had lost 7-0 away at Stradey, and Llanelli Youth had won all of their 31 games that season, when the teams met in the Welsh Youth Knock-Out Cup (ESSO) Final at the National Stadium. The Cardiff Youth captain of four years previously, international Mark Ring gave the boys a talk before the game. It was 10-10 at half-time, and with some exciting rugby Cardiff won 29-14. *'In the Welsh Youth (ESSO) competition our record stands as having reached the final five times out of the last six years and we have been winners four times… We see the departure of Elwyn Williams our coach, this season, and all thanks for the good work he has contributed to the success of Cardiff Youth.'* More on Elwyn's career after leaving Cardiff is included in a later section upon Taff's Well, where he also coached with great success. Elwyn married the sister of John Humphrys, the BBC personality, and cared for both her mother and her when they developed dementia.

Welsh Rugby June 1973 carried the following, all too short, article: '**Elwyn Williams says "Goodbye"** - Elwyn Williams, currently Cardiff's longest serving player and a member of the famous Williams clan of brothers, is to leave the club and join his home village team of Taff's Well. He joined Cardiff as a member of their youth team in season 1958-59, the year his elder brother Lloyd was vice-captain of the First XV. His departure means that only Tony now remains of the eight brothers who have played for Cardiff. He is the last of the line started by Gwyn, Brinley, Bleddyn and Vaughan, and carried on by Lloyd, Cenydd and Elwyn. A polished flank forward, Williams has rarely wavered from a high standard of consistency. This season he was still good enough to make the occasional first team appearance. He goes out on a high note, because the "Rags", under the captaincy of his younger brother Tony, have ended a brilliantly successful campaign with a record points total for the club. They have totted up 1,165 points while conceding 400 in 38 games. He announced his decision to sever his 15-year link with the Arms Park, after helping the "Rags" finish their record-breaking season with a 44-12 win over Ebbw Vale Athletic. *"It's time I made way for younger players"*, he said, *"I've had a great run with a great club, but I don't want to finish altogether. I want to go on playing by turning out for Taff's Well"*.'

Carey Collings reminisced about Elwyn's effect at Taff's Well, making the team train hard, and remembered two incidents. Firstly, a big Number 8 from Blaengarw, recently out of the Army and very fit, swung a punch at a Taff's Well player. Elwyn raced over, grabbed him by the front of his shirt collar, drew the errant player towards him, and shouted in his face, *'You don't need to do that! You're a good player. There's no need to do that!'* and released him. Most players would have piled into him, but not Elwyn, he defused the situation, and telling him he was 'a good player' calmed the Number 8 down for the rest of the game. Carey said, *'It shows the type of player Elwyn was, a gentleman.'* However, against Blaengarw someone 'booted' Carey in the head, and nearby Elwyn instinctively clobbered him. A kick in the head can be life-threatening. The referee sent Elwyn off, but 'Rugger' Jones, club secretary and a WRU member, ran onto the pitch shouting, *'You can't send him off! He's a Williams! Not one of them has ever been warned, let alone sent off! Please don't send him off.'* It seems the referee relented as Elwyn apologised to the ref, completed the game and served no two-match ban. Between them the brothers played more than 2,500 games – with a spotless record.

CHAPTER 46 - CARDIFF SEASON 1973-74

TONY WILLIAMS AGAIN CAPTAINS THE ATHLETIC – *'THE RAGS CAPTURE THE LIMELIGHT'* - TONY RETIRES TO PLAY WITH ELWYN FOR TAFF'S WELL – CARDIFF'S SECOND-CHOICE SCRUMHALF IS FIRST CHOICE FOR THE LIONS' TEST TEAM - CARDIFF'S FOUR INTERNATIONAL SCRUM-HALVES – TONY WILLIAMS RUGBY PROFILE

Tony Williams – his last season played 5 First-team games, won 5; 4 tries 16 points. Captain of the Athletic. Played in 32 of 35 Athletic fixtures 11 tries 44 points Made over 150 Athletic appearances. First XV record P328; W218, D24, L81. Tries 66, Points 228. Tony captained the Athletic in his last two seasons, and Danny Davies records of Tony's leadership: *'Never have I had to record such fantastic scoring in the club's official records as those of the past two seasons.'* Indeed, he captioned season 1973-74. *'The Rags capture the Limelight'.*

P53, W40, L11, D2. Points 1,186-511 Tries 190-61 Pens 47-64

We will end the reporting upon Cardiff at the end of this season, as the last Williams, Tony, returned to play with his brother Elwyn for Taff's Well and, with Elwyn, to coach them to the Silver Ball Trophy. Hooker Garry Davies played 12 seasons for Cardiff Firsts, from 1963-64, following Billy Thomas, and was to play in 281 First XV matches until 1974-75. He was now elected captain after many years of loyal service, and Davies chose as vice-captain wing Alec Finlayson. Newport centre Paul Evans joined, along with Llanharan wing forward Trevor Worgan and Pyle hooker Alan Phillips, a future Wales player. The forward Mark McJennett, son of the immediate post-war forward Ian McJennett, also joined, along with a great scrum half Brynmor Williams from Cardigan. Davies called him *'the find* of the season, the scrum half Brynmor Williams who was to show ability of international class.' With Gareth Edwards missing many games, Brynmor was a real favourite with spectators. On the 1977 Lions Tour to New Zealand, he played in the first three Tests – he was injured in the third – **before** being capped for Wales. He would have played in all four Tests otherwise. **Cardiff's second choice scrumhalf was first choice for the British Lions.** Because of the presence of Gareth Edwards, Brynmor had to wait for his Wales cap until 1978, scoring against Australia, and only had two more caps in 1981. Not many men can play in only three internationals and in three Lions Tests. Bryn's brother Gwynfor played 60 times, also at scrumhalf for Cardiff between 1973 and 1985. Brynmor's son Lloyd, yet another scrumhalf, for Cardiff Blues, has 31 Welsh caps and is a Barbarian. A younger son, full-back or wing Tom Williams has also played for Scarlets, Cardiff Blues and now plays for Jersey Reds.

Brynmor recounts how the Williams brothers helped him, a young West Walian from outside the normal catchment area, get into the Cardiff team: '*As a young local lad, I was always playing rugby with friends on Mwnt beach as a 13/14 /15-year-old. The Williams brothers were all holidaying there, and would play touch rugby with us. I was born two miles from Mwnt and it was 'lucky for me' that the famous Taff's Well family had a caravan there. I knew their sister the late Enid Pritchard and her daughter Mary. Enid was a lovely lady and massive Cardiff supporter and, believe it or not, helped me on my way when I came through the schoolboy ranks. I got connected to Cardiff RFC in early 70's through the Williams family. I also knew Bleddyn's daughters Lynne and Leslie very well. There was a period in my development where Bleddyn, Tony, Lloyd and Enid were very influential and helpful. I met all the brothers, real gentlemen, but was closer to Bleddyn, Tony and Lloyd from the days down at Mwnt, where Bleddyn had a caravan and later a cottage. I used to cycle to Mwnt to keep fit and play rugby on the beach with Bleddyn, Tony and Lloyd, and knew Edith Pritchard, their sister, down there. I played Welsh trials and for the Wales under 15s and under 18s, and used to buy 'the Pink un,' the Football Echo, based in Cardiff, as that had all the reports, so I knew what the opposition was like. It helped to know who the other scrum halves were in the trials, as Cardigan was out of the way of all the clubs whose boys played in trials. At Cardiff Training College, I met Roy Bish and got into the Athletic and played lots of times for the Firsts, as Gareth often had injuries or other commitments.*'

To be honest, Cardiff has often been blessed with overlapping international scrum halves. In the post-war period of this book, we have Haydn Tanner (73 games, 1947-48 to 1948-49); Rex Willis (208 games 1947-48 to 1957-58); Lloyd Williams (310 games, 1952-53 to 1963-64); Billy Hullin (152 games 1963-64 to 1968-69) before his banking job took him to London where he played 7 seasons for London Welsh; Gareth

Edwards (150 games 1966-67 to 1974-75); and Brynmor Williams (98 games 1972-73 to 1977-78). As mentioned, Brynmor was so good that he was chosen for the Lions before he played for Wales, and Gary Samuel played 112 games from 1965-66 to 1974-75, substituting for internationals Hullin, Edwards and Brynmor. Davies writes in 1974-75 – *'But the glut of top-class scrum halves could not, last and after serving Cardiff so loyally since 1965-66, Gary Samuel left to join and serve the Pontypridd Club with much distinction.'* In 1966-67, Samuel played 13 times, Hullin 37 and Edwards 10; 1967-68 Samuel 11, Edwards 12, Hullin 23; 1968-69 Samuel 13, Edwards 10, Hullin 16; 1969-70 Samuel 11, Edwards 17; 1970-71 Samuel 18, Edwards 19; 1971-72 Samuel 12, Edwards 19, Gwilym Treharne 22; 1972-73 Samuel 18, Edwards 25; 1973-74 Samuel 10, Edwards 14, Brynmor Williams 25; 1974-75 Samuel 2, Edwards 19, Williams 22; 1975-76 Edwards 15, Williams 22, Terry Holmes 6; 1976-77 Edwards 20, Williams 16, Holmes 12; 1977-78 Edwards 15, Williams 2, Holmes 26. In his 12 seasons with Cardiff, Edwards' injuries and other appearances meant that his top appearances were 20 and 25 games, averaging 15 games a season. In Lloyd Williams' 12 seasons, interrupted by National Service, he only played 44 times in his first four seasons, but in his next eight years he played 37, 21, 36, 33, 32, 34, 34 and 38 times, averaging 33 games each season.

Hullin, Gareth Edwards, Brynmor Williams and Terry Holmes gave Cardiff four overlapping Welsh international scrum halves and three British Lions. Brynmor Williams left for Newport for a couple of years, but in the years 1973-74 to 1976-77, played for Cardiff 85 times to 70 by Edwards, and was much-loved by supporters. After such a long service as Gareth's deputy, and faced with British Lion Brynmor's form, Gary Samuel went to play for three seasons at Pontypridd. He had also seen the emergence in Cardiff of a player who won a record number of Wales Youth caps, who in 1974-75 aged just 17 played for Cardiff. Terry Holmes was a truly inspiring rugby player, and like Lloyd Williams, had the strength and build to act like another wing forward. He used to hand off second rows, for Heaven's sake. *'Holmesy'*, with a bunch of Cardiff 'mates' who had played together in Cardiff school and youth teams, became the mainstay of a great Cardiff team in the 1980s. It would be remiss not to add a little about my joint-favourite Cardiff scrumhalf, who played 193 times for Cardiff, scoring 123 tries. Terry Holmes' team won the Welsh Cup in 1981, 1982 and 1984 and were finalists in 1977 and 1985. Holmes was club captain 1984-95, aged only 21, Holmes succeeded Gareth Edwards as Wales scrumhalf, scoring a try against Australia, in 1978. Terry Holmes won the Triple Crown in 1979, and played 25 times for Wales, captaining the team 5 times in 1985. Holmes was first-choice scrumhalf for the British and Irish Lions on the 1980 tour to South Africa and the 1983 tour to New Zealand, but was injured and returned early from both tours. In late 1985, Holmes joined Bradford Northern for a fee worth around £450,000 today, but injury meant that he had to retire after only 40 games. He was a devastating attacker and defender.

Cardiff began the season scoring 11 tries in beating Cognac in Cardiff 56-0, avenging the previous year's away loss when Cardiff had fielded a very weakened team. Then the touring Northern Suburbs of Sydney were defeated in October, 9 tries to nil, in a 44-6 win, despite Ian Robinson being sent off. Newport were beaten 16-6 away in October, then 38-14 at home under floodlights, 8 tries to 2. Cardiff then lost on penalties 6-3 away at Rodney Parade before winning at home 12-4. The season finished 13-4 on tries to Cardiff, yet another year when neither of the two rivals could not quite pull off the 'quadruple'. The following season Cardiff again won 3 and lost 1. Bristol were beaten with 5 tries to nil, 30-3; Pontypridd by 6 tries to nil, 34-6; Coventry by 6 tries to 1, 36-13 and Harlequins also by 6 tries to 1, 33-10. Cardiff, on their day, with a full team, were a real handful when they were running the ball. With Cardiff missing some players on the morning of the Wales-Scotland game, they outscored Heriots F.P. by 7 tries to 1 in a 35-9 win. And Davies records that '*On the morning of the England/Wales international, London Welsh were thrashed by 34 points to four through some great attacking Rugby. The Welsh were without John Dawes and Gerald Davies on duty for Wales, but they still turned out six internationals, Jim Shanklin, Keith Hughes. Jeff Young, T. G. Evans, Mike Roberts and John Taylor. Cardiff were without Gareth Edwards and Ian Robinson on duty at Twickenham.*' It was yet another win, 34-4, 7-1 on tries. In this season, as always in their history, Cardiff scored more tries, 190-61, and we again see their incredible recurring statistic of scoring fewer penalties, 47 against 64, although winning far more games.

Davies rarely describes any games in detail, but this account shows what many games were like: '*There was the victory over Bridgend (A) by 21 points to 18, it was in the third round of the W.R.U. Challenge Cup. It was a cracker of a game. Cardiff starting off with a bang, scoring two excellent tries - one involving a run of 75 yards in which six players handled. But Bridgend struck back with three penalty goals from Ian Lewis, then a try and conversion, then a dropped goal which put them into the lead at half time by 18 points to 8. Cardiff pulled back in the second half. P. L. Jones scored a very good try, which was followed by a brilliant solo one from Paul Evans, which, converted by Keith James equalled the scoring. At this stage there was only one side in it, and from a quick heel on the Bridgend twenty-five the ball was fed to Keith James who dropped the goal - suffering a late tackle - to give Cardiff victory by 21 points to 18 shortly before no-side. A great win this.*' Cardiff scored 4 tries to 1 in this cup game, but lost at home to Bridgend 13-11, each side scoring 2 tries, with a penalty by Steve Fenwick in the last minute deciding the game. However, half of Cardiff's First XV were playing for East Wales against Australia at

Newport, winning 19-11. And away Cardiff lost 13-7 to Bridgend, with a try apiece.

Away at Llanelli on 24 November, Cardiff suffered some injuries, and were hammered 26-0, an event that Danny Davies records – *'Up to this point in the meetings between our two clubs, Llanelli had never scored more than 20 points against the Blue & Blacks... In Cardiff's programme notes for the home match, Dai Hayward our programme editor recalls receiving Christmas cards from some of his Llanelli friends. The frontispiece showed the scoreboard after the November match Caerdydd 0, Llanelli 26, and below this, the cryptic words, "The scoreboard tells the story"'*. Llanelli's top scores in all the 179 non-cup fixtures between 1880-81 and 1972-73 had been 20, 17, 19, and 20. Cardiff had recorded scores against the Scarlets over the same period of 42, 22, 34, 40, 17, 18, 17, 22, 19, 17, 20, 19, 22, 35, 27, 19, 21, 19, 19, 22 and 19, with a try tally up to 1972-73 of Cardiff 336 – Llanelli 212. Despite Llanelli's proud history as an open, running team, Cardiff leads all clubs in the United Kingdom in its records of tries being more important than penalties. Plus, it needs repeating that Cardiff had the hardest fixture list in Europe.

Gareth Edwards won his 36th consecutive Welsh cap, surpassing the 35 gained by Swansea's R. M. 'Dicky' Owen in 1901-02. Edwards was the youngest Welsh captain ever, leading Wales for the 16th time in the win against England at Twickenham in March. Davies notes: *'Gareth, the greatest of all scrum halves, followed three other great Cardiff inside halves of post-war seasons, Haydn Tanner (earliest caps with Swansea) 1935-49, 25 caps, Rex Willis 1950-55 with 21 and Lloyd Williams 1957-62, 11 caps. In the summer of 1974, Gareth was vice-captain of the most successful and unbeaten British Lions team, which toured South Africa. It was his third Lions tour.'* Leading try scorers were wing Alec Finlayson 31 (four against Newport in November under floodlights), wing P. Lyn Jones 21, centre Paul Evans 15, Brynmor Williams (who Davies calls *'our third scrum half'*) 13, Roger Lane 12 and Mervyn John 11. Outside half Keith James scored 135 points from 5 tries and 46 goals, including 10 dropped goals. Full back John Davies achieved 108 points from 3 tries and 37 goals. Paul Evans, John Luff, Barry Nelmes and Brynmor Williams had 1st XV caps.

In his last season, Tony Williams only played 5 times for the First XV, touching down 4 times, and all his games were won. He captained the Rags again, his team scoring 40 points and over, on 12 occasions. The record was: P35, W30, L5. **Points 1,106 - 273. Tries 209 - 34. Penalties 27 - 42.** The average score was 32-8, and the try differential was 6:1. As Davies notes: *'it **was a splendid season in which Tony's leadership played a major part**...*

The Athletic were so good that Davies set a precedent by listing the 12 matches in which they scored over 40 points and over (SG = Sophia

Gardens):

Sept 15 H – CG6 T2 Pts 44 – Coventry Extra Firsts PG1 Pts 3
Oct 27 H – CG6 T2 Pts 44 – Newport H.S.O.B. PG1 Pts 3
Nov 3 H - CG6 T5 Pts 56 – Llantwit Major nil
Nov 24 H - CG12 T6 Pts **96** – Llanelly Wanderers PG1 Pts **3**
Dec 22 A – CG4 T9 Pts 60 – Cardiff H.S.O.B. PG1 Pts3
Dec 29 SG - CG6 T10 Pts 76 - Chepstow CG1 Pts 6
Jan 19 SG – CG5 T6 Pts 54 – Pontyclun CG1 T1 PG1 Pts 13
Jan 26 SG – CG6 T4 Pts 52 – Aberavon Quins nil
Feb 23 A – CG3 T5 PG1 Pts 41 – Llanelli Wanderers PG1 Pts 3
March 9 SG – CG3 T8 Pts 50 – Cardiff TC 2nd CG1 T1 Pts10
Apr 13 A – CG 4 T4 Pts 40 Ebbw Vale Athletic T2 PG1 Pts 11
Apr 24 A – CG6 T5 Pts 56 – St. Joseph's nil

Cardiff <u>CG67 T66 PG1 Pts 669</u> - Opponents <u>CG3 T4 PG8 Pts 58</u>

In these 12 fixtures, there were **133 tries**, of which 67 were converted, and **a single penalty goal**, against **7 tries**, 3 converted, and **8 penalty goals**. The stats show what a well-oiled, running machine this team was. Davies writes of the games: *'The first of these was the massacre of Llanelli Wanderers by Cardiff's record score of 96 points to three… One victory which gave more satisfaction than others higher up the points scale was the 44-3 win over Coventry Extra 1sts who, at home in 1972-73, thrashed "The Rags" by 42 points to three. In that season, 1972-73, when 40 points or more were scored in eleven matches, the points totalled 663 to 104 and tries 119 to 11. Never have I had to record such fantastic scoring in the club's official records as those of the past two seasons. It must be remembered, however, that from 1971-72 the try value was increased to four points. But these high scores surely indicate that Cardiff's traditional attacking standards were followed, **a tribute to the leadership of Tony Williams** who must rank as one of the very best of all Cardiff Athletic XV captains. The five defeats were from the strongest of clubs, Senghennyd 9-6, Pontypool Utd. (twice) 7-3 and 7-6, Bristol Utd. 9-6 and Swansea Athletic 17-6'.*

Brian 'Smokey' Coles scored 20 tries, Steve McCann 17, Mark McJennett and Gary Samuel 12 each and Tony Williams 11, playing in 32 out of the 35 games. Tony could have spent another season or two, 'bringing along' newcomers to the Athletic, but decided to help his home village club. Fly-half Dave Barry scored 110 points from 4 tries and 39 goals and Leighton Davies scored 97 from 9 tries and 27 goals. David Barry, Paul Kerrigan, John Manfield (son of Les), Mark McJennett (son of Ian), Alan Phillips and Trevor Worgan won Athletic caps. Cardiff Juniors' record was P26, W20, L6. Points 721-248. Full-back and captain Paul Simmonds, vice-captain and flanker Tony Brahim and Terry Holmes all gained Welsh Youth international caps.

In the following season, 1974-75, John Hickey led the Athletic to a fabulous season, losing only 2 games, to Pontypool United away 4-3, and Swansea Athletic away 15-7, with *'a very weak and rearranged team'*. 10 Youth players had to be drafted into the 65 players used in Hickey's season, and no less than 52 men scored points. 6 games were cancelled, which makes the season record all the more extraordinary. In 36 games, 34 were won and 2 lost, with 1,218 points against 246. The stats were Cardiff CG115 T105 DG9 PG27 Pts 1,218: opponents CG7 T18 DG2 PG42 Pts 246. **The try record of 220-25 is incredible**. On average, Cardiff were winning games by 6 tries to 0.7 of a try. Wins scoring 40 points and over were Chepstow 104-0; Llanelly Wanderers 94-0; Welsh Guards 86-3; Maesteg Celtic 64-6; Taibach 62-6; Barry 56-10; Fishguard 45-0; Harlequins Wanderers 42-12 and Llanharan 40-15.

The Five Nations Championship ended with all five teams on 4 points, but Wales on top with points difference. Wales started off with a bang against England, scoring 5 unanswered tries to win 25-9 at home, and there were instant thoughts of another Grand Slam. However, it was followed by a 10-9 loss at Murrayfield, a 16-12 home win against Ireland, and a 12-3 away loss to France. Gareth Edwards, Gerald Davies and John Bevan were the Cardiff players involved in all matches. Alec Finlayson and Ian Robinson gained their first Welsh caps. Gareth Edwards led Wales to a 24–0 win over Australia in November 1973. And in 1974, Gerald Davies decided to return to Cardiff from London Welsh. Edwards and Davies were picked for the 1974 Lions tour to South Africa, although Davies, like John Taylor, refused to go in protest against *apartheid*. Edwards started all four Tests, where the Lions went unbeaten through all 22 matches and would probably have won all their games, but in the final Test the South African referee blew the final whistle four minutes early with the scores level and the Lions camped on the South African line. Ah, memories...

CARDIFF SCRUMHALVES

If we may just mention the following season, 1974-75, from Davies' history of the club: *'Where the club was strong was at scrumhalf. It was able to call upon no less than six for that position, Gareth Edwards after his return from the Lions South African tour, Brynmor Williams, Gary Samuel, Robin Morgan, Terry Holmes and Nick Rose, the latter two from our Juniors XV. Brynmor Williams played for Wales v. Tonga, R. C. Shell of Aberavon having withdrawn, but his appearance with those of Gareth Edwards in the other Wales internationals, created what is probably unique in international Rugby, that of a club having* **two international scrum half-backs in the same season.**' (Tonga was an unofficial international with no caps awarded, so Brynmor had to wait until after his

1977 Lions tour, playing in 3 tests, before playing for Wales between 1978 and 1981 and being capped.) '*But the glut of top-class scrum halves could not last and after serving Cardiff so loyally since 1965-66, Gary Samuel left to join and serve the Pontypridd Club with much distinction. Robin Morgan also left the club after assisting it since 1971-72, and Pontypool R.F.C. was pleased to acquire this first-class player. On 22nd March at short notice, Terry Holmes, Cardiff Juniors captain made his first team debut for the Seniors against Newport (A) and shared in a notable victory. Nick Rose, the Juniors second scrum half choice, made his first team debut for Cardiff against New Brighton in April, a winning match for the Blue and Blacks which young Rose will ever remember.*'

1973-74 Best friends, Bledyyn and Jack in the Cardiff clubhouse

Simon Thomas, in *walesonline* 29 December 2021 interviewed Terry Holmes: *"I was born in Churchill Way in Cardiff and then lived in Fairwater. I suppose I was probably about 14, 15, when I was playing for Cardiff Schools, that I first realised I was quite good at rugby. I was at Bishop Hannon School in Fairwater at the time. That's long since closed. I played outside-half for a bit, but the teachers wanted to get me nearer the ball. I was small when I was younger, but then from about 16 to about 19, I had a growth spurt. I probably wasn't the ideal build for scrumhalf at that point, but I never thought of moving. That was my position by then."* It was in March 1975 that he made his senior debut for Cardiff, just days after his 18th birthday, and up against arch-rivals Newport, of all teams. *"I played on the Friday night for Cardiff & District and then they phoned me Saturday morning, because there were a few injuries, and told me I was playing,"* he recalls. In theory, the young Holmes could hardly have had a

595

more daunting task - for Cardiff and then Wales - stepping into the boots of Gareth Edwards. In theory, that is. *"I didn't really see it as that, to be honest, I don't think anyone could follow him, could they really? It was my home club, my hometown, so just playing for them was something I always wanted to do.* *"Being Cardiff born-and-bred definitely made it that more special for me."* Holmes soon made his presence felt, with his power, his raw strength and his predatory nature near to the line. He was like a ninth forward and, at times, simply unstoppable. *"Probably, technically, I wasn't as good as people like Dave Loveridge,"* he acknowledges. *"But I played a different game. If you were picking someone technically, you probably wouldn't have picked me. I just played the way that came naturally to me."*

As previously mentioned, Brynmor Williams is much-loved by older Cardiff supporters – when Gareth was unavailable, it was Brynmor donning his boots in Abertillery on a stormy Wednesday night. He was incredibly unfortunate to have been sandwiched between Edwards and 'Holmsey', and like Elwyn Williams could have 'walked' into any other first-class team or international side. Cardiff have been blessed with half-backs, and a *walesonline* article by Mark Orders, 28 January 2018, noted the top Welsh scrum-halves of the past 50 years. At number 10 is Ray 'Chico' Hopkins, a lovely man who was unfortunate, like Brynmor Williams, of playing at the same time as Gareth Edwards. *'The Maesteg product made only two appearances in Test rugby, but they will resonate with all who were around to witness them. He came off the bench to inspire Wales to rally from 13-6 down to a 17-13 victory over England at Twickenham, setting up a try for JPR Williams and scoring one himself. He was Wales's player of the year in 1970s. Hopkins's other Test outing saw him feature as a replacement in the ninth minute for Edwards, for the Lions in their 9-3 win over New Zealand in 1971. He beat the All Blacks with Llanelli the following year, meaning he boasted a 100 per cent record against them. Hopkins was strong and a bundle of energy, a player who took on back rows and made things happen. He switched to rugby league at the age of 26.'* 'Chico' was to be seen sitting with the late Phil Bennett after all Llanelli's home games, a great, and unlucky, character. At 9 is Rhys Webb, sadly left out of the Welsh 2019 World Cup squad as he was playing for the best team in Europe, Toulon, instead of lower-class rugby in Wales – a truly moronic decision. Number 8 is Llanelli's British Lion Dwayne Peel, who played in 76 games for Wales, and at 7 is Cardiff's Brynmor Williams. *'Maybe Brynmor Williams was the most unfortunate of Wales No.9s. After shadowing Gareth Edwards for so long with club and country, he then saw Terry Holmes rise to prominence. But Williams was a terrific player in his own right, a scrumhalf with a long pass who understood the game and could make searing breaks. He started three Tests for the Lions in New Zealand in 1977 and his tally of just three caps for Wales didn't reflect his talent.'*

Mark Orders places Mike Phillips, at his best playing for Cardiff, at 6th:
'There are many who have described Phillips in his pomp as being a great rugby player, with his will to win, supreme fitness, remarkable defensive play and ability to lift his performance level in big games. Was he a great scrumhalf? The supremely confident man himself would have said so, tongue just a little bit in cheek. He didn't have a classical pass and some said he didn't marshal a game through expert box-kicking, but the 6ft 3in, 16st Bancyfelin product was massively physical and often inspirational to those around him. Phillips stood tall on the Lions tours of 2009 and 2013 and was widely seen as best scrumhalf at the 2011 World Cup.' Fifth was Robert Jones of Swansea and Cardiff, who suffered from being in a poor Welsh side, and fourth was a magical, hard player from Cardiff, *'Bish'*, who never played for the club but was friends with most of its players, especially schoolfriends Mark Ring and Paul 'Pablo' Rees: *'Neath's then rugby supremo Brian Thomas rated David Bishop the finest rugby player in the northern hemisphere at one point during the 1980s. That the Pontypool player was capped just once says more about the Wales selectors than about him. He could fairly be described as a one-man army on a rugby pitch. Bishop bossed games with unshakeable self-belief; he won matches with breath-taking interventions; he galvanised those around him to believe they could win. But he was too hot for the Welsh selectors to handle. He famously wiggled his backside at them after landing a winning penalty out of the mud for Pontypool against Swansea, and some of his off-field exploits weren't guaranteed to endear him to everyone. But Bishop was an extraordinary player.'*

In third place is Cardiff's Rob Howley – *'Those fortunate enough to have been at the Arms Park for the Worthington Sevens in the summer of 1995 would have witnessed Rob Howley pulling off three try-saving tackles in the final, on Swansea's flying wing Simon Davies. Few scrum-halves would have had the pace to get near Davies that day, but Howley did. Wales let him wait until he was 26 for his first cap; few understood why, for he had been consistently excellent at club level for many years before. Welsh player of the year in 1996 and 1997, he scored spectacular tries and was on top of the basics. It was his misfortune to have played during a largely bumpy era for Wales, though he led the side during a period of respite under Graham Henry, when they strung together 10 consecutive wins. Injuries cost him more than the two Lions Test caps he pocketed on the 2001 tour of Australia, when a broken rib robbed him of a spot in the decider. He really didn't deserve such a fate. Some called him the finest British and Irish scrumhalf since Gareth Edwards. Whether that was right or not, he was a top-class operator, a match-winner.'*

Second was my favourite Cardiff scrumhalf, along with Brynmor, Terry Holmes. I was at *Holmesy's* last away game at Leicester, where the referee was, how shall I put this? Bad beyond belief. Holmes knew that the only way to win was to grab the ball and not pass it, otherwise a forward pass would be called or any other infringement that the ref could think of at the time. Come halftime, Holmes decided that there was only one way to win the game. Terry just ran in two tries from near halfway, refusing to pass, in case a forward pass was called, and from long range broke and made another try, for Cardiff to beat the referee. Awesome. *'If Gareth Edwards was the toughest of acts to follow, Terry Holmes still made some fist of it. Wales's forward play had started to retreat from the heights of previous years, when the 6ft 1in, 13st 3lb Cardiff youngster came through in the summer of 1978, but if you wanted someone to play for your life behind a beaten pack, that person would surely be Terry Holmes. He had the strength to take on opposition back rows, an iron will and was blessed with a ferociously competitive spirit. In some games, he appeared to be taking on the opposition on his own. He scored tries and was consistently outstanding for club and country, notwithstanding that backrows identified him as a threat and targeted him. Identified as an outstanding prospect when coming through with Cardiff in 1973-74, he lived up to expectations. Oh, and he was also a gentleman on and off the pitch who had a reputation for fair play. Injuries may have punctuated his career, but he was the genuine article.'*

Number 1 is, of course, Gareth Edwards, still voted *'the best player of all time'*: *'Maybe Wales will one day produce a better scrumhalf than Gareth Edwards. But probably not. Will Carling once wrote: "He was outstanding at running, passing, kicking and reading the game. He played in the 1970s but if he played now, he would still be the best." There is no exaggeration there. A schoolboy gymnast and athlete who could play football, Edwards had the strength, power, athleticism and skill to shape and win rugby matches. His tactical display in the wind and rain against England at Twickenham in 1978 saw him produce one of the greatest displays of kicking out of hand the game has seen from a scrumhalf, with the ball often raking 50 metres upfield, skidding along the ground before heading into touch. There were the miracle tries, but so much more. The Welsh Rugby Union's official history called him "a back amongst backs" but also "a forward amongst forwards." He remains the gold standard.'* So there we have it, in a 70 year period, **Rex Willis** and **Haydn Tanner** would have been included, but Cardiff scrum-halves included are **Gareth Edwards** (1), **Terry Holmes** (2), **Rob Howley** (3) (– and it is a pity we cannot include Dai Bishop at 4 because he was Cardiff through and through), **Robert Jones** (also Swansea 5) – **Mike Phillips** (6) and **Brynmor Williams** (7). Six of the top seven scrum-halves were Cardiff players, and in fourth place was Dai Bishop, from Cardiff who wanted to play for the club. It could easily have been 7 out of 7.

ANTHONY DAVID 'TONY' WILLIAMS 1 February 1941 – 3 September 2014
Christ College, Brecon
Cardiff Youth
Wales Youth
15 seasons Cardiff 1ˢᵗ XV from 1959-60 to 1973-74 Fly-half, centre, sometimes wing and stand-in captain
328 games and 67 tries for Cardiff Firsts
Barbarians 30 March 1970 vs Swansea, won 24-8
Crawshays XV
A Record 16 Sevens Tournaments for Cardiff, 11 as captain, twice *'Player of the Tournament'*. 1969 captained Cardiff to win the Harlequins, Snelling and Welsh National Sevens. Snelling Sevens - 1963, 1965, 1966, 1967, 1968, 1969. Gala 1965 – Newport 1969, Harlequins 1968, 1969 - WRU National 1968, 1969, 1970, 1971, 1973 – Aberaeron 1973.
Captain Cardiff Athletic 1972-73 and 1973-74
182 games for Cardiff Athletic = **510 games for Cardiff** plus charity and other Cardiff matches
Taff's Well RFC 1974-75 to 1975-76
Silver Ball Trophy 1975, with Elwyn Williams
East District Cup 1976, with Elwyn Williams

Tony spent his last two seasons captaining the Athletic before joining Taff's Well again. However, in 1972-73 he played 8 times for the Firsts, scoring 4 tries and a drop goal. In his final season, 1973-74 Tony again scored 4 tries, in 5 fames – not a bad return for a centre, 8 tries and a drop goal in 9 games. He was in the same splendid vein of form when he joined his brother Elwyn at Taff's Well. Under Tony's captaincy, the Athletic set a club record of over 1,165 points in 1972-73. The highest season's points of the Firsts were 1,058 and 1,086 in 1971-72 and 1973-74, in 39 and 40 fixtures respectively. In the Athletic, despite constantly losing players to the Firsts, Tony led the team in fewer fixtures to:
1972-73 Played 38 Won 33 Lost 5 - Points 1165-400 Tries **213-49**
1973-74 Played 35 Won 30 Lost 5 - Points 1106-273 Tries **209-34**
Thus in 1972-73, the Rags scored an average of 5.6 to 1.3 tries per game, 4.3 times as many tries as their opponents. In 1973-74, **they scored 6 to 1 tries** per game, obviously a factor of 6. In those two seasons, Cardiff scored 25 penalties against 47, and then 21 against 35, so their opponents scored almost twice as many penalties. Tony's team ran opponents ragged and refused easy penalties, preferring to score tries. And remember, this was before the days when we saw penalties being kicked, to enable a driving maul from the five-yard line to go over. The present Irish team scores 70% of their tries within three phases of line-out possession. This is not exactly spectacular rugby, but a forward falling or being pushed over

the line from a distance of up to a metre. Cardiff tries came from flowing, running rugby wherever possible. Indeed, many of today's driving mauls, with the ball being transferred backwards to the last man, would have been illegal, as all the forwards in front of the ball would have been judged offside. (To be honest, a man with the ball connected to a fellow player in front of him should mean that the man in front is deliberately offside. It used to be so, before different laws were enacted – which enable the ball to be held and transferred back in a driving maul. If a player runs into one of his team-mates in front of him it is accidentally offside, so why the difference? The game would open up dramatically. Then again, we could have a differential penalty, giving more points to tries scored from open play).

1973-74 Tony scoring

In a Taff's Well Rugby Club display cabinet there is the following tribute to the '*irrepressible*' Tony Williams, in which he may well have had an input into the opening sentences: '*TONY – The youngest of the "Clan" and possibly the best-looking, Tony inevitably followed his brothers to Cardiff. He graduated to the Senior Team via Christ College, Brecon, and made a name for himself as a "Sevens" player. Well-informed people at the Cardiff Club insist that Tony was robbed of international honours. Like*

600

Elwyn, Tony is a Taff's Well man through and through, and when he returned from "First-Class Rugby" in 1974, he was keen to give something to the Village Club. He brought technical expertise and steadiness to our back division, and showed the rest of the team how to tackle properly. Tony's approach to playing can be summed up in one word, "honesty". He never shirked anything in his time with Taff's Well. He became very popular among the players, many of whom were in awe of his reputation when he first came to the club. When Tony retired from playing, he returned to Cardiff to join the rugby committee, and such was his standing in the Club that he was honoured with the Chairmanship in 1978.'

The Cardiff RFC history site records: '*Tony Williams was the youngest of the Williams family from Taff's Well and played 328 games for the first team. One of eight brothers that played for Cardiff he was, like his better known and more illustrious brother Bleddyn, a centre. After progressing through Christ College, Brecon and Cardiff Juniors, he played for Cardiff Athletic in 1959-60 winning his Athletic cap in 1961. His first team debut came against Penarth in 1959 and he was awarded his First XV cap in 1962. Tony was captain of the Athletic XV in 1972-73 and again the following season and he was elected to the Rugby Committee for 1975-76 season.'* Danny Davies writes: '*After fifteen seasons of dedicated service and 328 1st XV matches to his credit, Tony, like his brother Elwyn, decided to sever his links with Cardiff and join his village club, Taff's Well, before finally hanging up his boots. Tony's retirement ended a great era of the Williams family as **one or more of the brothers played for Cardiff in every season since the first of them, Gwyn, made his debut in 1935-36**. A link however is maintained as Lloyd, chairman of the club this season, still serves on the Rugby committee. Tony's service will long be remembered gratefully by the Cardiff Rugby Club and its statistician "Massa" Dan.'* (- Danny Davies).

In '*The Williams Family (More than a Rugby Dynasty)*' there is a press cutting entitled "*Another Bleddyn*"- 'The smallest team ever to ever wear the famous blue and black colours of Cardiff – the "Under 11" Cardiff XV – served up some of the most attractive rugby of recent months, against a similar side drawn from Bridgend and District, as a "curtain-raiser" to the Cardiff-Coventry game on Saturday. There were many famous names represented amongst these pint-sized toddlers; there was a Judd, a Gooding, a Nelson and a Williams… and it was this T. Williams who had the crowd rubbing its eyes in sheer, downright disbelief as he capped a superb display with a 40-yard run in which side-steps, changes of pace and double-shuffles were included. "*Look!*" shouted one delirious fan, "*It's the 'jink' – the Bleddyn 'jink' – all over again!*" And, quite soberly, it was! "T. Williams", the diminutive Cardiff "Under 11" fly half, was none other than Tony, youngest of the famous Williams clan. If the pitch had been smaller, (and a full-sized international pitch is too large for such tiny tots!) we might have seen that 40-yard run end in a try, which would have very favourably compared with the sensational 70-yard dash of "big brother" Bleddyn. One thing for certain, Wales can look forward in 10 years or so to another "*Jink*" Williams to confound her international rivals!'

Regarding Tony, in his review of the 1972-73 Cardiff season, Davies records: '*The sad event was the passing of A. T. Thomas after quite a long and painful illness. Popularly known as "Akka", a splendid wing three-quarter, he played 118 games with distinction in the period 1928-36, subsequently gaining a degree at Aberystwyth, and then serving H.M. Forces as an officer in the Royal Navy during the war. He served on the Cardiff Committee from 1947-48 until he died, although for a number of reasons he reluctantly resigned, to take up a post as sports master at Christ College, Brecon, from where he was to predict that one of his Juniors would become a great player - none other than Tony Williams.*'

Tony Williams

Tony played an astounding total of 510 games for the First and Athletic teams of the most successful rugby team in Europe. Unfortunately for Tony, who always played with a smile on his face, the Welsh fly half and centre roles of his era were occupied by some of the nation's greatest players. And remember these were amateur days of settled international teams, very few games and no, ad then few substitutes. From 1964-71, at the peak of Tony's powers, when he was possibly the best Sevens player in Wales, those positions were occupied by outside halves David Watkins, Barry John and Phil Bennett. And centres were Keith Bradshaw, John 'Dick' Uzzell, D. Ken Jones of Cardiff, John Dawes, Gerald Davies (a centre until 1969, then wing), Maurice Richards (a Cardiff centre, then

602

wing), Billy Raybould, Ian Hall, Arthur Lewis and Roy Bergiers – these were all wonderful players.

In '*The Williams Family*' we read: 'Tony, born in 1941, the youngest of the Williams brothers, graced the football field for fifteen years. Yet another product of that remarkable rugby nursery, Taff's Well School, Tony played for Cardiff under-elevens and then Cardiff Juniors. During his secondary education at Christ's College Brecon, he continued to polish his rugby skills and went on to win Welsh Youth cps. It was almost inevitable that he would quickly become part of the Cardiff set-up and aged just 18 years and one month he played his first game for the 'Rags'. Cardiff Rugby Club must have seemed like '*home from home*' to Tony Williams, for he had watched his illustrious brothers in action there many times. Even when he was very young, he used to go and see Bleddyn play, and he was allowed to sit in a corner of the home changing room before matches. He would be instructed by Tom Holley the trainer to "*sit there and be quiet!*" Watching those Cardiff games from the old dog-track, his ambition to emulate the brothers grew and grew.

In the 1959-60 season, at barely 19, Tony made the first of his 328 appearances for the Cardiff Firsts team. He would also play on 182 occasions for the Athletic, of which he was captain towards the end of his first-class career in 1972-73 and 1973-74. It was a particular pleasure for Tony to be one of four Williams brothers in the same Cardiff side, in matches against Newport, Aberavon, Ebbw Vale and Neath. Also, to have followed his brothers in being selected for the Barbarians was another highlight of his career. Among the disappointments was the injury he sustained, leading up to Cardiff's game against the touring Wallabies in 1966. Torn ligaments kept him out of the game for several weeks, causing him bitter disappointment. However, there was some compensation at the end of the season, in the fact that he was able to go on the club's first overseas tour to South Africa. One of the toughest games Tony can recall is the match against the touring Springboks in 1969, in which he remembers having to defend for 80 minutes!' John Harding, who played for Cardiff between 1966-67 and 1971-72, recalled: '*I first met Tony on the Llandaff RFC rugby field. The event was a Cardiff and District Youth 7's competition Spring 1959. Sevens tournaments were usually arranged to conclude a busy rugby season. Tony was captain of an impressive star-studded Cardiff Youth Team. Coming from the Williams stable, Tony had a lot to live up to. He trained hard, practised basic skills repeatedly, and centre three-quarter moves time and time again. Practice made perfect. As well as being an outstanding centre for the CRFC First XV he was also an outstanding Captain of many 7's campaigns. I joined Cardiff RFC in 1965 and trained and played alongside Tony for many years. Touring with such a determined team player was a deligh*t.'

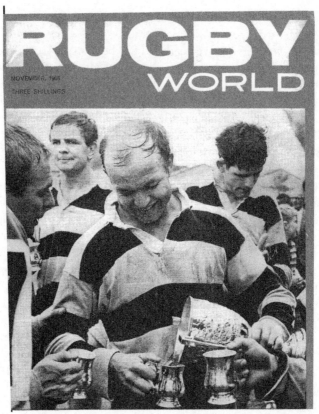

RUGBY WORLD

NOVEMBER, 1968
THREE SHILLINGS

Tony captaining to win yet another Sevens trophy. In 1969 he captained Cardiff win the Snelling, Harlequins and National Sevens. John Huw Williams and Elwyn are on the left, and John Hickey on the right.

'Tony Williams earned a reputation for being a 'master-craftsman' when it came to the seven-a-side version of rugby. Hs ability to 'read' a game, his sudden bursts of speed and his high distribution skills made him a natural for sevens. Despite his phenomenal successes which included leading Cardiff to victories at the Harlequins, the Snelling, and the WRU Sevens Tournaments (in recognition of which the club presented him with an engraved silver plate), he admits to having dreaded those events as the dates came closer. "*The thing about Sevens rugby*" says Tony, "*is that there's no hiding place. If you were out of form, you would be found out!*" Jack Davies told me: '*I had the pleasure of playing for London Welsh against Lloyd in Cardiff in 1963-64 and served with him on the Cardiff Committee from 1971 to the 1990's. On my return to Cardiff in 1964, I became a member of CRFC and played many games with Elwyn and Tony for the First Fifteen and 'The Rags'. All three were highly talented players, great sportsmen and great club representatives. The great Bleddyn Williams was a wise mentor and adviser to me when I joined the CRFC*

Committee in 1971. I am honoured to have been associated with such a marvellous rugby family.'

Tony was the best 'Sevens' player in Wales for a few seasons, and Davies writes of his great success as the Athletic Captain over two seasons: '*Tony Williams was captain, well worthy of the honour. This versatile outside-half learned his Rugby at Taff's Well School and at Christ College, Brecon. He had already played in 315 games for the 1st XV since his debut in 1959-60. He was a great leader, a real driver, with skill and courageous example. At "sevens" he had proved himself as Cardiff's captain and tactician. In this splendid season (1972-73)* **his team was the first to score more than 1,000 points**, *four points for a try of course. Even so, his team scored more than 40 points in no less than eleven matches, including a points record for the club of 93 to 9 over the unfortunate Tonyrefail Club, in the opening match of the season at Sophia Gardens. What a spur to other successes, a 74 points to 12 win over St. David's, Pembs. (A), Llantwit Major beaten 70-13 at Sophia Gardens, Old Illtydians (A) 69-12, Risca (A) 66-4, Milford Haven (A) 62-12, Llanelli Wanderers (S.G.) 54-10 and 52-14 (A), Harlequin Wanderers (S.G.) 52-15, Ebbw Vale Athletic (S.G.) 44-12 and Newport Utd. (S.G.) 41-0. I doubt whether any club of comparable standing has ever scored 228 points in its initial three matches as did Tony's team against Tylorstown, Old Illtydians and Risca. The scoring was fantastic, unparalleled. Seventy-eight players were called upon and 53 took part in the scoring.*'

Bowing out gradually from the first-class game, Tony did what many star players had done previously: he played a couple of seasons for the 'Rags. Tony played a few First Team games, but also captained a terrific Athletic team. In *Welsh Rugby* April 1980, there is a feature celebrating the team's centenary celebrations. Fred Croster reported: '*Some of the scoring records, despite a formidable fixture list, speak for themselves: 72-73 under Tony Williams, they amassed 1,165 points in winning 33 of the 38 matches played. The following season, again with Tony as an inspiring leader, it was 30 wins out of 35, with 1,106 on the board. There was one spell, from November to April, which produced at least 40 points from every game.*' Then it was a matter of honouring his promise to return to Taff's Well where he thoroughly enjoyed his last days of rugby, in the company of his brother Elwyn, who had already made his move to the village side. After his playing career ended, Tony Williams served on the Cardiff committee and in 1994 was elected to the General Committee of the WRU. He is proud, that at this time he was team manager of the Welsh Students. For someone as modest as Tony, it must have come as a shock when one day he was stopped by a complete stranger, walking along Westgate Street who said: "*Thank you for all the enjoyment you gave me when you played for Cardiff*". Tony admits that the remark made him feel "*ten feet tall!*' And here we will end the brothers' contribution to Cardiff

RFC teams, which lasted from Gwyn in 1934-35 to Tony in 1973-74 – **forty years of playing for *"the greatest"*.**'

Tony now joined Elwyn for two years to help Taff's Well to another glorious period in its history. Peter Thomas told me '*I have fond memories of my playing days with Cardiff, but I came at the end of Lloyd's career. I played more with Elwyn and Tony. Both great players with great skills and as fit as any player at their time. One game I remember playing with Tony was against the Harlequins on the old Arms Park (now the Principality Stadium) in 1967, the year we went to South Africa. The reason I remember was I had a pass off Tony on our 25, with the line in front of me, but got tackled from behind and dislocated my shoulder, but thanks to Tony controlling the game playing at 10 we won.*'

In the Cardiff-Harlequins programme of 11 April 1966, won by Cardiff 8-6, Tony Williams or Billy Raybould were down to play outside half, with Elwyn number 6, John Davies number 8 and Dai Hayward or Tony Pender at number 7. In the programme there is a '*Players' Who's Who*' – *Tony Williams. Tony is the youngest of the remarkable Williams family and perhaps the best tribute to their rugby ability lies in the fact that the most memorable game in which he has played was that against Newport in 1961-62 when no fewer than four brothers viz. Lloyd, Cenydd, Elwyn and Tony himself appeared in the Cardiff side that day. This is a record of which any parents would be justly proud. A married man of twenty-five, he weighs 12st. and is 5' 10" tall. He began his rugby career at Christ's College, Brecon and then went on to win Welsh Youth caps in 1958-59 against the Welsh Secondary Schools, France and the Midlands. He was awarded his Athletic XV cap in 1960-61 and the First XV cap in 1961-62. He considers that one of the best players he has played against is David Watkins because of his ability to turn defence very quickly into attack. An office-manager for a wholesale chemist, Tony's form of relaxation in the summer is swimming and tennis. One of the outstanding features of his play is the determined tackling and when broached about what he considers to be the best position he paused a moment before hinting that **he would even play hooker to gain a place in the Cardiff side.***'

SEASON	P	W	D	L	TRY	CON	PEN	DG	PTS
1959-1960	1	1	0	0	0	0	0	0	0
1960-1961	8	5	1	2	4	0	0	0	12
1961-1962	30	19	5	6	1	0	0	0	3
1962-1963	20	10	1	9	5	0	0	0	15
1963-1964	13	11	1	1	1	0	0	1	6
1964-1965	25	16	4	5	5	0	0	0	15
1965-1966	34	25	1	8	5	0	0	2	21
1966-1967	31	19	4	8	5	0	0	0	15
1967-1968	36	24	2	10	6	0	0	1	21

1968-1969	40	28	3	9	9	0	0	0	27
1969-1970	25	19	2	4	10	0	0	0	30
1970-1971	36	22	5	9	3	0	0	0	9
1971-1972	16	10	0	6	4	0	0	1	19
1972-1973	8	4	0	4	4	0	0	1	19
1973-1974	5	5	0	0	4	0	0	0	16
TOTAL	**328**	**218**	**29**	**81**	**66**	**0**	**0**	**6**	**228**

Cardiff R.F.C. Epilogue

Danny Davies added an *Epilogue* to his wonderful history *Cardiff Rugby Club – History and Statistics 1876-1975*, from which we read:
'Last year I read a report by Arthur Trembath, writer to the *"Sunday People"*, on a match between Neath and Cardiff in April 1974. He opened his report by saying, *"If there's one club calculated to bring the best out of the opposition, it's Cardiff"*. A tribute to greatness? A club is not "Great" because of its age, or because of its periods of Rugby brilliance during its history. It must have a traditional standard of Rugby in the spirit of the game, pleasing both to its players and public. **A club is "Great" only if it retains the admiration of its adversaries and all clubs, for its standard of sportsmanship**, whilst at the same time retaining its hospitable and administrative reputation in the Rugby world… The players enjoy facilities second to none in the matter of equipment, modern dressing rooms, social rooms and travelling arrangements. They are *privileged to play on the Cardiff Arms Park* – the Mecca of the Rugby world! If, as I have often heard them describe Cardiff as *"the greatest club in the world"* they must *"play up, play up and play the game"*, and help to maintain its greatness.'

Eight Brothers - and all... Cardiff players! J.B.G. Thomas (Chief Rugby critic 'Western Mail') Rugby World, July 1961

The great rugby writer, known to one and all as 'JBG' wrote the following, 13 years before the last two brothers, Elwyn and Tony, retired, and the remarkable Cenydd 'went North'. Although our full attention upon Cardiff RFC finishes with this chapter, season 1973-74, his article serves as an elegant resume of the brothers' careers and the love of their parents.
'Number 11, Moy Road, Taff's Well, is the home of Britain's proudest rugby family. Here, in this small village seven miles north of Cardiff in the heart of Glamorgan, live Mr. and Mrs. Arthur Williams, whose boast to sporting fame is that their eight sons all play or have played or Cardiff Rugby Club. Seven of them have performed with distinction for the first XV, and two, indeed, have led Wales. A search through the records reveals this as unparalleled, and it must be a tremendous source of pride for the two likeable and modest parents who, unless cross-questioned, are most

reluctant to sing the praises of their family. I called at the Williams' home some weeks ago and discussed the "boys" with their parents. I wrote down their names and age in order, and the honoured list reads as follows: Gwyn (43 years old), Brinley (40), Bleddyn (38), Vaughan (29), Lloyd (27), Cenydd (22), Elwyn (21) and Tony (20). There are also four daughters to complete a happy family of 12.

As I sat chatting to the parents, Mrs. Williams was preparing high tea for two of the sons still living at home, Vaughan and Elwyn, and Mr. Williams commented: "*Much of the reason for their success has been the wonderful care and cooking of my wife.*" All eight sons attended the local school at Taff's Well, where the now-retired headmaster, Captain W.S. Trigg, played an important role in their Rugby development. I spoke to him recently about the family, and he told me: "*I have never known a sequence of brothers take to the game so easily. The eldest boy, Gwyn, was basically one of the greatest schoolboy players I have ever seen, and so mature was he **at 13 years old that he had no difficulty in holding a place in the village senior side**. He turned professional when on the brink of a great international career in the Union code, and it was left to Bleddyn to prove himself the top Union player in the family. I hoped that Gwyn would win a schoolboy cap but, as my school was not then in a district organisation, he was recommended for international honours only at the last moment. Then, when his birth certificate weas produced, it was found that he was three weeks over age.*" It sufficed to say that **Gwyn was in the Cardiff first XV at the tender age of 16 as a forward**, and this record is likely to remain unique in the club's history.

Seven of the eight brothers passed through the guiding hands of Captain Trigg, and when he handed over the reins as headmaster of the village school, his faithful successor, the late Mr. Del Harries, carried on the tradition and looked after the youngest, Tony, before he left for Christ's College, Brecon. The village of Taff's Well is proud of the Williams family, and the former secretary of the village club, W.R.U. referee Mr. David Millward, once commented: "*It was always a great relief for me as club secretary to know that I could call on one of the younger members of the family to fill a gap in the side on Saturday morning, and never once did they let me down!*" Gwyn was one of the two forwards among the eight brothers, and he played for Cardiff in the backrow of the scrum before turning professional just before World War II. He was a police constable in Bargoed and unable to obtain leave regularly to play for Cardiff. Gwyn quickly established himself in Rugby League football and earned a "cap" playing for Wales. When war was declared in 1939, he volunteered for the Welsh Guards and took part in many Service international matches, in which League and Union players joined together to form strong Welsh XVs. Unfortunately, Gwyn was badly wounded in North Africa and had to spend much time in hospital recovering from a wound in the head. That

608

ended his Rugby career, but he still follows the game he loves and the activities of his brothers.

While Gwyn was achieving glory as a League player just before the war, the third son, Bleddyn, was a pupil at Rydal College in North Wales. He had been accepted on the recommendation of a former pupil, Wilfred Wooller, who was then a successful member of the Cardiff and Wales XV's. Bleddyn served his school with distinction and appeared for Cardiff while on holidays in the last official season before the war. Bleddyn was top scorer for the School XV, but failed to win a place in the Welsh Secondary Schools XV because of a broken ankle. Prior to this, while a member of the Taff's Well school team, he had won a Welsh schools cap at full-back for boys under 14 years of age. When his schooldays ended, Bleddyn volunteered for the R.A.F. in 1942, but there was a waiting list for pilot training, and he returned to Cardiff to find temporary employment before the final call came. He went into the war-time Cardiff XV under the captaincy of Hubert Johnson, the club's present vice-chairman, and, with other young players like Billy Cleaver and Jack Matthews, developed rapidly. He had joined the R.A.F. in December 1942, and a few weeks later refused an invitation to play for the Barbarians, in the hope that he would get leave to go home for Christmas.

He did not get his leave and thought he would never be asked to play for the Barbarians again, but he did, and played many times with distinction for them. Bleddyn appeared for Rosslyn Park, as well as in the Welsh Services XV, before doing his pilot's training in America. On gaining his wings, he returned to play for R.A.F. representative sides, and then came the first full season after the war, 1945-46, when Bleddyn was one of the Cardiff 'stars'. He appeared in Victory internationals, and in January 1947 got his first full cap for Wales at outside half against England at Cardiff. England lost, but Bleddyn decided he was a centre, and from then onwards appeared 21 times for his country in that position to earn the title of one of the great players of modern times. His fine play for Cardiff, with W.B. Cleaver, J. Matthews and H. Tanner during the record season of 1947-48 is now legendary, as are his later performances for Cardiff and Wales, particularly in 1953-54, when he was captain of the only two British sides, Cardiff and Wales, to beat the All Blacks.

Bleddyn Williams was vice-captain of the 1950 British Lions in Australia and New Zealand and a member of the memorable Barbarians XV which defeated the Wallabies in 1947-48. He retired in 1955, having won all the honours in the game he had adorned so well, but another son, Lloyd, was knocking at the door of fame. Lloyd played for the Taff's Well School and the successful Cardiff District Schools XV in the Dewar Shield competition before graduating to the Cardiff Youth XV and winning a Welsh Youth "cap". A tall, slim scrumhalf, he was earmarked for Cardiff as a successor to the powerful W.A. "Rex" Willis. He first played for the

Cardiff first XV at the age of 18 against the Barbarians, and there could not be a harder "baptism" for anyone. But he showed the true Williams touch in that 1952-53 season. When the great Willis retired, Lloyd, after serving as his deputy, got the job to partner Cliff Morgan, then at his zenith, and freshly back from the South African tour. In 1957 Wales dropped D.O. Brace after the England match to give Lloyd his first cap, and the two players, vastly different in style, have been great rivals for the scrumhalf position in the Welsh XV. Brace retired after playing against Lloyd, in his last match for Llanelly last season at Cardiff, and was chaired off the field to end the great and friendly rivalry. Brace led Wales several times, while Lloyd was first honoured with the captaincy against France in Paris in March, which was his 11th appearance in international rugby.

Lloyd was captain of Cardiff last season and will do the same duty next winter. Number two son, Brinley Williams, played for Cardiff Athletic before the war, and for Cardiff after, and No. 4, Vaughan, appeared at centre after the war. Number Six son, Cenydd, who is now in the R.A.F., has played for Cardiff 1st XV as centre as well as for the R.A.F. A sound player with a touch of the Bleddyn genius, he is young enough to climb higher. Son number seven in wing-forward Elwyn, who looks a future Welsh forward. He was a big boy as a schoolboy when he led Welsh Schools in 1955. Then he moved into the Cardiff Youth XV, and, like Lloyd, played for the Welsh Youth XV. He is a tall, rangy player, with sound anticipation and good hands, specialising in blind-side play, from which he scored several excellent tries last season, including two "specials" against the Barbarians. Quiet and unassuming, he may well appear in trial matches next winter and in a year or two join the Welsh back row. Forwards take a shade longer to reach their prime than do backs, but it will come as a big surprise to all if Elwyn is not the third owner of a Welsh cap in the Williams family. Bleddyn and Lloyd have both captained Wales, and there is an outside chance that yet another brother may do so, to create a record that will be difficult to emulate.

Son Number Eight, Anthony, is the "baby", but he, too, was blooded last season in the Cardiff first XV. He has the advantage of special school training at Christ College, Brecon, after leaving Taff's Well School, and looks a centre of considerable promise. He is now just 20 years of age and the last of a long line of rugby footballers, although Bleddyn's son, Ashley, may make the grade later.

The Cardiff Club is almost as proud of the Williams brothers as are their parents, who are regular spectators in the stand at the Arms Park when their sons are playing.' (Arthur Williams used to 'stand' in the terraces however, not 'sit' in the stand. Strange language, English.) 'Mr. Williams gave me this recipe for success: "*Look after your sons in body and mind and encourage them at home; but outside let them get on with the game, and do not chase committee men or the Press for special 'help'. If the boys*

610

have the ability, the game will develop it. *The Cardiff Club has done a great deal for my sons, but my wife and I have not embarrassed the boys in any way, and as a family we have remained tremendously loyal."* When the sons were young, there were regular discussions about the game on Sundays after the previous day's matches. *"We would all sit round in a circle and talk Rugger while passing a ball around. Mother used to join in, and there developed a wonderful family spirit. All the boys are tremendously loyal to each other, and no parents could wish for better sons."* It is said that Taff's Well may be changed to "Williams-ville" in the near future. Certainly, it is doubtful if any village in the world has a family to match the Williams, even if the great Clarkes of Waikato in New Zealand come near to it.'

1973-74 Former captains, Jack and Bleddyn, together as usual, on the far left standing together, Lloyd eighth in line

CHAPTER 47 - ELWYN AND TONY JOIN TAFF'S WELL

ELWYN TRAINS AND PLAYS FOR TAFF'S WELL - TAFF'S WELL BEATS A FIRST-CLASS CLUB HOME AND AWAY – PLAY SWANSEA – LOSE AGAINST LLANELLI WHEN ELWYN IS OFF THE FIELD – WIN THE SILVER BALL TROPHY – WIN THE EAST DISTRICT SEVENS – WIN THE EAST DISTRICT ON 3 CONSECUTIVE SEASONS - PLAY ULSTER, CARDIFF AND THE BAA-BAAS AT SEVENS

Most of what follows is taken from Peter Thomas' absorbing '*A View from the Garth – 100 Years of Taff's Well Rugby 1887-1987.*' I am utterly indebted, and hope that someone will take up the pen (- shows how old I am -), to continue recording the history of this splendid institution. We left the rugby club in the 60s and with 'Ike' Stephens, a future Wales, Barbarian and Lions player, moving on to Bridgend in 1975. The playing strip had changed from all white to black and white hooped shirts in 1970, and the current black shirt with a white V was adopted in 1974. In 1970, the great Lions centre Steve Fenwick was in the Taff's Well Youth Team, which won the Pontyclun Sevens that year. The Youth had also won the Cardiff and District Sevens in 1963. Steve moved on to Beddau and then Bridgend, leaving his brother Chris, who could play flanker or centre, at Taff's Well. The club was transformed with the return of Elwyn Williams to play and coach, after 15 splendid seasons with Cardiff. Peter Thomas, who played with him at Taff's Well, records: '*During the summer of 1973, the players of Taff's Well trained with a newfound enthusiasm in anticipation of the coming season. The reason for this can be summed up in one name – 'ELWYN.'*

Elwyn Williams had returned to Taff's Well to play and coach. The last but one in line of the famous Williams family, he had spent his rugby playing life with the Cardiff Club. There, he had become ingrained with their way of thinking, which was 'professional' in the best sense of the word. The committee, of course, were delighted that one of 'The Clan' had come home.' In 1973-74, Jack Jones was again captain, after what he called a 'mediocre' first season, and the team's nucleus were Taff's Well, Nantgarw and Tongwynlais boys, what Thomas calls a TNT team. Elwyn joined and took over at number 8, but there were three equally good wing forwards, Chris Fenwick (brother of international Steve), Les 'Poacher's Dog' Hancock and the 'destructive' Roger Watkins. An Arms Park groundsman Dick Stevens, who Elwyn had played with at Cardiff Athletic, was persuaded to join the club.

In 1900 Sid Richardson played scrumhalf for Taff's Well, as did his son, another Sid, in the 1920s. Carey Richardson Collings played wing, centre, fly half and wing forward for Taff's Well, but by the start of 1973-74 was the regular scrumhalf, like his grandfather Sid from 1900. Carey won an East District cap, scored a try for Pontypridd when they were short of a scrumhalf, and with his marvellous spin pass could have played at a higher level, but stayed loyal to his village. Centre Colin Riley was the team's star player, having progressed from the youth, and played for Pontypool and Pontypridd. The Welsh centres during his time at Pontypridd were Steve Fenwick and Ray Gravelle, but many thought he deserved a cap.

Colin Riley introduced Martin 'Maxi' Rickard to Taff's Well, as an excellent outside half and kicker, who could bring his centres into play. In November 1973 Peter Thomas came to play a few games in the seconds before forming a terrific first-team centre partnership with Riley. Wings were the very fast East District players Gwyn Davies and Dai Owen, and the fullback was Clive Day or Geoff Morgan. It was a great set of backs, getting better by the game, and Elwyn ensured a far higher standard of fitness for all players, focusing upon the forwards giving fast ball to the backs. Carey Collings recalls much running up hills to build stamina – 'Ken "Blackie" Blackman, a legend in local rugby circles, was the best distance runner in the club, and in 1974-75 Player of the Year, and later captain. Usually the backs are the athletes but this second-row forward showed us the way, on those interminable road runs that Elwyn dreamed up for wet, winter nights. The 1973-74 season, Elwyn's first, saw some brilliant rugby from the team, with a lot of pressure from players in the Seconds side trying their hardest to get into the Firsts. The Taff's Well's trainer and sponge-man was George Herman, a Polish refugee from the Nazis, who loved working with the players, providing liniment in the changing rooms, and "strink" for players' tie-ups. He loved to hear the boys singing in Welsh, getting them started by imploring them to "Sink a Welsh Sonk".'

With Elwyn now playing and coaching, in his first season Taff's Well beat Pontyclun in the WRU Challenge Cup and were drawn away against the first-class club Glamorgan Wanderers. Carey Collings, and wings Gwyn Davies and Dai Owen scored a try apiece, Colin Riley converting one and kicking 2 penalties. Wanderers scored 3 penalties. Score 20-9. Then it was away to a very good Amman United at Cwmamman Park. 'Geoff Wilson recalls "It was trench warfare". There is no doubt that they were out to intimidate. Second-row Alf Healan got raked and kicked, time and time again. He just kept bouncing back into the fray. They gave up on him in the end.' 'The old warhorse' was displaced by the taller and more mobile Dick Stevens towards the season's end. Taff's Well won 32-12. In the next round, there was a home draw – against Swansea, one of the best teams in Britain. Swansea's back row was Trevor Evans (Wales), the great Mervyn Davies (Wales) and Mark Keyworth (England). Its second row was Geoff Wheel and Barry Clegg, not just internationals, but massive men.

Elwyn arranged a training session with Cardiff, to get the feel of playing against bigger, fitter opponents, especially in scrummaging. The game was recorded by BBC Wales, and attended by rugby correspondents Bleddyn Williams, Wilf Wooller, JBG Thomas, Clem Thomas and Barry John. Swansea played a kicking game for their forwards to enjoy, while Taff's Well played 'more imaginative' rugby and lost 13-6. The club then reached the East District Cup Final against Newport HSOB, played at Cardiff Arms Park. Newport had former internationals like Stuart Watkins playing, and in training Colin Riley pulled a hamstring and fly half Martin Rickard was also unfit. Colin Richards was recalled at fly half and Chris Fenwick was reluctantly pulled out of the back row to play centre.

Taff's Well scrum half Carey Collings gets the ball away clear of Wanders scrum half Billy James.

Scrum-half Carey Collings in the win
over First-Class Glamorgan Wanderers

On 18 April 1974, *'The match night came, and Geoff Morgan kicked off for Taff's Well. From the first line-out, a 'move' was called among the backs. Chris Fenwick was involved, but when the ball reached him, he stopped, looked at the opposing centre, and ran through him with a very unsubtle 'Maori Sidestep'. From then on, every time Chris got the ball he did the same thing and the Newport Old Boys centres became completely demoralised, as this was a type of approach with which they were completely unfamiliar and not very fond. The former Newport outside-half Eddie Mogford kept probing, but the match could have gone either way, until Taff's Well were awarded a penalty. Geoff Morgan converted, with the last kick of the game, to win the East District Championship Cup, its first major trophy.'* Peter Thomas records that: *'these then were the men who produced the goods through this 1973-74 season, and played the kind of rugby that could arguably have been the best seen in Taff's Well. Elwyn Williams was always in evidence, playing, coaching, motivating, supporting, while the committee supported him in his aims.'* Tony Williams' arrival meant that he trained the Taff's Well senior sevens side of Peter Thomas, Tony and his brother Elwyn, 'Ike' Stephens, Les Hancock, Peter Flood and Carey Collings to win the District Cup twice and the Vale of Glamorgan Tournament in 1974.

Taff's Well East District Champions

Elwyn now set the club's sights upon the prestigious Glamorgan County 'Silver Ball'. Luckily, as centre Colin Riley left for Pontypridd, centre Tony Williams returned to his home club from Cardiff. Taff's Well rugby history book author Peter Thomas played outside centre when Riley was inside centre, but switched to inside centre when Riley left and Tony Williams re-joined Taff's Well for two years. An article, *'These are the Most Talented Players never to Play for Wales'* by Anthony Woolford, 2 January 2016 in *walesonline,* places Riley as unlucky not to get a full Welsh cap. Colin *'spent 12 productive years in the centre at Sardis Road from 1970 onwards and enjoyed some heady days with the club. In his time in the Ponty midfield he accumulated 78 tries, and as no mug with the boot landing 105 conversions, 89 penalties and four drop goals.'* In Pontypridd's *'Hall of Fame', 'Colin Riley was a mainstay of the Pontypridd midfield for over a decade, contributing hugely to the club's league and cup successes... Centre 236 appearances 1970-1982.'*

At the end of the 1974-75 season, Tony began to train with, and get accustomed to his new team-mates. Peter Thomas, his co-centre, was amazed that, like Elwyn, Tony did not let his training or playing standards slip when dropping down from a great first-class club. The utility back Peter Flood joined the squad – he had known Tony and Elwyn at Cardiff, and had also played for Neath and captained Abertillery. The main line-out forward Dick Stevens had to move with his work, and the team was left

615

with only front-line jumpers Cilfynydd's Ken Blackman and Nigel 'Jughead' Stevens. Luckily, Simon 'Sam' Fear from Penarth joined, after Colin Richards met him on a train. Considered by his mam *'too tall for his cot'*, he took a degree in economics and wanted to travel, so became a Cardiff Corporation bus driver, but one day lost his bus. He then served as crew on luxury sea voyages before learning computer-programming. Taff's Well had kept its nucleus but improved its team, and decided to play more of a kicking game. Thomas says *'There is no doubt that this tighter control made us a more difficult side to beat and a very good bet to win a trophy.'*

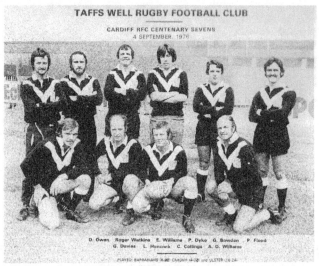

Taff's Well centenary 1976

In the Welsh Cup, Pontyclun and Newport Saracens were beaten, to enter the draw against the 'big clubs'. After the high of playing Swansea in the previous season, there was an even bigger draw – Llanelli - with these current Welsh internationals: Lions centres Ray Gravell and Roy Bergiers; wings the Lion JJ Williams and Andy Hill, scorer of a club record 454 games, 312 tries and around 3,300 points in modern scoring; second row the legendary British Lion Derek Quinnell; and openside wing forward the Wales international Gareth Jenkins. This was the team that in October 1972 had beaten the All Blacks at Stradey Park! Only Phil Bennett, who travelled with the team, was unfit to play, being replaced by Wales 'B' international Bernard Thomas. For the village, Chris Fenwick, like his brother Steve, was a superb tackler, and along with Clive 'Dayo' Day had a superb game. Everyone tackled for their lives, with Tony Williams marshalling the backs in defence and Elwyn leading the forwards by example, as usual.

However, in the first half, with matters even, Elwyn had to leave the field with a bad scalp wound, to be stitched. In his absence, a backrow move was called by Llanelli and Gareth Jenkins went over to score. Then Martin Rickard made a break and passed to Peter Thomas, who was held by Roy Bergiers. Fellow centre Tony Williams called for the ball... *'The ball, however, never reached Tony. A red flash appeared between our two centres and snapped it up. J.J. Williams, an international sprinter, was away, running the length of the field to score. Amazingly, Carey Collings made a covering run and managed to get a despairing hand on J.J. pushing him towards the touch line. Many supporters, who were near the line, swear that J.J. put his foot into touch. The Llanelli linesman however, disagreed and kept his flag down. So what should have been four points for us at one end, turned into four points for Llanelli at the other. The team kept the score to 10-0 until Elwyn returned, heavily bandaged. In the second half, Llanelli fell away – Elwyn's fitness regime came into its own – and Clive Day kicked two penalties – 10-6!*

Then wing Gwyn Davies almost scored before the end, kicking on a ball that trickled over the dead ball line. Llanelli went on to win the cup, and this was the closest margin of any of their cup victories. J.B.G. Thomas reported *'Courage is one of Rugby's ideals and the men of Taff's Well revealed this in a match that was hard but played in the best spirit'.* The next day's headlines in the press included: *'It's Glory in Defeat for Taff's Well'*, *'Holders Llanelli have to Struggle'*, *'Scarlets Ride out the Storm' 'Taff's Well run Llanelli Close'*, and *'Super-Tacklers Rock Llanelli – Scarlets Snatch Two Tries when Taff's Well have Man Off'.* With Elwyn on the pitch – who knows what would have happened – Taff's Well beating the conquerors of the All Blacks?

Lucky Llanelli headlines 'Scarlets snatch two tries'
when Taff's Well have Elwyn off the field

What a game, and the Llanelli players praised the boys in the clubhouse afterwards. I met some of the players in that match, 48 years later, in Taff's Well Rugby Club, and they all say that Elwyn was kicked in the head, and with him on the pitch, the team would have won. Llanelli only scored their 10 points when Elwyn was off for 18 minutes with a try from a deliberate back-row move to exploit his absence, and an interception by the fastest wing in Welsh rugby – which was disputed by spectators. There was a Llanelli linesman who disagreed with the crowd, Carey Collings and the village team. It is hard to doubt it – and **it would have been the greatest giant-killing act in Welsh rugby**.

Barry John, now a rugby writer, and living nearby in Radyr, came to report on the Swansea and Llanelli games, and wrote to the club that it had *'become very dear to my heart... my car finds itself readily moving and with effortless ease to that little acre on the banks of the Taff where, on Sunday mornings, the real experts emerge. Their wisdom is something to behold – and they don't charge for it! ... these unbelievably enjoyable episodes owe in part to 2 memorable Welsh Cup games against Llanelli and then Swansea in the 1970s which I covered for the "Daily Express". They were two remarkable games, and to this day, when I think back of all the David and Goliath games I've see, they are the ones that linger longer in the memory and provide a real yardstick for other such clashes. Jack Jones and his team not only did the village proud on the field of play by really giving it a go; but the club's attitude to the whole occasion was a "breath of fresh air" and illustrated perfectly how the Club approaches rugby and, indeed, life. It was like Henley on Taff (2 majestic marquees) and the best press set-up going – Rhys Davies's wagon! It all made for carnival time – but above all, it was the genuine, very warm, and sincere welcome that came over loud and clear, which captivated everybody. Since then, I've been a guest at their dinner. From what I can remember, it was a tremendous evening, and just to prove that they are very sensitive people, everybody had a Cup!'*

The disappointed team kept playing well, progressing to the both the East District Championship and the Silver Ball finals. The East District Cup Final was a repeat of the previous season, again against Newport HSOB, and unlike the previous hard-fought last-minute victory, Taff's Well won easily. The team was Clive 'Dayo' Day, Peter Flood, Elwyn Williams, Peter Thomas, Gwyn Davies, Martin Rickard, Carey Collings, Jack Jones, Gwyn Bowden, Ian 'Ike' Stevens, Blackman, Sam Fear, Chris Fenwick, Tony Williams and Roger Watkins. In the Silver Ball, the club won 9 and drew 1 of ten games – with Taff's Well now being 'the team to beat'. The Silver Ball final, under captain Carey Collings, was the next target. The Silver Ball final was played at the Brewery Field, Bridgend, with Pyle expected to win, as they had won at Taff's Well earlier in the season, and included the much-feared forward John Richardson, soon to play for Wales. Pyle were defeated 9-6, all penalties, by the team of Clive Day, Les

Hancock, Martin Rickard, Elwyn Williams, Simon 'Sam' Fear, Ken Blackman, Ian 'Ike' Stephens, Gwyn 'Curly' Davies, Gwyn Bowden, Tony Williams, Jack Jones, Peter Thomas, Peter Flood, Carey Collings and Chris Fenwick.

Taff's Well Silver Ball Winners 1974-75

It had been some season, winning two major cups, and Taff's Well also won the District 'B' Sevens in Barry, earning the right to play against major teams in the Snelling Sevens, the main tournament in Wales, at the Arms Park. In the preliminary round the team was drawn against mighty Swansea and <u>won 16-6</u>. Next up was another top club of the time, Penarth, who called upon some great players from Cardiff College of Education, and the game was 12-12 at full time, Penarth then scoring in a sudden-death playoff to go through. The team were applauded loudly at the end – these games used to be a highlight of the season for many of us, despite no beer being available during the 'day out'. The team's performance fell off a little in 1975-76, although the East District Champions ship, with a perfect 11 wins out of 11 matches, was won again – for a third successive year. St Peter's RFC in Cardiff website records: '*The team was successful in the various competitions winning eight out of ten Silver Ball matches and the same number of East District games. The latter was sufficient to take the side to its first East District final where they lost to a very fine Taff's Well team 17-4.*' Gwyn Davies scored 2 tries.

At the season's end, Cardiff announced it was to hold a Centenary Seven-a-Side Tournament, in which the Barbarians would be playing and just one East District club could take part. It was to be the William brothers' swansong. After a season of 35 games, Tony and the 35-year-old Elwyn decided to retire from playing. Tony joined the committee at Cardiff and later was chairman. Taff's Well won the East District Sevens tournament, beating Llanharan in the final, so were to appear in the Centenary Sevens at the Arms Park. There were two pools of four teams, and on 4 September 1976, the club was drawn to play in the hardest pool. Apart from Taff's Well, the other seven teams were Stewarts Melville, Newport, Bridgend, Loughborough Colleges, Ulster, Cardiff and the Barbarians. Taff's Well were in the 'pool of death' playing the last three teams. The squad was Elwyn and Tony, Dai Owen, Roger Watkins, P. Dyke, Gwyn Bowden, Peter Flood, Gwyn Davies, Les Hancock and Carey Collings.

1974-75—Winners East District and Vale of Glamorgan Sevens

1974-75 Sevens Winners

In game one, '*Taff's Well shook the Barbarians by showing the better sevens technique for a while*'. Peter Flood scored a try, but the game was lost 22-6 to a wonderful team including Tony Neary, Ian McGeechan, Peter Wheeler, Alan Martin and Andy Ripley. In the second game Gwyn Davies raced away, scoring the first try of the game against a Cardiff side captained by Gerald Davies and including Brynmor Williams, Alan Phillips and Stuart Lane. Cardiff got on top after halftime and won 26-4. Ulster was a closer match, but Ulster won 24-10. Tony and Elwyn, especially, had a huge cheer when their names were read out. '*The years 1922-25 have been referred to as the "Golden Years" of Taff's Well RFC. The years of 1973-76 therefore, must surely be the "Silver Years"*'.

620

From 1972, Taff's Well arranged exchange visits with French clubs. In 1972, playing at Borderais (Bordères-sur-l'Échez, Hautes-Pyrénées), Jack Edwards lost a plate juggling competition. There followed overseas trips to La Nicolaite in Tarn et Garonne (1974), Bizanos F.C. in the foothills of the Pyrenees, near Lourdes (1976) and in 1978 to F.C. Baronnies - now Entente Sportif des Baronnies (ESB) Sarlabous, Midi-Pyrenees, with the Welsh boys slightly embarrassed at all venues by their French counterparts' *'lavish hospitality'*. Indeed, by 1978 Jack Edwards was said to be on first name terms with the customs officials at Toulouse Airport. The team's second French cultural tour was to St. Nicolas de la Grave, in the Tarn et Garonne Departement, Southwest France in 1974. They travelled cheaply on the plane taking French supporters back from the international in Cardiff. They were obviously attracted to St. Nicolas by the Chateau Richard Coeur de Lion, a French castle conquered, and added to, by the English king. Richard I is extremely popular amongst the Welsh, as while he was building 16 castles in France, he was the first English king since the Anglo-Saxons, Normans and the Plantagenet-Angevins not to invade Wales. He was killed, by a crossbow wound turning gangrenous, in France in 1199, having spent hardly any of his adult life in England, with his heart, entrails and rest of his body buried in various places across his homeland of France. (He could not speak English – the first English king to use the language was Henry IV, the usurper who tried to kill Owain Glyndwr, Prince of Wales, from 1400 to 1418.) Richard's killer was flayed alive. Under his successor John, the invasions restarted, only really ending when Henry Tudor landed in Wales and raised an army to kill Richard III in 1485.

Elwyn in Taff's Well colours

One would also expect that Elwyn and Tony Williams and the team would have also visited the Musée Lamothe-Cadillac, where Antoine

Laumet de la Mothe, Sieur de Cadillac was born, the explorer and founder of modern-day Detroit. When Detroit became the centre of world car construction, the founders of the Cadillac company honoured him by naming the company after him. In 1970 the Historical Society of Detroit gave the town $20,000 to buy the house where Cadillac was born to turn it into a museum devoted to him and Cadillac cars. During the day, members of the local rugby team, La Nicolaite, took Taff's Well on a long tour of local hostelries, and the boys were quite content, knowing that they could out-drink their opponents, who were all ages, shapes and sizes, and still win the game. However, treachery was afoot. Kick-off was under floodlights at 9pm. Peter Thomas recounts: *'We had given the grape a good bashing all day. Then, when we emerged into the glare of the floodlights, like inebriated black and white moths, we were surrounded by fit-looking strangers. I personally felt like screaming for help.'* Somehow the French could not score, and *'with minutes to go, Gwyn Davies intercepted a pass and raced the length of the field for the winning try.'*

1977-78 saw Elwyn finally retire from the Firsts, and it was called a disappointing season, with results of Played 38, Won 23, Drew 2, Lost 13. In the previous season, Bishopston of Bristol had just been beaten 11-8, but in this season, after losing key players, lost 104-0, a Taff's Well record. Most appearances were Roger Watkins 36, Dai Owens, Mike Bonetto, Peter Dyke and Ken Blackman 34, and Laurence Bonetto 33. Gwyn Davies scored 20 tries in 23 matches. A new clubhouse with adequate changing and showering facilities was built, and Steve Fenwick agreed to bring an international XV to celebrate the opening by Bill Clement, RWU Secretary. On 4 September 1978, Taff's Well scored a terrific try, but were well beaten by a team containing six British Lions - Terry Holmes, John Bevan, their own 'Ike' Stephens, Tommy David, David Burcher and Elgan Rees. Peter Thomas's lovely history of Taff's Well RFC ends in January 1987, but we must quickly mention a few events about the club that gave us the Williams brothers, Roy Roberts, Steve Fenwick and Harry Rees.

Big clubs were finding it difficult to balance the books before the pandemic, owing to tiny crowds. And declining attendances are because of ever-shifting kick-off times and the unappealing nature of biff-bash-bosh big-bloke modern rugby. I can honestly say that there is usually far more open rugby played by a team like Llanybydder in National League Division 3 West A, than in any of the big fixtures. Small clubs have always faced financial problems. In the past bar takings used to pay for the team coach, kit, rent, rates, utilities, insurances and the like. However, many players today hardly drink after a game. I have witnessed many a team, after a game, nearly all having meal and a Coke before heading back home in their cars or on the coach. And throughout their history small clubs have relied upon unpaid volunteers, male and female, to keep the clubs in existence. They get virtually nothing from the WRU, in fact some get a third of what they were receiving 20 years ago. In many villages, the rugby team has been the heart of the community for decades – a tradition that must not die. In fact, Llanybydder set a world record in one match playing Aberystwyth – in the starting 30, there were five players christened Llyr.

A player through the 50s and 60s, Alan 'Rugger' Jones, the brother of Iorrie, reluctantly took up Dai Millward's mantle as 'Honorary Secretary' of Taff's Well RFC in 1961. Iorrie, Chairman of the club, proposed his brother, who protested, saying that he was left-handed, was not the man for the job, had no experience and could not write properly. Iorrie said that 'Rugger' could not make a worse mess than when he had played scrumhalf. At this point 'Rugger' capitulated, admitting the 'irrefutable fact' that his service had turned Clive Day's hair prematurely grey when he was just 24. Rugby cannot exist without unpaid 'servants' like Alan Jones and former players across the British Isles. 'Rugger' recalls: *As well as performing all the traditional duties of a club secretary, I now had to call bingo numbers, compere dances and shows and eventually learn to order stock, bank money, and virtually become a businessman.'* He then praises the dedicated men who have helped him ensure the smooth running of the club *'uncomplainingly and of course free of any financial reward. For me life became a continual routine of committee meetings, writing letters, making phone calls and organising functions etc., and, although this may sound monotonous, it was always interesting due to the challenge of ever-changing situations. The work was demanding but often exciting, although the hours needed to do the job – I was putting in between 25-30 hours a week – left little time for other things'.*

Exhausted, Alan had to give up the post for a few years. He thanked his wife – like him she had a full-time job – for her patience and understanding while bringing up two children in his long absences. In 1986, 'Rugger' returned to the role, by now retired and able to put in the hours required. I feel I must add an anecdote by 'Rugger', to demonstrate to non-rugby people the dangers of the demon drink; *'Of course it was not all work and I remember after one particularly hectic session it would be prudent to get home and into bed as quietly and surreptitiously as possible. I switched off the car engine some distance from the house, and once inside closed it very slowly, it only took an instant to remove my shoes and I tiptoed up the stairs. I decided to sleep in the spare room, then "her indoors" would never know what time I came in. I crept into the spare room, sat on the bed and started to undress. It was only then that I realised that somebody was already in the bed and I was startled to hear a female voice with a heavy West Wales accent exclaim, "Is that you Alan?" It was my mother-in-law who had arrived on a surprise visit while I was out. Around this time my health started to deteriorate (were the gallons of various brews beginning to take their toll?) and I developed heart trouble.'* Alan had a heart bypass, with the stresses and strains of 20 years holding down a full-time job and work at the club leading to his retirement from the Secretary's post. He wrote *'I only hope that my contribution to the club played a part in making true what I have always believed, that Taff's Well Rugby Club is the best club in the world.'*

At Easter 1983, the team took on another overseas trip, their first full week trip, playing The Hague, Den Helder and The Hook of Holland, only losing to Den Helder, a team that was all over six foot tall, and whose scrumhalf was taller than any Taff's Well player – this is from Peter Thomas' history of the rugby club, so it must be correct. In 1983, the extremely capable Mike Bonetto was captain, and the club was drawn against first-class side Penarth in the cup. 'Ike' Stephens 'physically and mentally' prepared the team but could not play. Playing into the wind at Penarth, the team were 6-0 down at halftime, but Ian Mapstone, Geraint Jones and Gareth Philips scored tries, the veteran Colin Riley converting one, to win 14-6. In the 1985-85 cup, Penarth were drawn again, this time at Taff's Well, and the home team scored a try after five minutes. Penarth answered with a try, but were down 10-7 at halftime. Taff's Well missed a penalty in front of the posts, but Dave Mason, who had hit the post with the penalty, then touched down. *'By the final whistle, Taff's Well had won 11-10 and we believe that Taff's Well are the only small club to beat on of the "Big 16" home and away in consecutive seasons.'*

Jack Edwards had developed a relationship with Nantes, a city twinned with Cardiff, in the 1960s when he met a Nantes man. He invited him to Taff's Well where he played a token game for the club. In 1981, the Frenchman asked for a game of over-35s veterans, and a scratch team of *'Taff's Well War Babies'*, lost 30-20. In April 1984, a Taff's Well team was ready for a rematch, taking the long journey by coach, ferry and bus to Nantes. Nantes claimed themselves veteran 'world champions', having seen off Cardiff, Newport, Swansea, Bristol and the Royal Navy, as well as Taff's Well over the years. The team of village elders was not in the best condition upon arrival, having demolished *'a mountain of IPA* (beer) *the Common Market would be proud of.' 'The match itself was a victory for Welsh stoicism. We flogged our tired and saturated bodies into the fray. Play was immediately held up for treatment to Paul (Boomer) Williams. The first four passes he had received bruised his ankles. He was replaced by that Mexican-faced swine Hywel Davies. He made one run, feigned double vision and left the pitch. Eventually we ran out winners, by 38-24. We were* **World Champions***! The highlights of the game were some fine tries by Gwyn Davies and Colin Riley and a few fine cases of assault by Bob Davies and Geoff Wilson.*

"LORD WILLIAMS" After the match we were entertained at the Hotel de Ville where the mayor made a speech welcoming us and making particular reference to Lord Williams. He meant Lloyd Williams, who was with us. We had mentioned to Nantes' players that Lloyd was a famous ex-

international and they were impressed. The mayor had somehow become confused as to the reason for Lloyd's eminence. He mistakenly believed him to be a member of the aristocracy, confusing Lloyd with Lord. Lloyd seemed quite happy with the arrangement. We drank our fill of Muscadet and also a purple liqueur which can only be described as a mixture of Ribena and Harvey-Wallbanger. Led by Alun 'Rugger' Jones we sang superbly.' (The 'purple liqueur' mush be crème de cassis, made from blackcurrants, often mixed with Muscadet to make a '*kir*' cocktail. With sparkling wine, preferably champagne, it is a '*kir royale*'.) In 1984, there were also two wins in Spain, against Benidorm and El Cer. In the latter game, *'things livened up no end when the Spanish referee walked off, complaining that the Spanish team would not listen to him. A replacement was found, however…'* At the award ceremony after the tour, the '*Injury of the Tour*' went to Keith Clash, for breaking his leg. This occurred when falling off a pool table. Another award, '*The Spanish Tummy Cup*' was presented to Mark (*Twtty*) Bowden who was badly sick … <u>before</u> boarding at Cardiff Airport.

Viva Espana – The Bonettos sample the 'Good Life'
in Benidorm, cartoon by Carey Collings

There is a cartoon in *One Hundred Years of Taff's Well Rugby* depicting the Bonetto brothers in Benidorm… *'The beach at Benidorm was the particular stamping ground of Mike and Lawrence Bonetto, who with hankies knotted on theirheads and their white legs hanging out of very baggy shorts, were the talk of the town. Our boys nicknamed them "The Clampetts" after the television "Hillbillies". They cut fine figures as they strolled among the jet-setters and posers on the beach.'* In 1985-86, Taff's Well Youth reached the quarterfinals of the Esso Welsh Youth Cup, the semi-finals of the East District Youth Cup, and won the club's first trophy since 1976 at Cardiff Arms Park, beating St. Albans in the Cardiff and District Youth Cup Final. The Youth team had playing Eifion and Huw Williams playing, the sons of Tony and Vaughan, but Darren, son of Elwyn, was absent through injury. Six other players were sons of former players. In 1985-86 the senior team had another good run in the Silver Ball, losing to St Peter's in the semi-final, and Peter Thomas's history of the club, and its players from the village and its neighbours Tongwynlais and Gwaelod-y-Garth ends here.

One of the greatest, if not the greatest joy from playing rugby at junior levels is that a few times a season one cannot speak for laughing, tears run down your face – there are always characters who make you laugh from the pit of your stomach. I would like to add a few Taff's Well players' remarks collected by Peter Thomas: '1962 *"I'm not fit enough to train" (- Brian Lancaster); 1969 "As suave as a bucket of shit" (- Clive Day); 1970, when asked how he would like his steak "Knock his horns of and wipe his arse" (- Brian Lancaster); 1973 "I'll try a bottle of the Italian stuff. I think it's called Carafe" (- Alan Thomas, aka 'Archie Wheelbrace'); 1974 "I want 80 per cent for 100 minutes" (- Elwyn Williams); 1975 "Remember boys, the bigger they are, the further they hit you" (- Calvin Howlett);* 1975, referring to Cardiff Brains Brewery putting its beers in the clubhouse *"Four of the committee thought they would have to have an operation when we said we were having Brains in" (- Brian Lancaster); 1975 "I love playing at Abercynon, I always get two free meals for nothing" (- Ken Blackman); 1976 on tour at St. Nicolas in France "Leslie! You are not bringing that thing into bed with you!" (- Martin Rickard); 1978 "A tiger never changes his spots" (- Lenny Pearce); 1978 "My favourite music is that Town and Country stuff" (- Lenny Pearce); 1978 at Lourdes on tour "Did you see that? That man went in there in a wheelchair and came out with a new set of tyres!" (- Clive 'Dayo Day); 1986 "Dai Millward refereed before the First World War – on horseback" (Tony Bonetto); 1986 "My great-grandfather was not a bullfighter, he was a well-known pirate (- Tony Bonetto); 1987 "If I'm fighting four blokes on the floor, there's bound to be an overlap" (- Alan Jones,* not Alan 'Rugger' Jones, but also variously known as Rambo, Bonehead and then universally as the overlapping *Rambonehead*).

A recent Llantwit Major (Llanilltud Fawr) RFC programme previewed its upcoming match and the respect with which Taff's Well commands: *'On Saturday the 1st XV travel to Taff's Well which is home to Scrum V pundit and part time comedian Phil Steele who refers to his home village as "Equatorial Taff's Well". They were formed in 1887 and have been a full member of the Welsh Rugby Union since 1900. As a club they quite rightly boast a no mean feat for a village side, in that they have produced 3 Welsh Captains, 7 Full internationals and 3 British Lions: Welsh Captains*

626

– Steve Fenwick, Bleddyn Williams, Lloyd Williams; Internationals – Steve Fenwick, Bleddyn Williams, Lloyd Williams, Harry Rees, Elwyn Williams, Ian Stevens and Gwilym Beech.

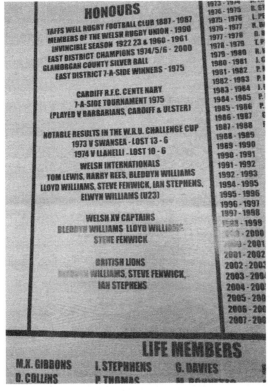

Taff's Well Honours Board

British Lions – Steve Fenwick, Bleddyn Williams and Ian Stevens. Taff's Well are also former Silver Ball winners having been successful in the 1974/1975 season.' Taff's Well's 100th Anniversary in 1987 saw Jack Edwards, a great friend of Bleddyn, arranging games against Cardiff, Bridgend and Pontypridd. It was also the anniversary of its first game with its great 'rival' from over the Garth Mountain, Pentyrch. The teams play annually for the John Llewellyn Cup – the great Pentyrch player who was fullback in the Cardiff team that beat the All Blacks in 1953. John was also instrumental in 'untiring efforts' to obtain the new ground, which was named Cae'r Afon, (River Field) adjoining the River Taff. (After the clubhouse fire in 1968, the pitch was sold for housing to finance a new clubhouse, a new floodlit pitch and pay off the club's debts, the ground being renamed Cae Gwyn, Gwyn's field, in tribute to Gwyn Davies' enormous effort in helping his club to move and rebuild).

Taff's Well pitch

CHAPTER 48

THE BROTHERS' PARENTS, GRANDPARENTS, GREAT-GRANDPARENTS. THE LINK WITH THE TAMPLIN FAMILY

Father - Arthur Lougher Williams, born September quarter 1891 at 123 King's Road, Cardiff, was birth registered as simply Arthur Williams. He had six siblings: Philip Williams, b. December quarter 1874, who played for Taff's Well and Cardiff Athletic; Susanna b. December quarter 1878; Jessie b. June quarter 1881 (Jessie is probably the child noted as Miriam or Marian on the 1881 Census, and her name altered by the time she was registered); Elizabeth b. September 1884; and Herbert b. June quarter 1893. In 1911 Arthur, aged 19, was a clerk in a Cardiff 'coal office', while his father Charles had risen to be the Clerk of Works for Cardiff Corporation. However Arthur soon became a coal tipper at Cardiff Docks, presumably for more money.

The 1930s were a difficult time for unemployment, with a world-wide Depression until aggression by Hitler, Mussolini, Osami Nagano and Isoroku Yamamo and others caused a global increase in jobs. In 1939 Britain suddenly moved to full-time employment in manufacturing, and job vacancies because of men being called up for war. According to Gwyn, the reason he left the Police Force and went North in November 1938 was that his father **Arthur had been unemployed for six years** – moving to Wigan would give Gwyn a double income to help his family. Gwyn never mentioned his intention also to help pay Bleddyn's school fees until two decades later, to a close friend. Dilys (b.1915) had married in 1934. However, probably still living in Moy Road in the 1930s were Gwyn (b.1915); Bryn (b.1920, m.1939); Bleddyn (b.1923, left for Rydal School in 1937); Enid (b.1925); Joan (b.1928); Vaughan (b.1931); Lloyd (b.1933); Mair (b.1936) and Cenydd (b.1938). So Dilys had left, and perhaps nine children were at home, less Bleddyn for most of the year at Rydal, and perhaps Gwyn if he had a police house allocated. That leaves seven children at home, and to be born shortly were Elwyn (b.1939) and Tony (b.1941).

Arthur's father was **Charles Williams***** a stone mason and Clerk of Works, but only a 'dock labourer', when Arthur was born in 1891. Born 1850 in Cardiff, Charles was the son of John Williams and Elizabeth Jones. Arthur's mother was Susan Griffiths, born 1854 in Bonvilston, christened in March, the daughter of Richard Griffiths and Margaret Lougher. Charles had 6 siblings, all born in Cardiff; Edward b.1838; John b.1840; Josiah b.1842; Elizabeth b.1842; Henry b.1847 and Matilda b.1858.

Arthur's paternal grandfather, John Williams, was born in St Andrews, a hamlet near Dinas Powys in the Vale of Glamorgan in 1812. On 18 March 1839 he married Elizabeth Jones, born 1813 in Laleston in the Vale of Glamorgan.

Arthur's maternal grandparents were Richard Griffiths of Pendoylan and Margaret Lougher of Bonvilston. This century saw mass emigration from the Vale and other agricultural areas to new jobs in the mines and ports of South Wales. (In turn there was an influx of displaced farm workers from the West Country into the Vale of Glamorgan to replace these labourers.)

Mother - Mary Ellen 'Nellie /Nell' Roberts was born September 1898 in Risca, the eldest daughter of collier Edward 'Ted' George Roberts and Susan Roberts, née Lewis. She was born at Main Road, Gwaelod-y-Garth. Her five siblings were: Lily May b.1901; Ada b.1904; Tom Albert b.1906 and Leslie Roydon **'Roy' Roberts**, b. 3 June 1917 – d. 2 November 1988. Tom Albert Roberts may well be the Tom Roberts who played 3 games for Cardiff in 1927-28. Roy Roberts was born in 1917 at 11 Moy Road, ???Taff's Well, from 1918 also the home of the 12 Williams brothers and sisters. The older Roberts children, including 'Nell', were born in Risca. Over 26 years 'Nell' had 12 known children – there may well have also been still-births and miscarriages, as with many mothers in these days: 1915 (Dilys), 1918 (Gwyn), 1921 (Brinley/Bryn), 1923 (Bleddyn), 1926 (Enid), 1928 (Joan), 1931 (Vaughan), 1933 (Lloyd), 1935 (Mair), 1938

(Cenydd), 1940 (Elwyn) and 1941 (Tony).

Nell Roberts' father was **Edward George 'Ted' Roberts**, born in Newchurch East, Monmouthshire in 1879. Newchurch East, or Yr Eglwys Newydd ar y Cefn (New Church on the Ridge). This is a small village clustered around the fourteenth-century St. Peter's Church, between Usk and Chepstow. 'Ted' was the son of Mary A. Roberts, with an unnamed father, so may have well been illegitimate. In the first quarter of **1898 he married Susan Lewis** in Newport. **Ted Roberts was incredibly important in the early years of Taff's Well rugby.** In the 1901 Census Edward and Susan Roberts were listed as living at Ochrwyth, Risca, Monmouthshire, where he is a 'woodcutter's agent' born at Chepstow, Monmouth. (Ochrwyth is spelt Ochenwyth in records, but Ochrwyth is the name of a long-abandoned quarry on Machen Mountain. *Ochr* means side and *chwith*, normally meaning left, not right, can also mean 'wrong'. From early times, the left has had bad connotations, e.g. the Latin 'sinister' for left and 'dexter' for right, giving us 'dextrous'. The village, near Risca, was in the parish of Machen, in other words the village was 'on the wrong side' of Machen Mountain from its parish church. Over the years the name Ochrwith has been corrupted into Ochrwyth.)

Their first two children, born at Pontymister, were listed as Ellen aged 2 (our Nellie Roberts) and Lily May, under 9 months. However, in the 1911 Census, Edward 'Ted' altered his place of birth to Newchurch East, and he was now a *'coal miner, hewer'* living at Bristol Terrace, Gwaelodygarth, Taff's Well, Glamorgan. 'Ellen' now aged 11 has now been altered to Mary Helen, with an altered birthplace of Machen, and 10-year-old Lily May is also allotted to Machen. There were two more children, both born in Machen, Ada aged 7 and Tom Albert aged 5. This Census states that Edward and Susan had five children, four living and one deceased. Their last child was Leslie Roydon 'Roy' Roberts, born 3 June 1917 at the house, 11 Moy Road where Gwyn Williams would be born the following year, followed by 11 brothers and sisters. The eldest of Nell Williams' children, Dilys, was born at Gwaelod-y-Garth.

It seems that Edward 'Ted' Roberts was illegitimate. Lynne Barry found him in the 1881 Census at Raglan Road, Newchurch East, Monmouthshire, at the home of William Simmonds, a 67-year-old general labourer, born in Lydney, Gloucestershire, and his wife Anne, aged 47, born in Newchurch. At the same address was their 12-year-old son John, a scholar, and their unmarried daughter a 'domestic', 22-year-old Mary A. Roberts. Their grandson was noted as Edward G. Roberts. His birth is registered in the December quarter of 1879 as Edward George Roberts, and the blank entry for his mother's maiden name means that she was unmarried.

Nell Robert's mother Susan Lewis was born in Risca, birth registered in the June quarter 1881, the daughter of Thomas Lewis of Risca, born 1847 and Sarah Ann Bright of Abersychan, born 1848. They married 26 November 1870 in Machen Parish Church, and both were registered as living in Machen. Thomas Lewis was a 24-year-old 'hammerman', son of James Lewis, a 'stock taker'. Saran Ann was 23, daughter of labourer Benjamin Bright. Susan Lewis' six siblings were: Elizabeth Lewis b. 1872 Machen; Charlotte b. 1874 Machen; Edgar James birth registered December quarter 1875 Machen; Amy b.1879 Risca; Benjamin E. b.1886 Pontymister and Mabel Ann b 29 October 1891 Pontymister. Mabel's birth was not registered until March quarter 1892, possibly because she was a sickly baby.

We first come across Susan Lewis as a 1-month-old baby in the 1881 Census, where her parents are noted as Tom Lewis, a 34-year-old 'Hammerman' born in Risca, and 43-year-old Sarah A. Lewis, born in 'Abercarne' Monmouthshire. They are living at 2 Goulds Houses, Pontymister, Risca, Monmouthshire. Their first three children were born in Machen – Elizabeth aged 9; Charlotte aged 7 and Edgar J., 5. Amy aged 2, and baby Susan were born in Risca. In the 1891 Census the family had moved to 'Ochenwyth', Risca, and Tom was now listed as a 'Coaching skillworker' aged 44 with wife Sarah A., whose birthplace had altered from Abercarne to Abersychan. Charlotte, now 17, was an 'opening tinplater', and Edgar J. a 'catcher, tin rolls'. The eldest girl, Elizabeth, may have gone into service or married. 12-year-old Amy and 10-year-old Susan now had a brother Benjamin E. Lewis, born at Beachan, Monmouthshire. By 1901, Susan Lewis had left home and her father Tom had died. However, there was one additional child, Mabel, now aged 9. Mabel married William Ewart Tamplin, and their son of the same name played for Cardiff, Wales and with the Williams' brothers, his second cousins.

PARENTS' MARRIAGE

Arthur Lougher Williams married Mary Ellen 'Nellie' Roberts on 1 March 1915, at Cardiff Registry Office instead of church. It may well have been a 'hurried' affair, as their first child, Dilys, was born 32 weeks later, on 5 October 1915. Arthur was then a trooper in the Glamorgan Yeomanry, living at 123 Kings Road, Canton, Cardiff, and 'Nellie' was at Main Road, Gwaelod-y-Garth. His father Charles was a dock labourer and her father Edward 'Ted', a collier. Upon the marriage certificate, Mary Ellen is described as Nellie Williams. Arthur was 23 and Nellie was 17.

*A digression upon Arthur Williams' father, **Charles Williams,** a dock labourer when Arthur was born in 1891. He married Susan Griffiths, born in Bonvilston in 1854, the sibling of Alice b.1851; Catherine b.1853; Matilda b.1856 and Harriet b. 1848. All the five girls were born in the village of Bonvilston in the Vale of Glamorgan. Their parents were Richard Griffiths, born in Pendoylan, in 1816, and Margaret Lougher of

Bonvilston, born 1821. They married in Cardiff in 1842. The story of Charles Williams is an amazing one, as evidenced by his occupation upon his children's birth and marriage certificates. In the 1881 Census he was a stone mason aged 31, living in 46 Wellington Street, Canton, Cardiff, with a 6-year-old son Philip and two small daughters. In 1891 Charles Williams was a stone mason living at 12 Smeaton Street, Canton, Philip was a 16-year-old carpenter and there were four daughters. In the same year, 1891, Arthur was born at 123 Kings Road, Canton, but Charles Williams was only described as a Dock Labourer on the birth document. In the 1901 Census, Philip had left home, daughter Jessie was a schoolteacher and daughter Edith a tailoress. Elizabeth was 14, Arthur 9 and Herbert 7. Still at Kings Road, Charles was now the 50-year-old **Clerk of Works and Buildings, Cardiff Corporation**, quite an advancement from being a dock labourer ten years previously. In the 1911 Census we are told that Arthur is 61, his wife Susan (née Lewis) 58, Elizabeth has no occupation, aged 24 and Arthur is a Clerk, Coal Office. The parents spoke both Welsh and English, but the children only English. Of their ten children, three had predeceased them. Charles' previous occupation is given as Stone Mason, but he is still the Clerk of Works, Cardiff Corporation.

Cardiff had grown at a phenomenal pace in the 19th century, with the population growing from around 1,850 in 1801 to over 18,000 in 1851. The railway reached Cardiff in 1841, vastly improving transport links. By 1851 the population had passed 18,000, in 1871 it was nearly 60,000, and the number of residents exploded to over 160,000 by 1900. The growth was driven by exports of iron and coal, along with grain, with the Bute West Dock being built in 1839, East Dock in 1855, Roath Basin in 1874 and Roath Dock in 1887. In 1886 a Coal and Shipping Exchange was built. Shipbuilding, rope-making, iron and steel, brewing, milling and paper manufacture flourished, and from 1821 there was gas street lighting, and from 1902 there were electric trams. In the early twentieth century, Charles Williams rose to virtually oversee much of Cardiff's building programme in this incredible time, being Clerk of Works from at least 1901 to 1911.

In the 1871 census, Charles Williams is a 21-year-old had been a stone-cutter, living with his parents John, an 'Iron Weigher' aged 59 and 58-year-old Elizabeth Williams, formerly Jones. John was from St. Andrews near Dinas Powys and Elizabeth from Laleston in the Vale of Glamorgan. (Incidentally, a witness to the wedding of John and Elizabeth on 18 March 1837 was Thomas Lougher – Arthur Williams adopted the Lougher middle name after he was christened, but it probably came from another source). They were all now living at 20 North Church Street, St Mary's, Cardiff. All Charles' siblings were born in Cardiff and were living at the same address: John aged 31, an O.D. Officer, Customs; the widower Josiah, aged 29, labouring with timber; and 13-year-old Matilda, a scholar (i.e. at school). Also at the address were granddaughter Elizabeth J. Williams, aged 6; and grandsons John B. and John, both aged 5. They were possibly the children of the widower Josiah, with his wife dying in childbirth, after the second John Williams was born so soon after John B. Williams. The 1861 Census gives John Williams as a railway labourer, at the same address as in 1871, living with wife Elizabeth and 23-year-old Edward, a railway brakeman; John, 21, a sailmaker; Josiah, 19, labourer; Elizabeth 15; the scholars Henry and Charles, 14 and 12; and Matilda, aged 3.

On the maternal side of Charles Williams' family, his wife Susan Griffiths was baptised in Bonvilston 24 February 1854, the daughter of Richard and Margaret Griffiths who farmed at Tregroes, Bonvilston. They married in Cardiff in 1842, and Margaret's maiden name was Lougher, born 24 February 1854 at Bonvilston. Their youngest child was born in Bonvilston in 1857, but it appears that the family later moved to 46 Wellington Street, Canton, Cardiff, where her father was registered as a labourer, born in Pendoylan in the 1871 Census. He was 55 and Elizabeth 50, and their first five children were born in Bonvilston. They were Margaret, a tailoress aged 21; Alice, a domestic servant, 19; Susan, a seamstress, 17; Matilda, a scholar aged 14; and 23-year-old daughter Harriett Thomas. Living with her and her parents was her husband, engine driver Joseph Thomas, aged 25, born in Peterston-super-Ely near Cardiff. There was also a 1-year-old 'nurse child' named John Driscoll at the address. Thus, five children, a son-in-law and a foster baby were living with Richard and Margaret Griffiths. There is an anomaly in the Marriage Record for Richard Griffiths in the District of Cardiff in that four spouses are listed in order – Sarah Jenkins, Anna Marie Jonathan, 'our' Margaret Lougher and Mary Morris. Arthur Williams therefore probably acquired his middle name from his grandmother. There is some sort of family legend that there should have been money passed down from the Lougher family.

THE LINK WITH THE TAMPLIN FAMILY

The link is Susan Lewis, the mother of Nell Williams, née Roberts. Her youngest sister was Mabel Ann Lewis b.29 October 1891 at Pontymister. Mabel married William Ewart Tamplin b.10 February 1886, at Bethesda Chapel, Rogerstone on 4 July 1908. We have covered the Lewis side of the family above and there is a little confusion on the Tamplin side with a father giving his son the same Christian names of William Ewart, the son being our famous post-war rugby player and Welsh captain. James Tamplin, born in Machen in 1854, married Elizabeth Russell of Bassaleg, born 1851, in 1879. In the 1881 Census, James is a baker aged 27, and he and Elizabeth have an 8-month daughter, Mabel. M. They are living at Tidw Road, and for the next two censuses. In 1891, James is a 35-year-old stationary boiler stoker, and he and Elizabeth have four children all born in

Risca – Mabel M., Edward J., Percess A., and William E., aged 10, 8, 6 and 5 respectively.

Their children were Mabel M. Tamplin b.1881; Edward J. b.1883; Percess Ada b.1885 and William Ewart Tamplin (snr.) in 1886. All were born in Risca. In the 1901 Census, James is a 'stationary engine stoker' aged 45, and his wife Elizabeth is aged 52. Their children are Mabel, 20; Edwards, railway worker, 17; Percess Ada, 16; and William Ewart Tamplin, aged 15, a 'coal miner, hewer'. William Ewart snr. married Mabel Ann Lewis on 4 July 1908 at Bethesda Chapel, Rogerstone. Her father Tom was a deceased hammerman at the steelworks. Her husband was a 22-year-old coal miner of Tydw Road, Pontymister. Mabel gave her age as 18 on the wedding certificate, but in fact she was not yet 17, being born on 29 October 1891, and the wedding being on 4 July 1908.

In the 1911 Census, James Tamplin was living at 5 Station Road, Pontymister, Risca, a stationary boiler stoker, aged 55 and born in Machen, with his 63-year-old wife Elizabeth, born in Bassaleg. With them was their son William Ewart Tamplin (snr.), a 25-year-old 'miner, hewer', born in Risca; their daughter-in-law Mabel Anne, born in Machen; and their 2-year-old grand-daughter Iris Ruby, also born in Machen. The census states that James and Elizabeth had been married for 31 years, having 5 children, 4 living, one deceased.

William Ewart and Mabel Anne's son was the rugby player, let us call him William Ewart Tamplin jnr., for the present, born on 10 May 1917 at 12 Dixon's Place, Risca. His siblings were Violet D. b. 7 September 1911 (registered blind); Jack N. Tamplin b. 6 March 1920 and Edgar J. Tamplin b. 6 March 1923. By 1939 William Ewart snr. and Mabel were living at 54 Garden Suburbs, Risca. William, born 1886 was still a colliery worker, his wife Mabel was listed down for 'domestic duties, and their daughter Violet D. was noted as being born on 7 September 1911, on the blind register and later married to someone called Nicholas. Jack N. Tamplin and Edgar J. Tamplin are still at home, listed as a 'Blacksmith (heavy work) and a 'Blacksmith's striker'.

Thus Susan Lewis's children included 'Nell' Williams, the mother of the 8 rugby-playing sons and 4 daughters; and Leslie Roydon 'Roy' Roberts. The son of Susan Lewis's youngest sister Mabel was William Ewart Tamplin. 'Roy' Roberts was thus the uncle of the Williams brothers, and 'Bill' Tamplin was their first cousin once removed. The oldest of the Williams boys, Gwyn (b. 20 May 1918) played before the war with his uncle Roy (b. 3 June 1917) for Cardiff. Roy Roberts also played after the war for Cardiff, alongside his nephews Bill Tamplin (b. 10 May 1917), Bleddyn Williams (b. 22 February 1923) and possibly Bryn Williams (b. 23 December 1920). The wonderful Gwyn Williams (b. 20 May 2018) first played for Cardiff in 1934-35, two years before his slightly older uncle Roy (b. 3 June 1917). International Bill Tamplin (b. 10 May 1917) did not play for Cardiff until 1945-46, winning his 1st XV cap in that season. Roberts and Tamplin played 150 and 252 games for Cardiff, which puts Gwyn's precocious talent, with 103 appearances, into perspective.

Williams Family Tree

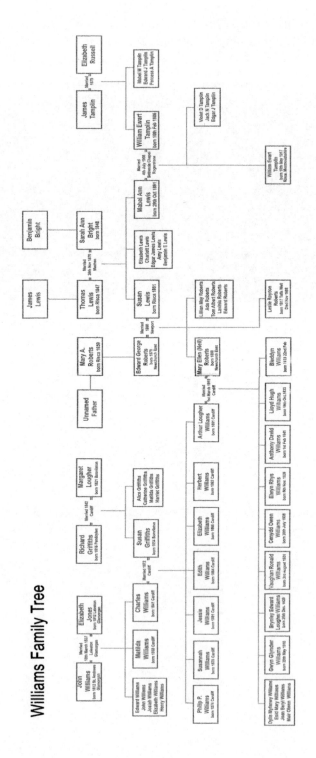

CHAPTER 49 – AFTERWORD

Toward the end of the period of this book, there was an issue given over to Cardiff Rugby Club, in *Welsh Rugby* November 1971. One article was captioned '*Where the Best is Never Good Enough!*' - 'How is greatness measured? A question that is often asked but seldom when referring to a rugby football club. As this story, necessarily mainly factual because of space limitations, unfolds, it will become obvious why in 1945, the Rt. Hon. Jim Callaghan said in Parliament, *"Undoubtedly Cardiff is THE first rugby club"*. What are the special qualities then which have merited such praise? Players of high quality, dedicated officials ensuring sound administration, and progressive policy, supporters who through thick and thin with the targets set as high as possible have all contributed to make this club really great and spoken of with the utmost respect throughout the world, synonymous with all that is best in sport generally, and Cardiff in particular.*

Facts Speak
Let me illustrate with some facts. They can speak for themselves. Nearly 150 international players; sixteen Lions with Barry John, Gareth Edwards and John Bevan writing their names in the history books this year (1971) and Gerald Davies, Gareth, Barry, Keri Jones, John O'Shea and Maurice Richards making what was then an all-time record representation in 1968 with Billy Raybould, a former Cardiff player also in the party; victories over ALL the Tourists, victories in 'Sevens', some of which may surprise you – Middlesex, at Twickenham in 1939, for the first time of asking, winners of the Snelling's, three times, the W.R.U. National twice, the special Harlequins, Lord Wakefield Tournament in 1968-69, the formidable Gala Competition in 1963-64; plus victory four times in a season over old rivals Newport on four occasions; twenty-four teams have yielded more that forty points in a game, the full list of achievements is long and impressive.

Add to this the galaxy of stars who have worn the Blue and Black shirt throughout the long years to make their contribution to what is known throughout the world as the "Cardiff" style of play. Yes, there is certainly something that bit special! Something to be proud of.'

Welsh Rugby had a special issue in 1976, devoted to the club, with a cover of '*Cardiff R.F.C. – A Toast to the Vintage Years – 1876-1976.*' The centre page spread was entitled '*The Ace of Clubs – The world pays tribute to Cardiff R.F.C.*' The subheading was '*THERE IS AN AURA, a status about some clubs, that never dies. They attract attention and jealousy, respect and envy. When they have their lean periods, as do most clubs at some time or other, they may be criticised and there's talk of decline, but they still remain one of the sides that everyone wants to beat. And all clubs want them on their fixture list.*' An article by John Reed of the Sunday Express was titled '*THE ROLLS-ROYCE OF RUGBY – Such a Club is Cardiff, who this season celebrate their centenary, and I am sure that all their English opponents and friends will wish them a memorable and successful year. They have been called the Rolls-Royce club of Welsh rugby and Johnny Matthews, post-war England forward and Harlequins captain, sums up English attitudes to Cardiff when he says: "They are a great bunch of chaps. They stand for all that is best in football, on and off the field... We regard Cardiff more as an international club. They always had great players and were very good socially after the match."*

C.G.R. Harris added an article '*Believe It Or Not*' about Cardiff's statistics. Cardiff in 6 seasons were unbeaten at home: 1879-1880 (captain W.D. Phillips) 1886-87 (W.M. Douglas); 1898-99 (Erith Gwyn Nicholls); 1906-07 (Percy Bush); 1911-12 (Louis Meredith Dyke); and 1947-48 (Haydn Tanner). Unbeaten away records were in 3 seasons: 1885-86 (Frank Hancock); 1905-06 (Percy Bush); and 1948-49 (Haydn Tanner). (Harris adds unbeaten seasons home and away in 1939-1940 (Wilfred Wooller), but only 3 games were played).

'*100 TRIES AND OVER IN A SEASON' (EXCLUDING 1976-77)*
Cardiff have accomplished this feat in 58 seasons. This obviously means that they concentrate more on crossing the line. In the seasons 1885-86 and 1892-93 no Penalty Goals were scored. In 1895-96, 1896-97, 1900-01, 1913-14 and 1919-1920 only ONE Penalty Goal was scored and very many of the other seasons up to 1939-40 only show that two or three Penalty Goals were scored. This, no doubt, avoided the irritating delay in modern rugby given to goal kicking. Many of the so-called Top Teams would have very poor records without Penalty Goals.

SIX ALL-WALES THREEQUARTER LINES
The only club in Wales to have had this honour.
1 - vs Ireland, Belfast 10th March 1894 – Norman Biggs, Dai Fitzgerald, 'Jack' Elliott, Tommy Pearson – Ireland won by a penalty goal to nil.
2 - vs Ireland, Dublin 12th March 1910 – Reggie Gibbs (captain), Louis Dyke, W. Spiller, Johnny Williams; plus outside half Percy Bush and forward Joe Pugsley – Wales 19 – Ireland 3 (try). All of Wales's points were scored by Cardiff players – Percy Bush (drop goal); Louis Dyke (try); Reggie Gibbs (try); Johnny Williams (3 tries).
3 - vs Scotland at Inverleith, 4th February 1911 – Reggie Gibbs, W. Spiller, Louis Dyke, Johnny Williams plus forward Joe Pugsley. Wales 32 – Scotland 10 (2 tries, 1 drop goal). Cardiff players scored 29 of the Welsh team's points – Gibbs, Spiller and Williams each bagged 2 tries; Spiller dropped a goal and Dyke converted 2 tries.
4 - vs France at Parc des Princes 28th February 1911 – Gibbs, Spiller, Dyke, Williams plus Joe Pugsley – Wales 3 (Johnny Williams try) France 0
5 - vs Ireland at Arms Park 11th March 1911 – Gibbs, Spiller, Dyke and Williams again. Wales 16 (2 goals, 1 penalty, try by Gibbs) – Ireland 0.

638

*Note: In this 1911 series England were defeated at Swansea on 21ˢᵗ January 1911, when R.A. Gibbs, W. Spiller and J. Pugsley each scored a try, so this made 44 points by Cardiff players, made up with 12 tries, 2 conversions and 1 drop goal. **Unequalled in Welsh history**.*

6 - vs Scotland at Murrayfield 1ˢᵗ February 1930 – Gwyn Davies, Bernard Turnbull, Graham Jones, Ronnie Boon, plus outside half Frank Williams and forward Archie Skym. Wales 9 – Scotland 12 (goal, drop goal, try). Graham Jones scored all the points with a try, conversion and drop goal.'

There was also an unofficial international:

'vs France at Arms Park 23ʳᵈ December 1945 – Graham Hale, Bleddyn Williams, Dr. Jack Matthews, Dr. Glyn Jones, plus outside half Billy Cleaver, scrumhalf Billy Darch, and forwards Maldwyn James and Selby Davies. Wales 8 – France 0. All points scored by Cardiff players - Jack Matthews and Selby Davies a try each, 1 conversion by Maldwyn James.'

Wales captain Percy Bush captained Cardiff three times in a 'Golden Era' from 1903-04 to the end of 1909-1910. In 1904 he played all 4 Tests in the British Isles tour of Australasia. In 1905-06 Cardiff, under Bush, only lost one game, to the All-Blacks, owing to his mistake. In 32 games they won 29, drew 2, and just lost 10-8 to New Zealand, two goals to a try and a goal. However, he was outside half in the so-called '*Match of the Century*' or '*World Championship*' when Wales beat New Zealand, their only defeat in 35 matches. It was an Invincible Inter-Club season, scoring 404 points to 83, 92 tries to 20, and 21 Cardiff players were presented with gold watches, one of which is in the Cardiff club's museum. In the following season, Bush was again Cardiff captain, and the club inflicted the only defeat of the South African tourists. At the end of the 1909-1910 season, Percy was appointed British Consul in Nantes, Cardiff's twin-town, then in Brittany. (The central government hated Breton nationalism so much that it was a criminal offence to give children Breton names, or speak Breton in schools and churches. De Gaulle legalised the Vichy Government's new department, Loire-Atlantique, to move the Breton capital of 1,500 years out of Brittany. To non-Welsh readers, the Breton language is very similar to Welsh. British saints and other Britons headed there in the 6th and seventh centuries to escape the Germanic Anglo-Saxon invasions, taking the language.) Harris writes, '*On 9ᵗʰ April, 1910, he figured prominently in the win by Nantes over Le Havre, by the huge score of 66-6. Percy Bush contributed, what was in those far-off days, **a world record number of points, 54 in all**, made up with **10 tries**, eight of which he converted, and also dropped two goals, valued at 4 points each, to complete this fantastic scoring.*' After a couple of seasons, Percy Bush returned to play for Cardiff, retiring at the end of the 1913-14 season. His art teacher father was one of the founders of Cardiff Rugby Club in 1875.

Wilfred Wooller was a forthright rugby and cricket reporter for the Sunday Telegraph after his cricketing days ended. He summed up what it meant to play for Cardiff in an article *Those were the Days*, in *Welsh Rugby* May 1977. It begins, '*THERE IS A TRADITION and discipline inherent in belonging to a great club akin to serving in a crack regiment. There is none of this puerile dogma of levelling down to the mediocre, a diffusing of precious talent among the many, like yeast in flour to raise the whole to edible proportions. It is precisely the reverse.* **Great clubs earn their reputation by the cult of excellence. The best only is good enough for them. Sports players by instinct want to be the best, club supporters by their nature require their club to be the top. To gain a cap for Cardiff is to gain esteem throughout the rugby world.** *Cardiff is, of course, not unique in this respect. Great Welsh clubs have their fine traditions, like Newport, Swansea or Llanelli, or in England the Harlequins, Coventry and Northampton, to mention some, but with due respect to my friends in many fine clubs, there is something a little different about Cardiff. Maybe it is because the club has been so closely linked with a National XV at Cardiff Arms Park, or perhaps it is because it played such an important part in the evolution of the rugby game, but whatever the cause it does have its special niche in the HALLS OF RUGBY FAME.*'

Cardiff treasured their games against the best English clubs, and the records up to 1974-75 (1972 Leicester) are:

Team	First played	Pl	W	L	D	Pts	Tries	Pens
Blackheath	1889	98	73	22	3	1325-586	306-123	20-24
Bristol	1888	142	108	27	7	1874-791	419-148	55-56
Coventry	1891	85	53	27	5	1099-654	217-122	63-44
Gloucester	1882	157	104	35	18	1661-781	285-146	45-58
Harlequins	1882	91	66	16	9	1131-612	248-115	39-39
Leicester	1890	72	50	14	8	808-387	183-73	33-23
London Welsh	1885	78	66	10	2	1198-395	269-70	39-29
Moseley	1880	65	53	10	2	956-225	230-40	17-12
Wasps	1903	44	39	3	2	721-225	160-39	25-13
Totals		832	612	164	56	10773-4656	2317-876	336-298

Of these 832 fixtures, Cardiff won 612 (74%), lost 164 (20%) and drew 56 (6%). They were thus unbeaten in 80% of games. They scored 10,773 points against 4,656, 2.3 times as many points as their opponents. The try count was 2,317 to 876, a 2.6 times factor. However, the penalty count was 336 to 298, just a ratio of 1.1. In the 832 games played, the average score was 13-6 and average tries per game 2.8-1. In 91 matches against the Barbarians, dating from 1891, Cardiff won 58, lost 29 and drew 4, scoring 1,208 points against 708, with a very impressive 269 tries against 168.

Cardiff have supplied more British Lions/British Isles Tourists than any other club, but also have supplied many Welsh captains. From 1875 to 1975, the period of this book, they are: H.J. 'Joe' Simpson; Frank E. Hancock; Arthur Frank Hill; Erith Gwyn Nicholls; Rhys Gabe; Herbert 'Bert' Benjamin Winfield; 'Reggie' A. Gibbs; 'Johnny' Lewis Williams; J. M. 'Clem' Lewis; Tom 'Codger' Johnson; R. Arthur Cornish; W.J. 'Bobby' Delany; Bernard R. 'Lou' Turnbull; B.O. 'Ossie' Male; Harry M. Bowcott; Wilfred Wooller; Cliff Jones; Bill Tamplin; Haydn Tanner; Dr. Jack Matthews; Bleddyn Williams, Rex Willis; Cliff Morgan; Lloyd Williams and Gareth Edwards. We then have from 1975: T.G.R. Gerald Davies; Gareth Davies; Terry Holmes; Robert Norster; Mike Hall; Jonathan Humphries; Gwyn Jones; Robert Howley and Dai Young. Martyn Williams was captain for Cardiff R.F.C. and then when the club was sadly renamed Cardiff Blues. Other Cardiff Blues who captained Wales were: Gareth Thomas, Gethin Jenkins; Matthew Rees; Sam Warburton, Bradley Davies; Ellis Jenkins and Josh Navidi. Warburton holds the record for captaining Wales, 49 times. The Blues are now again Cardiff Rugby and the 'Rags' are Cardiff Athletic.

In the process of 'regionalisation', the longstanding Welsh tradition of club rivalry was replaced by four leading 'regions', intensely disliked by many grass-roots followers. Sadly, Cardiff RFC became Cardiff 'Blues' in 2003, with the Athletic/Rags renamed as Cardiff. A declining number of supporters still chanted 'Cardiff', while the BBC only ever called the team 'Blues'. However, from the 2021-22 season, the 'Blues' were renamed Cardiff Rugby/Rygbi Caerdydd, the traditional 'the Blue and Blacks'. The second team, the much-loved 'Rags', will be called Cardiff RFC, and both teams will wear the customary colours of Cambridge Blue and Black, not the recent pastel shades of blue or pink. Speaking on the Cardiff Blues official website, chief executive Richard Holland said, '*We see this change as a key step in the evolution of top-flight rugby in Cardiff. We are proud to embrace our rich heritage and history, which goes back more than 145 years, and encompasses greats of the game including Bleddyn Williams, Cliff Morgan, Gareth Edwards, Terry Holmes and Gethin Jenkins. Cardiff Rugby is a world-renowned brand and we simply have to leverage that to build sustainable success on and off the field. Not only is Cardiff globally recognised in rugby circles, it is also the commercial powerhouse of Wales and one of the fastest growing cities in the UK and Europe. Over a long period, our supporters and sponsors have been very clear that this is what they want and I am pleased that we have been able to respond to them in such a positive way, especially at a time when they have stood beside us.*

*This is also the best way forward for the development of players, with much closer alignment between all of our teams and Cardiff RFC now returning to be the traditional 'Rags' to Cardiff Rugby. We are enormously excited to see what the future holds and look forward to seeing the blue and blacks run out at the iconic Arms Park, whether in the Regional Age Grade competitions, Indigo Group Premiership, Guinness PRO14 or European competition. We have a long-standing commitment to developing from within and have seen our representation at all levels grow. **Ninety-five per cent of our senior squad is Welsh and almost 70 per cent are products of our rugby development pathway**. We are continuing to invest with our biggest academy squad and there is fantastic work being done through the age-grades. Prior to the Covid-19 pandemic, we were engaging with more than 50,000 people per year through our Community Foundation. This involves people of all ages and backgrounds, from Barry to Builth Wells, and we will continue to do this using the Cardiff Rugby brand. While there are still challenges to navigate due to the pandemic and further work to achieve our goals on and off the pitch, this is a hugely exciting time for Cardiff Rugby.'*

The game in Wales is struggling financially, and fewer and fewer are taking up the game. Paying spectators at club level are low and falling, with regions and clubs finding it difficult to balance the books. Unequal financial resources, and a small number of professional players compared to France, England and Southern Hemisphere teams mean that Cardiff can only hope to regain its reputation as *'the greatest'* team in rugby union, which it held for decades. (The Welsh team nearly always performs above expectation, camouflaging deep troubles beneath the surface). The Welsh Rugby Union is ploughing money to develop women's rugby, whereas rugby is now a more dangerous sport for boys and men, let alone for girls and women. This is not being 'sexist' – I believe that the game has become too dangerous and violent, with too much emphasis upon contact. Rule changes are desperately needed to make the game more flowing and attractive, taking out the 'big hits' that enthuse coaches and commentators alike. There is a major problem with concussion that is causing multiple health claims in the sport. Alterations in the rules take place at a glacial pace, and are, like the British legal system, leading to accretion, confusion and obfuscation, whereas the rule book needs to be ripped up. A start would be to go back to 1970's rules and take it from there. When Cardiff were in their pomp, in amateur days, the game was easy to understand and explain. The game was far better if teams wished to play open rugby. Perhaps we need a discretionary try – one scored from distance involving passing should score more than driving over from a line-out, or bashing at the try-line for perhaps ten attempts.

I know no person, from former internationals to club players, who thinks that the modern professional game is more attractive than when it was amateur. Unless sides are badly mis-matched, it is boring and emphasises physical contact. The game has to change. Internationals may be money-spinners, but there are far too many, swelling the coffers of international rugby bodies, but causing many injuries and hurting the major clubs' incomes as fixtures are cancelled for international 'windows' outside the Six Nations Championship. One final note. Men used to play over forty times a season for Cardiff, not including charity and some representative games. Spectators could see up to 25 homes games in a season, mainly on Saturday afternoons. From 1920-21 to 1938-39, Cardiff played between 42 and 47 official games each season. From 1945-46 to 1974-75 they played from 40-53 games, at an average of 46 games a season. (In four years from 1971-72, fixtures were 53, 49, 53 and 51 games.) These Cardiff teams rarely changed. In 1971-72 there were 53 fixtures. Flanker Mervyn John played 51 games, Roger Beard 46, Carl Smith 43, Garry Davies 41, In Robinson 39, Roger Lane 35, John Regan 33, Lyn Baxter and Wayne Lewis 31. In today's game, there is no way that players could play that many times, season by season.

For years, Wales have been down to the bare bones in many games, owing to long-term injuries to first-choice players. In some games they have been missing up to 12 first choices for the international team. As mentioned previously, in the 2015 World Cup pool game against England at Twickenham, Wales were without 10 backs through injury, forced to play a scrumhalf, Lloyd Williams on the wing. Yet somehow, they scraped a win. Wales does not have the necessary pool of, say, 45 top class rugby players to give cover in every position. Injuries dictate the make-up of the Welsh team, whereas in the past, including the golden era of the 1970s the team picked itself. The greatest Wales and Cardiff teams hardly changed week-in, week-out, except for trial and international calls. Over-training, full-contact training, 'clearing-out' and full-collision rugby have caused the game to deteriorate in safety to players. In 1999, that splendid rugby writer John Billot wrote in his foreword to his splendid 'History of Welsh International Rugby' – 'My saddest day in rugby was when it turned professional. We were not prepared, and it has done little for the game. We need time to adapt, to create a recognisable structure that will provide responsible, vibrant and attract back the lost thousands to our club matches.' He could not have foreseen Cardiff's away games being in South Africa, Ireland, Scotland and Italy. That is no way forward. This book has been about a better time and a better game – with men playing for the love of the sport. And it pays homage to a unique band of brothers who played

clean, attractive rugby at the highest levels of expertise and sportsmanship.
Heaven only knows what will happen to the game.

---

¹ Just before publication, Cardiff's new change strip was announced as being red.
A red change strip for all clubs, without red as their main colour, could bring in
some necessary income as Wales supporters would buy them.

REFERENCES

PRIMARY SOURCES

Davies, D.E. 'Danny': *Cardiff Rugby Club – 'The Greatest' – 100 Years at Cardiff Arms Park: History and Statistics 1876-1975* (1975)

Llewellyn, Don and Edwards, Gerald: *The Williams Family (More than a Rugby Dynasty), The Garth Domain* No.26 December 2004

Thomas, Peter: 1887-1987 - *A View from the Garth – One Hundred Years of Taff's Well Rugby* (1987)

Cardiff Rugby Football Club has a wealth of detail, for example: *cardiffrfc.com/player-archive*

SECONDARY SOURCES

Baldwin, Bernard, *Mountain Ash Remembered* 1984

Bowen, Bleddyn Keith, son of Jack Bowen, for information upon Gwyn Williams at Wigan and his input upon Welshmen in rugby league

Billot, John: *History of Welsh International Rugby* 1999

Cardiff Rugby Museum digital archive – *cardiffrugbymuseum.org*

Evans, Howard: *Welsh International Matches 1881-2011*, Y Lolfa 2011

Evans, Alan: *Taming the Tourists – How Cardiff Beat the All Blacks, Springboks and Wallabies*, Vertical Editions 2003

Evans, Alan and Duncan Gardiner: *Cardiff Rugby Football Club 1940-2000*, Tempus Images of Sport 2001

Evans, Howard: *Welsh International Matches 1881-2011*, Y Lolfa 2011

Gardiner, Duncan and Evans, Alan: *Cardiff Rugby Football Club 1876-1939*, Tempus Images of Sport 1999

Harries, Ross: *Behind the Dragon – Playing Rugby for Wales*, Polaris 2019

Hignell, Andrew: *Turnbull – A Welsh Sporting Hero*, Tempus 2001

Hignell, Andrew: *The Skipper – A Biography of Wilf Wooller*, Limlow Books 1995

Llewellyn, Arthur and Don: *Pentyrch R.F.C. – A Club for All Reasons 1883-1983*, pub. The Authors and Pentyrch R.F.C. 1983

Parry-Jones, David (ed): *Taff's Acre – A History and Celebration of Cardiff Arms Park*, Willow Books (Collins) 1984

Rugby Relics, based in Glynneath and founded and run by Dai Richards – *'the Leading Supplier of Rugby Memorabilia Worldwide'* is a great source of information - *rugbyrelics.*

Thomas, J.B.G.: *Springbok Glory*, Stanley Paul 1961

Smith, David and Williams, Gareth: *Fields of Praise – The Official History of the Welsh Rugby Union 1881-1981*, University of Wales Press 1980

Thomas, J.B.G.: *Rugger in the Blood – Fifty Years of Rugby Memoirs*, Pelham 1985

Williams, Bleddyn, *Rugger, My Life*, Stanley Paul and Co. Ltd 1956

Welsh Rugby November 1971, cover is *CARDIFF RUGBY CLUB – Full Length Feature with Photos*, with articles by reporters from *The People, The Mirror* and *The Evening Post*
Welsh Rugby 1976 'special issue', cover is *CARDIFF R.F.C. A TOAST TO THE VINTAGE YEARS 1876-1976*
Welsh Rugby May 1977 *– Cardiff's Centenary Year issue*

GENEALOGY
Many thanks to Lynne Barry for some amazing research into the history of the Williams family and especially for uncovering the familial link with the Tamplins.
Also thanks to Mike Roberts, for information upon his father Roy Roberts MM, uncle of the Williams brothers, and for digitising the complex family tree into understandable form.

PICTURES
Courtesy of Cardiff Rugby Museum, Glamorgan Archives, Keith Bowen (son of Jack), Mike Roberts and Taff's Well RFC

Terry Breverton is a Fellow of the Royal Historical Society, the Institute of Consulting, the Chartered Institute of Marketing and the Royal Society of Arts. He has spoken on Wales at the North American Festival of Wales at Vancouver and Washington and across Wales, given academic papers in Paris, Thessaloniki, Charleston and Seattle and taught in Milan and Reggio Emilia. He has given the Bemis Lecture at Lincoln, Massachusetts and been awarded a Helm Fellowship at the University of Indiana. Breverton has appeared in several television documentaries about the Welsh, including in Los Angeles, and has worked and consulted in over thirty countries.

After a career in international business and acadaemia, he is a full-time non-fiction writer of over fifty books, and has won five Welsh Books Council 'Book of the Month' awards. He has spoken across Wales upon Welsh heritage, a particular interest being Welsh pirates and privateers such as 'Black Bart' Roberts and Admiral Sir Henry Morgan. His A to Z of Wales and the Welsh was an acclaimed 'first Welsh encyclopaedia', and Archbishop Rowan Williams commented upon his The Book of Welsh Saints: 'this book is a really extraordinary achievement: a compilation of tradition, topography and literary detective work that can have few rivals. I have enjoyed browsing it immensely, and have picked up all sorts of new lines to follow up... an enormous work of research.'

Richard Booth MBE, (King Richard Coeur de Livre, the 'King of Hay'), states that 'Breverton has done more for Welsh tourism than the Welsh Tourist Board.' His books have been published across the world, and translated into over twenty languages from Polish and Turkish to Chinese and Japanese. Breverton played rugby until he was 38, and says his proudest achievement is being on the committee of Llanybydder Rugby Football Club. Breverton's 100 Great Welshmen (2001) was a Welsh Books Council Book of the Month reviewed as 'a fascinating compendium' with 'painstaking research'. His second edition of 2006 was called: 'a veritable goldmine of a book'; and 'a massive treasure chest of facts and figures which no collector of books on Wales can overlook'.

Published by Glyndŵr Publishing

Printed in Great Britain
by Amazon

44442413R00364